Cases on Semantic Interoperability for Information Systems Integration:
Practices and Applications

Yannis Kalfoglou
RICOH Europe plc & University of Southhampton, UK

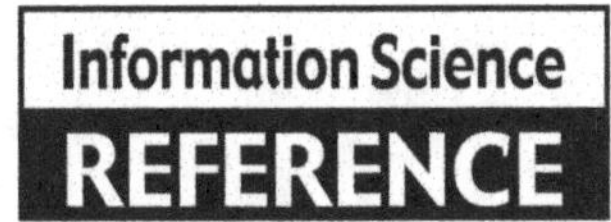

INFORMATION SCIENCE REFERENCE
Hershey · New York

Director of Editorial Content: Kristin Klinger
Senior Managing Editor: Jamie Snavely
Assistant Managing Editor: Michael Brehm
Publishing Assistant: Sean Woznicki
Typesetter: Kurt Smith, Sean Woznicki
Cover Design: Lisa Tosheff
Printed at: Yurchak Printing Inc.

Published in the United States of America by
Information Science Reference (an imprint of IGI Global)
701 E. Chocolate Avenue
Hershey PA 17033
Tel: 717-533-8845
Fax: 717-533-8661
E-mail: cust@igi-global.com
Web site: http://www.igi-global.com/reference

Library of Congress Cataloging-in-Publication Data

Cases on semantic interoperability for information systems integration : practices and applications / Yannis Kalfoglou, editor.
p. cm.

Includes bibliographical references and index.
Summary: "This book presents the use of semantic interoperability for a variety of applications ranging from manufacturing to tourism, e-commerce, energy Grids' integration, geospatial systems interoperability and automated agents interoperability for web services"--Provided by publisher.

ISBN 978-1-60566-894-9 (hardcover) -- ISBN 978-1-60566-895-6 (ebook) 1. Semantic integration (Computer systems) I. Kalfoglou, Yannis, 1970-
TK5105.88815.C364 2010
005.7--dc22
2009021593 uti

British Cataloguing in Publication Data
A Cataloguing in Publication record for this book is available from the British Library.

All work contributed to this book is new, previously-unpublished material. The views expressed in this book are those of the authors, but not necessarily of the publisher.

Editorial Advisory Board

List of Reviewers

Table of Contents

Foreword xi

Preface xiii

Acknowledgment xxiv

Section 1
Novel Concepts for Engineering Semantic Interoperability Solutions

Chapter 1
Entity-Centric Semantic Interoperability 1
Paolo Bouquet, University of Trento, Italy
Heiko Stoermer, University of Trento, Italy
Wojcech Barczyński, SAP AG, Germany
Stefano Bocconi, Elsevier B.V., The Netherlands

Chapter 2
The Ontological Stance for a Manufacturing Scenario 22
Michael Gruninger, University of Toronto, Canada

Chapter 3
Use of Semantic Mediation in Manufacturing Supply Chains 43
Peter Denno, National Institute of Standards and Technology, USA
Edward J. Barkmeyer, National Institute of Standards and Technology, USA
Fabian Neuhaus, National Institute of Standards and Technology, USA

Chapter 4
Service Integration through Structure-Preserving Semantic Matching 64
Fiona McNeill, University of Edinburgh, Scotland
Paolo Besana, University of Edinburgh, Scotland
Juan Pane, University of Trento, Italy
Fausto Giunchiglia, University of Trento, Italy

Detailed Table of Contents

Foreword xi

Preface xiii

Acknowledgment xxiv

Section 1
Novel Concepts for Engineering Semantic Interoperability Solutions

Chapter 1
Entity-Centric Semantic Interoperability 1
Paolo Bouquet, University of Trento, Italy
Heiko Stoermer, University of Trento, Italy
Wojcech Barczyński, SAP AG, Germany
Stefano Bocconi, Elsevier B.V., The Netherlands

This chapter introduces the concept of entity centric semantic interoperability. The authors distinguish two distinct approaches to semantic interoperability: schema centric and entity centric.

Chapter 2
The Ontological Stance for a Manufacturing Scenario 22
Michael Gruninger, University of Toronto, Canada

The author argues that in order to achieve complete semantic integration, we need to enable the automated exchange of information between applications in such a way that the intended semantics of the applications' ontologies are preserved by the receiving application. The ontological stance is an operational characterization of the set of intended models for the application's terminology.

Chapter 3
Use of Semantic Mediation in Manufacturing Supply Chains 43
Peter Denno, National Institute of Standards and Technology, USA
Edward J. Barkmeyer, National Institute of Standards and Technology, USA
Fabian Neuhaus, National Institute of Standards and Technology, USA

This chapter argues for the use of semantic mediation to achieve semantic interoperability. The authors elaborate on the central role that system engineering processes and their formalisation and automation play in facilitating semantic interoperability.

Chapter 4
Service Integration through Structure-Preserving Semantic Matching 64
Fiona McNeill, University of Edinburgh, Scotland
Paolo Besana, University of Edinburgh, Scotland
Juan Pane, University of Trento, Italy
Fausto Giunchiglia, University of Trento, Italy

This chapter presents the structure preserving semantic matching algorithm (SPSM). The domain of application is integration of services. The authors argue that in large, open environments such as the Semantic Web, huge numbers of services are developed by vast numbers of different users.

Chapter 5
Streamlining Semantic Integration Systems 83
Yannis Kalfoglou, Ricoh Europe plc & University of Southampton, UK
Bo Hu, SAP Research CEC Belfast, UK

The authors of this chapter argue for the use of a streamlined approach to integrate semantic integration systems. The authors elaborate on the abundance and diversity of semantic integration solutions and how this impairs strict engineering practice and ease of application.

Chapter 6
Sharing Resources through Ontology Alignments in a Semantic Peer-to-Peer System 107
Jérôme Euzenat, INRIA & LIG, France
Onyeari Mbanefo, INRIA & LIG, France
Arun Sharma, INRIA & LIG, France

This chapter presents an application of peer-to-peer to enable semantic interoperability. The authors point to the bootstrapping problem of the Semantic Web: benefit will emerge when there is enough knowledge available; however, people are not willing to provide knowledge if this will not return immediate benefits.

Chapter 7
Quality-Driven, Semantic Information System Integration: The QuaD^2-Framework 127
Steffen Mencke, Otto-von-Guericke University, Germany
Martin Kunz, Otto-von-Guericke University, Germany
Dmytro Rud, Otto-von-Guericke University, Germany
Reiner Dumke, Otto-von-Guericke University, Germany

This chapter elaborates on the need for a framework for quality driven assembly of entities. The authors argue that although automation is an important aspect of integration solutions, quality must be of substantial interest as it is an inherent characteristic of any product.

Section 2
Domain Specific Semantic Interoperability Practices

This chapter elaborates on a case study in the domain of medical image annotation and patient data management. Their work is drawn from a large scale nationally funded project, THESEUS MEDICO. The objective of this large scale collaborative project is to enable seamless integration of medical images and different user applications by providing direct access to image semantics.

This chapter presents a case of semantic interoperability in the electricity generation domain with emphasis on the uses and evolution of the International Electrotechnical Commission (IEC) framework 62357.

The authors of this chapter elaborate on how to provide dynamic semantic synchronisation between business partners using different e-business standards. Their approach is based on ontology mapping with interactive user participation.

This chapter presents the XAR framework that allows for free text information extraction and semantic annotation. The language underpinning XAR, Ashish and Mehrotra argue, allows for the inclusion of probabilistic reasoning with the rule language.

Chapter 12
CRUZAR: An Application of Semantic Matchmaking to e-Tourism 255
Iván Mínguez, Fundación CTIC, Spain
Diego Berrueta, Fundación CTIC, Spain
Luis Polo, Fundación CTIC, Spain

This chapter presents the CRUZAR system which is used for semantic matchmaking in the e-Tourism domain. CRUZAR is a web application that uses expert knowledge in the form of rules and ontologies and a comprehensive repository of relevant data to build custom routes for each visitor profile.

Chapter 13
Data Integration in the Geospatial Semantic Web 272
Patrick Maué, Westfälische Wilhelms-Universität,Münster, Germany
Sven Schade, Westfälische Wilhelms-Universität,Münster, Germany

This chapter presents insight and applications of semantic integration in the domain of geospatial information systems.

Chapter 14
An Ontology-Based GeoDatabase Interoperability Platform 294
Serge Boucher, Université Libre de Bruxelles, Belgium
Esteban Zimányi, Université Libre de Bruxelles, Belgium

This chapter presents a platform for interoperating geographical information sources. The authors elaborate on the lessons learnt from deploying a prototype system to tackle interoperability needs between different cartographic systems from the domain of military operations.

Compilation of References 316

About the Contributors 336

Index 344

Foreword

The modern digital world contains a deep paradox that is unnoticed by most users, but is keenly appreciated by designers and systems architects. The world is becoming increasingly connected while simultaneously becoming increasingly fragmented. The increasing connectivity is easy to understand: All those computers, all those smart phones, and all those massive server farms in the cloud are connected by ever-faster and (we hope) ever-more-reliable wireless and wired links. So where does the fragmentation occur? Fragmentation occurs because effective communication happens not when bits are transferred but when meanings are shared.

The principal technical approach to sharing meanings across heterogeneous systems is based on ontologies. Ontologies provide a way of explicitly defining the meanings of information entities, so that systems designed, implemented and maintained independently of each other can interoperate to solve human problems. For example, how can multiple health-care providers share information effectively to serve a patient? How can supply chain participants collaborate to increase efficiency? How can electrical grids fed by both conventional and green generating stations be operated effectively? Solutions to the problem of semantic heterogeneity are needed.

This book brings together some of the best current thinking on the conceptual foundations and domain-specific practices of semantic interoperability. It is an essential resource for all those concerned with resolving the paradox noted above.

Peter E. Hart
RICOH Innovations Inc., USA

***Peter E. Hart** has contributed to the theory, practice, and leadership of artificial intelligence for more than 40 years. He invented, and developed the theory, of some of the most widely used algorithms in modern computing. He co-authored one of the most-cited textbooks in the field of computer science, and holds dozens of issued patents in the US, Europe, and Japan. He founded and/or led half a dozen companies and international research centers. Hart is currently Chairman of Ricoh Innovations, Inc., in Menlo Park, California. He is a Fellow of the IEEE, the ACM, and the AAAI.*

Foreword

A part of formal knowledge representation that we once took as a given turns out to be a major stumbling block to the development of reasoning systems on a global scale. Twenty years ago a well trained "knowledge engineer" understood how to represent certain forms of knowledge but took it for granted that the validity of things said about any particular domain would be ensured by "experts" with consensus in that domain. Then the Internet changed the problem. Instead of having to drag information out of people, the tide of information became unstoppable; but nobody much cared about consensus on what was meant. On the contrary, the sheer inconsistency and variety of points of view nourishes the Web. We now have a system composed of small islands of (relative) consistency connected by bridges and aquifers of many different kinds; people are moved between different sources of knowledge via their Web browsers or knowledge sources import information from others via feeds. The media of expression of knowledge also differs hugely, from natural language and images through to curated data. The big problem is that there are too many islands; too much information and too varied media for us to build by hand all the bridges and aquifers that we need. In this context, automated reasoning changes from being something that might possibly work to being the only thing that could possibly work. Heterogeneity in knowledge representations and in reasoning is now a given, and those who want to attempt large scale systems that take advantage of the scaling properties of the Internet must find ways to make this heterogeneity reinforce (rather than undermine, as we had traditionally assumed) the systems we build. This book looks at ways in which theoreticians and engineers have managed, so far, to come to terms with heterogeneity.

Dave Robertson
University of Edinburgh, UK

***Dave Robertson** is the Director of the Centre for Intelligent Systems and their Applications, part of the School of Informatics at the University of Edinburgh. His current research is on formal methods for coordination and knowledge sharing in distributed, open systems - the long term goal being to develop theories, languages and tools that out-perform conventional software engineering approaches in these arenas. He was coordinator of the OpenKnowledge project (www.openk.org) and was a principal investigator on the Advanced Knowledge Technologies research consortium (www.aktors.org), which are major EU and UK projects in this area. His earlier work was primarily on program synthesis and on the high level specification of programs, where he built some of the earliest systems for automating the construction of large programs from domain-specific requirements. He has contributed to the methodology of the field by developing the use of "lightweight" formal methods - traditional formal methods made much simpler to use in an engineering context by tailoring them to a specific type of task. As an undergraduate he trained as a biologist and continues to prefer biology-related applications of his research, although methods from his group have been applied to other areas such as astronomy, simulation of consumer behaviour and emergency response.*

Preface

Today's information systems are becoming too complex. Managing their complexity has been a theme of interest and considerable contribution from a variety of communities, practitioners and enterprises since the mid eighties. This resulted in information systems that can manage massive amounts of data, complex transactions and serve a multitude of applications across global networks. Nowadays, however, we face a new challenge that undermines information systems' productivity: *heterogeneity*. As information systems become more distributed and open to serve the needs of an ever increasing distributed IT environment, heterogeneity, which is naturally inherited in independently constructed information systems, comes across as an obstacle. The crux of the problem with heterogeneity is that it impedes productivity as it makes integration of information systems difficult. Integration of information systems is deemed as a prerequisite for operating in different market segments, geographic regions and across different information systems. The properties of distributiveness, seamless connectivity, and omnipresence of information in a global scale are the norm in today's business environment and information systems have to support and enable them.

Heterogeneity occurs in many levels in an information system; however, the most important source of heterogeneity is in the conception, modelling and structuring of information. There are cultural, regional, and organisational variations of the same piece of information. This results in heterogeneity: it is common to encounter different forms of information regarding the same entity of interest across different information systems. To overcome this burden, interoperability solutions have been proposed and used extensively in the past three decades. From the early days of Electronic Data Interchange to XML solutions in recent times, interoperability solutions aim to glue together heterogeneous information data sets and increase productivity. Despite the plethora of interoperability solutions though, we observe that most are focused on one aspect of heterogeneity: *syntax*. That is, they tackle syntactic variations in the representation of information.

SEMANTIC INTEROPERABILITY

However, as systems become more distributed and disparate within and across organisational boundaries and market segments, there is a need to preserve the *meaning* of entities used in everyday transactions that involve information sharing. In order for these transactions to be successful, we need to be able to uncover and expose the semantics of the elements taking part in these transactions. That goes beyond detection of simple syntactic variations and tackles the issue of information entities expressed in syntactically similar manner but have a different meaning. Solutions that take into account the meaning of information entities are often characterised as *semantic integration* or *semantic interoperability*. Semantic interoperability and integration is concerned with the use of explicit semantic descriptions to facilitate information and systems integration. Semantic technologies, primarily ontologies and the use of Semantic Web, provide the means to attach meaning to conventional concepts. That makes it possible to automatically process and integrate large amounts of information without human intervention.

But there exist various perceptions of what semantic interoperability and integration stands for. These notions are much contested and fuzzy and have been used over the past decade in a variety ways. Moreover, as reported in (Pollock, 2002), both terms are often used indistinctly, and some view them as the same thing.

The ISO/IEC 2382 Information Technology Vocabulary defines interoperability as "the capability to communicate, execute programs, or transfer data among various functional units in a manner that requires the user to have little or no knowledge of the unique characteristics of those units." The ISO/IEC 14662 IT Open EDI reference model International Standard emphasizes the importance of agreed semantics: "user groups have identified the need to agree on information models at the semantic level before agreeing on specific data structures and data representations to be exchanged between parties," and further on the benefits of agreed semantics: "agreement on semantics of data is needed to reconcile and co-ordinate different data representations used in different industry sectors; agreed information models allow completeness and consistency controls on data exchanged between parties."

In a debate on the mailing list of the IEEE Standard Upper Ontology working group, a more formal approach to semantic interoperability was advocated: use logic in order to guarantee that after data were transmitted from a sender system to a receiver, all implications made by one system had to hold and be provable by the other, and there should be a logical equivalence between those implications[1]. With respect to integration, Uschold and Gruninger argued that "two agents are semantically integrated if they can successfully communicate with each other" and that "successful exchange of information means that the agents understand each other and there is guaranteed accuracy, " (Uschold & Gruninger, 2002).

IMPACT AND OUTREACH

Interoperability has also been the focus of high profile governmental, industrial and scientific endeavours in recent years. For example, the US Government Healthcare Information Technology Enterprise Integration Act[2] calls for interoperability solutions to increase efficiency and productivity of heterogeneous healthcare IT systems. Similarly, the European Commission is working on a number of initiatives for the knowledge economy, like the well publicised i2010 initiative, and interoperability is a focal point of that initiative as it aims to achieve interoperable systems for e-government services across Europe. The IDABC[3] (Interoperable Delivery of European eGovernment Services to public Administrations, Business and Citizens) programme and the SEMIC.EU[4] platform are two exemplars of interoperability work in Europe's public sector. According to David White, Director, European Commission, Enterprise and Industry Directorate General: "the realization of i2010 goals will very much depend on platforms, services and applications being able to talk to one another and to build an economic activity on the information retrieved. This is what we understand as interoperability. It is complex, not limited to the infrastructure level but encompasses semantic interoperability, organisational interoperability, and even regulatory interoperability." In sciences, the high profile E-Science programme praises the role and highlights the need for interoperability: "Interoperability is key to all aspects of scale that characterize e-Science, such as scale of data, computation, and collaboration. We need interoperable information in order to query across the multiple, diverse data sets, and an interoperable infrastructure to make use of existing services for doing this." (Hendler, 2004).

Financially, the value of interoperability has been praised recently by (Schrage, 2009) "Look no further than the internet for the inspiration for interoperable innovation. The misunderstood genius of the internet is that interoperability makes "networks of networks" possible. Protocols permitting diverse data to mingle creatively explain why the internet's influence as a multimedia, multifunctional and multidisciplinary environment for innovation remains unsurpassed."[5] Although the "data mingle" that Schrage calls for is evident in today's large data mashup ventures, the design and execution of protocols to support such activity are hard to build.

SOLUTIONS AND TRENDS

Semantic interoperability solutions are using a variety of technologies; however, the dominant paradigm is to use technologies that are geared toward the management and exploitation of codified semantics, often attached to information entities as descriptors. Such technology is the ontology. According to the infamous quote from (Gruber, 1995), an ontology is "a shared conceptualisation of a specification" and it aims to enable knowledge sharing. Early ontology work suggested that they are suitable for achieving interoperability between disparate systems. In the mid nineties, the seminal article from Uschold and Gruninger provided supportive evidence of this claim (Uschold & Gruninger, 1996). This is best illustrated in the compelling Figure of the authors which we redraw in Figure 1.

Figure 1.

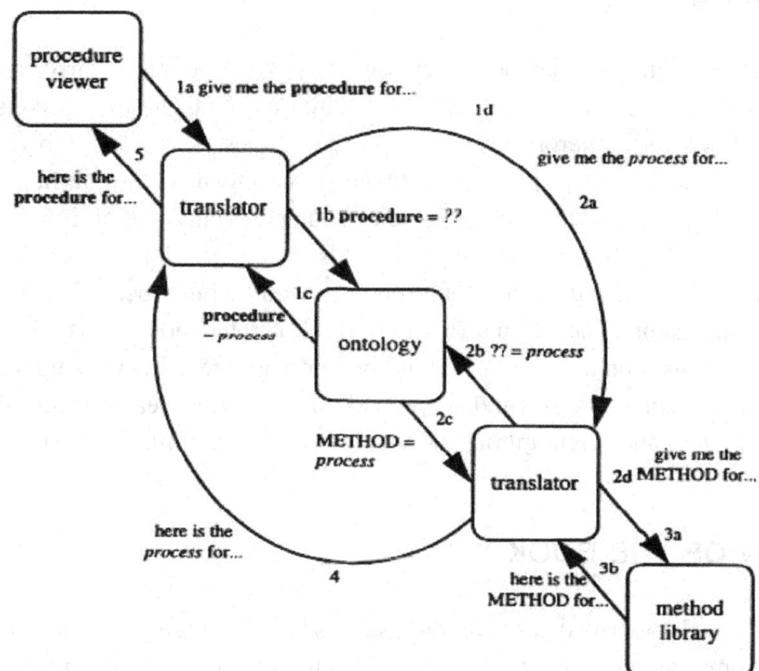

As we can see from that Figure, the presence of an ontology makes it possible for two disparate systems (in this example, a method library and a procedure viewer) to communicate, and ultimately share knowledge albeit they use different vocabularies. This has been the dominant approach in the nineties. It has been applied to some of the long lasting knowledge sharing projects, as well as to a plethora of smaller knowledge sharing tasks. It is effective, once the ontology is up and running, and evidently has a knock-on effect on sharing and design costs (Uschold et.al., 1998). However, it is not efficient: designing the "perfect" ontology that will accommodate all needs is not an easy task. There are irreconcilable arguments among engineers about how and what knowledge should be modelled when trying to build a comprehensive ontology for a given domain. Even when an overcommitted group normally resolves the disputed issues and releases the ontology, there are often inappropriate interpretations of its constructs by users or simply lack of appropriate tools to reason over it.

We also observe changes in the environment and practice of knowledge and ontology engineering: ontologies have transformed from a knowledge representation experiment in the artificial intelligence community in the early nineties, to a mainstream technology that transcends community boundaries and increasingly penetrates the commercial world. Furthermore, the emergence of the Semantic Web, made it possible to publish and access far more ontologies than knowledge engineers ever thought that it would be possible to build! Consequently, ontologies proliferated and made publicly available and accessible by large audiences. This brought forward a number of issues regarding scalability, authoring, deployment, and most importantly: interoperability of ontologies themselves. This is different from having a single, consensual ontology upon which interoperability will be based and engineers have to work out on how their systems will communicate with that ontology. Hence, there is a call for ontology to ontology interoperability, which includes the acknowledged problem of ontology mapping (Kalfoglou & Schorlemmer, 2003).

THE ROAD AHEAD

Semantic interoperability solutions that tackle heterogeneity will continue to thrive and attract interest from a variety of communities. In fact, the diversity of solutions and techniques used is one of the most fascinating factors of semantic interoperability work. Ontologies, Semantic Web techniques, syntax matching algorithms, natural language processing, text engineering, machine learning and standards are all used in one way or another to tackle heterogeneity and enable automation in information systems integration. This book is carefully structured to present this variety of solutions from an engineering and practicing perspective. This also reflects a recent trend in semantic interoperability solutions: a holistic approach that draws on best practices from a variety of fields and technologies is often preferred over a vertical approach that focuses on a specific technology. For example, a heavy weight knowledge engineering approach with formal ontologies and automated inference can greatly benefit from light weight text engineering techniques and serendipitous knowledge acquisition utilizing Web 2.0 practices.

ORGANISATION OF THE BOOK

The book contains 14 well presented cases on the use of semantic interoperability for a variety of applications ranging from manufacturing to tourism, e-commerce, energy Grids' integration, geospatial systems interoperability and automated agents interoperability for web services. The book is split in two main sections; section 1 covers novel concepts for engineering semantic interoperability solutions whereas section 2 focuses on domain specific interoperability solutions.

Novel Concepts for Engineering Semantic Interoperability Solutions

This section introduces novel concepts advocated for engineering semantic interoperability solutions: entity centric design of semantic interoperability solutions; ontological stance as an operational characterisation of the intended models used for enabling interoperability; the role of message structures and semantic mediation; structure preserving semantic matching; unified frameworks for streamlining multiple semantic integration solutions; semantic peer-to-peer design principles; and the role of quality frameworks in the design of semantic interoperability solutions.

In Chapter 1, "*Entity-Centric Semantic Interoperability*", Paolo Bouquet, Heiko Stoermer, Wojcech Barczyński and Stefano Bocconi introduce the concept of entity centric semantic interoperability. The authors distinguish two distinct approaches to semantic interoperability: schema centric and entity centric. The former, is by far the most popular and tackles the problem of heterogeneity by finding alignments and mappings across heterogeneous schemata which are used to structure information. In contrast, the latter focuses on the identification and manipulation of the entities that made up the information space, and it is less investigated. The authors point to issues that hinder interoperability: (a) a proliferation of identifiers is taking place, because the same object is potentially issued with a new identifier in several information systems, therefore, applications need to keep track of a growing amount of identifiers; (b) reference to entities across information systems is very complicated or impossible, because there are no means to know how an entity is identified in another system; (c) injectivity of identifiers is in general not guaranteed, since the same identifier can denote different entities in different information. Bouquet and colleagues argue that for large scale, heterogeneous information systems, entity centric semantic interoperability solutions are better suited due to unprecedented proliferation of uniquely identified entities which do not necessarily adhere to a predefined schema. The authors also elaborate on how entity centric solutions to the semantic heterogeneity problem can support various forms of interoperability without the need to achieve schema level interoperability. The supporting case is drawn from the European Commission funded consortium OKKAM with focus on two applications in the domains of corporate information management and online publishers' information extraction and annotation; the exemplar applications are drawn from SAP and Elsevier, respectively. The authors put the idea of entity centric semantic interoperability into practice using a proposed infrastructure, Entity Name System (ENS), built under the auspices of the OKKAM consortium.

In Chapter 2, "*The Ontological Stance for a Manufacturing Scenario*," Michael Gruninger presents the notion of ontological stance. When software applications communicate with each other, there needs to be some way to ensure that the meaning of what one application accepts as input and output is accurately conveyed to the other application. Since the applications may not use the same terms to mean the same concepts, we need a way for an application to discover what another application means when it communicates. In order for this to happen, every application needs to publicly declare exactly what terms it is using and what these terms mean. This meaning should be encoded in a formal language which enables a given application to use automated reasoning to accurately determine the meaning of other applications' terms. The author argues that in order to achieve complete semantic integration, we need to enable the automated exchange of information between applications in such a way that the intended semantics of the applications' ontologies are preserved by the receiving application. The ontological stance is an operational characterization of the set of intended models for the application's terminology. When the ontological stance methodology is used in conjunction with an interlingua ontology it is possible to axiomatize the implicit ontologies of software applications. Gruninger presents a set of compelling example cases drawn from manufacturing interoperability scenarios: ILOG Scheduler, SAP ERP data model and the process planning software MetCAPP. The interlingua ontology used was the Process Specification Language (PSL). One of the benefits of such an approach is that we can achieve correctness and completeness of the axiomatization with respect to the intended models of the application ontology since the interlingua ontology is verified. The correctness and completeness of the axiomatization with respect to the software application, as well as the correctness and completeness of the semantic mappings, is demonstrated through the use of the ontological stance.

In Chapter 3, "*Use of Semantic Mediation in Manufacturing Supply Chains*," Peter Denno, Edward J. Barkmeyer and Fabian Neuhaus argue for the use of semantic mediation to achieve semantic interoperability. The authors elaborate on the central role that system engineering processes and their formalisation and automation play in facilitating semantic interoperability. Systems engineering is any methodical approach to the synthesis of an entire system that (a) defines views of that system that help elicit and elaborate requirements, and (b) manages the relationship of requirements to performance measures, constraints, risk, components, and discipline-specific system views. The authors continue that providing semantic interoperability solutions can be achieved by reconciling differences of viewpoint that may be present in the system components whose joint work provides a system function. Reconciling differences in viewpoint that are exposed in component interfaces is a systems engineering task. Consequently, Denno and colleagues do not link semantic interoperability to models and truth conditions, but to behaviour or lack of intended behaviour: the absence of semantic interoperability between components is the inability to achieve some joint action of the systems components which is the result of the inability of a component to respond with the intended behaviour if provided by the appropriate message. Thus, the essential form of their solution entails a relation of message structure elements to elements of ontologies. The authors present three exemplar research projects in the domain of semantic mediation.

In Chapter 4, "*Service Integration through Structure-Preserving Semantic Matching*," Fiona McNeill, Paolo Besana, Juan Pane and Fausto Giunchiglia present the structure preserving semantic matching algorithm (SPSM). The domain of application is integration of services. The authors argue that in large, open environments such as the Semantic Web, huge numbers of services are developed by vast numbers of different users. Imposing strict semantics standards in such an environment is useless; fully predicting in advance which services one will interact with is not always possible as services may be temporarily or permanently unreachable, may be updated or may be superseded by better services. In some situations, characterised by unpredictability, the best solution is to enable decisions about which services to interact with to be made on-the-fly. To achieve that, McNeill and colleagues propose a method that uses matching techniques to map the anticipated call to the input that the service is actually expecting. This must be done during run-time, which is achievable with their SPSM algorithm. Their algorithm underpins a purpose built system for service interaction that facilitates on-the-fly interaction between services in an arbitrarily large network without any global achievements or pre-run-time knowledge of who to interact with or how interactions will proceed. Their work is drawn from the European Commission funded consortium OpenKnowledge and the system has been evaluated in an emergency response scenario: a flooding of the river Adige in the Trentino region of Italy.

In Chapter 5, "*Streamlining Semantic Integration Systems,*" Yannis Kalfoglou and Bo Hu argue for the use of a streamlined approach to integrate semantic integration systems. The authors elaborate on the abundance and diversity of semantic integration solutions and how this impairs strict engineering practice and ease of application. The versatile and dynamic nature of these solutions comes at a price: they are not working in sync with each other neither is it easy to align them. Rather, they work as standalone systems often leading to diverse and sometimes incompatible results. Hence, the irony that we might need to address the interoperability issue of tools tackling information interoperability. Kalfoglou and Hu also report on an exemplar case from the field of ontology mapping where systems that used seemingly similar integration algorithms and data, yield different results which are arbitrary formatted and annotated making interpretation and reuse of the results difficult. This makes it difficult to apply semantic integration solutions in a principled manner. The authors argue for a holistic approach to *streamline* and glue together different integration systems and algorithms. This will bring uniformity of results and effective application of the semantic integration solutions. If the proposed streamlining respects design principles of the underlying systems, then the engineers will have maximum configuration power and tune the streamlined systems in order to get uniform and well understood results. The authors propose a framework for building such streamlined system based on engineering principles and an exemplar, purpose built system, CROSI Mapping System (CMS), which targets the problem of ontology mapping.

In Chapter 6, "*Sharing Resources through Ontology Alignments in a Semantic Peer-to-Peer System,*" Jérôme Euzenat, Onyeari Mbanefo and Arun Sharma present an application of peer-to-peer to enable semantic interoperability. The authors point to the bootstrapping problem of the Semantic Web: benefit will emerge when there is enough knowledge available; however, people are not willing to provide knowledge if this will not return immediate benefits. To overcome this problem, Euzenat and colleagues propose a semantic peer-to-peer system in which users can start develop, locally, the annotation scheme that suits them best. Once this is done, then they can offer their resources to their friends and relatives through peer-to-peer sharing. Then using global social interaction infrastructures, like Web 2.0 applications, the body of knowledge can quickly spread, thus overcoming the bootstrapping problem. However, the authors argue that heterogeneity can occur as resources, often described in ontologies, are developed locally and are prone to terminological variations across peers. The remedy to this problem is to use semantic alignment in conjunction with a native peer-to-peer system. The authors describe a working example of this in the context of the PicSter system, an exemplar case for heterogeneous semantic peer-to-peer solution. PicSter is a prototype for ontology bases peer-to-peer picture annotation that allows to users' needs the ontologies used for annotation.

In Chapter 7, "*Quality-Driven, Semantic Information System Integration: The QuaD²-Framework*" Steffen Mencke, Martin Kunz, Dmytro Rud and Reiner Dumke elaborate on the need for a framework for quality driven assembly of entities. The authors argue that although automation is an important aspect of integration solutions, quality must be of substantial interest as it is an inherent characteristic of any product. Mencke and colleagues continue that existing quality related information can be reused to optimize aggregation of entities by taking into account different characteristics like quality attributes, functional requirements or the ability for automated procedures. To this end, the authors propose a quality driven framework for assembly of entities. The QuaD² framework is a first attempt to provide a holistic consideration of quality and functional requirements with a substantial semantic description of all involved elements. This could enable an automated procedure of entity selection and execution on one hand and a substantial support of quality evaluation of involved entities on the other hand. The presented quality driven approach proposes the usage of semantic descriptions for process automation and supports different quality models and quality attribute evaluations. The easy extensibility of process models, entities, interfaces and quality models makes the presented framework deployable for many fields of application. The authors present a comprehensive application case of the QuaD^2 framework in the domain of e-learning.

Domain Specific Semantic Interoperability Practices

This section describes semantic interoperability uses in a variety of domains: medical domain for the annotation of images and management of patient data, standards interoperability with respect to the electrotechnical domain, e-commerce with emphasis on business-to-business transactions, annotation and extraction of Web data, e-tourism with annotation and integration of heterogeneous e-tourism resources, and geospatial information sharing.

In Chapter 8, "*Pillars of Ontology Treatment in the Medical Domain*", Daniel Sonntag, Pinar Wennerberg, Paul Buitelaar and Sonja Zillner elaborate on a case study in the domain of medical image annotation and patient data management. Their work is drawn from a large scale nationally funded project, THESEUS MEDICO. The objective of this large scale collaborative project is to enable seamless integration of medical images and different user applications by providing direct access to image semantics. Semantic image retrieval should provide the basis for help in clinical decision making support and computer aided diagnosis. In particular, clinical care increasingly relies on digitized patient information. There is a growing need to store and organise all patient data, such as health records, laboratory reports and medical images, so that they can be retrieved effectively. At the same time, it is crucial that clinicians have access to a coherent view of these data within their particular diagnosis or treatment context. The authors argue that with traditional applications, users may browse or explore visualized patient data, but little help is given when it comes to the interpretation of what is being displayed. This is due to the fact, the authors continue, that the semantics of the data is not explicitly stated. Sonntag and colleagues elaborate on how this can be overcome by the incorporation of external medical knowledge from ontologies which provide the meaning of the data at hand. The authors present a comprehensive case from the MEDICO project and elaborate on the lessons learnt: that only a combination of knowledge engineering, ontology mediation methods and rules can result in effective and efficient ontology treatment and semantic mediation. They argue that clinician's feedback and willingness to semantically annotate images and mediation rules play a central role.

In Chapter 9, "*A Use Case for Ontology Evolution and Interoperability: The IEC Utility Standards Reference Framework 62357*," Mathias Uslar, Fabian Grüning and Sebastian Rohjans present a case of semantic interoperability in the electricity generation domain with emphasis on the uses and evolution of the International Electrotechnical Commission (IEC) framework 62357. The authors argue that the landscape for electricity delivery has changed a lot in recent times and with the upcoming distributed power generation, a lot of interoperability challenges lie ahead. In particular, deploying new generation facilities like wind power plants or fuel cells, energy is fed into the grid at different voltage levels and by different producers. Therefore, Uslar and colleagues argue, the communication infrastructure has to be changed: the legal unbundling leads to separation of systems, which have to be open to more market participants and this results in more systems that have to be integrated and more data formats for compliance with the market participants. The authors then focus on a key aspect of streamlining integration in this domain, the IEC standards framework, a working practice in today's electricity generation domain.

They introduce a specific methodology, COLIN, whose aim is to overcome problems with adoption of IEC family of standards and the heterogeneity of different providers. COLIN uses mediator ontologies and the CIM OWL ontology as a basic domain and upper ontology. Uslar and colleagues show an example case from integrating the IEC 61970 and IEC 61850 standards family.

In Chapter 10, "*Semantic Synchronization in B2B-Transactions*," Janina Fengel, Heiko Paulheim and Michael Rebstock elaborate on how to provide dynamic semantic synchronisation between business partners using different e-business standards. Their approach is based on ontology mapping with interactive user participation. The need to achieve semantic integration arose from the wish to enable seamless communication through the various business information systems within enterprises and across boundaries. This need is becoming more acute in a business context where a company needs to dynamically work in an ad-hoc fashion with changing partners in a global market. In such an environment, it is time and cost-wise impossible, the authors argue, to provide the ramp-up efforts for predefining each information exchange before being able to conduct a business. So, Fengel and colleagues state that interoperability of the information to be exchanged is required as the basis for focusing on the business instead of concentrating on technological issues. To this end, the authors developed the ORBI (Ontology Based Reconciliation for Business Integration) Ontology Mediator, which is a scalable solution to providing semantic synchronisation. The authors linked this work with a system for partition-based ontology matching. The proposed semantic synchronization approach is used in an example case with the e-business negotiation system, M2N.

In Chapter 11, "*XAR: An Integrated Framework for Semantic Extraction and Annotation*", Naveen Ashish and Sharad Mehrotra present the XAR framework that allows for free text information extraction and semantic annotation. The language underpinning XAR, Ashish and Mehrotra argue, allows for the inclusion of probabilistic reasoning with the rule language, provides higher level predicates capturing text features and relationships, and defines and supports advanced features such as token consumption and stratified negotiation in the rule language and semantics. The XAR framework also allows the incorporation of semantic information as integrity constraints in the extraction and annotation process. The XAR framework aims to fill in a gap, the authors claim, in Web based information extraction systems. XAR provides an extraction and annotation framework by permitting the integrated use of hand-crafted extraction rules, machine-learning based extractors, and semantic information about the particular domain of interest. The XAR system has been deployed in an emergency response scenario with civic agencies in North America and in a scenario with an IT department of a county level community clinic.

In Chapter 12, "*CRUZAR: An Application of Semantic Matchmaking to e-Tourism*," Iván Mínguez, Diego Berrueta and Luis Polo present the CRUZAR system which is used for semantic matchmaking in the e-Tourism domain. CRUZAR is a web application that uses expert knowledge in the form of rules and ontologies and a comprehensive repository of relevant data to build custom routes for each visitor profile. It has been deployed in collaboration with the city council in the Spanish city of Zaragosa. The authors use semantic technologies to integrate and organise data from different sources, to present and transform user profiles and tourism profiles and to capture all the information about the generated routes and their constraints. Since the information sources originate from different providers, a problem of heterogeneity occurs and CRUZAR uses a matchmaking algorithm to merge all the relevant information in a consistent user interface. Minguez and colleagues elaborate on the lessons learnt from using Semantic Web technologies at CRUZAR and their experiences with the pilot application at the city of Zaragosa tourism services.

In Chapter 13, "*Data Integration in the Geospatial Semantic Web*," Patrick Maue and Sven Schade present insight and applications of semantic integration in the domain of geospatial information systems. In particular, the authors elaborate on the heterogeneities that occur with multiple resources of geospatial information and argue that it impairs discovery of new information and decreases the usefulness of geographic information retrieval; a notion that summarizes all the tasks needed to acquire geospatial data from the web using search or catalogue data. Maue and Schade describe their solution which is drawn from the European Commission funded consortium, SWING, and aims to facilitate discovery, evaluation and usage of geographic information on the internet. The authors present an example case from BRGM, the French geological survey which is responsible for the exploration and management of potential quarry sites in France. The authors also present their findings on deploying semantic web technologies to support geospatial decision making.

In Chapter 14, "*An Ontology-Based GeoDatabase Interoperability Platform*," Serge Boucher and Esteban Zimanyi present a platform for interoperating geographical information sources. The authors elaborate on the lessons learnt from deploying a prototype system to tackle interoperability needs between different cartographic systems from the domain of military operations. Boucher and Zimanyi provide an analysis of the issues involved with integrating heterogeneous data silos from a cost-effective perspective and the beneficial role that knowledge representation could play in the field of geographical databases.

REFERENCES

Gruber, T. (1995). Towards principles for the design of ontologies used for knowledge sharing. *International Journal of Human-Computer Studies, 43*, 907-928.

Hendler, J., & De Roure, D. (2004). E-Science: The Grid and the Semantic Web. IEEE Intelligent Systems, 19(1), 65.

Kalfoglou, Y., & Schorlemmer, M. (2003). Ontology mapping: the state of the art. The *Knowledge Engineering Review, 18*(1), 1-30.

Pollock, J. (2002). The Web Services Scandal: How data semantics have been overlooked in integration solutions. *eAI Journal*, 20-23

Schrage, M. (2009, February 5). Interoperability: the great enabler. *Financial Times*. Retrieved from http://www.ft.com/cms/s/0/08794a70-f3be-11dd-9c4b-0000779fd2ac.html

Uschold, M. & Gruninger, M. (1996). Ontologies: principles, methods and applications. *The Knowledge Engineering Review, 11*(2), 93-136.

Uschold, M. & Gruninger, M. (2002). Ontologies and Semantic Integration. *Software agents for the Warfighter, the first in a series of reports sponsored by the US Government Information Technology Assessment Consortium (ITAC)*.

Uschold, M., Healy, M., Williamson, K., Clark, P. & Woods, S. (1998). Ontology reuse and application. In *Proceedings of the 1st International Conference on Formal Ontology in Information Systems* (pp. 179-192). IOS Press.

ENDNOTES

1. message thread on the SUO mailing list initiated at http://suo.ieee.org/email/msg07542.html
2. http://science.house.gov/legislation/leg_highlights_detail.aspx?NewsID=1853
3. http://ec.europa.eu/idabc/en/chapter/3
4. http://www.semic.eu/semic/view/snav/About_SEMIC.xhtml
5. http://www.ft.com/cms/s/0/08794a70-f3be-11dd-9c4b-0000779fd2ac.html

Acknowledgment

The editor would like to acknowledge the help of all involved in the collation and review process of the book, without whose support the project could not have been satisfactorily completed.

Most of the authors of cases included in this book also served as referees for articles written by other authors. Thanks go to all those who provided constructive and comprehensive reviews: Steffen Mencke, Fiona McNeill, Patrick Maue, Peter Denno, Michael Gruninger, Jerome Euzenat, Mathias Uslar, Daniel Sonntag, Janina Fengel, Heiko Stoermer, Serge Boucher and Bo Hu.

Special thanks also go to the publishing team at IGI Global. In particular to Tyler Heath, who continuously prodded via e-mail for keeping the project on schedule and to Nicole Gerhart and Megan Childs for their support in the production of the manuscript.

Special thanks go to Dr. Peter Hart and Professor Dave Robertson who read the final draft of the manuscript and provided helpful suggestions for enhancing its content. Dr. Hart and Professor Robertson also kindly agreed to write insightful forewords for the book.

In closing, I wish to thank all of the authors for their insights and excellent contributions to this book.

Finally, I want to thank my beloved wife, Steph Esther, for her eternal love and wholehearted support throughout this project.

Yannis Kalfoglou
Southampton, UK
April 2009

Section 1
Novel Concepts for Engineering Semantic Interoperability Solutions

Chapter 1
Entity-Centric Semantic Interoperability

Paolo Bouquet
University of Trento, Italy

Heiko Stoermer
University of Trento, Italy

Wojcech Barczyński
SAP AG, Germany

Stefano Bocconi
Elsevier B.V., The Netherlands

EXECUTIVE SUMMARY

This chapter argues that the notion of identity of and reference to entities (objects, individuals, instances) is fundamental in order to achieve semantic interoperability and integration between different sources of knowledge. The first step in order to integrate different information sources about an entity is to recognize that those sources describe the same entity. Unfortunately, different systems that manage information about entities commonly issue different identifiers for these entities. This makes reference to entities across information systems very complicated or impossible, because there are no means to know how an entity is identified in another system. The authors propose a global, public infrastructure, the Entity Name System (ENS), which enables the creation and re-use of identifiers for entities. This a-priori approach enables systems to reference entities with a globally unique identifier, and makes semantic integration a much easier job. The authors illustrate two enterprise use cases which build on this approach: entity-centric publishing, and entity-centric corporate information management, currently being developed by two leading companies in their respective fields.

INTRODUCTION

The use of semantic techniques for interoperability and integration has been gaining momentum for several years, not to a small extent driven by the efforts in the area of the Semantic Web which, since the beginning of the new millenium, has been occupying scientists and practitioners alike to explore methods that originated from traditional AI,

DOI: 10.4018/978-1-60566-894-9.ch001

with the goal of more intelligent and larger-scale information integration.

Substantial efforts have been devoted to effect a similar transition of what the Web achieved with respect to traditional hypertext systems, in the area of semantic representation, integration, and interoperability.

There is however a very important difference between traditional knowledge-based systems and modern approaches that attempt to achieve semantic computing at web scale: the notion of global interlinking of distributed pieces of knowledge.

At the base of such interlinking - and the resulting semantic interoperability of fragments of data - is the notion of identity of and reference to *entities*. Systems that manage information about entities (such as objects or individuals) commonly issue identifiers for these entities, just in the way relational databases may need to issue surrogate keys to uniquely identify records. If these identifiers are generated by the information system itself, several issues arise that hinder interoperability and integration considerably:

- a proliferation of identifiers is taking place, because the same object is potentially issued with a new identifier in several information systems; therefore, applications need to keep track of a growing amount of identifiers;
- reference to entities across information systems is very complicated or impossible, because there are no means to know how an entity is identified in another system;
- injectivity of identifiers is in general not guaranteed, since the same identifier can denote different entities in different information.

To this end, we propose a global, public infrastructure, the Entity Name System (ENS), which fosters the systematic creation and re-use of identifiers for entities. This a priori approach enables systems to reference the entities which they describe with a globally unique identifier, and thus create pieces of information that are semantically prealigned around those entities. Semantic search engines or integration systems will thus be enabled to aggregate information from distributed sources around entities in a precise and correct way. We call this the entity-centric approach to semantic interoperability.

The ENS is currently under creation in a large European Integrated Project (IP) named OKKAM[1]. Part of this project are two enterprise use cases which build on this approach: entity-centric publishing, and entity-centric corporate information management, which are covered by two major companies in their respective fields, and which we are going to describe in detail in this document.

ENTITY-CENTRIC SEMANTIC INTEROPERABILITY

Information systems are full of valuable information about entities[2] which are relevant for the business of an organization. This is evidently true for systems based on structured information (like relational databases), but is also true for much less structured types of data, like email folders, text documents, slide presentations, web portals, forums and discussion lists. Being able to collect information about one of these entities, or about their relations with other entities, is a task which would help in many strategic processes, from knowledge management to decision making. However, as we said in the introduction, modern organizations are so complex that there is no centralized control on how and where information is produced and published. This is true not only within the organizational boundaries, but also across organizations and across networks, including of course the Internet. This is why, much more than in the past, the concepts of data interlinking and semantic integration and interoperability become more and more important, and in some situations a real necessity. On the other hand, in such a distributed and decentralized scenario, different people use different conventions for naming things, and different schemas for structuring information.

In general, information-level interoperability is therefore difficult for two different reasons:

1. on the one hand, information may be heterogeneous at the structural level (for example, the databases of people and projects in the same company may be based on different schemas, and therefore their integration may require a form of *ad hoc* mapping between the two schemas);
2. on the other hand, the same real-world entity may be named in many different ways, including: different primary keys in different databases, variations of their name in natural language, different descriptions, different URIs (Uniform Resource Identifier) in web-oriented information sources (e.g. RDF/OWL knowledge bases).

The first problem, which we call *schema-level heterogeneity*, has been attracting much attention and resources for many years. Indeed, the attempts of addressing this type of heterogeneity have produced a good amount of important research, from schema matching in databases to more recent work on ontology alignment in the Semantic Web. We call this work a *schema-centric* approach to semantic interoperability, as the core idea is that interoperating information across sources presupposes that their respective schemas have been mapped onto each others or onto a global schema used for mediation.

The second problem, which we call *entity-level heterogeneity*, has received much less attention, maybe because people thought this issue should be addressed only after the schema-level integration issue had been solved. It is true that some work has been done in related fields under the headings of *record linkage, object consolidation, data cleansing, de-duplication*, etc., but for sure it does not compare to what has been done in the other area. We call this an *entity-centric* approach to semantic interoperability, as the core idea is that the main aggregators for interoperating information across heterogeneous sources are not primarily schemas, but uniquely identified entities, intuitively corresponding to the "things" which different sources provide information about.

It is quite clear that a complete solution to the problem of semantic interoperability must take into account both issues. That the two approaches need each other is easy to show: if the first problem is solved (i.e. two or more schemas are aligned), then it is still the case that we do not know when two records, for example, refer to the same real world entity; if the second problem is solved, then one can answer queries like "For any table, select any record where the identifier is X" (where "X" is some kind of global key which is used to identify the same entity across any relational table), but it is still the case that we do not know which properties are the same, or comparable, in different records. Arguably, both approaches can benefit from each other: once schemas are mapped onto each other, it can be easier to detect that entities are the same. Conversely, once entities are found to be the same, some relations can be inferred between the schemas they belong to. However, we claim that it makes sense to address the second independently from the first, especially now that the Semantic Web has revamped the popularity of an object-based representation model like the Resource Description Framework (RDF) in which resources (and not schemas) are the main building blocks; and that the entity-centric approach may lead to results which are very interesting *per se*.

A first argument is straightforward: very often, information about an entity is not stored in a structured data source, but in a text, in an email message or in a slide presentation; in this case, there is no schema to be mapped; still, being able to automatically link information about an entity (say, a customer) from all these sources is very valuable, and may enable interesting services. The cases described in the second part of this chapter are just two examples.

A second argument is that weak – but still interesting – forms of semantic interoperability can be achieved even without solving the schema-level problem. Indeed, just having entities uniquely identified across different sources (e.g. relational databases) allows to resolve queries like: "Select * from T_1, ..., T_n where EID=id", which can be read as: select any information you have from any table T_1, ..., T_n where a record is identified with the entity ID "id". This, of course, is not a typical SQL query, and results cannot be arranged into a single table (this would require a global schema and the mappings from each local schema to the global one), but is a request for collecting data which may have a value by itself, and which can anyway be understood by a human agent.

The third and last argument we bring forward is that making sure that an entity is unambiguously recognized wherever it occurs makes a huge economy of scale possible in using background knowledge in large-scale information systems. For example, imagine that we know that two entities E1 and E2 are named in thousands of different documents in a corporate document management system; if we know from a structured source (e.g. an RDF/OWL knowledge base) that the known relationships between the two entities are R1, ..., Rn, then this single piece of information can be used to make inferences across thousands of documents without any unnecessary replication.

Realizing entity-centric semantic interoperability is not easy, and requires appropriate processes and services. Some examples are: methods for detecting any mention of an entity in different types of formats, in different locations of a network and through different applications; methods for assigning entities a unique identifier; methods for recognizing when two entity names or descriptions indeed refer to the same entity (and when it is not the case, though it looks like); methods for annotating different formats of content with entitiy identifiers. All together, this is tantamount to saying that we need some kind of *entity management system* within a network viewed as a collection of potentially interlinked data sources.

In the next part of this chapter, we will present a possible approach to realize entity-centric semantic interoperability in large networks based on a service called *Entity Name System*. We will briefly explain how it works, and then we will show how it has been used in two relevant scenarios within Elsevier and within SAP.

A SOLUTION APPROACH: THE ENTITY NAME SYSTEM (ENS)

Any alignment task for interoperability, in our context the alignment of identifiers for entities described in (semantic) information systems, can either be effected a-priory or ex-post. While schema-level interoperability suffers from several issues that make alignment very hard (and the acceptance of such approaches very low), we argue that in a majority of situations, there is very little potential for disagreement or subtle differences about the identity of *entities*. Take the example of human beings: even though a human being can have many different roles (and thus be categorized differently in different formalizations), there is no doubt that the human being is actually itself, and can unambiguously be identified, e.g. by demonstration (pointing).

In this document, the term "entity" is restricted to refer only to a subclass of resources (or entities in other contexts) which corresponds to individuals, as opposed to entity-types or to abstract concepts. Individuals are sometimes called particulars (formal ontology) or instances (web ontologies). Beyond this restriction, the notion of entity endorsed here is quite liberal, and includes tangible things like people, buildings, cars, mountains, books, etc., as well as non tangible things like organizations, countries, and events. It may also include fictional objects (e.g., Pegasus), objects from the past (e.g., Plato), and abstract objects (e.g., the Goedel Theorem).

We concentrate on entities that have names (named entities), such as authors, proteins and software products. In same cases, named entities can refer to two things at the same time:

- to an individual (e.g. p53_HUMAN is an instance of the class Protein)
- to a class of individuals (e.g. p53_HUMAN is the class of all the existing p53 proteins in human organisms)

Generally speaking, we assign an ID to the individual the name refers to, and not to the class (so to the first case in the above list). This is motivated by the fact that some individuals do not have specific names, and therefore, taking language as a criterion to define what we want to refer to and what we do not, do not need to have global identifiers. Specific individuals can be described in terms of the named entity (e.g. the protein of type p53_HUMAN contained in a particular human organism). In case it is important to refer to a particular individual of a named entity class, that particular individual can get an ID. For example, we assign an ID to the Aston Martin DB5, and not to each instance of that car. An exception can be the Aston Martin DB5 featured in the movie "Goldfinger". The situation is different for other entity types, such as people. Named entities can refer to individuals (e.g. Paolo Bouquet) and not to classes of individuals.

This approach has both a theoretical and a practical justification:

- **Theoretically**, we believe that - at the abstraction level needed for most web applications - individuals can be assigned a name (and therefore an ID) which identifies them in a context-independent way, whereas this is quite tricky for abstract concepts (e.g. there is no single concept which can be assigned as the standard reference for the word "organization").
- **Practically**, this way we fill a gap which is not filled by other ID-based services (e.g. openGUID, WordNet, even Swoogle), which are mainly oriented towards creating identifiers for terminologies and not for data instances.

Following this argumentation, we believe that agreement on the identity of entities is in fact possible for a significant number of situations, and can contribute considerably to semantic interoperability. A consequence is that if two or more information sources are able to agree on the same electronic placeholder (identifier) for the same entity, and thus reach *a priori interoperability* due to the fact that if there is an overlap between their domains of discourse, this will be syntactically evident and can ease alignment or interlinking substantially.

Consequently, we have developed a back-bone infrastructure ENS (the Entity Name System (Bouquet et al. 2008)) which enables information systems to extend their information set with entity references in a structured and re-usable way. This infrastructure can be used in an information creation or enhancement process, to issue the entities that are being described with stable, re-usable and unique identifiers. This situation is very much in line with the "global graph" vision of the Semantic Web, but can equally be applied to relational databases were these identifiers can serve as primary keys, or to web site annotations with Microformats. The obvious benefit is that whatever data source or format is chosen, if two systems contain information about the same entity, then this information can be directly interlinked. This is what we call *entity-centric semantic interoperability*, as illustrated in Figure 1.

The Entity Name System can be imagined as a very large "phone book" for entities, whose sole purpose is to return an identifier for the entity at hand, potentially creating a new entry if the

Figure 1. Entity-centric interoperability across systems and data sources: accessing information in a variety of distributes sources via the entities that the information is about. The same entity (highlighted in yellow) can be interlinked across data sources.

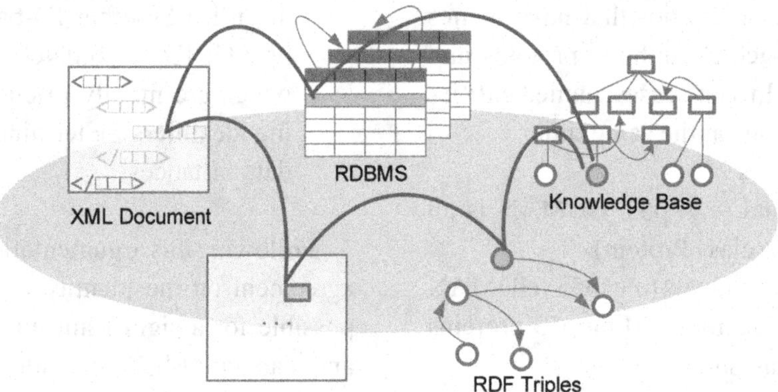

entity had not been added before. This may seem a trivial task at first sight, but bears a number of challenges that have partially been addressed or are ongoing work, and are represented by individual components of the ENS architecture in Figure 2 (see also Bouquet et al. 2008). First, the process of finding out whether an entity already has a record in the system is harder than for example in a traditional database system, because the description of an entity is not following a fixed schema, and search requests are more in the style of information retrieval searches; this is handled by the *matching* component. Secondly, the *lifecycle* of an entity needs to be managed, for example to avoid garbage data and duplicate entries the creation of a new record needs to go through a thorough, automated duplicate and quality check. Thirdly, the scalability of the system is a big challenge, both from the point of view of *storage* size (we are preparing for billions of records), as well as in terms of workload (*core* component), because the system is expected to answer a very large amount of concurrent requests. And finally, secure, trustworthy and privacy-respectful operation of the infrastructure is a complex issue which cannot be neglected, and consequently is addressed on several levels inside the infrastructure, most prominently by the *access management* component.

ENS-enabled applications access the infrastructure through a set of services, which provide for entity search, the retrieval of entity information, and the creation of new entities, as illustrated in Figure 2. This provides for loose coupling with the ENS, and facilitates a situation in which the applications can create content that is annotated with entity identifiers, but remain independent from the ENS. This holds true also for the data themselves: even in the absence of the ENS, the data would still be aligned on entity identifiers, because the Entity Name System is not required for a syntactical alignment that bases on entity identifiers.

In the field of the Semantic Web, a very related effort to the ENS is the Linked Data initiative[3], which describes a recommended best practice for exposing, sharing, and connecting pieces of data, information, and knowledge on the Semantic Web using URIs and RDF. Entity identifier alignment is performed using the construct owl:sameAs, which the OWL reference defines as following: "Such an owl:sameAs statement indicates that two URI references actually refer to the same thing: the individuals have the same 'identity'"[4]. A main difference with the ENS is that the owl:sameAs approach aims at ex post integration between different identifiers, while the ENS supports an a priori agreement on a single identifier, therefore

Figure 2. The ENS architecture and service-oriented use

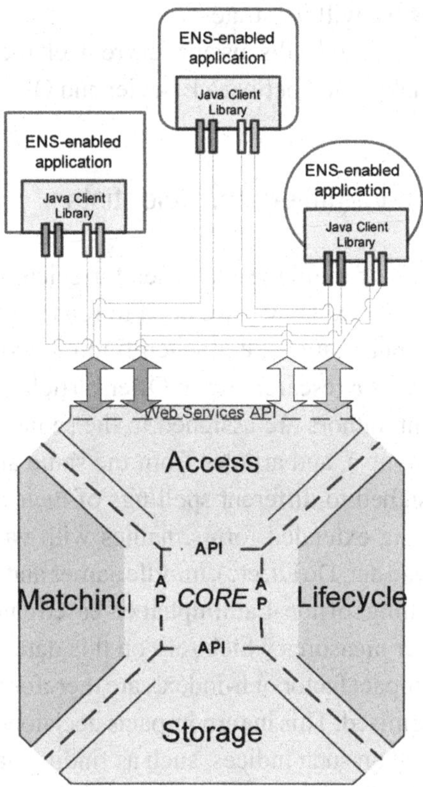

trying to prevent the proliferation of identifiers. Another difference is that the ENS offers a general matching functionality to get from named entities to their ID, while in Linked Data this mechanism depends on the type of entities (e.g. using the email hash in matching FOAF profiles).

One of the key functionalities of the ENS is of course the matching part, which plays a crucial role not only in finding an entity identifier in the system, but also internally to help maintain data quality in the repository by avoiding duplicate or non-distinguishable entries. One aspect that makes the requirements of the ENS quite unique and places possible solutions between methods from Information Retrieval and de-duplication (entity consolidation, merge-purge, …) is the fact what really counts is the top-1 success rate of the system in retrieving one single entity from a large collection (or none if no entry exists), by applying matching techniques that are much related to the ones studied in de-duplication, but on un- or semi-structured data the representation of which is unknown. This is definitely an interesting problem, and not to be underestimated. For this reason, a substantial investment is being made in the course of a large-scale European research project to address exactly these issues on an appropriate scale. The results – and more details that would go beyond the scope of this chapter – can be evaluated in the public deliverables of the OKKAM project[5].

In the following sections we are going to illustrate two application scenarios that benefit clearly from the existence of the ENS, and the resulting possibility of creating entity-centric interoperability.

CASE 1: ENTITY-CENTRIC AUTHORING

Background about the Organization

Elsevier is a multiple media publisher of scientific, technical and medical information, providing the broadest and deepest coverage of health sciences, life sciences, physical sciences and social sciences. Elsevier products and services include journals, books, reference works, textbooks and e-products written and edited by international scholars with outstanding professional credentials in their respective fields.

Setting the Stage

In the following we consider data integration as composed of the following steps:

- univocally assign identifiers to entities such as people (authors) or research objects (proteins)

- annotate all information about a certain entity with its identifier.

Although this can be seen as a very simple form of semantic integration (or even a non-semantic integration at all), having a one-to-one mapping between identifiers and entities is necessary to enable and facilitate other forms of semantic integration, especially in fields such as experimental sciences where entities are the focus, e.g. in biology (Goble, 2006).

In general, when using unique identifiers, the following steps are crucial:

- determining what (new) entities are present in the field, enter them in a database and assign them a unique identifier;
- maintaining the database: check for wrong entries, entries that should be merged together since they refer to the same entities, or split since they refer to different entities;
- annotating every occurrence of the entity in any information source with its identifier.

All tasks are performed as much as possible in an automatic way: entities are either imported from already existing entity databases (such as UniProt[6] for proteins) or inserted automatically by tools that parse natural text sources (such as Wikipedia[7]). Database maintenance is done in an automatic fashion (for example checking for duplicates is performed by similarity algorithms), although this is still subject of research.

We discuss two cases: the first is related to the publishing process, and it therefore concerns Elsevier's core activity, the second is related to one of the scientific communities that Elsevier serves, namely the biologists. For the second case we present an editorial experiment an Elsevier journal has started in order to better integrate literature and information sources, and how the ENS is contributing to this experiment. Both cases have in common the fact that some sort of unique identifiers already exist. Nonetheless, they are not yet providing a satisfactory solution for the reasons we will illustrate.

We conclude discussing current challenges the collaboration between Elsevier and OKKAM is facing.

Unique Identifiers for Scientists

The lack of a unique identifier for scientists is problematic whenever we need to relate authors to their publications, e.g. when finding good reviewers for a research paper. Often, articles from different authors are assigned to the same name (homonymy), and articles from the same author are assigned to different spellings of their name (including extended forms, names with various parts (van der, De La, etc), middle names and various spellings of non-Latin alphabet- based names). All other measures which rely on this data, such as the impact factor or h-index[8], are therefore also compromised. This in turn impacts decisions that are based on such indices, such as finding names of qualified editors or reviewers.

Elsevier has the possibility to use unique identifiers for authors in Scopus[9]. Scopus is Elsevier's abstract and citation database of research literature and it contains also information about authors. Even though Scopus has unique IDs for authors, the records are not extensively checked for duplicates. Scopus tries to let authors check their own data but many authors are reluctant to do so, because of the time and effort involved. Consolidating a database of people is generally hard since it is very difficult for anybody except the author to understand whether a record refers to the same person. Affiliation and spelling can change considerably, especially when translated to English from another language and alphabet.

Trying to establish unique identifiers for scientists on a company-wide scale (i.e. without each journal having to maintain its own database) would in general facilitate editorial tasks. Obsolete information would not be left in the database if an updated record is added for the same person, and publication records would not be related to the same author entry when in fact the authors are more than one. The Scopus IDs are a good starting point to establish unique identifiers but there is the need for a robust mechanism able to detect duplicates and eliminate them.

The Data Integration Problem in Biology

Biology, as well as many other experimental sciences, is experiencing an exponential growth in the amount of data. This data is generated by experiments that occur at a very high pace, such as through high-throughput screening methods. To be of value, this data needs to be stored in such a way as to be easily found by biologists, and so it must be analysed, encoded and stored in a database that can be queried by scientists. In some cases, scientists can directly submit information to a database, but more often the publications that describe the experiment and the data produced need to be analyzed. The analysis must determine whether new entities are defined in the articles, such as new proteins or new interactions between proteins. If new entities are found, they are entered in the relevant database and they get an accession number, i.e. their unique identifiers.

These operations require qualified personnel (i.e. curators), and have a very high cost. As a consequence, a first bottleneck for the availability of data is that there are not enough curators to examine all the data that is produced, and enter it in searchable databases. For example, the ratio between curated publications versus the total number of publications in the field of protein interactions is about 1:4 (Ceol, 2008).

Entering information in the databases is one part of the necessary step to make knowledge accessible, articles also need to be annotated. These annotations link the entities contained in the article to the entries in the databases that describe them. To link an entity it is sufficient to indicate the unique identifier and the database containing it. This operation can be done manually by curators, or automatically by text mining tools.

Having all experimental data encoded in a database would only partially solve the information need of biologists. Knowing an entity's unique identifier would make searching for relevant information in literature very easy, assuming all relevant information would be annotated with each entity's identifier. The problem is that there are more identifiers for the same entity. Therefore, even though a scientist might have the identifier of an entity they are interested in according to a particular database, it is not straightforward to access more information from a different database since the ID is different.

According to Galperin (2008), there are 1078 biological databases. With these numbers, it is hard to believe there is no redundancy of records in those databases. For example, Goble claims there are more than 231 different pathway[10] databases. Since biologists often need to access information for which they are not necessarily specialist, it can sometimes be difficult to find out whether a particular record in a database actually describes the same entity as another record in another database.

To integrate data, records (and therefore identifiers) that refer to the same object need to be matched together. This is of course only one aspect of data integration, namely the syntactical one, but it is a fundamental step to get to a shared understanding of what different pieces of data mean, i.e. the semantic data integration.

Case Description

The OKKAM project by design chose to provide an enabling technology for data integration, and therefore to focus on the syntactic data integration. More specifically, the OKKAM project is relevant in all the areas where there are no unique identifiers for entities yet, or where there are more unique identifiers for the same entities. In the latter, the ENS can provide the infrastructure to resolve alternative identifiers, i.e. to map a particular identifier in a particular database to another identifier in another database.

In fact, the approach chosen by OKKAM is to import, when possible, the entities contained in commonly used databases and to assign them OKKAM identifiers (OKKAMids). The unique identifier of the imported database is then saved as an alternative ID, and it can be used to access the information contained there.

In the domain of scientific publishing, the Scopus database and the DBPL database are the initial candidates for importing entities, matching records when they refer to the same author. In the domain of biology, we imported into the ENS UniProt[11] entries. UniProt is the main, freely accessible protein database.

When inserting an entity into the ENS, the record created must contain enough information to make the matching possible when a client application queries for the ID of that particular entity. Nevertheless, the ENS does not store knowledge, being only a unique ID provider. The information about an entity resides in external information sources. Via the OKKAMid or one of the alternative IDs, the user can access those information sources. For proteins, this can be the UniProt database, as well as the DDBJ[12], the EMBL[13] and the GenBank[14] databases.

To integrate different sources of information, the occurrences of an entity in literature should be annotated with the entity's unique ID. There can be two possible approaches to annotate articles with the entities identifiers:

- at authoring time
- after authoring time

When identifiers for entities started to be available, there was already a considerable amount of published resources. Therefore, most efforts have focused on adding annotations to published articles, i.e. after authoring time. The main technique used is text-mining, where large corpora of text are automatically processed to detect candidate entities for annotations.

Text-miners currently have trouble with detecting "entities" which are not verbally in the text, such as relations between other entities. In fact, relation types (for example interactions between proteins) are well specified in biology and have unique identifiers, but are not always literally present in the text.

To quantify the performance of text miners in biology, the BioCreative[15] challenge has been launched, providing a platform to evaluate several text mining tools. The evaluation included document classification tasks, the identification of biological entities (Name Entity Recognition or NER), and the detection of relationships between those entities. Run for the last time in 2006, the challenge yielded good results for the NER (almost 90% of the entities correctly detected), but far less positive results for the relationship detection (the authors do not mention figures (Leitner, 2008)).

Text-mining tries to guess the authors intentions when they wrote the text. As we can see from the result of the Biocreative challenge, some entities such as protein interactions are very hard to detect. To tackle this problem, the editors of the molecular biology journal FEBS Letters[16] launched their Structured Digital Abstract (SDA) experiment. This consisted in asking the authors of accepted papers for the journal to describe the proteins, their interactions and the method used to discover their interactions in an abstract to be put at the beginning of the paper. The SDA only encodes novel information from the article, mostly new proteins interactions, i.e. the article contribution. Such abstract has a formal structure and each entity is annotated with its unique identifier, together with a link to the database where the entity information is contained. The initial results (Ceol et al, 2008) showed that authors were willing to collaborate (on a test set of 7 articles, 5 authors accepted to try the experiment) and they were able to complete the task without intensive help from the curators (4 out of 5)

Figure 3. The Word plugin – (The Word plugin has been developed by Expert System)

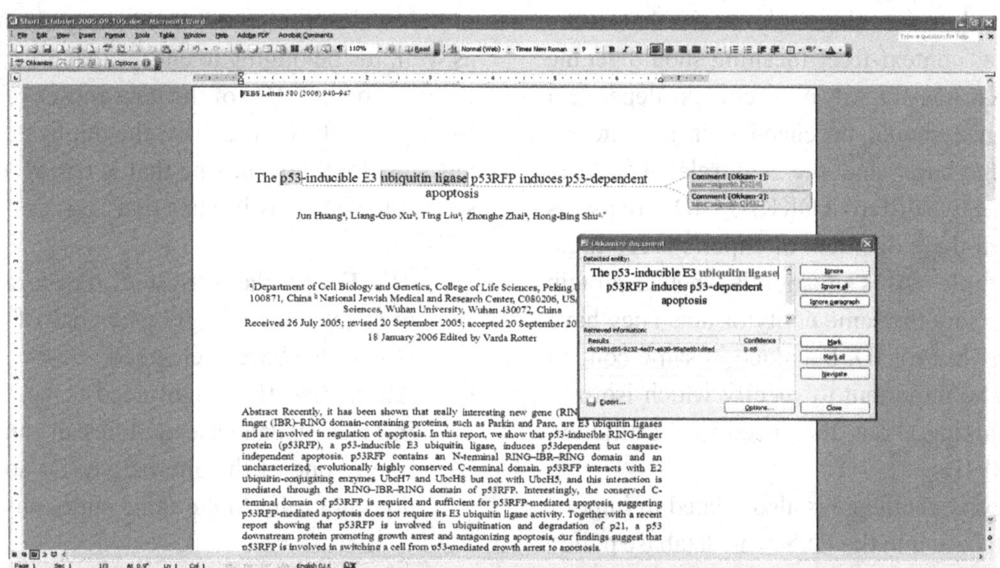

The time spent in annotating is crucial for the adoption of the SDA approach. In order to facilitate the annotation process, the OKKAM project in collaboration with FEBS Letters curators has developed a plugin for Microsoft Word that performs entity recognition (see Figure 3). The plugin parses the file loaded in the editor and highlights the entities (initially only proteins) it finds in a popup window. Once an entity has been detected, the ENS is queried to retrieve the OKKAM-ID or one of its alternative ID (in this case the UniProt ID). In the figure, the ubiquitin ligase protein is found and highlighted. In case there are more candidates, the user is asked to disambiguate the result by choosing one item. A selected word can also be ignored if the user thinks it is not a (relevant) entity. When the user selects "Mark", the plugin inserts a comment containing the UniProt ID of the entity.

Microsoft product screen shot reprinted with permission from Microsoft Corporation.

After this phase, the plugin can generate a section where all found entities are reported together with their identifiers. FEBS Letters authors and curators can use this section as a start to compose the SDA. They still need to check for correctness, but this is usually faster than having to detect each entity in the text.

The identifiers associated to entities in the text allow the user to jump from the article to other sources of information: together with the UniProt ID the ENS can provide all the other alternative IDs, for example the DDBJ, EMBL and GenBank IDs.

In case there are other online information sources annotated with the OKKAM-IDs, the user can also do a search using an entity's OKKAM-IDs on Semantic Search Engine such as Sindice[17], which harvests the Web for semantic relations.

Current Challenges Facing the Organization

The challenges the collaboration between Elsevier and the OKKAM project concern each step described in the Setting the Stage section: inserting entities into the ENS, maintaining the database and annotating the sources.

When inserting entities, a first challenge is to determine when two entities are really the same, or when under some circumstances they can be viewed as the same thing. Only entities that are the same in a "context-free" meaning should get the same OKKAM-ID. Any other context-dependent equivalence should be encoded in an external knowledge-base, and the two related entities should get two different OKKAM-IDs. To assess this, often the judgement of experts is required. One example of this situation is whether protein isoforms[18] are the same entity or not. They have a unique UniProt ID, but since in same context it might be important to specify which isoform we are talking about, they need to get different OKKAM-IDs.

A second challenge is also related to importing a database into the ENS. The database policy should guarantee the fundamental properties of a unique identifier, which are:

- Persistency: the database must not cease to exist and its IDs must not become obsolete
- The database must be checked for errors, especially duplicates, so that there is a one-to-one mapping between entities and identifiers
- Id life cycle management: the same entity must keep the same ID unless it is found to be a duplicate, or it is split in more fine-grained entities. In both cases, the database policy must be clear what concerns old identifiers

Another challenge is therefore to match the policy of the imported database/identifier system with the above-mentioned requirements. For ex. the Scopus database contains duplicates. The ENS is developing strong matching algorithms in order to detect when two entities are the same, and this information can be fed back to the original database (Scopus in this case) in order to correct the records. On the other hand, the Uniprot database is constantly being curated to remove duplicates, split entries that are found to correspond to different proteins, correct information and add new proteins. UniProt has a sort of history mechanism as well. Ids belonging to entries that are split become secondary IDs of the new entries resulting from the split. Analogously, the duplicate that is left gets the ID of the one that is removed as its secondary ID. This implies that:

- The Entity Name System database needs to change accordingly when one of the imported database is changed
- Alternative IDs might need to be revised, in case one database modifies an entry relative to one of the alternative IDs so that it does not refer to the same entity anymore

The highest maintenance cost will probably come from the entries belonging to different databases, since for each import of a new version of one database the ENS will need to be checked to verify that alternative IDs are still valid or that no duplicates has been created.

As we said earlier, this relies on a good matching algorithm. The latter is also needed when annotating sources such as articles. Once an entity in the text is detected client applications, such as the Word plugin, query the ENS to retrieve its unique identifier. The results must have sufficient precision and recall. Too many hits would force the user to examine them all to find the good candidate, whereas a low recall would make the client application (e.g. the Word plugin) useless.

CASE 2: ENTITY-CENTRIC ORGANIZATIONAL IKM

Background about the Organization

SAP has grown to become the world's leading provider of e-business software solutions. With 12 million users, 96.400 installations, and more than 1.500 partners, SAP is the world's largest inter-enterprise software company and the world's third-largest independent software supplier, overall. The goal of SAP solutions is help to enterprises of all sizes around the world to improve customer relationships, enhance partner collaboration and create efficiencies across their supply chains and business operations. SAP employs more than 51.800 people in more than 50 countries.

Setting the Stage

In this global setting, SAP maintains a number of portals, such as SAP Developer Network[19] (SDN), SAP HELP[20], and SAP Marketplace[21] in order to provide technical support and other services to the large community of SAP customers and end-users. Every day, more than one million SDN users access the portals in order to consume and enrich the content of the portals by searching for needed information and contributing to problem-solving discussions. This results in several hundreds of thousands of contributions (e.g., questions, answers, downloads) which are being added to the community on a daily basis. At this stage, the SDN and HELP sources already contain a vast amount of documents which contain problem-solving knowledge (6000 posts per day in SDN forum, 20.000 Wiki pages, and 500.000 help pages).

There is also big amount of unstructured data inside SAP: manuals, corporate wiki, project wikis etc. Almost every day SAP employees share best practices, ideas and hand-on experience in unstructured form. Enterprise Web 2.0 improves performance, shape work, and improve collaboration but it causes that more and more of a company's hand-on know-how becomes unstructured.

There are also many SAP users' communities, such as DSAG[22] and ASUG[23], many technical portals like *ittoolbox.com* or *techtarget.com* and blogs/articles of individual developers. Moreover there are even more data sources talking about SAP Solutions.

As a consequence, there is a huge business potential for SAP to exploit the knowledge readily available in such unstructured sources in order to provide better and faster services to the SAP community. Unfortunately, all this information becomes futile if there is no appropriate support available such that it would enable the users to retrieve the correct answers for their queries. Even in case of SAP there is no semantic integration between portals. The semantic integration means that we know that two sources are talking about the same entity such as *SAP product, error message*, etc. Such integration could help to search for solutions across different data sources to retrieve precise results. Complexity of nowadays programs is growing in general and SAP software is not an exception. Thus having access to aggregated and high quality information is crucial for finding solutions and new usage scenarios.

Our analysis of query logs from SDN shows that existing search infrastructures do not provide sufficient support for the end users. In previous work (Loeser, 2008) we have examined query logs from March 2007 to recognize the most common user intentions behind the queries (Broder, 2002). In parallel we have manually checked the results from two search engines, Google[24] and TREX[25], for the 400 queries extracted from query logs. We have considered as correct results those containing the given strings and that were relevant for the user intention behind the query. For example, if the user commits query 'XI', he expects to get as the result a pointer to the "Exchange Infrastructure". We found out that for 10 most popular queries the correct result did not appear on the first three answer pages (or 30 result links) returned by these two search engines. We have learnt that the recognition (a part of which is entity recognition) of user intention implicitly given with the search query could improve the precision for keyword-based search queries in corporate portals.

We have also examined the forum's content from SDN. In the forum more than one million users contribute each day more than 5000 postings on approximately 60 moderated sub-channels. On a sample of 219.000 postings we measured that in average a user needs to wait nearly one day after the first response (not necessarily a correct one) has been posted as a follow-up. Even worse, for only 27% of the threads such a response will be created by another community member. During manual examination we learnt also that in general users answer question by pointing to resources on the web (e.g. *sap.techtarget.com*) and to other portals maintained by SAP such as SAP HELP and SAP Notes.

In the next step we have investigated the issue of duplicates in SDN forum. Our analysis built on a user study and on interviews with experienced forum administrators shows that it is a serious and worrying problem. It lowers the quality of the search result and causes that users think about the forum as of an unstructured bag for throwing questions, instead of contributing to the creation of an organized and structured source of information. The issue of duplicates shows that many users are neither able nor willing to search for existing solutions. In fact, it is actually estimated that around 50% of the forum questions have already been answered at the time they are posted.

In the next sections, we present our approach that aims to help the users to find relevant answers in a shorter time span by providing them aggregated and high quality content. We realized our approach in our Self-Support Application prototype. It is a proposal of additional forum functionality for SDN that assists the user in obtaining an answer for his question before submitting it to the forum. Such functionality could make a SDN a hub for finding solutions related to SAP Solutions. The Self-Support system uses OKKAM infrastructure (private and public nodes) to integrate different data sources provided by SAP (SAP HELP, SAP NOTES, etc.), SAP community (SDN forum, SDN wiki, SDN blogs etc.) and by third party portals.

Case Description

In this section we present the Self-Support Application prototype. Based on this prototype we explain how the problems mentioned in the previous section have been addressed. We assume that ENS reaches critical mass and the structured data about SAP Products is already OKKAMized.

The prototype application is based on information extraction technology. First we need to pre-processed all available information sources in SDN, such as wiki, forum data and blog, etc. and to recognize entities (e.g. *SAP Products*, *3rd party products*, *error messages*) and relations (e.g. *Error occurs in Product*, *Products are used together*). Information extraction is performed in SAP private OKKAM node which provides OKKAM-IDs for found entities. If we cannot resolve an entity using a private ENS node, we use the public ENS to get relevant OKKAM-ID. As a result of the pre-processing we obtain an index which maintains the relation between the found entities or the relation to the original documents.

The solution we illustrate in this showcase, gives you immediate access to aggregated and

Figure 4. Request for support in natural language

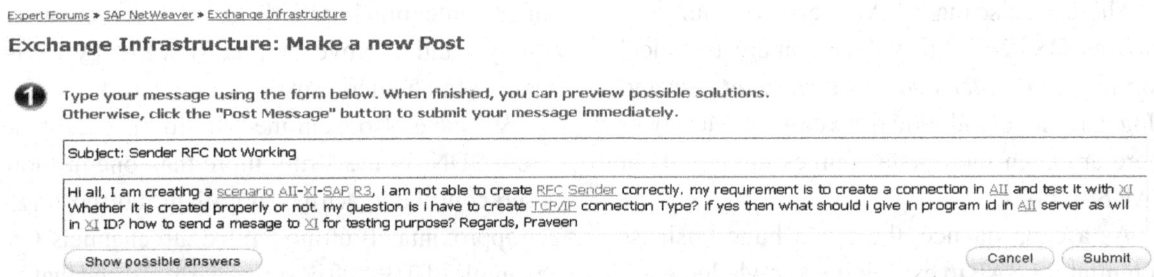

Expert Forums » SAP NetWeaver » Exchange Infrastructure

Exchange Infrastructure: Make a new Post

1 Type your message using the form below. When finished, you can preview possible solutions.
Otherwise, click the "Post Message" button to submit your message immediately.

Subject: Sender RFC Not Working

Hi all, I am creating a scenario AII-XI-SAP R3, i am not able to create RFC Sender correctly. my requirement is to create a connection in AII and test it with XI Whether it is created properly or not. my question is i have to create TCP/IP connection Type? if yes then what should i give in program id in AII server as wll in XI ID? how to send a mesage to XI for testing purpose? Regards, Praveen

Show possible answers | Cancel | Submit

Figure 5. The interpretation of the AII term and OKKAM profile

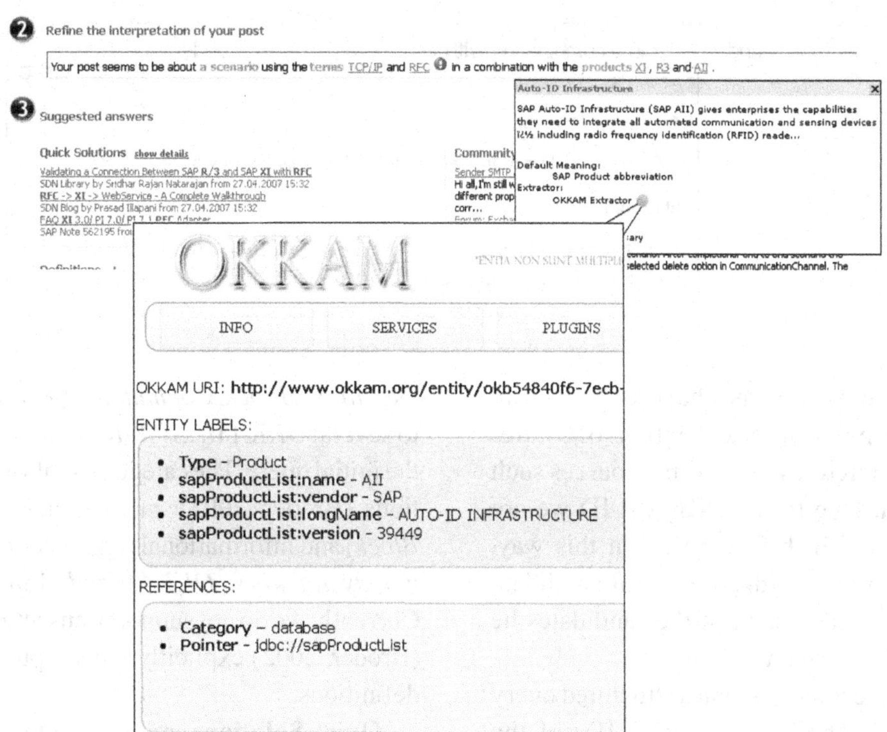

high quality support content. Figure 4 shows an input field similar to the one used in forums to post queries. The developer can simply start by typing a complete request in natural language as if he would like to post it into the experts' forum.

But instead of directly contributing it to the forum, the system is able to understand the request and to directly provide pointers to the content related with the original natural language request (an *interpretation* of the request). This functionality is based, as mentioned before, on the ability to recognize entities, such as SAP components, SAP Products, SAP terminology, error messages, and so on.

Figure 5 shows the interpretation for the *AII*, which stands for the *SAP Auto-Id Infrastructure*. The description of *AII* comes from SAP Terms[26] database. SAP Terms is a taxonomy which contains an SAP components' hierarchy including terms and their variants related to them. This is part of the user feedback mechanism, which is able to help the user to use the proper abbreviations and product names. In this way, we want introduce implicitly and not restrictively a control vocabulary (Raghavan, 2008), similar to approach used in medical databases, where users can use only certain terms understandable by a search engine.

Additionally, a link to the entity profile of the product is provided. The user can connect to an ENS node and retrieve the profile of the product.

In case of ambiguous entities, the system will propose several candidates and the user has the possibility to select the interpretation that fits the best (see Figure 6). This feature is realized by using the matching capabilities of the ENS. Application posts query "RFC" with restriction that one of a profile's references has to point to some page at *wikipedia.com*. User can disambiguate "RFC", in such case the user feedback is captured by the system and it is used to train the algorithms and influence further results.

Figure 6. Multiple Candidates for the ambiguous "RFC" term

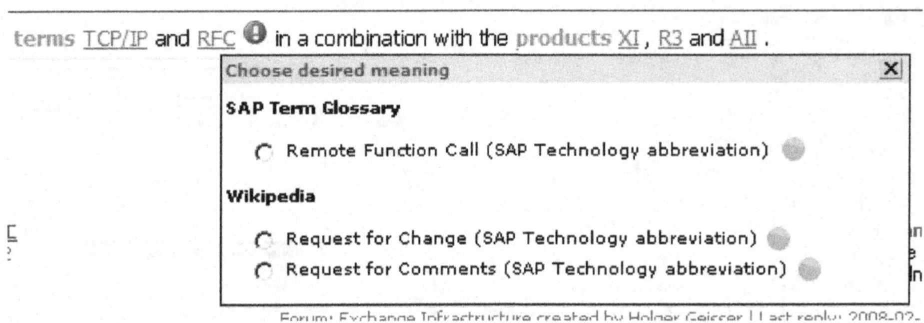

Additionally, the candidates have associated an OKKAM-ID, pointing to descriptions of entities from various OKKAMized Web resources such as Wikipedia. Due to the OKKAM-ID we are able to distinguish these entities. In this way, the user can analyze a disjoint set of candidate profiles and decide which of the candidates he was actually referring to.

Based on the interpretation a structured query is constructed. The query contains IDs of the recognized entities and is run against the pre-processed data sources to get the answers that are to be shown in the third step: *Suggested Answers* (see Figure 7).

Figure 7 shows step three. The result set is divided in several categories: *Quick Solutions*, *Definitions Block*, *Community Answers*, and links to several *OKKAMized Web resources* relevant to the initial query. The categories follow user intentions (Broder, 2002): navigational (*Definitions Block*) and informational (*Quick Solutions*, *Community Answers, OKKAMized Web resources*). Currently we do not support transactional queries (Broder, 2002) explicitly but we put them under definitions.

Quick Solutions area aggregates links to high quality sources, such as Blogs or SAP Notes, pointing to resources that most likely contain the solution of the initial problem. This kind of resources is provided by experts; therefore we expect to get answers which at least point users to relevant materials existing in the SDN.

Figure 7. Suggested answers

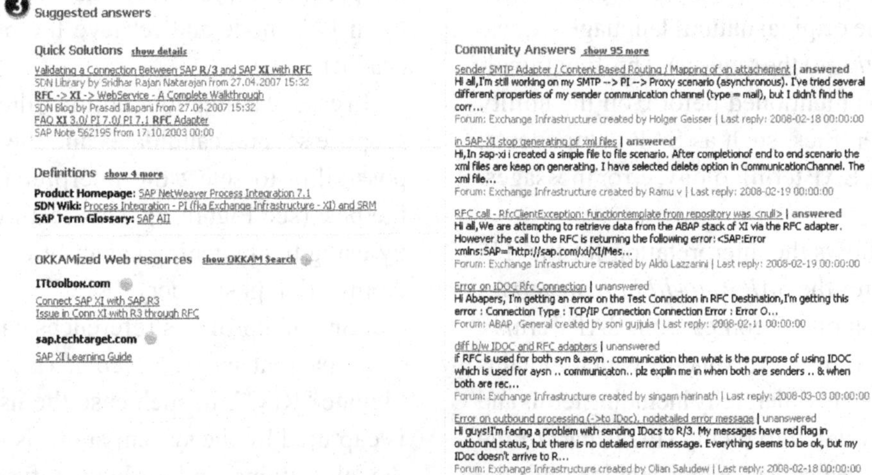

Definitions Block groups several types of hub pages such as homepages of Products, wiki sites, help pages or structured knowledge based like SAP Terms. Sometimes users, especially beginners, ask simple queries which could be answered just by reading materials on the products homepages. There are also users that do not want or do not know how to search for information and just flood the forum with the questions like "What is..." or "What for I need...". The definition block is addressing these kinds of users.

Community Answers are searched based on extracted entities and not only by matching keywords to the full text index of all these information sources. In this fashion, it does not matter whether abbreviations, deprecated terms or orthographical variants of the same entity are used. If one is using "XI" in the natural language question, there are pages shown containing either "Exchange Infrastructure" or "Process Integration". In this way, the result set is very concise. Therefore we expect to get higher precision then classical information retrieval engines. Additionally, we currently work on thread duplicates detection which helps to increase accuracy since the duplicate entries are filtered out and the similar content is grouped together.

OKKAMized Web resources provide reference from third party portals. The main aim of SDN is to build a strong community around SAP solutions, to solve problems and to collect information about where to find them. In this context, OKKAM provides support for integration. Thus we use the search service provided on top of the ENS, to retrieve pages containing the recognized entities (SAP Product: "XI", "R3", "AII") in order to also include the potential answers provided by the third party sources. We use for querying the OKKAMids of the entities and benefit from the high precision of OKKAMid-based search by finding not only simple syntactic matches like "XI", but the actual desired meaning, e.g. SAP Product "XI" as provided by the users through disambiguation.

In the case the user still does not find a satisfactory solution for his problem, he has still the option to post his/her request to the experts' forum and to wait for the appropriate answer.

Current Challenges Facing the Organization

The described scenario in the previous section incorporates several technologies and therefore raises many research questions. The Self-Support Application prototype is still under development and many issues have to be solved before we can introduce it to the end user. We describe the most important directions of work.

Main Challenges

Entity Matching/Recognition. In our approach for extracting SAP Products, we exploit the business terminology SAP Terms for finding software components within the software forums of the SAP Developer Network (SDN). Interpretations of forum postings are derived from mappings between the linguistic representation of a forum post (in terms of the underlying noun groups) and the structured representation of the relevant segment of the terminology (in terms of sub graphs over SAP Terms). Our first investigation of the SDN forums using the conventional dictionary-based approach (with an excerpt of the SAP Terms database containing 888 component names and their abbreviations) led to 36,951 direct Component matches in 120,000 forum entries. This implies that on average only every third forum entry can be linked to a software component. This result clearly indicates the shortcoming of this approach for forums used mainly to discuss software component related issues. In addition, heavy usage of ambiguous acronyms (e.g., "PM" used both as an acronym for "Plant Maintenance" and as a qualifier for a time stamp) limits the precision at one of the dictionary approach to about 11%. On the other hand a full exploitation of structured data can lead to construction of hyper graphs for entity resolution. We target this problem in (Brauer, 2008) but there is still much space for improvement in precision and performance.

Quality of integration based on ENS. Let's consider an integration scenario between two databases from different companies. Data integration has high business value so ENS should provide clear message about consequences and hazards of using it in this scenario. Almost important aspect is a consistency guarantee. Consistency means that every entity that occurs in both data sources gets the same OKKAM-ID (OKKAM-IDs if we retrieve also alternatives). Unfortunately it is not easy to achieve since ENS has to cope with uncertainty on many levels e.g. uncertainly data (entity profile) and matchers with different precision. Therefore, processes to integrate data based on ID-provider, such as ENS, have to be developed. The process should include user's actions, e.g. performing test on sample data and matchers' selection, and usage of other ENS services such as: get alternative OKKAM-IDs.

User/Application feedback handling. As achieving high precision for Information Extraction is not a trivial problem (Feldman, 2006), it is important to be able to collect the user/application's feedback. In the presented scenario we consider user's feedback, which is used in improving results of the prototype and can be sent back to ENS. The UI for explicit user's feedback collection is shown on Figure 5. There is ongoing investigation in SAP on how leverage user's feedback in improving of entity recognition process and entity centric search.

Threads grouping and duplicate detection. We expect that a grouping algorithm will help users to spot the right answers in the search results immediately. Furthermore, contributors will be able to focus on unanswered threads and will be able to create answers of higher quality by searching existing threads. Common methods to detect duplicates on non user-generated content are near-duplication detection approaches, such as (Broder, 2000; Charikar, 2002). These methods are developed for automatic replicated web pages or web pages describing the same entity (e.g., a product) but presented by different agents (e.g., vendors). However, unlike replicated web-pages, forum threads with the same question intention often differ significantly in the syntax and language. That is, in our initial experiments we could observe that these existing metrics result in only a decent precision of ca. 50% and are not directly applicable to forum content. Therefore we work on a new algorithm for detecting thread duplicates.

Future Directions

The OKKAM approach and ideas cannot only be used to improve the information extraction results but everywhere where a global identification system is beneficial. As such, OKKAM-IDs can be associated to all kind of entities, from published entities on the World Wide Web to transactions in business software systems. The benefits are multiple at all levels, from simple search and retrieve operations to more sophisticated queries such as "Which are all the transactions (and their parameters) related to entity A?"

Our future work will focus on the Self-Support scenario to increase the precision of results and performance. We will target precision twofold: we will mine user's feedback and enhance entity recognition process based on structured data. But the very next step is to perform usability test of the prototype on large group of users i.e. SDN members. We have already validated our concepts and prototype based on limited number of use cases (e.g. subset of available channels, selected questions from SDN forum) but comprehensive and methodic evaluation is needed. The goal will be to learn how users interact with the system and find out how presented solution helps them in solving their problems. All collected information will be a base for definition of further tests.

We investigate also scenario Business Intelligence over unstructured data across different data sources. It will be an extension of prototype's back end by analytics functionality. We want to provide user information about a popularity of given problem over time. It would help user to recognize if the problem is new one or it was solved long time before e.g. after release of a service pack. In the Business Intelligence scenario we will examine quality of information aggregation over data integrated by ENS.

CONCLUSION

In this chapter, we argued that there are two approaches to the problem of semantic interoperability and information integration in information systems: the first, by far the most popular, is called *schema-centric* approach and stresses the problem of finding alignments/mappings across schemas which are used to structure information; the second, so far less investigated, is called *entity-centric* approach and stresses the identification and manipulation of the entities which "inhabit" the information space. We also argued why, in our opinion, in large-scale, heterogeneous and decentralized information systems the second approach is very interesting and promising. This claim is also supported by the two applications we described in the chapter, namely the authoring application within Elsevier and the application for information and knowledge management at SAP. In both scenarios, the entity-centric approach enables services which otherwise would have been very difficult.

Before closing the chapter, we want to draw a few general conclusions from our experience:

1. Finding an agreement on a common annotation for single entities in a complex information space is much easier than finding an agreement on a common vocabulary or conceptual schema. Indeed, at the right level of analysis, we can say that an identifier for an entity is almost context-free, namely does not need to change from context to context (for example, the ID used for an author in Elsevier can be the same as the ID used for the same person as a professor in their university, if the two information/knowledge sources are clearly distinguished). The advantage is that, when cross-context interoperability is needed, the same ID can be used as an aggregator of different bodies of information about the same "thing". In general, this is not true for schemas, as people tend to use many implicit assumptions in schemas (see Bonifacio at al., 2002 for a more general discussion of this point from a technical and a managerial standpoint), and therefore it is very unlikely that the same schema (e.g. an ontology) may be re-used for annotating concepts even in two organizational contexts which – from outside – look very similar;
2. The entity-centric approach can be applied also to content which is not based on any schema, e.g. text documents or multimedia assets. Entities occur everywhere, and connecting them is always very useful (even when the connection is very loose). The integration of information stored in structured, semi-structured and unstructured content is something which is not easy to achieve, and the usage of entity identifiers as aggregators is a first step. One of the contributions of this chapter is a vision in which these identifiers are globally unique, both companywide and worldwide. This approach has the potential of triggering a network effect which is not triggered by the use of local identifier in different applications and in different content repositories;
3. The entity-centric approach is very suitable for the creation of tools which may support the annotation of content at authoring time (and not only *ex post*). Having the humans in the loop is always an advantage for quality,

though of course the overhead should not be greater than the expected advantage. The ENS we described in this chapter provides an example of how such a process of entity-aware content creation can be made easy and global.

That an entity-centric approach is a promising direction for the future is also shown by the high number of new initiatives and tools which are based on such a vision. Here we mention only two examples. The first is the Reuter-sponsored tool suite called *OpenCalais* (see http://www.opencalais.com/), which provides APIs and tools for identifying entities in different types of content, for extracting relations between them, and for storing the extracted information in machine-readable form. The second is the German magazine *Der Spiegel* (see http://www.spiegel.de/), which provides additional information and links about entities named in their articles. These two examples show that making use of general information about entities and linking entities (wherever they appear) to such a body of knowledge is very valuable from a business perspective, and seems very suitable for decentralized environments (like the Web, but also like a complex organization) than other (perhaps more sophisticated) approaches which require considerable conceptual work from the content creators.

ACKNOWLEDGMENT

This work is partially supported by the FP7 EU Large-scale Integrating Project "OKKAM – Enabling a Web of Entities" (contract no. ICT-215032). For more details, please visit http://www.okkam.org.

REFERENCES

Bazzanella, B., Bouquet, P., & Stoermer, H. (2009). *A cognitive contribution to entity representation and matching* (Tech. Rep. DISI-09-004). Ingegneria e Scienza dell'Informazione, University of Trento.

Bonifacio, M., Bouquet, P., & Traverso, P. (2002). Enabling distributed knowledge management. Managerial and technological implications. *Informatik/Informatique, 3*(1).

Bouquet, P., Stoermer, H., Niederee, C., & Maña, A. (2008). Entity name system: The backbone of an open and scalable Web of data. In *Proceedings of the IEEE International Conference on Semantic Computing, ICSC 2008, number CSS-ICSC*. Washington, DC: IEEE.

Brauer, F., Schramm, M., Barczyński, W., Loeser, A., & Do, H.-H. (2008). Robust recognition of complex entities in text exploiting enterprise data and NLP-techniques. In *Proceedings of the ICDIM '08*.

Broder, A. (2002). A taxonomy of Web search. *SIGIR Forum, 36*, 3–10. doi:10.1145/792550.792552

Broder, A. Z. (2000). Identifying and filtering near-duplicate documents. In *COM0: Proceedings of the 11th Annual Symposium on Combinatorial Pattern Matching* (pp. 1-10). Berlin, Germany: Springer-Verlag.

Ceol, A., Chatr-Aryamontri, A., Licata, L., & Cesareni, G. (2008). Linking entries in protein interaction database to structured text: The FEBS letters experiment. *FEBS Letters, 582*(8-9), 1171–1177. doi:10.1016/j.febslet.2008.02.071

Charikar, M. S. (2002). Similarity estimation techniques from rounding algorithms. In STOC 02: Proceedings of the thirty-fourth annual ACM symposium on Theory of computing (pp. 380-388). New York: ACM.

Feldman, R. (2006). *Tutorial: Information extraction, theory and practice*. Tutorial presented at the ICML.

Galperin, M. Y. (2008). The molecular biology database collection: 2008 update. *Nucleic Acids Research, 36*, D2–D4. doi:10.1093/nar/gkm1037

Goble, C., & Stevens, R. (2008). State of the nation in data integration for bioinformatics. *Journal of Biomedical Informatics, 41*(5), 687–693. doi:10.1016/j.jbi.2008.01.008

Leitner, F., & Valencia, A. (2008). A text-mining perspective on the requirements for electronically annotated abstracts. The FEBS letters experiment. *FEBS Letters, 582*(8-9), 1178–1181. doi:10.1016/j.febslet.2008.02.072

Loeser, A., Barczyński, W., & Brauer, F. (2008). What's the intention behind your query? A few observations from a large developer community. In *Proceeding of the IRSW*.

Manning, C. D., Raghavan, P., & Schütze, H. (2008). *Introduction to information retrieval*. Cambridge, UK: Cambridge University Press.

Naumann, F. (2002). *Quality-driven query answering for integrated information systems* (LNCS 2261). Berlin, Germany: Springer-Verlag Inc.

ENDNOTES

1 See http://www.okkam.org for more information.

2 By "entity", in this paper we mean objects, individuals, particulars, instances. Examples can be: organizations, projects, people, locations, events. We discuss the concept of entities further in the next section.

3 http://linkeddata.org/

4 The current use of owl:sameAs in the Linked Data community is not always in line with this definition. owl:sameAs is also used as a link to related resources with a much weaker semantics.

5 At the time of this writing, e.g. "D5.2 Integration Prototype OKKAM V1", or "D6.1 Entity Management Fundamentals", to be found at: http://www.okkam.org/deliverables

6 http://www.uniprot.org/

7 http://www.wikipedia.org/

8 The ***h*-index** is an index that quantifies both the actual scientific productivity and the apparent scientific impact of a scientist. The index is based on the set of the scientist's most cited papers and the number of citations that they have received in other people's publications.

9 http://www.scopus.com

10 A pathway is a series of chemical reactions occurring within a cell.

11 http://www.uniprot.org/

12 http://www.ddbj.nig.ac.jp/

13 http://www.ebi.ac.uk/embl/

14 http://www.ncbi.nlm.nih.gov/Genbank/

15 http://biocreative.sourceforge.net/

16 http://www.elsevier.com/wps/find/journaldescription.cws_home/506085/description#description

17 http://sindice.com/

18 A **protein isoform** is any of several different forms of the same protein.

19 http://sdn.sap.com/

20 http://help.sap.com/

21 https://websmp207.sap-ag.de/

22 http://www.dsag.de

23 http://www.asug.com/

24 http://google.com

25 http://help.sap.com/search/sap_trex.jsp

26 http://help.sap.com/content/additional/terminology

Chapter 2
The Ontological Stance for a Manufacturing Scenario

Michael Gruninger
University of Toronto, Canada

EXECUTIVE SUMMARY

The semantic integration of software systems can be supported through a shared understanding of the terminology in their respective ontologies. In practice, however, the author is faced with the additional challenge that few applications have an explicitly axiomatized ontology. To address this challenge, we adopt the Ontological Stance, in which we can model a software application as if it were an inference system with an axiomatized ontology, and use this ontology to predict the set of sentences that the inference system determines to be entailed or satisfiable. This chapter gives an overview of a deployment of the Process Specification Language (PSL) Ontology as the interchange ontology for the semantic integration of three manufacturing software applications currently being used in industry—a process modeller, a process planner, and a scheduler.

MOTIVATION

The necessity for software applications to interoperate has become crucial to the conduct of business and operations in organizations. In practice, however, interoperability is difficult to achieve, since each of these applications utilizes information in a different way, and the knowledge representation formalisms inherent to these applications differ. In particular, existing approaches to interoperability lack an adequate specification of the semantics of the terminology used by the software applications, which leads to inconsistent interpretations and uses of knowledge.

The development of ontologies has been proposed as a key technology to support semantic integration. Ontologies are logical theories that provide a set of terms together with a computer-interpretable specification of the meanings of the terms in some formal logical language. In this way, we can support the semantic integration of software systems through a shared understanding of the terminology in their respective ontologies, in the sense that a semantics-preserving exchange of information between ontologies requires mappings between logically equivalent concepts in each ontology. The challenge of semantic integration is therefore equivalent to the problem of generating such mappings, determining that they are correct, and providing a vehicle for executing the mappings, thus translating terms from one ontology into another. The emphasis in this article will be on the verification of the correctness and completeness of semantic mappings rather than on the specification of the mappings (as in (Giunchiglia et al., 2007), (Kalfoglou & Schorlemmer, 2003)).

In practice, we are faced with the additional challenge that few applications have an explicitly axiomatized ontology. To address this challenge, we adopt the Ontological Stance, in which we can model a software application *as if* it were an inference system with an axiomatized ontology, and use this ontology to predict the set of sentences that the inference system determines to be entailed or satisfiable.

In the first part of this article, we discuss a set of sufficient conditions that a neutral interchange ontology must satisfy in order to support this approach to the generation and validation of semantic mappings. In the second part of the article we give an overview of a deployment of the Process Specification Language (PSL) Ontology as the interchange ontology for the semantic integration of three manufacturing software applications currently being used in industry—a process modeller, a process planner, and a scheduler. The semantic mappings between the applications' ontologies and PSL are semi-automatically generated from invariants (properties of models preserved by isomorphism) and verified prior to integration. The correctness of the application ontologies are validated using the notion of the Ontological Stance.

FORMALIZATION OF SEMANTIC INTEGRATION

When software applications communicate with each other, there needs to be some way to ensure that the meaning of what one application accepts as input and output is accurately conveyed to the other application. Since the applications may not use the same terms to mean the same concepts, we need a way for an application to discover what another application means when it communicates. In order for this to happen, every application needs to publicly declare exactly what terms it is using and what these terms mean; this specification is commonly referred to as the application's *ontology*. Moreover, this specification must be accessible to other software applications. Thus, we require that the meaning be encoded in a formal language, which enables a given application to use automated reasoning to accurately determine the meaning of other applications' terms. For example, if application 1 sends a message to application 2, then along with this message is a pointer to application 1's ontology. Application 2 can look in application 1's ontology to see what the terms mean, the message is successfully communicated and the application's task is successfully performed. Complete understanding will occur between the applications only if they share the semantics of all the terminology used in the content of the messages that they exchange or the information sources that they access.

We can therefore say that two software applications will be interoperable if they share the semantics of the terminology in their corresponding ontologies. Sharing semantics between applications is equivalent to sharing models of their ontologies; two ontologies are equivalent if they have isomorphic sets of models. Nevertheless, applications do not explicitly share the models of their theories; instead, they exchange sentences in such a way that the semantics of the terminology of these sentences is preserved.

Formally, we will say that an ontology T_A is sharable with an ontology T_B if for any sentence Φ_A in the language of T_A, there exists an exchange that maps to a sentence Φ_B such that there is a one-to-one mapping between the set of models of T_A that satisfy Φ_A and the set of models of T_B that satisfy Φ_B. We will say that a theory T_A is interoperable with a theory T_B if any sentence Φ that is provable from T_A, there exists an exchange that maps Φ to a sentence that is provable from T_B. We make the following assumption to restrict our attention to domains in which sharability and interoperability are equivalent.

Interoperability Assumption

We are considering interoperability among software applications that are equivalent to complete first-order inference engines that exchange first-order sentences.

The soundness and completeness of first-order logic guarantees that the theorems of a deductive inference engine are exactly those sentences which are satisfied by all models, and that any truth assignment given by a consistency checker is isomorphic to a model. If we move beyond the expressiveness of first-order logic, we lose completeness, so that, for any deductive inference engine there will be sentences that are entailed by a set of models but which are not provable by that engine. We could therefore have two ontologies that are sharable but not interoperable.

VERIFIED ONTOLOGIES

For applications to completely understand each other, we require that all of the terms that one application uses are completely understood by the other application. From one application's perspective, the actual meaning of the terms is exactly what is specified by the axioms in the other application's ontology. It cannot know what was in the mind of the human who designed the application's ontology. For successful understanding to take place, this *actual* meaning of a term has to be the same as the meaning that was *intended* by the designer of the application's ontology. For convenience instead of the cumbersome phrase: 'the meaning that was *intended* by the designer of the application's ontology', we will simply say 'the intended semantics of the application's ontology'. Thus, to achieve complete semantic integration, we need to enable the automated exchange of information between applications in such a way that the intended semantics of the applications' ontologies are preserved by the receiving application.

The challenge here is to guarantee that the intended semantics of an ontology is equivalent to the actual semantics of the ontology. The actual semantics is defined by the axioms of the ontology in conjunction with the semantics of the ontology representation language. We must therefore explore the ramifications of explicit formally specified semantics and the requirements that this approach imposes on both the ontology designer as well as the application designer. We need to characterize the relationship between the intended semantics of an application's terminology and the actual semantics of the application's ontology that must hold to support complete semantic integration.

An additional problem is that we cannot directly access the intended semantics of an application's terminology. We can however examine the behavior of the application; this is completely dependent on the inferences it makes, which in turn is completely dependent on the semantics of its axioms. In effect, an application's behavior is constrained by the semantics of its ontology, because any inferences made by the application must conform to the semantics of its internal knowledge together with any information acquired by the application from the environment or other applications. If an application does not do the right thing, or retrieve the right information, or make correct inferences, then it does not share its semantics with other applications. So, while we cannot peek inside an application to directly examine its semantics, we can observe what it does, and infer information about the semantics of the application's terminology.

In this operational characterization of semantics, we must make the link between inference and the semantics of the application's ontology. An application's behavior is characterized by the inferences that it makes, that is, the sentences that can be deduced from its knowledge or the sentences that are consistent with its knowledge. Remember that with a formal ontology, the application's knowledge is specified as a theory, so that a sentence is consistent if there exists a model of the theory that satisfies the sentence and that a sentence can be deduced if it is satisfied by all models of the theory. Therefore, the application's behavior (and hence the semantics of the application's terminology) can be characterized by this implicit set of models, which we will call the set of *intended models*.

Given this framework, we can say that two applications completely share semantics if their sets of intended models are equivalent. However, applications cannot exchange the models themselves – they can only exchange sentences in the formal language that they use to represent their knowledge. We must be able to guarantee that the inferences made with sentences exchanged in this way are equivalent to the inferences made with respect to the application's intended models – given some input the application uses these intended models to infer the correct output.

We can use this characterization to evaluate the adequacy of the application's ontology with respect to these intended models. We will say that an ontology is *verified* if and only if the set of models of the axioms of the ontology is equal to the set of intended models for the application's terminology.

Once we have specified the class of structures M and characterized it up to isomorphism, we can formally evaluate an ontology with respect to this specification. In particular, we want to prove two fundamental properties:

- *Satisfiability*: every structure in M is a model of the ontology.
- *Axiomatizability*: every model of the ontology is elementary equivalent to some structure in M.

We only need to show that a model exists in order to demonstrate that a theory is satisfiable, but in the axiomatization of domain theories, we need a complete characterization of the possible models. For example, since we are considering the domain of activities, occurrences, and timepoints, to show that a theory is satisfiable, we need only specify an occurrence of an activity which together with the axioms are satisfied by some structure. The problem with this approach is that we run the risk of having demonstrated satisfiability only for some restricted class of activities. For example, a theory of activities that supports scheduling may be shown to be consistent by constructing a satisfying interpretation, but the interpretation

Figure 1. Methodology for the evaluation of ontologies

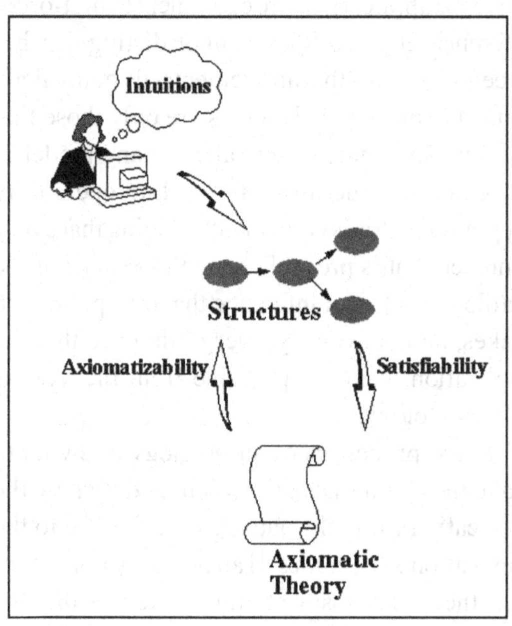

may require that resources cannot be shared by multiple activities or it may require all activities to be deterministic. Although such a model may be adequate for such activities, it would in no way be general enough for our purposes. We want to propose a comprehensive theory of activities, so we need to explicitly characterize the classes of activities, timepoints, objects, and other assumptions that are guaranteed to be satisfied by the specified structures.

Note that we are not imposing the requirement that the ontologies themselves be categorical or even complete. The two applications must simply share the same set of models (up to isomorphism). Ambiguity does not arise from the existence of multiple models for an ontology – it arises because the two applications have nonisomorphic models, that is, the ontology for application A has a model that is not isomorphic to any model for the ontology of application B.

The purpose of the Axiomatizability property is to demonstrate that there do not exist any unintended models of the theory, that is, any models that are not specified in the class of structures. By the Interoperability Hypothesis, we do not need to restrict ourselves to elementary classes of structures when we are axiomatizing an ontology. Since the applications are equivalent to first-order inference engines, they cannot distinguish between structures that are elementarily equivalent. Thus, the unintended models are only those that are not elementarily equivalent to any model in the class of structures. By the Interoperability Hypothesis, this is equivalent to saying that every sentence that is provable from the axioms of the ontology is also an inference that the application makes, and conversely, every inference that the application makes is provable from the axioms of the ontology.

These properties of an ontology allow us to make the claim that any inferences drawn by the application using the ontology are faithful to the application's semantics. If an ontology is not verified, then it is possible to find sentences that the application infers based on its intended models, but which are not provable from the axioms of the ontology. For example, automated inference cannot be used to determine that two applications can in fact be completely semantically integrated. In the next section, we will consider in some detail the challenges that must be addressed in achieving semantic integration with unverified ontologies.

It may seem unreasonable to require that verified ontologies be used for complete semantic integration. Unverified ontologies allow for the existence of unintended models that are a potential source of semantic heterogeneity; the critical question is to determine whether or not they prevent semantic integration in a particular application. One may take heuristic approaches in which the applications only need to match their semantics "well enough" to make "good enough" decisions based on the information exchanged; however, such approaches implicitly assume metrics for integration, and these metrics arise by considering the possibly unintended models that are allowed by unverified ontologies.

Through the Satisfiability and Axiomatizability Theorems, verified ontologies characterize the relationship between the intended models for the ontology and the actual models of the ontology's axiomatization. This does not address the relationship between the intended models and the original intuitions of the user; it is possible that an ontology can be verified yet the intended models do not correspond to models of the user. What is needed is a methodology for validating the ontology.

THE ONTOLOGICAL STANCE

When integrating software applications, we are faced with the additional challenge that almost no application has an explicitly axiomatized ontology. Nevertheless, we can model a software application as if it were an inference system with an axiomatized ontology, and use this ontology to predict the set of sentences that the inference system decides to be satisfiable. This is the Ontological Stance (Gruninger & Menzel, 2003), and is analogous to the intentional stance (Dennet, 87), which is the strategy of interpreting the behavior of an entity by treating it as if it were a rational agent who performs activities in accordance with some set of intentional constraints.

The Ontological Stance is an operational characterization of the set of intended models for the application's terminology. In this sense, it can be treated as a semantic constraint on the application. It does not directly postulate a specific set of axioms, but rather a set of intended models:

Given an application A, there exists a class of models M^A such that any sentence Φ is decided by A to be satisfiable iff there exists M in M^A such that M entails Φ.

The Ontological Stance also addresses the relationship between the intuitions and the intended models; this is, of course, informal, but we can consider the domain intuitions as providing a physical interpretation of the intended models. In this sense, we can adopt an experimental or empirical approach to the evaluation of the class of intended models in which we attempt to falsify these models. If we can find some objects or behaviours within the domain that do not correspond to an intended model, then we have provided a counterexample to the class of model. In response, we can either redefine the scope of the class of models (i.e. we do not include the behaviour within the characterization of the models) or we can modify the definition of the class of models so that they capture the new behaviour.

It is important to realize that the Ontological Stance is not a methodology for specifying semantic mappings between ontologies, nor is it a methodology for designing ontologies for software applications; rather, it is used to evaluate the correctness and completeness of any proposed application ontology.

DOMAIN THEORIES AND ONTOLOGIES

Although we consider semantic integration from the perspective of the relationship between ontologies, we must be careful to distinguish the ontologies from the domain theories that use them. For example, if two software applications both used an ontology for algebraic fields, they would not

Figure 2. We can model a software application as if it were an inference system with a formal ontology, and use this ontology to predict the set of sentences that the inference system decides to be entailed or satisfiable.

Intended Models
INPUT
OUTPUT
"Using the ontology, I can infer the output from the input"

exchange new definitions, but rather they would exchange domain theories that consist of sentences that expressed properties of elements in their models. For algebraic fields, such sentences are equivalent to polynomials. Similarly, the software applications that use a process ontology do not exchange arbitrary sentences, such as new axioms or even conservative definitions, in the language of their ontology. Instead, they exchange process descriptions, which are sentences that are satisfied by particular activities, occurrences, states, or other objects.

An n-type for a theory is a consistent set of formulae (each of which has n free variables) that is satisfied by a model of the theory. Domain theories for an ontology are Boolean combinations of n-types that are realized by some model of the ontology. In the algebra example, polynomials are n-types for elements in an algebraic field. In PSL Ontology (Gruninger, 2003), formulae that specify the constraints under which subactivities of an activity occur are types for complex activities. In the axiomatization of situation calculus in (Reiter, 2001), precondition and effect axioms are types for actions.

This distinction between ontologies and their domain theories has important consequences for semantic integration. Both the inputs and outputs of a software application are axiomatized as domain theories. In the context of the Ontological Stance, we never actually "see" the application ontology, but we can verify that the axiomatization of the inputs and the outputs of the application are the types of elements that are realized in models of the application ontology.

Given a model M, we say that Th(M) is the first-order theory of M, that is, the set of sentences that are entailed by M. A domain theory for an ontology T is a subtheory of Th(M) for some model of T. Using this approach, domain theories can also be considered to be axiomatizations of specific models of an ontology. As a result, we can use the domain theories that are either the inputs or outputs of a software application to represent the intended models that are otherwise implicit.

VALIDATING APPLICATION ONTOLOGIES

If a software application already has an ontology, then the Ontological Stance can be used to evaluate the ontology with respect to the application's intended models. This is distinct from the methodology proposed in the preceding section can be used to evaluate verified ontologies. Even if an application ontology is verified (so that we have a complete characterization of all models of the ontology's axiomatization), the models of the ontology may not be intended models. Using the Ontological Stance, if the models of the application ontology are not equivalent to the intended models, then there are two possibilities.

In the first case, the application ontology is incorrect since the axioms have unintended models. We can formalize this in two ways:

- There exists a model M of the ontology's axioms T that is not an intended model.
- The intended models entail some sentence Φ that is not entailed by the axioms T.

In the second case, the application ontology is incomplete since there are intended models that do not satisfy the axioms. This can also be formalized in two ways

- There exists an intended model M that does not satisfy the axioms of T
- The intended models do not entail the axioms of T.

We consider two alternative formalizations because they each give rise to a different set of techniques for evaluation of the application ontology. We can either search for a model (either an intended model or a model of the axioms) that has certain properties, or we can search for a sentence that is supposed to be entailed by either the intended models or the models of the axioms.

Following the discussion of the preceding section, we can use domain theories to axiomatize specific models of the ontology. Thus, rather than search for models with certain properties, we are actually searching for domain theories with the corresponding properties. In regards to application ontologies, domain theories are equivalent to the possible inputs and outputs of the software application.

The second kind of formalization corresponds to the notion of competency questions (Gruninger & Fox, 1995), which are classes of queries used to characterize the adequacy of an ontology to support a set of tasks, such as decision support, search, or semantic integration. Essentially, the sentences that are entailed by intended models are competency questions for the application ontologies.

The above conditions can also be rephrased in a more positive way by stating analogues of the Satisfiability and Axiomatizability theorems for verified ontologies. We will say that an application ontology is correct iff any sentence that is entailed by the axioms T is also satisfied by all intended models. We will say that an ontology is relatively complete iff any sentence that is satisfied by all intended models is also entailed by the axioms T. We will say that an application ontology is validated if it is both correct and relatively complete with respect to the intended models of the application.

AXIOMATIZING APPLICATION ONTOLOGIES

In cases where the software applications do not have explicit ontologies, existing techniques for generating semantic mappings to achieve integration are not applicable. In addition, current work on semantic mapping addresses the generation of semantic mappings between axiomatized ontologies, but they do not emphasize the evaluation of the correctness of the mappings.

One can, of course, axiomatize the application ontologies before specifying mappings between them. Alternatively, we can use an existing mediating ontology as the basis for the axiomatization for the application ontologies; this approach has the advantage that the axioms in the mediating ontology can also play the role of semantic mappings between the application ontologies.

This raises one seemingly obvious question—what is the terminology whose intended interpretations are being axiomatized? In the methodology of the Ontological Stance, we only focus on the terms that are used in the specification of inputs and outputs; we do not provide axioms for any terms that arise from internal data structures. This technique arises from the demands of semantic interoperability scenarios, in which it is the ambiguity in the sentences exchanged between software applications that cause problems. Communication between software applications consists of their input and outputs, and not their internal data structures.

Translation definitions (Gruninger & Kopena, 2004) were originally proposed to specify the semantic mappings between the mediating ontology and application ontologies. Translation definitions have a special syntactic form—they are biconditionals in which the antecedent is a class in the application ontology and the consequent is a formula that uses only the lexicon of the mediating ontology. We can also use translation definitions as the axiomatization of the intended models of the software application's ontology.

We can axiomatize the intended semantics of the terminology that a software application uses to specify its input and output sentences by writing sentences that are conservative definitions of the terminology. In other words, all of the axioms in the application ontology will have the syntactic form

```
(forall (x1 ... xn)
    (iff (appi x1 ... xn)
        (Φ x1 ... xn)))
```

where app_i is an n-ary relation in the lexicon of the application ontology and Φ is a sentence in the language of the mediating ontology. Such sentences have the same syntactic form as translation definitions.

The generation of axioms through the specification of invariant values for models has been implemented in the PSL project's Twenty Questions mapping tool. By guiding and supporting users in creating translation definitions without requiring them to work directly with first order logic, the Twenty Questions tool provides a semi-automated technique for creating axioms. It also captures the application's set of intended models, since the translation definitions generated by the tool together with the mediating ontology define an explicit axiomatization of the application's previously implicit ontology.

This approach also works in the case where the application ontologies exist but they are not verified; however, it does require that models of the application ontology together with the translation definitions are equivalent to the intended models of the application. In other words, even though there exist unintended models of the application ontology's axioms, if the mediating ontology is powerful enough, then it can be used to augment the application ontology so that it is verified. In this way, the translation definitions eliminate the unintended models of the application ontology.

Axiomatizing the intended models of the application ontologies requires that the mediating ontology be verified. If it is not, then there is no guarantee that the translation definitions are faithfully capturing the intended models of the application ontologies. Thus, even if it is possible in principle to preserve semantics directly between the application ontologies, the translation definitions will fail to guarantee semantic integration, even though it is logically possible.

It is possible that the intended models of the application ontology are definable in the mediating ontology, but the translation definitions are incorrect. In such a case, the translation definitions that axiomatize the application ontologies can be validated using the Ontological Stance. This can be done by demonstrating that the class of models of the application ontology are axiomatized by the mediating ontology together with the translation definitions. To verify this axiomatization of the application ontology, the generated translation definitions may be treated as falsifiable hypotheses and tested empirically. By the Ontological Stance, the application decides some sentence Φ to be provable iff the translation definitions and mediating ontology entails Φ. In this way, it may be evaluated whether or not the attributed ontology correctly predicts inferences made by the software, and consequently whether or not the translation definitions accurately capture the semantics of the application.

One potential problem with this approach is that there may be cases in which the intended models of the application ontology are not definable in the mediating ontology. Intuitively, this is equivalent to the case in which the mediating ontology is not expressive enough to capture all of the concepts in the application ontology.

MANUFACTURING INTEROPERABILITY SCENARIO

In this section, we present the use of an interlingua ontology (the Process Specification Language) for the axiomatization of the ontologies of a set of manufacturing software applications (ILOG Scheduler, SAP ERP data model, and the process planning software MetCAPP). None of the software applications in the scenario had a pre-existing axiomatized ontology. For each of the software applications, we consider a subset of the translation definitions (written using the Common Logic Interchange Format, as specified ISO/IEC

JTC 1/SC 32 (2005) ISO/WD 24707—Common Logic—Framework for a family of logic-based languages) that axiomatize the intended models of the application ontology and discuss how the Ontological Stance was used to evaluate the correctness and completeness of the definitions. This scenario also provides a validation of the PSL Ontology, in the sense that it demonstrates that it is sufficiently strong to specify definable interpretations of the application ontologies.

Semantic Mappings

A semantics-preserving exchange of information means that there are mappings between logically equivalent concepts in each ontology. The challenge of semantic integration is therefore equivalent to the problem of generating such mappings, determining that they are correct, and providing a vehicle for executing the mappings, thus translating terms from one ontology into another.

The approach used in the scenario is known as the Interlingua architecture for semantic mapping. Its distinguishing feature is the existence of a mediating ontology that is independent of the applications' ontologies, and which is used as a neutral interchange ontology (Ciociou et al., 2001). The semantic mappings between application and interlingua ontology are manually generated and verified prior to application interaction time (Schlenof et al., 1999). This process of creating the mapping between the application ontology and the interlingua ontology is identical to the process of creating a mapping directly between two application ontologies. As such, we can consider the application ontologies to be integrated with the interlingua ontology.

This architecture is much more powerful than specifying direct mappings between application ontologies. We only need to specify one mapping for each application ontology, whereas the direct mapping approach requires a semantic mapping for each pair of application ontologies, making the creation and maintenance of mappings becomes unmanageable. The existence of the pre-defined mappings between the application ontologies and the interlingua ontology enables the automatic generation of the point-to-point mapping between the applications' ontologies. If one application's ontology changes, then only one mapping need be affected, rather than one for each application. New applications can subscribe to the community of applications using this interlingua merely by creating a mapping to and from the interlingua. With no changes to their own mappings, all other applications now can translate between their ontology, and the new application's ontology. This was not possible in the manual mapping case because every point to point mapping has to be pre-specified.

Semantic mappings can be expressed as formal definitions or rules between application ontologies and interlingua ontologies. In the interlingua approach, there are two steps in translation: the execution of the mapping from the application ontology to the interlingua, and from the interlingua to the other application's ontology. The translation can be accomplished by applying deduction to the axioms of the interlingua ontology and the formal mapping rules. If these rules have already been verified to preserve semantics between the application and interlingua ontologies, we are guaranteed that translation between the applications also preserves semantics. In effect, a direct mapping rule from one applications ontology to the other applications ontology is inferred from the two separate rules. If run-time translation efficiency is important, then the point to point mapping rules could be cached as explicit rules; otherwise they need only be implicit. When they are implicit, then the otherwise distinct processes of creating and executing a mapping is conflated – it happens at the same time, rather than being two separate steps.

If the application ontologies are axiomatized, then the semantic mappings can be verified by proving that they do indeed preserve the models of the ontologies. If the application ontologies have been axiomatized as definitional extensions of a mediating ontology, then the direct semantic mappings between different application ontologies are sentences that are entailed by the application ontologies.

Process Specification Language

The Process Specification Language (PSL) (Bock & Gruninger, 2005; Gruninger & Menzel, 2003; Schlenoff et al., 1999) has been designed to facilitate correct and complete exchange of process information. The primary purpose of PSL is to enable the semantic interoperability of manufacturing process descriptions between manufacturing engineering and business software applications such as process planning, scheduling, workflow, and project management. Additional applications of PSL include business process design and analysis, the implementation of business processes as web services, and enterprise modelling. PSL has been published as an International Standard (ISO 18629) within the International Organisation of Standardisation. The full set of axioms in the Common Logic Interchange Format is available at http://www.mel.nist.gov/psl/ontology.html.

The PSL Ontology is a modular set of theories in the language of first-order logic. All core theories within the ontology are consistent extensions of a theory referred to as PSL-Core, which introduces the basic ontological commitment to a domain of activities, activity occurrences, timepoints, and objects that participate in activities. Additional core theories capture the basic intuitions for the composition of activities, and the relationship between the occurrence of a complex activity and occurrences of its subactivities.

The PSL Ontology is verified – the models of all core theories within the ontology have been characterized, and the Satisfiability and Axiomatizability theorems have been proven for these theories. A fundamental structure within the models of the axioms of the PSL Ontology is the occurrence tree, whose branches are equivalent to all discrete sequences of occurrences of atomic activities in the domain. The basic structure that characterises occurrences of complex activities within models of the ontology is the activity tree, which is a subtree of the legal occurrence tree that consists of all possible sequences of atomic

Figure 3. Semantic integration using an interlingua ontology. The thin arrows represent manually generated mappings created by the application designers prior to application integration. The thick arrows represent the [possibly implicit] application-to-application mapping that is automatically generated.

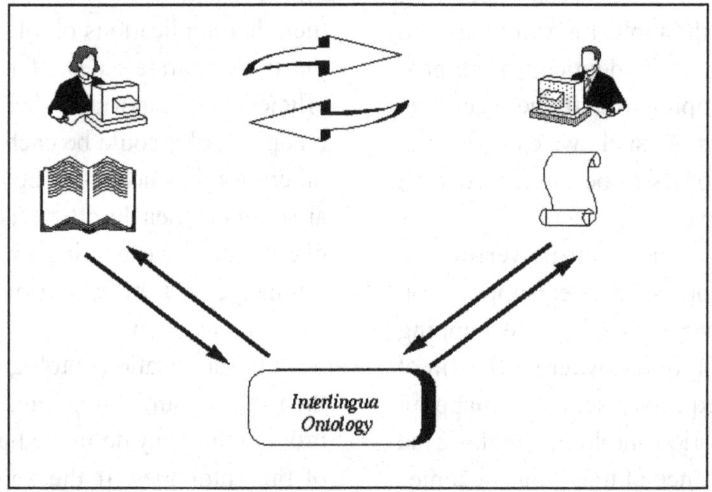

subactivity occurrences; the relation *(root ?s ?a)* denotes that the subactivity occurrence *s* is the root of an activity tree for the activity *a*. Elements of the tree are ordered by the *min_precedes* relation; each branch of an activity tree is a linearly ordered set of occurrences of subactivities of the complex activity. In addition, there is a one-to-one correspondence between occurrences of complex activities and branches of the associated activity trees.

The fundamental intuition in the ontology of process plans is the notion of a partial ordering that is embedded within the activity trees of a complex activity. Different classes of process plans are defined by characterising the relationship between the partial ordering and the set of possible occurrences of a process plan.

Three new relations are introduced to specify the relationship between the partial ordering (referred to as the subactivity occurrence ordering) and the activity tree. The relation *(soo ?s ?a)* denotes that the activity occurrence *s* is an element of the subactivity occurrence ordering for the activity *a*. The relation *(soo_precedes ?s1 ?s2 a)* captures the ordering over the elements.

There are three basic classes of process plans, each of which impose different occurrence constraints on the elements of the partial ordering:

- strong poset activities, in which there is a one-to-one correspondence between branches of the activity tree and the linear extensions of the partial ordering;
- choice poset activities, in which there is a one-to-one correspondence between branches of the activity tree and the maximal chains in the partial ordering;
- complex poset activities, each of which is the union of the strong poset activities corresponding to a set of linear extensions for suborderings of the partial ordering.

Two relations are introduced that allow one to specify whether or not two incomparable elements in the partial ordering correspond to subactivities that occur in any order or whether they are subactivities that never occur on the same branch of the activity tree. The *same_bag* relation is used to specify the sets of subactivity occurrences that are elements of strong poset activity trees that are subtrees of the activity tree. The *alternate* relation is used to specify the sets of subactivity occurrences that can never be elements of the same branch of the activity tree.

The partial ordering in Figure 4(a) has four linear extensions, which correspond to the branches of the strong poset activity tree in Figure 4(c). The partial ordering in Figure 4(a) has four maximal chains, which correspond to the branches of the choice poset activity tree in Figure 4(b). the activity trees in Figure 4(d) and 4(e) are complex poset activities.

ILOG Scheduler

ILOG Scheduler (ILOG 2008) consists of an extensible library of C++ classes and functions that implement scheduling concepts such as activities and resources. The library enables the representation of scheduling problems as a collection of scheduling constraints, such as activity durations, release dates and due dates, precedence constraints, resource availability, and resource sharing. These constraints in turn are used as input for ILOG Solver, which can solve the constraints to provide schedules, in which activities are assigned to resources over different time intervals.

Translation Definitions

There are three main classes within ILOG Scheduler's ontology:

- *IlcActivity*
- *IlcResource*
- *IlcSchedule*

Figure 4. Examples of poset activities in PSL

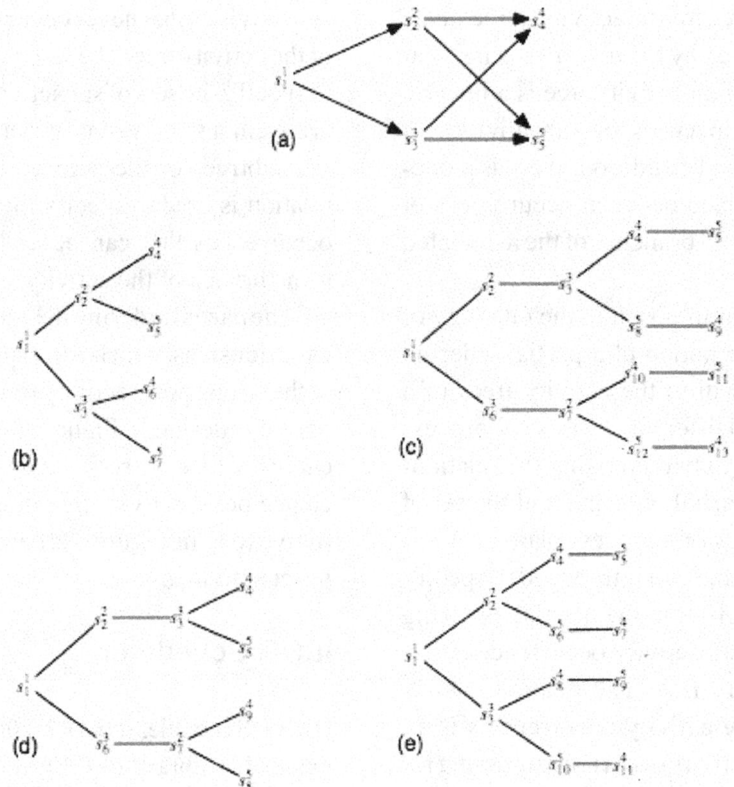

An instance of the class *IlcSchedule* is an object that represents a schedule. Any schedule is associated with a time interval, during which all activities in the schedule must occur.

```
(forall (?a)
  (iff (IlcSschedule ?a)
    (forall (?o)
      (if (occurrence _ of ?o ?a)
        (and (or (permuted ?o)
            (folded ?o))
          (ordered ?o)
          (amorphous ?o)
          (uniform ?o)
          (universal ?o)
          (schedule ?o)
          (strong _ poset ?a))))))
```

(1)

The class *IlcActivity* is the root class for all activities that may occur in a schedule. All activities have a start time and an end time; the duration of an activity is the difference between these times.

```
(forall (?a)
  (if (iff (nondet _ res _ activity ?a)
      (primitive ?a))
    (iff (ilcActivity ?a)
      (activity ?a))))
```

(2)

ILOG Scheduler provides two predefined classes of activities: *IlcIntervalActivity* and

IlcBreakableActivity. An instance of *IlcIntervalActivity* is an activity which occurs without interruption from its start time to its end time and which requires the same resources throughout its occurrence. An instance of *IlcBreakableActivity* is an activity whose occurrence can be interrupted.

```
(forall (?a)
  (iff (ilcIntervalActivity ?a)
    (uninterruptable ?a)))
                                                  (3)

(forall (?a)
  (iff (ilcBreakableActivity ?a)
    (interruptable ?a)))
                                                  (4)

(forall (?occ1 ?occ2)
  (iff (getSchedule ?occ1 ?occ2)
    (subactivity_occurrence ?occ1
?occ2)))
                                                  (5)
```

Activities within a schedule satisfy precedence constraints, which are used to define orderings over the occurrences of the activities. The translation definitions for the complete set of precedence constraints defined in ILOG Scheduler is shown below:

```
(forall (?occ1 ?occ2 ?d ?a)
  (iff (endsAfterEnd ?occ1 ?occ2 ?d ?a)
    (exists (?s1 ?s2)
      (and (leaf_occ ?s1 ?occ1)
      (leaf_occ ?s2 ?occ2)
      (soo_precedes ?s2 ?s1 ?a)
      (= ?d (delay ?s1 ?s2))))))
                                                  (6)

(forall (?occ1 ?occ2 ?d ?a)
  (iff (endsAfterStart ?occ1 ?occ2 ?d ?a)
    (exists (?s1 ?s2)
      (and (leaf_occ ?s1 ?occ1)
      (root_occ ?s2 ?occ2)
      (soo_precedes ?s2 ?s1 ?a)
      (= ?d (delay ?s1 ?s2))))))
                                                  (7)

(forall (?occ1 ?occ2 ?d ?a)
  (iff (startsAfterEnd ?occ1 ?occ2 ?d ?a)
    (exists (?s1 ?s2)
      (and (root_occ ?s1 ?occ1)
      (leaf_occ ?s2 ?occ2)
      (soo_precedes ?s2 ?s1 ?a)
      (= ?d (delay ?s1 ?s2))))))
                                                  (8)

(forall (?occ1 ?occ2 ?d ?a)
  (iff (startsAfterStart ?occ1 ?occ2 ?d
?a)
    (exists (?s1 ?s2)
      (and (root_occ ?s1 ?occ1)
      (root_occ ?s2 ?occ2)
      (soo_precedes ?s2 ?s1 ?a)
      (= ?d (delay ?s1 ?s2))))))
                                                  (9)

(forall (?occ1 ?occ2 ?a)
  (iff (endsAtEnd ?occ1 ?occ2 ?a)
    (exists (?s)
      (and (leaf_occ ?s ?occ1)
      (leaf_occ ?s ?occ2)
      (soo ?s ?a)))))
                                                  (10)

(forall (?occ1 ?occ2 ?a)
  (iff (endsAtStart ?occ1 ?occ2 ?a)
    (exists (?s)
      (and (leaf_occ ?s ?occ1)
      (root_occ ?s ?occ2)
      (soo ?s ?a)))))
                                                  (11)

(forall (?occ1 ?occ2 ?a)
  (iff (startsAtStart ?occ1 ?occ2 ?a)
```

```
    (exists (?s)
      (and (root _ occ ?s ?occ1)
        (root _ occ ?s ?occ2)
        (soo ?s ?a)))))
                                          (12)
```

```
(forall (?occ1 ?occ2 ?a)
  (iff (startsAtEnd ?occ1 ?occ2 ?a)
    (exists (?s)
      (and (root _ occ ?s ?occ1)
        (leaf _ occ ?s ?occ2)
        (soo ?s ?a)))))
                                          (13)
```

Domain theories for the ILOG Scheduler Ontology consist of conjunctive formulae consisting of precedence constraints that use the above eight relations.

Validation of Translation Definitions

The reasoning problem associated with ILOG Schedule is schedule existence: an executable schedule is the output of the software application iff the following sentence is consistent with the application ontology and the domain theory that axiomatizes the input to the software application:

$$\exists o, a \ IlcSchedule(a) \wedge occurrence\_of\ (o, a)$$

The first attempt at providing translation definitions between ILOG Schedule and the PSL Ontology was described in (Ciociou et al., 2001). Through the methodology of the Ontological Stance, however, these definitions have been shown to be incorrect. In particular, the translation definitions did not capture the correspondence between possible schedules and branches of the activity trees that satisfied the precedence constraints; as a result, none of the domain theories were consistent, even though schedules were generated by ILOG Scheduler.

It is also instructive to see how a slight modification of the above translation definitions would also be incorrect. For example, consider the following:

```
(forall (?occ1 ?occ2 ?d ?a)
  (iff (startsAfterStart ?occ1 ?occ2 ?d
?a)
    (exists (?s1 ?s2)
      (and (root _ occ ?s1 ?occ1)
        (root _ occ ?s2 ?occ2)
        (soo _ precedes ?s2 ?s1 ?a)))))
```

This sentence is incorrect, since there exist models of domain theories using this precedence relation that are not schedules produced by ILOG Schedule, namely, those in which the subactivity occurrences do not satisfy the delay constraint.

The final translation definitions were tested by the generation of random sets of precedence constraints. By the Ontological Stance, ILOG Schedule produces a schedule for these constraints iff the corresponding domain theories for the ontology are consistent; furthermore, there should be a one-to-one correspondence between solutions of the precedence constraints and branches in the activity trees that are axiomatized by the domain theories.

It should be emphasized that the experiments with random precedence constraints are used to evaluate the translation definitions; they are not used to generate the translation definitions. In general, the methodology for generating translation definitions requires more sophisticated techniques to elicit the sentences that are satisfied by intended models of the application ontology.

SAP Flow Models

SAP ERP (SAP 2008)is an enterprise resource planning solution that among many other capabilities can be used to design manufacturing processes and manage manufacturing operations. In this context the SAP ERP system can be viewed as the central repository for manufacturing process information. Production orders in the ERP system are used to represent the enterprise's demand on manufacturing operations to deliver a certain quantity of a specific product to be available by a give date and time.

Translation Definitions

The central construct in the SAP application ontology is the SAP production order. A production order can contain multiple "sequences" of operations. The sequences can be of three types: simple sequence, alternate sequence or parallel sequence. A simple sequence is a linearly ordered sequence of operations (see Figure 5(b)). Each production order has a main simple sequence called the standard sequence; branching off from the standard sequence can be parallel or alternate sequences. Each parallel or alternate sequence consists of a simple sequence, and it also has start and end branch points to indicate the subsequence of the standard sequence with which it is parallel or alternate (see Figure 5(b) and Figure 5(c)). Parallel sequences occur in parallel with the corresponding standard subsequence, but alternate sequences, if they are chosen for execution, will occur instead of the corresponding subsequence of the main sequence.

```
(forall (?a)
  (iff (production_order ?a)
    (or (simple_sequence ?a)
      (parallel_sequence ?a)
      (alternate_sequence ?a))))
```
(14)

Any activity tree for a *simple_sequence* process plan consists of a unique branch. None of the operations within a sequence overlap, there is no iteration, and all activity trees have the same structure.

```
(forall (?a)
  (iff (simple_sequence ?a)
    (forall (?o)
        (if (occurrence_of ?o ?a)
          (and (simple ?o)
          (rigid ?o)
          (ordered ?o)
          (amorphous ?o)
          (uniform ?o)
          (universal ?o)
          (unrestricted ?o)
          (strong_poset ?a))))))
```
(15)

Any activity tree for a *parallel_sequence* process plan consists of branches that are combinations of occurrences of the operations within a set of sequence process plans.

```
(forall (?a)
  (iff (parallel_sequence ?a)
    (forall (?o)
        (if (occurrence_of ?o ?a)
          (and (permuted ?o)
            (rigid ?o)
            (ordered ?o)
            (amorphous ?o)
            (uniform ?o)
            (universal ?o)
            (unrestricted ?o)
            (strong_poset ?a))))))
```
(16)

Any activity tree for an *alternate_sequence* process plan consists of a set of branches, each of which corresponds to the activity tree for a sequence process plan.

```
(forall (?a)
  (iff (alternate_sequence ?a)
    (forall (?o)
      (if (occurrence_of ?o ?a)
        (and (simple ?o)
          (rigid ?o)
          (nondet_ordered ?o)
          (amorphous ?o)
          (uniform ?o)
          (universal ?o)
```

```
        (unrestricted ?o)
        (choice _ poset ?a))))))
```
(17)

Domain theories for this application ontology consist of formulae that specify the branch points between different sequences within the production order. Two relations are used to specify these domain theories – *next_op* (which is the ordering relation among elements of the same sequence) and *branch_point* (which is the ordering relation between elements of different sequences).

```
(forall (?o1 ?o2 ?a)
  (iff (next _ op ?o1 ?o2 ?a)
    (exists (?a1)
      (and (subactivity ?a1 ?a)
        (simple _ sequence ?a1)
        (soo _ precedes ?o1 ?o2 ?a1)
        (soo _ precedes ?o1 ?o2 ?a))))
```
(18)

```
(forall (?o1 ?o2 ?a)
  (iff (branch _ point ?o1 ?o2 ?a)
    (exists (?a1 ?a2)
      (and (subactivity ?a1 ?a)
        (subactivity ?a2 ?a)
        (simple _ sequence ?a1)
        (simple _ sequence ?a2)
        (not (= ?a1 ?a2))
        (soo ?o1 ?a1)
        (root _ soo ?o2 ?a2)
        (soo _ precedes ?o1 ?o2 ?a)))))
```
(19)

Validation of Translation Definitions

The reasoning problem associated with the SAP Ontology is executability – a production order in the software application is executable iff the following sentence is consistent with the application ontology and the domain theory for the production order P:

$$\exists o\ occurrence\_of(o, P)$$

Since the class of production orders is axiomatized by a class of poset activities in the PSL Ontology, production orders in experiments were generated by the construction of random comparability graphs (which are a class of graphs that correspond to partial orderings). The initial set of translation definitions was found to be incorrect, since the production orders are actually restricted classes of poset activities. In particular, the second activity occurrence argument in the *branch_point* relation must be the initial element of the corresponding simple sequence subactivity. This error led to domain theories that did not correspond to production plans, that is, domain theories for which the above sentence is consistent, yet which the software application determined to be unexecutable.

MetCAPP

MetCapp™ (MetCAPP 1994) is a computer-aided process planning system that generates process plans, given a set of workstations, machines, setups, routing sequences, and generic part feature data. A machining capability database provides automated capabilities of cutting tools selection, speed and feed calculations, processing time estimation, and operation sequencing. In this article we are primarily be concerned with the operation sequencing concepts.

Translation Definitions

A *routing* in MetCAPP is a resource path whose underlying topology is a complex poset.

```
(forall (?a)
  (iff (routing ?a)
    (and (resource _ path ?a)
    (complex _ poset ?a))))
```
(20)

An *operation* is an activity that satisfies the following conditions:

- An operation is the superposition of a processor activity and a setup activity for the unique possibly reusable resource of the processor activity.
- All subactivities of the processor activity require the same possibly reusable resource.
- An operation is also a resource path composed of feature activities, with the topology of a strong poset activity.

```
(forall (?a1)
  (iff (operation ?a1)
    (exists (?a2 ?a3 ?a4 ?r)
      (subactivity ?a3 ?a1)
      (subactivity ?a1 ?a2)
      (processor _ activity ?a3)
      (possibly _ reusable ?r ?a3)
      (subactivity ?a4 ?a1)
      (setup _ activity ?a4 ?r)
      (resource _ path ?a3)
      (strong _ poset ?a3)
      (routing ?a2)
      (forall (?a5 ?r2)
        (if (and (subactivity ?a5 ?a3)
              (processor _ activity ?a5)
              (possibly _ reusable ?r2 ?a5))
            (= ?r2 ?r))))))
```

(21)

The *next_operation* relation is the coo_precedes relation of complex posets restricted to the operation subactivities of a routing.

```
(forall (?occ1 ?occ2 ?a)
  (iff (next _ operation ?occ1 ?occ2 ?a)
    (exists (?s1 ?s2 ?a1 ?a2)
      (and (coo _ precedes ?occ1 ?occ2 ?a)
        (routing ?a)
        (operation ?a1)
        (operation ?a2))))
```

(22)

The *concurrent_operation* relation is the same_bag relation for complex posets, restricted to the operation subactivities of a routing.

```
(forall (?occ1 ?occ2 ?a)
  (iff (concurrent _ operation ?occ1 ?occ2
?a)
    (exists (?s1 ?s2 ?a1 ?a2)
      (and (coo _ parallel ?occ1 ?occ2 ?a)
        (routing ?a)
        (operation ?a1)
        (operation ?a2))))
```

(23)

An *alternate* activity is a choice poset activity composed of operations.

```
(forall (?occ1 ?occ2 ?a)
  (iff (alternate _ operation ?occ1 ?occ2
?a)
    (exists (?s1 ?s2 ?a1 ?a2)
      (and (coo _ alternate ?occ1 ?occ2
?a)
          (routing ?a)
          (operation ?a1)
          (operation ?a2))))
```

(24)

Domain theories for this ontology specify routings, and consist of conjunctive sentences using the above three relations.

Validation of Translation Definitions

The reasoning problem associated with MetCAPP is equivalent to the consistency of the existence of an occurrence of a routing consisting of a set of operations:

As with the SAP application ontology, routings in MetCAPP are axiomatized by poset activities, so that experiments to verify the translation defini-

tions can be designed by randomly generating comparability graphs, which can then be translated into partially ordered sets.

Generation of Semantic Mappings

Using the above axiomatizations of the application ontologies, we can use the PSL Ontology to generate direct semantic mappings between the application ontologies. Since all translation definitions are sentences in PSL, we can entail sentences that characterize the relationships between concepts in the different application ontologies. In this section, we present some of the sentences that are entailed by the translation definitions in the scenario described above.

First, we can show that process plans in MetCAPP can be exported to SAP by showing that the following sentences are entailed by the translation definitions. Note that the sentences have the special property that the antecedent is a relation in the MetCAPP ontology, while all of the relations in the consequent in each formula are in the SAP ontology.

```
(forall (?a)
  (if (routing ?a)
    (or (simple_sequence ?a)
      (parallel_sequence ?a)
      (alternate_sequence ?a))))
                                        (25)
```

```
(forall (?a)
  (if (operation ?a)
    (or (simple_sequence ?a)
      (parallel_sequence ?a))))
                                        (26)
```

```
(forall (?occ1 ?occ2 ?a)
  (iff (next_operation ?occ1 ?occ2 ?a)
    (next_op ?occ1 ?occ2 ?a)))
                                        (27)
```

We can also show that the process plans in the SAP ontology can be exported to ILOG Schedule:

```
(forall (?occ1 ?occ2 ?a)
  (if (next_op ?occ1 ?occ2 ?a)
    (exists (?d)
      (startsAfterEnd ?occ1 ?occ2 ?d
?a))))
                                        (28)
```

```
(forall (?occ1 ?occ2 ?a)
  (if (next_op ?occ1 ?occ2 ?a)
    (exists (?d)
      (or (endsAfterEnd ?occ1 ?occ2 ?d ?a)
        (endsAfterStart ?occ1 ?occ2 ?d ?a)
        (startsAfterEnd ?occ1 ?occ2 ?d ?a)
        (startsAfterStart ?occ1 ?occ2 ?d ?a)
        (endsAtEnd ?occ1 ?occ2 ?d ?a)
        (endsAtStart ?occ1 ?occ2 ?d ?a)
        (startsAtStart ?occ1 ?occ2 ?d ?a)
        (startsAtEnd ?occ1 ?occ2 ?d
?a)))))
                                        (29)
```

In general, not all SAP process plans can be mapped to MetCAPP routings, and not all ILOG activities can be mapped to SAP process plans. The precise relationships between these classes of processes is still an open problem.

LIMITATIONS

At the beginning of this article, we introduced the Interoperability Hypothesis, by which we are considering interoperability among complete first-order inference engines that exchange first-order sentences. There are, of course, many knowledge-based systems that use nonmonotonic reasoning (such as logic programming) rather than first-order entailment. The Ontological Stance must be extended in order to work with such software applications. The primary problem in this case is that the semantics of logic programming systems requires second-order logic to fully characterize the intended models, whereas we restrict ourselves to first-order logic because it is sound and complete.

SUMMARY

One approach to the semantic integration of software applications is through the generation of semantics-preserving mappings between their respective ontologies. In practice, this approach does not succeed due to several problems – the applications do not have explicit ontologies, or if they do, then the ontologies are often incomplete, and the existence of unintended models prevents the specification of semantic mappings. Furthermore, there has been little work done to validate the proposed semantic mappings.

In this article, we have addressed these challenges by using an interlingua ontology and the methodology of the Ontological Stance to axiomatize the implicit ontologies of software applications. The correctness and completeness of the axiomatization with respect to the intended models of the application ontology is achieved since the interlingua ontology is verified. The correctness and completeness of the axiomatization with respect to the software application, as well as the correctness and completeness of the semantic mappings, is demonstrated through the use of the Ontological Stance -- any sentence that is satisfiable or entailed by the axiomatization and semantic mappings must be a possible output of the software application.

GLOSSARY

- *Axiomatizes*: A set of sentences in a logical language axiomatizes a class of structures iff every model of the sentences is in the class of structures and every structure in the class satisfies the set of sentences. A class of structures is axiomatizable in a language L iff there exists a set of sentences in L that axiomatizes the class.
- *Completeness* (of a logic): A representation is complete if for any sentence S and theory T, if S is satisfied by all models of T, then S is provable from T by some inference procedure. Equivalently, a representation is complete if for any sentence S and theory T, if S is consistent with T then there exists a model of T that satisfies S.
- *Definitional extension*: A theory T1 is a definitional extension of a theory T2 if all sentences in T1 are biconditionals that define the terms in the lexicon of T1.
- *Elementary equivalence*: Two interpretations are elementary equivalent iff they satisfy the same set of first-order sentences.
- *Entailment*: A theory T entails a sentence S iff S is satisfied by all models of T. A set of models entails a sentence S iff it is satisfied by all of the models in the set.
- *Interpretation*: An interpretation M of a first-order language L consists of the following:
    - a nonempty set D, called the domain of the interpretation;
    - for each constant symbol in L, the assignment of an element in D;
    - for each n-ary function symbol in L, the assignment of a mapping from D^n to D;
    - for each n-ary predicate symbol in L, the assignment of a truth value to sets of elements in D^n.
- *Lexicon*: The set of relation, function, and constant symbols in the terminology of an ontology.
- *Model:* An interpretation M is a model for a theory T if the truth value for each sentence in T with respect to M is true.
- *Satisfiable*: A theory T is satisfiable if there exists a model for T.

- *Soundness* (of a logic): A representation is sound if for any sentence S and theory T, if S is provable from T by some inference procedure, then S is satisfied by all models of T. Equivalently, a representation is sound if for any sentence S and theory T, if there exists a model of T that satisfies S, then S is consistent with T.

REFERENCES

Bock, C., & Gruninger, M. (2004). *PSL: A semantic domain for flow models, Software and Systems Modeling.*

Ciocoiu, M., Gruninger, M., & Nau, D. (2001). Ontologies for integrating engineering applications. *Journal of Computing and Information Science in Engineering, 1*, 45–60. doi:10.1115/1.1344878

Dennet, D. C. (1987). *The Intentional Stance*. Cambridge, MA, The MIT Press.

Giunchiglia, F., Yatskevich, M., & McNeill, F. (2007). Structure preserving semantic matching. In *Proceedings of the ISWC+ASWC International workshop on Ontology Matching (OM)* (pp. 13–24).

Gruninger, M. (2003). Ontology of the Process Specification Language. In S. Staab (Ed.), *Handbook of Ontologies and Information Systems (pp. 599-618).* Berlin: Springer-Verlag.

Gruninger, M., & Fox, M. S. (1995). Methodology for the Design and Evaluation of Ontologies. *Workshop on Basic Ontological Issues in Knowledge Sharing.* IJCAI-95, Montreal.

Gruninger, M., & Kopena, J. (2004). Semantic Integration through Invariants. *AI Magazine, 26*, 11–20.

Gruninger, M., & Menzel, C. (2003). Process Specification Language: Principles and Applications. *AI Magazine, 24*, 63–74.

Kalfoglou, Y., & Schorlemmer, M. (2003). Ontology Mapping: The State of the Art. *The Knowledge Engineering Review, 18*(1), 1–31. doi:10.1017/S0269888903000651

MetCapp Utilities Manual. (1994). *The Institute of Advanced Manufacturing Sciences.* Cincinnati, Ohio. SAP Library. Retrieved on November 17, 2008 from http://help.sap.com/saphelp_erp60_sp/helpdata/en/e1/8e51341a06084de10000009b38f83b/frameset.htm

Scheduler, I. L. O. G. 6.3 Reference Manual, ILOG, Inc. (2008).

Schlenoff, C., Gruninger, M., & Ciocoiu, M. (1999, December). The essence of the Process Specification Language. *Transactions of the Society for Computer Simulation, 16*(4), 204–216.

This work was previously published in the Journal of Cases on Information Technology, Vol. 11, Issue 4, edited by M. Khosrow-Pour, pp. 1-25, copyright 2009 by IGI Publishing (an imprint of IGI Global).

Chapter 3
Use of Semantic Mediation in Manufacturing Supply Chains

Peter Denno
National Institute of Standards and Technology, USA

Edward J. Barkmeyer
National Institute of Standards and Technology, USA

Fabian Neuhaus
National Institute of Standards and Technology, USA

EXECUTIVE SUMMARY

This chapter discusses lessons learned about enabling interoperability using semantic methods in three automotive industry projects spanning 8 years. In these projects the authors attempt to automate systems integration tasks typically performed manually. The essential form of the solution is to define ontologies of (1) the joint action of the required business process, (2) business domain objects from the viewpoints of the components playing roles in the process, and (3) the engineered interfaces through which the interaction occurs. The authors then use these ontologies, in semi-automated processes, to generate mediators that translate message content to the form required by message recipients. They discuss briefly how these methods suggest the need for a more methodical and rigorous systems engineering practice and semantically richer, computationally accessible exchange and interface standards.

INTRODUCTION

This chapter reports on our experience investigating issues of semantic interoperability through three related research projects. The common thread throughout our work is the central role that system engineering processes and their formalization and automation play in facilitating semantic interoperability. *Systems engineering* is any methodical approach to the synthesis of an entire system that (1) defines views of that system that help elicit and elaborate requirements, and (2) manages the relationship of requirements to performance measures, constraints, risk, components, and discipline-specific system views. The projects described in this chapter automate tasks traditionally performed by human systems engineers. Our perspective is that today's service-oriented architectures, tomorrow's semantic web, and other efforts in interoperability seek to do the same. In these efforts, the task to be

DOI: 10.4018/978-1-60566-894-9.ch003

automated determines the knowledge that needs to be formally represented. Qualities of that representation and the soundness of the process that automates the task will determine the characteristics of the solutions produced. Among these characteristics, confidence in the assessments of risk, and performance of the solution produced, stand out as key issues in determining the solution's effectiveness in a given problem space. The search for a new paradigm in systems integration is a search for an approach that provides a good return on the cost of producing the formal representation that enables the automation.

The three projects discussed in this chapter focus on providing semantic interoperability by reconciling differences of viewpoint that may be present in the system components whose joint work provides a system function. Reconciling differences in viewpoint that are exposed in component interfaces is a systems engineering task. Though the three projects differ with respect to the nature of the solutions that they deliver, they share important aspects of design.[1]

BACKGROUND

System components *interoperate* when they act jointly for the purpose of achieving a shared goal. Their joint work is coordinated through their communication with each other. This is as true for wholly mechanical systems as it is for information systems and agencies with human components. With respect to information systems particularly,

Figure 1. A message prompts a behavior, but the relationship between the message and behavior is hidden from the sender

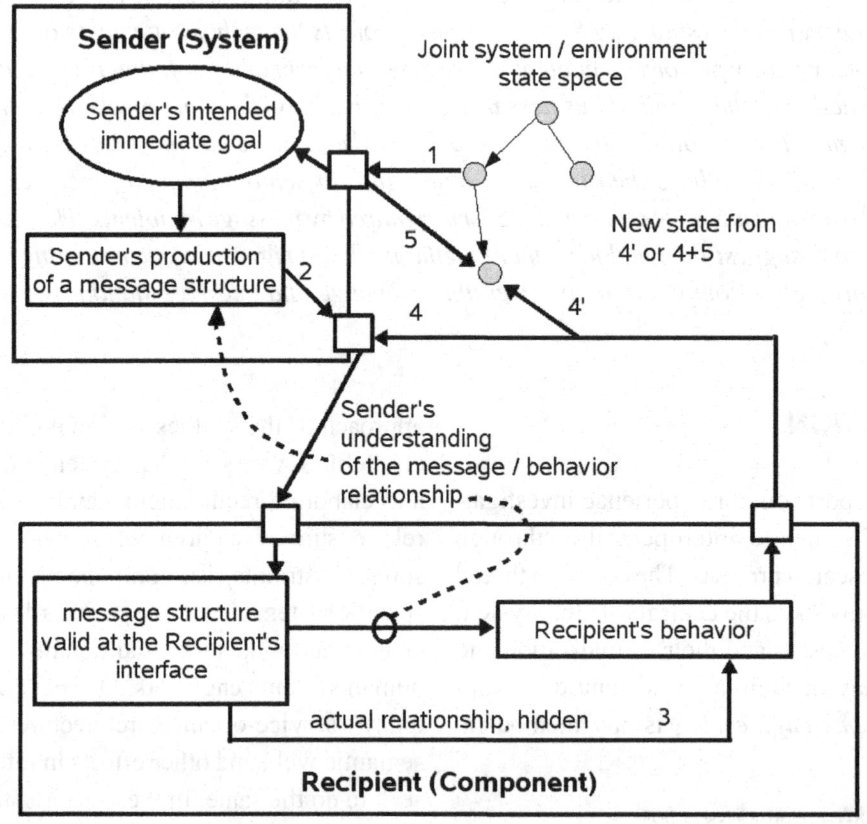

the communication is a message, which is the bearer of information that is necessary for the component to fulfill its role in the system.

The requirements conceived for a component are not necessarily a subset of the system requirements. The component may have been designed for use with another system, or without foreknowledge of the systems with which it might interact. What is necessary is only that when provided with an appropriate message, the component must respond with a behavior that serves the intended system requirement. Whereas system interoperability is the ability to do the joint work generally, *semantic interoperability* concerns what is meant by "intended" and "appropriate" here. (See *Figure 1.*) Semantic interoperability concerns the relationship between the intended immediate goal of the sender and its understanding of how it might elicit the response it requires from the component. The message is tailored by the sender based on its immediate goal and its understanding of this relationship.

Semantic interoperability then, is not a form of interoperability, but rather a term that brings attention to a failure mode of interoperability – one in which intended consequences are not achieved due to a misinterpretation of a message/behavior relationship.

The trichotomy of syntax, semantics, and pragmatics can be introduced in different ways. One that is widely accepted identifies the semantics of a sentence with its truth-conditions, which can be formally specified with the help of a model theory. Hence, the meaning of a sentence (or an axiomatic theory) is identified with the set of models that satisfy the sentence (axiomatic theory). This is the notion of "semantics" which is fundamental to the approach presented by Michael Gruninger in another chapter of this book. He embraces the Ontological Stance and models software applications as if they were axiomatic theories; thus the notion of semantic interoperability between two software applications is analyzed in his view in terms of constraints on satisfying models.

In contrast, we do not link semantic interoperability to models and truth conditions, but to behavior or, to be more specific, lack of intended behavior: the absence of semantic interoperability between system components has been defined above as the inability to achieve some joint action of the system's components, which is itself the result of the inability of a component to respond with the intended behavior when provided with the appropriate message. Within linguistics, the study of how speakers intend to bring about reactions of their listeners is part of pragmatics. Hence one could argue that we are not concerned with "semantic interoperability" but "pragmatic interoperability." However, we decided to follow the liberal use of the term "semantics" that seems to be prevalent in the literature

A purely semantic view of communication would relate structures (message structures) to structures (implemented in the component). The view depicted in *Figure 1* relates message structures to behaviors, and therefore admits a broader set of concerns and is more directly relevant to the goal of system integration. Relating message to behaviors enables recognition of quality of service issues, for example, that the response is timely and accurate to a degree defined by a requirement. Indeed, quality of service requirements may be included in what is communicated to the message recipient. Secondly, message/behavior relationships are a special case of stimulus/response relationships, the building blocks of every engineering endeavor. Aspects of behaviors recognized as sufficing particular system requirements are harnessed through stimulus/response (or message/behavior) relationships to serve system goals. It is the recognition of the sufficiency, inconsequentiality, and antagonism of behaviors that motivates the engineer's choice of design.

Messages are intended to elicit behaviors. As important as is understanding what must be included in the message is understanding what need not. To someone unfamiliar with the workings of a system, the content of its communications may appear starkly insufficient for the purpose of coordinating joint work. For example, an information system supporting a manufacturing supply chain may issue an order fulfillment request message containing little more than an order reference number, industrial code terms identifying the parties involved, and a list of part numbers and their quantities. The message might omit, for example, details describing the transport of the goods. This is possible because messages are not the sole source of information enabling the system to function. Messages serve to trigger a system function and to identify the individuals that are to participate in an occurrence of a process. But the pattern of activity that is the process, and the properties associated with the types of the individuals can be encoded into system components and elsewhere.

To the reader familiar with Service Oriented Architecture (SOA), a casual reading of the above paragraph, its mention of stark message content and static process definitions, may appear antagonistic to SOA's goals – that it entails opaque and idiosyncratic interfaces that are costly to establish and to evolve as requirements change. This is not the case. SOA and other methods that seek to mechanize semantic interoperability operate by exposing information about supported services and protocols to an infrastructure that can use it to dynamically build system solutions. In the problem space that SOA addresses, this information is sufficient. For other classes of problems, other systems integration knowledge may be more pertinent. For example, there may be a need to consider the "risk profile" for the composition of services (a plan) performing some high-level task. Knowledge of the risk of the plan, assessed in its social context, would determine the system solution's viability. In other classes of problems, ontology matching and meditation, or traceability and accountability to high-level goals might be critical. What SOA and these other examples share is that they select among the totality of systems engineering concerns those that are to be mechanized in their infrastructure. Characteristics such as stark message content and static process definitions are entailments of some selection, and might be completely appropriate for the problem at hand. In those cases, concerns not mechanized in the run-time infrastructure can be addressed outside it, using semi-automated tools, to perform systems integration. Business process modeling, when used by a human system integrator, is an example of this.

To automate tasks of systems integration, it is necessary to know what these tasks are. Unfortunately, what we might call the "systems integration body of knowledge" is relatively unexplored terrain. It encompasses some of the software engineering body of knowledge (SWEBOK) (IEEE, 2004) and some of the systems engineering body of knowledge (SEBOK) (INCOSE, 2009) and some elements not part of either of these.

Integration and Mediation

An integration problem can be stated as a requirement to provide an improved business result from a set of existing systems. The existing systems may be viewed as components of a new system that will provide new functions. (We use the term *component systems* to refer to these throughout the chapter.) Each component system contributes through interfaces it exposes to the new system. These interfaces are communication endpoints. Integration is the activity of enabling communication among the components so that they may coordinate their behaviors to perform *joint actions* that achieve the improved business result.

To enable the desired communication between the endpoints where differences in message syntax or interpretation exist, the engineer can either (1) generate the appropriate translators of the relevant messages between the two tools using the interfaces they already support, or (2) adapt existing interfaces or provide new interfaces to support the required communications directly. The former is analogous to the **mediator** design pattern of object-oriented programming (Gamma et al., 1995) and the latter to its **adapter** design pattern. However, our focus is on the general system organization for communication, and not object-oriented programming.

In practice, the choice of a mediator design versus an adapter design may be based on pragmatic logistical concerns of deployment in the environment in which the system will operate. If the components that must interoperate are numerous and loosely federated, as they are in, for example, supply chain logistics, an adapter design using agreed-upon messages may be preferred. On the other hand, if the components that must interoperate are few, there is little opportunity for modification of the interface, nor a desire to collaborate, a mediator design may be more appropriate.

The first project described in this chapter uses a mediator design, the second an adapter design based on a mediator architecture, and the third an adapter design. Nonetheless, the process by which the integration is achieved, and the information on which the mediation relies, remains substantially the same across the designs. In the following section we discuss the process from the viewpoint of a mediator design without loss of generality. The difference is primarily in where the reconciliation occurs.

Enabling Communication

In *Figure 2*, Tool A and Tool B represent existing systems that can contribute to a new business process by some joint action. Each exposes interfaces for communication, in the form of sharable files, application program interfaces (APIs) or middleware interfaces, such as webservices. A human engineer applies systems engineering techniques to obtain the improved business result. The systems engineer reasons from the desired business result to determine the behavior the new system must yield – the joint action the two systems are to perform. From knowledge of the required system behavior and the interfaces they expose, the system engineer determines the required communications between Tool A and Tool B.

Ideally, Tool A and Tool B were designed to support the target joint action and both were implemented to support that action using a common interface and identical interpretations of the interface elements. When that is the case, the systems engineer need only create the connection between them. In many cases, however, the two systems implement incompatible interfaces or interpret a common standard in differing ways, so that simply connecting them will not produce the joint action.

Figure 2. A high-level view of integration

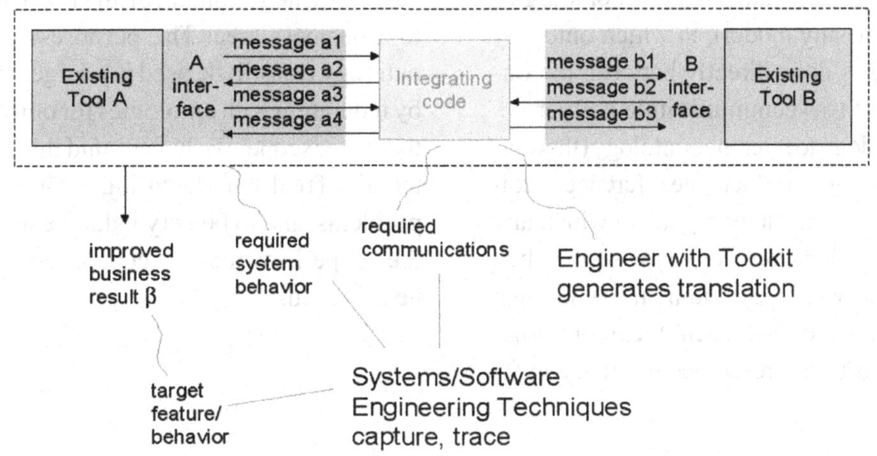

In order to enable the communication in the latter case, the engineer must identify the appropriate translation of the relevant messages between the two tools, using the interfaces they support. This is accomplished by first linking the concepts and functions that are pertinent to the new joint action to their representations in the exposed interfaces. The systems engineer then uses these links to specify the required interactions between the tools, and the translations of operations and messages that are needed to produce those interactions. From these specifications, software developers can generate integrating code to produce the necessary translations and obtain the new system behavior. The function of semantic mediation technologies is to assist the engineer in generating the integrating code, following the model s/he is implicitly using – matching interface elements based on common meaning.

The universe of discourse relevant to each component system can be represented in a **local ontology**. Likewise, the universe of discourse relevant to the required new business process can be represented in a reference ontology. Hameed (2004) makes the assumption that each system has its own local ontology, represented by its documentation, and the mediation problem is then a problem of matching independently developed ontologies. He identified three general architectures for ontology-based mediation systems:

(1) pair-wise reconciliation of local ontologies (the any-to-any model), in which ontology matching is done directly between the ontologies of two communicating partners
(2) local ontology to reference ontology (the any-to-one model), in which one reference ontology serves as an "interlingua" to which any participants local ontology may be matched
(3) hybrid, in which each domain has its own reference ontology, each local ontology is mapped to the reference ontology in its domain, and the reference ontologies are matched pairwise as needed to support inter-domain interactions

In our experience, the assumption that each system has its own local ontology is correct, but the available form of that ontology is largely text descriptions and software documentation. This requires then that any matching problem begin with converting an informal document to a formal form. To the extent that this process is manual, when it is done by the systems engineers to enable integration, the conversion itself obviates much of the subsequent mapping process.

Further, Hameed and a number of other academic efforts (Dell'Erbaa, 2002; Bicer, 2005) concentrate on the ontology mapping problem, ignoring the fact that aligning the terms used to describe the functions of system interfaces is only one step in achieving communication between them. It is as if two physicists who agree on the essential theory could communicate even though one speaks French and the other Chinese. Actual communication must be achieved at the expression level, which for software means at the interface. An equally critical issue in semantic mediation is the relationship between the interface elements and the ontologies.

Finally, the hybrid architecture highlights the idea that a reference ontology can be purpose-built for a domain of known interactions, rather than covering a large domain of all knowledge relevant to a business area. The purpose-built reference ontology can still be used in a larger environment by federation with ontologies for other domains in the larger scope. We have found this to be characteristic of real manufacturing software integration problems, and to be very valuable in establishing the scope in which conceptual agreement must be achieved.

THREE RESEARCH PROJECTS IN SEMANTIC MEDIATION

Project 1: AMIS

NIST began work on semantic mediation technologies with the Automated Methods for Integrating Systems (AMIS) project in 2001 (Libes, 2004). The project developed a semantic mediation architecture based on the idea that the enabling communication of a new business requirement must reference a shared viewpoint of the joint action. The enabling communication is analyzed to a set of *required flows* described in terms of an ontology of the business entities and properties of the joint action. *Available flows* are defined in terms of the messages the component systems send and receive. The mediation problem is to map the message structure data elements to the business entities and properties, and to provide the required flow as a transformation of one or more available flows. AMIS defines an approach to automating the generation of the software that performs this transformation.

The approach involves three major activities (See *Figure 3*):

- Formulation of the Joint Action Model - capturing the business and engineering concerns relevant to the joint action in a form suitable for machine reasoning.
- Semantic Mapping – capturing the relationships between the elements of the exposed interfaces and the concepts in the Joint Action Model.
- Connector Transformation – creating the physical mappings between the interfaces, by generating the integrating software component from the semantic relationships and knowledge of the engineering characteristics of the interfaces. The Message Converter generated by this activity is an ad hoc software component that implements runtime interface conversions between the selected systems.

The AMIS viewpoint identifies the following conceptual components: *local engineering models* (LEMs) of component systems, that describe the interfaces that support interactions with other components; *local conceptual models* (LCMs) of these components that each describe the entities and relationships relevant to the new interaction

Figure 3. The AMIS approach to integration

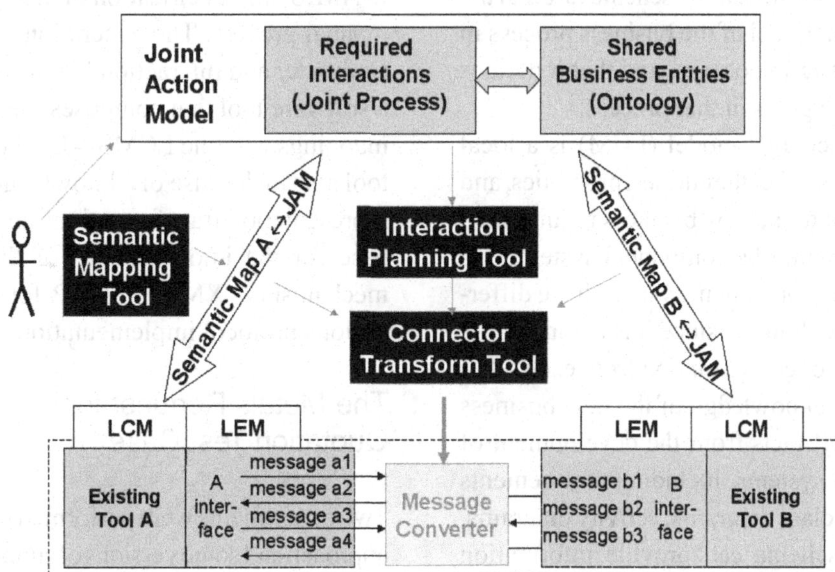

from the viewpoint of that component; and, a *joint action model* (JAM) that describes a shared viewpoint on the entities, relationship and actions of the required interaction.

The JAM provides the semantic foundation for the integration activity. It is a model of the concepts, rules, relationships, functions, and actions of the business domain. The conceptualization provided by the JAM sees the interacting agents as playing specific roles in the business process, such as buyer and seller. The model represents

- **business actions:** the functions and behaviors that implement the roles of each agent, or relate to those functions
- **business entities:** the objects that are discussed in the communications and used or modified by the joint action
- **transactions:** notifications, requests for information, requests for functions or services, and responses

Some other semantic mediation schemes see the semantic center as a reference ontology (Dell'Erbaa, 2002) for the business domain generally. The AMIS view of the JAM is that it need only include as much of the domain as is relevant to the intended joint action. Important differences with other semantic mediation schemes are that the JAM includes a model of the business process in which the joint action occurs, and that it defines the roles of the agents in that process.

A local conceptual model (LCM) is a local ontology that describes the entities, properties, and actions relevant to the new business requirement from the viewpoint of a component system. It is possible that the component systems have differing views of the domain, since it is assumed that they were developed in isolation from each other and without foreknowledge of the new business requirement. Artifacts from the development of the component systems, including requirements specifications, class diagrams, activity diagrams, and database schema can provide information that may be restated in the LCM. In AMIS, the specification of the LCM is a manual process.

A local engineering model (LEM) is a model that describes the interfaces supporting interactions with other components. These interactions could be performed as file transfers, database accesses, operation invocations, or message passing. For each unit of communication there is a mechanism, and each agent plays a specific role with respect to that mechanism; e.g., sender or recipient of a message. There is a further level of detail associated with engineering models that defines the detailed protocols for the communications and the binary representations for each data item exposed in the interface.

Generation of the Message Converter and the interaction plan requires knowledge of two forms of mapping. The first is a mapping that relates engineering elements of the interfaces (in a LEM) to corresponding element in the LCM. From the point of view of the development of that component system, these relationships are traces from implementation to intent. The second mapping is from elements in the LCM to corresponding elements of the JAM. This is a mapping from conceptual model to conceptual model (ontology to ontology). A LEM-to-LCM mapping and a LCM-to-JAM mapping is specified for each component system. In AMIS, the specification of these mappings is a manual process. The generation of the Message Converter and Interaction Planner is provided by a software tool that composes the JAM-to-LCM mappings with the LCM-to-JAM mappings. The tool also makes use of a knowledge base for data representation transformations and a knowledge base for the idiosyncrasies of the engineering mechanisms - XML or SOAP, for example - and various protocol implementation libraries.

The Metals Request for Quotation Test Case

Two experiments were performed using the AMIS approach and some versions of supporting technology. The first involved an exchange of "Request for Quote" and Quotation messages between an automotive manufacturer and a sheet metal supplier. The interfaces to the automotive system used standard messages defined by the Open Applications Group (OAG, 2003). The metals supplier used standard messages conforming to the Chemical Industry Data eXchange (CIDX) standards (CIDX, 2003). Both interfaces used compatible (proprietary) message-passing technologies. To simplify the problem, we used the XML version of CIDX, so that the generated connector had only to use the same message-passing library and convert XML message structures to XML message structures. This reduced the required background knowledge to understanding XML.

Each of the standards contained fairly rich documentation enabling the specification of Local Conceptual Models. These models, however, were expressed only in text and diagrammatic form. In the CIDX case, the relationships between the conceptual models and the XML engineering models were only traceable based on consistent naming of entities. In the OAG case, most of the information relevant to integration was provided in the documentation of the individual XML elements; only the outer process models were separate. So the local mappings were easy to formulate.

Since the local engineering models were represented in XML Schema, it was possible to use a tool to extract a representation of the engineering models suitable for use by a human engineer in performing the mappings.

In this exercise, the formal mapping from each LEM to the corresponding LCM was never performed. Instead, the project constructed tooling to allow a human expert to specify the mapping from the simplified engineering model of the XML elements to the corresponding JAM concepts, using the textual documentation of the local conceptual model as a guide. The "composed mappings" were thus generated outright. The Connection Generator Tool (Flater, 2004) was applied to the composed mappings to generate the runtime integrating components. After some additional work to fit the generated component to the proprietary message-passing library, the generated component was plugged into the runtime environment. The messages tested were transformed successfully.

The Automotive Dealership Test Case

The second test case investigated whether information about operations provided by the interfaces of components can be used to automatically compose a plan of joint action to satisfy a new business requirement. This work investigated issues in the development of an interaction plan using an Interaction Planning Tool. The example used was one in which a server of bulk used car buying information can be queried

1. for a list of cars of a given make, model and year – this operation returns vehicle identification numbers (VINs) of all such cars
2. for the dealer location of a car given its VIN

The challenge problem placed against these capabilities is that the client component needed the VINs joined with the corresponding dealer locations for every car provided in the response to its query. (The client may be interested in minimizing transportation costs, for example). As a consequence, the request the client would like to make did not correspond to a single (atomic) message in the bulk server's interface. Rather, the request required the composition of results from multiple messages that would need to be planned (atomic actions identified and the order of their execution determined).

In the exercise, relationships were defined between objects in the local conceptual models of the server and client. OASIS Business Process Specification Schemas (BPSS) (OASIS, 2001) of the client and server capabilities and object definitions were analyzed by software that could translate the operation specifications into operators of a **planning** domain to be used by the Interaction planning Tool. The Interaction Planning Tool was implemented as a usage of a domain-independent planning system, SHOP2 (Nau, 2001). The BPSS referenced XML Data Type Definitions (DTDs) to describe the form of the request and response structures.

The plan-generation software was able to generate a planning domain that the planner then used to produce a successful plan. However, the exercise revealed difficulties arising from the lack of useful information toward this task. One might reasonably expect to find this information in the business process specification, but it was not provided in the BPSS. Though BPSS provided definitions of the interface operators by way of the request and response object types, it did not contain provisions to qualify those types in ways that might be important to the user of the interface. For example, an interface operation that responds with junked cars is indistinguishable from one that responds with ordinary cars. Secondly, the BPSS did not indicate what properties may be used as identity conditions on the objects it returns in response. It was necessary to manually specify this in the planning domain.

Project 2: ATHENA

Via participation in an Automotive Industry Action Group (AIAG) project called "Inventory Visibility and Interoperability," NIST worked with semantic mediation tools independently developed in the EU Framework 6 ATHENA project (ATHENA, 2003). The test case developed automated mappings between the proprietary interfaces of three commercial "inventory visibility" tools and a proposed AIAG/OAG standard. This proved to be feasible, but not cost-effective. It had interesting intellectual property aspects, and it clarified the requirements for representation capabilities in the ontology, in the message models, and in the transformation rules.

The ATHENA semantic mediation architecture is shown in *Figure 4*. It involves the following components

Figure 4. The ATHENA semantic mediation architecture

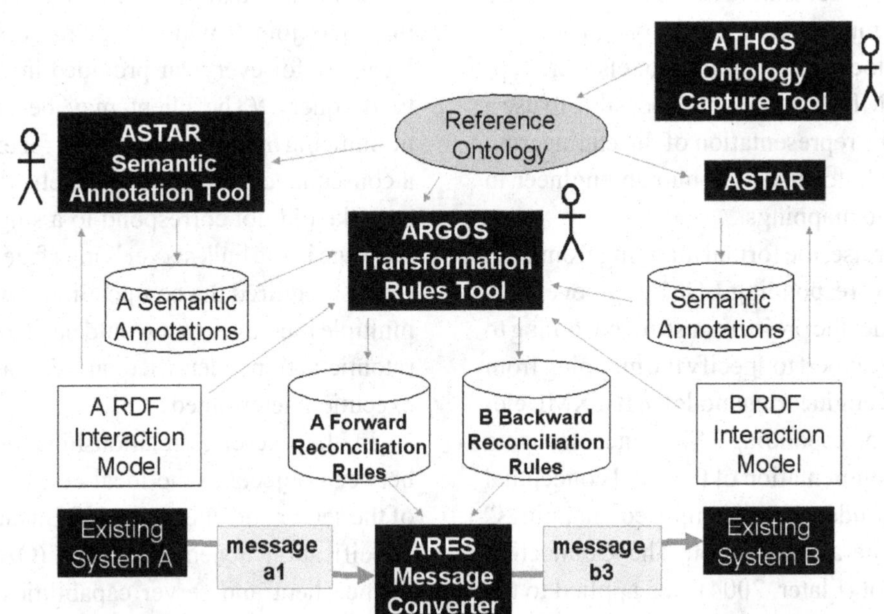

- A **reference ontology** captures the shared concepts of the business interactions that are to be enabled, including the business objects and their properties, the processes and activities, actors/agents. and messages. The ontology was created in the OPAL language, a knowledge representation language specialized for business processes, using the ATHOS tools (Missikof, 2000; Missikof, 2007).
- A **message model** for each type of message to be used at runtime. The message model is a simple RDF (World Wide Web Consortium, 2008) model of each actual message structure and its data elements. The RDF schema supports only the following concepts: *element has name*, *element contains element*, *element has data type* (from a standard list), *element has named value*.
- The **semantic annotation** set for each such message model. A human-interactive semantic annotation process, using the ASTAR tool, captures the relationships between the message structure elements (as captured in the RDF model) and the business concepts in the reference ontology. The related elements can be described as equivalent, or as functionally related. In the latter case, the function can be a standard one, such as extracting part of a text value, concatenating text strings, converting common date/time formats, or designated as user-defined.
- Two reconciliation rulesets for each such message model. Both rulesets are constructed by semi-automated process, using the ARGOS tool, the reference ontology, the message model, and the semantic annotation set. The *forward ruleset* is a set of executable rules that transform runtime message structure elements into individual RDF instances of classes and properties in the reference ontology. The *backward ruleset* is a set of executable rules that transform RDF instances of concepts in the reference ontology into runtime message structure elements.
- The **ARES runtime mediation engine.** A running instance of the ARES engine is configured to convert messages in the form output by the sending system (A) to the form expected by the receiving system (B), using the forward rulesets for the messages sent by the sending system followed by the backward rulesets for the messages expected by the receiving system. The rules themselves are written in the Jena rules language (Jena Rules Language, 2006). The open source Jena rules engine is the knowledge engineering engine for ARES.

Note that the development of the reference ontology for the interactions, the construction of the message models, the development of the semantic annotations, and the development of the reconciliation rulesets are all design-time software engineering activities in which the primary intelligence is the human engineer, somewhat supported by the ATHOS, ASTAR and ARGOS tools. They are applied to each component separately and require knowledge of only the reference ontology and that component system. However, once developed, the rulesets can be used with the rulesets for any other system to achieve effective communication.

There are strong similarities between the ATHENA model and the AMIS model – a single reference ontology (Joint Action Model), engineering models of the individual messages, and semantic mappings/annotations relating the message structure elements to the reference ontology. (While AMIS describes a two-step mapping process and a composition of the mappings, the actual test cases implemented direct mappings from the engineering models to the JAM; the ATHENA architecture posits that single-step approach.) They both depart from the Hameed architectures in the same

Figure 5. Inventory visibility and interoperability scenario

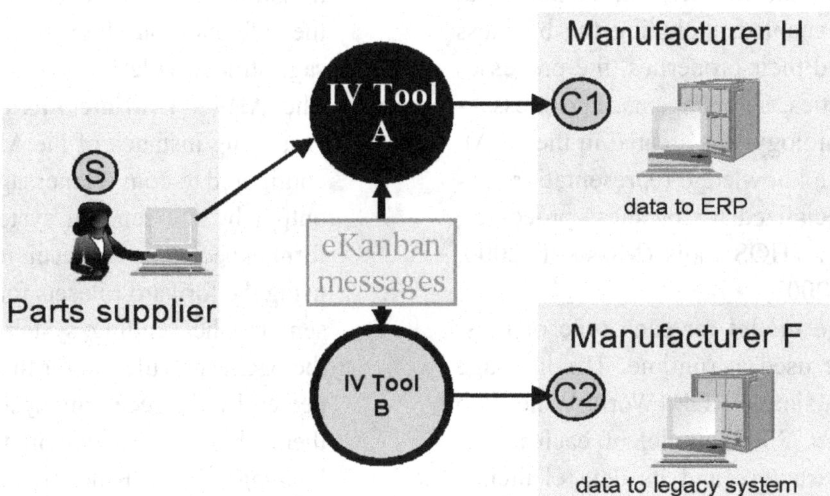

way – they are about mapping message models to ontologies, not matching ontologies.

The Inventory Visibility Test Case

The purpose of the ATHENA/AIAG project (Barkmeyer, 2007) was to evaluate the use of the ATHENA semantic mediation tools in an actual industrial application. The AIAG scenario deals with the automotive supply-chain situation in which a joint "electronic Kanban" business process regulates the flow of parts from the supplier to match actual consumption by the customer's automotive assembly plant. As conceived by their vendors, "Inventory Visibility" (IV) applications provide web-based interfaces to the parts suppliers and communicate with the specific ERP systems of the automotive manufacturer using proprietary messages. The problem arises when a supplier connected to one of these IV applications is also contracted to supply parts to a different manufacturer, who has a different IV application with a differing, proprietary interface. (See *Figure 5*). The AIAG solution was to develop a standard set of messages for communications between the IV applications. If each proprietary message can be converted to/from the corresponding standard message using semantic mediation tools, the IV applications themselves do not need to be modified. This was the test scenario.

This scenario had certain advantages. First, the joint electronic Kanban business process was standardized by AIAG, along with the messages that supported it. This meant that a reference ontology common to all such interactions could be developed from the AIAG standards. Second, because the standards were in the public domain, placing the reference ontology, the semantic annotations, and reconciliation rules in the public domain and making them available to all of the participating IV application vendors would allow effective collaboration. Further, the validity of the approach could be decided by whether each of the vendors could use the tooling to generate runtime reconciliation rules that mapped messages in their proprietary form to and from the standard form. Importantly, they would have exclusive access to the artifacts they created: the message models, the semantic annotations and the reconciliation rules. To the outside world, their tooling, inclusive of their uses of the ATHENA semantic mediation tools, would accept and produce the standard messages.

The e-Kanban business process involved 4 standard messages, loosely referred to as "authorize shipment", "shipment notification", "delivery notification", "consume Kanban notification". (The actual messages were derived from standard messages of the Open Applications Group suite.) The reference ontology supporting the entire e-Kanban business process (Bicer, 2005) comprised approximately 50 classes and 150 properties. There were 3 participating IV applications, plus interfaces to the systems of two major automotive manufacturers.

One problem became apparent immediately. The ATHENA toolkit did not include tools for converting XML Schema message models to the simple RDF message model used by the ATHENA tools. So additional tooling was created to do that. It was also necessary to convert the actual XML message structures to a simple RDF form of the message content, in order for the forward mappings to work, and to convert the simple RDF form back to XML for the backward mappings to be useful (Miletic, et al., 2007). Further, the ARES tool had to be embedded in a runtime module that implemented standard communication protocols. In the AIAG test case, the required protocols were "reliable webservices with addressing and security." Using additional ATHENA webservice tooling, this gave rise to the actual runtime architecture depicted in *Figure 6*.

The more serious problem with the ATHENA tooling was that the over-simplified RDF form of the message models was not rich enough to guide conversion to a valid XML message structure. The sequencing of elements, multiple occurrences of an element, and the concept of namespaces were not supported. To get this information captured and propagated through the ATHENA tools, and in particular, the ARES runtime engine, this information had to be encoded in the names. That, in turn, made the semantic annotation process much more difficult for the IV application engineers, because the names of their proprietary message structure elements had been significantly modified when they appeared in the tools and were difficult for them to recognize.

The lesson from this experience is that the semantic mediation toolkit is useless if it does

Figure 6. ATHENA / AIAG runtime adapter

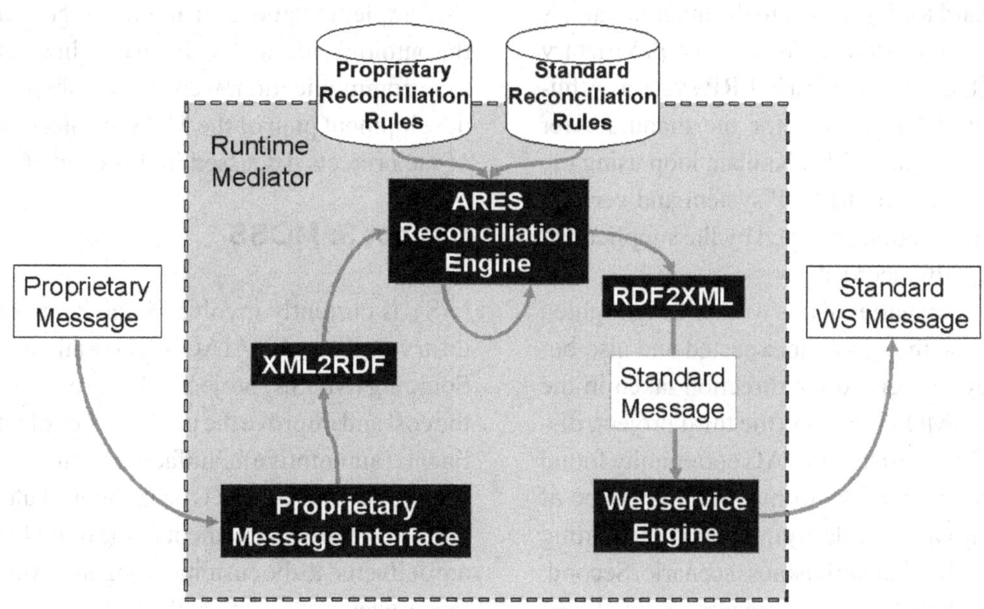

not include tools supporting the common message syntaxes and protocols used in industry. Today, support for XML message structures described by XML schemas and conveyed by SOAP (World Wide Web Consortium, 2000) or ebMS protocols (OASIS, 2002) is the minimum requirement. The academic favorite, RDF, is simply not used in industrial communications.

Ultimately, we were able to demonstrate exchange of one of the standard messages between two IV applications and between them and the manufacturers systems. It would not have been difficult to complete the set, but it was apparent to all involved that the name-tracking work-arounds had made the experience unpleasant for the IV vendors. With the "first-draft" ATHENA tooling, the development process using semantic mediation was not cost-effective, and they withdrew their resources after the first demonstration.

In addition, the ATHENA project conducted an end-user test of semantic interoperability involving one IV application and the automotive manufacturers ERP system. In this exercise, a supplier's shipment notification was created in the IV application and sent, in proprietary form, to the mediator for that application, which converted the message to the AIAG standard form. The standard form was sent to the manufacturer's mediator, which converted it to the proprietary form for the manufacturer's ERP system. A human "material manager" for the manufacturer inspected the state of that Kanban loop using the human interface to the ERP system and verified that the information provided by the supplier had been correctly recorded.

Three discoveries of this work are highlighted here because they were unexpected and also because they influenced the direction taken in the subsequent MOSS project (the third project, discussed below). First, the AIAG community found the development of the formal ontology to be of significant value in clarifying and documenting the intended e-Kanban business scenario. Second, they considered that the semantic annotations, viewed as a trace from the business concepts to the XML implementations, would be of significant value to the software engineers – if and when the noise introduced by the oversimplified RDF message model was eliminated. That is, they saw significant value in the capture of the business model as an ontology, and in the trace from the ontology to the XML implementation, independent of run-time semantic mediation.

The third discovery is that the ATHENA team was surprised that the test scenario involved conversion from proprietary message A to standard message, and from standard message to proprietary message B. The scenario they envisaged was direct conversion from proprietary message A to proprietary message B within the ARES tool. With the proprietary mappings actually developed, that pair of rulesets could have been loaded into ARES and the rulesets for the standard discarded. In that configuration, the value of the AIAG standard is the standard e-Kanban reference ontology, not the standard XML schemas for the exchange messages.

The ideas that development of the business ontology clarifies understanding of subject business scenarios, that trace relationships from messages to the business domain ontology served to guide tool implementations of the messages, and that the ontology might serve as an interlingua in message communication, were each embraced in the development plan of the MOSS project, the third of the projects discussed in this chapter.

Project 3: MOSS

NIST is currently involved in an automotive industry project, the AIAG's Materials Off-Shore Sourcing (MOSS) project, which seeks to reduce the cost and improve the performance of intercontinental automotive manufacturing supply chains. The scope of the project is ocean-going automotive parts from order placement to the point the goods are delivered to the customer. Begun in May, 2005, the project is on-going at the time of this writing.

There is not sufficient experience at this time to make practical evaluations, but the technical issues and planned work will be discussed.

The MOSS project was motivated by a survey of automotive industry stakeholders that showed that errors in the information coordinating the movement of goods was causing 15% of shipments to be delayed en route. Unanticipated delays can result in substantial variation in transit times. To ensure the availability of components despite this variation, manufacturers must carry additional, costly buffer stock. The survey also found that customers had limited visibility into the progress of a shipment as it moved through the supply chain.

The survey revealed some of the sources of the problems experienced. Oftentimes, processes involved paper documents, fax and email. These forms of communication proved error-prone and costly due to the need to manually copy information from one media to another. Electronic Data Interchange (EDI) technology is pervasive in the automotive industry, but messaging between the systems supporting the processes was hampered by inconsistent interpretation of the content. In summary, the study revealed that a lack of semantic interoperability (but also error-prone manual processes) resulted in costly inefficiencies.

The problem space of the MOSS project is distinguished from the others described in this chapter in that (1) its processes are supported by a large installation of legacy information technology; (2) the systems must support substantial variation in business processes and interact with many partners; (3) there are many roles to be played in the processes (customers, suppliers, freight forwarders, ocean carriers, pre-carriage and on-carriage carriers, customs brokers, import and export customs authorities, warehouse operators, and third-party logistics provider, among others); and, (4) MOSS is defining industry standard message definitions as well as participating in the NIST research.

Typically, the systems in the supply chain logistics community support EDI interfaces. XML messaging in this community is almost non-existent. The community is experienced in adapting its systems to support new business requirements by modifying the EDI messages and the systems that use them. These facts, the diversity of the ownership of the systems, and their loose federation, all worked against solutions that would deploy mediators.

MOSS-conforming systems interoperate through the standard EDI messages the project is developing. However, EDI has little semantic foundation, and its modeling methodology has serious shortcomings. To address these problems, the project is defining mappings from its EDI message structure elements to structures in a Supply Chain Logistics Conceptual Model, a reference model for MOSS. The conceptual model shall be mirrored by an ontology on which reasoning can be performed. Validation requirements are defined in terms of the business concepts in the ontology. Through this approach, we will use the ontology to investigate a new modeling methodology and to support the validation of implementations of the MOSS messages.

A commercial technology provider is collaborating on the project to address an additional problem with the current-state process: the high cost of establishing the communication channel among participants intending to collaborate in trade relationships. That software is implemented upon a viewpoint closely resembling the MOSS reference model.

EDI standards such as EDIFACT (CEFACT, 2009) and ANSI X12 (ASC, 2009) define widely-used message types covering processes in the scope of the MOSS project. A key task addressed in deploying EDI is that of tailoring the standard message type definition (the "directory message type") to the needs of the business process. EDI's directory message type definitions contain provisions for an immense spectrum of situations, only a small subset of which are likely to be relevant and supported in an actual usage of the message type. In EDI technology, a document known as a *Message Implementation Guide* (MIG) is used to identify a subset of the directory message structure elements that will be used in actual messages. A MIG is an engineering model of a file-based interface. The partners collaborating in the design of an EDI message supporting a new business requirement use the MIG to identify what information will be included in the exchange. In order to designate the business purpose of an element conveyed in a message, an EDI message designer may be required to associate with the element a term from a code list. A *code list* is a dictionary of terms and their associated natural language definitions that enumerates the values of some domain property. For example, EDIFACT provides a code list enumerating business process roles. This code list enumerates about 200 roles, and provides short English language descriptions of the intended semantics. For example, the code term "BY" is defined "Buyer. Party to whom merchandise and/or service is sold" (CEFACT, 2009).

In practice, EDI's code lists are a major contributing factor to its failure to provide a semantic foundation for messaging. Before the details of this problem are described, however, it is important to recognize that many of the code lists used in business serve important roles beyond their use in messages. For example, INCOTERMS (ICC, 2008) is a code list describing 13 patterns for the sharing of risk and transport responsibilities between a buyer and a seller. Stakeholders use these terms to concisely describe the logistics relationships they intend. Acceptance to operate under a given INCOTERM entails legal obligations consistent with its definition. Business processes are structured around some code lists; typically, process stakeholders are conversant in these.

Certain industrial and government organizations maintain registries of individual entities. In EDIFACT these registries are considered code lists, but they are in fact quite different. The registry identifies individuals of the type that is its concern. For example, a tax registry may identify a taxable organization in the context of a government's process for assessing a tax. Processes for which the registry's "Tax ID" identifier is a relevant property may treat the property as closed. Further, it may be impossible in the context of these processes for an entity not represented in the registry to play roles that one might casually associate with it. In essence, it would be of the type, but for its absence from the registry.

In practice, the principal problem with EDI code lists is that it is oftentimes not possible to determine from a code term's definition what business entity it designates. Thus when multiple parties independently create MIGs, they may choose differing code terms to describe identical entities, or they may use a single code term in a situation where a party with whom they communicate requires that a distinction be made, (perhaps using multiple code terms).

A second problem with the EDI modeling methodology is that there is nothing in it that provides knowledge of the correspondence (or "life-cycle") of its units of information across the messages in which they might appear – the methodology does not enable one to specify in what message and business process a unit of information is introduced, and in what messages and business processes it is reused. Lacking this, it is difficult to form a cohesive view of the business process at the level of message detail. Consequently, interpretation errors are made in implementing the messages.

The first step in the MOSS solution to these problems is to identify, through an analysis of the business process, the enabling business-relevant information. This analysis identified about 400 units of business information ("MOSS Properties") used across the 20 messages that were considered essential to managing the process ("MOSS Messages"). The 400 MOSS Properties are represented by about 1400 EDI information elements. The growth is due to the fact that the EDI encoding of a unit of business information may need to make reference to, for example, one code list to associate meaning to the value, and another to indicate the syntactic encoding of the value. For example, an instance of the MOSS Property "Requested Delivery Date" may be encoded as "DTM+2:20090803120000:204". In this structure, the "+" and ":" separate components of the structure. "DTM" indicates that this is an EDIFACT "Date Time" message structure element. The first position of this structure, containing the value "2," is a code term from an EDIFACT code list. "2" designates "Date on which buyer requests goods to be delivered." The value "20090803120000" is the timepoint noon, August 3, 2009 (Though it is ambiguous; the time zone has not been specified). "204" is a term from an EDIFACT code list describing various encodings for timepoints.

The 1400 EDI properties were mapped to EDI structures in the 20 MOSS Messages. Though this suggests that 28,000 units of mapping mappings may need to be specified, in practice only about one third of the business units are relevant to the process supported by the message. The mapping was performed manually, but automated tools were used to validate (1) the mapping consistency across messages, (2) the consistency of EDI encoding, and, (3) the correctness relative to the EDI directory message type. Mapping consistently across messages ensures that we do not introduce multiple message structure elements to represent a single business-level unit of information. Mapping to a consistent EDI encoding reduces the cost and complexity of implementing the messages. Mapping consistent to the EDI directory type ensures that implementers can use their usual EDI tooling in providing an implementation.

The end products of the process just described are MIGs, similar to what would be produced by the conventional EDI modeling methodology except that our process additionally provides (1) knowledge of the correspondence of the units of information across the messages in which they appear (life-cycle information), and (2) consistency across messages of the EDI encoding of the information. MIGs are similar in purpose to the Local Engineering Models of AMIS, but in MOSS they are more accurately "Reference Engineering Models" since they describe an AIAG MOSS standard interface. They are documented by web-based tools that are used by project participants implementing the MOSS standard (AIAG, 2009).

As in AMIS and ATHENA, the means by which we provide a semantic foundation for messaging is to relate message structure elements to a domain ontology. MOSS maps units of business information from the MIG engineering model (EM) message structures described above to the MOSS Supply Chain Logistics Conceptual Model (CM). In MOSS, the first role of these mappings is to provide engineers implementing the standard with knowledge of how the message structure elements should relate to structures in their implementations.

The MOSS Supply Chain Logistics Conceptual Model, currently under development, (AIAG, 2008) is similar to the AMIS Joint Action Model in that it describes business entities and transactions. However, it does not contain action descriptions, and it is scoped to the entire business process, not a single joint action. In MOSS, action descriptions are represented only informally, through activity diagrams that each reference multiple actions of typical scenarios. These scenario include, for example, Asia Pacific full container load shipments to the US, Europe less-than-container-load shipments consolidated and sent through Canada to the US, and so on.

Since MOSS is specifying a standard, "local" viewpoints (those of existing systems) are not represented. The mapping is done in one step, from the engineering models to the conceptual model (EM-to-CM).

Semantic Interoperability Testing in MOSS

Information systems conforming to the MOSS standard must be able to send and receive MOSS messages. Compliance with the standard requires that the data elements within the message structures be interpreted as defined, and that the interchange between the systems follows the business process as specified. Had the focus of MOSS, like AMIS and ATHENA been the automatic generation of mediators and adapters, testing could have been limited to assessing the soundness of the message transformations those mediators and adapters produced. MOSS does not specify a process by which mediators and adapters may be generated. MOSS tooling does not link to knowledge of local engineering models – it has no direct knowledge of how implementations view elements of the Trade Logistics Conceptual Model.

One strategy MOSS is pursuing to assess the correctness of implementations is to assess whether they can correctly populate a knowledge base mirroring the Supply Chain Logistics Conceptual Model. The EM-to-CM mappings described above are executable in the sense that a "mapping engine" can create from a message instance a population of entities and relationships conforming to the conceptual model. The mapping engine uses the Queries, Views and Transformations (QVT) relational language (OMG, 2009). The mapping performed by the QVT engine is not just a purely syntactical translation. During the mapping process, the information contained within the messages is enriched with additional information from a MOSS formal business process model and a reference ontology. The aggregate model consisting of the reference ontology and the formal business process model can be viewed as a representation of the MOSS standard in a formal language. A population of contingent facts are derived from messages produced by the implementation, representing its view of a challenge problem posed to it. These are placed in a message assertion base .(See *Figure 7*)

By enriching the information from messages presented to the validation tool with other information about the trade lane, defaults, closure properties, and other considerations, the reasoner can perform some validation tasks on the collection of messages presented to it. Messages describing a span of interactions in the supply chain.

The reference ontology contains a classification of all the entities that are relevant within a

Figure 7. Testing in the MOSS project

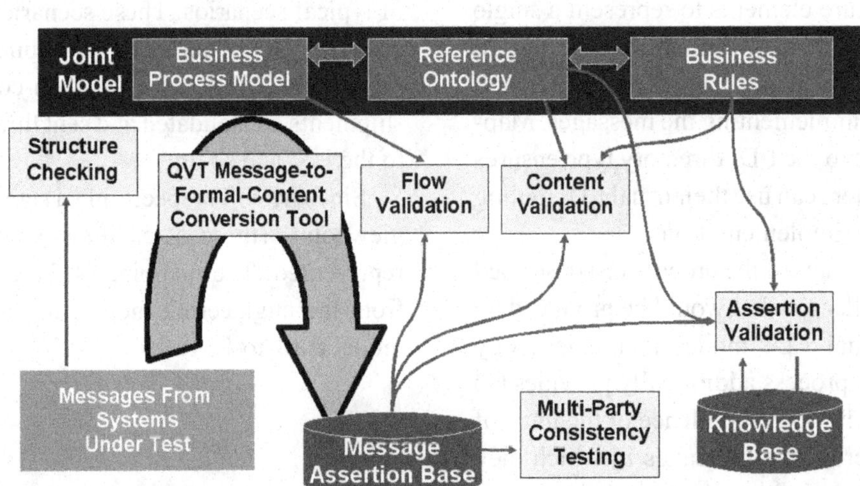

manufacturing supply chain, the relations among these entities, and an axiomatization of these relations. The formal business process model specifies the intended process flow for supply chain processes including the information flow; for example, how milestones within a supply chain process are linked to MOSS messages.

The logical representation of the messages in the message assertion base allows an inference engine to test for semantic interoperability. We distinguish five different kinds of tests:

1. **Content validation** contains tests that evaluates individual messages given the axioms of the reference ontology.
2. **Information flow validation** consists of test that determine whether the messages are sent and received in the appropriate order, and whether messages are missing.
3. **Process flow validation** consists of test that determine whether the events within the shipment process meet the requirements of the business process model. Since many of the messages are linked to milestones of the shipment process, information flow validation and process flow validation are closely linked.
4. **Consistency validation** utilizes the power of the reasoning engine to determine whether the available information is consistent within and across the messages. Inconsistencies might be explicit – for example, in the case where a value was copied wrongly from one message to another – but the inconsistencies might also be implicit and only discovered by the reasoner with by reasoning with the axioms within the reference ontology.
5. **Assertion validation** utilizes additional knowledge to evaluate the information. For example, one can use external knowledge bases to check DUNS numbers or postal codes.

CONCLUSION

This chapter reports on our experience investigating issues of semantic interoperability through three related research projects. We investigated architectures and procedures for the reconciliation of differences of viewpoint that are exposed in component interfaces. The essential form of our solution is to relate message structure elements to elements of ontologies.

The task to be automated determines the knowledge that needs to be formally represented. Much of the recent research in semantic interoperability concerns ontology matching ("reconciliation in the abstract"). Accordingly, these efforts make reference to ontologies that do not include representation of the supporting information technology and its interfaces. Another community, working in near isolation from the former, has produced service oriented architectures that provide scant reference to the domain ontology, and an inscrutable shorthand of the systems engineer's reasoning. The result is that practical automated semantic interoperability seems a long way off.

Achieving the results we sought required that we enrich message structures and interfaces with links to the domain ontology. Since these domain ontologies usually do not exist, they have to be developed as part of the integration process. One major obstacle is the poor quality or even lack of proper documentation, which required that we perform time-intensive "archeology" to recover engineering representations of interfaces capable of serving our goals. On the upside, our experience suggests that an ontology that serves to automate mediation has value beyond this narrow role; it may serve human system integrators in the manual process of system integration, and it may improve the quality of exchange specifications. Another lesson learned was that implementing so-called "semantic technologies" was only a small fraction of the actual work, because there was substantial technical minutiae to address. Overcoming these obstacles does not so much require a reconceptualization of how systems and interface standards are made, as it does a commitment to capture systems engineering rationale as it is established, and in a form that facilitates its use in future systems integration. In systems development, the technical and business-domain specific needs of future systems integration projects often cannot be foreseen, but the need for a methodical systems engineering practice, performed in advance, can be.

REFERENCES

AIAG MOSS Project. (2008). *MOSS conceptual model (a UML model).* Retrieved February 9, 2009, from http://syseng.nist.gov/poc/repo/trunk/conceptual-model/moss.mdxml

AIAG MOSS Project. (2009). *MOSS message mapping*. Retrieved February 9, 2009, from http://syseng.nist.gov/moss/moss-views/msgview?msg=DELJIT&select=1185&open=1202*1219#1185

ASC. (2009). *Accredited standards committee, ANSI X12*. Retrieve February 9, 2009, from http://www.x12.org

ATHENA. (2003). *A3 knowledge support and semantic mediation solutions (2004), European integrated project*. Retrieved August 2008, from http://www.athena-ip.org

ATHENA. (2007). *B5.10 - inventory visibility subproject: IV&I end-to-end interoperability demonstration including conformance testing demonstration.* Retrieved August 2008, from http://xml.aiag.org/athena/resources/WD.B5.7.6—InteropAndConformanceTestDemo.pdf

Barkmeyer, E. J., & Kulvatunyou, B. (2007). *An ontology for the e-kanban business process* (NIST Internal Report 7404). Retrieved August 2, 2008, from http://www.mel.nist.gov/msidlibrary/doc/NISTIR_7404.pdf

Bicer, V., Laleci, G. B., Dogac, A., & Kabak, Y. (2005). Artemis message exchange framework: Semantic interoperability of exchanged messages in the healthcare domain. *SIGMOD Record, 34*(3), 71–76. doi:10.1145/1084805.1084819

CIDX. (2003). *CIDX overview*. Retrieved February 2, 2009, from http://www.cidx.org/AboutCIDX

Dell'Erbaa, M., Fodor, O., Ricci, F., & Werthner, H. (2002). HARMONISE: A solution for data interoperability. In J. Monteiro (Ed.), *Proceedings of the Second IFIP Conference on E-Commerce, E-Business, E-Government (I3E 2002)* (pp. 433-445). Norwell, MA: Kluwer.

Flater, D. (2004). *Automated composition of conversion software.* Retrieved August 2, 2008, from http://www.mel.nist.gov/msidlibrary/doc/nistir7099.pdf

Gamma, E., Helm, R., Johnson, R., & Vlissides, J. M. (1995). *Design patterns: Elements of reusable object-oriented software*. Boston, MA: Addison Wesley.

Hameed, A., Preece, A., & Sleeman, D. (2004). Ontology reconciliation. In S. Staab (Ed.), *Handbook on ontologies* (pp 231-250). Berlin, Germany: Springer-Verlag.

ICC. (2008). *International Chamber of Commerce, INCOTERMS, rules at the core of world trade.* Retrieved November 10, 2008, from http://www.iccwbo.org/incoterms/id3045/index.html

IEEE. Computer Society. (2004). *Guide to the software engineering body of knowledge*. Retrieved February 10, 2009, from http://www.swebok.org/

INCOSE. (2009). *International council on systems engineering (INCOSE), guide to the systems engineering body of knowledge*. Retrieved February 10, 2009, from http://www.incose.org/practice/guidetosebodyofknow.aspx

Jena Rule Language. (2007). *Jena rule language*. Retrieved August 2008, from [REMOVED HYPERLINK FIELD]http://jena.sourceforge.net/

Libes, D., Barkmeyer, E. J., Denno, P., Flater, D., Steves, M. P., Wallace, E., & Feeny, A. B. (2004). *The AMIS approach to systems integration* (NISTIR 7101). Retrieved August 2, 2008, from http://www.mel.nist.gov/msidlibrary/doc/nistir7101.pdf

Miletic, I., Vujasinovic, M., Ivezic, N., & Marjanovic, Z. (2007). Enabling semantic mediation for business applications: XML-RDF, RDF-XML, and XSD-RDFS transformation. In R. J. Goncalves (Ed.), *Enterprise interoperability II, new challenges and approaches* (pp. 483-494). Berlin, Germany: Springer-Verlag.

Missikoff, M. (2000). *OPAL a knowledge based approach for the analysis of complex business systems* (Internal report). Laboratory of Enterprise Knowledge and Systems, IASI-CNR, Rome.

Missikoff, M., & Taglino, F. (2007). *athena document D.A3.1 - part 3, the ATHOS user manual* Retrieved February 2, 2009, from http://www.athena-ip.org

Nau, D. Muñoz-Avila, H., Cao, Y., Lotem, A., & Mitchell, S. (2001). Total-order planning with partially ordered subtasks. In B. Nebel (Ed.), *Proceedings of the International Joint Conference on Artificial Intelligence (IJCAI-2001)*. New York: Morgan Kaufmann.

OASIS. (2001). *Organization for the advancement of structured information systems (OASIS) ebXML business process specification schema version 1.01*. Retrieved February 7, 2009, from http://www.ebxml.org/specs/ebBPSS.pdf

OASIS. (2002). *Organization for the advancement of structured information standards. Message service specification version 2.0*. Retrieved February 9, 2009, from http://www.ebxml.org/specs/ebMS2.pdf

Object Management Group. (2009). *Meta object facility (MOF) 2.0 query/view/transformation, V1.0*. Retrieved February 9, 2009, from http://www.omg.org/spec/QVT/1.0/

Open Applications Group. (2003). *Open application group*. Retrieved February 1, 2009, from http://www.openapplications.org

UN/CEFACT. (2009). *United Nations directories for electronic data interchange for administration, commerce and trade*. Retrieved February 9, 2009, from http://www.unece.org/trade/untdid/welcome.htm

World Wide Web Consortium. (2000). *Simple object access protocol, (SOAP) 1.1*. Retrieved February 9, 2009, from http://www.w3.org/TR/2000/NOTE-SOAP-20000508/

World Wide Web Consortium. (2004). *RDF vocabulary description language 1.0: RDF schema*. Retrieved August 2008, from http://www.w3.org/TR/rdf-schema/

ENDNOTE

[1] References to proprietary products are included in this paper solely to identify the tools actually used in the industrial applications. This identification does not imply any recommendation or endorsement by NIST as to the actual suitability of the product for the purpose.

Chapter 4
Service Integration through Structure-Preserving Semantic Matching

Fiona McNeill
University of Edinburgh, Scotland

Paolo Besana
University of Edinburgh, Scotland

Juan Pane
University of Trento, Italy

Fausto Giunchiglia
University of Trento, Italy

EXECUTIVE SUMMARY

The problem of integrating services is becoming increasingly pressing. In large, open environments such as the Semantic Web, huge numbers of services are developed by vast numbers of different users. Imposing strict semantics standards in such an environment is useless; fully predicting in advance which services one will interact with is not always possible as services may be temporarily or permanently unreachable, may be updated or may be superseded by better services. In some situations, characterised by unpredictability, such as the emergency response scenario described in this case, the best solution is to enable decisions about which services to interact with to be made on-the-fly. We propose a method of doing this using matching techniques to map the anticipated call to the input that the service is actually expecting. To be practical, this must be done during run-time. In this case, we present our structure-preserving semantic matching algorithm (SPSM), which performs this matching task both for perfect and approximate matches between calls. In addition, we introduce the OpenKnowledge system for service interaction which, using the SPSM algorithm, along with many other features, facilitates on-the-fly interaction between services in an arbitrarily large network without any global agreements or pre-run-time knowledge of who to interact with or how interactions will proceed. We provide a preliminary evaluation of the SPSM algorithm within the OpenKnowledge framework.

BACKGROUND

The problem of automated integration of services is key to the successful realisation of the Semantic Web, or any other system where services interact with one another. So far, this has proved difficult. Global ontologies allow different services to be expressed using the same terms, which are thus understandable to all. But there are significant difficulties with the notion of a global ontology: both the relevance of terms and appropriate categorisation of those terms is very context dependent. An ontology that included all terms that could be relevant to any situation would be impossible to build, impossible to reason with and would allow no flexibility for different interpretations of situations.

However, integration of services using different ontologies is difficult. The difficulties arise at two levels: in the structure of the invocation to the service and in the values passed with the invocation. A service will expect some input parameters and will return an output. Consider for example, the web service measurement, whose WSDL description is shown in Figure 1. Its purpose it to provide the level of water registered by a particular sensor on a grid of sensors on a particular riverside area, which can be used during an emergency to assess the conditions. It expects as the input message the location, defined as the node identifier in the grid, and the id of the sensor, and returns in the output message the measured water level and the timestamp of the measurement.

The structure, or signature, provided by input parameters and output values must be respected by a process invoking the service. However, the invoking process may have a different signature for the caller function (parameters may have different names or they may have a different structure). For example, a caller process could be a BPEL workflow, originally developed to invoke a service called reading, that does not have the concept of location, but only of the reporter and node identities, and expects the level to be named differently. The invocation needs to be adapted to the new called service.

Even after the structural adaptation has been performed, the terminology used in the parameters may be defined in different ontologies in the caller process and in the service. This may cause misunderstandings or failure: for example, the water level may be returned in meters when the caller expected feet. Translation is required.

This case focuses on the problem of matching the signature of service invocation with that of the service when they are expressed in different ontologies. It is perfectly possible to solve this problem by manually matching the expected inputs and outputs of two services – the one that the caller expected and the one that is actually called – prior to interaction. For example, Altova MapForce[1] is a system which facilitates this manual mapping. However, performing this is time consuming and not scalable. Additionally, this presupposes that one knows in advance what calls will be necessary. This is perhaps feasible in a small, static system, but in a large, dynamic system where services may be temporary, may be updated, may suffer from occasional communication breakdown, and so on, we do not wish to limit the number of services with which it is possible to interact. A better solution in this sort of environment is to automatically integrate services on-the-fly as the need becomes apparent.

Using our matching approach we are able to map between the invocation of the service, written in the ontology of the caller, and the call the service is expecting, written in the ontology of the service. The goal of the matching is two-fold:

- to establish whether these services (the expected and the called) are *similar enough*: if the service is being asked to perform an action that is too different to the function it is equipped to perform, then the correct response is to refuse to interact;

Figure 1. WSDL code for a web service returning the water level measured by a sensor in a grid of sensor for preventing flooding

```
<wsdl>

 <xsd:element name="locationtype">
 <xsd:complexType>
  <xsd:sequence>
  <xsd:element name="reporterID" type="string"/>
  <xsd:element name="node" type="string"/>
  </xsd:sequence>
 </xsd:complexType>
 </xsd:element>

 <xsd:element name="datetype">
 <xsd:complexType>
  <xsd:sequence>
  <xsd:element name="month" type="int"/>
  <xsd:element name="day" type="int"/>
  <xsd:element name="hour" type="int"/>
  <xsd:element name="minute" type="int"/>
  </xsd:sequence>
 </xsd:complexType>
 </xsd:element>

 <message name="measurementRequest">
 <part name="term" type="locationtype"/>
 </message>

 <message name="measurementResponse">
 <part name="level" type="int"/>
 <part name="date" type="datetype"/>
 </message>

 <portType name="sensor">
 <operation name="measurement">
  <input message="measurementRequest"/>
  <output message="measurementResponse"/>
 </operation>
 </portType>

</wsdl>
```

- if the call is judged to be similar enough, then an adaptor is generated to bridge beween the caller and the invoked service .

Our technique is designed to work at runtime, without user interaction and without any pre-alignment of ontologies, as we believe that in a Semantic Web kind of environment, such an approach is vital. This is therefore a lightweight and flexible approach that can be employed on-the-fly if – and only if – the need arises.

SETTING THE STAGE

Structure-Preserving Semantic Matching

We have developed the *Structure-preserving Semantic Matching (SPSM)* technique, which allows us to find a map between two service descriptions and returns a score in [0 1] indicating their similarity.

The SPSM maps trees structures; we therefore first need to transform web services into trees. The name of the service becomes the root of the tree, while the parts in input and output messages become the children. As the WSDL description in Figure 1 shows, parts can contain complex structures (such as Location in the input message and Date in the output): the part itself becomes a subtree. For compactness, we will represent trees as formulae. The WSDL in Figure 1 can therefore be represented as:

```
measurement(location(ReporterID, Node),
Level,
date(Month, Day, Hour, Minute))
```

Note that in such formulae and in diagrams such as Figure 2, the names of the variables indicate the types expected. For example, the second level argument Level indicates that the argument is a variable that should be instantiated with a value of type level.

SPSM is a two-step process. Firstly, we make use of adapted conventional ontology matching techniques to investigate relationships between the individual words in the nodes of the trees. The second – novel – step matches the structure of the trees to discover an overall relationship. This is crucial because the structure of the tree itself contains a lot of semantic information that must be considered if we are determining whether two service calls are equivalent or similar. SPSM, therefore, needs to preserve a set of structural properties (e.g., vertical ordering of nodes) to establish whether two trees are globally similar and, if so, how similar they are and in what way. These characteristics of matching are required in web service integration applications, see, e.g., (Kluch et al., 2006; Li & Horrocks, 2006; Gooneratne & Tavi, 2008).

Moreover, SPSM allows us to detect not only perfect matches – which are unlikely to occur in an unconstrained domain – but also *good enough* matches. SPSM returns both a mapping between two trees and a numerical score in [0 1] indicating the degree of *global similarity* between them. A match between two trees is considered to be *good enough* if this degree of global similarity exceeds some threshold value. Since the concept of *good enough* is very context dependent – in safety critical situation perhaps only a near-perfect match will

Figure 2. Two approximately matched web services as trees – T_1: reading(ReporterID,Node,date(Time,Day,Month,Year),Water_level) and T_2: measurement(Level,location(ReporterID,Node),date(Month,Day,Hour,Minute). Functions are in rectangles with rounded corners; they are connected to their arguments by dashed lines. Node correspondences are indicated by arrows.

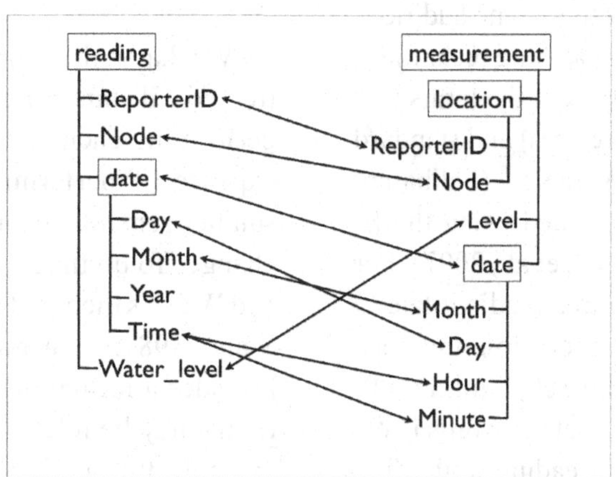

do but in other situations a much weaker match may suffice – this threshold is set by the user according to the particular interaction (Giunchiglia et al., 2008b). This approach greatly increases the range of services it is possible to interact with. This solution is lightweight enough to be done quickly on-the-fly, during run-time, so that we need have no expectations of which services we will want to interact with in advance of run-time.

Service descriptions that are not written in WSDL will need to have the conversion step to turn them into trees built for them, but we believe that it is possible to view most service descriptions as tree structures and that this conversion process will generally be straightforward. An example of two service descriptions, which have been converted into trees, being approximately mapped, can be seen in Figure 2.

Once the conversion to tree has taken place, the SPSM algorithm consists of two stages:

- **Node Matching:** this matches the nodes in one tree to the nodes of another tree. This will often be matching single words to one another, although nodes may be more complex (for example, they can be composed of more than one word) and our techniques are able to deal with this. These terms may be annotated with references to ontologies so that it is easier to determine their semantic meaning and, if so, our matching techniques take advantage of this. If there is no additional information then our matching techniques rely on syntactic properties of the terms (for example, suffixes and prefixes) and standard ontologies such as WordNet (Fellbaum, 1998). This step is performed using the S-Match system (Giunchiglia et al., 2007). For example, in matching a tree reading(date(Day,Month,Year),water(Level)) to a tree measurement(Liquid,Level,date(Month,Day)), this step would discover that the words Date, Day, Month, Level and Reading in the first term all have equivalent words in the second term (in the case of the first three, these are identical, whereas Reading is matched to the semantically equivalent Measurement).
- **Tree Matching:** once we have the correspondences between the nodes of the trees, the next step is to match the whole trees and determine the global similarity between them. This is achieved by considering the relationships, within the trees, of nodes identified as similar in the previous step. For example, if we were matching reading(Water,Level) and reading(Liquid,Level), we would expect the similarity score to be high, but the relationship between reading(water(Level)) and reading(Liquid,Level) to be much lower: the different structure of these trees indicates a difference in meaning. For this step, we make use of a tree-edit distance algorithm. Tree-edit distance algorithms are designed to determine the cost of translating one tree into another through the application of three operations: *(i)* vertex deletion, *(ii)* vertex insertion, and *(iii)* vertex replacement (Tai, 1979). However, tree-edit distance algorithms do not consider the semantics behind these operations: for example, according to the standard algorithm, replacing a vertex Water with a vertex Liquid would cost the same as replacing Water with Sandwich, although it is clear that a far greater change is occurring in the second case.

We have therefore augmented a standard tree-edit distance algorithm so that the cost of performing each operation is dependent on the expense of performing the change: that is, a smaller semantic change costs less than a large change. To do this, we make use of Giunchiglia and Walsh's theory of abstraction (Giunchiglia & Walsh, 1989; Giunchiglia & Walsh, 1992), which provides a formal theory of how two first-order terms may be related and yet non-identical. For example, the number of arguments of predicates may be different; the types of these arguments may be more or less general; the name of the predicate may be more or less general. Since it is trivial to convert first-order terms into trees, this theory is applicable to our tree matching step.

Thus the node matching step tells us in what way the node terms are related and the combination of the tree-edit distance algorithm and the abstraction operations tell us how similar two trees are by combining the steps that are necessary to convert one tree to another (which is functionally identical to providing a map between the two) with the costs that should be assigned to each of these steps. Taking one example from Figure 2, the node matching tells us that Water_level from Tree 1 is a more specific type of Level from Tree 2 (or Water_level is a subclass of Level), and the augmented tree-edit distance algorithm will map these two together (as part of the process of mapping the whole tree) and, using the abstraction operations, determine that the cost of this map should be low due to the relationship identified in the node matching step. Therefore, by combining semantic matching with structural matching, we obtain the SPSM (*structure-preserving semantic matching*) algorithm.

Of all the potential maps between two trees, the tree-edit distance algorithm will return the map with the least overall cost (calculated through the application of abstraction operations). The cost of the overall map is calculated by

$$Cost = min \sum_{i \in S} k_i * Cost_i \qquad (1)$$

where S stands for the set of the allowed tree edit operations; k_i stands for the number of *i-th* operations necessary to convert one tree into the other and $Cost_i$ defines the cost of the *i-th* operation. Our goal here is to define the $Cost_i$ in a way that models the semantic distance. We can then define the similarity between two trees T_1 and T_2 to be:

$$TreeSim = 1 - \frac{Cost}{\max(T_1, T_2)} \qquad (2)$$

This case is intended to outline the ideas and motivation behind our ideas; for full technical details of this process, together with implementation information, see (Giunchiglia et al, 2008a).

The OpenKnowledge Framework

Matching service descriptions is only one aspect of service integration: another important aspect is service selection: how a potentially suitable service is located, how a particular one is chosen from potentially many, and so on. In this section, we introduce the OpenKnowledge framework within which the SPSM algorithm was originally designed, in order to describe how this framework allows the full process of service integration to take place, and to show SPSM in action within a specific context. Note that although SPSM was designed within this context, it is nevertheless very widely applicable: in fact, it does not need to be restricted to matching service descriptions but can be used for matching any two artifacts that can be expressed as a tree.

The OpenKnowledge framework facilitates interactions between disparate peers or services, which generally do not share an ontology or have prior knowledge of one another. The key technology that makes this possible is the use of shared choreographies called *Interaction Models (IMs).* These IMs can be designed by any user on the network, and can then be shared across the network, so that determining an IM for a particular interaction is usually a case of finding the appropriate one for reuse rather than writing one from scratch. Note that in the OpenKnowledge context, services are proactive, signing up to IMs in which they wish to play a role. Calls to services therefore do not come out of the blue, from an unknown caller, but occur when that IM is enacted and are of the form described within the IM.

The OpenKnowledge framework enables this through providing an API that can be used by an application to become a peer in a network. The API exploits:

- a *distributed discovery service*, which searches for suitable IMs for a particular interaction;
- a *matching service*, which uses the SPSM algorithm to map between requirements in IMs and abilities in the peers to determine how similar they are;
- a *trust component* to allow users to assess with which peers they wish to interact with;

We will not address these components, other than the matching service, in any detail in this case. Further information about OpenKnowledge can be found on the project webpage[2].

Describing Interactions

An Interaction Model (IM) specifies the interaction between different peer in tasks that require their coordinated activities. Interaction Models are written in LCC (Robertson, 2004), a compact, executable language based on process calculus. An IM is composed by a set of *role definitions*: a peer enters an interaction by taking a role, and follows the unfolding of the interaction as specified by the role definition. The definition prescribes to a peer in a specific role what messages to send, which messages to expect and what other roles to adopt later if necessary. The coordination of the peers is obtained through message exchange between the roles they have adopted, while the behaviour of peers is defined by constraints on messages. Through constraints it is possible to set preconditions for sending a message and for changing role as well as describing the effects of receiving a message. A peer must solve the constraints in order to proceed. The IM makes no assumptions at to how constraints are solved and the operation is delegated to the peer. In LCC constraints are expressed as first order predicates, which can be easily transformed into trees for matching.

Figure 3 shows a simple IM for querying a sensor. The IM is performed by two peers, one taking the querier role and the other taking the sensor role. The querier needs first to satisfy the constraint needLocation(RepID,Nd) to select the interested reporter ID and the node, then send the request message to the sensor and wait for the reply. The sensor receives the request, satisfies the constraint reading(RepID,Nd,Lvl,Date) and sends back the reply. The IM execution is then concluded. Note that in an IM, there are no semantics in the message: the name of the message is merely a placeholder and the meaning of the arguments is determined within the constraints. Thus the ability to play a role depends on the ability to satisfy the constraints on the messages in that role. Any peer using the OK infrastructure can trivially pass any message if the constraints on that message are satisfied.

A constraint in an IM can be compared to the call to a web service in a BPEL workflow. In order to solve a constraint a peer needs to map it to its own local knowledge base, provided by an extensible set of plug-in components (Besana et al., 2007). The plug-in components expose

Figure 3. A simple Interaction Model for querying a sensor about the water level

```
a(querier,Q)::
 request(RepId,Nd) => a(sensor,S) ← needLocation(RepID,Nd)
 then
 level(Lvl,Date) <= a(sensor,S)

a(sensor,S)::
 request(RepID,Nd) <= a(querier,Q)
 then
 level(Lvl,Date) => a(querier,Q) ← reading(RepID,Nd,Lvl,Date)
```

methods, which can be simple wrappers for web services, or can be self-contained java methods. We have developed a tool that generates a wrapper component from a WSDL file: each operation in it becomes a method in the component.

In the constraint reading(RepID,Nd,Lvl,Date), the variables RepID and Nd are already instantiated (they are received with the request message), and are the input parameters; the variables Lvl and Date are instantiated by the peer when solves the constraint and are the output parameters.

While first order predicates are usually untyped, in OpenKnowledge, arguments can be annotated with their ontological type and, if desired, these types can be annotated with a reference to an ontology in which the semantics of that type are given. The annotations are used to create the trees that are then matched by SPSM. Figures 4 and 5 shows annotations for the parameters in the IM and for the method in the peer's component.

Lifecycle of Interaction in OpenKnowledge

The IMs are published by the authors on the *distributed discovery service (DDS)* (Kotoulas & Siebes, 2007) with a keyword-based description. Peers search and subscribe to roles in IMs in the DDS. The OpenKnowledge kernel provides the functionality needed to subscribe to a role and the framework for handling the plug-in components used to satisfy constraints. The peer can be a GUI-based application whose components interact directly with a user or a server application that solves the constraints automatically, possibly calling the web services wrapped by the components or accessing a database.

The lifecycle of an interaction is:

- **Interaction selection:** a peer searches, by sending a keyword-based query to the DDS, for published IMs for the task it intends to perform. The DDS replies with a list of IMs satisfying the query. The peer needs to compare the received IMs with its plug-in components, in order to select the one that best matches its capabilities. This is one instance – the most important one – where the SPSM algorithm comes into play. In order for a peer to decide whether it wishes to play a role, it needs to map every constraint on that role to one of the methods in its plug-in components. For each of these constraints, the SPSM algorithm will return a numerical score in [0 1] describing how close this constraint is to one of the peer's constraint, as well as a map detailing how this conversion must be done. To estimate how good the peer will be at performing that role, it must somehow aggregate these scores. The simplest

Figure 4. The annotations of the parameters used by the role sensor in the IM of Figure 3

```
@annotation(@role(sensor), @variable(RepID, reportedID)
@annotation(@role(sensor), @variable(Nd, node)
@annotation(@role(sensor), @variable(Lvl, water_level)
@annotation(@role(sensor), @variable(Date, date(day,month,year,time))
```

Figure 5. The annotations for the method measurement in the plug-in component of a sensor peer

```
@MethodSemantic(language="tag",
args={"location(reporterID,node)",
   "level",
   "date(month,day, hour, minute)"}
public boolean measurement(Argument Lc,Argument Lv,Argument D){...}
```

way to do this – and the way that is current implemented – is to average all scores over the number of constraints to be mapped. However, more sophisticated mechanisms could be devised which could incorporate user preferences and context-dependent information. Once this overall score has been calculated, the peer must decide whether or not to subscribe to the role. This is entirely up to the peer and it may subscribe even if it gets a very low score. In such a case, it would not usually be in the peer's interests to subscribe, as it is very likely to fail in the execution of the role. If it finds a role in an IM with an acceptably high matching score, it subscribes on the DDS, indicating its intention to perform the appropriate role in it. As part of the subscription process, it must declare a matching score.

Peers may subscribe to as many IMs as they wish, to play as many different roles as they wish. For example, in a vending scenario, a seller peer may subscribe to many different IMs in the seller role, as it may be content to act as a seller simultaneously in many different types of purchase interactions. A buyer would more typically only wish to buy once (though of course this depends on the exact situation), so would only wish to subscribe once in the role buyer, but may also be subscribed in other roles in different IMs for quite different goals. A peer may also be subscribed as seller in one purchase IM, and as buyer in another, as it may be interested in buying supplies for its production as well as in selling it.

- **Bootstrap:** when all the roles in an IM are subscribed to, the discovery service randomly selects a peer in the network, asking it to play the coordinator of the interaction. If it accepts, it becomes the IM coordinator and asks all the subscribed peers to select which other peers they are prepared to interact with. This matching score provided by peers as they subscribe is also useful to other peers deciding whether or not they wish to interact with that peer in that role. However, neither the system nor other peers have any way of checking this matching score: the peer's own capabilities and ontology are private. So peers must use this score with caution, for there are several reasons why it may not be accurate: the peer may be dishonest and may be trying to exaggerate its abilities; it may have a poor ontology, so the matching score returned may be a poor reflection of its actual ability to perform the role. This score is therefore most useful to others when it is moderated by some kind of trust score examining the peer's past behaviour: if the peer is dishonest or inept, it will repeatedly underperform and therefore trust scores are lowered. We therefore have developed a *good enough* algorithm, whose role is to moderate the matching score with respect to a trust score, resulting in the *good enough answers* score (GEA). OpenKnowledge provides a built-in mechanism for calculating trust, based on prior experience of interaction in the same, similar or non-similar contexts, and a way to combine this trust score and the matching score to obtain a single score reflecting how well that peer is likely to behave. This process is explained in (Giunchiglia et al., 2008b). Peers are free to use this built-in method or to use their own mechanisms as they please.

After receiving the peers' preferences, the IM coordinator creates a group of peers who are all willing to interact with one another in their proposed roles. If the group covers all the roles, it starts the interaction. If there is more than one way of filling roles such that all involved peers are satisfied, the choice of allocation is made arbitrarily. It is thus possible that peers subscribed for roles will not be chosen in a particular run of that interaction. In such a case, they must wait for a subsequent run of the interaction, perhaps weakening their choice criteria next time, as they may be ruling themselves out of potential allocations by refusing to interact with many of the other subscribed peers.

- **Run of the interaction:** the IM coordinator runs the IM locally: messages are exchanged between proxies of the peers, which are contacted in order to solve the constraints.
- **Follow-up:** after the run of the interaction, the IM coordinator sends the log of the interaction to all involved peer so that they can analyse it if they wish to. The analysis can be aimed at computing a trust value for the other peers (Giunchiglia et al., 2008b) to be used in selecting peers in future interactions or to create a statistical model for the content of the messages, in order to improve mapping (Besana & Robertson, 2007). If, interaction after interaction, a peer is consistently unreliable it will be selected less and less frequently by the other peers.

In a more orchestration-oriented model, the invocations to services are normally grounded at design time by the designer of the workflow. In this model, the peers decide to take part in interactions: they can look up an interaction for a specific task, they can be alerted when new interactions are published, or they can be asked to evaluate an interaction upon the request of another peer, but in all cases they evaluate the IMs they receive and then select those they want to subscribe to. The task of handling heterogeneity is therefore distributed among the peers.

CASE DESCRIPTION: FLOODING IN THE TRENTINO REGION

The OpenKnowledge system has been fully evaluated in two testbeds: Proteomics and emergency response. Here, we explain the emergency response testbed and explain the role that the SPSM algorithm took in providing the necessary functionality.

Emergency response was chosen as being a particularly knowledge-intensive and dynamic application domain, with many players and a high potential for unexpected developments. We briefly outline the general scenario and then describe a specific interaction in more detail, highlighting where the techniques discussed in this article will be utilised.

The general scenario we are exploring is the case of the flooding of the river Adige in the Trentino region of Italy, which presents a significant threat to the city of Trento and the surrounding area and which has occurred seriously many times before, most notably on November 4th, 1966. We have large amounts of data from the 1966 flood, as well as data concerning the emergency flooding response plans of the Trentino authorities. Around this data, we have developed scenarios of interacting peers: for example, coordination centres, emergency monitoring services, the fire brigade, sensor nodes, GIS systems, route finding services and weather services.

Emergency response is not inherently peer-to-peer: we would of course expect that the key players would have strategies worked out well in advance and would have established the infrastructure and vocabulary for communicating with other key players. However, the chaotic nature of an emergency means that many players who will not have been able to coordinate in advance, or who were not expected to participate, may become involved. Additionally, services which were part of an emergency response may be unexpectedly unavailable or may be swamped by requests, and in such a situation, it is crucial that the emergency response can carry on regardless. Additionally, services may develop and change and it is unrealistic to expect these changes would always be known and accounted for in advance.

The e-Response system we have developed for this testbed is used:

i. to model and execute interactions between peers involved in an emergency response activity, whether individuals, sensors, web services or others;
ii. to provide feedback about the environment at appropriate moments, in a way that mirrors the real world (for example, a peer attempting to take a road will be informed that the road is blocked only when it is actually at that road, and it can then share this information with other peers through the network).
iii. to visualize and analyze a simulated coordination task through a Graphical User Interface (GUI).

The developed e-Response system is composed of two major components: the e-Response simulator and the peer network (and related interaction models). The e-Response simulator provides the disaster scene and its evolution, thus representing the "real world" within which all the actors (network peers) acts. The idea is that once the simulator has been used to aid the development and thorough testing of the approach, it could be removed and the peer network could instead operate in a real world situation (using real peers rather than simulated ones).

Every peer (either simulator or network peer) has an OpenKnowledge plug-in component (the OpenKnowledge kernel) which enables it to publish and search for IMs and be involved in a coordination task with other participants. Some of the peers in the peer network interact with both the simulator and network peers: these are the peers that 'exist' in the physical location. These peers will usually receive sensory information and be able to directly influence the simulated world, though some can only do one or the other (for example, water-level sensors have some sensory ability (they will receive information about the water-level) but they cannot directly influence the world, they can only indirectly influence the world by sharing this information across the peer network). Other network peers communicate among themselves and never connect to the simulator: these are peers that are not physically involved in the simulation and cannot directly affect the world, such as geographical-map-provider peers.

The peer network reconstructs (in a limited form) the infrastructure of the emergency response: for example, the command centre that will control the whole response (except in unforeseen circumstances such as it becoming uncountable), the fire teams they will be commanding, the buses that are to evacuate the citizens, and so on. One important job of the command centre is to keep a picture of the changing environment that is as accurate as possible and this is done through gathering information from other peers.

Figure 6 illustrates a scenario in which some of the peers in the simulation are interacting in order to facilitate the evacuation of citizens by bus from the flooding area. The emergency coordinator (EC) communicates with the buses (Bs), informing them which area they should pick up from and which area they should evacuate the citizens to. It is up to the buses to determine an appropriate route for this. To do this, they can communicate with the route service (RS), which will tell them what possible routes there are, but since they are in a flooding situation, they must also try to establish which routes are closed. To do this, they communicate with the civil protection peer (CP), whose role is to continually poll the water-level sensors (r_1, r_2, …) as to the water level in their vicinity, and from this they can calculate whether a route suggested by a bus is accessible. As long as this process is functioning, it is perhaps reasonable to assume that there will be no difficulty with integration: this is part of the planned emergency response, and such service integration should have been calculated in advance (though even this much cannot be certain as the peers may be constantly evolving – perhaps the owners of the water-level sensors have upgraded their ontologies since the most recent coordination effort). However, in such an emergency situation, such structure is not necessarily reliable. Perhaps

Figure 6. Interactions of peers in evacuation scenario

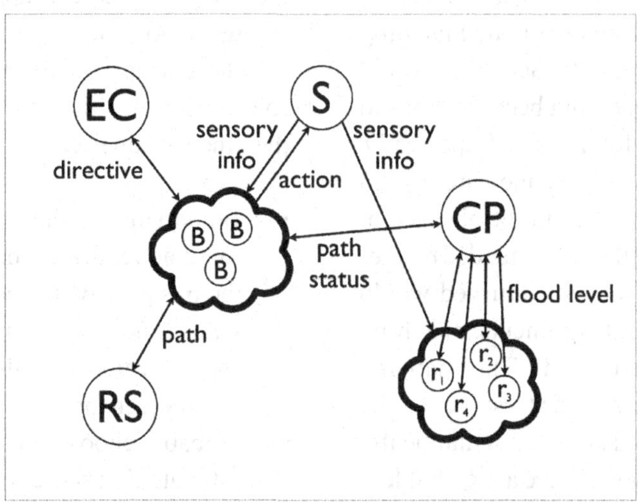

the civil protection peer will be swamped with requests from buses, citizens and others and be unable to respond to some of them; perhaps it will crash; perhaps it is housed in a building that is itself being flooded. If a bus peer cannot reach the civil protection peer, they must still do their best to reach their given destination. The OpenKnowledge system allows the seamless change from a centralised system to a decentralised one: instead of interacting with the civil protection peer, a bus can communicate with the water-level sensors directly and calculate for themselves which routes are possible. However, it is highly unlikely that such a scenario has been planned for in advance, and we are therefore forced to perform service integration on-the-fly.

We repeat the lifecycle of interaction described above for this particular interaction.

- **Interaction selection:** both the bus peer and the water-level sensor peers must be subscribed to an appropriate IM to play their relevant roles. Since the bus peer is taking the initiative here, this is most likely to happen through the bus peer searching for and subscribing to an IM in which many water-level sensor peers are already subscribed. A well-organised water-level sensor should subscribe to many such IMs so that it is ready to perform its role whenever requested. There may be many sensors at a single node, so in order to determine the water level at that node, it is necessary to choose one of potentially many with which to interact. The IM used in such a situation could be the one described in Figure 3, and let's imagine the process by which these water-level sensors have subscribed to their role. Since they wish to play the role sensor, they have only one constraint to satisfy: reading(RepID,Node,Level,Date). Imagine six sensors wish to sign up, and they describe their abilities in the following ways:

i. measurement(RepID,Node,Level,Date)
ii. reading(ReporterID,Level,Node,Date)
iii. reading(RepID,Level,UnitMeasure,Node,Date)
iv. reading(RepID,Water_level,Node,Date)
v. output(Level,Node)
vi. measurement(location(ReporterID,Node),Level,Date)

They would each use the SPSM algorithm to map their abilities to the constraint. Sensor

i) would discover that had a perfect match; all that is necessary is to consider measurement to be equivalent to reading and the node matching step reveals this is permissible. Sensor ***ii)*** would have less than perfect matching because it has to infer a match between RepID and ReporterID. Analysis of these terms would indicate a high similarity but it is not certain, in the absence of further information, that they are intended to refer to the same thing. The adapter returned would also switch the two central arguments, matching Level to Level and Node to Node. This mapping would not influence the similarity score, as the order of nodes is assumed not to be semantically significant. Sensor ***iii)*** would have a high but less than perfect matching score as it has an extra argument that would not be used: UnitMeasure, which is intended to make explicit the units in which the measurement is given. Sensor ***iv)*** would also have a lower matching score, losing points through the match between Water_level and Level. In this particular situation, we can see that these are functionally equivalent because what is meant by Level is the level of the water. However, the water-level sensor does not have this high-level view and therefore cannot be sure of this. Sensor ***v)*** would receive a very low score: the naming of its predicate is unintuitive and does not describe what it actually does, and it misses out key information such as its ID and the Date. Sensor ***vi)*** is a slightly simplified version of the one discussed earlier in the case and illustrated in Figure 2. There is a significant structural difference here, also illustrated in Figure 2, in that an extra predicate location is included, and the arguments ReporterId and Node become children of that predicate, and grandchildren of the top-level predicate measurement. The similarity score would be lower due to this: in fact, this is an 'organisational' detail and does not really affect the meaning of the arguments, but it is an indication that this meaning may be different. Nevertheless, every argument in the constraint can find a similar or exact argument to match to in ability, albeit in a different structure. Therefore the similarity score would be reasonable but not as high as for sensors ***i) - iv)***.

These sensors will all subscribe to play the role sensor and the bus peer will subscribe to play the role querier.

- **Bootstrap:** If these sensors are all at the same node, then, when the coordinator asks the bus peer which peer it wishes to interact with, it need only chose one. Unless it has any information to the contrary, and assuming the sensor peers are all honest, it will probably choose sensor ***i)***, as it has the highest matching score. However, if it has previously interacted with sensor ***i)*** and found it to be unreliable, it will have a low trust score, and so the GEA score, formed by combining its matching and trust scores, may be lower than the GEA scores of other sensors. The bus peer would normally choose the peer with the highest GEA score to interact with. Assuming the chosen sensor is happy to interact with the bus peer, the interaction will proceed.
- **Run of the interaction:** The appropriate messages are passed.
- **Follow-up:** The bus peer will update its trust model according to the outcome of the interaction. If the interaction was successful, the bus peer's trust in the sensor peer will increase. If it fails, it will be lowered. For example, sensor ***v)*** may claim to have a very high matching score and may come out top in the GEA calculation. However, it will fail to satisfy the constraint on its role and so will not be able to pass the message, leading to failure. The next time this interaction occurs, it is much less likely to be chosen even if it reports a high matching score, as the trust score will be low. Alternatively, the interaction may run smoothly – if, for example, sensor ***i)*** was chosen – but if sensor ***i)*** is faulty it will report a false level, leading to a

successful interaction but an unsatisfactory outcome. This will not be as obvious as a breakdown of the interaction, but once it has been noticed by the bus peer (perhaps when it finds its route unexpectedly flooded), the bus peer will update its trust model accordingly. The bus peer is also free to share its trust model with other peers if desired.

Evaluation

There are many reasons why heterogeneity can become a problem, even amongst services that were originally designed to interact. For example, drifting can cause heterogeneity between components and IMs: components that were designed for a particular interaction could be used in other interactions and can change over time to adapt to these, when they are reused in the original interaction, matching is required. Similarly, interactions designed for a specific context may be used for different aims and therefore adapted to better suit these aims. Moreover, new interactions or components can be developed by copying others.

Starting from these assumptions, we tried to evaluate how the matching mechanism, described previously, could cope with these sort of heterogeneity. The evaluation aimed at exploring the robustness of the SPSM approach towards both typical syntactic alterations (i.e. replacements of node names, modification of node names and misspellings) and typical meaning alterations (i.e. usage of related synonyms, hyponyms, hypernyms) of node names.

Since the tree alterations made are known, these provided the reference results. This allows for the computation of the matching quality measures, such as Precision (which is a correctness measure) and Recall (which is a completeness measure). The alterations are applied probabilistically on each node of the original tree: increasing the probabilities of the modifications it is possible to obtain trees that are statistically more and more distant from the original one. The tree alteration procedure has been inspired by the work in (Euzenat and Shvaiko, 2007) on systematic benchmarks.

Figure 7 shows how recall behaves when the probabilities of syntactic and semantic alterations are increased. Recall decreases slowly: only when both semantic and syntactic changes are extremely likely, recall drops to 0.1. In our experiments, precision was always very high. This is not uncommon in matching scenarios, where recall is often the problem.

Figure 7. Recall results for syntactic and meaning alterations

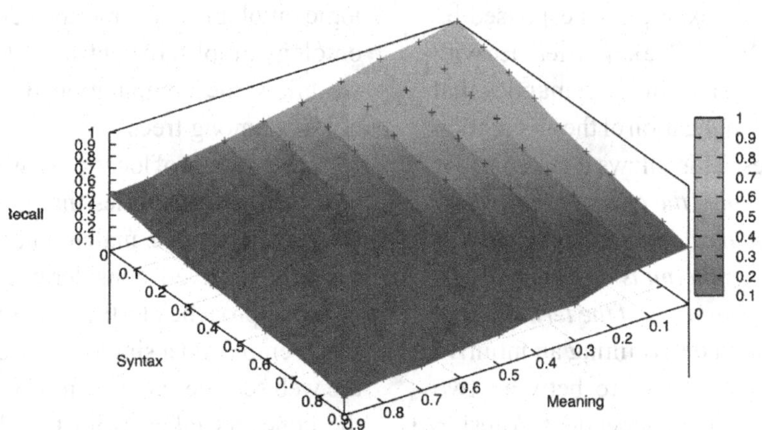

The evaluation is done by comparing the output of the SPSM algorithm with the output of a standard tree-edit distance algorithm, which does not consider the semantics. The fact that SPSM performs better, whilst a reassuring validation of the approach, is therefore not particularly surprising. A more powerful approach would be to compare our work against a 'state-of-the-art' system. However, as far as we believe there is no other approach currently existing that can be used to perform the same task as SPSM: matching trees whilst considering the semantics. Systems that perform semantic-free tree matching can be compared to SPSM in such experiments, as they are at least capable of performing the necessary tree matching. Other semantic-based approaches cannot do this, and therefore will fail completely in the task.

We are currently undertaking a much more thorough evaluation of the whole process of service integration within OpenKnowledge. These results may lend themselves more naturally to comparison with other service integration approaches because the scope will not be so limited as in the current experiments. We intend to publish these results shortly.

RELATED WORK

Our work builds on standard work in tree-edit distance measures, for example, as espoused by (Shasha and Zhang, 1997). The key difference with our work is the integration of the semantics that we gain through the application of the abstraction and refinement rules. This allows us to consider questions such as *what is the effect to the overall meaning of the term (tree) if node a is relabelled to node b?*, or *how significant is the removal of a node to the overall semantics of the term?* These questions are crucial in determining an intuitive and meaningful similarity score between two terms, and are very context dependent. Altering the costs assigned to the tree-edit distance operations enables us to provide different answers to these questions depending on the context, and we are working on giving providing even more subtle variations of answers reflecting different contexts.

Work based on these ideas, such as Mikhaiel and Stroudi's work on HTML differencing (Gligorov et al., 2005), tends to focus only on the structure and not on the semantics. This work never considers what the individual nodes in their HTML trees mean and only considers context in the sense that, for example, the cost of deleting a node with a large subtree is higher than the cost of deleting a leaf node; the semantic meanings of these nodes are not considered.

Many diverse solutions to the ontology matching problem have been proposed so far. See (Shvaiko & Euzenat, 2005) for a comprehensive survey and (Euzenat & Valtchev, 2004; Euzenat & Shvaiko, 2007; Noy & Musen, 2003; Ehrig et al., 2005; Gligorov et al., 2007; Bergamaschi et al., 1999; Kalfoglou & Schorlemmer, 2003; Straccia & Troncy, 2005) for individual solutions. However most efforts have been devoted to computation of the correspondences holding among the classes of description logic ontologies. Recently, several approaches allowed computation of correspondences holding among the object properties (or binary predicates) (Tang et al., 2006). The approach taken in (Hu & Qu, 2006) facilitates the finding of correspondences holding among parts of description logic ontologies or subgraphs extracted from the ontology graphs. In contrast to these approaches, we allow the computation of correspondences holding among trees.

The problem of location of web services on the basis of the capabilities that they provide (often referred to as the matchmaking problem) has recently received considerable attention. Most of the approaches to the matchmaking problem so far employed a single ontology approach (i.e., the web services are assumed to be described by the concepts taken from the shared ontology): see (Klusch et al., 2006) for example. Probably the most similar to ours is the approach taken in METEOR-S (Aggarwal, 2004) and in (Oundhakar, 2005), where the services are assumed to be annotated with the concepts taken from various ontologies. Then the matchmaking problem is solved by the application of the matching algorithm. The algorithm combines the results of atomic matchers that roughly correspond to the element level matchers exploited as part of our algorithm. In contrast to this work, we exploit a more sophisticated matching technique that allows us to utilise the structure provided by the first order term.

Web services composition follows two alternative approaches: *orchestration* or *choreography*. Their primary difference is their scope. An orchestration model provides a scope specifically focussing on the view of one participant. Instead, a choreography model covers all parties and their associated interactions giving a global view of the system. The OpenKnowledge system is closer to the choreography approach, since all services involved know – and can choose – with whom they are interacting and what these interactions will involve (once they have signed up to IMs; prior to run-time this may not be known). Other important service composition languages are BPEL[3] and YAWL (van der Aalst & ter Hofstede, 2005) (orchestration languages) and WS-CDL[4] (a choreography language). BPEL and YAWL benefit from the simplicity of the orchestration approach, but the OpenKnowledge system has advantages: services choose to take part in interactions and they know in advance both what these interactions will involve and which other services they may be interacting with, allowing them to make informed decisions as to whether this is in their interests and which other services they would prefer to participate with. Additionally, the interactions are not owned by any particular service and are therefore not biased towards any one service but rather allow free interaction for all. Crucially, this approach is also scalable, allowing a network of arbitrarily large size to interact on the OpenKnowledge system. WS-CDL is closer to the OpenKnowledge approach but, unlike OpenKnowledge, it is merely a specification and is not executable.

In summary, much work has been done on structure-preserving matching and much has been done on semantic matching, and our work depends heavily on the work of others in these fields. The novelty of our work is in the combination of these two approaches to produce a structure-preserving semantic matching algorithm, thus allowing us to determine fully how structured terms, such as web service calls, are related to one another.

CURRENT CHALLENGES

The current implementation of the SPSM algorithm, though it has proved effective in practice, does not have the full scope we believe to be necessary. For example, it assumes that matching between the abilities of a peer and the requirements of a role can be performed by considering a one-to-one relationship between arguments. If, for example, we were to match:

```
reading(RepID,Node,Date,Level)
to
reading(RepID,Node,Day,Month,Year,Level)
```

then, once RepID, Node and Level had been matched, a choice would need to be made as to whether to map Date to Day, Month or Year. In reality, a mapping of date to all three of these arguments would be the best solution. We would therefore like to include *one* $\rightarrow$ *many, many* $\rightarrow$ *one* and *many* $\rightarrow$ *many* mappings in the algorithm.

Another way in which the algorithm could be improved is to make the scoring system more sophisticated. Currently, there is a single score assigned for mapping one node to another where one node is an abstraction of the other node. For example, the relationships between tiger and feline and tiger and animal are both abstraction relations, as tiger is a sub-class of both feline and animal, and they would therefore score the same. However, there is clearly a closer degree of kinship in the first relation than in the second, and a scoring system that could reflect this would provide a more accurate notion of similarity. In addition, allowing user-set weightings to affect the scoring would provide a much more accurate estimation of whether a service would perform a job satisfactorily. For example, if the constraint to be satisfied is:

```
reading(RepID,Node,Date,Level),
the services
reading(RepID,Node,Date) and
reading(RepID,Node,Level)
```

would both receive the same (low) score because they both omit an argument. However, perhaps the querier is very concerned to receive a value for Level but is not very bothered to receive a value for date (maybe the call is done in real time and the querier assumes that the date on which the reading is returned is the date on which it is made, so that this value becomes obsolete). In this case, we would like to allow the user to give a high weight to the Level argument and a low weight to the Date argument, meaning that the first mismatched service would score very low, whereas the second mismatched service would have quite a high score, reflecting that the fact that is could, despite mismatches, satisfy the querier.

These are the challenges we have currently identified with the SPSM algorithm; perhaps more will become apparent as the evaluation continues.

For the OpenKnowledge system as a whole, the largest challenge is to provide a complete and thorough evaluation done on a large scale. This is difficult due to the bootstrapping problem: proper evaluation depends on large numbers of services acting as OK peers in a natural and organic way – i.e., not set up by us solely for the purpose of evaluation. However, we cannot expect large numbers of services to become OK peers before we provide a full evaluation of the system. This problem is currently being made much more tractable as there are already many users of the OK system, and we intend to perform evaluation on their experience. Details of these early adopters can be found on the project webpage[2].

RUNNING THE OK SYSTEM

The full OpenKnowledge system, complete with full instructions and demonstrations, is available to download free from the project webpage. Details of the emergency response testbed and simulator can also be found, together with complete documentation for the project. Once the full evaluation is completed, the results will be posted here as well as in the relevant publications.

CONCLUSION

The key contributions of this case are two-fold:

i. the introduction of the SPSM algorithm, which is broadly applicable and can be used in any situation where semantic tree-matching is necessary, making it applicable for service integration in most circumstances but also for many other forms of matching such as database integration;
ii. the introduction of the OpenKnoweldge system, which itself provides a major contribution to the problem of service integration by providing a complete framework in which this integration can occur, and also provides a demonstration of SPSM in action.

We have described a scenario in which both the full OpenKnowledge system and the SPSM algorithm have been demonstrated in action and evaluated. We briefly described an evaluation of the SPSM algorithm; further evaluation is currently taking place.

We believe that our approach offers a solution to a problematic and important issue: that of automatically integrating services in the many situations where hard-coding service calls is impractical or impossible. Whilst any solution to this problem that does not depend on a shared ontology must be an imperfect solution, it is nevertheless a solution that can be used in real-world, large-scale situations where the use of fully shared semantics is impossible.

ACKNOWLEDGMENT

We appreciate support from the OpenKnowledge European STREP (FP6-027253).

REFERENCES

Aggarwal, R., Verma, K., Miller, J. A., & Milnor, W. (2004). Constraint driven web service composition in METEOR-S. In *Proceedings of IEEE SCC.*

Bergamaschi, S., Castano, S., & Vincini, M. (1999). Semantic integration of semistructured and structured data sources. *SIGMOD Record, 28*(1). doi:10.1145/309844.309897

Besana, P., & Robertson, D. (2007). How service choreography statistics reduce the ontology mapping problem. In *Proceedings of ISWC.*

Ehrig, M., Staab, S., & Sure, Y. (2005). Bootstrapping ontology alignment methods with APFEL. In *Proceedings of ISWC.*

Euzenat, J., & Shvaiko, P. (2007). *Ontology matching.* Springer.

Euzenat, J., & Valtchev, P. (2004). Similarity-based ontology alignment in OWL-lite. In *Proceedings of ECAI.*

Fellbaum, C. (1998). *WordNet: an electronic lexical database.* MIT Press.

Giunchiglia, F. McNeill, F., Yatskevich, M., Pane, J., Besana, P., & Shvaiko, P. (2008a, November). Approximate Structure-Preserving Semantic Matching. In *Proceedings of "ODBASE 2008"*, Monterrey, Mexico.

Giunchiglia, F., Sierra, C., McNeill, F., Osman, N., & Siebes, R. (2008b). Deliverable 4.5: Good Enough Answers Algorithm. *Techincal Report, OpenKnowledge.* Retrieved November 2008 from www.openk.org.

Giunchiglia, F., & Walsh, T. (1989, August). Abstract theorem proving. In *Proceedings of "11th international joint conference on artificial intelligence (IJCAI'89)* (pp 1372-1377).

Giunchiglia, F., & Walsh, T. (1992). A theory of abstraction. *Artificial Intelligence, 57*(2-3). doi:10.1016/0004-3702(92)90021-O

Giunchiglia, F., Yatskevich, M., & Shvaiko, P. (2007). Semantic matching: Algorithms and implementation. *Journal on Data Semantics, IX.*

Gligorov, R., Aleksovski, Z., ten Kate, W., & van Harmelen, F. (2005). Accurate and efficient html differencing. In *Proceedings of the 13th IEEE International Workshop on Software Technology and Engineering Practice (STEP)* (pp. 163–172). IEEE Press.

Gligorov, R., Aleksovski, Z., ten Kate, W., & van Harmelen, F. (2007). Using google distance to weight approximate ontology matches. In *Proceedings of WWW.*

Gooneratne, N., & Tari, Z. (2008). Matching independent global constraints for composite web services. In *In Proceedings of WWW* (pp. 765–774).

Hu, W., & Qu, Y. (2006). Block matching for ontologies. In *Proceedings of ISWC.*

Kalfoglou, Y., & Schorlemmer, M. (2003). IF-Map: an ontology mapping method based on information flow theory. *Journal on Data Semantics, I.*

Klusch, M., Fries, B., & Sycara, K. (2006). Automated semantic web service discovery with OWLS- MX. In *Proceedings of AAMAS.*

Kotoulas, S., & Siebes, R. (2007). Deliverable 2.2: Adaptive routing in structured peer-to-peer overlays. *Technical report, OpenKnowledge.* Retrieved November 2008 from www.openk.org.

Li, L., & Horrocks, I. (2003). A software framework for matchmaking based on semantic web technology. In *Proceedings of WWW.*

Noy, N., & Musen, M. (2003). The PROMPT suite: interactive tools for ontology merging and mapping. *International Journal of Human-Computer Studies, 59*(6). doi:10.1016/j.ijhcs.2003.08.002

Oundhakar, S., Verma, K., Sivashanugam, K., Sheth, A., & Miller, J. (2005). Discovery of web services in a multi-ontology and federated registry environment. *Journal of Web Services Research, 2*(3).

Robertson, D. (2004). A lightweight coordination calculus for agent systems. In Declarative Agent Languages and Technologies (pp. 183–197).

Shasha, D., & Zhang, K. (1997). Approximate tree pattern matching. In *Pattern Matching Algorithms* (pp. 341–371). Oxford University Press.

Shvaiko, P., & Euzenat, J. (2005). A survey of schema-based matching approaches. *Journal on Data Semantics, IV.*

Straccia, U., & Troncy, R. (2005). oMAP: Combining classifiers for aligning automatically OWL ontologies. In *Proceedings of WISE.*

Tai, K.-C. (1979). The tree-to-tree correction problem. *Journal of the ACM, 26*(3). doi:10.1145/322139.322143

Tang, J., Li, J., Liang, B., Huang, X., Li, Y., & Wang, K. (2006). Using Bayesian decision for ontology mapping. *Journal of Web Semantics, 4*(1).

van der Aalst, W. M. P., & ter Hofstede, A. H. M. (2005). YAWL: Yet Another Workflow Language. *Information Systems, 30*(4), 245–275. doi:10.1016/j.is.2004.02.002

ENDNOTES

1. http://www.altova.com/products/mapforce/data_mapping.html
2. www.openk.org
3. Web Services Business Process Execution Language Version 2.0, http://docs.oasis-open.org/wsbpel/2.0/wsbpel-v2.0.pdf
4. Web Services Choreography Description Language Version 1.0, http://www.w3.org/TR/2005/CR-ws-cdl-10-20051109/

This work was previously published in the Journal of Cases on Information Technology, Vol. 11, Issue 4, edited by M. Khosrow-Pour, pp. 26-46, copyright 2009 by IGI Publishing (an imprint of IGI Global).

Chapter 5
Streamlining Semantic Integration Systems

Yannis Kalfoglou
Ricoh Europe plc & University of Southampton, UK

Bo Hu
SAP Research CEC Belfast, UK

EXECUTIVE SUMMARY

Yannis Kalfoglou and Bo Hu argue for the use of a streamlined approach to integrate semantic integration systems. The authors elaborate on the abundance and diversity of semantic integration solutions and how this impairs strict engineering practice and ease of application. The versatile and dynamic nature of these solutions comes at a price: they are not working in sync with each other neither is it easy to align them. Rather, they work as standalone systems often leading to diverse and sometimes incompatible results. Hence the irony that we might need to address the interoperability issue of tools tackling information interoperability. Kalfoglou and Hu also report on an exemplar case from the field of ontology mapping where systems that used seemingly similar integration algorithms and data, yield different results which are arbitrary formatted and annotated making interpretation and reuse of the results difficult. This makes it difficult to apply semantic integration solutions in a principled manner. The authors argue for a holistic approach to streamline and glue together different integration systems and algorithms. This will bring uniformity of results and effective application of the semantic integration solutions. If the proposed streamlining respects design principles of the underlying systems, then the engineers will have maximum configuration power and tune the streamlined systems in order to get uniform and well understood results. The authors propose a framework for building such streamlined system based on engineering principles and an exemplar, purpose built system, CROSI Mapping System (CMS), which targets the problem of ontology mapping.

DOI: 10.4018/978-1-60566-894-9.ch005

THE NECESSITY FOR SEMANTIC INTEROPERABILITY

"We need interoperable systems."

Time has long gone when manufacturers designed and assembled artefacts as stand-alone objects, ready to be used for whatever purpose they had been originally conceived. The necessity for more and more complex devices and the industrialisation/standardisation of manufacturing processes have led to the engineering of very specialised components that can be reused for a variety of component-based systems, which neither have been designed nor assembled by a sole manufacturer and for a unique purpose.

Analogously, in our *information age*, a similar phenomenon has occurred to the "manufacturing" of information technology (IT) artefacts. Originally, software applications, databases, and expert systems were all designed and constructed by a dedicated group of software or knowledge engineers who had overall control of the entire lifecycle of IT artefacts. But this time has gone too, as software engineering praxis is shifting from the implementation of custom-made, stand-alone systems to component-based software engineering (COTS, ERP, etc.). Databases are gradually deployed in distributed architectures and subsequently federated, and knowledge-based systems are built by reusing more and more previously constructed knowledge bases and inference engines. A compelling example on this front is SAP Business One™, which contains 14 core modules specialised in the immediate and long-term needs (e.g. customer relationship management, finance, purchasing, etc.) of small or medium-sized enterprises (SMEs). Individual SMEs then decide which fields of business activity they want to support and align the relatively independent modules into an integral framework. While accessing a raft of functionalities through one seemingly unified interface, the users normally are not aware of the underlying integration effort that seamlessly juxtaposes heterogeneous data from different units of an organisation and different business policies.

Moreover, the World Wide Web, and its ambitious extension the Semantic Web, has brought us an unprecedented global distribution of information in the form of hypertext documents, online databases, open-source code, terminological repositories (like for example Wikitionary), web services, blogs, etc., all of which continually challenge the traditional role of IT in our society. As a result, the distributed nature of IT systems has experienced a dramatic explosion with major IT suppliers starting to provide on demand web-based services (empowered by Service Oriented Architectures) instead of all-in-one boxed products and localised solutions (fine-tuned against the legal system, currency, and accountancy policy in each country) instead of universal solutions.

But in contrast to traditional industrial manufacturing and composition of artefacts, the composition and interaction of IT components at the level of distribution on the Web is still at its infancy, and we are just grasping the scope of this endeavour: successful IT component interoperability beyond basic syntactic communication is very hard. Unlike with industrial manufacturing, our era's basic commodity around which all IT technology is evolving, namely *information*, is not yet well understood. While industrial and civil engineers know how to apply well-established mathematical models to derive an artefact's characteristics from the physical properties of its components, software engineers and knowledge workers lack the machinery that will enable them to do the same with information assets. The problem with understanding information is that we need ways with which we can reveal, expose and communicate the meaning (semantics) of information. But this has eluded any mechanistic approach to interoperability. Putting together different databases has proved to be successful only for closed environments and under very strong assumptions; the same holds for distributed artificial intelligence applications and interaction in multi-agent systems. While we were staying on entirely syntactic issues, it has been relatively easy to achieve component interoperability. For example, in the case of the Web, standardisation of hypertext representation using HTML, of hypertext location by means of URL/URIs, and of data transfer protocol via HTTP has boosted it to the great success it is today. But as soon as we try to deal with the meaning of information, looking for intelligent management of the information available on the (Semantic) Web, interoperability becomes a hard task.

The crux of the problem lies in the *heterogeneity* which is naturally inherited in independently constructed information systems. As most of the interoperability tasks faced today in distributed IT environments deal with integration of legacy and proprietary systems, the quest of engineers is to devise effective and practical solutions that leverage the existing assets. This is the state-of-the-practice as we are in financially challenging times and re-usability of existing assets, maximising their value and efficiency is a top priority from a cost-reduction perspective.

Solutions to the problem of heterogeneity are commonly dubbed, *integration* at a system level or *interoperability* at a task level. When the solution takes into account the "meaning" of information that needs to be integrated or used in support of interoperability, we often further refine the terminology as semantic integration or semantic interoperability. For example, a database schema matching algorithm that uses purely syntactic features of the schema (like table/column names) is not semantic whereas an ontology alignment algorithm that takes into account the codified meaning of ontology constructs that need to be aligned, it is. These comparisons are simplified views of what has become a versatile and dynamic mix of techniques and algorithms borrowed from a multitude of domains – like information retrieval, artificial intelligence, semantic web, database management – with a common goal: utilising as much semantic information as feasibly possible to enhance and improve the integration process of heterogeneous systems.

But, the versatile and dynamic nature of these solutions comes at a price: semantic integration solutions are available in abundance in both academic and commercial settings[1i]; however, these solutions are not working in sync with each other neither is it easy to align them. Rather, they work as standalone systems often leading to diverse and sometimes incompatible results leading to the irony that we might need to address the interoperability issue of tools tackling information interoperability. For example, in (Kalfoglou and Hu, 2006) the authors report an exemplar case from the field of ontology mapping where systems that used seemingly similar integration algorithms and data, yield different results which are arbitrary formatted and annotated making interpretation and reuse of the results difficult. This makes it difficult to apply semantic integration solutions in a principled manner.

One way to alleviate this problem is to apply a holistic approach and *streamline* by gluing together different integration systems and algorithms. This will bring uniformity of results and effective application of the semantic integration solutions. If the proposed streamlining respects design principles of the underlying systems, then the engineers will have maximum configuration power and tune the streamlined systems in order to get uniform and well understood results. This is the proposal we put forward in this work. Our working prototype is described in sections 3 and 4. Initially though, in the next section, we will provide a brief account on the historical context of semantic integration solutions with regards to their origins, state-of-practice and modern trends.

HISTORICAL CONTEXT AND TECHNOLOGY LANDSCAPE

Early work to tackle the semantic heterogeneity problem emerged in the eighties from the database community. In particular, the notion of federated databases where schemata are treated globally and exchanged between designers and among disparate systems, informed the requirements for techniques which assist database administrators to do schema matching.

Most of these techniques were based on syntactic features of the schemata used, and employed a variety of heuristics to kick off similarity measure algorithms, borrowed from the information retrieval community. A dominant technique has been the use of correspondence values, typically in the range 0..1, which supposedly captures the intended overlap of two mapped elements. These approaches had their deficiencies though, as it was often observed that schemata with virtually similar syntactic elements were describing different real world concepts. The crux of the problem was the lack of semantic information carried by the designated database schema elements. This information is important for the validity of the proposed mapping which made verification check of the proposed mappings by a human user, a necessity. This is one of the reasons why these approaches could not scale up.

In the mid to late nineties, more complex and richer knowledge representation models, namely ontologies, became popular and the advent of a global infrastructure for sharing semantics, the Semantic Web, necessitated the need to share ontologies. Sharing ontologies though presupposes some mapping between heterogeneous ontologies. Ontology mapping practice employs a variety of techniques: use of syntactic similarity, correspondence values (though sometimes more elaborated than a numerical range 0..1), and more advanced semantically rich techniques, mainly due to the knowledge representation origin of ontologies. For example, there are ontology mapping systems that exploit the hierarchical lattice found in ontology structures (partially ordered lattices), take advantage of ontology formalisms which allow certain semantic information to be attached to a particular element (from formal axioms to informal textual descriptions), and some use the underlying deductive mechanism to infer mappings (for example, use of Description Logics reasoning).

A popular technique has been the use of instance information. As both ontologies and database schemata are expected to be instantiated in the application domain (either directly with declared ontology instances or indirectly with an instantiated knowledge base that adheres to the ontology or a database that adheres to the schema).

Recently, the use of machine learning for computing correspondences has gain popularity. The underlying reason for that is that ontology or database schema mapping is, nowadays, an expensive endeavour. The proliferation of ontologies on the (Semantic) Web and the sheer number of database schemata call for automated support to compute correspondences in acceptable time. It appears that machine learning could be a solution to the problem of automating the matching task but there are some open issues, especially with regards to sourcing and training the background data used to feed the learning algorithms.

Finally, the use of heuristics was always an easily applicable and preferable choice for engineers. This is not a surprise to everyone who has attempted to do mapping: heuristics are cheap to develop, easy to deploy, and support automation. However, the main problem with heuristics is that they are easily defeasible. Even well-crafted heuristics that work for a particular case can fail in similar situations. Attempts to solve this problem go beyond the use of syntactic features, linguistic clues, and structural similarities and use as much semantic information as possible when building heuristics. They use the intended meaning of the concepts to be mapped. However, this is not always feasible as semantics are often not captured in the underlying formalism and a human expert is needed to provide their precise meaning.

To motivate the importance of semantic integration, we briefly present some key application areas where semantic heterogeneity occurs and there is a need for resolving it. This is not an exhaustive list but merely an indication of the diversity for the application domain of semantic integration[2].

Database schema integration: "Given a set of independently developed schemas, construct a global view." (Rahm and Bernstein, 2001). The schemata often have different structure and the process of integration aims to unify matching elements. Matching is a whole field in its own right and is the core operation of schema integration.

Data warehouses: this a variation of the schema integration where the data sources are integrated into a data warehouse: "A data warehouse is a decision support database that is extracted from a set of data sources. The extraction process requires transforming data from the source format into the warehouse format." (Kalfoglou and Schorlemmer, 2003) These transformations could be assisted by database schema matching operations.

E-Commerce: Trading partners frequently exchange messages that describe business transactions. As each trading partner uses its own message format, this creates the problem of heterogeneity. That is, message formats may differ in their syntax (EDI structured, XML formatted, etc.) or use different message schemata. To enable systems to exchange messages, application developers need to convert messages between the formats required by different trading partners.

Semantic query processing: "A user specifies the output of a query (e.g., the SELECT clause in SQL), and the system figures out how to produce that output (e.g., by determining the FROM and WHERE clause on SQL)' (Kalfoglou and Schorlemmer, 2003). The heterogeneity arises when the user specifies the query output in terms which are different from those used in the schema.

Ontology integration (or merging): Given two distinct, and independently developed ontologies, produce a fragment which captures the intersection of the original ontologies. This area is similar to that of schema integration but more difficult in nature due to the rich and complex knowledge representation structures found in ontologies.

Ontology mapping: This is a subset of the previous area, mapping ontologies is a step towards integration and it is often the case that mapping ontologies is adequate for most interoperability scenarios on the Semantic Web.

Semantic Web agents' interoperability: A pre-requisite for Semantic Web agents to collaborate is their ability to understand and communicate their mental models. These are often model in the form of ontology and it is very likely to be distinct albeit modelling the same universe of discourse. Mapping their ontologies is a major area of interest where automated and scalable solutions are also sought due to the sheer size of agents involved in these scenarios.

In the next section we present the underlying principles for a unifying integration framework that aims to streamline and leverage on different integration systems.

SEMANTIC INTENSITY SPECTRUM

We observe a common trend for semantic integration practitioners to progress from semantically-poor to semantically-rich solutions. We therefore, use the metaphor of *semantic richness* to classify integration techniques along a *semantic intensity spectrum*. We mark several interim points to address string similarity, structure, context, extension, and intension awareness as different layers of semantic intensity (see Figure 1)

String similarity: occupying the semantically-poor end of the spectrum, compares names of elements from different semantic models. A refinement of such techniques enhances the result

Figure 1.

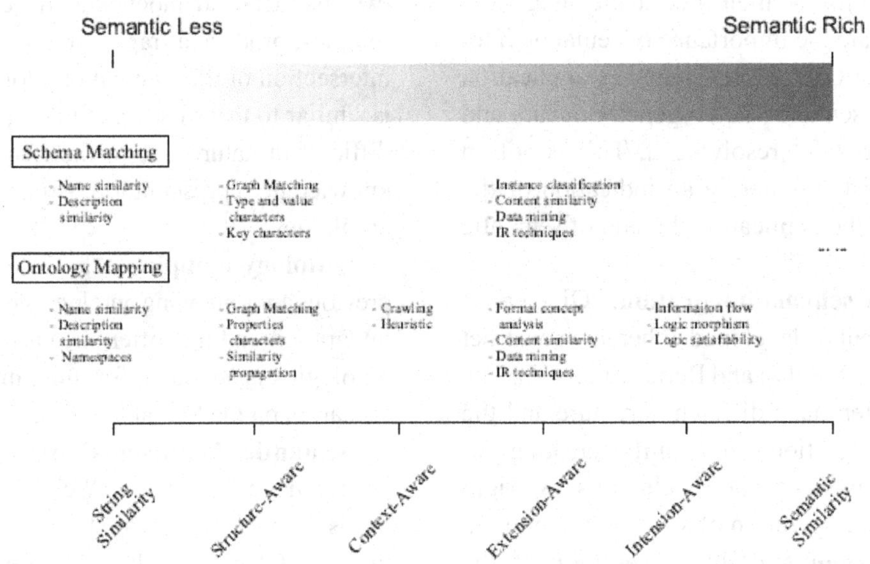

by taking into account the textual descriptions (a.k.a., comments) associated with concepts and properties. These techniques are based on the assumption that concepts and properties names representing semantic similarity will have similar syntactic features. A string matcher usually first normalises the input string of names and/or descriptions via stemming and tokenisation. In the simplest form, the equality of tokens will be obtained and combined to give a score of the equality for the whole string. In a slightly more complicated form, similarity of two strings is computed by evaluating their substrings, edit distance, etc. Nowadays, pure string similarity measures are seldom used in practice, but rather in combination with external resources, like user-defined lexica and/or dictionaries.

Linguistic Similarity: at a position very close to the semantically-poor end, is an example of string similarity measures blended with some sense of semantics. For instance, pronunciation and soundex are taken into account to enhance the similarity when based purely on strings. Also, synonyms and hypernyms will be considered based on generic and/or domain-specific thesauri, e.g. WordNet, Dublin Core[3]. In many cases, user-defined name matches are often treated as useful resources. For lengthy descriptions, information retrieval techniques can be applied to compare and score similarities. As a basic group of matching techniques, linguistics usually are the initial step to suggest a set of raw mappings that other matchers can work with.

Structure-aware: refers to approaches that take into account the structural layout of ontologies and schemata. Going beyond matching names (strings), structural similarity considers the entire underlying structure. That is, when comparing ontologies there is a hierarchical, partially ordered lattice where ontology classes are laid out. Similarly, database schemata also use a lattice of connections between tables and classes, but not necessarily in a hierarchical fashion. Structure-aware techniques are seldom used solely in real-life mapping and matching applications. For instance, *PromptDiff* (Noy and Musen, 2002) leverages a series of heuristics to identify differences between two versions of ontology. Amongst the heuristics used are those based on structure information, e.g. the "single unmatched sibling" heuristic rule states

Figure 2.

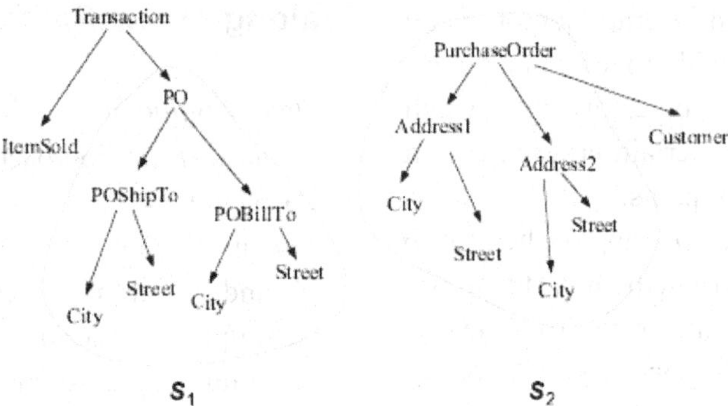

that if two nodes, N1 and N2 are matching and each of them has exactly one unmatched child, N(C1) and N(C2), respectively, then N(C1) and N(C2) match.

In pure structural matching techniques, ontologies and schemata are transformed into trees with labelled nodes, thus matching is equivalent to matching vertices of the source graph with those of the targeted one. Similarity between two such graphs, G1 and G2 is computed by finding a subgraph of G2 that is *isomorphic* to G1 or vice versa. Although nodes of such graphs are labelled, their linguistic features rarely play a significant role in computing the similarity. Furthermore, labels of edges are normally ignored with the assumption that only one type of relation holds between connected nodes. For instance, suppose we have two fragments of e-Commerce schemata, one describing an arbitrary Transaction and the other one a PurchaseOrder (see Figure 2). Graph's isomorphism then gives us, among other possible mappings: PO ↔ PurchaseOrder, POShipTo ↔ Address1, and POBillTo ↔ Address2.

Analogous to pure *string similarity* methods, structure matching approaches, such as the one presented in (Wang et. al., 1994) are not common in practice, but they are usually enhanced with other matching techniques. We deliberately use the notion of *structure similarity* in a broad sense in order to accommodate many relevant methods that relate to each other, and which could, and sometimes are used in such a combined fashion.

Typically, algorithms that do structure to structure comparison use the properties found in these structures (transitivity, cardinality, symmetry, etc) as well as their tree form similarity (for example, similar branches). Other algorithms use information at the nodes other than label, for example, attributes such as datatype, property range and property domain, etc, (Milo and Zohar, 1998). These are used as if they were labels (strings) with the range of methods discussed above available for comparing them.

- **Context-aware**: in many cases there are a variety of relations among concepts or schema elements which makes it necessary to differentiate distinct types of connections among nodes. This gives rise to a family of matching techniques which are more semantically rich than *structure similarity* ones.

Both database schema and ontology can be transferred into a labelled directed graph of which nodes could be elements and concepts, and edges, could be attributes and properties, respectively, with the names of attributes and properties as labels. A *context* defined in graph jargon, is an arbitrary node together with nodes that are connected to it via particular types of edges which at the same time satisfy certain criteria, e.g., a threshold of the length of paths.

Sometimes, *context-aware* approaches group and weigh the edges from and to a node to impose a view of the domain of discourse from the end user perspective. Depending on whether importing external resources is allowed, there are two types of context-awareness.

In the simplest form, algorithms that compare nodes from two schemata also traverse downwards several layers along the direction of edges from the node under consideration, or upwards against the direction of edges to the node under consideration. All the visited nodes, together with the information about edges connecting them (taxonomic relationships like part-of, subclass-of, etc) are evaluated as a whole to infer further mappings between nodes in the context. For instance, in Figure 3, the issue of whether "Norway" in S1 corresponds to "Norway" in S2 is evaluated together with the information provided by their ancestors along the part-of relationship path. It is evident that these two nodes do not match, as "Norway" in S1 refers to a map of this country while "Norway" in S2 refers to the country itself.

Anchor-Prompt (Noy et. al., 2001) is an example of exploiting context information in detecting and refining mappings between ontologies. If one sees ontologies as labelled graphs with nodes as concepts and edges as hierarchical relationships (superclass/subclass) and properties that have concepts as their domains and ranges, Anchor-Prompt can be understood as follows: it takes as input a set of mapping nodes, referred to as "anchors", and traverses the paths of the same sorts (with the same labels) between the anchors.

Similar Concepts are Identified by Comparing the Nodes along These Paths

Similarity flooding (Melnik, 2002) is an example of a *context-aware* approach. An arbitrary schema S_n is first transformed into a directed labelled graph. The initial mappings between two schemata, S_1 and S_2, are obtained using certain mapping techniques, e.g., a simple string matcher comparing common prefixes and suffixes of literals, and captured to a Pairwise Connectivity Graph (PCG). Nodes of a PCG are elements from $S_1 \, x \, S_1$, denoted as $N_{S1 \, x \, S2}$. An edge labelled $a : (m \times k) \rightarrow (n \times l)$ where ($m, n \in S_1$ and $k, l \in S_2$) of a PCG means that an a edge is present in the original schemata between m and n as well as k and l, i.e. $a : m \subset n; a : k \subset l$.

Figure 3.

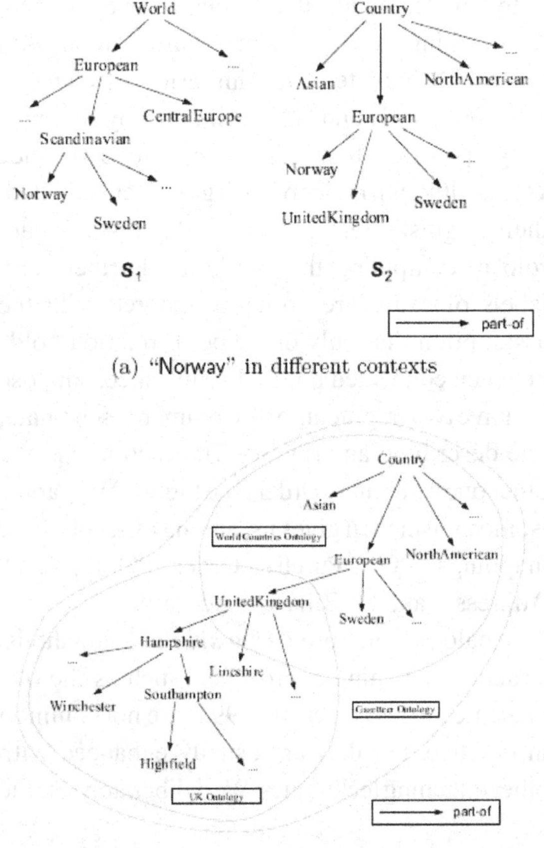

(a) "Norway" in different contexts

From a PCG, a similarity propagation graph is induced which assigns to each edge in the PCG a propagation coefficient to indicate the influence between nodes of the PCG. In other words, the weighted edges indicate how well the similarity of a given PCG node propagates to its neighbour. The accumulation of similarity is performed until a pre-set threshold is reached or terminated by the user after some maximal number of iterations. A series of filter methods are then adopted to reduce the size of the resultant mapping candidates and select the most plausible ones.

Following the same philosophy—similarity propagation, (Palopoli et. al., 2003) integrated multiple entity relationship (ER) schemata by using the following principle: similarity of schema elements depends on the similarity of elements in their vicinity (nearby elements influence match more than those farther away). ER schemata are first transformed into graphs with entities, relationships, and attributes as nodes. The similarity coefficient is initialised by standard thesauruses and re-evaluated based on the similarity of nodes in their corresponding vicinities.

With the use of *namespaces*, along comes another type of *context awareness*. As illustrated in Figure 3, "United Kingdom" belongs to both "World Countries Ontology" and "UK Ontology". Articulating these two ontologies summons the resolution of different namespaces that might involve string matchers in certain forms. An example of dealing with co-reference resolution of such namespaces is given in (Alani and Brewster, 2005).

Extension-aware: when a relatively complete set of instances can be obtained, semantics of a schema or ontology can be reflected through the way that instances are classified. A major assumption made by techniques belonging to this family is that instances with similar semantics might share features (Madhavan, 2003), therefore, an understanding of such common features can contribute to an approximate understanding of the semantics.

Formal Concept Analysis (FCA (Ganter and Wille, 1999)) is a representative of instance-aware approaches. FCA is a field of mathematics emerged in the nineties that builds upon lattice theory and the work of Ganter and Wille on the mathematisation of concept in the eighties. It is mostly suited for analysing instances and properties of entities (concepts) in a domain of interest. FCA consists of formal contexts and concept lattices. A formal context is a triple $K = \langle O, P, S \rangle$, where O is a set of objects, P is a set of attributes (or properties), and $S \subseteq O \times P$ is a relation that connects each object o with the attributes satisfied by o.

The intent (set of attributes belonging to an object) and the extent (set of objects having these attributes) are given formal definitions in (Ganter and Wille, 1999). A formal concept is a pair $\langle A, B \rangle$ consisting of an extent $A \subseteq B$ and an intent $B \subseteq P$, and these concepts are hierarchically ordered by inclusion of their extents. This partial order induces a complete lattice, the concept lattice of the context. FCA can be applied to semi-structured domains to assist in modelling with instances and properties in hierarchical, partially ordered lattices. This is the main structure most the mapping systems work with. Thus, FCA albeit not directly related to mapping, it is a versatile technology which could be used at the early stages of mapping for structuring a loosely defined domain. Data mining and information retrieval techniques are frequently exploited to winnowing away apparent discrepancy as well as discover the hidden correlations among instances. Some recent efforts along this line of research are presented in (Doan et. al., 2002) and (He and Chang, 2003).

Intension-aware: refers to the family of techniques that establish correlations between relations among extent and intent. Such approaches are particularly useful when it is impossible or impractical to obtain a complete set of instances to reflect the semantics.

Barwise and Seligman propose a mathematical theory, *Information Flow*, that aims at establishing the laws that govern the flow of information (Barwise and Seligman, 1997). It is a general theory that attempts to describe information flow in any kind of a distributed system. It is based on the understanding that information flow results from regularities in a distributed system, and that it is by virtue of regularities among the connections that information of some components of a system carries information of other components. As a notion of a component carrying information about another component, Barwise and Seligman followed the analogy of types and tokens where tokens and its connections carry information. These are classified against types and the theory of information flow aims to capture this aspect of information flow which involves both types and tokens.

When integration is our major concern, the same pattern arises: two communities with different ontologies (or schemata) will be able to share information when they are capable of establishing connections among their tokens in order to infer the relationship among their types. Kalfoglou and Schorlemmer argued for the relation of information flow to a distributed system like the (Semantic) Web, where the regularities of information flowing between its parts can be captured and used to do mapping (Kalfoglou and Schorlemmer, 2003). The mathematical background of information flow theory ensures that the corresponding types (concepts) respect token (instance) membership to each of the mapped types. Their approach is community-oriented, in the sense that communities on the (Semantic) Web own and control their data (instances) and they use them (i.e., classify them) against ontologies for the purpose of knowledge sharing and reuse. It is precisely this information of classifying your own instances against ontologies that is used as evidence for computing the mapping relation between communities' heterogeneous ontologies. It is evident that *information flow* goes beyond *extension-awareness* towards the tick marked by *intension-aware*.

Semantic similarity, very close to the semantically-rich end lays the family of *logic satisfiability* approaches which focus on the logic correspondences. Logic constructors play a significant role in expressive formalisms, such as DLs, implying that the discovery of similarity is more like finding logic consequence. There has been a long debate regarding "semantics" (Ogde and Rich, 1923), (Smith, 2004) and (Uschold, 2003). Although none of the approaches has been unanimously agreed upon, in ontology engineering, capturing semantics with logic based (mainly DL-based) modelling languages and interpreting the formulae with model theories seem promising (c.f. the de facto standards, OWL/OWL1.1). The rationale behind such a phenomenon is that by formalising the definitions using constructs with clear interpretation, preferably machine-understandable, we prescribe the way how others, being human users or intelligent software agents, approach the semantics encoded in the definitions. There is a major assumption that enables such a vision: the intended semantics can be formalised by DLs or other logic languages and the formalisation can be uniformly interpreted. This gives rise to techniques reducing the matching/mapping problem to one that can be solved by resorting to logic satisfiability techniques. Concepts in a hierarchical structure are transformed into well-formed logic formulae (*wffs*). To compute the relationships between two set of *wffs* amounts to examine whether $\left(\phi, wffs_1, wffs_2\right)$ is satisfiable. ϕ is the set of relationships normally containing not only equivalence but also "more general than", "less general than", "disjoint with", etc.

The major difference among these approaches is on how the *wffs* are computed with respect to each concept (and/or label of concept). Bouquet, et. al. (2003) introduced an algorithm with the notions of *label interpretation* and *contextualization*, called CtxMatch. Each concept in a concept hierarchy is associated with a formula based on the WordNet senses of each word in the label of the concept. The senses associated with each label are refined according to the information provided by its ancestors and direct descendants. Matching of two concepts, C_1 and C_2, is then transformed into checking the satisfiability of a formula composed by contextualised senses associated with their labels and the known WordNet relations among senses expressed in logic formulae, e.g. $art\#1 \subseteq_{WordNet} humanities\#1$ denotes that, according to WordNet, the first sense of the word "art" is less general than the first sense of the word "humanities" where "art" and "humanities" are words from the labels of C_1 and C_2 respectively.

(Guinchiglia et. al. 2004) went one step further by distinguishing two different notions of concept, namely the *concept of label* and the *concept of node*. *Concept of a label* is context insensitive concerning only the WordNet senses of the labels of a concept. On the other hand, *concept of a node* is context-sensitive, its logic formula is computed as the "intersection of the concepts at labels of all the nodes from the root to the node itself." (Guinchiglia et. al., 2004). The concept of label matrix is constructed containing the relations exist between any two concepts of labels in the two hierarchies of which the matching is to be obtained. Based on such a matrix the concept of node matrix is calculated.

A significant caveat to this approach is that in real-life settings, humans tend to view the same things from different perspectives and thus formalise their knowledge in, possibly, fundamentally different ways. Therefore, logic-based approaches, though very close to the semantic rich end, still have a long way to go to faithfully capture the meaning of information. Technologies go beyond logic-based ones in SIS are yet to reach their maturity and will be discussed in Section 5. But first, we present a flexible modular architecture that enables a seamless integration of multiple ontology mapping strategies and combines arbitrary numeric similarities in a systematic manner.

A MULTI-STRATEGY APPROACH TO ONTOLOGY MAPPING

It is evident that current approaches demonstrate a wide diversity in terms of mapping capabilities and mapping results that cover all layers in the SIS mentioned in the previous section. Hence, we need to combine different technologies in order to achieve effective and efficient mapping. One way of doing this, is by using an architecture which is capable of accommodating diverse systems without sacrificing their functionality. We therefore proposed such an architecture that is characterized as a multi-stage and multi-strategy system comprising of four modules: *Signature Generation*, *Signature Selection* and *Processing*, *Aggregation* and *Evaluation*. We formalised that architecture in the CROSI system (Section 4.3) in which, different signatures of the input data (be it ontologies or other knowledge models) are generated. A subset of these signatures are selected to trigger different sorts of matchers. The resultant similarity values are compiled by multiple similarity aggregators running in parallel or consecutive order. The overall similarity is then evaluated to initiate iterations that backtrack to different stages. At multiple stages feedback loops enable fine-tuning of the system. A schematic depiction of the system is illustrated in Figure 4.

Unifying the Efforts

If sim() is defined to compute similarity between two ontology signatures, the multi-strategy approach that we envisioned can be formalised as follows:

$$sim(\mathrm{O},\mathrm{O}') = aggregator\left(sim_i\left(sig_j(\mathrm{O}), sig_j(\mathrm{O}')\right)\right)$$

where $sig_j(\mathrm{O})$ extracts a particular signature j from ontology O.

Similarity functions $sim_i(\mathrm{O},\mathrm{O}')$ instantiate one of the similarity measures discussed in

Figure 4.

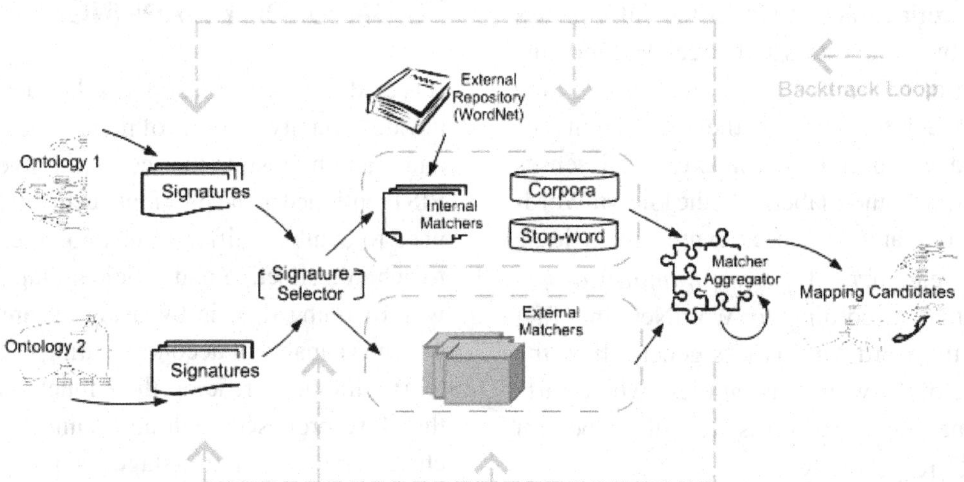

Section 3. To show a full coverage of mapping capabilities, for individual similarity measures that are not ready at the moment, we implement a local copy as the "internal matchers"; while for those that are provided by existing systems, we integrated them as "external matchers".

A multi-stage and multi-strategy approach is demonstrated by many systems, e.g. COMA (Do and Rahm, 2002), GLUE (Doan et. al., 2002), and QoM (Ehrig and Staab, 2004). Our approach, as illustrated in Figure 4, is different in that it allows: 1) multiple matchers: several heterogeneous matchers run independently producing intrinsic, yet different but complementary results; 2) use of existing systems which are treated as standard building blocks each of which is a plug and play component of the overall hybrid mapping system; 3) multiple loops: the overall similarity is evaluated by users or supervised learners to initiate iterations that backtrack to different stages of the process.

There are a number of challenges which we need to consider when building such a system: in ideal situations, each independent matcher considers an identical set of characteristics of the input ontologies and produces homogeneous output for further processes. However, this is seldom true in practice. There is currently no standard or common agreement on how an ontology mapping system should behave, i.e. no formal specification on what should be the input and how the system should output. If we consider some recent OWL based ontology alignment systems, we see intrinsic diversities: some take as input only names (URIs) of classes while others take the whole taxonomy; some generate as output abstract relationships (e.g. *more general than*, *more specific than*, etc) while others produce pairwise correspondences with or without confidence values; and some are stand-alone systems when others operate as Web services. Thus, the first and most imminent task for us was to derive a set of common ontology *signatures* that would cover all candidate ontology matching systems included in the CROSI framework and conceive a mechanism to unify heterogeneous outputs. For matchers that utilize specific aspects of ontologies, we fed them with ontology signatures that fully characterize the input ontologies no matter which representation language is used. In cases that matchers are treated as black-boxes—signature selection is not visible—the entire ontologies are used. We parsed and lifted up all output using an extended SKOS representation (enriching SKOS with extra constructs for numeric similarities).

Making Combined Sense

Equally difficult to build are methods which process and aggregate results from different mapping systems (also refer to as *external matchers*). An unbiased measure is to run in parallel componential matchers each of which produces its own results. The output is then normalized and unified to facilitate accumulation and aggregation with numeric and non-numeric methods. A rift of aggregation methods were implemented and evaluated.

Weighted Average

When accumulating results, weighted average algorithms assumes the returns from different algorithms are in compatible formats and assign each algorithm a numeric weight that is decided manually based on the characteristics and the user's confidence in the algorithm.

$$sim_{overall}(\varepsilon, \varepsilon') = \frac{\sum_i w_i \bullet sim_i(\varepsilon, \varepsilon')}{\sum_i w_i}$$

where w_i is the weight of the *i*th similarity algorithm/tool and $sim_i()$ gives the mapping candidates of the *i*th algorithm.

Sigmoid Function

Instead of using predefined and static values, one can also adjust weights using Sigmoid function [12]. The rational behind such approach is that candidate alignments with higher similarity value should be emphasized and thus their contribution to the final result is amplified while the effects of least similar candidates should be largely diminished. Given function sig(x) = 1/(1 + e−x), one can define the sigmoid function based similarity aggregation method as

$$sim_{overall}(\varepsilon, \varepsilon') = \sum_i w_i \bullet sig_i(sim_i(\varepsilon, \varepsilon') - n)$$

where n is between [0..1) used to fine-tune the output from the sigmoid function and w_i is defined as in the previous section.

Rank Aggregation

When aggregating heterogeneous results, however, weighted average is not strictly applicable. First, the selection of weights is a highly subjective activity that requires experience and background knowledge, which are not always available when mapping ontologies on the Semantic Web. Second, there might be algorithms that produce mapping candidates whose relations are described with high-level abstract descriptors, e.g. "more general than", "subsuming", etc. Such abstract relations cannot be soundly and precisely converted into numeric values. We therefore adopt rank aggregation methods in processing mapping candidates. Historically speaking, issues of how to aggregate ranking have been intensively studied since the late 18th century, and extensively applied in different voting systems as well as in improving search engines (Dwork et al., 2001). Our approach is rooted in the observation that results from many ontology mapping techniques can be sorted according to a predefined preference, e.g. sorting candidates in a decreasing order of their similarity values.

We implemented two rank aggregation approaches. We use *Borda* count when a weight of each ontology mapping algorithm can be confidently acquired to adjust the significance of its votes towards the final aggregated ranking By taking into account the weights, a *Borda* count of a particular mapping candidate is computed as:

$$bc(\varepsilon) = \frac{\sum_i w_i \bullet rank_i(\varepsilon)}{\sum_i w_i}$$

where $rank_i()$ returns the rank of E from the *ith* algorithm as an integer. For instance, if one method considers a candidate alignment α as the best and another ranks the same α at the 3rd position, the overall *Borda* count of α is then $1w + 3w = 4w$. In the initial implementation, $w_i = 1$ is used.

Weights, however, are *ad hoc* and subjective and cannot be systematically computed. In such occasions, we implement the aggregation optimizing the *Spearman's* foot rule-distance. Lets assume that we have n different ontology mapping algorithms each producing a sorted list of candidates ε_j', $1 \leq j \leq k$ with respect to ontology entity ε, the final rank is a permutation of ε_j' that minimizes

$$\arg\min_{\varepsilon'} \sum_{\varepsilon_j} (\sum_{i=1}^{n} abs(rank_i(\varepsilon_j') - rank_{final}(\varepsilon_j')))$$

where abs () returns the absolute value, ε' is a mapping candidate of ε whose position in a the final ranking is given by $rank_{final}()$ as a non-negative integer, and $rank_i()$ is defined as above. By leveraging *minimum-cost perfect matching*, such an optimal rank can be found in polynomial time (Dwork et al., 2001). *Foot rule* optimal aggregation is particularly useful when incompatible results from heterogeneous algorithms need to be combined.

CROSI: A Multi-Strategy Modular System for Ontology Mapping

We realised the architecture described in the previous sections in a working prototype, CROSI Mapping System (CMS), which was developed in the context of the industrially funded CROSI (Capturing, Representing and Operationalising Semantic Integration) project (Kalfoglou et al., 2005). We depict the entry point of CMS in Figure 5. CMS has been deployed in a variety of scenarios[4], and successfully tackled the problem of aligning ontologies (Kalfoglou and Hu, 2005) in the context of the 2005 Ontology Alignment Evaluation Initiative (OAEI) contest[5]. Our experience with devising a purpose-build modular

Figure 5. CMS user interface

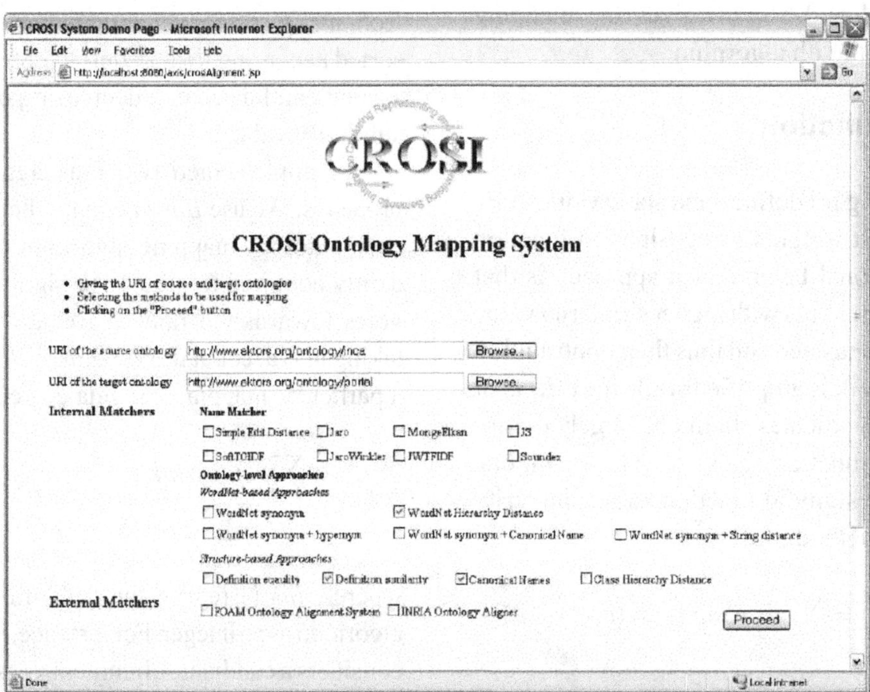

architecture and instantiating it with an ontology mapping system, CMS, helped us to understand better ways in which ontology mapping practice can be improve. First, results from multi-matchers are aggregated using multiple aggregators. Thus far, the selection of aggregation methods is left to the experience and domain knowledge of end users who would have to derive such knowledge from vast test data and the context of individual applications. Although labour-intensive, we see this as a sensitive approach as different matchers might focus on different aspects of ontologies and emphasise different outputs. A knowledgeable user of CMS would have to evaluate and justify such idiosyncrasies to make informed decisions. So far, this process is difficult to automate. Our experience indicates that in many cases the simple weighted average aggregator works, if not better than, as well as other approaches, especially when matcher weights are learnt from past performance based on user feedback. Alternatively, users can be assisted with sophisticated machine learning techniques to work out the most appropriate aggregator with respect to recurrent and largely similar tasks and data.

Second, the heterogeneous nature of different matchers – some external matchers produce pairwise equivalence with numeric values stating the similarity score while others output high level relationships, e.g. *same entity as*, *more specific than*, *more general than* and *disjoint with* expressed in high level languages such as OWL and RDF, and utilised in specialised vocabularies such as SKOS[6]. This suggests that output from different matchers has to be lifted to the same syntactical and semantic level. A unified representation formalism equipped with both numeric and abstract expressivity can facilitate the aggregation of heterogeneous matchers. In CMS, we extended SKOS with numeric similarities. A dedicated converter/parser acts as the interface of individual matchers (signature-specific ones and those adopted in a black-box fashion).

Third, multiple matchers give CMS a board coverage of many ontology signatures ranging from simple name/URL to the exact position of concepts in the concept hierarchy. Users are given the freedom to make adjustments according to their preferences and the task at hand by switching on and off certain signature processors and by including or excluding certain external matchers based on their past performance. Matchers designed for handling heavy-weight ontologies are obviously an over-kill for simple taxonomies and flat vocabularies. CMS provides an "omni-directional" framework to satisfy different requirements.

CONCLUDING REMARKS AND FUTURE DIRECTIONS

It is evident from the increasing number of participants in recent OAEI contests[7], there is a lot of interest and demand for semantically enriched ontology matching or semantic similarity tools due to: (i) the Semantic Web has grown out of its infancy with a large amount of data and services being annotated with one RDF model or another resulting in an imminent quest for aided data manipulation and service composition; (ii) techniques such as those reviewed in the previous sections have fallen into the incompatibility dilemma of "semantics or syntax" with the former as the ultimate goal to pursue and the latter as a compromise; and (iii) "semantics" has been ushered into a new territory with the Web 2.0 philosophy leading to a suite of new matching methodologies to be conceived and developed. Top-down semantics capture approaches start to give way to versatile grass-root initiatives allowing semantics to become explicit in collaborative activities. Instead of being imposed with a pre-defined unsolicited conceptual model, a community is given the freedom to negotiate and gradually build its consensus. Real world examples of this trend is the "schema last" metaphor used in building one of the largest sharable knowledge bases today in a true bottom up fashion[8]. Although arguably, we contend that such a "negotiating-reseeding-and-expanding" approach is an analogue of human learning and thus provide a high fidelity replica of human assigned meanings of information. A common term used to label these approaches as "emergent semantics".

Emergent Semantics

The promise of emergent semantics is that, as communities of users are getting more involved in the setting up of collaborative networks with the help of social software, then that very software, social software, should help us to capture the semantics used by communities as these emerge from social interactions. This promise has been put to work, to a certain extent and in certain scenarios. For example, (Zdhanova, 2005) proposed the involvement of user communities in ontology engineering, in particular, to validate ontology alignments. Furthermore, we saw that a dedicated event recently, (Dzbor et.al., 2005), focussed on the user aspects of the Semantic Web with emphasis on how users can be involved in certain engineering tasks. It is also an appealing prospect from the systems' maintenance point of view, as users, the ultimate target of information systems when they deployed, could be involved in their maintenance thus making sure that the system stays current and up to date. Sparse examples of this can be found in the software engineering literature with the engineering of experiences gathered throughout the life cycle of a project (see, for example, the work of (Basili et. al., 1999) on Experience Factory and Experience Bases). Similarly, organisational memories practitioners have experimented with user participation in their engineering tasks with some degree of success. For example, in the KnowMore system of (Abecker et.al., 2000) and the OntoProPer system of (Sure et al., 2000).

However, there are a number of issues which could potentially render the emergent semantics promise useless.

First, it relies on a relatively smooth and uniform representation of a community's interests. But, real world practice tells us that communities rarely employ uniform and common representations. In fact, they use a variety of norms and manifestations (Wenger, 1998). If we, the engineers, are to take advantage of the emergent semantics, then these manifestations should be analysed (ideally automatically), and represented in commonly agreed formats (like, for example, in an ontology) so that they can be shared in a distributed environment like the World Wide Web, and its extension the Semantic Web.

Second, little work has been done in resolving possible conflicts of representation. It is not uncommon for similar communities to use seemingly similar representations of the same domain concepts. Even if the sheer number of members that belong to these communities is a good enough indicator that these concepts are prevailing and should be part of a prospective ontology for the emerging domain, the fact that there are slight variations in representing or using the concept, calls for ontology mapping technology to resolve it.

Third, emergent semantics rely heavily on the use of machine learning technology and other statistical techniques, like OLAP. We do not despise the use of these technologies, but we are sceptical about the practicalities of deploying machine learning to capture and extract prevailing semantics from a community's log of information exchanges. As we know from machine learning theory, supervised learning methods are probably the most reliable ones (Wilks et al., 2005). But, they also require a lot of engineering in order to make sure that the right learning data set is fetched into the system, proper and timely updates to the learning strategy are made, timely maintenance of the learning rules is executed, etc. All these tasks are time consuming and require specialised knowledge of not only machine learning, but also of the domain in question. We do not see how this could scale up when we deal with subtle concept definitions where only a human expert in the domain is most likely to be capable to decode the information and associate the correct meaning to concepts.

This leaves us with other methods of machine learning which scale up dramatically well, but they also have serious flaws: unsupervised learning has seen some remarkable performance highs in recent years but the domains that it has been applied are well understood and devising the initial set of learning rules is not difficult, even with little knowledge of the domain in question. But in domains where a wide variety of concepts should be extracted and learned it is difficult to see how this approach could be applied with success.

One of the promising efforts in the context of emergent semantics is the use of collaboratively contributed web encyclopaedias, in particular Wikipedia. There has been an increasing research interest in deriving (formal or informal) semantics from Wikipedia (Weber and Buitelaar, 2006) (Wu and Weld, 2008). Equally, there is a growing but less mainstream approach that tries to maintain the formality of ontologies while, at the same time, exploit the flexibility, visibility and low overhead of mass contributions. Along this line of research, we discuss the approach deriving common background knowledge from Wikipedia.

Wikipedia as Background Knowledge

"*How can we find out the semantics of a concept?*" has been a question that plagues researchers of the conventional knowledge representation/engineering as well as the rapidly growing Semantics Web community. The diversity of human cognition has long been widely accepted. Even though we restrict the envisaged application to software agents, human factors cannot be ignored due to the fact that ontology creation and resource annotation tasks are still human labour intensive. For example, human reasoning is needed when the intended meanings of primary concepts and properties are less evident and difficult to be formally derived—all the concerned parties must agree upon a list of words as the most basic building blocks to be the semantics carriers and the meanings of these words must "pick out the same individuals in the same context" (Steels and Kaplan, 1999). In other words, we should not hope that with a common language, formal or otherwise, the semantics and the way we understand them just become evident thereafter.

Discovering semantics requires understanding of idiosyncrasies and particulars in using the concept constructs so as to reproduce as faithfully as possible the context wherein ontological entities are created. Hence, in establishing a common understanding of ontologies, human factors have to be explored and somehow captured. In other words, when trying to grasp the semantics that the original modelers deliver, one needs to project his/her domain knowledge upon to those possessed by other modelers. In doing so, we accept a certain degree of imperfectness and replace the rigid model theory based semantics with one emerging from large scale collaborative contributions, such as Wikipedia[9]. The assumption is that tolerating approximation is more close to how humans observe and understand our surroundings. The merit of Wikipedia is evident from its scale, the versatile background of its contributors, and the structure of both its categories and the contents. Wikipedia is probably the biggest and most appealing collaboratively created source of encyclopaedic knowledge. It is a freely accessible, peer-reviewed Web encyclopaedic repository. Up to November 2008, it collects more than 7 million articles in more than 250 different languages (among them are about 2,700,000 English ones). It contains both conventional encyclopaedias and articles about current affairs. The latter is constantly updated on a daily basis and usually by several contributors with different writing skills, story-telling techniques, and perspectives. This great diversity of the background of wikipedians (connotation for people who contribute to Wikipedia, among them about 10,000 are very active contributors) naturally reflects the variations of human cognition. Meanwhile, as an open access repository, Wikipedia articles are frequently reviewed and revised to ensure that the content is generally better and more comprehensive than other non-peer-reviewed web sources (Giles, 2005). In order to take advantage of such resource, we developed the following algorithm:

- project a concept together with its conceptual context upon to Wikipedia as a well selected document repository which we treat as the background knowledge where the concept is defined;
- identify the association between the Wikipedia articles and a concept's defining context (its conceptual neighbours) using conventional information retrieval methodologies;
- distill a signature vector for each concept as the topics/titles of such articles whose weights may subject to a further refinement with the help of Singular Value Decomposition (SVD) to reveal hidden associations (Deerwester et al., 1990).

The resultant vector provides a simple and scalable method for measuring the semantic similarity between concepts from different ontologies. It might be of particular interest in ontology mapping aiming to facilitate knowledge sharing in distributed and peer-to-peer environments. In this scenario, dynamic and on-the-fly methods for establishing on demand consensus become more desirable and exact equivalences have given way to less perfect ones. Assuming each party has generated semantics-capturing vectors using Wikipedia, by passing such vectors, we can approximate ontology mapping with cosine distance between semantics-capturing vectors.

Towards Certified Ontologies

Despite the advantages and disadvantages of using emergent semantics and some encouraging results we mentioned above, we are cautiously optimistic about them. We believe that emergent semantics will continue to grow as more and more people will be drawn into these online communities using social software. We would like, therefore, to make the most out of their interactions and information exchanges on the Web and Semantic Web by capturing the semantics underlying their actions with respect to the pertaining problem of evaluation.

Communities alone though, will not be able to provide us with practical input with respect to evaluation unless we have ways of regulating and vetting their input. One way that this could be mechanised is with the use of certification. In the knowledge engineering domain, the issue of certification has been debated in the past (Shadbolt, 1999) in the context of certified knowledge bases. Recently, the issue of using ontologies as a commodity, and the commercial interest it has attracted has also been debated (O'Hara, 2001). We have also witnessed efforts that aim to certify and validate domain specific ontologies, like the work of (Eysenbach, 2001) with medical ontologies.

All these representative pieces of work emerge from different contexts and application domains but point to a workable approach: evaluation could be done by professionals and adhere to standards and practices approved by recognized bodies of prominence. We should also point to efforts that already exist in the commercial world, especially those that apply to the Web. For example, the commercial importance of the Web and the volume of trading online brought us technologies like SSL certificates for encrypting financially sensitive information and certification mechanisms like VeriSign's "verified by" trademarked certificates.

Similarly, at the syntactical level, some of the W3C family of languages, and other products related with the consortium's efforts, have clearly identifiable stickers on compatible web pages ("XHTML checkers", etc.) pointing to syntax validators and checkers or simply stating conformance to a standard.

Despite these activities though, the certification of ontologies, especially with respect to evaluation remains an issue largely unresolved and ignored by big standardisation bodies. We might have witnessed high profile efforts in ontology development, like the commercialisation of CyC (Lenat, 1995) or the IEEE sponsored work on SUO[10] but this does not mean that we have evaluation bodies that provide certificates of ontology quality assurance.

The problem with issuing certificates of ontology quality is two fold: on the technological level, we do not have a clear idea of what quality criteria and tests ontologies should satisfy in order to be accredited. On the political level, there is an issue of authority. Who will certify ontologies and how? How trustworthy will that organisation be and what, if any, will be the cost of certification. Will there be licensing issues and restrictions of use with respect to the ontology? How likely it is to reach at a standardisation level when talking about ontology evaluation?

Experience and industry reports on standardisation tells us that standards are hard to debate, difficult to enforce in an open-ended environment, hard to reconcile conflicting commercial interests, and take years to materialize. But, for ontology evaluation efforts to have more credible profile some sort of standardisation would be needed. One way of combining the strengths of emergent semantics we reviewed before and ideas from commercial efforts on certification and standards could be to use simple cataloguing technologies, like ranking.

Classification and Ranking

In (Alani et al., 2005), the authors reported on early efforts to come up with ranking mechanisms that allow us to classify ontologies according to their usage. Their domain of application is on searching for appropriate ontologies but the ranking mechanism is simple and could be adopted to support evaluation. Assuming that a community is willing to participate in a common effort to rank ontologies, such an approach could provide us with a majority's view on what is best and what to avoid. This is the premise of the ranking approach.

We do however, have certain issues to resolve before making it practical for evaluating ontologies: (a) how to monitor and regulate rankings in an open-ended environment? Reports that examined well crafted commercial efforts on using communal ranking (like for example the eBay feedback mechanism) has shown that it is easy to deceive authoritative systems in order to achieve personal gains (Resnick and Zeckhauser, 2002) (in the case of eBay feedback, a positive one could mean better deals for auctioneers). (b) What sort of features in an ontology users will be called upon to evaluate? That issue is related to the certification content discussed above and we see efforts such as in (Uschold, 1999) as an early step towards a consensual set of features that evaluated ontologies should demonstrate. Furthermore, in (Lozano-Tello, 2004) a more detailed and extensive list of characteristics for ontology classification has been proposed. (c) Will all participating users have equal opinion weighs? For example, in the case of the FMA ontology, should an anatomist's opinion have greater importance than an ontology engineer's? Common sense might dictate that he should, but there might be subtle knowledge representation related issues that only the ontology engineer will be qualified to resolve.

Evaluation of ontologies themselves is a difficult issue. It cannot be seen as orthogonal to other ontology development and use issues, especially not in an environment like the Web and the Semantic Web. The promise of accessing, retrieving, and re-using a variety of ontologies in these environment necessitates an evaluation strategy that is (a) open to users, transparent in nature and with references to the standards it adheres to or certificates it holds, (b) amendable, easy to change and adopt to different use cases, (c) domain specific, and reflect opinions of various stakeholders, not only of ontology engineers.

But, these are hard to achieve goals. In the short to medium term we should look for mid term solutions that we can build and experiment with, before engaging to long term evaluation research. In the last part of the paper, we elaborate on a rough roadmap of the short to medium future. Standards and certification is an area that needs more work. In fact, when it comes to ontology evaluation, it is in its infancy. However, we want to avoid the painfully slow process of standardisation. There are lessons learnt and experiences we can build upon. For example, in the context of the IEEE SUO effort, there have been debates on using ISO standards to evaluate the content and appropriateness of ontologies[11]. Despite the fact that views and opinions expressed there are subjective, it is a good start.

We also see an increasing interest in using emergent semantics and engaging user communities. That could prove to be a useful and practical input to the evaluation problem. The commercial interest in ontologies nowadays also brings us closer to certification and standards. As academic and neutral interest stakeholders we should inform possible attempts for certification as to what the quality features that ontologies need to exhibit should be and leave the prolong arguments on how to enforce them to the politicians. Licensing is also an issue that should be considered closely with evaluation. Appropriate licensing should provide certain assurances on evaluation.

The practical research questions on what sort of evaluation technology we need should be part of the ontology development and language communities. The Semantic Web community at the moment focuses on applications and infrastructure issues. Having closed a successful circle on developing languages to materialise the Semantic Web, researchers and practitioners are focussing on attracting commercial and public interest by demonstrating Semantic Web technology and its advances. But, evaluation of ontologies, a cornerstone for achieving the full potential of the Semantic Web, is not complete yet.

Last, but not least, in an era where user communities matters the most, we need to raise the awareness of this issue and demonstrate its importance. As researchers, we need to share experiences, good and bad, on related efforts and learn from each others mistakes. Open source and publicly available tools should be on the agenda so that we can reach to a consensus quicker. We should not be afraid to constructively critique and despise ill-defined ontologies as this will raise the quality standards. Most importantly, we should work with examples, tools, and use cases that are easy to replicate in neutral settings. One of the fruitful directions is that of using Wikipedia as background knowledge.

ACKNOWLEDGMENT

The work described in this manuscript is a result of many years of research and development by the authors under the auspices of a multitude of programmes and projects: CROSI, a Hewlett Packard Laboratories sponsored project (2004-2005); Advanced Knowledge Technologies (AKT) Interdisciplinary Research Collaboration (IRC) programme (2000-2007) sponsored by the UK EPSRC under Grant number GR/N15764/01; OpenKnowledge, a European Commission funded Specific Targeted Research Project (STREP) under contract number FP6-027253. The views and conclusions contained herein are those of the authors and should not be interpreted as necessarily representing official policies or endorsements, either expressed or implied, of the HP CROSI, UK EPSRC AKT IRC, EC OpenKnowledge, RICOH Europe Plc or SAP institutions.

REFERENCES

Abecker, A., Bernardi, A., Hinkelmann, K., Kuhn, O., & Sintek, M. (2000). Context-aware, proactive delivery of task-specific knowledge: The KnowMore project. [ISF]. *International Journal on Information Systems Frontiers*, *2*(3/4), 139–162.

Alani, H., & Brewster, C. (2005). Ontology ranking based on analysis of concept structures. In *Proceedings of the 3rd International Conference on Knowledge Capture (K-Cap'05),* Banff, Canada (pp. 51-58).

Alani, H., Dasmahapatra, S., Gibbins, N., Glasser, H., Harris, S., Kalfoglou, Y., et al. (2002). Managing reference: Ensuring referential integrity of ontologies for the Semantic Web. In *Proceedings of the 13th International Conference on Knowledge Engineering and Knowledge Management (EKAW'02),* Siguenza, Spain (pp. 317-334).

Barwise, J., & Seligman, J. (1997). Information flow: The logic of distributed systems (Cambridge Tracts in Theoretical Computer Science 44). Cambridge, UK: Cambridge University Press.

Basili, R. V., Shull, F., & Lanubile, F. (1999). Building knowledge through families of experiments. *IEEE Transactions on Software Engineering*, *25*(4), 456–473. doi:10.1109/32.799939

Bouquet, P., Magnini, B., Scrafini, L., & Zanobini, S. (2003). A SAT-based algorithm for context matching. In *Proceedings of the 4th International and Interdisciplinary Conference on Modeling and Using Context (Context03)*.

Deerwester, S., Dumais, S., Landauer, T., Furnas, G., & Harshman, R. (1990). Indexing by Latent Semantic Analysis. *Journal of the American Society for Information Science American Society for Information Science*, *41*(6), 391–407. doi:10.1002/(SICI)1097-4571(199009)41:6<391::AID-ASI1>3.0.CO;2-9

Do, H.-H., & Rahm, E. (2002). COMA: A system for flexible combination of schema matching approaches. In *Proceedings of the 28th International Conference on Very Large Databases (VLDB'02),* Hong Kong, China.

Doan, A., Madhavan, J., Domingos, P., & Halevy, A. (2002). Learning to map between ontologies on the Semantic Web. In *Proceedings of the 11th International World Wide Web Conference (WWW 2002)*, Hawaii, USA.

Dwork, C., Kumar, S., Naor, M., & Sivakumar, D. (2001). Rank aggregation methods for the Web. In *Proceedings of the 10th International Conference on World Wide Web* (pp. 613-622).

Dzbor, M., Takeda, H., & Vargas-Vera, M. (Eds.). (2005). *Proceedings of the UserSWeb: Workshop on End User Aspects of the Semantic Web (UserSWEB'05), CEUR (137) WS.* Retrieved from http://sunsite.informatik.rwth-aachen.de/Publications/CEUR-WS//Vol-137

Ehrig, M., & Staab, S. (2004). QOM - quick ontology mapping. In *Proceedings of the 3rd International Semantic Web Confernece (ISWC'04)*, Hiroshima, Japan (LNCS 3298, pp. 683-697).

Euzenat, J. (2004). An API for ontology alignment. In *Proceedings of the 3rd International Semantic Web Confernece (ISWC'04),* Hiroshima, Japan (LNCS 3298, pp. 698-712).

Eysenbach, G. (2001). An ontology of quality initiatives and a model for decentralized, collaborative quality management on the (semantic) World Wide Web. *Journal of Medical Internet Research*, *3*(4), e34. doi:10.2196/jmir.3.4.e34

Fagin, R., Kumar, R., & Sivakumar, D. (2003). Efficient similarity search and classification via rank aggregation. In *Proceedings of the ACM SIGMOD International Conference on Management of Data.*

Ganter, B., & Wille, R. (1999). *Formal concept analysis: Mathematical foundations*. Berlin, Germany: Springer.

Giles, J. (2005). Internet encyclopaedias go head to head. *Nature*, *438*(7070), 900–901. doi:10.1038/438900a

Guinchiglia, F., Shvaiko, P., & Yatskevich, M. (2004). S-Match: An algorithm and an implementation of semantic matching. In *Proceedings of 1st European Semantic Web Symposium (ESWS'04),* Crete, Greece, (pp. 61-75).

He, B., & Chang, K. C. (2003). Statistical schema matching across Web query interfaces. In *Proceedings of SIGMOD Conference* (pp. 217-228).

Kalfoglou, Y., & Hu, B. (2005). CMS: CROSI mapping system - results of the 2005 ontology alignment contests. In *Proceedings of the K-Cap'05 Integrating Ontologies workshop,* Alberta, Canada.

Kalfoglou, Y., & Hu, B. (2006). Issues with evaluating and using publicly available ontologies. In *Proceedings of the 4th International EON workshop,* Edinburgh, UK.

Kalfoglou, Y., Hu, B., Reynolds, D., & Shadbolt, N. (2005). *CROSI project: Final report* (CROSI project deliverable). University of Southampton and HP Labs Bristol.

Kalfoglou, Y., & Schorlemmer, M. (2003). Ontology mapping: the state of the art. *The Knowledge Engineering Review*, *18*(1), 1–31. doi:10.1017/S0269888903000651

Kalfoglou, Y., & Schorlemmer, M. (2003b). IF-Map: An ontology mapping method based on information flow theory. *Journal on Data Semantics*, *1*, 98–127.

Lenat, D. (1995). Cyc: A large scale investment in knowledge infrastructure. *Communications of the ACM*, *38*, 11.

Lozano-Tello, A., & Gomez-Perez, A. (2004). ONTOMETRIC: A method to choose the appropriate ontology. *Journal of Database Management*, *15*(2), 1–18.

Madhavan, J., Bernstein, P. A., Kuang, C., Halevy, A., & Shenoy, P. (2003). Corpus-based schema matching. In *Proceedings of the IJCAI'03 Workshop on Information Integration on the Web (IIWeb-03),* Acapulco, Mexico.

Melnik, S., Garcia-Molina, H., & Rahm, E. (2002). Similarity flooding: A versatile graph matching algorithm and its application to schema matching. In *Proceedings of the 18th International Conference on Data Engineering (ICDE)* (pp. 117-128).

Miller, G. A. (1990). WORDNET: An online lexical database. *International Journal of Lexicography*, *3*(4), 235–312. doi:10.1093/ijl/3.4.235

Milo, T., & Zohar, S. (1998). Using schema matching to simplify heterogeneous data translation. In *Proceedings of the 24rd International Conference on Very Large Data Bases (VLDB'98),* New York, NY, USA (pp. 122-133).

Noy, F. N., & Musen, M. (2002). PROMPTDIFF: A fixed-point algorithm for comparing ontology versions. In *Proceedings of the 18th National Conference on Artificial Intelligence, (AAAI'02),* Edmonton, Alberta, Canada (pp. 744-751).

Noy, N., & Musen, M. (2003). The PROMPT suite: Interactive tools for ontology merging and mapping. *International Journal of Human-Computer Studies*, *59*(6), 983–1024. doi:10.1016/j.ijhcs.2003.08.002

Noy, N., Sintek, M., Decker, S., Crubezy, M., Fergeson, W., & Musen, M. (2001). Creating Semantic Web contents with Protege-2000. *IEEE Intelligent Systems*, *16*(2), 60–71. doi:10.1109/5254.920601

O'Hara, K., & Shadbolt, N. (2001). Issues for an ontology for knowledge valuation. In *Proceedings of the IJCAI'01 workshop on E-Business and the Intelligent Web,* Seattle, WA, USA.

Ogden, C., & Richards, I. (1923). *The meaning of meaning: A study of the influence of language upon thought and of the science of symbolism.* San Diego, CA: Harcourt Brace Jovanovich.

Palopoli, L., Terracina, G., & Ursino, D. (2003). DIKE: A system supporting the semi-automatic construction of cooperative information systems from heterogeneous databases. *Software. Practice, 33*(9), 847–884.

Rahm, A., & Bernstein, A. (2001). A survey of approaches to automatic schema matching. *The Very Large Databases Journal, 10*(4), 334–350. doi:10.1007/s007780100057

Resnick, P., & Zeckhauser, R. (2002). Trust among strangers in Internet transactions: Empirical analysis of eBay's reputation system. *Advances in Applied Mircroelectronics, 11.*

Shadbolt, N., O'Hara, K., & Crow, L. (1999). The experimental evaluation of knowledge acquisition techniques and methods: History, problems, and new directions. *International Journal of Human-Computer Studies, 51,* 729–755. doi:10.1006/ijhc.1999.0327

Smith, B. (2004). Beyond concepts: Ontology as reality representation. In *Proceedings of the International Conference on Formal Ontology and Information Systems (FOIS 2004),* Turin.

Steels, L., & Kaplan, F. (1999). Bootstrapping grounded word semantics. In T. Briscoe (Ed.), *Linguistic evolution through language acquisition: Formal and computational models.* Cambridge, UK: Cambridge University Press.

Sure, Y., Maedche, A., & Staab, S. (2000). Leveraging corporate skill knowledge - from ProPer to OntoProPer. In *Proceedings of the 3rd International Conference on Practical Aspects of Knowledge Management (PAKM2000),* Basel, Switzerland.

Uschold, M. (2003). Where are the semantics in the Semantic Web? *AI Magazine, 24*(3), 25–36.

Uschold, M., & Jasper, R. (1999). A framework for understanding and classifying ontology applications. In *Proceedings of the IJCAI-99 Workshop on Ontologies and Problem-Solving Methods (KRR5),* Stockholm, Sweden.

Wang, J. T.-L., Zhang, K., Jeong, K., & Shasha, D. (1994). A system for approximate tree matching. *IEEE Transactions on Knowledge and Data Engineering, 6*(4), 559–571. doi:10.1109/69.298173

Weber, N., & Buitelaar, P. (2006). Web-based otnology learning with ISOLDE. In *Proceedings of the Workshop on Web Content mining with Human Language, International Semantic Web Conference (ISWC'06),* Athens, USA.

Wenger, E. (1998). *Communities of practice: The key to knowledge strategy.* Cambridge, UK: Cambridge University Press.

Wilks, Y., Webb, N., Setzer, A., Hepple, M., & Capitzone, R. (2005). Machine learning approaches to human dialogue modelling. In *Advances in natural multimodal dialogue systems.* Amsterdam: Kluwer Academic Publishers.

Wu, F., & Weld, D. (2008). Automatically refining the Wikipedia infobox ontology. In *Proceedings of the 17th International Conference on World Wide Web* (pp. 635-644).

Zdhanova, A., & Shvaiko, P. (2006). Community-driven ontology matching. In *Proceedings of the 3rd European Semantic Web Conference (ESWC'06),* Budva, Montenegro.

ENDNOTES

1. See, for example the list in http://www.ontologymatching.org/
2. A more elaborate list appears in the CROSI project report accessible from: http://www.aktors.org/crosi/deliverables/
3. http://dublincore.org/
4. The project's software is available as open source and accessible from: http://sourceforge.net/projects/ontologymapping/
5. Source data and reference alignments are available from: http://oaei.inrialpes.fr/2005/
6. http://www.w3.org/TR/skos-reference/
7. http://oaei.ontologymatching.org/
8. The Freebase knowledge base from Metaweb technologies - http://www.metaweb.com/8
9. http://en.wikipedia.org/.
10. http://suo.ieee.org/
11. http://suo.ieee.org/email/msg12376.html

Chapter 6
Sharing Resources through Ontology Alignments in a Semantic Peer-to-Peer System

Jérôme Euzenat
INRIA & LIG, France

Onyeari Mbanefo
INRIA & LIG, France

Arun Sharma
INRIA & LIG, France

EXECUTIVE SUMMARY

In heterogeneous semantic peer-to-peer systems, peers describe their resources through ontologies that they can adapt to their particular needs. In order to interoperate, queries need to be transformed with respect to alignments between their ontologies before being evaluated. Alignments are thus critical for sharing resources in such systems. The authors report an experiment that explores how such alignments can be obtained in a natural way. In particular, asking users to provide alignments is a heavy constraint that must be relaxed as much as possible. This can be attempted through automatic matching. However, the authors suggest other possible solutions.

BACKGROUND: SEMANTIC PEER-TO-PEER SYSTEMS

The semantic web can be described as a web for machines. For that purpose, it requires the expression of formalised knowledge on the web (in languages like RDF). This is aimed at bringing more precision to the knowledge gathered from the web than automatically indexing text documents. However, the semantic web suffers from a bootstrap problem: it can only start providing benefits when there is enough knowledge available and people will not provide knowledge if this does not return benefits.

DOI: 10.4018/978-1-60566-894-9.ch006

In order to overcome this problem, we want to provide tools that allow people to start using semantic web technologies locally, for personal purposes and personal benefits, and that can spread through global and social communication. On the one hand, peer-to-peer (P2P) systems are suited for this purpose since their use for sharing resources on the web is widespread and such systems can be used by many untrained users. On the other hand, such tools are restricted in the freedom of expression given to the user: most of them do not provide much expressiveness in resource annotations or they rely on a one-size-fits-all metadata vocabulary. This restricts the precision of shared item descriptions and thus prevent their full retrieval, e.g., "Finding all recordings in which Eric Dolphy is playing flute" or "All pictures featuring a member of your family and a horse".

We describe a kind of semantic peer-to-peer system in which users can start locally to develop the annotation scheme that suits them best. They can customise ontologies, either imported from the web or home made, so as to organise their resources the way they want. Then, users can offer their resources and annotations to their friends and relatives through peer-to-peer sharing. However, because ontologies have been designed locally, it is more difficult to interoperate between peers: therefore, alignments between ontologies are necessary. An alignment is a set of assertions, called correspondences, which express the relation between entities of two ontologies. They can be used for translating queries from one ontology to the other, as well as for other purposes (Euzenat and Shvaiko, 2007). With alignments, interaction and sharing can take place, and users do not have to abandon their own view on resources.

This chapter presents the PicSter system as a case of heterogeneous semantic peer-to-peer system. It aims to illustrate the need for ontology alignments in such systems and the difficulties of providing such alignments.

After briefly presenting the field of semantic peer-to-peer systems, we describe extensively the PicSter picture sharing system. This description highlights the need for alignments in such systems. Then we elaborate on several possible solutions for obtaining these alignments and the difficulties facing these solutions. We do so through the description of an experiment.

Related Work

In principle, peer-to-peer systems are distributed systems which do not rely, in their communication, on centralised resources. In practice, they often rely on some directory for joining a network. Once they have joined, all communication goes through adjacent peers. Peer-to-peer systems are well known as resource sharing devices in which peers offer resources and can query other peers for particular resources. We are concerned with this type of systems (other systems may be built on a publish and subscribe protocol, for instance).

Semantic peer-to-peer systems are peer-to-peer systems using semantic technologies for describing shared resources. The use of ontologies allows a richer description framework for resources than tags and simple categories. In particular, it allows querying the other peers with more precise queries ("Give me the Portraits depicting Paul Cezanne") instead of ("Portrait" and "Cezanne"). It also allows peers to draw inferences from the query and their ontology. For instance, something classified as a "Self-portrait" will be qualified as an answer for the above query if a "Self-portrait" is defined as a "Portrait". Similarly, a "Painting displaying Paul Cezanne" may be considered a "Portrait of Paul Cezanne" if "Portrait" is defined as a "Painting displaying some person". In summary, semantic peer-to-peer systems aim at providing a more complete and more precise answer to the queries that are exchanged between peers.

There have been several such systems. (Staab and Stuckenschmidt, 2006) provides a good overview of issues in such systems.

Edutella (Neijdl et al., 2002) was an early project for sharing educational resources. The system used the JXTA protocol to query over the network RDF annotation of these resources. One problem addressed by Edutella was to have more precise resource descriptions and queries while avoiding the fragmentation of niche P2P systems. The use of general purpose technologies such as those of the semantic web was the solution to this problem.

A first semantic peer-to-peer system was BibSter (Haase et al., 2004) developed in the framework of the SWAP European project. In BibSter, resources are bibliographic entries. They are expressed in RDF with regard to the same RDF schema (built from BibTeX). Hence queries are unambiguous. However, peers may have different ways to describe the same entry within BibTeX (using more or less information and more or less the same categories). Hence, the project has developed techniques for matching similar items (Haase at al., 2006).

In this chapter, we focus on open semantic peer-to-peer systems in which peers are free to use any ontologies they estimate suitable to their purposes.

Peer Data Management Systems (PDMS) are peer-to-peer systems whose shared resources are data. They have gone through some popularity in database. As data management systems, they are usually made of peers supporting a database that can be queried through an query language such as SQL. Peer databases are defined by a known schema which can be different from peer to peer. Although they do not provide a particularly expressive ontology, PDMSes address the problem of heterogeneity of the schema used by each peer through the use of mappings which are usually correspondences between queries.

Piazza (Ives et al., 2004) is such a PDMS based on XML and Xquery. SomeWhere (Rousset et al., 2006) is another such system initially based on Datalog with a well-defined query evaluation procedure. It has been extended towards RDF and OWL over the years. Most of the PDMSes are made of autonomous peers, non controlled by human beings. Other systems, such as BibSter and most of the well-known internet sharing systems, are directed by someone manipulating the system. This is also the context of the system we consider here.

Semantic peer-to-peer systems are confronted with important challenges such as routing queries in the network for efficiency or accuracy, replicating resources across peers, decomposing queries or finding the correct matching between two peers. These issues are well described in (Staab and Stuckenschmidt, 2006; Zaihrayeu, 2006). This chapter considers exclusively the issue of establishing alignments between ontologies and offering solutions to end users who are not ontology nor matching specialists.

SETTING THE STAGE: THE PICSTER SYSTEM

PicSter is an experimental semantic peer-to-peer picture annotation and sharing system developed in 2006 at INRIA (Sharma, 2006). In PicSter, both the semantic sharing aspect and the annotation aspects are important: this is because users have more freedom in modifying their ontologies that the system is heterogeneous and this makes answering queries difficult.

Semantic Peer-to-Peer Framework

This case study considers a particular framework that we call semantic peer-to-peer. This framework involves the following elements:

- Peers: are the agents which describe and share a set of resources, e.g., pictures.
- Resources: are the resources that will be shared among peers. These resources can be stored in peer directories or available on the web.
- Ontologies: define the vocabulary used for annotating resources. They can be found

on the web or be locally available at each peer.

- Instances: are individuals described by the ontologies. They are stored separately in each peer. They can also be referred from the web through URIs.
- Annotations: describe resources or resource fragments using the ontologies. Agents annotate resources by indicating that they belong to particular classes of the ontology, e.g., Picture, or they have relations with particular instances, e.g., depicts Grenoble.
- Queries: are expressions used for selecting resources with regard to their annotations. They are usually expressed in a dedicated query language.
- Alignments: express relationships between ontologies so that an annotation expressed with regard to one ontology can be understood with the vocabulary of another ontology. For instance, a "Lilium" under one ontology can be understood as a subclass of "Fleur" in another ontology.

Each peer can work independently of the others as a fully functional system. As far as content is concerned, this framework covers the examples of peer-to-peer systems that we have considered previously.

This framework provides the basic functions of semantic desktops (Schumacher et al., 2008):

- annotating a resource with elements from ontologies, and
- searching for resources annotated by particular elements.

Semantic desktops provide two additional and advanced features:

- extending ontologies, and
- sharing annotations.

In this framework, resources are identified by URIs, they are annotated in RDF (Carroll and Klyne, 2004) through vocabularies defined by ontologies in OWL (Dean and Schreiber, 2004) or RDF Schema (Brickley and Guha, 2004). Ontologies can be related by alignments and queries are expressed in SPARQL (Prud'hommeaux and Seaborne, 2008). Hence, this framework takes the maximum advantage of standard semantic web technologies.

This framework is instantiated in PicSter that we describe in the remainder.

PicSter Overview and Architecture

Our working example is the use of semantic web technologies for annotating resources (and particularly pictures) on one's computer. This is already a very helpful application since it can help people querying their data with respect to very precise and personal vocabularies (this is more powerful than simple schemes such as those used in Web 2.0 picture sharing sites).

We have developed PicSter, a prototype for ontology-based peer-to-peer picture annotation that allows accommodating users' needs in the ontologies used for annotation. PicSter provides the ability to annotate pictures in RDF by selecting individuals and classes in chosen ontologies. The ontologies can be modified on the fly by users as they need to refine the classification, e.g., that a Fjording is a Horse, or to add individuals, e.g., that Tony is a particular Fjording. This requires very little overhead.

Since users can select and evolve ontologies as they need it, their ontologies are necessarily different from each others. Hence, when connecting to the peer-to-peer system, users have to provide (partial) alignments between the ontology they use and those of the peer they are connected to. These alignments are used for transforming queries from one peer to another so that the query can be interpreted with regard to the other peer's ontology. These alignments may be stored in an alignment server and can be retrieved on demand.

PicSter peers can be used off-line, for annotating local pictures and querying them, or online, when a peer accepts incoming queries from authorised peers and can issue queries to these peers. In order to properly work off-line, PicSter peers cache most of the information they deal with. Hence, peers store:

- List of authorised peers,
- Resources (here pictures),
- Ontologies, as well as local extensions to these ontologies,
- Instances,
- Annotations.

These resources are stored in several separate silos (actually file system directories) of individual PicSter repositories according to the following rules:

- pictures: contains all the resources as individual files, unchanged.
- ontologies: contains the original ontologies as unchanged files and the extension of these ontologies as separate prefixed files.
- instances: contains all the individuals described with regard to the ontologies. They are stored as one file per concept containing all its instances.
- annotations: contains picture annotations expressed in RDF. There is one file per picture containing all its annotations.

An example of annotation is given in appendix. These directories are inspected when launching PicSter so that it can load ontologies and pictures. Annotations and individuals are loaded at query and annotation time.

PicSter offers two main functions (see Figure 1):

- Annotation editor allowing to (1) annotate artefacts with elements of the ontology, and (2) evolving the ontology to meets the annotator's need.
- Query interface allowing to answer queries (1) against the local store, and (2) by submitting them to connected peers through their alignments.

Figure 1. Architecture of a PicSter peer and relations to other elements. Simple arrows correspond to invocation and data flow. Double arrows correspond to query/answer interface. Aserv corresponds to the Alignment server, providing alignments to the mediator. It is in dashed lines because it is not available in PicSter's current implementation

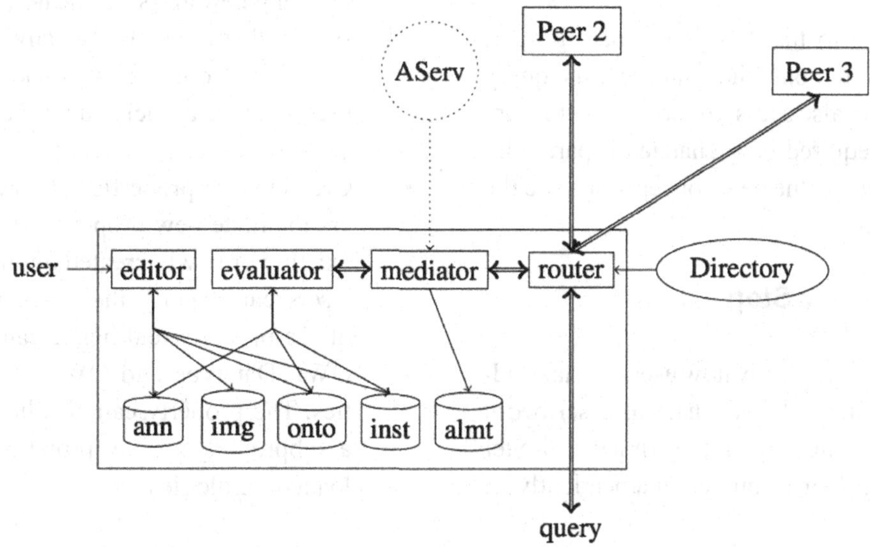

The goal of PicSter is to share the annotations and resources with other peers. For that purpose, peers are connected together and can send queries about their annotations to other peers and receive replies (under the form of lists of picture URIs satisfying the query). The queries are thus either evaluated locally or routed to other peers.

PicSter is based upon a peer-to-peer model without any centralised authority, but directories for finding peers. It is also an autonomous model: a PicSter peer without neighbours is a fully functional software. This authorises the off-line use of the tool: nothing pertaining to the peer is stored on the peer network.

The PicSter annotation tool is based on the PhotoStuff software (Halaschek-Wiener et al., 2005) that has been developed at MindLab (University of Maryland). PhotoStuff already had the ability to load images and ontologies, display images, select image areas, annotate pictures and zones with ontology concepts and properties, store the annotations in RDF and query them with SPARQL. We added the possibility to:

- modify ontologies on the fly and to store and reload these ontologies;
- load several ontologies;
- route queries to other peers and declare related peers;
- transform queries through alignments.

With regard to the description of Figure 1, PhotoStuff offered only the editor and the query evaluator. It had also a less rigourous way to store the data. This required many changes, in particular about how to name the new concepts or store the new ontologies.

PicSter Step by Step

We describe progressively how users can take advantage of PicSter in the way that was described at the beginning of the chapter: they first use PicSter for annotating their resources independently of any other peers. The first feature of PicSter is to help user organising their own resources without constraints. Then, users can connect to other peers and benefit from the work of others

Users start with an empty PicSter instance in which they can load "pictures" and "ontologies". Both images and ontologies can come from their file system or the web. Under the hood, PicSter copies them in the images and ontologies directories, but it always maintains the initial URI identifying each of these objects.

In order to annotate pictures, users can either select several pictures, one picture or a particular area in a picture. Then from the ontology panel, they can select a class for annotating the selected item with this class. For instance, in Figure 3, the user has selected the "Rose" class in ontology "World". Instead of choosing classes, users can choose instances, i.e., individual objects. For instance, on Figure 2, the image has been annotated with the instance "GrenobleCoursliberation63Arriere".

It may be that the ontology is not precise enough, in which case, the user can, on the fly, extend it. PicSter provides some basic ontology edition functions which are useful for quick personalisation of the picture annotation process. In particular, it allows users to extend the ontologies they use by:

- Creating new classes: The new class can be specified as a subclass of any class among the loaded ontologies. Labels and comments can be associated with it (see Figure 5).
- Creating new properties: PicSter allows users to create new properties for any of the existing or newly created ontology classes. Users can specify the range and domain of the property and hence can create both OWL Datatype and OWL Object properties. The property can also be specified as a subproperty of any property among the loaded ontologies.

Figure 2. Main PicSter edition interface. On the top panel, pictures can be selected; on the left panel, a selected picture is displayed and subareas can be selected; on the right panel, annotations, ontology and instances can be displayed and selected. The bottom panel is used for expressing queries.

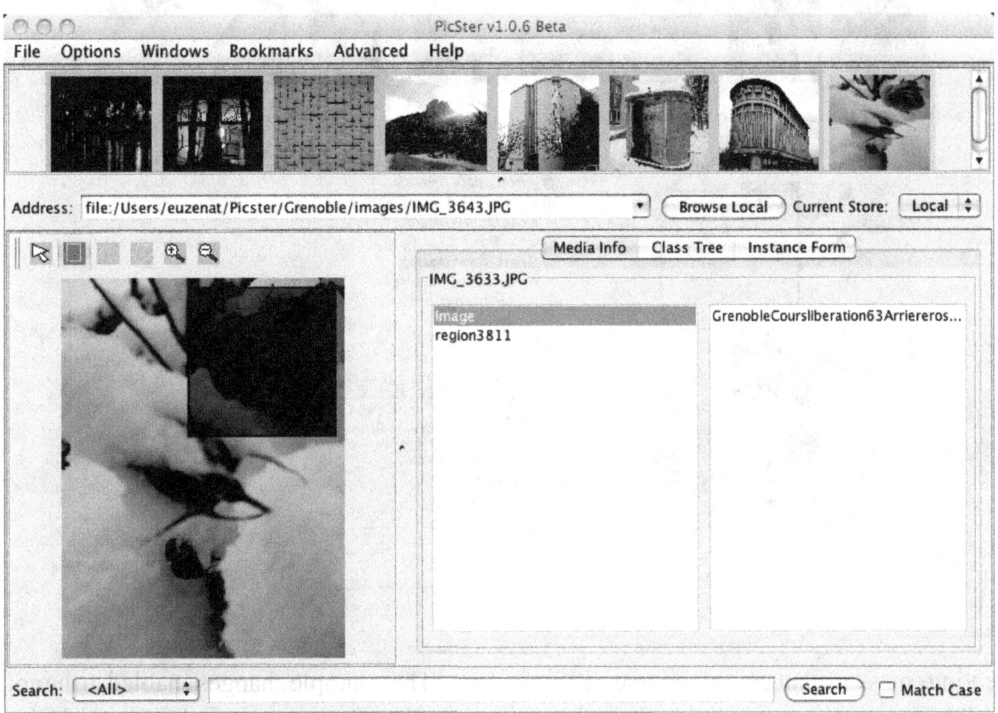

Figure 3. Ontology representation and concept selection

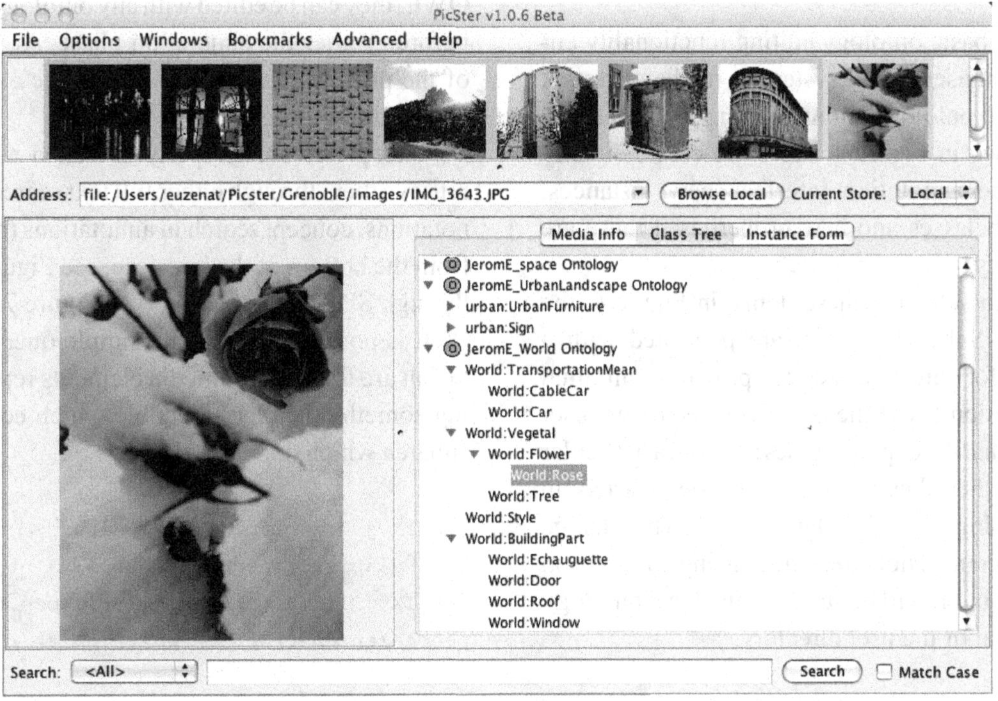

Figure 4. Addition on the fly of an instance, a subclass or a property to an existing ontology

- Creating new instances: of course, it is possible to create new individuals and to fill their properties, relating them to other individuals.

This basic ontology editing functionality ensures that users of the system do not have to stick to a base ontology for annotating their pictures. As shown in Figure 4, users can create directly from the annotation interface new instances, new subclasses and new properties if these are necessary.

When selecting these items, in Figure 4, the "Create Subclass", users are presented with a straightforward interface for providing minimal information about the new items. Here, the user knows that the depicted roses are from a particular variety, then they can create this new variety in the ontology as "PinkFlamingo12". This change will, of course, not affect the existing ontology on the web but it will be stored in the local ontology extension of the user directory.

These simple changes enabled in the annotation interface free users from having to design elaborate and extensive ontologies before annotating. However, since the ontologies are stored in genuine OWL, they can be edited with any ontology editor before or after the annotation phase. At the end of the process, the user has set up the elements depicted in Figure 6.

Once pictures are properly annotated, users can retrieve them through either full text search in annotations, concept search in annotations (directly from the bottom of the interface, see Figure 4) or through SPARQL querying (see Figure 7).

It is possible to evaluate simple queries like "what are the URIs of media elements representing something called Grenoble which contain a subarea which depicts a flower":

```
PREFIX j.0: <http://www.mindswap.
org/~glapizco/technical.owl#>
PREFIX j.1: <http://exmo.inrialpes.fr/
people/euzenat/JeromE_world.owl#>
```

Figure 5. Required information for class creation

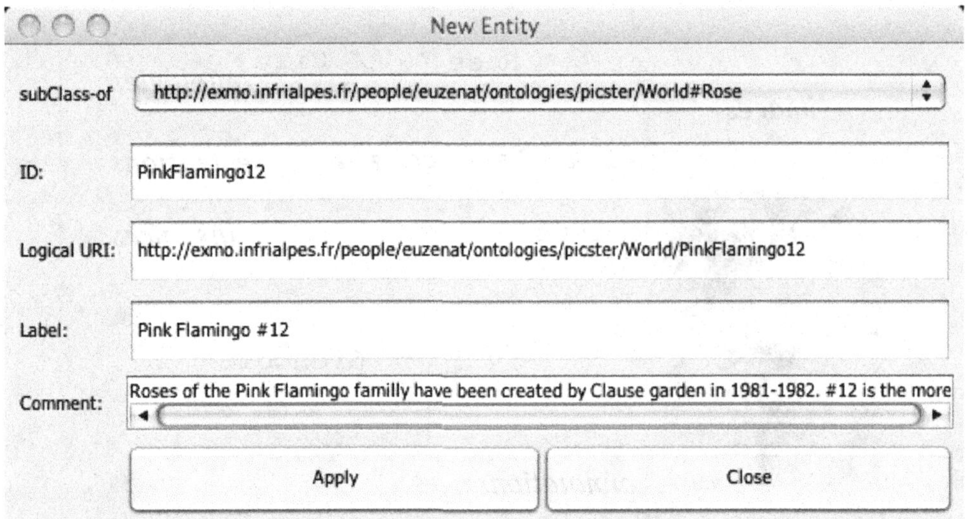


```
PREFIX j.2: <http://exmo.inrialpes.fr/
people/euzenat/JeromE_space.owl#>
SELECT ?uri
WHERE
{
    ?x j.0:depicts ?y.
    ?y rdf:type j.1:Flower.
    ?x j.0:subAreaOf ?uri.
    ?uri j.2:isIn ?z.
    ?z j.2:name "Grenoble".
}
```

This query returns the results provided in the right panel of Figure 7. The answer is provided in terms of instances and in terms of pictures. Thanks to the available ontologies it will also retrieve pictures which are not even annotated by "Flower" but by "Pink flamingo12".

Query evaluation is implemented by using the ARQ SPARQL processor for the Jena API.

Resource Sharing

PicSter enables more than semantically annotating resources. It offers sharing resources and annotations among peers. For that purpose, peers are connected through the Java JXTA Protocol (Oaks et al., 2002). PicSter, through JXTA support, performs the tasks which are related to peer-to-peer communication. The design principles for this component are the ones which are typical of peer-to-peer systems, namely:

- A peer announces its presence to other peers when joining the network;
- Peer advertisements are sent and received in an asynchronous manner;
- All peers maintain a local cache of known peers, so that they can send queries to known peers even if they have not received an advertisement for these peers.

This peer-to-peer interface allows to declare some of the peers as friends. The support is visible in Figure 1 through the "Directory" component. It is dealt with, in each peer, through a "router" whose purpose is to route queries and answers from one peer to another.

Once a peer is connected to the network, it can evaluate its queries locally or against other peers. The interface provides the ability to send queries to all other peers or to select a subset of these (see Figure 7, left). A peer also enables other peers to send it queries to evaluate.

Figure 6. Resulting links between elements

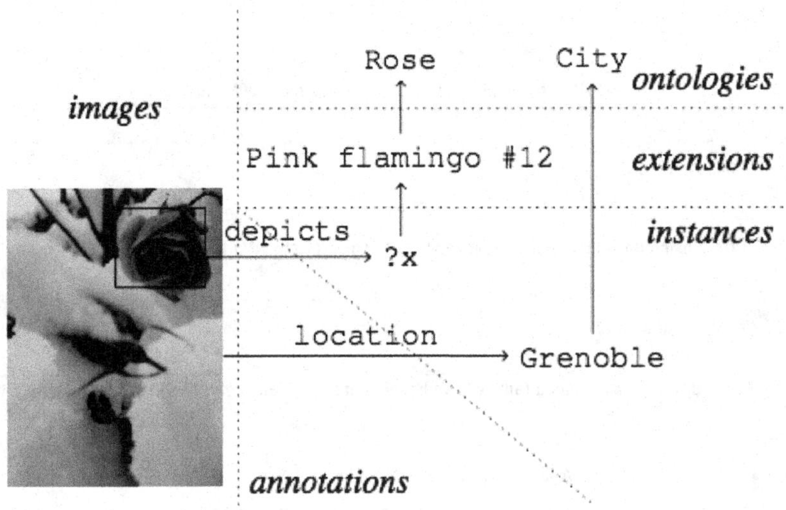

Figure 7. On the left hand side, the query panel of PicSter 1.2.1. It allows to select if the query will be evaluated only locally or sent to related peers. On the right hand side, the results of query evaluation. Here these results can be either instances (I) or pictures (M).

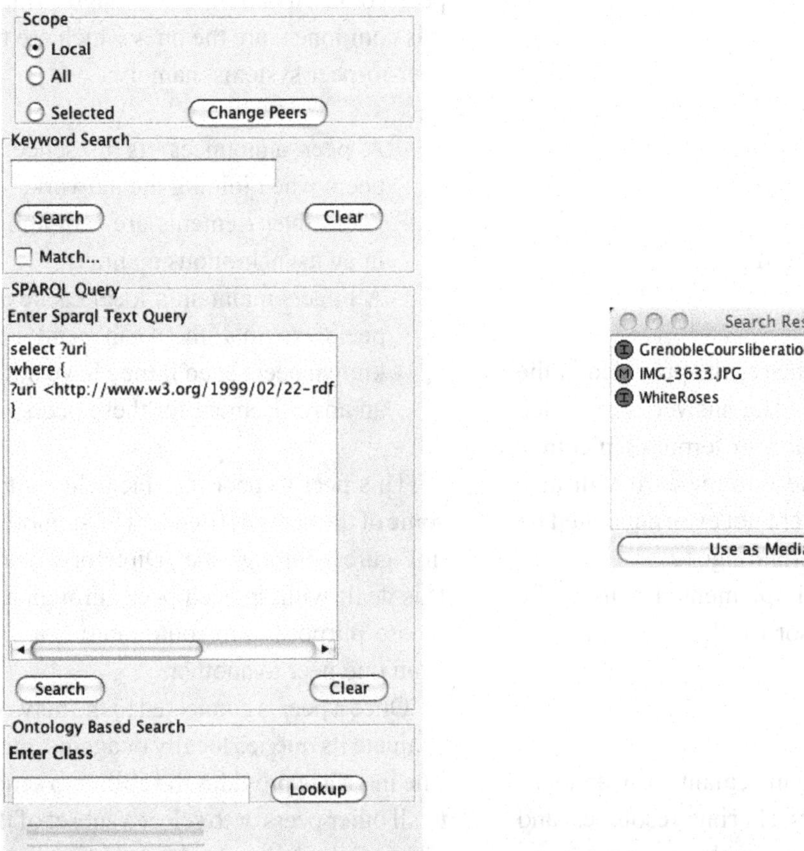

However, more is needed in order to evaluate queries. Indeed, since users are allowed to choose the ontology they use and to adapt them to their needs, they will end up having different ontologies. Hence, simply evaluating queries in others peers' context is deemed to fail. For solving this problem, PicSter uses mediators (see Figure 1) which transform queries with regard to a source ontology into queries with regard to a target ontology. Mediators themselves take advantage of alignments between the ontologies. Alignments are expressed using the Alignment API (Euzenat, 2004): an alignment is a set of correspondences between entities found in the ontologies. In our context, these entities could be classes, properties or individuals. For instance, the property "isIn" in one ontology may be more general than the property "city" in another one.

Query mediators translate queries. For this purpose, they take an ontology alignment and a query as input and generate the rewritten query with regard to the alignment. The current version of the mediator performs translations on the basis of equivalent correspondences given by the input alignment. The URI references within a query are replaced by their corresponding equivalent URI as mentioned in the input alignment. A further improvement would be to allow translations based on more elaborate correspondences. The mediator is implemented for queries written in the SPARQL (Prud'hommeaux and Seaborne, 2008) query language.

For instance, the following query returns the URI of all the resources which depicts some instance of "Fleur" in ontology Arun_sumo and which is situated in a "city" named "Grenoble".

```
PREFIX j.0: <http://www.mindswap.
org/~glapizco/technical.owl#>
PREFIX j.1: <http://exmo.inrialpes.fr/
people/sharma/Arun_sumo.owl#>
PREFIX j.2: <http://daml.umbc.edu/ontolo-
gies/space-basic#>
SELECT ?uri
WHERE
{
    ?x j.0:depicts ?y.
    ?y rdf:type j.1:Fleur.
    ?x j.0:subAreaOf ?uri.
    ?uri j.2:city ?z.
    ?z j.1:id "Grenoble".
}
```

In this query, the ontology j.0 is the internal ontology of PicSter providing the notions of depiction and areas. The subAreaOf relation is reflexive (so that a picture is a subarea of itself). The two other ontologies are the local extensions of respectively the SUMO and DAML space ontologies.

If the target peer also uses two ontologies, JeromE_world.owl and JeromE_space.owl, then four ontologies are involved apart from the PicSter ontology itself. If the peer finds an alignment between the ontologies providing the correspondences stating:

```
Arun_sumo.owl#Fleur = JeromE_world.
owl#Flower
Arun_sumo.owl#id = JeromE_space.owl#name
space-basic#city < JeromE_space.owl#isIn
```

The first correspondence relates two concepts and the latter relates properties. It is noteworthy that the ontologies do not coincide one by one.

The mediator rewrites the input query according to these correspondences. This will yield the query presented in the previous section:

```
PREFIX j.0: <http://www.mindswap.
org/~glapizco/technical.owl#>
PREFIX j.1: <http://exmo.inrialpes.fr/
people/euzenat/JeromE_world.owl#>
PREFIX j.2: <http://exmo.inrialpes.fr/
people/euzenat/JeromE_space.owl#>
SELECT ?uri
WHERE
{
```

```
    ?x j.0:depicts ?y.
    ?y rdf:type j.1:Flower.
    ?x j.0:subAreaOf ?uri.
    ?uri j.2:isIn ?z.
    ?z j.2:name "Grenoble".
}
```

The rewritten query is able to find pictures which are not annotated by "Fleur" but by "Flower".

This process works with SPARQL queries but it also works with more simple queries (such as those using only one concept name: "Fleur").

CASE DESCRIPTION: OBTAINING ALIGNMENTS IN PEER-TO-PEER NETWORKS

So far, we have described how annotating pictures by ontology elements and altering ontologies themselves is made easy for end-users. This feature is important for the comfort of users but it raises the important problem of heterogeneity.

Hence, one important problem of a semantic peer-to-peer system such as PicSter is to obtain alignments so that queries can be transmitted from one peer to another. In order to solve this problem, users must obtain alignments between their ontologies. There are different ways to do this:

- manually: users can provide themselves the alignments by comparing the relevant ontologies;
- by automatic matching: users, or the system itself, can rely on matching algorithms in order to establish alignments (Euzenat and Shvaiko, 2007);
- by invert and composition: if enough alignments are available across ontologies, it is possible to combine them through algebraic operations (converse, composition, union, intersection) in order to obtain an alignment between the exact two ontologies that we have;
- by retrieving them from an alignment store: if high-quality alignments are available between ontologies, it is then possible to retrieve alignments from these stores;
- by local and aggregative interaction: it is possible to ask users for partial alignments which is sufficient for evaluating the query, then, as more queries are issued, the alignment between two ontologies will grow and eventually provide a full alignment.

It is possible to classify these techniques with regard to their expected quality and the effort required from the users, like in Table 1.

In order to evaluate if PicSter is a viable system and if Table 1 is an accurate picture of reality, we ran an experiment that we report here.

Experimental Setting

In PicSter, autonomous semantic peers share resources by relying on alignments. In 2006, we ran an experiment in order to investigate the practicality of this framework. There were several goals of this experiment in relation to the work of our team:

- Test and evaluate the PicSter application and infrastructure;
- Provide experimental data for knowledge-based social network analysis;
- Provide experimental data for alignment algorithm evaluation;
- Provide experimental data on which to test alignment composition.

We have experimented PicSter on a set of pictures and users free to choose and modify the ontologies they use. Users where asked to provide an alignment with one of the other users' ontologies. These alignments were used to generate new

Table 1. Solutions for obtaining alignments classified according to their quality and difficulty. Since, they depend on existing alignments, the algebraic and storage methods need a critical mass of alignments to be usable .

	Expected quality	Effort on the user
Manual	high	high
Automatic	low	low
Algebraic	medium (depends in input)	low
Store	high (depends on input)	low
Local	medium (correct but incomplete)	medium

alignments through inverse and composition, and to evaluate simple automatic matching systems against the given alignments.

The experiment was made among 7 researchers of the Exmo team (named here: P, E, L, A, Z, J, S) during January and February 2006. They had a set of 133 pictures taken by themselves on the topic of Grenoble and the INRIA centre to annotate. A common subset 47 randomly selected pictures was compulsory to annotate in order to ensure a common coverage of the data set and relations in annotations.

Participants were totally free to choose the way to annotate the pictures, they were only required to use the PicSter interface to do this work. In particular, they could use existing ontologies, design their own or extend existing ones.

In the end of the experiment, this provided us with a set of ontologies per participants, a set of annotated images per participants, and a set of annotations per participants. Participants were also asked to evaluate the time they spent in annotating and to name the other participants to whom they feel to be the closest ontology-wise. This is summarised in Table 2.

Participants took a relatively long time to provide the annotations. This was mostly due to the instability of the prototype.

What is surprising to us is that very few of the users (among the ontology-savvy) created their own ontologies. This is a good news for the semantic web showing that people are willing to reuse the existing resources if they are available. This can also be explained by the short time schedule or by the will of using the sharing philosophy of the web. Because this was possible in the interface, users used Swoogle (Ding et al., 2004) for finding ontologies related to the annotation they had in mind and extended them.

The second remark is that users have used upper-level ontologies (SUMO, AKT) rather than more specialised ontologies (SPACE, FOAF). This resulted in very large ontologies to be used.

After this step, each participant had been asked to evaluate and provide one alignment between his ontologies and those of another participant. In that step, we wanted to limit the burden put on users for providing alignments and yet preserve the possibility to compose alignments. The participants were organised in a circle (P → J → S → A → E → L → Z → P) in order to allow some manipulations related to reciprocity — inverse — and transitivity — composition. No interface was provided to perform this task.

The resulting alignments were used for two distinct purposes:

- As reference alignments to compare with (simple) automatic matching techniques;
- As seeds for obtaining other alignments through converse and composition.

Additionally, we used the assessment by participants to evaluate the usability of the system and to compare their self-assessed affinity with distances on their ontologies.

Analysis

We analyse the results of this experiments with respect to several criteria. The usability of the PicSter system itself was considered fair by users. It was only a first prototype. Let consider the results concerning alignments and their computation.

Table 2. Data from the participants in the experiment: #pic is the number of annotated pictures, #onto, the number of used ontologies, #inst, the number of instances that have been created, #class, the number of classes in the ontologies and their local extensions, #prop, the number of properties, and time, the approximate time spent for this annotation work. The closest column corresponds to the other participant, they felt their annotations would be the closest.

Participant #pic #onto #inst #class #prop time closest
S 47 3(SUMO,FOAF,SPACE) 66 158 242
Z 47 5(AKT,office,SPACE+2) 87 141 45 18h E
A 37 2(earthrealm,Travel) 81 738 38 11h E+S
E 49 6(SPACE,FOAF+4) 78 390 30 35h Z+L
J 47 1(SUMO) 49 1468 208 6h S+L
P 30 1(SUMO) 27 1449 208 5h L+Z
L 25 2(SUMO) 24 1395 416

Manual Provision of Alignments

The size of the resulting alignments is provided in Table 3. It shows a relatively low ratio of correspondences with regard to the size of the ontologies (especially if one compares with the number of potential one-to-one correspondences expressed in the third column). This easily confirms what was expected: users are not particularly willing to align ontologies by hand. This applies even if they have chosen themselves the ontologies. As a qualitative remark we had a lot of difficulties to obtain these alignments: while people have annotated pictures and altered ontologies within a few weeks, they spent several months providing the alignments.

As a result, there has been several workaround used by participants: some of them did not do the task, some of them did use very simple matchers (string equality), some of them did the task only partially. In particular, there were several people using SUMO which contains more than one thousand concepts. We could imagine that it is relatively easy to obtain an alignment from SUMO with itself and adding the few missing correspondences by hand. A simple program could be devised for doing most of this automatically. Unfortunately, these SUMO users found the task too overwhelming and returned very small alignments.

This shows that, according to our expectations, hand-made alignments indeed require a lot of effort, but, contrary to our expectations, the results were not of a high quality.

Evaluating Simple Matching Algorithms

We wanted to compare the results of simple matching algorithms on real world data in order to have an idea of which such algorithms were the most useful (Mbanefo, 2006). We designed and run a script that: (a) computed alignments between all pairs of ontologies, and (b) computed the alignments resulting from applying threshold to these alignments. This resulted in 588 alignments. Some of these alignments could be compared, through classical precision and recall to the reference alignments provided by users. We also performed a consensus analysis in which we took the best threshold for each method, we did the intersection of the resulting alignments and we compared them to the other results.

Unfortunately, the bad quality of our reference alignments prevented to obtain good evaluation of the quality of the alignment obtained automatically. When comparing the simple matchers with the result of the participants who had used the simplest automatic matchers, then the algorithms always had 100% recall and around a 10% precision. Worse, for those participants who had used SUMO, the precision of the automatic matchers was very bad (0%), while the results were indeed correct. This was a case where automatically computed alignments were better than those provided by human subjects, but our protocol was unable to find it.

In spite of these bad conditions, we can note that, for those users who did the matching work

Table 3. Characteristics of alignment returned by participants

Alignment	#Correspondences	#Potential correspondences
P→J	14	2.127.132
J→S	17	231.944
S→A	50	116.604
A→E	75	287.820
E→L		544.050
L→Z	19	196.695
Z→P	138	204.309

properly, we had significantly better results with our simple matchers that for others (yet around 30% precision and recall).

Evaluating Composition and Inverse

The third method that we had planned for obtaining alignments was to start from existing alignments and to obtain other alignments by algebraic operations. We wanted to check the quality of the results.

Since participants were randomly organised in a circular manner, each alignment (x → y) can be computed by (a) inverting all alignments provided by participants, and (b) composing these inverses in order to go from x to y. For instance, the alignment from P to E can be obtained by $(Z \rightarrow P)^{-1}.(L \rightarrow Z)^{-1}.(E \rightarrow L)^{-1}$ or through (P→J).(J→S).(S→A).(A→E). Figure 8 shows how to start computing inverse and composition from the set of alignments provided by participants.

Once this was achieved, it would have been possible to evaluate the results with simple measures:

- by comparing the result to the given alignment;
- by having users evaluating the result;
- by evaluating the amount of lost information.

We generated the alignments corresponding to the inversion method, unfortunately, our inverse operator was not working properly. This, conjugated with the poor alignments provided by participants, prevented us to exploit results.

The algebraic operations are so highly dependent on the quality of initial alignments that we did not even perform consensus tests like comparing the results that could be obtained by the two paths above.

Conclusion

In conclusion, computer experiment is a very delicate task. It requires many people available and this is not easy for complex experiments like this one. The experiment was interesting but non conclusive due to a number of problems:

- PicSter was not the most robust and easy going system in the world. This frustrated participants.
- There was a bug in the invert function of the Alignment API which reduced our confidence in the results.
- Providing alignments by hand is a very tedious task, thus some participants (with large ontologies) did not perform it with the required quality. Hence, results were not conclusive.
- Some of the instructions were not clear enough.

Figure 8. The set of participants and input alignments between them (plain arrows). In dotted arrows are examples of alignments obtained by composition (.) and inverse ($^{-1}$)

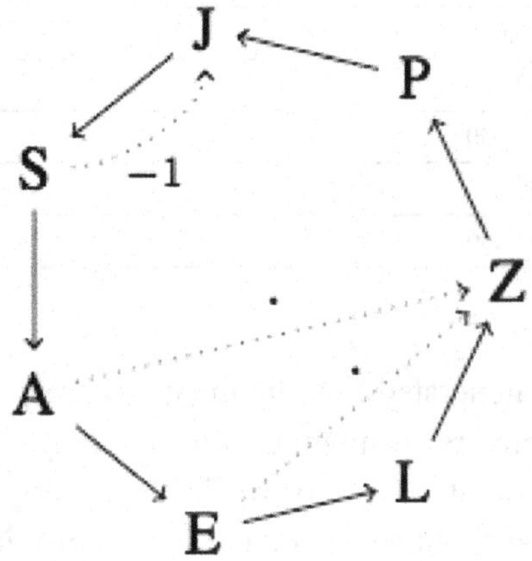

Most of these problems come from the data collection and not their exploitation, hence this kind of experiment could be run again with the above problems fixed.

A specific kind of evaluation that could have been performed is introduced in (Isaac et al., 2008): instead of evaluating alignments with regard to reference alignments, it consists of using the alignments for answering queries and asking users to evaluate the answers or having reference answers. More precisely, each participant would have to ask identified queries expressed in their ontologies and to identify the answers to these queries from the annotated pictures by anyone. Then, precision and recall could be given with regard to the answer returned by transformed queries with regard to the alignments. In the case of PicSter, such an evaluation would have been relatively natural since the only purpose of the alignments is querying. It would have had the advantage of showing to the users how bad their alignments were and enabled the evaluation of automatic alignments: automatic alignments would have provided better results than partial alignments. This would certainly have required more annotated pictures, but it would evaluate both the alignments, the ontologies and the annotations of all the peers.

However, the main problem is the need for good quality alignments.

Current Challenges Facing the Organisation

PicSter is an experimental semantic peer-to-peer system. Beside its prototype status, it is functional but not really stable. Its characteristics are:

Semantic

by using ontologies (as opposed to tags or keywords) for annotating and querying;

Serendipity

by extending ontologies through annotating pictures, non obtrusively;

Sharing

by connecting peers in a natural and personal way.

The peer-to-peer aspect of PicSter is highly relying on alignments for reducing heterogeneity. We have attempted to assess the possible ways to obtain alignments in systems like PicSter.

The main conclusion of this experiment is that the task of providing good alignments manually is very difficult for users, even if the ontologies have been chosen by them. Hence, other ways should be investigated.

In particular, it is critical for this application and, we guess, for many others to have automatic matching systems delivering alignments of reasonable quality. These alignments could, of course, be reviewed before being used, either by users when they issue queries or by curators before entering alignments in a store.

Moreover, composing alignments in such networks may be useful when one does not have a direct alignment of his or her ontology to those of another peer. On the one hand this is supposed to reduce the effort; on the other hand, composition degrades the results. It would be worth finding the paths between peers and compose the alignments along those paths which minimise the loss. It would also be useful to really measure how much is lost and to investigate the trade-offs involved in composing alignments. In any case, algebraic composition can only be achieved if there are sufficient high quality alignments it cannot rely on those provided on the spot by users.

Since good quality alignments are difficult to obtain, efforts should be devoted to maintain them. In particular, when one of the aligned ontologies changes, the alignment should not be rebuilt from scratch but the alignments should be evolved with regard to the change. This can be achieved with the help of composition of the alignment with a unique alignment between the new and the old version of the ontology. Alignment evolution should be integrated in an alignment management perspective (Euzenat et. al., 2008).

We planned from the beginning to store alignments in an Alignment server (Euzenat et al., 2008). However, at the time PicSter was developed the Alignment server was not ready so we stored the alignments within the peers themselves. There was one alignment covering all ontologies used by a pair of peers which was used for transforming queries between these two peers. An Alignment server can either store alignments or compute them on the fly with embedded matching methods. The advantages of using an Alignment server is that alignments may be shared by several peers (at least concerning the non altered parts of ontologies) and even shared with other applications of the semantic web. They can be retrieved from the server and modified with regard to the changes a peer has made to these ontologies.

Last, but not least a new trend recently emerged for facing the difficulty of obtaining high quality alignments. It consists of obtaining partial alignments from users while they accomplish their tasks (Conroy, 2008). In our case, the task may be either modifying the ontology or, more likely, querying. Instead of asking users for an alignment beforehand, the idea is to ask users for their help. When a query is issued, the system can ask the user for a partial alignment regarding the query, i.e., the terms in the query or the query as a whole. This can be done relatively easily by displaying the query and the target ontologies. Users who want to see their queries answered should show more willingness to help the system in this specific way. This local alignment could be recorded as a special type of alignment that can be reused when these alignments are necessary. The peer-to-peer system may collect many of these alignment fragments and the aggregation of many such partial alignments provided by many users over time will eventually provide high quality alignments between ontologies. Even partial, such alignments may be sufficient for answering a large proportion of the queries.

Hence, local query alignment is a cheap way to serendipitously obtain alignments from users: it seems to be a promising way to obtain the necessary alignments in semantic peer-to-peer systems.

The topic of finding alignments for heterogeneous semantic peer-to-peer systems is not closed yet. The problem of bootstrapping the semantic web with formal knowledge has resulted in that of bootstrapping with alignments. Once such alignments are available, we think that querying in semantic peer-to-peer systems will become easier. Like we promoted simple user interaction for stimulating ontology edition by users, the same could apply to alignments with local alignments: a simple interface for providing local and task-related clues to the system could go a long way.

The code of PicSter can be obtained fromftp://ftp.inrialpes.fr/pub/exmo/software/picster/PicSter-1.2.1m.zip

However, PicSter is an unsupported research prototype and is not suitable for use. The test results can be obtained from ftp://ftp.inrialpes.fr/pub/exmo/tmp/picster-tests.zip.

ACKNOWLEDGMENTS

We thank the PhotoStuff, Jena and JXTA teams for developing and making available the software that we have extended.

We thank Faisal Alkhateeb, Jason Jung, Sébastien Laborie, Jérôme Pierson and Antoine Zimmermann for their participation in this project.

REFERENCES

Brickley, D., & Guha, V. (2004). *RDF vocabulary description language 1.0: RDF schema*. W3C Recommendation.

Carroll, J., & Klyne, G. (2004). *RDF concepts and abstract syntax*. W3C Recommendation.

Conroy, C. (2008). Towards semantic mapping for casual web users. In *Proceedings of the 7th International Semantic Web Conference (ISWC) doctoral consortium, Karlsruhe (DE)* (LNCS 5318, pp. 907-913).

Dean, M., & Schreiber, G. (2004). *OWL Web Ontology Language: Reference*. W3C Recommendation.

Ding, L., Finin, T., Joshi, A., Pan, R., Cost, R., Peng, Y., et al. (2004). Swoogle: A search and metadata engine for the semantic web. In *Proceedings of the 13th ACM Conference on Information and Knowledge Management* (pp. 652-659).

Euzenat, J. (2004). An API for ontology alignment. In *Proceedings of the 3rd International Semantic Web Conference (ISWC), Hiroshima (JP)* (LNCS 3298, pp. 698-712).

Euzenat, J., Mocan, A., & Scharffe, F. (2008). Ontology alignments: An ontology management perspective. In M. Hepp, P. De Leenheer, A. De Moor, & Y Sure (Eds.), Ontology management: semantic web, semantic web services, and business applications (pp. 177-206). New York: Springer.

Euzenat, J., & Shvaiko, P. (2007). *Ontology matching*. Heildelberg: Springer-Verlag.

Haase, P., Ehrig, M., Hotho, A., & Schnizler, B. (2006). Personalized information access in a bibliographic peer-to-peer system. In S. Staab, & H. Stukenschmidt (Eds.), Semantic Web and peer-to-peer (pp. 143-158). Heidelberg: Springer.

Haase, P., Schnizler, B., Broekstra, J., Ehrig, M., van Harmelen, F., & Menken, M. (2004). Bibster – a semantics-based bibliographic peer-to-peer system. *Journal of Web Semantics*, *2*(1), 99–103. doi:10.1016/j.websem.2004.09.006

Halaschek-Wiener, C., Golbeck, J., Schain, A., Grove, M., Parsia, B., & Hendler, J. (2005). Photostuff - an image annotation tool for the Semantic Web. In *Proceedings of the 4th International Semantic Web Conference poster session*.

Isaac, A., Matthezing, H., van der Meij, L., Schlobach, S., Wang, S., & Zinn, C. (2008). Putting ontology alignment in context: usage scenarios, deployment and evaluation in a library case. In *Proceedings of the 5th European Semantic Web Conference (ESWC), Tenerife (ES)* (pp. 402-417).

Ives, Z., Halevy, A., Mork, P., & Tatarinov, I. (2004). Piazza: Mediation and integration infrastructure for Semantic Web data. *Journal of Web Semantics*, *1*(2), 155–175. doi:10.1016/j.websem.2003.11.003

Mbanefo, O. (2006). *Comparaison expérimentale d'algorithmes d'alignement d'ontologies*. Unpublished TER manuscript. Grenoble (FR): Université Joseph Fourier.

Nejdl, W., Wolf, B., Qu, C., Decker, S., Sintek, M., Naeve, A., et al. (2002). Edutella: A P2P Networking Infrastructure Based on RDF. In *Proceedings of the 11th Worldwide web conference, Honolulu (HA US)* (pp. 604-615).

Oaks, S., Travaset, B., & Gong, L. (2002). JXTA in a nutshell. Sebastopol, CA: O'Reilly.

Prud'hommeaux, E., & Seaborne, A. (2008). *SPARQL query language for RDF*. W3C Recommendation.

Rousset, M.-C., Adjiman, P., Chatalic, P., Goasdoué, F., & Simon, L. (2006). Somewhere in the semantic web. In *Proceedings 32nd International Conference on Current Trends in Theory and Practice of Computer Science (SofSem), Merin (CZ)* (LNCS 3831, pp. 84-99).

Schumacher, K., Sintek, M., & Sauermann, L. (2008). Combining metadata and document search with spreading activation for semantic desktop search. In *Proceedings 5th European Semantic Web Conference (ESWC), Tenerife (ES)* (pp. 569-583).

Sharma, A. (2006). Lightweight synchronization of ontologies. Unpublished Master's thesis. Aachen (DE): RWTH.

Staab, S., & Stukenschmidt, H. (2006). *Semantic Web and peer-to-peer*. Heidelberg: Springer.

Zaihrayeu, I. (2006). *Towards peer-to-peer information management systems*. PhD thesis. Trento, IT: University of Trento.

APPENDIX: RDF ANNOTATIONS

In annotations/IMG3833.JPG.rdf:

```
<rdf:Description rdf:about="http://exmo.infrialpes.fr/people/euzenat/elster/images/
IMG3833.JPG">
  <j.0:make>Canon</j.0:make>
  <j.0:resolutionUnit>Inch</j.0:resolutionUnit>
  <j.0:orientation>top, left side</j.0:orientation>
  <j.0:model>Canon PowerShot A80</j.0:model>
  <j.0:xResolution>180 dots per inch</j.0:xResolution>
  <j.1:depicts rdf:resource="http://exmo.infrialpes.fr/people/euzenat/elster/instances/
meteo/Condition.rdf#Clouds"/>
  <j.1:depicts
                rdf:resource="http://exmo.infrialpes.fr/people/euzenat/elster/instances/
euzenat/House.rdf#GrenobleCoursliberation38"/>
  <j.0:compression>JPEG compression</j.0:compression>
  <j.0:imageLength>1704</j.0:imageLength>
</rdf:Description>
```

In instances/House.rdf:

```
<rdf:Description
                    rdf:about="http://exmo.infrialpes.fr/people/euzenat/elster/instanc-
es/euzenat/House.rdf#GrenobleCoursliberation38">
  <rdfs:label>38, cours de la Liberation, Grenoble</rdfs:label>
  <rdf:type rdf:resource="http://space.frot.org/rdf/space.owl#House"/>
</rdf:Description>
In Ontologies/space.owl:
```

In Ontologies/space.owl:

```
<owl:Class rdf:about="http://space.frot.org/rdf/space.owl#House">
  <rdfs:comment xml:lang="EN">A (private) house.</rdfs:comment>
  <rdfs:label xml:lang="EN">House</rdfs:label>
  <rdfs:subClassOf>
    <owl:Class rdf:about="http://exmo.infrialpes.fr/people/euzenat#Inhabitation"/>
  </rdfs:subClassOf>
</owl:Class>
```

Chapter 7
Quality-Driven, Semantic Information System Integration: The QuaD²-Framework

Steffen Mencke
Otto-von-Guericke University, Germany

Martin Kunz
Otto-von-Guericke University, Germany

Dmytro Rud
Otto-von-Guericke University, Germany

Reiner Dumke
Otto-von-Guericke University, Germany

EXECUTIVE SUMMARY

The importance of automatic integration in every field of application is beyond controversy these days. Unfortunately, existing solutions are mainly focusing on the automation aspect. But for the success in the long run, the quality must be of substantial interest – it is an inherent characteristic of any product (Garvin, 1984). Existing quality-related information can be reused to optimize this aggregation of entities to thereby always provide the best possible combination (Kunz et al., 2008b). Such aggregation of entities can be done taking into consideration different characteristics like quality attributes, functional requirements, or the ability for automated procedures.

INTRODUCTION

Existing approaches for automatic entity assembly suffer from certain problems. There exists no common model that is applicable in every situation where small parts are assembled to form a complete architecture. Existing approaches focus on special domains like e.g. SOA or e-Learning. Another point of critique is the only sporadically emerging, throughout focus on quality. Existing knowledge

DOI: 10.4018/978-1-60566-894-9.ch007

is often not reused in contrast to information and data. Rarely expert knowledge is used to describe the assembly of entities (Meder, 2006; Pawlowski, 2005; Helic, 2005; Mencke & Dumke, 2007).

Sometimes individual quality requirements are taken into consideration (e.g. for services: Zeng et al., 2003; Lin et al., 2008). Their focus is on Quality of Service only. No product-related quality attributes are continuously used. A framework for the quality-driven assembly of entities, taking into account the derived need for better solutions, is proposed here. Besides this quality-oriented characteristic, the usage of semantic knowledge and structured process descriptions enable an automatic procedure. Especially the combination of both is a promising approach.

It will be shown, that the introduced framework is even more valuable due to the fact that it is not restricted to content aggregation, but also usefully applicable for all domains where a whole should be qualitatively assembled out of small parts. This work follows this point of view to not to restrict the scope of the framework. The concrete occurrence of the intended system uses elements that need to work together to provide the intended system functionality. These elements are abstractly defined as entities at this point.

High-flexible infrastructures have manifold advantages compared to monolithic products. Because of this, a lot of initiatives propose approaches for the integration of single components (e.g. services, content). Semantic metadata provide the basis for the automation of this process (Kunz et al., 2008a). But so far, either only functional requirements or single quality attributes are taken into consideration. A throughout consideration of existing and updated empirical data and the use of semantic descriptions of included functionality or reached quality of an entity promises better solutions (Kunz et al., 2008b).

THE FOCUS ON QUALITY

The better is the enemy of the good. Why should somebody be satisfied with something, if he has the need and resources to achieve a better result? The answer is: he should not. And this is entirely about quality. A product's perceivable quality is a key factor for the long term success of a company (Buzzell & Gale, 1987). Therefore, quality is defined according to the definition of the ISO 9000 standard (ISO/IEC, 2004b):

Definition: Quality is the "degree to which a set of inherent characteristics fulfils requirements" (ISO/IEC, 2004b).

A quality attribute is such a characteristic. To achieve quality in the field of software engineering, measurement is the fundamental basis: "*you cannot improve what you cannot measure.*" With software measurement it becomes possible to understand and communicate, to specify and achieve objectives, to identify and resolve problems as well as to decide and improve (Ebert & Dumke, 2007).

Definition: Software measurement is the approach to control and manage the software and to track and improve its performance (Ebert & Dumke, 2007).

Figure 1 comprises general software measurement phases and methods.

Measuring certain attributes is only the first step. The interpretation of the results is important, too. It is necessary because the human mankind is rarely capable to directly comprehend the meaningful information of the real world (see Figure 2).

Certain international activities were and are performed in order to standardize the expertise in this field. That ensures the usage and improvement of the current state of art on a global scale. The most important standards for software measurement are:

How to do things (described in life cycle processes):

Figure 1. Software measurement phases and methods (Ebert & Dumke, 2007)

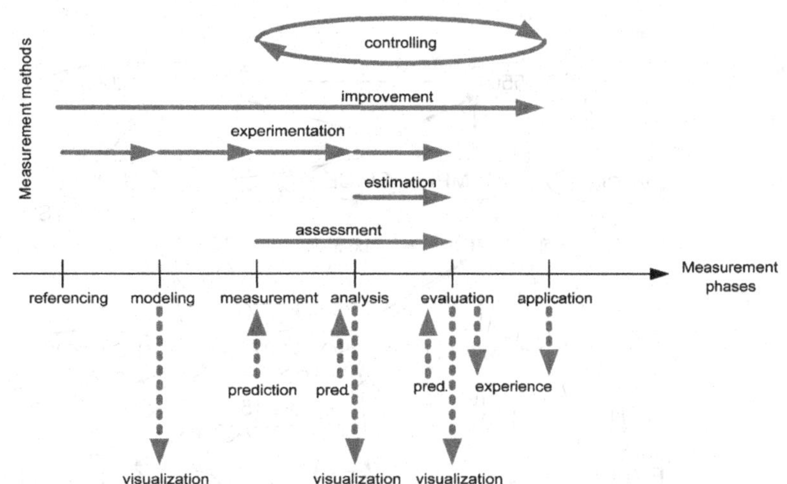

- ISO/IEC 12207: Software Life Cycle Processes (ISO/IEC, 1995)
- ISO/IEC 15288: System Life Cycle Processes (ISO/IEC, 2008)
- SWEBOK: Software Engineering Body of Knowledge (Abran et al., 2001)
- PMBOK: Project Management Body of Knowledge (Project Management Institute, 2004)

How to do better (described in management systems and process improvement frameworks):

- CMMI: Capability Maturity Model Integration (Ahern et al., 2008)
- ISO 15504: Software Process Capability Determination (ISO/IEC, 2004a)
- ISO 9001: Quality Management System (ISO/IEC, 2000)
- ISO/IEC 9126: Software Product Quality (ISO/IEC, 2001)

How to measure both:

- ISO/IEC 15939:2002: Software Measurement Process (ISO/IEC, 2002)

Figure 3 shows the major software engineering standards and their relations. ISO standards are marked in grey.

The most important quality-related standard for this work is ISO/IEC 15939:2002: Software Measurement Process (ISO/IEC, 2002). It is about the improvement of measurement itself. The standard is depicted in Figure 4.

Figure 2. Measurement helps to comprehend the real world (Ebert & Dumke, 2007)

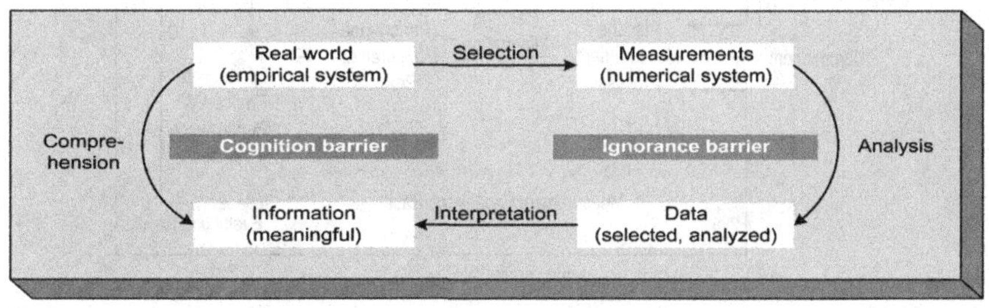

Figure 3. The Standards quagmire: Standards increasingly line up and cross-fertilize (Ebert & Dumke, 2007)

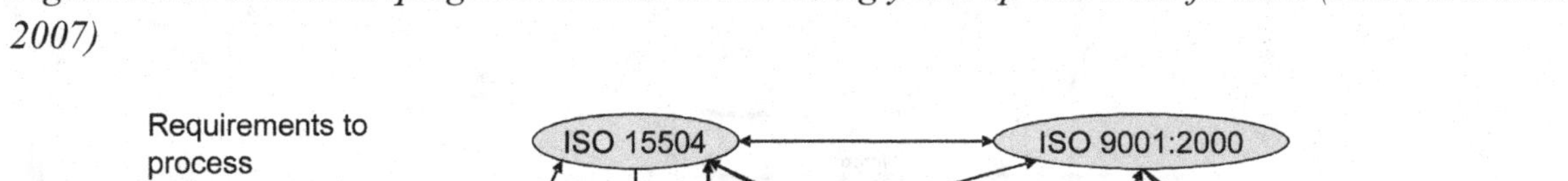

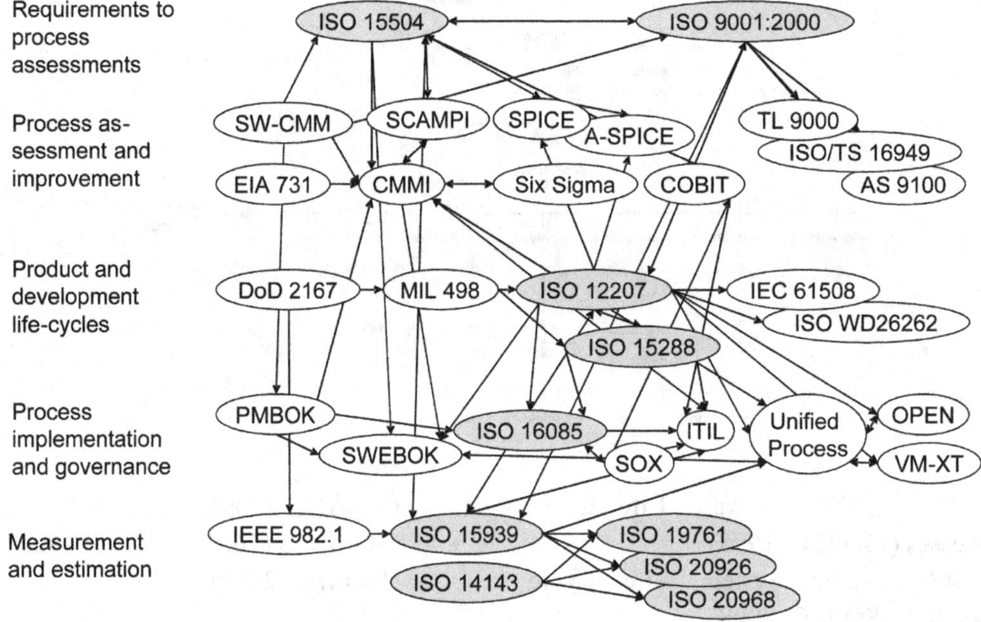

The *Establish and Sustain Measurement Commitment* is about the acceptance of the measurement requirements. Therefore, the scope of measurement needs to be identified. An agreement for this procedure must be achieved between management and staff. Next to this, the needed resources must be assigned.

The *Planning of the Measurement Process* is the next step. It is about the identification of relevant organizational units and the important

Figure 4. The ISO/IEC 15939 measurement standard

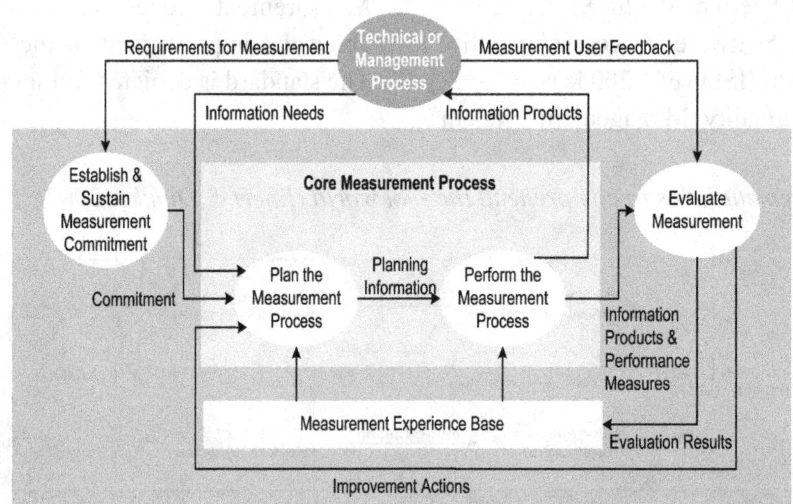

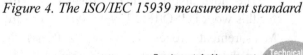

information needs. Afterwards, the planning of the measurement procedure itself starts with the selection of measurement procedures as well as data collection, analysis and reporting procedures. In order to be able to appropriately evaluate acquired data, the criteria for the information products and the measurement process must be identified (Dumke et al., 2006): Acquiring supporting technologies and additional resources as well as the planning of the evaluation review process are other tasks of this step.

For *Performing the Measurement Process*, the substep of measurement procedure integration into the relevant processes is the first one. The collection of data, their analysis and the communication of the results follow as next steps (Braungarten et al., 2005; Wille et al., 2006).

After having performed the measurement, the *Result Evaluation* follows. It targets information products as well as the measurement process. Starting points for further improvement should be identified as well (Farooq et al., 2006; Dumke et al., 2007).

The ISO/IEC 15939 standard is widely accepted (Dumke et al., 2005) and its focus on measurement makes it an ideal basis for quality-driven development. It is a cyclic process with the main steps of measurement agreement, measurement preparation, measurement performance and measurement evaluation. Evaluation results are the input for the next – now improved – cycle.

TOWARDS QUALITY-DRIVEN SEMANTIC INTEROPERABILITY AND INTEGRATION

Such continuous improvement is also the goal for semantic interoperability and integration as described here. Therefore, the quality-driven QuaD^2-Framework (Quality Driven Design) was developed to reach this goal.

In contrast to existing approaches, the presented framework reveals a holistic orientation on quality aspects. It combines Semantic Web technologies for the fast and correct assembly of system elements and quality attribute evaluations for making the best assembly decisions possible. Therefore, complex quality models are considered as well as empirical evaluations. Both contain existing information that can be used to improve the assembly process. Furthermore, different types of quality evaluation like simulation as well as static and dynamic software measurement provide additional data. Combining them delivers a holistic quality view on entities and the flexibility enables a quality improvement of the targeted system by the exchange of single components, if the evaluation of their quality attributes decreases and fails quality requirements.

It is shortly sketched and introduced below (see Figure 5).

The presented QuaD^2-Framework reveals the same inner structure as the ISO/IEC 15939 standard. Only the *Establish and Sustain Measurement Commitment* is not explicitly modelled, because the framework's usage already implies this substep.

The *entity provision initialization* focuses on the functional preparation. Based on expert knowledge an appropriate process model is selected. It describes the functional flow of the proactive, semantic entity provision. A first agreement, about the quality that should be achieved, is made by the selection an appropriate quality model (set of quality attributes). Both, functional and quality-related information are used to *determine the best entity*.

In the standard, the measurement subprocess follows. QuaD^2 also performs its *execution* in the next step. *Measurement* is performed in parallel in order to allow evaluations. In both frameworks, *evaluation* is the last step. It is the basis for continuous improvements. The measurement and evaluation are not focus of this work.

Figure 5. Quality-driven entity provision

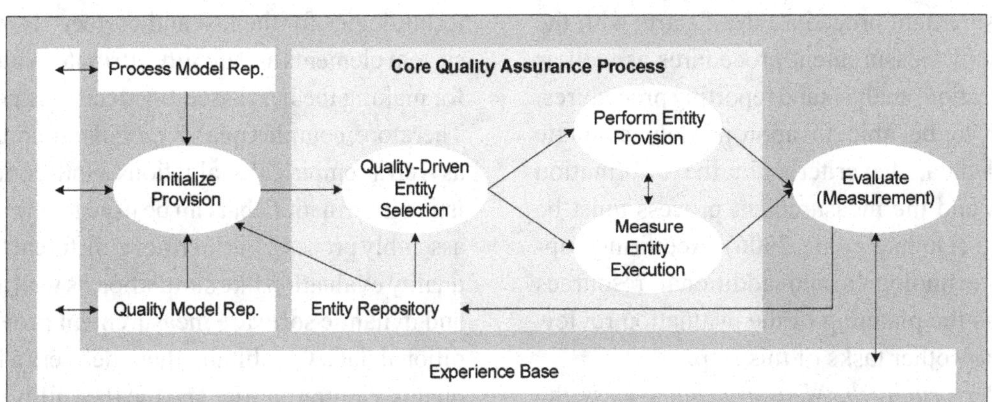

The QuaD²-Framework

The presented general QuaD²-Framework can easily be adapted to a lot of different fields of application, e.g.: e-Learning content provision, service-oriented architectures and enterprise application integration. In general, the subprocesses of this empirical-based assembly process are the initialization, the feasibility check (checking the functional coverage), the selection process based on empiricism as well as the operation of the established application. Quality assurance is achieved by certain subprocesses that allow optimizations at initialization time as well as during runtime. Furthermore, measurement subprocesses are performed to update evaluation data – to get further information that can be reused to optimize the next application assembly. The major goal of the described core process is an architecture consisting of single entities. Such an entity is metadata-annotated functionality and may be depicted by for example services, agents or content fragments in concrete applications. In order to achieve the sketched goals, a special process is developed below. Its major use cases are introduced in Figure 6.

The basis of the presented framework is a collection of semantically-annotated sources: the process model repository, the entity repository, a quality model repository and furthermore an experience factory.

The process model repository is the source for process models that serve as descriptions for the functionality of the aspired distributed system. They depict a set of activities that are performed in coordination in an organizational and technical environment. These activities jointly realize a goal. Each process is enacted by a single organization, but it may interact with processes performed by other organizations (Weske, 2007). Examples for such processes can be ISO/IEC 15939 (ISO/IEC, 2002) for the software measurement process or didactical approaches (Mencke & Dumke, 2008). Technological realization may vary, too. That can result in UML (Object Management Group, 2004), BPMN (Object Management Group, 2005), ontologies (Lin et al., 2005; Mencke & Dumke, 2007), etc. QuaD² essentially bases on ontology-based descriptions of process models. They depict the general aspects of a process – a set of activities associated with a set of events (Wang & King, 2000) – and support the semantic annotation of those aspects. Thereby, the needed basis for a semantic-based and adequate entity selection is provided. A more descriptive example is presented in section 4.1.

Important foundations for the intended reuse of quality-related information are quality models being provided by a quality model repository. The basis of a quality model's definition is an extensible list of quality attributes. The specification

Figure 6. Use case diagram: Empirical-based entity assembly process

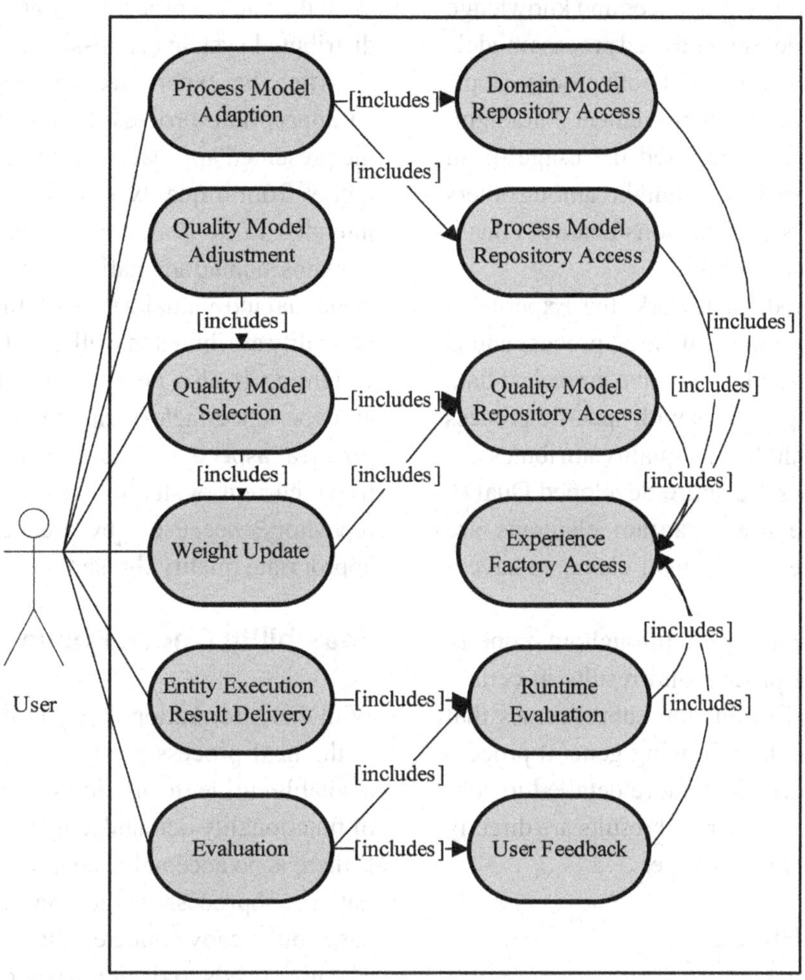

of a certain quality model is realized by selecting and weighting appropriate attributes. The evaluation and selection of appropriate entities bases on evaluation criteria for each included attribute. Such attributes can be e.g. cost, performance, availability, security and usability. The attributes and corresponding evaluation formulas are standardized e.g. in ISO/IEC 9126 (ISO/IEC, 2001). Quality models are not a new concept. They have been extensively described in literature, e.g. (McCall et al., 1977), (Boehm, 1978), (Hyatt & Rosenberg, 1996) or (ISO/IEC, 2001). A throughout usage of ontologies provides the possibility for a whole new class of quality attributes. They base on the semantic structure of the knowledge that is depicted within the structure of the ontologies. Section 4.2 introduces some exemplified novel approaches.

The entity repository contains entities, their semantic description and up-to-date empirical quality evaluations regarding all defined quality attributes. Together with ontology-based process models the semantic meaning of entities grounds the possibility of an appropriate selection. Thereby only those entities are chosen for a certain process step that semantically fit for the intended purpose.

The selection and adoption of process models and quality models are difficult tasks which constitutes the need for guidance and support.

Because of this, the presented framework proposes the usage of existing experiences and knowledge about previously defined and used process models and quality models to support both process steps. Based on the Quality Improvement Paradigm, Basili and Rombach proposed the usage of an Experience Factory which contains among others an Experience Base and Lessons Learned (Basili et al., 1994), (Basili, 1999).

In the presented framework, the Experience Factory is fed from the evaluation process and is the major building block to save empirical data and the user's experiences with specific process procedures or with distinct quality attributes.

Figure 8 shows the entire developed QuaD²-Framework. The used diagram elements are defined in Figure 7 – optional elements have a grey border.

The focus on quality is a throughout property of the developed process and results in certain measurement and evaluation subprocesses that are introduced in the following general process description and described more detailed in subsequent sections. The derived results are directly used for optimization purposes.

Initialization Phase

The selection of an appropriate process model that defines the functional requirements for the parts of the later distributed system is the first step of this phase. Due to the fact, that such a choice can be a manual process, it should be supported by an experience factory providing knowledge and experiences – lesson learned – for the decision for or against a specific process model for the current need. Information about previous assembly process' success factors are too important than to not use them for the next assembly process. The concept of an experience factory provides an appropriate basis for this purpose. The process model should essentially base on semantic metadata to allow the later automatic mapping of semantically-described entity functionalities to the functional requirements as specified by the process model. With the chosen process model, a set of concrete distributed systems is possible.

After the experience-supported selection of an appropriate process model, the next step of the presented approach is a selection of a quality model from a quality model repository. This is intended to be done automatically. For certain domains manual adaptations can be more efficient. A manual individualization of this predefined set of quality attributes as well as of their importance weighting is also possible. For these purposes, an experience factory can be helpful again. For practical aspects it is necessary to be able to retrieve current evaluation values from the entity repository, because they are needed to define appropriate quality thresholds.

Feasibility Check Phase

With this information, it is possible to determine in the next process phase, if there exist enough available entities to provide an acceptable amount of functionality demanded by the process model. If there is no acceptable coverage after the negotiation subprocesses, then an abort probability based on already collected data can be computed. The user needs to decide whether he accepts the probability or not. If not, the distributed system provision process will be aborted. An automatic approach aborts the process, if the probability falls below a certain threshold.

In the case of an acceptable coverage, the runtime subprocesses of step 4 can start. The first of them determines the next process step to be executed following the process model. Therefore, information about the last process steps can be taken into consideration to optimize the next process step execution. Exception handling in case of aborted pre-subprocesses is a functional requirement and thereby should be covered by the process model itself.

Due to the fact that new entities can be added to the entity repository, another coverage check

Figure 7. Definition of used diagram elements

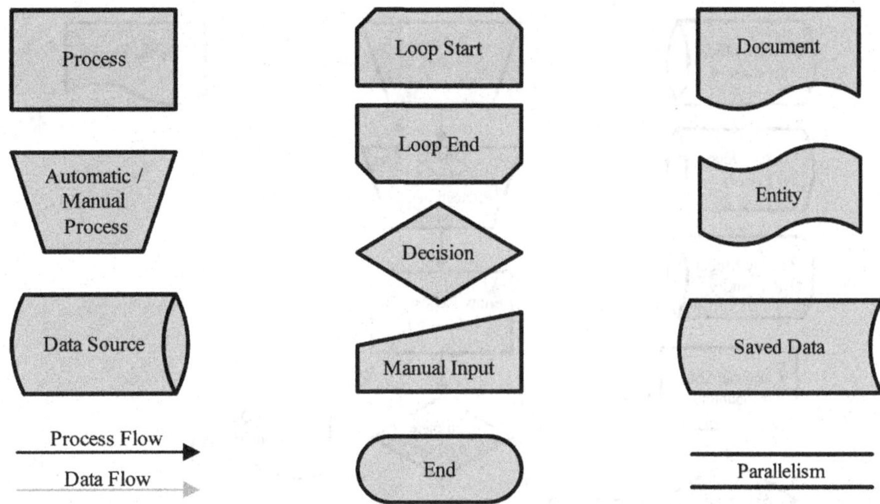

for the next process step is performed. Now, up-to-date entity information, their evaluation values as well as the data of the quality model are available to identify the best entity possible.

Selection Phase

In general, the entity selection has several steps. The first (Entity Repository Query) identifies possible entities according to the functionality defined within the process model. An additional step selects the identified quality model (Quality Model Selection and Update) that specifies what quality aspects are useful for the intended usage and how important they are for the initiator of the application to be assembled. Manual adjustments are possible, but not necessary and are performed during initialization, too. In exceptional cases a manual adjustment during runtime is reasonable.

Step three (Entity Selection in Selection phase) is the most important one and identifies the most appropriate entity for the next process step to be performed. It takes into account the weighted quality attributes as well the candidate entity set whose elements fit the functional requirements of the current process step. Figure 9 shows a diagram presenting the underlying process flow of this special Entity Selection Process.

For the Entity Selection Process, several approaches were analyzed. In general, they all focus on ranking several entities following several quality attributes to determine the one entity that fits best. The basic set of entities is determined by the selection of subprocesses focusing on the required functionality (defined by the process model).

A first decision to be made was: either to perform a pure ranking of entities based on an importance-ordered list of quality attributes or to decide based on relations between the quality attributes. The second approach was chosen because a more detailed specification of importance is possible. That means that the quality attributes (QA_i) defined in the quality model are weighted in the way that the sum of all weights is 1. The higher the defined weight is, the more important the related quality attribute is (example: three quality attributes weights $QA_1 = 0.7$, $QA_2 = 0.2$ and $QA_3 = 0.1$).

The weighted quality requirements matrix is manually created by selection needed quality attributes from a predefined set during initialization. Amongst others, the calculation formula and normalization directive are stored for all quality

Figure 8. The QuaD²-Framework (Kunz et al., 2008b)

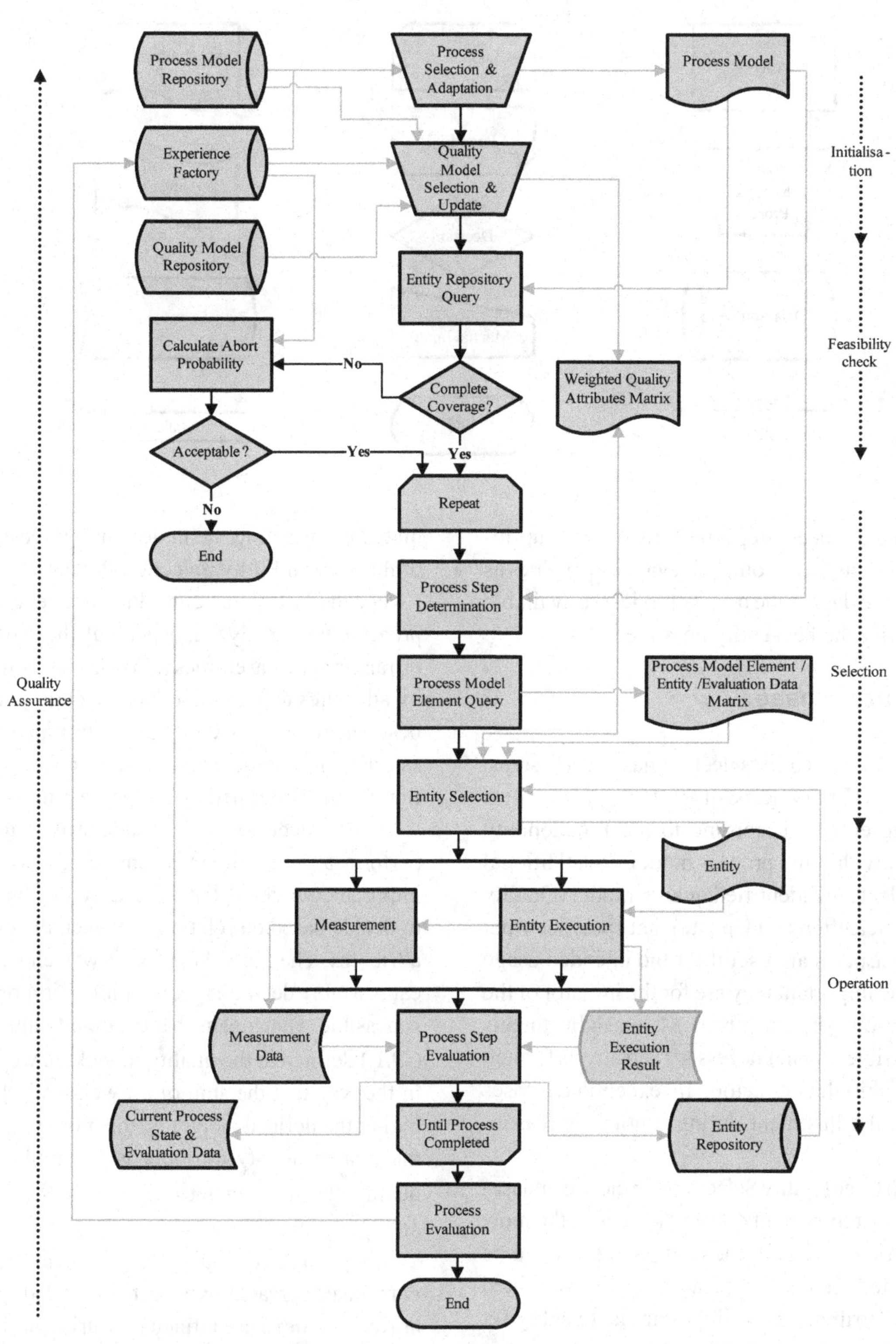

Figure 9. Entity selection process

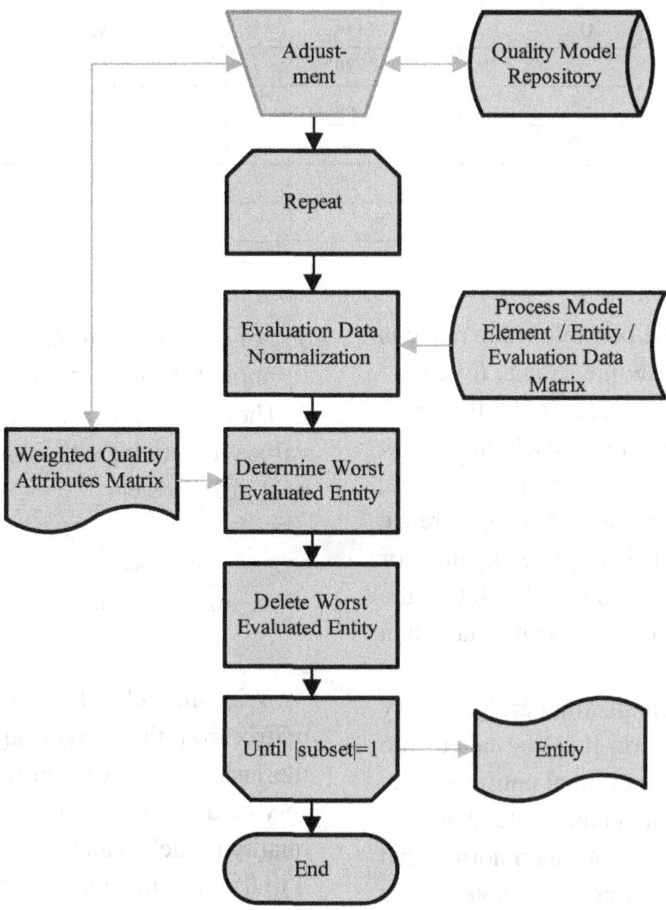

attributes to be able to determine the qualitatively best entity for the current need.

A next decision targeted the determination the correct interval for the normalization of the evaluation values. Normalization is necessary because the data have different ranges. A first approach is to normalize the entity evaluation data over the whole set of entities within the entity repository. The observed problem is, that entities having never been used and maybe having nothing to do with the current required functionality get an influence to the selection process. Furthermore outliers get an extreme influence to the weighting procedure, because they cause major changes in the normalization procedure.

The next and better step is to normalize over the identified entity subset and to identify the best entity. Here, another classic ranking problem occurs. The addition of an entity with the same functionality but worse evaluation data changes the normalized values of better fitting entities. The ranking of better entities may change although their evaluation data remain the same (check the example in Table 1). This problem arises due to a needed re-normalization, which becomes necessary because the worse quality attribute evaluation value is beyond the range determined by the other entities.

Within the example, at first the evaluation and ranking of the first three entities is performed. Later a new entity 4 is included. The table shows, that the re-normalization due to the bad entity 4 causes a ranking change of entities 1 and 2.

Table 1. Re-normalization Problem

	QA_1	QA_2	QA_3	
ENTITY 1	10	20	20,000	
ENTITY 2	5	80	5,000	
ENTITY 3	100	4	4,000	
ENTITY 4	*50*	*200*	*10,000*	

A predefinition of the possible value range is also not useful. How to define a range for costs? Is 1,000,000 the maximum cost or 100,000,000? A re-normalization may happen each time a new entity is added to the repository. Furthermore, extreme interval borders neglect the difference between the evaluation data values again. For example, in an interval from 0 to 1,000,000 the difference between 1 and 2 is less important than in an interval from 0 to 5.

So, ranking and normalization are necessary – because multiple criteria must be taken into account to determine the optimal entity and because the domains of the quality criteria are not comparable. An additional reason for normalized weights is the desired assurance of stable weight influences. In the end the following algorithm is chosen as an adaptive, normalized, weighted indicator model.

Following the defined necessities and given data the entity selection is formally described below. For the following formulas let PM be the chosen process model. Function $f^{funct}(PM)$ specified in Formula 1 is used to determine the set of entities E from the entity repository. Each of them can deliver the functionalities specified within the chosen process model (see Formula 2).

$$f^{funct} : ProcessModel \mapsto \left\{Service, \ldots\right\}. \quad (1)$$

$$E = f^{funct}\left(PM\right). \quad (2)$$

Using the classic normalisation approach presented in Formula 3, the evaluation values $v_{i,j}$ of quality requirements j defined in the quality model must be normalised for each service i. These $v_{i,j}$ are the measurement/simulation values to anticipate the optimal decision for the next process step.

$$v_i^{norm} = \frac{v_i - \min\left(v\right)}{\max\left(v\right) - \min\left(v\right)} * \left(\max_{norm} - \min_{norm}\right) + \min_{norm} \quad (3)$$

With the help of the weighted requirements matrix from the (maybe adjusted) quality model the last step – the identification of the optimal service according to the empirical data and the quality model – can be performed (see Formulas 4 to 8). Formula 4 adjusts the normalized evaluation values to ensure proper calculation. If $v=1$ describes the best quality level then no adjustments are necessary, otherwise a minimum extremum is desired and $1\text{-}v$ must be calculated.

$$f^{mm}(v) = \begin{cases} v & \text{,if a maximal } v \text{ is the best} \\ 1 - v & \text{,if a minimal } v \text{ is the best} \end{cases} \quad (4)$$

$$f^{eval}(e_i) = \sum_{j=0}^{n-1} f^{mm}\left(v_{i,j}^{norm}\right) \,\middle|\, e_i \in E \wedge n = \left|QM\right| \quad (5)$$

$$V = \left\{f^{eval}\left(e_i\right) \middle| \forall e_i \in E\right\}. \quad (6)$$

$$e^{worst} = e_{index} \,\middle|\, index = \min\left(\left\{x \middle| v_x = \min\left(V\right)\right\}\right) \wedge e_{index} \in E \quad (7)$$

$$E' = E \backslash e^{worst} . \quad (8)$$

To determine the best evaluated entity, Formulas 5 to 8 are repeated until E' contains only 1 element. It provides the needed functionality and is the most appropriate one according to the specified quality model.

After the entity's selection it can be executed and measurement about runtime behaviour will be captured to get additional quality evaluations for this entity.

Operation and Evaluation Phase

Once the most optimal entity is identified, it can be executed. In parallel to execution, measurement can be performed. These data are used to evaluate the last process step. The runtime subprocesses are repeated until: either all process steps of the process model are successfully executed or an abort due to missing entities took place. The last phase of the presented approach covers the evaluation of the entire process – serving as an input for the experience factory. It compares the achieved results with the desired ones.

QUALITY ASSURANCE

Following ISO/IEC 9126 (ISO/IEC, 2001), quality assurance can be distinguished into internal, external and quality in use. The latter is covered by the quality assurance during runtime. Internal as well as external quality is measured by the iterative Entity Evaluation Process as part of the Entity Repository Management Processes.

The focus on quality is a throughout characteristic of the developed process and results in certain measurement and evaluation subprocesses. The derived results are directly used for quality-driven improvement purposes, e.g.:

Evaluation points:

- Quality attribute measurement during entity execution
- Entity execution result (in case its functionality was to test/evaluate)
- Process step evaluation
- Process evaluation
- Entity consistency checks
- Continuous entity evaluation process
- Meta-evaluation processes (e.g. usage of experience factory, entity update, . . .)

Quality-driven improvement approaches:

- Use of process model repository
- Use of quality model repository with quality models (quality attributes and weights)
- Use of entity repository with evaluation data about the entities
- Experience factory for process model selection
- Experience factory for quality model selection
- Update of quality requirements and weights in experience factory in case of aborted process steps (automatic and manual)
- Process step determination based on success and evaluation data about the last process step (and experience factory data in case of aborted last process step)
- Update and extension of process model repository
- Update and extension of quality requirements
- Update and extension of entity repository
- Update and extension of interfaces and wrapper
- Entity standardization with appropriate wrappers
- Continuous entity evaluation process

Quality requirements are evaluated from the user's point of view. The provider of the distributed system defines a subset of acceptable requirements using the selection of available entities within the entity repository. The described process uses these available entities to create an as optimal as possible result for the user.

Quality Attributes

Although most quality attributes are entity- and thereby domain-specific, there exist some common ones. In addition to cost, some selected ones are presented below.

Quality of Service:

- Availability (especial partial availability)
- Performance
- Accessibility
- Stability
- (Data) security
- Capacity
- Integrity

Quality Determination

The Entity Evaluation Process uses the defined formulas for each quality attribute being stored in the Quality Attributes List to calculate the evaluation values for every entity. Not for every attribute a mathematical formula is available, but at the attribute's definition time an evaluation procedure must be specified to allow quality assessment. Such evaluation procedures can be e.g. experiments, user surveys or certain simulations. Ensuring quality is fundamentally based on measurement. Figure 10 classifies formal measurement approaches.

For the proactive determination of quality aspects (Wille, 2005) is recommended for further reading. There fundamental information and approaches about measuring of and measuring with agent technology is presented.

USE CASE E-LEARNING

Especially e-Learning is nowadays one of the most interesting of the "e-"domains available through the Internet (Anghel & Salomie, 2003). In general, it refers to a wide range of applications and processes designed to deliver instruction through computational means (Juneidi & Vouros, 2005). It is seen as a technology-based learning alternative respectively extension to the classic classroom model (Giotopoulos et al., 2005). E-learning is only one chosen application domain for QuaD^2.

Ontological Process Model

The term "process" has manifold significances within each domain. Formally it is defined as a set of activities associated with a set of events, where an event is an internal or external signal, message, variable, scheduling, conditional change, or timing that is specified in association with specific activities in a process (Wang & King, 2000).

An e-Learning process thereby is a special process, whose domain is e-Learning and the process transitions involve e-Learning-related activities to change certain states within this domain (Mencke et al., 2008d).

There exist many possibilities for the implementation of process models as required for the QuaD^2-Framework. In the following ontology-based approaches are described. They guarantee applicability, reusability and extensibility. Ontologies as described in (Mencke & Dumke, 2007) and (Mencke & Dumke, 2008) are suggested to fulfil these requirements. Their usage in e-Learning can be useful for numerous goals (Mencke & Dumke, 2007) – for example they serve as:

- Didactical ontologies for the categorization of learning goals,
- Thematic ontologies for the thematic categorization of learning material,
- Rhetoric-semantic ontologies for categorization of learning material for the creation

Figure 10. Classification of formal measurement approaches (Ebert & Dumke, 2007)

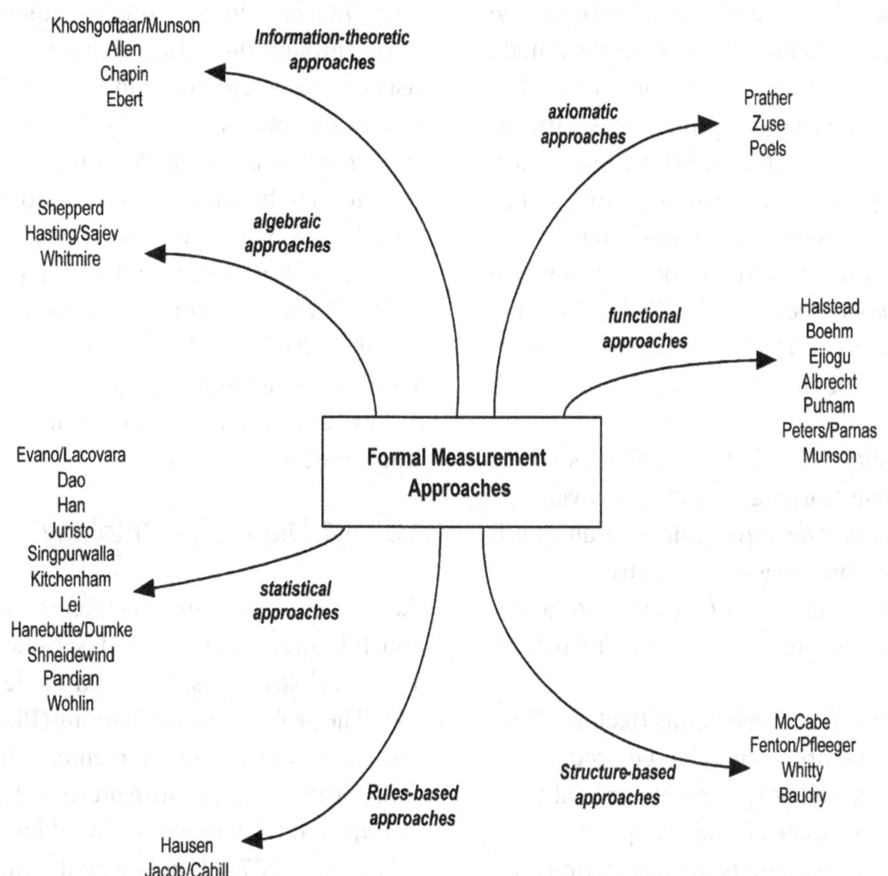

- of meaning contexts,
- Relational ontologies for the description of contextual dependencies and
- Curricular ontologies for the organizational categorization of learning material.

In the following a hierarchy of ontologies for e-Learning content aggregation is introduced. For the hierarchy of ontologies, a 5-level structure is proposed to reach the intended advantages.

Level 0 Didactical Ontology

Level 0 contains the most general ontology of the proposed set. It depicts a general description of a didactic strategy. Its purpose is to define the scheme for an ontology-based realization of the order of learning content to achieve an optimal learning result as well as the description of didactical expertise. Human experiences with the learning and teaching processes can be integrated in those ontologies. These implicit quality aspects result in a substantial quality gain. Timed strategic elements need to be adaptively chosen to fit certain context, learner or teacher-defined requirements: an abstract class for a learning step, a definition of an order of learning steps, conditions for multiple learning paths and metadata inclusion for runtime support.

Figure 11 presents the developed top-level ontology. The central concepts are the *LearningStep* and *Condition* class. A *LearningStep* is the reference to a part of a didactical approach. Further refinement is supported by the possibility to divide a learning step into several sub learning steps. Therefore, the relation *leadsToSubLearningStep* is created to point to the first *LearningStep* node that will compound the sub learning steps. The property *isFirstLearningStep* must be set true to mark this first node. According to this, the property *isLastLearningStep* must be set true for the last node. To permit a return to the main didactical flow, the sub nodes reference to their root node through the relation *hasAsRootLearningStep*. Additional relationships point to describing (sometimes taxonomic) ontologies.

- *hasActivityType* points to activities which the current learning step should cover.
- *hasLearningObjective* points to an ontology describing learning objectives
- *hasIntendedStudentRole* points to a description, where possible student roles a listed
- *hasIntendedResource* points (technical) resources that are intended to be used
- *hasIntendedTechnique* points special techniques/approaches for teaching
- *hasAssessment* points to suggestions for certain assessment types
- *hasIntendedCardinality* describes the type of interaction according to the number of participants

The condition concept is used to model restrictions to a path, permitting the runtime environment of an e-Learning system to decide the next appropriate path through the learning content for the current user in his specific context. Both main concepts are used to model a didactic in this way: identify the first *LearningStep* and then follow the learning path for the first condition that delivers a true result.

Therefore, a *LearningStep* points to a *Condition* with a *learningStepLeadsTo* relationship. A *Condition* itself redirects the learning path to one other *LearningStep* with the *conditionLeadsTo* relationship, if its result is true. Multiple learning paths can be modelled by integrating multiple *Condition* individuals. To support those alternative ways through the e-Learning course, additional aspects are integrated into the ontology. A first one is a hierarchy of conditions. If one fails, the *conditionLeadsTo* relationship points to the next condition to be checked. Another one is the possibility to depict sequences of conditions by using the *hasAsNextCondition* relationship; the last condition of a sequence must point to a *LearningStep*. The default relationship *DefaultNextLearningStep* between two learning steps provides an alternative for the case where no condition is fulfilled and must appear only once.

Level 1 Didactical Ontology

Level 1 may reveal an inner hierarchical structure, too. It is directed toward to description of general didactical strategies, based on the level 0 ontology. The problem-based learning (PBL) approach was chosen for further implementation. PBL is a didactic that begins with a presented problem and is followed by a student-centred inquiry process (Trevena, 2007). Fundamental principles base on the work of Barrows and Schmidt (Barrows, 1986; Schmidt, 1983). Figure 12 visualizes the ontology focusing on Schmidt's seven steps in problem-based learning.

This implemented PBL ontology describes the seven basic steps that a PBL didactical approach should have according to (Trevena, 2007), clarify terms and concepts, define the problem, analyze the problem, draw systematic inventory, formulate learning objectives, collect additional information and synthesize and test the new information.

These steps are defined as individuals of a *LearningStep* and, as there is no special condition to the transition between them, only the *defaultNextLearningStep* relationship is used. The activity types for each *LearningStep* are chosen based on what should be performed by the learner.

Figure 11. Level 0 didactical ontology (Mencke & Dumke, 2007)

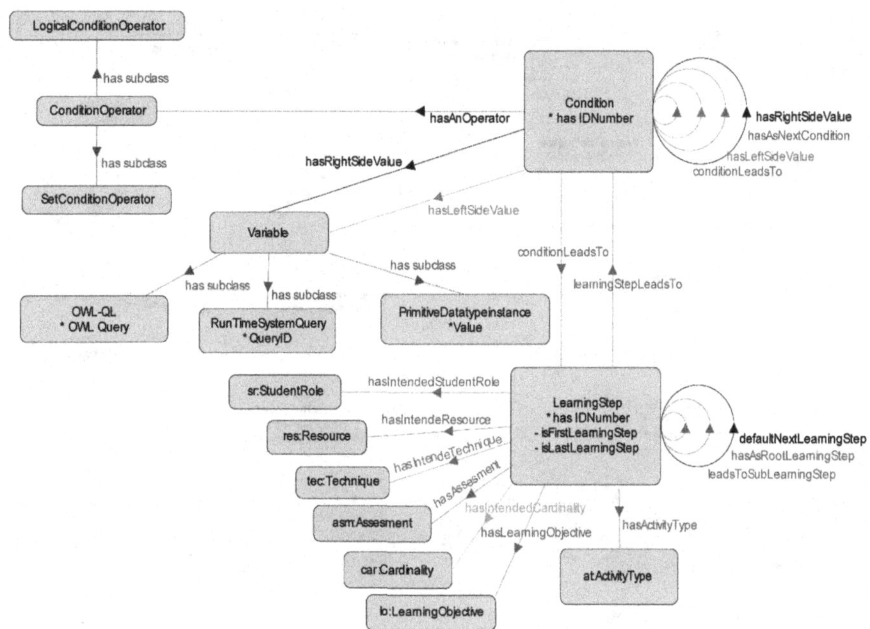

Level 2 Didactical Ontology

Level 2 contains the leaf nodes of the hierarchy, each describing an applicable didactical approach. Here, for example the micro didactics of Meder (Meder, 2006) or the didactical models of (Flechsig, 1996) are integrated. Figure 13 defines an ontology for a special problem-based learning didactic. It is adopted from (Mertens, 2002) and bases on (Hahn, 1971).

Level 3 Didactical Ontology

Level 3 is directed to the approach of individual (recombined) adapted didactics. The idea behind is, that individual approaches of specific teachers, tutors or scientists should be made available and usable, too. The trivial usage is to identify sub elements of the course that are didactically decoupled or only loosely coupled. These (sub-) *LearningSteps* are affiliated with each other with the standard *defaultNextLearningStep* relationship or reusable relationships that for example point forward, if the current learning step was successfully completed. The more complex problem is the identification of inter-didactic relationships within certain contexts and their ontology-based modelling.

Level 3 ontologies are still an open field of research.

Level 4 Didactical Ontology

To be able to depict the specific structure of an e-Learning course, the level 0 ontology is extended by an additional concept and certain properties (see Figure 9).

The *LearningObject* is integrated based on a developed Learning Object Metadata-Ontology comprising metadata instances of existing e-Learning entities – Learning Objects (LOs). This ontology forms the basis of the Entity Repository in this exemplified instantiation of the QuaD^2-Framework. Next to the *hasIDNumber* variable, storing an *ID* of the currently described Learning Object, this concept has two datatype properties –

Figure 12. Problem-based learning didactic level 1 ontology (Mencke & Dumke, 2007)

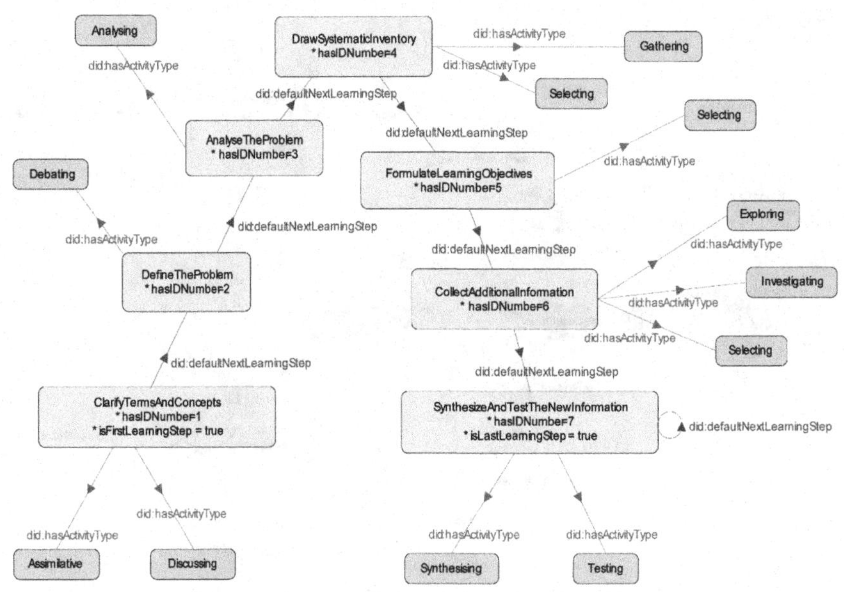

namely *isFirstLearningObject* and *isFirstLearningObject*. In addition to them object properties are integrated to point from a *LearningStep* to a *LearningObject* as well as from a *LearningObject* to another *LearningObject*. By this procedure, it is possible to refine a *LearningStep* as a sequence of *LearningObjects*.

Quality Attributes and Ontology-Based Quality Metrics

The QuaD²-Framework's next step is about the selection of a quality model. Therefore, the definition of appropriate quality attributes is necessary. Although quality was already defined above, the term quality needs to be interpreted in a special way in the context of e-Learning content provision. Its interpretation is fluid due to the involvement of a human within the whole process. His individual characteristics sometimes determine what is good and what is bad. For example, the amount of pictures of a LO can be a quality attribute of an e-Learning entity. But maybe a certain learner learns better on pure text-based descriptions – the quality-oriented interpretation of certain attributes is not constant. These facts lead to certain consequences that are defined in the following.

- User characteristics are important
- Every requirement that is seen as important for the author of the course must be modelled within the process model and thereby becomes a functional criterion for the selection of LOs for the next process step.
- Every requirement that is not explicitly modelled within the process model can serve as quality attributes and will lead to quality-driven decisions about the LO to be presented.

Another facet of human involvement is that not everything can be determined with automatically-processable metrics. Human experiences sometimes elude automatic observations. Examples are human experiences with learning processes. Those quality aspects can be integrated during the creation of didactical ontologies and provide a substantial additional value that exists but cannot be determined automatically.

Figure 13. Problem-based learning didactic level 2 ontology (Mencke & Dumke, 2007)

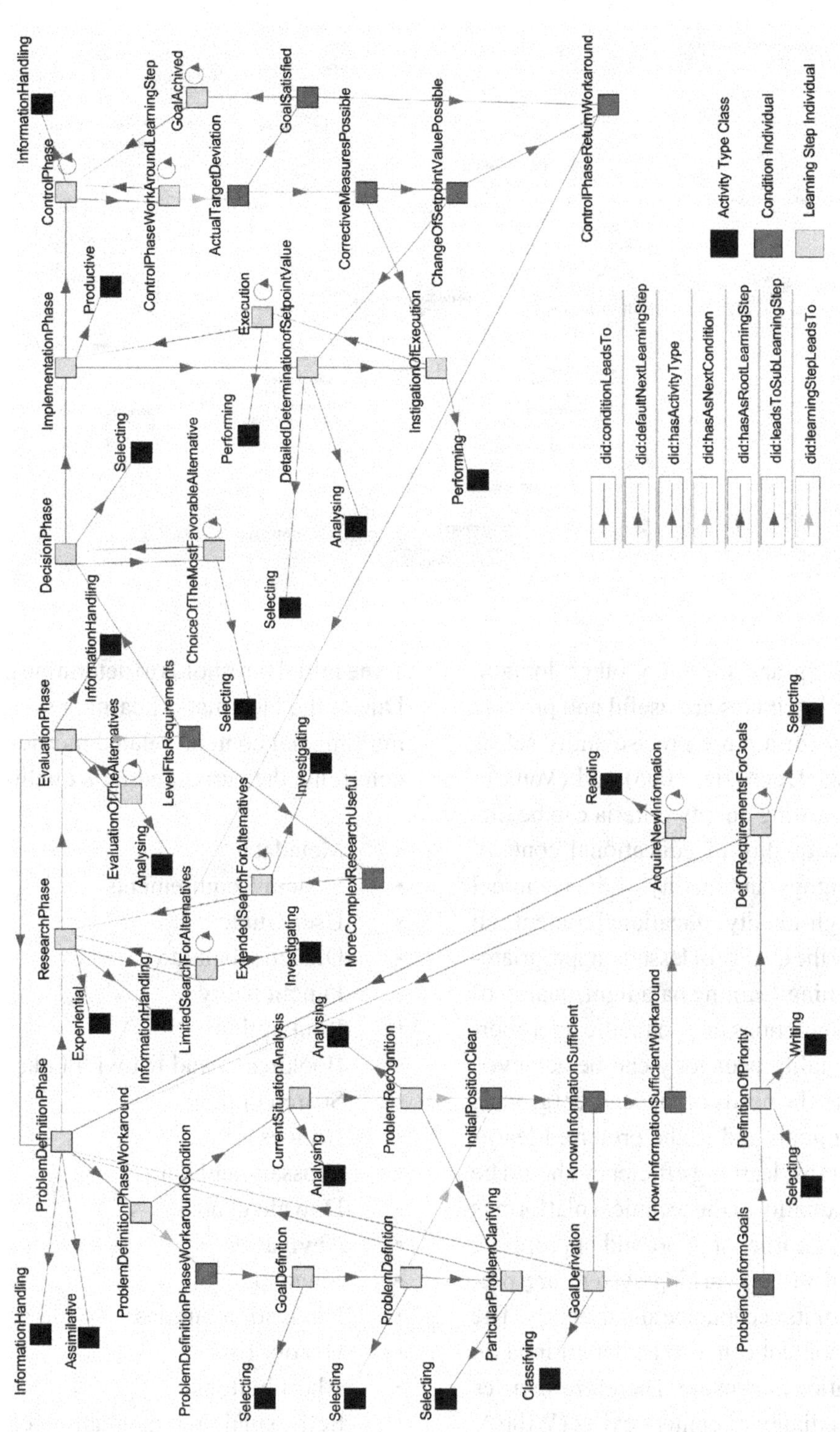

Figure 14. Level 4 didactical ontology (extended from (Mencke & Dumke, 2007))

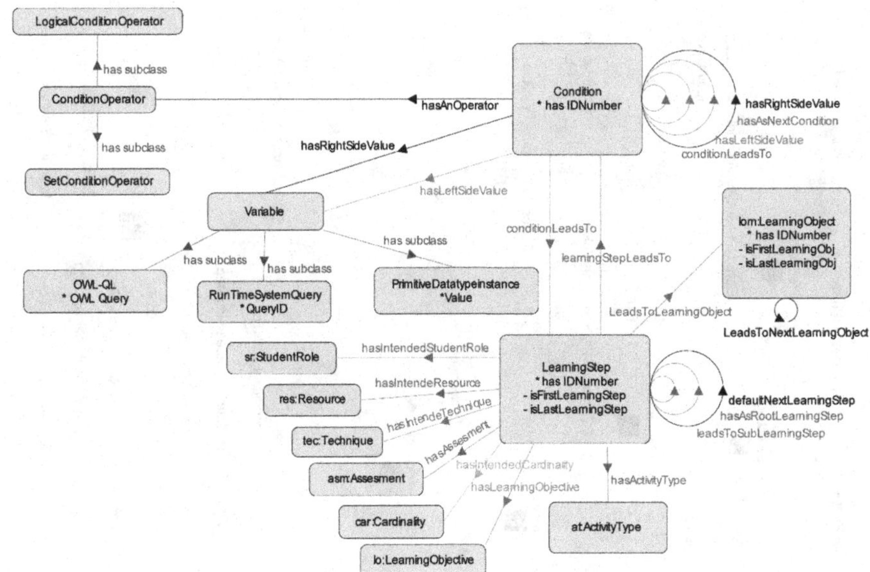

For e-Learning and for every other domain, specific quality attributes are useful and provide the opportunity for a more precise entity selection. Following (Devedžic, 2006) and (Vouk et al., 1999), e-Learning quality criteria can be differentiated into quality of educational content, quality of pedagogy and quality of the technical framework. High-quality educational content can be expressed by the quality of lessons, appropriateness of the teaching/learning paradigm, quality of user-system interactions and semantic interoperability. High-quality pedagogy can be achieved by adaptation to the needs of the learner (group), to the learning goals and to the preferred learning styles. Thereby, learning efficiency should be increased. The quality of the technical platform is important, too. Learner support and appropriate performance of the e-Learning system are prerequirements for its acceptance and usability. The quality of the content can also be determined on an implementation dimension. Therefore, metrics for the multimediality of content exists (Wille & Dumke, 2007).

In (Hametner et al., 2006) some quality criteria based on a slightly different classification are listed. An advantage is their presentation of some initial thresholds to determine good quality. Due to the fact, that e-Learning systems provide multimedial content, related metrics can used to determine the current entity's quality.

- Metadata
- System Requirements
- User Guide
- Didactical Guide
- Functionality
- Print option
- Bookmarks and list with links
- Search option
- Notices
- Glossary and help
- Download area
- Navigation
- Sitemap
- Navigation buttons
- History lists
- Abort buttons
- Self-explaining navigation elements, e.g. self-explaining symbols, expectancy conformance, rollover effects, highlight effects, …

Text-based recommendations are for example: font (no serifs), font sizes (min. 12 pt), highlighting (better bold than italic), line spacing (for displays 1.5 to 2), line length (eight to ten words = 60 to 80 characters) or paragraph alignment (better left-aligned).

For each of these requirements, the evaluation procedure as well as a measurement frequency must be available within its description. The entity's runtime evaluation data regarding quality requirements are determined using those evaluation procedures. Options for the measurement frequency are: only at entity functional core/version change (e.g. inheritance graph, maintainability), after every entity execution (e.g. performance of a database) or always and permanent (e.g. performance, availability). All information together forms the quality model that is stored within the quality model repository.

Certain common and special quality attributes exist. For the use case presented here, an excerpt of possible attributes was introduced above in a common manner. In the following, some selected novel approaches for the measurement of domain-specific quality attributes are introduced more detailed. These examples base on ontology-based entity descriptions.

Didactical Appropriateness (DA) Didactical appropriateness is about how good the current didactical approach fits to the desired one. The more equal they are, the better it is for the quality of the entire learning process. The metric bases on the taxonomy of didactical approaches as well as ontological distances as specified in (Mencke & Dumke, 2007) and (Mencke et al., 2008c). Formula 9 presents the developed metric, C_F is the desired didactical approach and C_j is the current one. An additional limitation to $c^{abs}\left(C_F, C_j\right)$, $c^{spec}\left(C_F, C_j\right)$ and $c^{sib}\left(C_F, C_j\right)$ is that 0 is defined as a result, if no such distances exists.

$$DA\left(C_F, C_j\right) = c^{abs}\left(C_F, C_j\right) + c^{spec}\left(C_F, C_j\right) + c^{sib}\left(C_F, C_j\right) \quad (9)$$

This metric sum up all applicable distance measures to define the distances of the concepts within the proposed taxonomy of didactical approaches. The lower the result is, the closer the concepts are related. A future extension may result in the addition of values, describing the similarity of the didactical approaches to each other.

Learning Object Consistency (LOC) Learning Object Consistency is about changes of a Learning Object. For the application of this quality attribute, a metadata history and the introduction of a special update process are necessary. The update process should continuously check the LO for consistency. History information should describe each check and update. The idea is that a continuously maintained LO has a higher quality. The metric delivers back *true* for a positive consistency check and otherwise *false*.

Learning Object Success Indicator (LOSI) Learning Object Success Indicator may reveal some information about LO quality as well. It relates the successful learning processes of available courses $F_{success}$ to the not successful ones $F_{notsuccess}$. Each course must contain the LO under survey.

$$LOSI\left(LO\right) = \frac{\left|F_{success}\right|}{\left|F_{notsuccess}\right|}. \quad (10)$$

This metric can be a possible indicator, that the current LO has a high quality and is a key factor for learning success. The higher the result is, the better the quality is indicated.

Learning Object Interest Factor (LOIF) Learning Object Interest Factor indicates an implicit user evaluation about the interest that the LO can cause at the learner's side. It compares the LO's anticipated acquisition time t^{ant} (taken from the LO metadata) with the average acquisition time whenever it was presented to a learner in any course t^{avg}.

$$LOIF\left(LO\right)=\frac{t^{ant}}{t^{avg}}. \quad (11)$$

LOIF indicates high quality, if the result is close to 1. Much higher and lower values indicate bad LOIF quality.

Domain Coverage of the Course (DCC) Domain Coverage of the Course indicates how much percent of the domain knowledge is covered by the e-Learning course. The results serve as a basis for other metrics. The formula is based on an ontology-oriented domain and entity description. For the metric, the numbers of several ontological elements being covered by the course are counted: number of concepts C, number of attributes A, number of non-taxonomic relationships R and the number of instances I.

$$DCC\left(course, domain\right)=\left|C\right|+\left|A\right|+\left|R\right|+\left|I\right|. \quad (12)$$

Domain Coverage of the Learning Object (DCLO) The Domain Coverage of the Learning Object describes how much percent of the domain knowledge of the course is covered by the current Learning Object. Each LO is about a subset of the domain of the e-Learning course. Because the LO is part of the course, the covered domain subsets of the LO is completely within the subset covered by the course. For the metric, DC the number of several ontological elements being covered by the LO are counted: number of concepts C, number of attributes A, number of non-taxonomic relationships R and the number of instances I.

$$DC\left(LO, course, domain\right)=\frac{DCC\left(course, domain\right)}{\left|C\right|+\left|A\right|+\left|R\right|+\left|I\right|} \quad (13)$$

A quality indicator can be that all Learning Objects have a similar DC value. Therefore, the DC of the current LO_i is compared to the average DC^{avg} of all LOs of the current course.

$$DCLO\left(LO, course, domain\right)=\frac{DC^{avg}}{DC\left(LO_i, course, domain\right)} \quad (14)$$

$DCLO$ indicates high quality, if the result is close to 1. Much higher and lower values indicate bad $DCLO$ quality.

Semantics-Supported Content Enrichment

With an ontology-based process descriptions and quality metrics as defined above, a throughout ontology-oriented QuaD²-Framework instantiation for the domain of e-Learning becomes possible. In the following, the main QuaD²-process is defined for the selected use case of content enrichment – the provision of semantically related information.

Cost-Based Semantic Window Approach

For the enrichment the concept of a 'Semantic Window' is defined. This term describes a set of elements of a given ontology within a certain multi-dimensional distance. Dimensions for its definition are related to the concepts of an ontology as well as to the datatype properties. Furthermore, instances and taxonomic as well as non-taxonomic relations are taken into consideration (Mencke et al., 2008b).

The function f^{cost} returns the "cost" of the transition between two nodes, given their types as well as the sequence of already accepted nodes (Formula 15). For the combinations of ontological elements' types, between which no transition is possible, the cost function is assumed to return the positive infinity.

$$f^{cost}: Type, Type, \left\langle Node, \ldots\right\rangle \mapsto Integer. \quad (15)$$

Function f^{type} returns the type of a given ontological element (a member of the enumeration 6.17). New types of ontological elements can be introduced by splitting the sets of ontological elements of a particular type on the basis of some constraints (subclassing). The domain of f^{cost} for these new types obviously cannot be broader as for the original type.

$$f^{type} : OntolElement \mapsto Type. \quad (16)$$

$$Type \in \{ParentConcept, ParentObjectProperty, ChildConcept, ChildObjectProperty, Concept, ObjectProperty, DatatypeProperty, ConceptInstance, ObjectPropertyInstance, DatatypePropertyInstance\} \quad (17)$$

Elements of a tuple $\langle n_0,\ldots,n_m\rangle, n_i \in O, m \in N$ are included to the Semantic Window, if n_0 is the enrichment point of the enrichment and inequality 18 resolves to true, where A is the cost restrictor ("the size of the Semantic Window").

$$\sum_{i=0}^{m-1} f^{cost}\left(f^{type}\left(n_i\right), f^{type}\left(n_{i+1}\right), \left\langle n_0,\ldots,n_i\right\rangle\right) \leq A. \quad (18)$$

In Figure 15, an example for the Semantic Window is given. Concept C_6 is the enrichment point around which the Semantic Window is created. For the sake of simplicity datatype properties are not taken into consideration. The cost function f^{cost} is given in Table 2 and the maximum cost is A = 3. Filled circles represent concepts, filled squares represent instances and filled diamonds on arrows represent object properties, all being located within the range of the Semantic Window around C_6.

Distance-Based Semantic Window Approach

Next to the cost-based approach described above, a distance-based solution for Semantic Windows is possible (Mencke et al., 2008c). For the further detailing, the description starts with a specialized redefinition of an ontology $O = \left(C, R, D, I\right)$, where C is the set of ontological concepts following a taxonomic structure, $R = R^{tax} \cup R^{ntax}$ is the set of object properties/relations taxonomically and non-taxonomically relating two concepts $R_{ij}\left(C_i, C_j\right)$ and D is the set of datatype properties/attributes of the ontology. I is the set of instances. An ontological component of each of these types can be the enrichment point for the Semantic Window. This is a generalization of the cost-based approach because also taxonomic ob-

Table 2. Example of transition costs between ontological elements (Mencke et al., 2008b)

	Parent concept / object property	Child concept / object property	Concept	Object property	Datatype property	Concept instance	Object property instance	Datatype property instance
Concept	1	1	∞	2	2	3	∞	∞
Object Property	1	1	2	∞	∞	∞	3	∞
Datatype property	∞	∞	2	∞	∞	∞	∞	3
Concept instance	∞	∞	3	∞	∞	∞	2	2
Object property instance	∞	∞	∞	3	∞	2	∞	∞
Datatype property instance	∞	∞	∞	∞	3	2	∞	∞

Figure 15. Example of a semantic window with enrichment point C_6, cost restrictor $A = 3$ and the transition costs given in Table 2

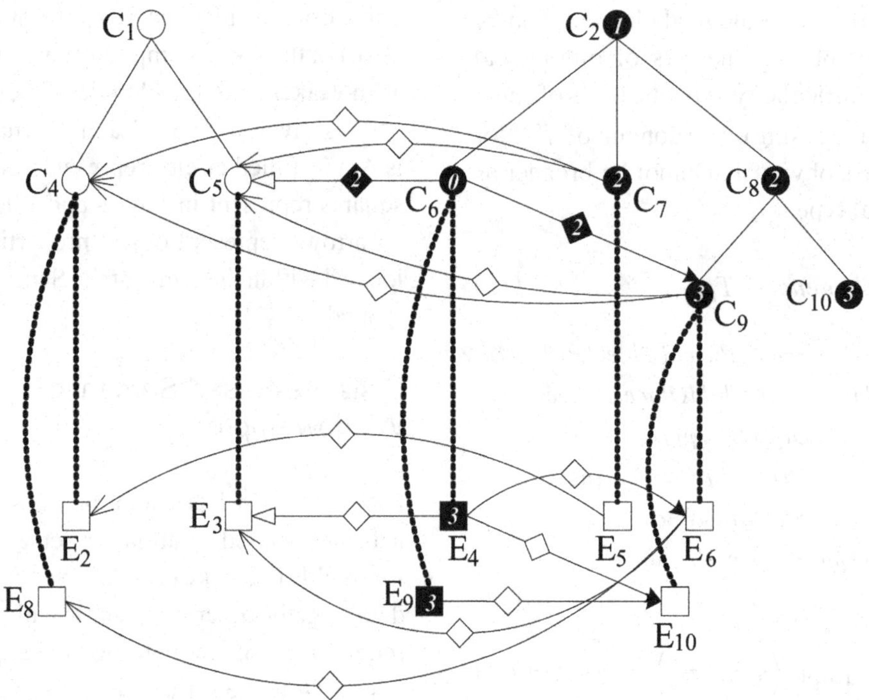

ject properties are taken into account now. From this, four different aspects, the dimensions of the Semantic Window, can be derived.

- Concept view
- Datatype property view
- Object property view
- Instance view

For each of the four views, distance measures are defined for the existing dimensions.

A help function is $f^{niv}\left(C_i\right)$ describing the level of the concept according to its taxonomic level with $f^{niv}\left(C_{root}\right)=0$ (Formula 19). Function $f^{parent}\left(C_i,C_j\right)$ delivers back the first more abstract concept shared by C_i and C_j, if it exists and is connected to them only via $R \in R_{tax}$ (Formula 20). $f^{tax}\left(C_i,C_j\right)$ (Formula 21) and $f^{ntax}\left(C_i,C_j\right)$ (Formula 22) determine the length of the taxonomic or non-taxonomic path of object properties from C_i to C_j (the result is -1, if there does not exist such a path).

$$f^{niv} : Concept \mapsto Integer\,. \tag{19}$$

$$f^{parent} : \left\langle Concept, Concept\right\rangle \mapsto Concept\,. \tag{20}$$

$$f^{tax} : \left\langle Concept, Concept\right\rangle \mapsto Integer\,. \tag{21}$$

$$f^{ntax} : \left\langle Concept, Concept\right\rangle \mapsto Integer\,. \tag{22}$$

f^{tax} and f^{ntax} can be realised as described in the equations 23 and 24.

$$f^{tax}\left(C_i,C_j\right)=\begin{cases}0 & if\ C_i \equiv C_j,\\ 1 & if\ \left|f^{niv}\left(C_i\right)-f^{niv}\left(C_j\right)\right|=1 \wedge R_{ij}\left(C_i,C_j\right)\in R_{tax},\\ f^{tax}\left(C_i,C_k\right)+1 & if\ f^{tax}\left(C_i,C_k\right)=n \wedge f^{tax}\left(C_k,C_j\right)=1,\\ -1 & otherwise.\end{cases} \tag{23}$$

$$f^{ntax}\left(C_i,C_j\right)=\begin{cases}0 & if\ C_i\equiv C_j,\\ 1 & if\ R_{ij}\left(C_i,C_j\right)\in R_{ntax},\\ f^{ntax}\left(C_i,C_k\right)+1 & if\ f^{ntax}\left(C_i,C_k\right)=n\wedge f^{ntax}\left(C_k,C_j\right)=1,\\ -1 & otherwise.\end{cases} \tag{24}$$

In the following, the concept dimensions of the concept point of view are described. Detailed formulas for the object property dimension, the datatype property dimension, the instance dimension as well as the dimensions from the other listed point of views are presented in (Mencke, 2008).

The dimensions of the distance related to the ontology's concepts having a concept as the focusing point are defined in equations 25 to 28. The single distance measures relate to the abstraction dimension distance c^{abs}, to the specialization dimension distance c^{spec}, to the sibling dimension distance c^{sib} and to the non-taxonomic dimension distance c^{ntax}. They measure the distance between the focusing point concept C_F and another concept C_j of the ontology.

$$c^{abs}\left(C_F,C_j\right)=f^{niv}\left(C_F\right)-f^{niv}\left(C_j\right). \tag{25}$$

$$c^{spec}\left(C_F,C_j\right)=f^{niv}\left(C_j\right)-f^{niv}\left(C_F\right). \tag{26}$$

$$c^{sib}\left(C_F,C_j\right)=f^{niv}\left(C_F\right)-f^{niv}\left(f^{parent}\left(C_j\right)\right). \tag{27}$$

$$c^{ntax}\left(C_F,C_j\right)=f^{ntax}\left(C_F,C_j\right). \tag{28}$$

The equations above are restricted by: $C_F, C_j \in C$. Equation 25 is restricted by: $f^{niv}\left(C_F\right)>f^{niv}\left(C_j\right)$ and $f^{tax}\left(C_F,C_j\right)\neq -1$. Equation 26 is restricted by: $f^{niv}\left(C_F\right)<f^{niv}\left(C_j\right)$ and $f^{tax}\left(C_F,C_j\right)\neq -1$. Equation 27 is restricted by: $f^{niv}\left(C_F\right)=f^{niv}\left(C_j\right)$ and $f^{niv}\left(f^{parent}\left(C_F,C_j\right)\right)<f^{niv}\left(C_F\right)$.

Within a Semantic Window, from any ontological element's point of view, all distances as well as the ontological element being the focusing point are given and used to determine a set of ontological elements W containing all ontological elements those distance are smaller than the given ones. The distances are summarized in vectors as demonstrated below.

The focusing point is a concept and the concept distances are given in vector 29, datatype property distances in vector 30, object property distances in vector 31 and the instance distances are given in vector 32.

$$dist^{C}\left(C_6\right)=\begin{pmatrix}c^{abs}\\ c^{spec}\\ c^{sib}\\ c^{ntax}\end{pmatrix}=\begin{pmatrix}1\\0\\1\\0\end{pmatrix}. \tag{29}$$

$$dist^{D}\left(C_6\right)=\begin{pmatrix}d^{abs}\\ d^{spec}\\ d^{sib}\\ d^{ntax}\end{pmatrix}=\begin{pmatrix}0\\0\\0\\0\end{pmatrix}. \tag{30}$$

$$dist^{R}\left(C_6\right)=\begin{pmatrix}r^{abs}\\ r^{spec}\\ r^{sib^{abs}}\\ r^{sib^{spec}}\\ r^{ntax}\end{pmatrix}=\begin{pmatrix}0\\0\\0\\0\\1\end{pmatrix}. \tag{31}$$

$$dist^{I}\left(C_6\right)=\begin{pmatrix}i^{abs}\\ i^{spec}\\ i^{sib}\\ i^{ntax}\end{pmatrix}=\begin{pmatrix}0\\0\\0\\0\end{pmatrix}. \tag{32}$$

In the following, an example is sketched to show the usage of distances to determine a Semantic Window. A graphical representation of the result is shown in Figure 16. Filled circles represent concepts, filled squares represent instances and filled diamonds represent datatype properties, all being located within the Semantic Window.

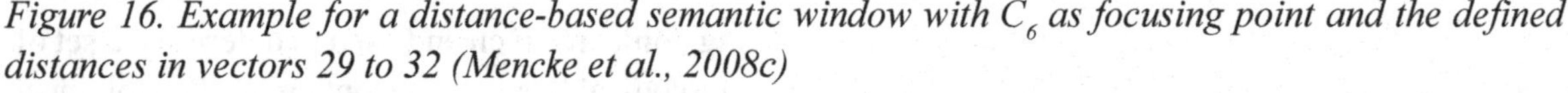

Figure 16. Example for a distance-based semantic window with C_6 as focusing point and the defined distances in vectors 29 to 32 (Mencke et al., 2008c)

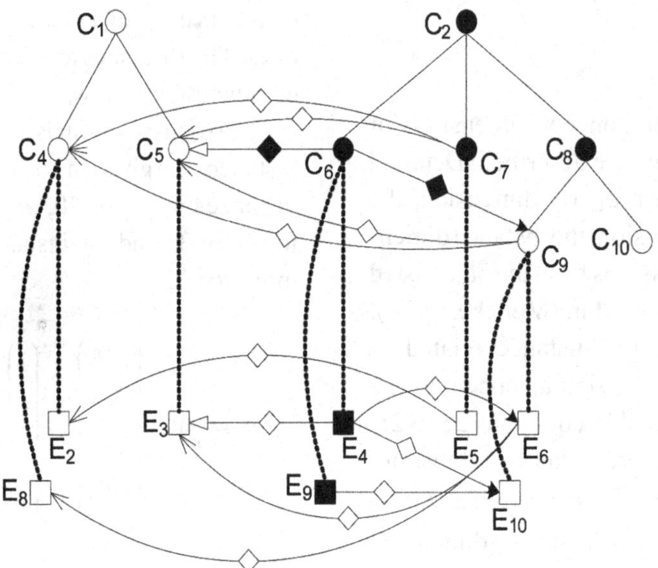

Content Enrichment Algorithm

E-Learning-related content is any portion of data that can be displayed to a user by the runtime part of an e-Learning system. According to this, content enrichment describes the process of searching and displaying additional information, being semantically related to the information of the e-Learning content.

For the identification of starting points for enrichment in an educational content an 'Enrichment Algorithm' is developed in (Mencke et al., 2008b).

In the first step, an identification of appropriate ontological elements within the ontology $O(C,P)$ with its concepts C and properties P is performed. The function $f^{naming}(a)$ (Formula 33) delivers a human readable name of an ontological element a. The tuples, containing ontology elements a_i and their names determined using $f^{naming}(a_i)$ constitute the set T^O as shown in Equation 34.

$$f^{naming} : OntolElement \mapsto String. \tag{33}$$

$$T^O = \left\{ \left\langle a_i, f^{naming}(a_i) \right\rangle \middle| a_i \in \left(C \cup \left(P \setminus P_{tax} \right) \right) \right\}. \tag{34}$$

At this point, taxonomic relations within the ontology (P_{tax}) are neglected, because $f^{naming}(a)$ cannot deliver any useful results for them.

A second step is the inflation of T^O with appropriate additional terms, for example taken from the WordNet specifications for the English language (Princeton University, 2006). The function $f^{syn}(a)$ delivers additional terms (synonyms) (Formula 35). The tuples of the extended set T^{O+SYN} connect ontology elements a_i with their synonyms (Equation 36).

$$f^{syn} : String \mapsto \{String, \ldots\}. \tag{35}$$

$$T^{O+SYN} = T^O \cup \left\{ \left\langle a_i, b_i \right\rangle \middle| a_i \in \left(C \cup \left(P \setminus P_{tax} \right) \right), b_i \in f^{syn}\left(f^{naming}(a_i) \right) \right\} \tag{36}$$

The function $f^{concept}(x)$ (Formula 37) applies to both, metadata LO^M and the content LO^C of learning objects LO (Formula 38) and extracts names of concepts contained in them. A particular implementation of $f^{concept}$ can use classic mining algorithms. For each learning object LO_i, the initial set T_i^{L+SYN} of concept names and their synonyms, that can serve as starting points of the enrichment, can be determined as shown in the Equation 40.

$$f^{concept} : DataObject \mapsto \{String, ...\}. \tag{37}$$

$$LO = \{LO_i\} = \{\langle LO_i^M, LO_i^C \rangle\}. \tag{38}$$

$$CN_i = f^{concept}\left(LO_i^M\right) \cup f_i^{concept}\left(LO_i^C\right). \tag{39}$$

$$T_i^{L+SYN} = CN_i \cup \bigcup_{x \in CN_i} f^{syn}(x). \tag{40}$$

The next step is to match the identified concepts of the learning objects with the human readable names of ontological elements (Equation 41). T_i^S maps ontological elements to possible enrichment points within the learning objects.

$$T_i^S = \left\{ \langle c, d \rangle \middle| d \in T_i^{L+SYN}, \langle c, d \rangle \in T^{O+SYN} \right\}. \tag{41}$$

T_i^S is a set of tuples $\langle c, d \rangle$ where d is a concept of the educational content and c is the associated ontological element. The set of all d is D (Equation 42).

$$D = \left\{ d \middle| \langle c, d \rangle \in T_i^S \right\}. \tag{42}$$

The algorithm's next part is the selection of identified enrichment points $D' \subseteq D$ within the learning object. Possible implementations can limit the set of enrichment points, for example by the selection of the first appearance of the enrichment points. The semantic relevance is proposed as the key factor. For its determination several approaches can be (combined) implemented: (a) choose those enrichment points that are most relevant based on certain mining algorithms, (b) choose those enrichments points that are most relevant based on the semantic relevance according to the metadata of the LO, (c) choose those enrichment points that are most relevant based on the ontological relevance of the associated ontological elements. For the last option, certain ontology metrics can be useful (Mencke et al., 2008a).

On the basis of the set RO (Equation 44) containing all ontological elements related to the selected enrichment points, and the Semantic Window approaches described above, an additional set of ontological elements can be computed. It will be referred to as W.

$$f^{onto} : String \mapsto \{OntolElement, ...\}. \tag{43}$$

$$RO = \bigcup_{d \in D'} f^{onto}(d). \tag{44}$$

The next step determines the amount of additional information EC that is used to enrich the educational content (Formula 45 and Equation 46).

$$f^{enrich} : OntolElement \mapsto \{EnrichmentContent, ...\} \tag{45}$$

$$EC = \bigcup_{r \in RO \cup W} f^{enrich}(r). \tag{46}$$

The presentation is not part of the algorithm above, but results in the highlighting of all selected $d \in D'$ and the selective displaying the prepared enrichment content $EC \subseteq EC'$ as described in the next section.

Prototype

The enrichment component described in (Mencke et al., 2008b) proactively scans the requested e-Learning resources, integrates new semantically related information and thereby adapts the presented information. A three-tier architecture was developed to implement this information system. The structure is shown in Figure 17.

The presentation tier displays the content of a resource, for example e-Learning course material or a web page. It invokes a request for new data from the proxy server of the second tier. Afterwards, they are displayed to the user for further usage. On this level, existing presentation components are used. They are not changed with the proposed solution.

The second tier with the proxy server contains the application logic. It analyzes the request of the presentation front-end and forwards the request to the content provider, too. Additionally, it queries the data tier that contains the ontology. Based on both data sources, the e-Learning resource to be displayed is enriched and sent to the visualization front-end.

The data tier is responsible for the structuring and access of the semantic information within the ontology as well as the storage of enrichment content.

The prototype focuses on a selected aspect of the QuaD^2-Framework – the semantic-based selection of entities. One advantage of the Semantic Window approach in this context is the well-defined definition of a semantic range around an entity. By this, not only the selection of semantically-fitting entities is realised. It also becomes possible to identify additional content based on the semantic and the knowledge structure of the targeted domain.

Figure 18 presents a screenshot of a tool that uses distance-based Semantic Windows for Web content enrichment (see Figure 19). Users can add new enrichment content in order to complete the available data sources and thereby collaborate on quality improvement.

Figure 17. Three-tier architecture for e-learning content enrichment (Mencke et al., 2008b)

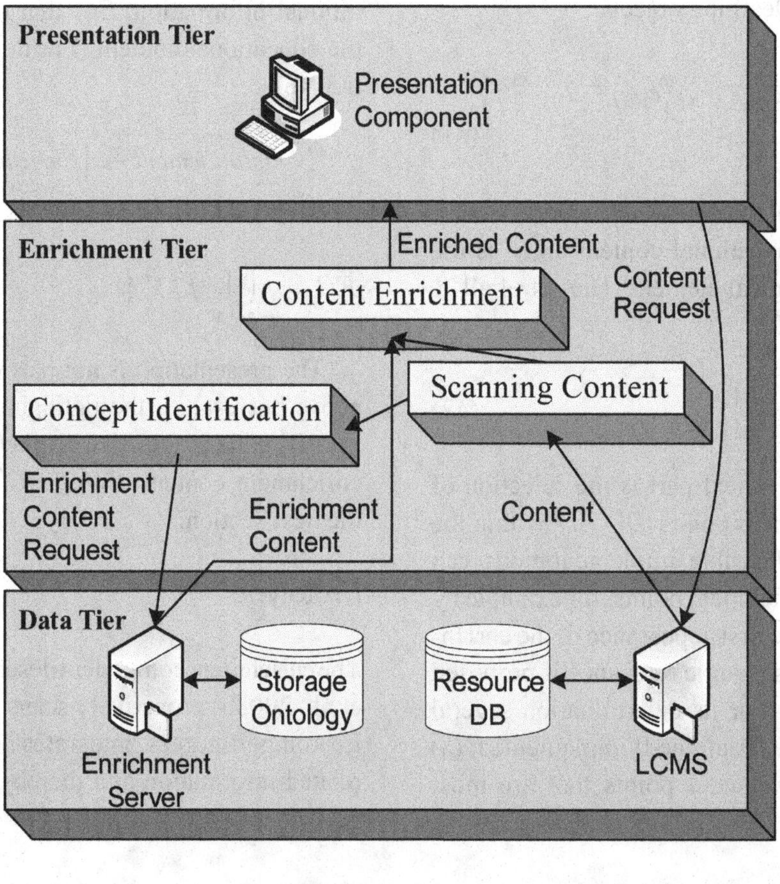

Figure 18. Distance-based semantic windows for content enrichment

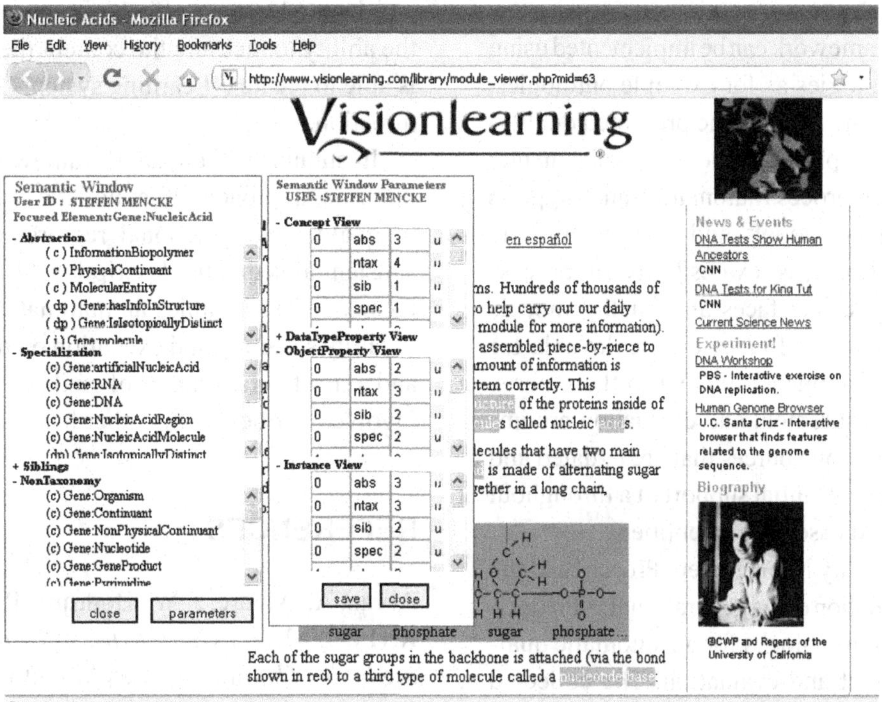

Figure 19. Enriched web page based on semantic windows

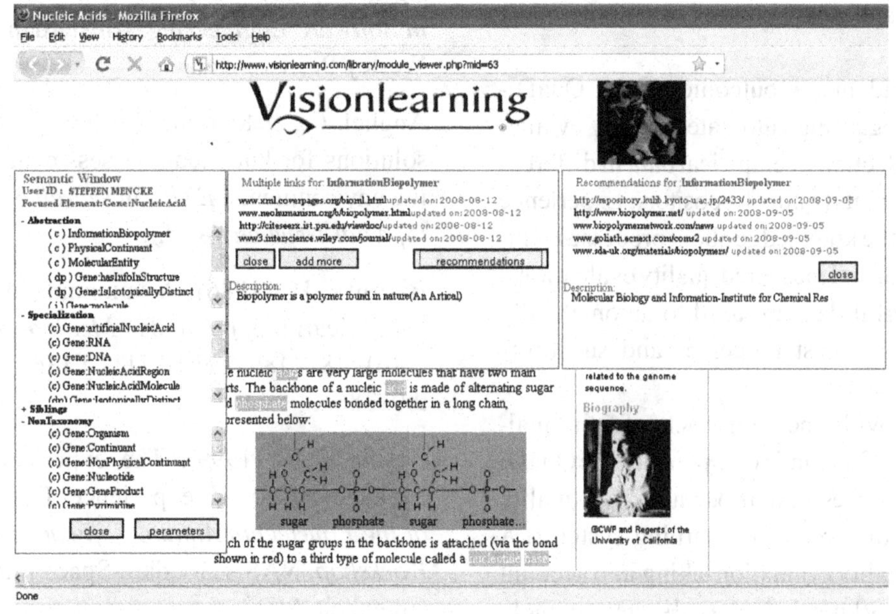

DISCUSSION

The QuaD²-Framework can be implemented using various technologies as for example ontologies, Web Services and agents. The presented quality-driven approach proposes the usage of semantic descriptions for process automation and supports different quality models and quality attribute evaluations. The easy extensibility of process models, entities, interfaces and quality models makes the presented framework deployable for many fields of application. Next to these parts, permanent measurement and evaluation are important information sources that are updated and reused for the substantial support of a throughout quality-oriented assembly of entities.

Both, the Entity Management Process and the Runtime Evaluation of the general QuaD²-Process, are major building blocks for an automatic quality measurement and evaluation. The collected measures about the runtime behaviour of entities bears the capability of reducing manual evaluation processes especially where automated metrics-based evaluation before runtime is difficult or not possible and user opinions at runtime make more sense.

The second major outcome of the QuaD²-Framework regarding automated quality evaluation is the collection of empirical data in different model components (Entity Repository, Experience Factory) like the knowledge about processes, runtime behaviour and measured quality evaluations. This meaningful data are used to automatically select entities, adjust processes and substitute elements.

Having provided new approaches for the quality evaluation of semantic components, the QuaD² framework enables new procedures for quality assurance in the area of e-Learning systems. A substantial quality evaluation taking into account the core of every knowledge based system, namely the semantic content description, can provide a new level of quality for content based systems and in this case enable a higher acceptance rate and better learning effects for users. And with the ability to measure the content the framework is able to create e-Learning systems in a specific direction.

In summary, the QuaD² framework provides the first approach of a holistic consideration of quality and functional requirements with a substantial semantic description of all involved elements. This enables an automated procedure of entity selection and execution on the one hand and a substantial support of quality evaluation of involved entities on the other hand.

REFERENCES

Abran, A., Moore, J. W., Bourque, P., & Dupuis, R. (Eds.). (2001). *Guide to the software engineering body of knowledge*. Los Alamitos, CA: IEEE Computer Society Press.

Ahern, D. M., Clouse, A., & Turner, R. (2008). *CMMI distilled: A practical introduction to integrated process improvement. The SEI Series in Software Engineering*. Amsterdam: Addison-Wesley Professional.

Anghel, C., & Salomie, I. (2003). JADE based solutions for knowledge assessment in eLearning environments. *EXP - in search of innovation (Special Issue on JADE)*.

Barrows, H. (1986). A taxonomy of problem-based learning methods. *Medical Education, 20*(6), 481–486. doi:10.1111/j.1365-2923.1986.tb01386.x

Basili, V. R. (1999). The experience factory: Packaging software experience. In *Proceedings of the Fourteenth Annual Software Engineering Workshop*. NASA Goddard Space Flight Center, Greenbelt, MD.

Basili, V. R., Caldiera, G., & Rombach, H. D. (1994). The experience factory. In J.J. Marciniak (Ed.), *Encyclopedia of SE* (Vol. 1, pp. 511-519). John Wiley & Sons.

Boehm, B. W. (Ed.). (1978). *Characteristics of software quality*. Amsterdam: Elsevier.

Braungarten, R., Kunz, M., Farooq, A., & Dumke, R. (2005). Towards meaningful metrics data bases. In A. Abran, & R. Dumke (Eds.), In *Proceedings of the 15th Workshop on Software Measurement (IWSM05)* (pp. 1-34), Aachen: Shaker Publ.

Buzzell, R. D., & Gale, B. T. (1987). *The PIMS principles: Linking strategy to performance*. New York: The Free Press.

catalogue_detail.htm?csnumber=21823

catalogue_detail.htm?csnumber=29572

catalogue_detail.htm?csnumber=43564

Devedžic, V. (2006). *Semantic Web and education*. Springer's Integrated Series in Information Systems. New York: Springer.

Dumke, R., Abran, A., & Buglione, L. (2006). Suggestion for improving measurement plans: First results from a BMP application. In *Proceedings of the 3rd Software Measurement European Forum (Smef 2006)* (pp. 209-224): Dumke, R., Braungarten, R., Mencke, S., Richter, K., & Yazbek, H. (2007). Experience-based software measurement and evaluation considering paradigm evolution. In *Proceedings of the DASMA Metric Congress (Metrikon 2007)* (pp. 47-62), Aachen: Shaker Publ.

Dumke, R., Braungarten, R., Kunz, M., & Hegewald, H. (2005). An ISO 15939-based infrastructure supporting the IT software measurement. In *Praxis der Software-Messung –Tagungsband des DASMA Software Metrik Kongresses (MetriKon 2005)* (pp. 87-106), Aachen: Shaker Publ.

Ebert, C., & Dumke, R. (2007). *Software measurement*. Heidelberg: Springer.

Farooq, A., Kernchen, S., Kunz, M., Dumke, R., & Wille, C. (2006). Complexity and quality evaluation of basic Java technologies. In A. Abran, M. Bundschuh, G. Büren, & R. Dumke (Eds.), *Proceedings of the International Workshop on Software Measurement and DASMA Software Metrik Kongress (IWSM/MetriKon 2006)*. Aachen: Shaker Publ.

Flechsig, K.-H. (1996). *Little handbook of didactical models* (in German). Eichenzell: Neuland.

Garvin, D. A. (1984). What does 'Product Quality' really mean? *MIT Sloan Management Review, 26*(1), 25–43.

Giotopoulos, K. C., Alexakos, C. E., Beligiannis, G. N., & Likothanassis, S. D. (2005). Integrating agents and computational intelligence techniques in e-learning environments. In *International Enformatika Conference (IEC'05)* (pp. 231-238).

Hahn, D. (1971). Decision process and case method (in German). In K. Alewell, K. Bleicher, & D. Hahn (Eds.), *Decision Cases in Business Practice* (in German) Wiesbaden: Gabler Publ.

Hametner, K., Jarz, T., Moriz, W., Pauschenschwein, J., Sandtner, H., Schinnerl, I., Sfiri, A., & Teufel, M. (2006). *Quality criteria for e-learning – A guide for teachers, lecturers and content creators* (In German).

Helic, D. (2005). An ontology-based approach to supporting didactics in e-learning systems. In *Proceedings of the 5th IEEE International Conference on Advanced Learning Technologies* (pp. 174-176), Kaohsiung, Taiwan.

Hyatt, L. E., & Rosenberg, L. H. (1996). A software quality model and metrics for identifying project risks and assessing software quality. In *Proceedings of the 8th Annual Software Technology Conference,* Salt Lake City, USA.

ISO/IEC. (1995). ISO/IEC 12207*: Information technology – Software life cycle processes*. Retrieved August, 2008 from http://www.iso.org/iso/iso_catalogue/catalogue_tc/ catalogue_detail.htm?csnumber=21208

ISO/IEC. (2000). ISO/IEC 9001: *Quality management systems – Requirements*. Retrieved August, 2008 from http://www.iso.org/iso/iso_catalogue/catalogue_tc/

ISO/IEC. (2001). ISO/IEC 9126-1:2001: *Software Engineering – Product Quality – Part 1: Quality Model*. Retrieved August, 2008 from http://www.iso.org/iso/iso_catalogue/ catalogue_tc/catalogue_detail.htm?csnumber=22749

ISO/IEC. (2002). ISO/IEC 15939: *Software Engineering – Software Measurement Process*. Retrieved August, 2008 from http://www.iso.org/iso/iso_catalogue/catalogue_tc/

ISO/IEC. (2004a). ISO/IEC 15504*: Information technology – Process assessment*. Retrieved from: http://www.iso.org/iso/iso_catalogue/catalogue_tc/catalogue_detail.htm?csnumber= 38932

ISO/IEC. (2004b). ISO/IEC 9000: *Quality Management Standards*. Retrieved August, 2008 from http://www.iso.org/iso/iso_catalogue/management_standards/iso_9000_iso_14000.htm

ISO/IEC 15288: *Systems and software engineering – System life cycle processes*. Retrieved August, 2008 from http://www.iso.org/iso/iso_catalogue/catalogue_tc/

Juneidi, S. J., & Vouros, G. A. (2005). Engineering an e-learning application using the ARL Theory for agent oriented software engineering. In *2005 AAAI Fall Symposium*, Arlington, Virginia. MIT Press.

Kunz, M., Mencke, S., Rud, D., Braungarten, R., & Dumke, R. R. (2008a). From QoS towards quality-driven orchestration. In *Proceedings of the 3rd Workshop Bewertungsaspekte serviceorientierter Architekturen (BSOA 2008)*, Leinfelden, Germany.

Kunz, M., Mencke, S., Rud, D., & Dumke, R. (2008b). Empirical-based design – Quality-driven assembly of components. In *Proceedings of the IEEE International Conference on Information Reuse and Integration (IRI 2008)*, Las Vegas, Nevada, USA.

Lin, F., Esmahi, L., & Poon, L. (2005). A human collaborative online learning environment using intelligent agents. In F. Lin (Ed.), *Designing distributed learning environments with intelligent software agents*. Hershey, PA: IGI Global.

Lin, N., Kuter, U., & Sirin, E. (2008). Web service composition with user preferences. In S. Bechhofer, M. Hauswirth, J. Hoffmann, & M. Koubarakis (Eds.), *Proceedings of 5th European Semantic Web Conference – The Semantic Web: Research and Applications (ESWC 2008)* (pp. 629-643), Tenerife, Canary Islands, Spain.

McCall, J. A., Richards, P. K., & Walters, G. F. (1977). *Factors in software quality* (Technical report). Rome Air Development Center Air Force Systems Command.

Meder, N. (2006). *Web-didactic*. Bielefeld: Bertelsmann Publ.

Mencke, S. (2008). *Proactive ontology-based content provision in the context of e-learning*. Doctoral dissertation. Otto-von-Guericke University of Magdeburg, Germany.

Mencke, S., & Dumke, R. (2008). Didactical ontologies. In *Emerging Technologies in e-Learning, 3*(1), 65-73.

Mencke, S., & Dumke, R. R. (2007). A hierarchy of ontologies for didactics-enhanced e-learning. In M. E. Auer (Eds.), *Proceedings of the International Conference on Interactive Computer aided Learning (ICL2007)*, Villach, Austria.

Mencke, S., Kunz, M., & Dumke, R. (2008a). Towards metrics for ontology balance. In *Proceedings of the Twentieth International Conference on Software Engineering and Knowledge Engineering (SEKE 2008)*, Redwood City, USA.

Mencke, S., Rud, D., Zbrog, F., & Dumke, R. (2008b). Proactive autonomous resource enrichment for e-Learning. In *Proceedings of the 4th International Conference on Web Information Systems and Technologies (WEBIST 2008)* (Vol. 1, pp. 464-467), Funchal, Madeira, Portugal. INSTICC Press.

Mencke, S., Wille, C., & Dumke, R. (2008c). Measuring distances for ontology-based systems. In *Proceedings of the 18th International Workshop in Software Measurement in conjunction with the Mensura and the DASMA Software Metric Kongress (ISWM/Mensura/Metrikon 2008)* (LNCS 5338, pp. 97-106).

Mencke, S., Zbrog, F., & Dumke, R. (2008d). Useful e-Learning process descriptions. In *Proceedings of the 4th International Conference on Web Information Systems and Technologies (WEBIST 2008)* (pp. 460-463), Funchal, Madeira, Portugal. INSTICC Press.

Mertens, H. (2002). *Conception and development of a problem-oriented interaction component for the depiction of economic case studies in hypermedia teaching/learning systems* (in German). Doctoral dissertation, University of Würzburg.

Object Management Group. (2004). *Unified Modeling Language*. Retrieved August, 2008 from http://www.uml.org/

Object Management Group. (2005). *Business Process Modelling Notation (BPMN)*.

Pawlowski, J. M. (2005). The didactical object model: Managing didactical expertise. In *The 5th IEEE International Conference on Advanced Learning Technologies* (pp. 788-792), Kaohsiung, Taiwan.

Princeton University. (2006). *WORDNET - A Lexical Database for the English Language*. Retrieved August, 2008 from http://wordnet.princeton.edu/

Project Management Institute. (2004). *A guide to the project management body of knowledge (PMBOK Guide)*. Project Management Institute.

Schmidt, H. G. (1983). Problem-based learning: Problem and definition. *Medical Education, 17*, 11–16. doi:10.1111/j.1365-2923.1983.tb01086.x

Trevena, L. J. (2007). Problem-based learning in public health workforce training: A discussion of educational principles and evidence. *New South Wales Public Health Bulletin, 18*(1-2), 4–8.

Vouk, M. A., Bitzer, D. L., & Klevans, R. L. (1999). Work-flow and end-user quality of service issues in Web-based education. *IEEE Transactions on Knowledge and Data Engineering, 11*(4), 673–687. doi:10.1109/69.790839

Wang, Y., & King, G. (2000). *Software engineering processes: Principles and applications*. Boca Raton: CRC Press, Inc.

Weske, M. (2007). *Business process management: Concepts, languages, architectures*. New York: Springer.

Wille, C. (2005). *Agent measurement framework*. Doctoral dissertation, Otto-von-Guericke University of Magdeburg.

Wille, C., Braungarten, R., & Dumke, R. (2006). Addressing drawbacks of software measurement data integration. In *Proceedings of the 3rd Software Measurement European Forum (Smef 2006)* (pp. 209-224), Rome, Italy.

Wille, C., & Dumke, R. (2007). Recording and evaluation of metrics about Web pages (In German). In G. Büren, & M. Bundschuh (Eds.), *Proceedings of the DASMA Software Metrik Kongress (MetriKon 2007)* (pp. 241-252), Aachen: Shaker Publ.

Zeng, L., Benatallah, B., Dumas, M., Kalagnanam, J., & Sheng, Q. Z. (2003). Quality driven Web services composition. In *Proceedings of the Twelfth International World Wide Web Conference (WWW 2003)* (pp. 411-421), Budapest, Hungary.

Section 2
Domain Specific Semantic Interoperability Practices

Chapter 8
Pillars of Ontology Treatment in the Medical Domain

Daniel Sonntag
DFKI - German Research Center for Artificial Intelligence, Germany

Pinar Wennerberg
Externer Dienstleister der Siemens AG, Germany

Paul Buitelaar
DERI - National University of Ireland, Galway

Sonja Zillner
Siemens AG, Germany

EXECUTIVE SUMMARY

In this chapter the authors describe the three pillars of ontology treatment in the medical domain in a comprehensive case study within the large-scale THESEUS MEDICO project. MEDICO addresses the need for advanced semantic technologies in medical image and patient data search. The objective is to enable a seamless integration of medical images and different user applications by providing direct access to image semantics. Semantic image retrieval should provide the basis for the help in clinical decision support and computer aided diagnosis. During the course of lymphoma diagnosis and continual treatment, image data is produced several times using different image modalities. After semantic annotation, the images need to be integrated with medical (textual) data repositories and ontologies. They build upon the three pillars of knowledge engineering, ontology mediation and alignment, and ontology population and learning to achieve the objectives of the MEDICO project.

INTRODUCTION

Clinical care and research increasingly rely on digitized patient information. There is a growing need to store and organize all patient data, such as health records, laboratory reports and medical images, so that they can be retrieved effectively. At the same time it is crucial that clinicians have access to a coherent view of these data within their particular diagnosis or treatment context.

With traditional applications, users may browse or explore visualized patient data, but little to no help is given when it comes to the interpretation of what is being displayed. This is due to the fact that the semantics of the data is not explicitly stated, which therefore remains inaccessible to the system and therefore also to the user. This can be overcome by the incorporation of external medical knowledge from ontologies which provide the meaning (i.e., the formal semantics) of the data at hand.

Our research activities are in the context of the THESEUS MEDICO project. MEDICO addresses the need for advanced semantic technologies in medical image and patient data search. The objective is to enable a seamless integration of medical images and different user applications by providing a direct access to image semantics. A wide range of different imaging technologies in various modalities exist, such as 4D 64-slice Computer Tomography (CT), whole-body Magnet Resonance Imaging (MRI), 4D Ultrasound, and the fusion of Positron Emission Tomography and CT (PET/CT). All these image modalities have the common property that their semantic contents include knowledge about human anatomy, radiology, or diseases.

One important requirement for advanced applications in semantic image retrieval, clinical decision support and computer aided diagnosis is the comparative exploration of similar patient information. For this purpose, we envision a flexible and generic image understanding software for which semantics of the images plays the major role for access and retrieval. However, currently, large amounts of medical image data are indexed by simple keywords to be stored in distributed databases without capturing any semantics.

The objective of MEDICO is to build the next generation of intelligent, scalable and robust search engines for the medical imaging domain, based on semantic technologies. With the incorporation of higher level knowledge represented in ontologies, different semantic views of the same medical images (such as structural aspects, functional aspects, and disease aspects) can be explicitly stated and integrated. Thus, the combination of formal semantics with image understanding helps building bridges between different but related domains that can be used for comparative exploration of patient data. MEDICO is a consortium research project funded by the German Federal Ministry of Economics with several R&D sites and the Erlangen University Hospital as a clinical partner. Visit http://theseus-programm.de/scenarios/en/medico.

Within the MEDICO project, one of the selected scenarios aims for improved image search in the context of patients that suffer from lymphoma in the neck area. Lymphoma, which is a type of cancer affecting the lymphocytes, is a systematic disease with manifestations in multiple organs. During the course of lymphoma diagnosis and continual treatment, image data is produced several times using different modalities. As a result, the image data consist of many medical images in different formats, which additionally need to be associated with the corresponding patient data. Hence, the lymphoma scenario is particularly suitable to demonstrate the strength of a semantic search engine as we envisioned in MEDICO.

To address the challenges of advanced medical image search, different medical resources need to be semantically integrated. Consequently, the following four research questions arise:

1. How is the workflow of the clinician, i.e.,
    a. What kind of information is relevant for his daily tasks?

   b. At what stage of the workflow should selected information items be offered?
2. What are the particular challenges and requirements of knowledge engineering in the medical domain?
   a. Can those challenges be addressed by a semi-automatic knowledge extraction process based on clinical user interactions?
   b. Can we embed the semi-automatic extraction process into the clinician's workflow?
3. How can different possibly overlapping data sources (i.e., ontologies) be aligned?
4. How can we learn and populate ontologies?

MEDICO's vision of the semantic medical search relies on ontology-based annotation of medical images and the related patient data. This allows us to mark-up the content at a higher level of granularity that goes beyond simple keywords. To realize this, the use of metadata from multiple, disparate but nevertheless related ontologies is required.

We will describe the three pillars of ontology treatment in the medical domain in a comprehensive case study within MEDICO. These pillars are knowledge engineering, ontology mediation and alignment, and ontology population and learning. We build upon these pillars to achieve the objectives of MEDICO.

The contribution of this book chapter is this description of the pillars of ontology treatment in the medical domain and the overview of our implementations of these pillars. For example, the approach for realizing a medical image search scenario based on semantic technologies within an industry setting represents one of the pillars (knowledge management). We put the focus on the challenges, requirements, and possible solutions related to ontology alignment.

The remainder of this book chapter is organized as follows. Section 2 outlines the pillars of ontology treatment. Section 3 describes our implementations of the knowledge engineering requirements of a clinician in the context of his daily work along three clinical scenarios. We will also discuss the medical knowledge engineering workflow. Section 4 addresses the challenges and possible solutions for mediating and (semi-automatically) aligning different medical ontologies. In section 5 we discuss and analyze how MEDICO ontologies can be populated in a semi-automatic way. The final section concludes and describes our future work in the THESEUS MEDICO use case.

PILLARS OF ONTOLOGY TREATMENT IN THE MEDICAL DOMAIN

According to the clinical knowledge requirements, we can identify three pillars of ontology treatment in the medical domain. These pillars should allow us to improve the clinical reporting process, the patient follow-up process, and the clinical disease staging and patient management process. This is achieved by the use of metadata from multiple, related medical ontologies. In the following, we will describe the pillars of ontology treatment: knowledge engineering; ontology mediation and alignment; and ontology population and ontology learning.

Knowledge Engineering

What is the recommended medical information management and ontology engineering process and what semantic-driven recommendations can be given to enhance existing medical knowledge repositories? Which recommendations can support building up new medical knowledge repositories? A knowledge engineering methodology (KEMM) helped us to formalize these requirements. How this relates to the doctor's practical interest in using a semantic search engine or dialogue interface is one major part of the practical case study. For example, consider a radiologist at his daily work: The diagnostic analysis of medical images typically concentrates around three questions: i) what is the anatomy? ii) what is the name of the body part? iii) is it normal or is it abnormal? To satisfy the radiologist's information need, this scattered knowledge has to be gathered and integrated from disparate dynamic information sources.

Ontology Mediation and Alignment

Information integration is concerned with access to heterogeneous information sources (in MEDICO: text patient data, medical images, relational databases) to be mediated in order to provide an integrated view of the data. In addition, we have specific information needs that must be satisfied by these information sources (which should be expressed by query patterns defined over a set of ontologies). In medical imaging and MEDICO, a single ontology is not enough to support the required complementary knowledge from different perspectives, for example anatomy, radiology, or diseases. Ontology mediation and alignment is therefore a key aspect of the semantic information integration task in the MEDICO use case.

We investigate linguistic-based, corpus-based, and speech-dialogue-based ontology alignment approaches in the main part of this case study. We will also discuss the methods that are required for interactive and incremental ontology mapping in the MEDICO use case, and their applicability.

Ontology Population

Given the set of identified relevant and aligned ontologies, one important aspect of our approach is the automatic extraction of knowledge instances (entities, facts) from text data. This data is widely available in the medical domain in the form of patient records as well as scientific articles. The important aspect is the semantic integration of these mainly unstructured data instances with those derived from other resources (medical images, relational databases) through ontology population across ontologies. In this connection, we describe an interactive GUI environment for the medical expert.

KNOWLEDGE ENGINEERING IN THE MEDICAL DOMAIN

MEDICO covers a particularly sensitive domain, i.e., human health. In this domain, the reuse of medical knowledge, which is already present in readily available standardized, high quality medical ontologies engineered by domain experts, is crucial.

In our context, we use the term "knowledge engineering" in the sense it is discussed by Grüninger and Uschold (1996). It is refer to *"methods for creating an ontological and computational basis for reuse of product knowledge across different applications within technical domains."* Consequently, we understand ontology treatment (i.e., ontology mediation and ontology population) as specific knowledge engineering tasks.

Various challenges exist in medical knowledge engineering. One challenge is that the knowledge engineer is not familiar with the complex and comprehensive medical terminology in the medical ontologies. As a result, the application domain remains opaque to him and he cannot verify the knowledge engineering process. Other challenges are the size of the medical ontologies, which overwhelms a non-medical person, not to mention the technical challenges of the software engineering process, for example runtimes.

The major challenge, however, is the so-called "knowledge acquisition bottleneck." We cannot easily acquire the necessary medical knowledge that ought to be used in the software application as it is hidden in the heads of medical experts. Our experience with the MEDICO project shows that common interview methods are neither efficient nor effective enough to acquire the domain knowledge (due to misunderstandings in the communication).

Therefore, we view medical knowledge engineering as an *interactive process* between the knowledge engineer and the clinician. The first essential step requires the knowledge engineer to gather and pre-processes available medical knowledge from various resources such as domain ontologies and domain corpora, whereupon the domain expert, i.e., the clinician, evaluates the outcome of the process and provides feedback.

Thus, we address the "knowledge acquisition bottleneck" problem by concerning ourselves with the question how a bottom-up ontology engineering approach can be established based on a data-driven knowledge pre-processing step (that is followed by a user interactive evaluation step). Here, our focus is on the development of semantic-driven recommendations to enhance existing medical knowledge repositories according to KEMM (Knowledge Engineering Methodology in the Medical Domain).

Clinical Knowledge Engineering Requirements

Today, medical images provide important information for identifying the patient's diagnosis and appropriate treatment. As medical imaging technologies progress and more and more medical details become more clearly visible, it happens quite often that clinicians discover some suspicious or unknown alteration of particular body parts in medical images. In such situations, the most valuable and relevant information for clinicians can be gained by comparing the non-routine results to other but nevertheless "similar" images. By comparing a given image to other scans and records of patients with similar visual symptoms, e.g., an enlargement of the lymph node of the neck, clinicians can learn about the meaning of the unknown alteration in the context of the progress of the disease.

In contemporary, daily hospital work, clinicians can only manually search for "similar" images. After considering the relevant categories of similarity, they subsequently set one filter after the other. For instance, a clinician first sets a filter for the imaging modality (e.g., CT angiography), the second filter for the procedure (e.g., coronary angiography), and so on. Beside the fact that this approach is quite time-consuming, it is neither possible to formulate complex and semantically integrated search queries, nor can valuable knowledge of external knowledge resources be integrated.

This is the situation we face today. Thus, in intensive discussions with clinicians we analyzed how the use of semantic technologies can support the clinician's daily work tasks. In particular, we discussed the medical case of lymphoma from the perspective of medical imaging and revealed three typical clinical scenarios that are of interest for further analysis of clinical knowledge requirements:

1. The clinical reporting process;
2. The patient follow-up treatment (i.e., monitoring the patient's health condition and the development of the disease);
3. The clinical disease staging and patient management.

Each scenario induces a list of relevant tasks with particular clinical questions to be answered. Each answer is again based on particular medical data that is (or is not) available and that is typically stored in distributed knowledge and data repositories. The three clinical scenarios require the acquisition of various types of domain knowledge:

1. The *clinical reporting process* focuses on the general question "What is the disease?" (or, as in the lymphoma case, "which lymphoma?") To answer this question, *semantic annotations* on medical image contents are required. These

are typically anatomical parts such as organs, vessels, lymph nodes, etc. Image parsing and pattern recognition algorithms can extract the low-level image feature information. The low-level information is used to produce higher-level semantic annotations to support tasks such as differential diagnosis.

2. Within the *patient follow-up process,* the clinician's concern is whether his former diagnosis hypothesis is confirmed by the outcome of the treatment or not. In other words, a clinician can only know what he is treating until he sees how the patient responds (Starbucks, 1993). The questions relevant for this scenario are, "Is the drug effective?", "Has the lesion shrunk?", and "Do the symptoms persist?" Therefore, the clinician is particularly interested in finding out if his prior diagnosis hypothesis can be verified or refuted.
3. In the *clinical staging* and *patient management process* the general concern is with the next steps in the treatment process. The results of the clinical staging process influence the decisions that concern the later patient management process. (*External medical knowledge* comes into play, in the sense that the disease staging results need to be mapped onto the standard clinical staging and patient management guidelines.)

To satisfy the radiologist's information need, this scattered information has to be gathered, semantically integrated and presented to the user in a coherent way. Finally, external resources such as medical guidelines or medical recommendations need to be integrated as well in order to achieve compatibility with the standard decision making and management procedures.

KEMM METHODOLOGY

From the knowledge engineering requirements, we derived a knowledge engineering methodology that is specific for the medical domain (Wennerberg, 2008). Consequently, KEMM (Figure 1) defines seven tasks. The initial task, called *Query Pattern Derivation,* supports the communication between the knowledge engineer and the clinician during the knowledge elicitation process. All other tasks (explained further down) support the medical ontology engineering process.

Query Pattern Derivation

This task is based on generating a set of hypothetical user queries using domain ontologies and domain corpora that are subsequently evaluated

Figure 1. Knowledge engineering methodology for the medical domain (KEMM)

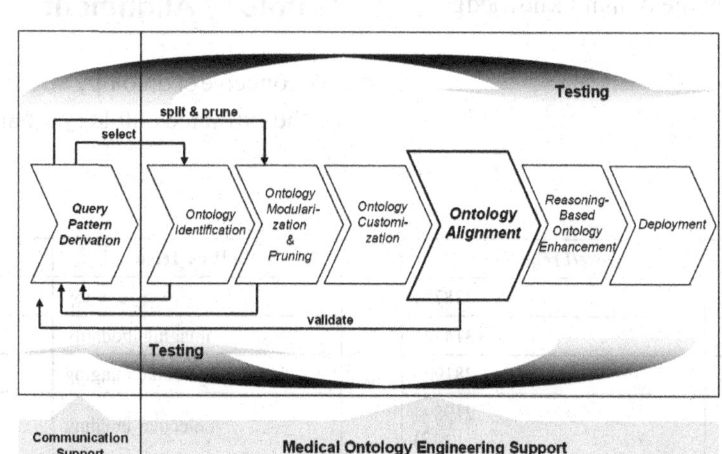

by the clinicians. A combination of various techniques from natural language processing to text mining are employed to derive patterns (described in detail in Buitelaar (2008) and Wennerberg (2008a)). In the MEDICO study, we focused on the patterns for typical clinical queries given the domain ontologies and use case corpora; concept-relation-concept triplets are identified. The pattern derivation can be viewed as a function that takes the domain (sub)ontologies and the corpora as input and returns a partial weighting of the ontologies, whereby the terms/concepts are ranked according to their weights. A complex query pattern example is: (ANATOMICAL_STRUCTURE *located_in* ANATOMICAL_STRUCTURE) **AND** ((RADIOLOGY_IMAGE) Modality *is_about* ANATOMICAL_STRUCTURE) **AND** ((RADIOLOGY_IMAGE) Modality *shows_symptom* DISEASE_SYMPTOM).

The top 4 concepts we identified for the generic query pattern above in the corpora are shown in Table 1.

Ontology Identification

As the medical image contents essentially relate to human anatomy, radiology, pathology, and/or diseases, we require identifying ontologies from these domains. Consequently, the Foundational Model of Anatomy[1], the Radiology Lexicon[2], and the NCI Cancer Thesaurus[3] were set as semantic resources that provide the domain knowledge.

Ontology Modularization and Pruning

Based on these patterns, the ontologies to be reused are identified, pruned, and modularized; the relevant modules are customized and finally integrated. For an effective reuse of the large medical ontologies, we have to construct modular ontology subsets that can be easily navigated by humans and reasoned by machines. The derived set of query patterns determines the criteria for pruning and modularizing the large medical ontologies that were identified in the previous step. These pruned (and modularized) ontologies are then presented to the clinical experts to confirm their relevance and validity.

Ontology Customization

Quite often, the modules extracted from the ontologies have either redundant or missing knowledge; only customized knowledge in terms of domain ontologies meets the requirements with respect to the applications. For example, we defined a relationship *has_nci_code* which relates the concepts in the lymphoma module to the entities in the NCI thesaurus. Another customization was the conversion of the lymphoma related section of the NCI Thesaurus from the flat text format to OWL.

Ontology Alignment

We conceive of ontology alignment as an operation on the extracted ontology modules (rather than the

Table 1.

FMA Term	Score/Frequency
lateral	338724
anterior	314721
artery	281961
anterior spinal artery	219894 (2)

RadLex Term	Score/Frequency
x-ray	81901
imaging modality	58682
volume imaging	57855
molecular imaging	57850

ontologies as a whole). The objective of the alignment is to obtain a coherent picture of separate but related ontology modules. Each customized ontology module represents a piece of knowledge that is necessary to realize the entire application. These knowledge pieces are not arbitrary but they need to be interrelated within the context of the application. The different ontology alignment and mediation approaches will be discussed in more detail in Section 2.

Reasoning-Based Ontology Enhancement

The MEDICO use case is characterized by the reuse and integration of distributed ontological knowledge that may introduce inconsistencies. With the KEMM methodology we concentrate on two specific reasoning services. In our lymphoma use case one objective is to be able to deduce the relevant image modalities (MR, CT scan etc.) given the symptoms of head and neck lymphoma. Via deductive reasoning we target the discovery of valid relationships—spatial, pathological, and physiological—between anatomical structures. ***Testing and Deployment:*** To avoid the propagation of inconsistencies and modeling mistakes, each and every task should be tested for validity, completeness, and coherence.

With the KEMM methodology, our intention is to provide a theoretical framework for the knowledge engineer, whose application domain is healthcare. Based on our experience, we assume that knowledge engineers, who have no or little background knowledge in biomedical sciences, will face similar challenges. Therefore, the goal of KEMM is to inform the knowledge engineers about both domain specific technical challenges and potential communication difficulties with the domain experts. Ontology alignment is the most important ontology treatment pillar in practical terms, and we discuss it next to explain *why* it is necessary. Additionally, we give details on *how* it can be implemented.

ONTOLOGY MEDIATION AND ALIGNMENT

We regard ontology alignment as an important building block of knowledge engineering in the medical domain. Medical knowledge engineering typically requires semantic integration of different medical knowledge, which can be supported by ontology alignment. KEMM demonstrates our view on *when* this should happen within the entire medical knowledge engineering process. Ontology alignment is an increasingly active research field in the biomedical domain, especially in association with the Open Biomedical Ontologies (OBO)[4] framework. The OBO consortium establishes a set of principles to which the biomedical ontologies shall conform to for purposes of interoperability. The OBO conformant ontologies, such as the FMA, are available at the National Center for Biomedical Ontology (NCBO) BioPortal[5].

Information integration is concerned with the access to heterogeneous information sources (in MEDICO: text patient data, medical images, and relational databases) to be mediated in order to provide an integrated view of the data. We also have specific information needs to be answered by these information sources, which may be expressed by a query pattern defined over a set of ontologies. As already mentioned, in MEDICO, a single ontology is not enough to provide the required complementary types of knowledge, i.e., the anatomy, radiology, or diseases.

There is a need for clinicians, in particular for radiologists, to be able to have access to coherent information from a single access point. At the center of their search are the medical images of patients, i.e., starting from a specific medical image, the radiologists wish to find all the information that is related to the case. Currently, this is not possible and the radiologist needs to use several systems at different locations.

Semantic annotations can help integrate the related data that is stored in distributed repositories by using commonly agreed annotation vocabularies. Consequently, radiologists can use the same vocabularies (i.e., those used for annotations) for their search and obtain the information from a single access point.

Hence, one of our goals within the context of the MEDICO use case is to offer clinicians and radiologists an integrated view of different kinds of information that is all centered around the medical images. We conceive of a radiology expert as an end user who looks, starting from a certain medical image, for all related information such as patient data, lab reports, treatment plans etc. Obtaining this kind of heterogeneous information from a single access point requires the data to have been previously integrated appropriately. The integration can be achieved while annotating the data with the relevant vocabularies. Nevertheless, during the search the radiologist prefer to use "his vocabulary" (i.e., a radiology specific vocabulary) for convenience. To be able to cover all relevant information by using only one vocabulary as a starting point therefore requires an alignment with other vocabularies that are relevant for image contents and patient data.

De Bruijn et al. (2006) offer terminological clarification for all the related research activities around ontology alignment. Accordingly, the reconciliation of differences between ontologies is defined as *ontology mediation*, whereby *ontology mapping* and *ontology merging* are considered as two specific cases of ontology mediation. In the case of ontology mapping the set of correspondences between different ontologies is not a part of the ontologies themselves. Ontology alignments, in this respect, are the results of the (semi-) automatic discovery of these correspondences in a suitable descriptive format. Others have a slightly different but non-contradictory definition. The difference between ontology mapping and ontology alignment according to Johnson et al. (2006) is that the former deals with the identification of equivalent concepts in multiple ontologies, whereas the latter specifically focuses on making the overlapping concepts in multiple ontologies compatible.

Our goal is to identify and post-process the correspondences between the concepts of different medical ontologies that are relevant to the contents of the medical images. This is how we define ontology mediation and alignment. The following scenario illustrates how the alignment of medical ontologies facilitates the integration of medical knowledge from multiple ontologies which are relevant for medical image contents. Suppose we want to help a radiologist who searches for related information about the manifestations of a certain type of lymphoma on a certain organ (e.g., the liver) on medical images. The three types of knowledge that help him would be about the human anatomy (liver), the organ's location in the body (e.g., upper limb, lower limb, neighboring organs etc.), and whether what he sees is normal or abnormal (pathological observations, symptoms, and findings about lymphoma).

Once we know what the radiologist is looking for, we can support him in his search in that we present him with an integrated view of only the liver lymphoma relevant portions of the patient health records, scientific publications abstracts (such as those of PubMed[6]) as a reference resource, drug databases, experience reports from other colleagues, treatment plans, notes of other radiologists, or even discussions from clinical web forums. From the NCI Thesaurus we can obtain the information that *liver lymphoma* is the synonym for *hepatic lymphoma*, for which holds:

'Hepatic lymphoma' (NCI term),*'disease_has_primary_anatomic_site'* (NCI relation),
'Liver' (NCI term and FMA term),
'Hematopoietic and lymphatic system' (NCI term),
'Gastrointestinal system' (NCI term).

With this information, we can now move on to the FMA ontology to find out that *hepatic artery* is a part of the liver (such that any finding that indicates lymphoma at the *hepatic artery* would also imply the lymphoma at the *liver*). RadLex, on the other hand, informs us that *liver surgery* is a *treatment procedure.* Various types of this *treatment procedure* are *hepatectomy, hepatic lobectomy, hepatic segmentectomy, hepatic sub-segmentectomy, hepatic trisegmentectomy,* or *hepatic wedge excision,* all of which can be applied to treat the disease.

Consequently, the radiologist, who searches for information about liver lymphoma, is presented with a set of patient health records, PubMed abstracts, radiology images etc. that are annotated using the terminology above. In this way, the radiologist's search space is reduced to a significantly small portion of the information available in multiple data stores. Moreover, he receives coherent data, i.e., images and patient text data that are related to each other, from a single access point without having to log in to several different data stores at different locations. In what follows, we will discuss related work in medical ontology mediation and alignments and we will propose our three approaches for the medial domain, i.e., linguistic-based, corpus-based, and dialogue-based to overcome some of the difficulties.

Johnson et al. (2006) take an information retrieval approach to discover relationships between the Gene Ontology (GO) and three other OBO ontologies (ChEBI[7], Cell Type[8], and BRENDA Tissue[9]). GO ontology concepts are treated as documents, they are indexed using Lucene[10] and are matched against the search queries, which are the concepts from the other three ontologies. Whenever a match is found, it is taken as evidence of a correspondence. This approach is efficient and easy to implement and can therefore be successful with large medical ontologies. However, it does not account for the complex linguistic structure typically observed in the concept labels of the medical ontologies and may result in inaccurate matches.

The main focus of the work by Zhang et al. (2004) is to compare two different alignment approaches that are applied to two different ontologies about human anatomy. The subject ontologies are the FMA and the Generalized Architecture for Languages, Encyclopedias and Nomenclatures for Medicine[11] (GALEN). Both approaches use a combination of lexical and structural matching techniques. One of them additionally employs an external resource (the Unified Medical Lexicon UMLS[12]) to obtain domain knowledge. In their work the authors point to the fact that medical ontologies contain implicit relationships, especially in the multi-word concept names that can be exploited to discover more correspondences.

The linguistic-based ontology alignment approach, which is described in the next section, builds on this finding and investigates further methods to discover the implicit information observed in concept labels of the medical ontologies. Furthermore, domain-independent ontology alignment methods are discussed by Kalfoglou and Schorlemmer (2005), Doan et al. (2003), Bruijn et al. (2006), Rahm and Bernstein (2001) and Noy (2004). We adapted techniques from all these approaches for the linguistic-based, corpus-based, and dialogue-based approach as discussed in the following.

Linguistic-Based Ontology Alignment

Drawing upon our experience with the medical ontologies throughout the MEDICO project, we have identified some of the common characteristics which are relevant for the alignment process. These can be summarized as follows:

1. They are very large models.
2. They have extensive *is-a* hierarchies up to ten thousands of classes, which are organized according to different views.
3. They have complex relationships, in which classes are connected by a number of different relations.

4. Their terminologies are rather stable (especially for anatomy) meaning that they should not differ too much in the different models.
5. The modeling principles for them are well defined and documented.

Both these observations and the fact that most medical ontologies are linguistically rich suggest that linguistic-based processing of ontology concept labels (and possibly also relations) can support the alignment process. The FMA ontology, for example, contains concept names as long as *'Anastomotic branch of right anterior inferior cerebellar artery with right superior cerebellar artery'*. The linguistic processing assumes that such long multi-word terms are usually rich with implicit semantic relations (e.g., equivalences) which can be exploited to identify additional alignments.

We argue that these relations can be made explicit by observing common patterns in the multi-word terms that are typical for the concept labels in the medical ontologies. Transformation grammars[13] can help to detect the variants of the ontology concept labels. In other words, with the help of rules, the concept labels can be transformed into semantically equivalent but syntactically different word forms.

There some naming conventions for the complex labels of the FMA concepts. For example, the order of adjectives in the term *'Left fifth intercostal space'* is based on the rationale that the noun in the term is *'space'*; its primary descriptor is *'intercostal'*, further specified by a sequence of numbers (enhanced by the *'laterality'* descriptor).

In a similar way, the term *'Right upper lobe'* is not the preferred name of the concept, although the FMA includes it as a *'synonym of' 'Upper lobe of right lung'* because of its common usage in radiology reports (Rosse and Mejino, 2003). This means that in this example each concept label (in most cases multi-word expressions) will terminate with a noun. Some examples of the complex FMA concept labels with their lexical categories are shown in Table 2.

One observation here is the use of prepositions (used to convey spatial information in most cases) to indicate *location* as in *'Pancreatic impression on spleen'*. The prepositions we observed in these concept labels are shown in Table 3 together with their frequencies.

A similar statistic can be observed for RadLex. The prepositions we observed in the concept labels are shown in Table 4, together with their frequen-

Table 2. Examples of FMA concept labels (preferred names and their lexical types)

Bile canalicular domain of plasmalemma of hepatocyte **(noun adjective noun preposition noun preposition noun)**
Blood in aorta **(noun preposition noun)**
Periventricular nucleus at the tuberal level **(adjective noun preposition determiner adjective noun)**
Organ with organ cavity **(noun preposition noun noun)**
Pancreatic impression on spleen **(adjective noun presposition noun)**
External carotid arterial subdivision **(adjective adjective adjective noun)**

Table 3. Prepositions observed in the FMA with their frequencies and example concept labels

Rank	Prep.	Freq.	FMA Concept Label
1	of	119886	Bile canalicular domain **of** plasmalemma **of** hepatocyte
2	to	3167	Branch of median nerve **to** opponens pollicis
3	for	438	Atlas **for** vertebral arterial groove
4	with	263	Organ **with** organ cavity
5	in	145	Blood **in** aorta
6	between	47	Intermetatarsal joint **between** first and second metatarsal bones
7	from	42	Inferior petrosal sinus **from** pons tributary
8	on	24	Pancreatic impression **on** spleen
9	over	19	Parietal peritoneum **over** left suprarenal gland
10	within	9	Nerve ending **within** taste bud
11	behind	6	Cutaneous branch to scalp **behind** auricle
12	by	4	Esophageal impression **by** arch of aorta
13	around	3	Nodes **around** cardia
14	at	2	Periventricular nucleus **at** the tuberal level
15	below	1	Trapezoid area **below** prostate

Table 4. Prepositions observed in RadLex with their frequencies and example concept labels

Rank	Prep.	Freq.	RadLex Concept Label
1	of	2180	aspiration **of** lipid
2	to	58	response **to** embolization
3	with	32	dementia **with** Lewy bodies
4	for	28	marking **for** intervention
5	in	21	carcinoma **in** situ
6	from	8	satisfactory drainage **from** catheter
7	by	6	metastasis **by** lymphatic and interstitial infiltration
8	on	5	images printed **on** paper
9	around	3	out of plane wrap **around** artifact
10	at	2	loss of signal **at** interface voxels
11	between	2	partial volume averaging **between** slices
12	within	2	refocusing of selected gradients **within** one TR interval
13	behind	0	
14	over	0	
15	below	0	

cies. Table 5 shows the transformation grammar we wrote for parsing complex medical terms.

For example, if we take the concept label *'Blood in aorta'* from the FMA and its lexical pattern (noun preposition noun), we can apply the transformation rule,

Table 5. The transformation grammar used to generate semantic equivalences for the common patterns in FMA and RadLex

ConceptLabel → NounPhrase
NounPhrase → Noun
NounPhrase → Adjective NounPhrase
NounPhrase→ NounPhrase (-) Token
NounPhrase → PrivateName Noun
PrepositionalPhrase → Preposition NounPhrase
NounPhrase → NounPhrase PrepositionalPhrase

Adjective → corneal|celiac|bifurcate|selected|printed|lymphatic…
Nounn → hepatocyte|prostate|gland|intervention|embolization…
Preposition → of|in|on|at|for|within…
PrivateName → Bochdalek|Lewy…
Token → 1|2|3|4|alpha|beta|1st|2nd|X|IV|…

noun1 preposition:'in' noun2 → noun2 noun1 (1)

and generate a syntactic variant for this concept label that nevertheless has equivalent semantics, i.e., *'Blood in aorta'* == *'Aorta blood'*. In RadLex, this rule transforms *'Carcinoma in situ'* to *'Situ carcinoma'*. The case with the preposition 'of' in the next transformation rule is similar.

noun1 preposition:'of' noun2 → noun2 noun1 (2)

applies to *'Protoplasm of lymphocyte'* to generate the syntactic variant *'Lymphocyte protoplasm'*. For RadLex the same rule generates *'Lipid aspiration'* from *'Aspiration of lipid'*. This is profitable for at least two reasons. First, it can help resolve possible semantic ambiguities (if one variant is ambiguous, it can be replaced by the other one). Second, identified variants can be used to compare linguistic (textual) contexts of ontology concepts in corpora. This leads to the corpus-based ontology alignment aspect of our approach.

Corpus-Based Ontology Alignment

The basic idea of the corpus-based alignment approach[14] is to compare the textual and linguistic contexts of ontology classes in large corpora. We hereby assume that ontology classes with similar meanings (originating from different ontologies) will appear in similar linguistic contexts. The linguistic context can be characterized by text characteristics and computed from texts directly. These characteristics describe the data instances (i.e., the words) and attributes (i.e., the part-of-speech tags) by applying descriptive statistical measures.

Then, we will learn statistics about words and their attributes (e.g., simple occurrence frequencies or supervised information gain statistics) and use them to infer constraints that we use to associate two terms. The association is then interpreted as a candidate mapping. Corpus-based linguistics focused not only on the distribution of words, but also on the distribution of linguistic features (i.e., part-of-speech tags) which we can derive from these words in context, i.e., features about the sentences, paragraphs and texts in which a specific word or word group occurs. Analogously, the linguistic context of an ontology class to be matched to another class can be defined as:

- the document in which it appears;
- the sentence in which it appears;
- a window of size N in which it appears.

For example, a window of size +5/-5 (including stop words) for *'Antidiuretic hormone'* would be "A syndrome of inappropriate secretion of antidiuretic hormone (SIADH) was diagnosed, and bortezomib was identified as its cause." In our approach, linguistic contexts are represented by token/word vectors, (e.g., <syndrome, of, inappropriate, secretion, of, (SIADH), was, diagnosed>), <token -5, token -4, ... token +4, token +5> or the following three alternative vector representations:

- Binary over set of context tokens/words (e.g., 10): < 0, 0, 0, 0, 1, 0, 1, 0, 0, 0 >
- Frequency over set of context tokens/words (e.g., 10): < 1, 5, 0, 0, 6, 7, 18, 1, 0, 1 >
- Frequency over set of context tokens/words (e.g., 10): < 1, 5, 0, 0, 6, 7, 18, 1, 0, 1 >
- Mutual Information/InformationGain over set of context tokens/words (e.g., 10): < 1.7, 0.5, 0, 0, 1.1, 3.5, 0.5, 1.2, 0, 1.5 >

The data sets for our corpus-based experiments consisted of context data collected from the PubMed corpus on Mantle Cell Lymphoma with 1,721 scientific abstracts. 38,853 tokens matched the simple or complex terms provided by FMA, Radlex, or Image terms (the resulting set of representative image features identified by parsing a liver image showing symptoms of lymphoma) (Figure 2).

811 different types (terms that may represent classes) were found (FMA: 320; RadLex: 562; Image terms: 20). This means the token/type ratio for FMA is 19.28, 43.44 for RadLex, and 413.3 for the Image Terms. This means that FMA terms were not used as frequently as RadLex terms, but vary twice as much. Image terms do not show a lot of variety; a specific term (type) is used almost 414 times on average. In addition, 6,800 different context words/tokens were found. Therefore, the non-sparse vector representation for the context of each token has a dimensionality of 6,800. We then used the TnT part-of-speech tagger[15] to annotate the POS classes (Penn Treebank Tagset[16]). Figure 3 shows the distribution of term tokens and the distribution of POS tags (categories).

After some experimentation with exploratory data mining methods and the medical experts, we agreed on an applicable model generation and interpretation process to be used by the medical expert. First, he generates term clusters by applying a hierarchical clustering method automatically. Then, he searches for interesting patterns in the clusters. Hierarchical clustering returns a hierarchy structure that is more informative (rather than a flat unstructured set of clusters). It does not require us to pre-specify the number of clusters or any other supervised criterion on the input data. Furthermore, it allows the expert to indicate similar meaning of corresponding ontology classes with the following procedure. He specifies a target value of interest and then searches the hierarchy for cluster boundaries.

For example, Figure 4 shows an excerpt of the cluster tree generated for the full data set #38852. The target value was set to the terms themselves (which correspond to a source value); this allows

Figure 2. The distribution of term tokens that stem from the image descriptors (Image terms), FMA, and Radlex

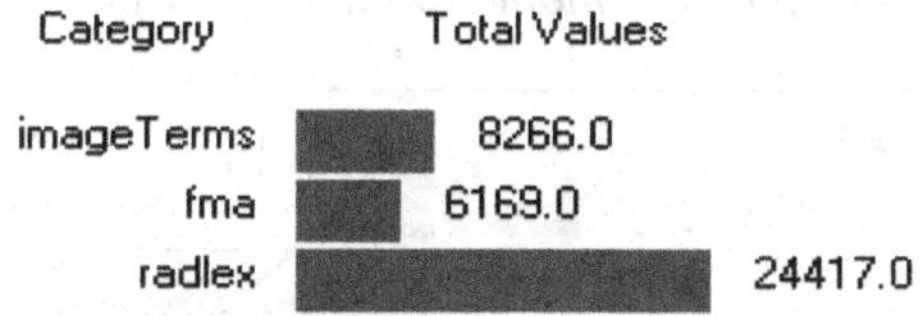

us to find new candidates for alignment because a) different terminologies are assumed to have similar terms and b) similar terms are represented in the same cluster (or cluster boundaries) per definition. The medical expert skims the clusters (which normally refer to either FMA or RadLex) and draws attention to the shift of FMA to RadLex or RadLex to FMA as illustrated. Then, he inspects the terms of the shift (in this case *Antibody* and *Monoclonal antibody*).

As a result, a mapping between those terms can be detected. Most importantly, this mapping was not found with a string comparison of the terms, but by clustering and interpreting the context vectors. In this way, a corpus-based method for alignment could be implemented which complements (string-based) term comparison methods and structure-based ontology alignment methods. The next step is to automize the method in order to find candidates without the expert visually mining the cluster results. Adequate measures for automatic processing are straightforward.

Dialogue-Based Ontology Alignment

The ontology matching problem can be addressed by several techniques as introduced in the section on related work. Advanced incremental visualisations have also been developed (e.g., see Robertson et al., 2006) to do better than merely calculate the

Figure 3. (Left) The distribution of term tokens that stem from the image descriptors (Image terms), FMA, and Radlex. (Right) The distribution of POS tags that stem from the image descriptors (Image terms), FMA, and Radlex.

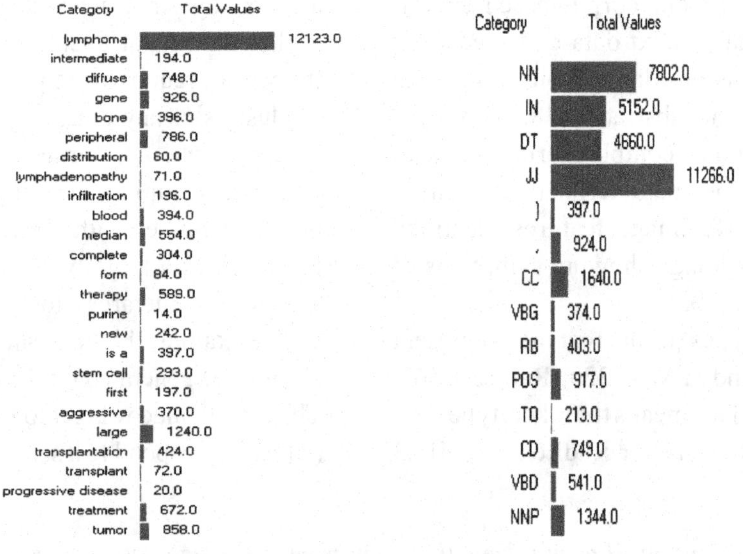

Figure 4. Hierachical clustering results. The medical expert inspects the shifts from, e.g., FMA to Radlex and the corresponding terms (antibody and monoclonal antibody).

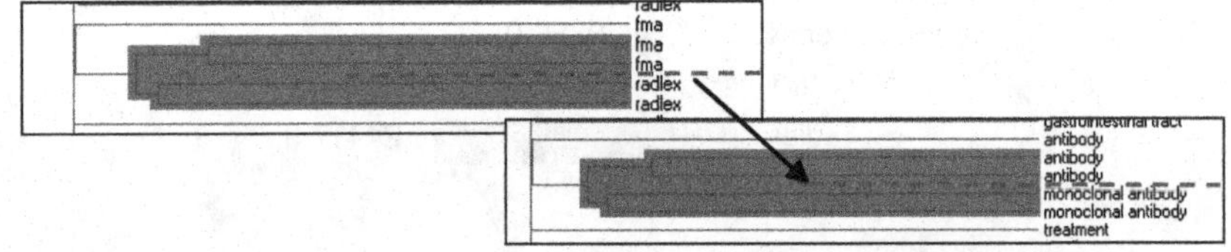

set of correspondences in a single shot; cognitive support frameworks for ontology mapping really involve users (Falconer et al., 2006). A dialogue-based approach could make more use of partial mappings in order to increase the usability in dialogue scenarios where the primary task is different from the schema matching task itself.

Recent work in incremental interactive schema matching stressed that users are often annoyed by false positives (Bernstein et al., 2006). This is a big problem when the user is actively engaged in the alignment process. Dialogue-based ontology alignment should provide a solution for that problem by providing a framework to elicit and interpret task-based user utterances. Task-based means that the user is not engaged in a tedious alignment dialogue where he judges proposed mappings. Instead, the doctor should use a dialogue shell to perform an intelligent image search as anticipated in MEDICO and answer only a few alignment questions if this step is not avoidable at all.

Our basic idea is as follows. Consider the methods that are required for interactive and incremental ontology mapping and evaluate the impact of dialogue-based user feedback in this process. While dialogue systems allow us to obtain user feedback on semantic mediation questions (e.g., questions regarding new semantic mediation rules), incrementally working matching systems can use the feedback as further input for alignment improvement.

In order to compute and post-process the alignments, we use the PhaseLibs library.[17] This platform supports custom combinations of algorithms and is written entirely in Java which allows us to directly integrate the API into the dialogue shell. In addition, the API supports individual modules and libraries for ontology adapters, similarity measures (e.g., string-based, instance-based, or graph-based), and alignment generators.

Subsequently, we focus on interactive ontology matching and dialogue-based interaction. Rather than focussing on the effectiveness of the interactive matching approach, we describe a suitable dialogue-level integration of the matching process by example. Our interactive ontology matching approach envisions the following three stages:

1. Compute a rudimentary partial mapping by a simple string-based method;
2. Ask the user to disambiguate some of the proposed mappings;
3. Use the resulting alignments as input for more complex algorithms.

Figure 5. Dialogue-based ontology alignment approach. The user is actively involved in the alignment creation and verification process. The architecture should be particularly useful for ad hoc mappings of medical disease databases.

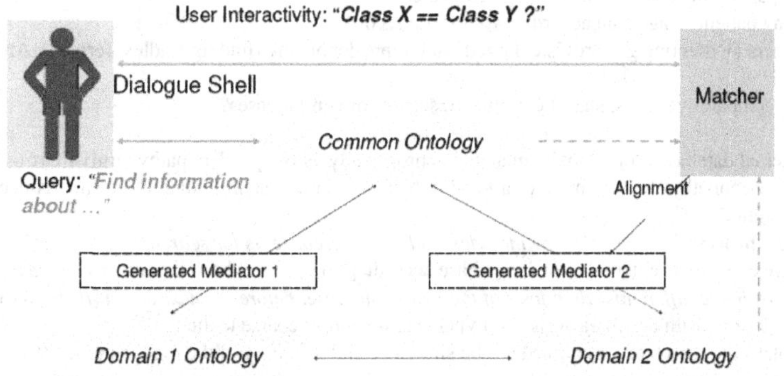

In regard to the first point, we hypothesise that the rudimentary mapping based on the concept and relation signs can be easily computed and obtained in dialogical reaction time (less than 3 seconds even for large ontologies). Second, user interactivity is provided by improving the automatically found correspondences through filtering the alignment. Concerning the third point, we employed similarity flooding since it allows for input alignments and fixpoint computation in PhaseLib's implementation following Melnik et al. (2002). The interactive semantic mediation approach is depicted in Figure 5.

In order not to annoy the user, he is only presented with the difficult cases for disambiguation feedback; thus we use the application dialogue shell basically for confirming or rejecting pre-considered alignments. The resulting alignments are then serialised as instances of an RDFS alignment format. Assuming that subsequent similarity computations successfully use the partial alignment inputs (to produce query-relevant partial alignment output), the proposed mediator can be said to be a light-weight but powerful approach to supporting incremental ontology matching and alignment generation (Sonntag, 2008).

Figure 5 also shows the architecture of the dialogue-based ontology alignment approach. An example dialogue of the speech-based interaction between the doctor and MEDICO (we plan to implement completely in summer 2009) is shown on in Table 6.

Example Dialogue

The example dialogue shows that the doctor is engaged in a task-based image retrieval dialogue. He follows the official procedure of the lymphoma finding guidelines when examining the organs. This is very important; the doctor cannot easily be asked to do anything else but search for images and complete the finding.

Fortunately, some feedback questions are allowed. With our dialogue shell (we use an upgraded version of the dialogue system for question answering on the Semantic Web we developed at DFKI, see Sonntag et al., 2007b), we try to smoothly embed the relevant question into the dialogue initiated by the MEDICO system. Most importantly, the user answers and utterances in general can be exploited for alignment judgement. Keywords, such as "so" and "equivalent to" can be interpreted to infer relations of interest, in addition to explicit user confirmations like, "Yes, that could be said."

Our datasets for a first evaluation of the three stage method as an integral part of a sensible dialogue initiative for alignments consisted of

Table 6. Possible dialogue between the clinician and MEDICO

1. U: "Show me the internal organs: lungs, liver, then spleen and colon."
2. S: Shows corresponding patient image data according to referral record.
3. U: "This lymph node here (+ pointing gesture) is enlarged; **so** lymphadenopathy (finding Radlex Term A). Are there any comparative cases in the hospital?"
4. S: "Sorry, there are no comparative cases, shall I continue to search for similar cases?"
5. U: "Ah okay."
6. S: "Unfortunately, external databases could not be matched appropriately. Is lymphadenopathy **equivalent to** lymph node enlargement (Radlex Term B) or adenopathy (NCI Term C) or **a kind of** hematopoietic system finding (NCI superconcept)?"
7. U: **"Yes, that could be said,"**
8. U: **"a pathophysiologic process**." *(MEDICO now includes RadLex superconcepts for search.)*
9. S: "I found comparative cases in an external knowledge base according to your feedback." *Medico switches to the comparative records to help the radiologist in the differential diagnosis of the suspicious case, before the next organ (liver) is examined.*
10. U: "Find similar liver lesions with the characteristics: hyper-intense and/or coarse texture ..."
11. S: Medico again displays the search results ranked by the similarity and matching of the medical terms that constrain the semantic search.

ontologies and alignment examples (manually annotated alignments for Radlex and NCI). For the first test in the medical domain, we annotated 50 alignments, 30 perfect positives and 20 perfect negatives. In the medical domain, the precision was 92% and the recall was 50% for simple string-based methods. (Corresponding concept names may differ substantially in their syntactic form.) The best matches were taken as alignment input for similarity flooding after manually confirming their validity (which simulates positive user feedback).

Our first experiments towards dialogue-based alignment generation suggest that we can use the three stage architecture as well as dialogue to do better than simply calculating the set of correspondences automatically and in a single shot. We are quite sure that in the medical domain, we cannot achieve acceptable precision and recall measurements without the expert feedback of the clinician. We are also sure that we have to obey the constraints of the doctor's task, i.e., we have to embed the alignment dialogue into the image retrieval dialogue, and, most importantly, not distract the doctor from the finding process. Furthermore, we do not start the interactive and incremental process from the refined corpus-based algorithms; it is possible to rely more on the corpus-based pre-selection by lowering the acceptance threshold of the string-based methods. But, since the dialogue-based approach is query-based, the differences cannot easily be observed. As a consequence, the linking only makes sense when the query is a "typical corpus query". According to Zipf's law, this is improbable at least for the included terms.

In future work, we are trying to provide evaluation methods to estimate the contribution of partial alignment inputs when the retrieval stage is more complex than simple name comparison, as is the case for most of our medical query patterns; user-confirmed perfect mappings can be used in simple name matching retrieval contexts with perfect precision, but this does not reflect the nature of real-world industrial requirements (in particular, where the user cannot be supposed to deliver a reliable judgement). Further, we are investigating techniques to better translate formal mapping uncertainties into appropriate dialogue-level questions for the radiologist and to address the general difficulty that users might not be able to provide helpful feedback in the course of a dialogue.

ONTOLOGY POPULATION

In this section, we will deal with the semi-automatic population of ontologies from unstructured text. We will propose a methodology to semi-automatically populate the FMA medical ontology by new instances that we will derive from medical texts. We will use the query pattern mining approach explained earlier to extract relation triples from the anatomy corpus. This pattern extraction step is helped by Wikipedia-based corpora and domain ontologies; the extracted relations consist of the relation type (e.g., *known_as*, *devided_into*, or *associated_with*) and the concept instances of the relation domain and range (e.g., "vein" is associated with "artery").

The extraction of patterns corresponds to the extraction of rules from annotated text. Finally, we will apply those rules to new articles to populate the ontology. To speak from our own experience, this step cannot be achieved directly and automatically. High user input is required in order to detect and discharge the false positives.

Semi-Automatic Knowledge Acquisition

Knowledge acquisition in the medical domain depends heavily on high precision. But automated ontology population provides little support for knowledge acquisition because one cannot rely on the results in terms of precision. In literature, several approaches have been proposed for, e.g., automated discovery of WordNet relations (Hearst, 1998) or discovering conceptual relations from text (Maedche and Staab, 2000).

In the medical domain, early approaches deal with the automatic knowledge acquisition from MEDLINE (Cimino and Barnett, 1993). In previous work, we evaluated potential linguistic context features for medical relation mining and designed a methodology of how to model relations and determine the parameters that distinguish relations (Vintar et al., 2003). However, all these approaches have two things in common. Either the precision values of acquired concepts and relations needed to populate a medical ontology were too low, or the task itself was too easy for the population of medical ontologies, as was the case for learning context models of medical semantic relations (Hirst and Budanitsky, 2006). Therefore, the ontology population process is time consuming and a clever semi-automatic procedure is very much in demand. To address this issue, we adapted the relation extraction approach discussed in Schutz and Buitelaar (2005) to our context in MEDICO, where the steps we took and the initial results are explained in Buitelaar et al. (2007). Having identified the statistically most relevant domain terms (i.e., ontology concepts), those about anatomy, given the domain ontology (FMA) and domain corpora (Wikipedia), we searched for relations that occur between them. For this purpose we implemented a simple algorithm that traverses each sentence, looking for the following pattern:

Noun: Verb + Preposition: Noun
(Term) (Relation) (Term)

This pattern enables us to identify possibly relevant relations between terms. The following table (Table 7) presents some early results of this work. In future work we will apply further statistical measures and linguistic heuristics to identify the most salient relations within each corpus, with an emphasis on relation identification in a more specific lymphoma corpus obtained from PubMed.

As a result, we were able to identify 1,082 non-unique relations (i.e., including syntactic variants such as *analysed_by* and *analyzed_by).* One important requirement that comes naturally at this stage is to assess the quality and the relevance of these relations, which should be done by the clinician. Upon the clinician's approval, these relationships can be used to enrich the ontology at hand and populate the found relation instances. As discussed earlier, according to our experiences throughout the MEDICO project, the ontologies at hand do not match the requirements

Table 7. Semi-automatically extracted term-relation-term triples

Term	Relation (Verb+Prep.)	Term
anterior	known as	anterior scalene muscle
dentate nucleus	subdivided into	anterior
muscle	situated between	anterior
body	divided into	anterior
anterior	continued over	zygomatic arch
hand	used for	anterior
artery	supplied by	medulla
artery	released if	ulnar
vein	associated with	artery
bronchopulmonary segment	supplied by	artery

set by the application (see Ontology Customization under KEMM). (Most of the times there are redundancies, or important information is missing.) Semi-automatic relation extraction helps overcome this difficulty. Having identified the statistically most domain-relevant relations (about anatomy, radiology, and diseases in our case), we can customize the ontologies we use according to our domain specific needs by populating them with these relations.

More concretely, if we take the FMA, this is an ontology about the human anatomy. Similarly, RadLex provides terminology about radiology. In MEDICO, we need all this information but we need it in a specific way, i.e., in a way that relates most to the medical image semantics. As this is a very specific need, it cannot be expected that FMA, RadLex, or any other medical ontology will provide us with these relations out-of-the-box. Therefore, the relationships we have extracted from our specific domain corpora are valuable in the sense that they enable us to enhance the ontologies we use (or fragments thereof) according to our specific needs.

As an example, even though FMA comes with many relation instances, it does not contain relationships such as *'stimulated by'*. However, this relationship is present within the pattern "gastric acid *stimulated by* distention". This pattern demonstrates how terms from different ontologies (or terminologies) relate to each other specifically within the medical imaging context. Hence, including these kinds of domain specific or *custom* relationships is necessary to be able to adapt the ontologies according to our domain specific needs. In this way, we find ourselves within the portion of the FMA we use in our application. We are, however, gaining an additional radiological (and disease) perspective that comes with the relations. As important as it is to be able to extract the domain specific relations, their accuracy and relevance still need to be assessed. As our relation extraction is a semi-automatic process, it is not possible to expect no noise. Thus, correct and relevant relationships are identified as well as wrong or irrelevant ones. Sometimes, correct relationships combine with wrong terms yielding a wrong pattern altogether as in 'gene *derived from* antibody'.

The ultimate solution to avoid such noise (especially in a sensitive domain like human health) is, in our opinion, to involve the expert in the process. An effective way to involve the clinical expert in the process is to present him the relationships and their combinations with the terms (i.e., our query patterns) and ask him for feedback. In this way, the clinical expert can say whether what has been identified is correct or false. One important aspect to keep in mind is that the clinical expert is not a computer scientist. Therefore, his involvement within the process needs to be as user friendly and least technical as possible. This requirement can be fulfilled by providing him with a simple, easy-to-use and easy-to-understand interface that displays the results of the relation extraction. Upon explaining the overall objective of our task, i.e., populating (or customizing) the ontologies with what will be displayed, we can show our results using the interface. Driven by this motivation, we developed an interactive clinical query browser that displays the results of the relation extraction to the clinical expert. The next subsection gives an overview of this browser and explains its functionality.

Interactive GUI Environment for Medical Experts

The purpose of the interactive clinical query browser is to display the semi-automatically extracted domain relations and the related terms (i.e., the patterns) to the user and receive his feedback. We expect two different types of feedback. First, the expert accepts or rejects the relationships either because they are wrong or they are irrelevant. Second, he types in or dictates his general comments as free text. The relationships that he confirms will be stored and used to populate the ontology in the next step. The rest will be deleted. His free text general comments remain reference to the knowledge engineer. (In the future, however, this text may also be processed to extract further valuable information.) Figure 6 displays the views of the interface that the user sees. On the left hand side (Figure 6, (1)) all domain resources that have been used are displayed in a tree form. The first node on top 'Clinical Query Patterns' has, as of now, three children 'Foundational Model of Anatomy', 'Radiology Lexicon' and 'Image Features'. Clicking on these children nodes will display the term-relation-term triples (i.e., the query patterns that have been identified by using the corresponding ontology or terminology).

One exception is the Image Features, where we have obtained a list of features from our partners that characterize the medical image that was automatically parsed by the image recognition algorithms. Clicking on the 'Foundational Model of Anatomy' node displays the second view as shown in Figure 6 (2). Here the patterns are displayed along with their calculated relevance scores that we explained earlier. The user has the possibility to sort this list according to any column he chooses. In the example they are sorted according to the relevance score. Each pattern can be deleted upon the user's request. The bottom pane allows the user to enter his general assessment and comments.

The 'Corpora' node of the tree has two children, which are 'Wikipedia' and the 'PubMed'. When clicked, they display the domain corpora that have been used to extract the patterns that include the relationships. Figure 6 (3) shows the Wikipedia Anatomy Corpus with the links to the corpus files and the corresponding Wikipedia pages where the files were obtained. The next example, Figure 6 (4), displays what the corpus file looks like after it has been processed to include the linguistic information that is necessary for the relation extraction algorithm. The final example in Figure 6 (5) shows the original Wikipedia page. We proposed a methodology for the population of

Figure 6. (1) First view that the clinician sees from the browser. The tree on the left reveals the contents available for browsing. (2) Second view of the browser that displays the query patterns as a sortable list. (3) Anatomy corpus files with links to original Wikipedia files. (4) Wikipedia Abdomen.xml with POS tagging. (5) Corresponding page in Wikipedia.

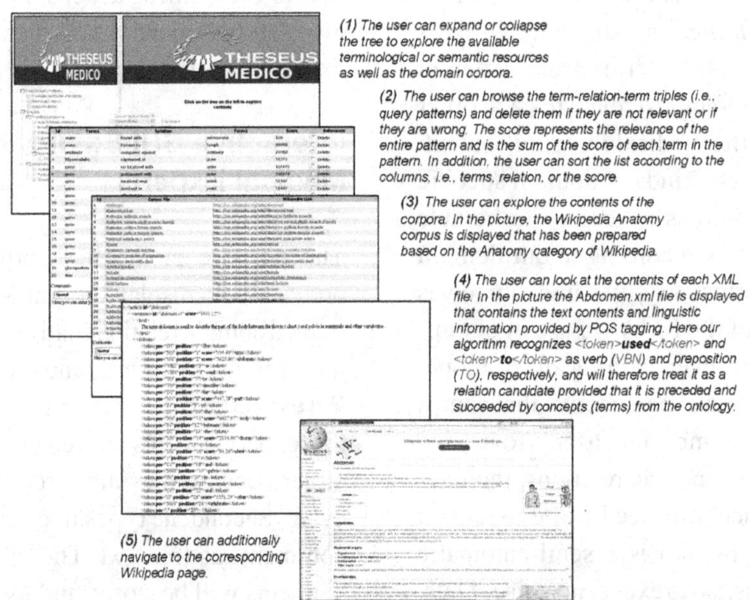

medical ontologies; we gave the user the control over the process while automatically offering the best suggestions for the ontology population according the relation extraction step.

CONCLUSION AND FUTURE WORK

We described the three pillars of ontology treatment of the medical domain in a comprehensive case study within the THESEUS MEDICO project. These pillars are knowledge engineering, ontology mediation and alignment, and ontology population and learning. Our ontology engineering approach was constrained by the clinical knowledge requirements upon which we developed the KEMM methodology.

Concerning ontology mediation and alignment, we investigated linguistic-based, corpus-based, and dialogue-based ontology alignment. We identified linguistic features and variants that can be used to compare linguistic (textual) contexts of ontology concepts in corpora leading to the corpus-based ontology alignment aspect of our approach. In addition, we considered methods that are required for interactive and incremental ontology mapping and evaluated the impact of dialogue-based user feedback in this process.

We hypothesise that only a combination of the knowledge engineering and ontology mediation methods and rules can result in effective and efficient ontology treatment and semantic mediation. In addition, the clinician's feedback and willingness to semantically annotate images and mediation rules plays a central role, just as our capabilities to follow the official procedure of the (lymphoma) finding guidelines. In this respect, we were particularly interested in semi-automatic approaches which we not only envisioned for ontology alignment, but also for the population of ontologies. We tried to provide a semi-automatic knowledge acquisition procedure and implemented an interactive GUI environment for the medical expert. In order to ease the task of determining whether the recommended instance to be populated is correct or not, we implemented a GUI environment for the medical expert and demonstrated its interactive use by example.

In future work, we will investigate techniques to better translate formal mapping uncertainties into appropriate dialogue-level questions or suggestions displayed in a GUI for the radiologist. Furthermore, we aim to address the general difficulty that users might not be able to provide helpful feedback in the course of a dialogue or an offline GUI environment session.

A nice GUI feature to have would be the possibility to use previously found instances or classes. For example, new instances could be populated when using previously found domain or range values. In this way, a partly correct relation instance (automatically found) could be effectively re-used. This would enable the user to provide even more constructive feedback, rather than a pure reject/accept signal. This would extremely enhance the usability of the GUI tool and the effectiveness of the expert user's involvement as anticipated, particularly by the dialogical interaction scenario. In addition, the efficiency of the semi-automatic annotation approach could be improved by increasing the precision of the mappings presented to the medical expert. As experimentation shows, most time gets lost when trying to single out the false positives. Additionally, the terminologies for existing medical knowledge might change or should be expanded. Both aspects require ontology evolution, which may be addressed by an ontology learning strategy, specifically from text data about contemporary medical issues that are available in the form of the incoming patient records and new scientific articles.

ACKNOWLEDGMENT

This research has been supported in part by the THESEUS Programme in the CTC WP4 and the MEDICO use case, both of which are funded by the German Federal Ministry of Economics and Technology (01MQ07016). The responsibility for this publication lies with the authors. Special thanks goes to our clinical partner Dr. Alexander Cavallaro, University Hospital Erlangen.

REFERENCES

Bernstein, P. A., Melnik, S., & Churchill, J. E. (2006). Incremental schema matching. U. Dayal, K.-Y. Whang, D. B. Lomet, G. Alonso, G. M. Lohman, M. L. Kersten, S. K. Cha, & Y.-K. Kim (Eds.), *Proceedings of the 32nd International Conference on Very Large Data Bases* (Vol. 32) (pp. 1167-1170). Seoul, Korea. PA: VLDB Endowment.

Buitelaar, P., Wennerberg, P. O., & Zillner, S. (2008). Statistical term profiling for query pattern mining. In D. Demner-Fushman, S. Ananiadou, K. B. Cohen, J. Pestian, J. Tsujii, & B. Webber (Eds.), *ACL BioNLP Workshop Current Trends in Biomedical Natural Language Processing* (p.114). Columbus, Ohio. PA: Association for Computational Linguistics.

Chalupsky, H. (2000). Ontomorph. A translation system for symbolic knowledge. In A.G. Cohn, F. Giunchiglia, & B. Selman (Eds.), *7th Intl. Conf. on Principles of Knowledge Representation and Reasoning KR'2000* (pp. 471-482). Breckenridge, Colorado. PA: Morgan Kaufmann Publishers.

Cimino, J. J., & Barnett, G. O. (1993). *Automatic knowledge acquisition from MEDLINE 32*(2). *Methods of Information in Medicine*, 120–130.

de Bruijn, J., Ehrig, M., Feier, C., Martín-Recuerda, F., Scharffe, F., & Weiten, M. (2006). Ontology mediation, merging and aligning. In J. Davies R. Studer, & P. Warren (Eds.), *Semantic Web Technologies: Trends and Research in Ontology-based Systems*. PA: Wiley.

Doan, A., Madhavan, J., Domingos, P., & Halevy, A. (2003). Ontology matching: A machine learning approach. In S. Staab & R. Studer (Eds.), *Handbook on ontologies in information systems* (pp. 397-416). Berlin Heidelberg, PA: Springer-Verlag.

Euzenat, J., & Shvaiko, P. (Eds.). (2007). *Ontology matching*. Berlin Heidelberg, PA: Springer-Verlag.

Grüninger, M., & Uschold, M. (1996). Ontologies: Principles, methods and applications. *The Knowledge Engineering Review, 1*(2), 93–155.

Hearst, M. A. (1998). Automated discovery of Wordnet relations. In Ch. Fellbaum (Ed.), *WordNet: An electronic lexical database*. Cambridge, PA: MIT Press.

Hirst, A., & Budanitsky, G. (2006). Evaluating Wordnet-based measures of lexical semantic relatedness. [Cambridge, PA: MIT Press.]. *Computational Linguistics, 32*(2), 13–47.

Johnson, H. L., Cohen, K., B., Baumgartner, W.,A., Jr., Lu, Z., Bada, M., Kester, T., Kim, H., & Hunter, L. (2006). Evaluation of lexical methods for detecting relationships between concepts from multiple ontologies. Pac. Symp. *Biocomputing*, 28-39.

Kalfoglou, Y., & Schorlemmer, M. (2005). Ontology mapping: The state of the art. In Y. Kalfoglou, M. Schorlemmer, A. Sheth, S. Staab, & M. Uschold (Eds.), *Ser. Dagstuhl Seminar Proceedings No: 0439. Semantic interoperability and integration*. PA: Internationales Begegnungs- und Forschungszentrum fuer Informatik (IBFI).

Madhavan, J., Bernstein, P., Chen, K., Halevy, A., & Shenoy, P. (2005). Corpus-based schema matching. In *21st International Conference on Data Engineering Proceedings* (pp. 57-68).Tokyo, Japan. PA: IEEE Computer Society.

Maedche, A., & Staab, S. (2000). Discovering conceptual relations from text. In W., Horn (Ed.),

Proceedings of the 14th European Conference on Artificial Intelligence (pp. 321-325). Amsterdam, PA: IOS Press.

Magnini, B., Speranza, M., & Girardi, C. (2004). A Semantic-based Approach to Interoperability of Classification Hierarchies: Evaluation of Linguistic Techniques. In *20th International Conference on Computational Linguistics* (p. 1133). Geneva, Switzerland. PA: Association for Computational Linguistics. Falconer, S., M., Noy, N., & Storey, M.A.D. (2006). Towards understanding the needs of cognitive support for ontology mapping. In P. Shvaiko, J. Euzenat, N.F. Noy, & H. Stuckenschmidt (Eds.), *Proceedings of the ISWC'06 International Workshop OM-2006* (Vol. 225). Athens, Georgia. PA: CEUR-WS.org

McGuinness, D., Fikes, R., Rice, J., & Wilder, S. (2000). The chimaera ontology environment. In *Proceedings of the Seventeenth National Conference on Artificial Intelligence and Twelfth Conference on Innovative Applications of Artificial Intelligence* (pp. 1123-1124.) PA: AAAI Press / The MIT Press.

Melnik, S., Garcia-Molina, H., & Rahm, E. (2002). Similarity flooding: A versatile graph matching algorithm and its application to schema matching. In *18th International Conference on Data Engineering* (pp. 117-128).

Noy, N. (2004). Tools for mapping and merging ontologies: In Staab, S & Studer, R, (Eds.). *Handbook on Ontologies* (pp. 365-384). Springer-Verlag.

Noy, N., & Musen, M. (2000). PROMPT: Algorithm and tool for automated ontology merging and alignment. Artificial Intelligence. In *Proceedings of the Seventeenth National Conference on Artificial Intelligence* Austin, TX. PA: AAAI Press.

Noy, N., & Musen, M. (2001). Anchor-PROMPT: Using non-local context for semantic matching. In *Proceeding IJCAI 2001 workshop on ontology and information sharing* (pp. 63-70). Washington, USA. PA: AAAI Press.

Rahm, E., & Bernstein, P. A. (2001). A survey of approaches to automatic schema matching. *The VLDB Journal, 10*(4), 334–350. doi:10.1007/s007780100057

Robertson, G., Czerwinski, M. P., & Churchill, J. E. (2005). Visualization of mappings between schemas. In *Proceedings SIGCHI Conference on Human factors in Computing Systems* (pp. 431-439).

Rosse, C., & Mejino, J., L. (2003). A reference ontology for bioinformatics: the foundational model of anatomy. *Journal of Biomedical Informatics*, (36): 478–500. doi:10.1016/j.jbi.2003.11.007

Shvaiko, P., & Euzenat, J. (2005). A survey of schema-based matching approaches. *Journal on Data Semantics*, (4), 146-171.

Sonntag, D. (2007a). Embedded Distributed Text Mining and Semantic Web Technology. In *Proceedings of the NATO Advanced Study Institute Workshop on Mining Massive Data Sets for Security*. PA: NATO Publishing.

Sonntag, D. (2008). Towards dialogue-based interactive semantic mediation in the medical domain. In *Proceedings Third International Workshop on Ontology Matching (OM-2008) collocated with the 7th International Semantic Web Conference*. Karlsruhe, Germany. PA: CEUR-WS.org

Sonntag, D., Engel, R., Herzog, G., Pfalzgraf, A., Pfleger, N., Romanelli, M., & Reithinger, N. (2007b). SmartWeb Handheld. Multimodal interaction with ontological knowledge bases and semantic web services (extended version). In T. Huang, A. Nijholt, M. Pantic, & A. Plentland, (Eds.), *LNAI Special Volume on Human Computing* (Vol. 4451). Berlin, Heidelberg, PA: Springer Verlag.

Starbucks, W. H. (1993). "Watch were you step!" or Indian starbuck amid the perils of academe (Rated PG). In A.G. Bedeion (Ed.), *Management Laureates* (Vol. 3) (pp. 65-110).

Vintar, Š., Todorovski, L., Sonntag, D., & Buitelaar, P. (2003). Evaluating context features for medical relation nining. In *Proceedings Workshop on Data Mining and Text Mining for Bioinformatics at the 14th European Conference on Machine Learning.* Berlin, Heidelberg: Springer Verlag.

Wennerberg, P., Zillner, S., Moeller, M., Buitelaar, P., & Sintek, M. (2008b). KEMM: A knowledge engineering methodology in the medical domain. In C. Eschenbach & M. Grüninger (Eds.), *Proceedings 5th international conference on formal ontology in information Systems (FOIS).* PA: IOS Press.

Wennerberg, P. O., Buitelaar, P., & Zillner, S. (2008a). Towards a human anatomy data set for query pattern mining based on wikipedia and domain semantic resources. *In Proceedings Workshop on Building and Evaluating Resources for Biomedical Text Mining at LREC.* Marakesch. PA:ELDA.

ENDNOTES

1. http://sig.biostr.washington.edu/projects/fm/FME/index.html
2. http://www.rsna.org/radlex
3. http://nciterms.nci.nih.gov/NCIBrowser/Connect.do?dictionary=NCI_Thesaurus&bookmarktag=1
4. http://www.obofoundry.org
5. http://www.bioontology.org/ncbo/faces/index.xhtml
6. http://www.ncbi.nlm.nih.gov/pubmed
7. http://www.obofoundry.org/cgi-bin/detail.cgi?id=chebi
8. http://www.obofoundry.org/cgi-bin/detail.cgi?id=cell
9. http://www.obofoundry.org/cgi-bin/detail.cgi?id=brenda
10. http://lucene.apache.org/java/docs
11. http://www.opengalen.org
12. http://www.nlm.nih.gov/research/umls
13. We use the term transformation grammar here to imply that given a set of rules, multiword expressions can be transformed into syntactic variants that nevertheless preserve their semantics. The concept of transformation grammar was first introduced by Noam Chomsky, where the focus was on obtaining passive sentences from the active ones.
14. Actually, related work on corpus-based methods for ontology alignment does not exist in literature, at least not under this name. In the ontology matching community (see Euzenat and Shvaiko, 2007, p. 65) using statistics of text corpora would best correspond to extensional matching techniques, where data analysis in the form of the frequency distributions is used. Sonntag (2007a) demonstrated the embedding of linguistic-based approaches for instance matching, such as matching the canonical word representations, into schema matching approaches.
15. http://www.coli.uni-saarland.de/~thorsten/tnt
16. http://www.cis.upenn.edu/~treebank
17. http://phaselibs.opendfki.de

This work was previously published in the Journal of Cases on Information Technology, Vol. 11, Issue 4, edited by M. Khosrow-Pour, pp. 47-73, copyright 2009 by IGI Publishing (an imprint of IGI Global).

Chapter 9
A Use Case for Ontology Evolution and Interoperability:
The IEC Utility Standards Reference Framework 62357

Mathias Uslar
OFFIS – Institute for Information Technology, Germany

Fabian Grüning
OFFIS – Institute for Information Technology, Germany

Sebastian Rohjans
OFFIS – Institute for Information Technology, Germany

EXECUTIVE SUMMARY

Within this chapter, the authors provide two use cases on semantic interoperability in the electric utility industry based on the IEC TR 62357 seamless integration architecture. The first use case on semantic integration based on ontologies deals with the integration of the two heterogeneous standards families IEC 61970 and IEC 61850. Based on a quantitative analysis, we outline the need for integration and provide a solution based on our framework, COLIN. The second use cases points out the need to use better metadata semantics in the utility branch, also being solely based on the IEC 61970 standard. The authors provide a solution to use the CIM as a domain ontology and taxonomy for improving data quality. Finally, this chapter outlines open questions and argues that proper semantics and domain models based on international standards can improve the systems within a utility.

DOI: 10.4018/978-1-60566-894-9.ch009

BACKGROUND

In the electric utility domain, several changes impose new requirements on the IT infrastructure of companies. In the past, the generating structure used to be very close aligned to the communication infrastructure. Electric energy was delivered top-down from the high voltage grid having large-scale generation attached to the lower voltage grid and the households. The corresponding communication infrastructure was arranged similar, as steering information be mainly passed down the vertical supply chain while data points from the field level were submitted to the SCADA (Supervisory Control and Data Acquisition System).

With the upcoming distributed power generation respectively the legal requirements imposed by federal regulation and the resulting unbundling, things have changed a lot. On the one hand, deploying new generation facilities like wind power plants or fuel cells, energy is fed into the grid at different voltage levels and by different producers – former customers having their own power generation can now both act as consumers and producers, which feed into the utilities' grid. Therefore, the communication infrastructure has to be changed. On the other hand, the legal unbundling leads to separation of systems, which have to be open to more market participants. Hence, this results in more systems that have to be integrated and more data formats for compliance with the market participants - the overall need for standards increases. This problem must be addressed by an adequate IT-infrastructure within the utility, supported by architectures like SOA (Service-oriented Architectures). Regarding this scope, the IEC (International Electrotechnical Commission) has developed data models, interfaces and architectures (Robinson, 2002) for both running the power-grid and automating the attached substations. Unfortunately, those standards have been developed by different working groups and therefore lack some harmonization although they have to be used in context (Uslar, 2006). Furthermore, the semantic techniques imposed by the CIM are not properly used. This contribution shows a possible solution for an integration based on semantic techniques for two use cases we would like to address, first general semantic ontology integration and second data quality management based on meta annotation.

The following contribution is as structured as follows. First, we give a brief introduction into the IEC TC 57 standards framework in Section 2 with a special focus on the two biggest domain ontologies available in the IEC TC 57 reference framework, the IEC 61970 family for IT integration with SCADA and the IEC 61850 family dealing with substation and distributed energy generation automation. We show the basic metrics for the two ontologies and excerpts on how they were developed and how their OWL serializations look like.

Afterwards, we summarize the current challenges imposed to the ontologies from practice. We argue that some of those challenges have already been addressed and outline the most striking problem when dealing with changing ontologies in the same domain, the need for constant integration and consistency.

Therefore, we introduce our domain specific alignment methodology, the COLIN framework and its results on the Common Information Model CIM and the IEC 61850 family in section 4.

Section 5 provides an example of using ontologies, especially, the CIM domain ontology to build an interoperable data quality management system called VDE and WDE comprising legacy systems using D2RQ.

Finally, the chapter concludes with a summary of the findings in this paper and an outlook of our future work. We emphasize on the actual benefits form using the ontologies as a technological basis and discuss both advantages and disadvantages.

SETTING THE STAGE

The IEC has the vision of enabling seamless integration of both data and functions for the electric utility domain using their standards reference framework. Within this standards framework, the so-called TC 57 seamless integration architecture, different working groups have developed several standards. Unfortunately, those groups have different ideas about what to standardize and the overall focus of the standardization efforts.

Two main standards families exist within the TC 57 framework, the so-called IEC 61970 family including the Common Information Model CIM and the IEC 61850 family for substation communication coping with the data exchanged between SCADA systems and the field devices. Those two families have been developed with a different technical background resulting in different serializations. The next section will give short introductions to those standards and provide a glimpse on the structure and sizes of the models to further understand the real world problem of integration of large structural heterogeneous ontologies.

The IEC 61970 Family – The Common Information Model CIM

The CIM (IEC, 2003) can be seen as the basic domain ontology for the electric utility domain at SCADA level. It is standardized in two different sub-families, namely the IEC 61970 family for the data model and OPC-based data models dealing directly with the day-to-day business of running the electric power grid.

Furthermore, the IEC 61968 family, which has to cover the needed objects to integrate the CIM into the overall utility having to exchange data with systems like GIS (Geographical Information Sys-

Figure 1. Top Level view on the CIM 11r_v00 packages

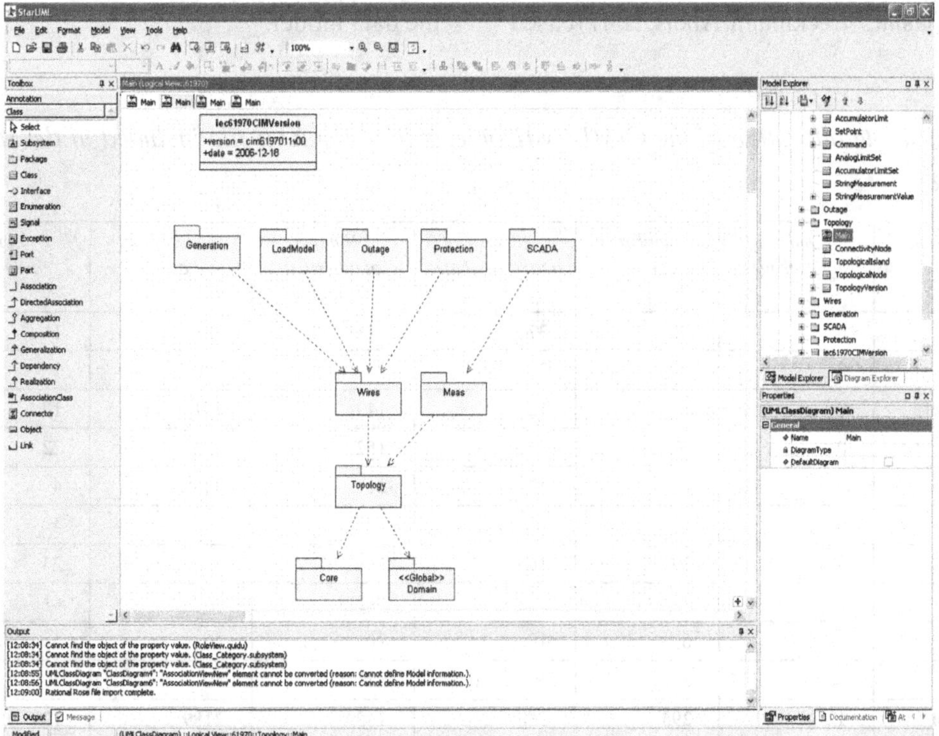

Table 1. Absolute allocation of the CIM11_v01-objects from the XMI-file

Package name	Number of sub packages	Number of classes	Number of native attributes	Number of inherited attributes	Number of total attributes	Number of associations
IEC 61970	12	293	780	1409	2189	126
IEC 61968	34	411	1021	4823	5844	502
Reservation	0	7	6	24	30	3
Market Operations	0	61	183	627	810	86
Financial	0	9	4	126	130	18
Energy Scheduling	0	19	25	198	223	35
IEC 61850	0	18	0	42	42	15
CIM11_v01	**53**	**819**	**2021**	**7249**	**9270**	**785**

tems), CSS (Customer Support System), or ERP (Enterprise-Resource Planning), is covered.

Overall, the CIM data model covers 53 UML packages covering roundabout 800 classes with more than 9200 attributes. A lot of effort and work has been put into the model to cover the most important objects for the electric utility domain. Furthermore, different serializations exist. First, XML and XML schema exist for building your own Enterprise Application Integration (EAI) messages (Uslar, Streekmann, Abels, 2007) based on the CIM and to use pre-defined messages built by the IEC.

Additionally, RDF serializations and RDF schemas used for modeling the graphs of power grids for electrical distribution exist, and, based on this work, an overall CIM OWL serialization for dealing with the concepts of the domain has been developed.

The following figures and tables 1, 2 and 3 show the extend and distribution of objects within the data model.

Table 2. Absolute allocation of the CIM11_v01-objects from the XMI-file included in the IEC 61970 sub packages

Package name	Number of sub packages	Number of classes	Number of native attributes	Number of inherited attributes	Number of total attributes	Number of associations
Core	0	28	37	144	181	11
Domain	0	118	249	0	249	2
Load Model	0	13	12	149	161	10
Meas	0	27	40	152	192	22
Outage	0	4	13	21	34	4
Topology	0	4	9	18	27	4
Wires	0	39	165	301	466	24
Generation	2	48	225	562	787	41
SCADA	0	6	10	30	40	4
Protection	0	5	18	32	50	4
IEC 61970	**12**	**293**	**780**	**1409**	**2189**	**126**

Table 3. Absolute allocation of the CIM11_v01-objects from the XMI-file included in the IEC 61968 sub packages

Package name	*Number of sub packages*	*Number of classes*	*Number of native attributes*	*Number of inherited attributes*	*Number of total attributes*	*Number of associations*
Assets	6	169	470	2959	3429	185
Consumers	0	16	59	193	252	29
Core2	7	52	116	383	499	45
Documentation	6	30	86	249	335	48
ERP_Support	0	41	64	393	457	44
Work	8	54	135	445	580	103
GML_Suport	0	48	89	201	290	48
IEC 61968	**34**	**411**	**1021**	**4823**	**5844**	**502**

Table 1 provides an overview of the absolute allocation of the CIM model in revision 11_v01. Looking at the numbers, you see that there are two main packages, the IEC 61970 and IEC 61968 package, all others packages are smaller and not the very core of the CIM. The CIM is a fully object-oriented data model using all UML mechanisms like inheritance and packaging. Due to strong use of inheritance, the absolute numbers of attributes for the classes is rather high. The absolute number of associations between the classes is rather high compared the metrics for the classes, the CIM model is not tree-like organized with some classes on top, broadening going down the model layers but rather broad at all levels starting at subpackage layers and a fully meshed graph. Classes are strongly interwoven and changes cascade trough the model when they occur. Tables 2 and 3 show

Figure 2. Subview of the load model package: main view

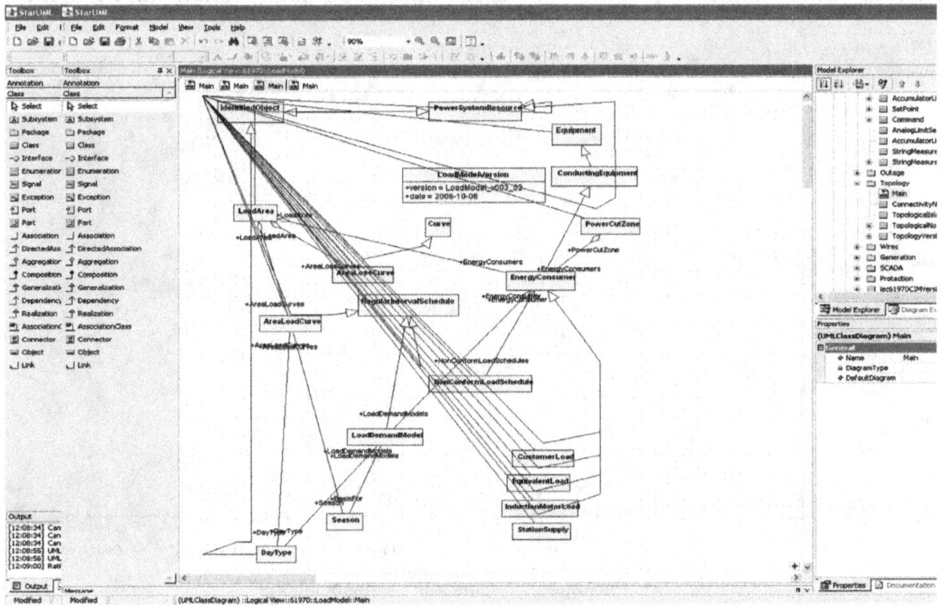

more detailed figures of the IEC 61970 and IEC 61968 packages.

The idea of tracking those metrics was to find out the focus of the CIM. When IEC WG experts were asked, they could not name the largest or most detailed class. They could not name the largest packages or the most interwoven one. They did not know the distribution of viewpoints for the power-grid in their data models, which makes it very hard to find starting points for a good integration with other standards like the IEC 61850 one.

Therefore, we argue that that those figures and metrics are essential to the domain engineers and new users since they provide a good overview where the most detailed parts of the models lie and where the focus of the overall model is. Discussions with experts working with the CIM for years have shown that even they have not been aware where the most detailed parts were and that the IEC's focus has shifted since the first model due to new stakeholders bringing in their objects and relations.

From these figures, we can realize that different scopes exist and changes in those dense parts of the model have a stronger impact since inheritance is used more than in parts where only little objects actually exist. Figures 3 and 4 show the development of the CIM's data within the last 6 versions, i.e. 5 years. We see bumps in the model where large projects have created new objects needed not previously incorporated in the CIM. The biggest one was the integration of the IEC 61968 family that was introduced in the 10_v003 version. The CIM does not grow continually like big taxonomies known to integration experts; a lot of effort has to be spent on manually updating existing applications that is a difficult process.

Figure 5 shows excerpts from the model loaded into our mapping bench for both having an overview of the model and creating the metrics needed for our evaluation and mapping approaches for CIM and IEC 61850. It provides some insights on how each individual class is handled in terms of attributes and associations in the CIM model.

For a better overview of how the CIM ontology is built, figure 6 provides an example of how the ontology is actually built and serialized.

Section 2.2 of this contribution is going to show how we adopted the techniques used by the

Figure 3. History of the number of packages, classes and associations included in the CIM

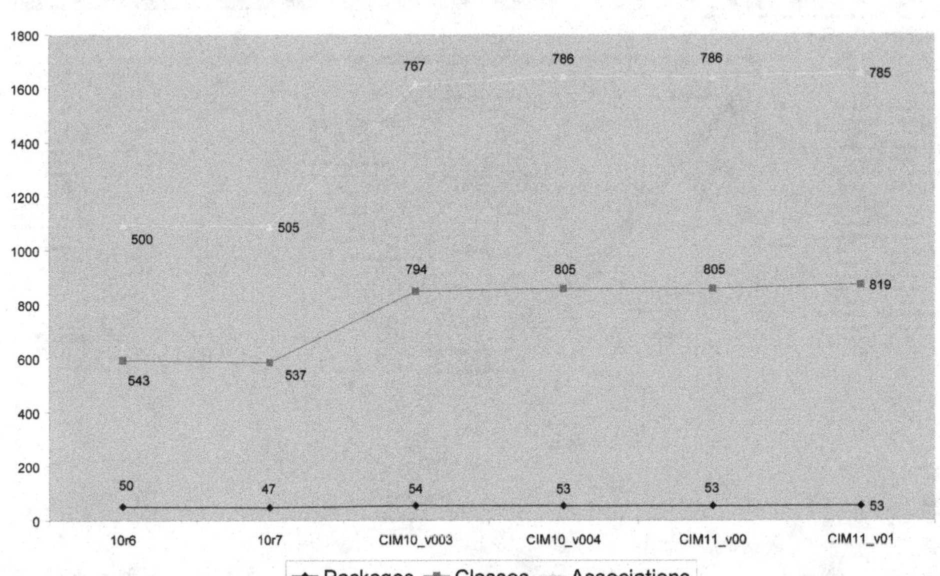

Figure 4. History of the number of native, inherited and total attributes included in the CIM

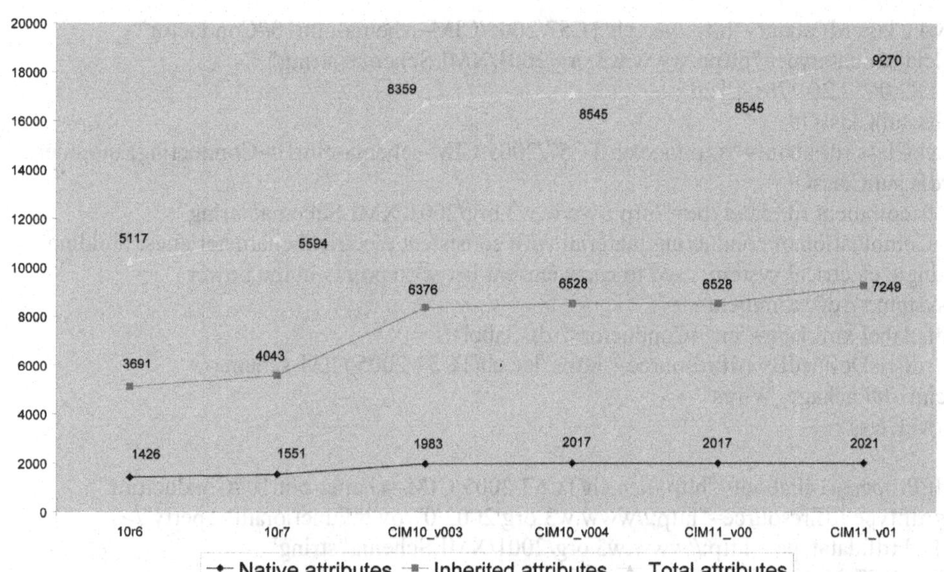

IEC and its working groups when dealing with the CIM to build a proper electronic model of the IEC 61850 family for substation communication. We will discuss why the overall data model is so different from the UML-model of the CIM and show the differences which make for difficult integration of both.

The IEC 61850 Family - Communication for Substations

The IEC TC 57 working group WG 10 has developed the IEC 61850 family dealing with substation automation systems and the corresponding communications. The standard itself is very large, comprising sub-standards of different kinds like communication protocols, data models, security standards etc.

Figure 5. CIMBench showing the conductor class

Class:	**Conductor**
Description:	Combination of conducting material with consistent electrical characteristics, building a single electrical system, use d to carry current between points in the power system.
Included in:	**61970 . Wires**
Inheritance Hierarchy:	BaseElement <- IdentifiedObject <- PowerSystemResource <- Equipment <- ConductingEquipment <- Conductor; LNodeContainer; SubEquipmentContainer
Attributes total (native / inherited):	**16 (9 / 7)**
Associations total (native / inherited):	**32 (3 / 29)**
Children:	**2**

Attributes

b0ch	**Susceptance**
bch	**Susceptance**
g0ch	**Conductance**
gch	**Conductance**
length	**LongLength**
r	**Resistance**
r0	**Resistance**
x	**Reactance**
x0	**Reactance**

Figure 6. The OWL Serialization of the Conductor type and the resistance property r

```
<owl:Class rdf:about="http://iec.ch/TC57/2005/CIM-schema-cim10#Conductor">
<j.1:id rdf:datatype="http://www.w3.org/2001/XMLSchema#string"
>S.082.0657.26.278</j.1:id>
<rdfs:subClassOf>
<owl:Class rdf:about="http://iec.ch/TC57/2005/CIM-schema-cim10#ConductingEquipment"/>
</rdfs:subClassOf>
<rdfs:comment rdf:datatype="http://www.w3.org/2001/XMLSchema#string"
  >Combination of conducting material with consistent electrical characteristics, building a
  single electrical system, used to carry current between points in the power
  system.</rdfs:comment>
<rdfs:label xml:lang="en">Conductor</rdfs:label>
  <rdfs:isDefinedBy rdf:resource="http://iec.ch/TC57/2005/CIM-schema-
  cim10#Package_Wires"/>
</owl:Class>

<rdf:Property rdf:about="http://iec.ch/TC57/2005/CIM-schema-cim10#Conductor.r">
  <rdf:type rdf:resource="http://www.w3.org/2002/07/owl#FunctionalProperty"/>
<j.1:id rdf:datatype="http://www.w3.org/2001/XMLSchema#string"
S.082.0657.26.284</j.1:id>
  <rdfs:domain rdf:resource="http://iec.ch/TC57/2005/CIM-schema-cim10#Conductor"/>
  <j.1:hasStereotype rdf:resource="http://langdale.com.au/2005/UML#attribute"/>
  <rdf:type rdf:resource="http://www.w3.org/2002/07/owl#DatatypeProperty"/>
  <rdfs:isDefinedBy rdf:resource="http://iec.ch/TC57/2005/CIM-schema-
  cim10#Package_Wires"/>
<rdfs:label xml:lang="en">r</rdfs:label>
  <rdfs:comment rdf:datatype="http://www.w3.org/2001/XMLSchema#string">Positive
  sequence series resistance of the entire line section.</rdfs:comment>
  <rdfs:range rdf:resource="http://iec.ch/TC57/2005/CIM-schema-cim10#Resistance"/>
</rdf:Property>
```

The overall control system domain for IEC 61850 is system automation (Kostic et al, 2004). While the CIM focuses on energy management systems, the IT domains here are substation intra-application communication and, for the CIM, control-center intra-application communication. Both standards have a basic data model but the serializations differ completely. While only a small subset for engineering of substations needs a XML-serialization in IEC 61850, all CIM objects can be serialized using XML, RDF or OWL. In addition, the IEC 61850 family lacks a significant support of APIs – only an abstract communication interface is provided. Those differences lead to problems when coping in real-world projects with the IEC TC 57 reference framework.

The data model used within the context of IEC 61850 is based on a strictly hierarchical system having a tree-like taxonomy structure with three levels and composed data types – so called CDCs. Functions are integrated into the data model with a special focus on set points for control by the SCADA and data reports have to be implemented using queues and buffers. Those two features are not included in the CIM data model and therefore make harmonization a bit more difficult – we have to distinguish between different viewpoints for integration like engineering time, run-time and basic data model. So far, our approach works for basic data model and engineering time both has performance withdraws at run-time. The data model for IEC 61850 consists of just about 100 classes (so-called logical nodes LN) which have over 900 attributes (so-called data objects DOs) from the variety of around 50 base types (so-called common data classes CDCs) consisting of more or less simple types. These figures show that the standard is about as big as the CIM data model mentioned above. Figure 7 shows the tree-like structure of the individual logical nodes for the XCBR (circuit breaker) node.

Based on those facts, we have created both an electronic model and a serialization in OWL for the IEC 61850 family strictly adhering to the hierarchical model for a better acceptance with the IEC 61850 community, however risking the chance that the different modeling approach leads to a slightly more difficult mapping with the OO-based CIM model. The following table shows the overall figures for the whole standard data model dealing with IEC 61850-like data models for substation automation (61850-7-4), distributed energy producers (61850-7-420) and wind parks (61400-25-2) or hydro power plants (61850-7-410).

Individual systems are built from several logical nodes that may be combined to provide the data representation for a real world system as shown in figure 8.

Next, we see a figure showing the tree-like hierarchy of our model of the standard in the CIMBench tool and a proper way to serialize the corresponding logical node (ZCAB) for a power cable. Please note already the difference between the modeling of a power line segment in the CIM where we have the syntax name "conductor" and the model for the IEC 61850 standard naming a line segment ZCAB.

In the later sections of this paper, we will see how we identified that both working groups of the IEC have built models which overlap and how to

Figure 7. The logical node circuit breaker XCBR from [22]

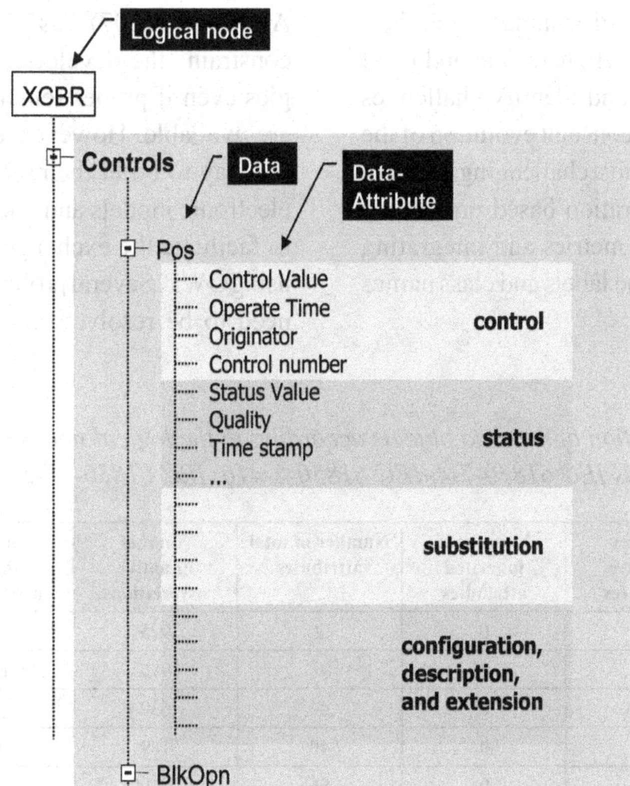

Figure 8. Model and real-world system from [22]

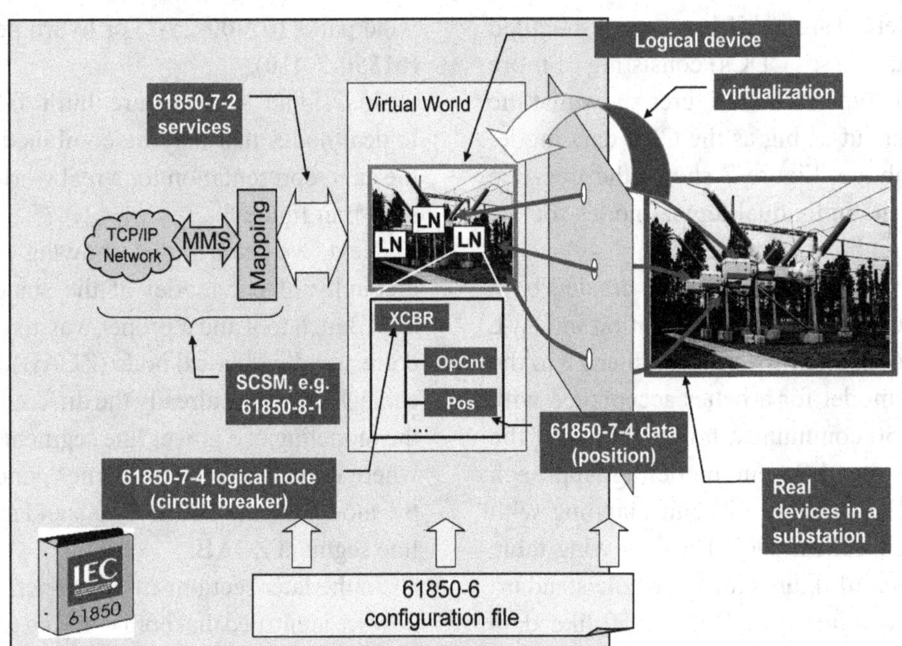

overcome this fallacy without having to change the whole standards.

In the next section, we will summarize our findings how the IEC and practioners deal and react to those two ontologies and identify challenges that are derived from the constant evolution of the domain ontologies. The most challenging problem will be the proper integration based on finding starting points form our metrics and integrating the semantics based on the labels and class names form the ontologies.

CURRENT CHALLENGES

As (Hepp, 2007) has already outlined, reality constrains the development of relevant ontologies even if proper semantics and serializations are available. However, the IEC still has taken the way to build their standards on rather large electronic models and taking modern techniques to facilitate the exchange of domain knowledge using OWL. Several problems have evolved which need to be resolved in order to further extend

Table 4. Absolute allocation of the data objects according to the logical nodes information model concerning the sub standards IEC 61850-7-4, IEC 61850-7-410, IEC 61850-7-420 and IEC 61400-25-2

Package name	Number of native attributes	Number of inherited attributes	Number of total attributes	Number of native associations	Number of inherited associations	Number of total associations
IEC 61850-7-4	2	0	2	925	900	1825
IEC 61850-7-410	0	0	0	980	1000	1980
IEC 61850-7-420	44	0	44	630	500	1130
IEC 61400-25-2	40	0	40	189	170	359
IEC 61850	**86**	**0**	**86**	**2724**	**2570**	**5294**

Figure 9. The CIMBench showing the power cable class

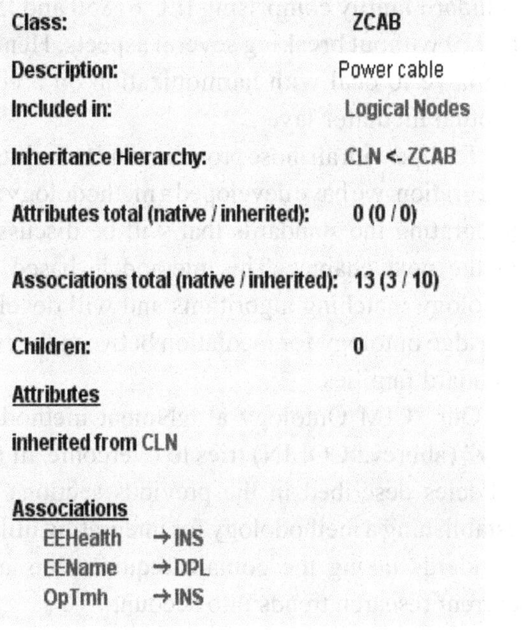

Class:	**ZCAB**
Description:	Power cable
Included in:	**Logical Nodes**
Inheritance Hierarchy:	**CLN <- ZCAB**
Attributes total (native / inherited):	**0 (0 / 0)**
Associations total (native / inherited):	**13 (3 / 10)**
Children:	**0**

Attributes
inherited from CLN

Associations
EEHealth →INS
EEName →DPL
OpTmh →INS

the use of such relevant early adopter projects for real-world OWL use. We have identified the following problems when dealing with our two large domain ontologies:

- Code-transformation techniques like MDSD (model-driven software development) have to be properly used to create both a holistic and, even more important, deterministic way to properly create the needed artifacts. Tooling is a key to deal with this problem.
- Visual editing is needed to help domain experts cope better with the formal semantics imposed by serializations like OWL – Protégé is not suitable for domain experts in the utility domain.
- A difference model to deal with new ontologies should be created to find out, what parts have changed in a new version of the ontology since it is far too large to find out manually.
- For finding out the impact of changes to individuals or interfaces, we have to deal with updates and additions to the model, deletions or changes in hierarchy and inheritance.
- A proper versioning of the ontologies (both schemes and instances) is needed.
- Checking instances for sub-profiles of the domain ontology should be done using standards reasoners like Pellet. The need for developing and updating custom reasoning and rule engines should not exist.
- The IEC has to create a maintenance process and a database format to deal with electronic models instead of using their processes originally developed for four-year maintenance cycles of paper standards.
- As more and more domain ontologies come up, more harmonization is needed since different groups see the world in a different manner. Since standards cannot easily be changed, federated and harmonized mapping ontologies should be created with least effort possible.

Challenges which are Nearly Solved

From the aforementioned problems and challenges, some have already been resolved by other projects. The model-driven development and transformation from the UML model to OWL and other serializations has been the focus of (Uslar, Streekmann, Abels, 2007). This lead to less efforts and a fast creation of needed serializations when changes to the model appeared.

A difference model to cope with changes to the CIM and finding out new parts for both instance data and schemes has been worked on in (Uslar, Dahlem, 2006). Currently, we built a checker for instance-based, mainly reasoning based CIM profile validation.

However, the most striking problem, which remains, is the fact, that the IEC versioning and standardization processes have not been adapted to the needs for electronic models. New versions of the standards are rolled out without having electronic models joining the bought paper documents and harmonization of the ontologies and models only gets little attention at all levels like engineering, basic data model and run-time. We argue that while the standards have overlapping semantics but different syntax and since products are already based on the standards, this fact leads to a resistance to fundamentally change the evolving standards while integration is necessary. Our solution is building mediation ontologies between the standards. The work conducted in this sector will be presented in section 4 of this contribution.

CASE DESCRIPTION 1: ONTOLOGY-BASED ALIGNMENT – THE COLIN FRAMEWORK

Of course, the data from both standards must be used in the same context, therefore, the SCADA and a mapping between structures from IEC 61850 must know a seamless integration of i.e. the functional description structure of a substation and IEC 61970. Furthermore, all data points and measurements from the field devices must be mapped from IEC 61850 semantics to IEC 61970 semantics. Without any doubt, those two scenarios are the most striking ones, but further scenarios exist.

Unfortunately, problems occur when trying to use the standards. The different working groups have used different naming schemes, object-oriented modeling vs. hierarchical modeling, different semantics, different tools and serializations and, the IEC 61850 model does not exist as an electronic model, just as tables within a proprietary text format (MS Word or PDF). Finally, all the standards have been made final international standards; therefore, they are being implemented by big vendors like ABB, Areva, or Siemens who rely on the stability of the standards and their products. The existing implementations cannot be harmonized at the meta-model level to a new, overall harmonized standard family comprising IEC 61850 and IEC 61970 without breaking several aspects. Hence, we have to deal with harmonization on a conceptual mediator layer.

To cope with all those problems and to facilitate integration, we have developed a methodology for integrating the standards that will be discussed in the next chapter. This method is based on ontology matching algorithms and will develop a bridge ontology for mediation between the two standard families.

Our "CIM Ontology aLigNment methodology" (abbrev.: COLIN) tries to overcome all the fallacies described in the previous sections by establishing a methodology for integrating utility standards taking the domain requirements and current research trends into account.

The approach taken to account as the scientific method was the design science approach by (Hevner et al, 2004). Our aim is to provide meaningful artifacts to evaluate the use of ontology-based integration and mediation in the context of the IEC standards. The artifacts e.g. the created mediation ontologies are rigorously evaluated and put into different contexts. We have to distinguish between harmonization at schema level or at instance level, for example. The relevance of each artifact being developed must be clear. Furthermore, the transfer of the solution found into practice and showing the importance to both scientific audience and managerial audience is of high importance.

We will briefly introduce the results for the mapping of the IEC 61970 CIM family and the IEC 61850 family based on our ontologies in the next section. Using the design science approach described by Hevner, we have identified several use cases dealing with ontology-based integration. Firstly, we had to identify the standards that had to be integrated, we did an overview and developed ontology to express the concepts and relations the different standards had in general. Secondly,

Figure 10. The OWL Serialization of the Cable logical node ZCAB and the operation time in hours property

```
<owl:Class rdf:ID="ZCAB">
        <rdfs:subClassOfrdf:resource="#Logical_Nodes"/>
        <rdfs:comment     rdf:datatype="http://www.w3.org/2001/XMLSchema#string"
        >Power cable</rdfs:comment>
</owl:Class>

<owl:ObjectProperty rdf:ID="_OpTmh_">
        <rdfs:comment rdf:datatype="http://www.w3.org/2001/XMLSchema#string"
        >Operation time
        </rdfs:comment>
        <rdfs:domain>
                <owl:Class>
                        <owl:unionOf rdf:parseType="Collection">
                                <owl:Class rdf:about="#ZCAB"/>
                        </owl:unionOf>
                </owl:Class>
        </rdfs:domain>
        <rdfs:range>
                <owl:Class>
                        <owl:unionOf rdf:parseType="Collection">
                                <owl:Class rdf:about="#INS"/>
                        </owl:unionOf>
                </owl:Class>
        </rdfs:range>
</owl:ObjectProperty>
```

we had to identify at what point the integration should take place. We mainly used the quantitative analysis from section 2 of this chapter for this to find where certain aspects like generation, grid topology, and basic data types were located in the standards.

Here, it is necessary to distinguish between run-time and engineering time integration. Run-time integration deals with the integration of messages and signal instances and is much more complicated due to complexity and time criticality. The engineering integration that means integrations of schemata or, in our case, integration of ontologies has to deal with larger amounts of data but is not time critical to the same extent – it is more tedious but does not need to be performed every time you use the system due to its nature. The first use case we developed therefore was the integration of the data models of the IEC 61970 and IEC 61850 families described in section 2 of this contribution.

The CIM could already be used as an electronic OWL model since the IEC provides it this way. Therefore, we chose the CIM as our basic domain ontology for the electric energy domain and tried to model all the other standards as OWL ontologies, too. For the IEC 61850 family, the electronic model provided by the national German IEC mirror committee DKE was used and transferred from the proprietary format to the OWL ontology format as shown in section 2.2. Afterwards, we had our two very large domain ontologies reflecting the standards that can be obtained for evaluation from (OFFIS, 2008). The next step was choosing the (better say a) proper way to integrate the two ontologies.

As argued in the sections before, international standards cannot be easily changed – implementations exist and have to be taken into account when it comes to drastic changes in the overall models and standards. Therefore, we chose to integrate the standards with a minimum of changes to the original data models. One possible solution with the minimum impact on the standards is to align them using a mediator ontology (Euzenat, Shvaiko, 2007). From the beginning, we chose to use the INRIA alignment format (Shvaiko, 2006) to cope with the mappings between the standards we needed. This format is very easy to apply and well supported by nowadays alignment tools like FALCON AO, HMatch or COMA ++ (Hong Hai, 2006).

One of our aims doing the integration was to find out whether the very large models could be integrated with minimum manual effort, e.g. mostly automatically. We tested the three aforementioned mapping tools with different configurations. In most cases, the results were not satisfying due to the different structures of the ontologies from the standards – the string matching approaches are very strong when strings are not abbreviated but as seen before, 61850: XCBR ist no good match for CIM:circuit breaker, we therefore had to rely on rdf:comments, labels and dictionaries using word stemming. Our idea was to keep the OWL ontologies as close as possible to the original standards, therefore reflecting their original hierarchies and depth structure. This has a strong impact on the overall mapping with automated matchers.

Based on the reference mediation ontology created by our domain experts, we got about 30 per cent of all the mappings correct in first place – therefore, we created a specialized mapping tool with a strong focus on the two standards, the so-called CIMBench. The main idea was to focus on string-based, lexical and dictionary-based methods. We integrated all the descriptions form the standards into the data model elements of each individual class in the OWL files and supported them by a dictionary containing the proper descriptions for each term contained in the IEC 60050 Electropedia (IEC, 2008). The OWL ontology of the Electropedia was created by scraping the website using a custom Ruby script. The overall size of the resulting upper ontology for the electric energy sector is 15 megabytes, containing descriptions in English, French and German for each concept/class like breaker or cable.

Furthermore, the original ontologies were analyzed in a semantic way to find out different parts that could be mapped better due to their original purpose having the same focus. The CIM is divided into UML packages whereas the IEC 61850 model is divided into twelve groups of (logical) nodes having the same starting letter from A-Z, this means there are about 26 packages. An analysis performed on the intentions of each package lead to the following results for a partitioning shown in Figure 12.

The packages in the middle have been sliced from the large ontologies and have been mapped with the custom CIMBench mapper. This led to promising results as many false positives and basic mappings could be ruled out from the resulting alignments. The other packages and elements were mapped afterwards in order to find alignments that were not that obvious based on the basic semantics identified before. Still the packages, which were not covered by the intersection, contained very important alignments. As a final result, our custom made alignment algorithms based on string matching methods (for the rdf labels, comments and class names) like Levenshtein distance, Hamming distance and Jaro-Winkler distance combined and the input dictionaries like Electropedia combined with a word stemming for the IEC 61850 short names for classes provided promising results, we found about 180 proper alignments out of the 210 estimated by the experts. Unfortunately, due to the heterogeneous structure of the two ontologies, structure and hierarchy based matching provides less good results. The alignments can be down-

Figure 11. The Mapping Bench Tool CIMBench

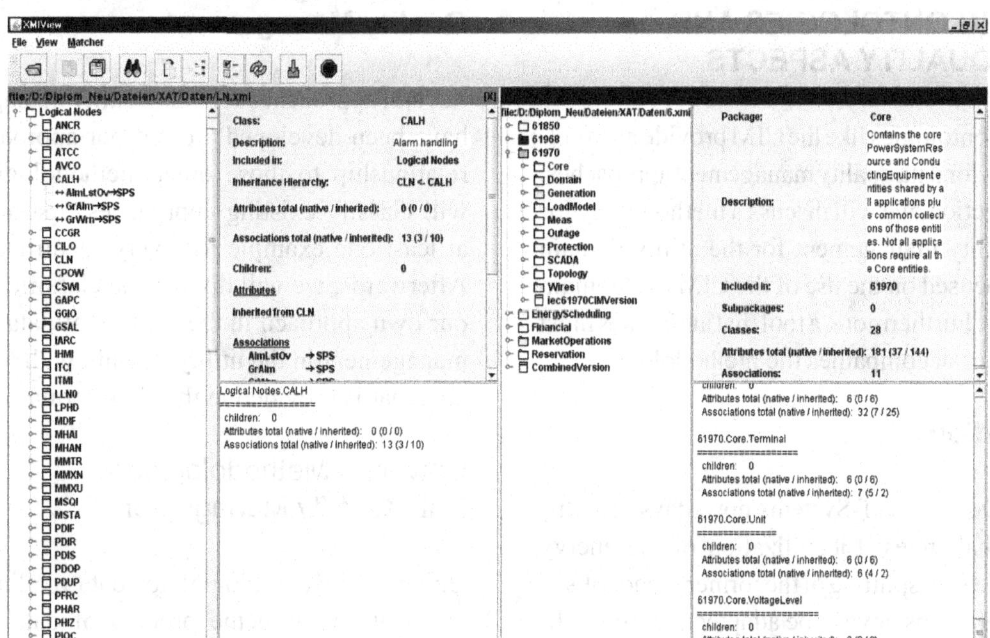

Figure 12. Intersection between the two standards

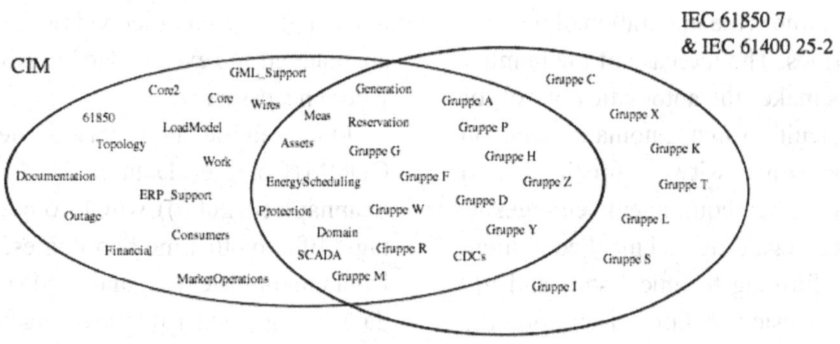

loaded at (OFFIS, 2008) or obtained from the authors. As future work, we want to specifically refine the packages and try to find better slicings for the pre-analysis of the standards. In addition, integration for engineering time based on instances is a further aspect of the framework.

Using this harmonized IEC standards as a foundation, we argue that this leads to an integrated data and function model that can be used as one model for semantic annotation for Web services in the electric utility domain. Both standards already have Web services as interfaces defined like the interface reference model (IRM) in the IEC 61970 CIM family and the Web services interface for IEC 61850 models based on the wind power plant standards and distributed generation standards. Still, the strong semantic imposed by the data models for annotation is not properly used.

CASE DESCRIPTION 2: DOMAIN ONTOLOGIES AND DATA QUALITY ASPECTS

Domain ontologies like the CIM provide an excellent basis for data quality management approaches. In this section, we will discuss a methodology for data quality management for the utility domain that is focused on the use of the CIM as a domain ontology. Furthermore, a tool that automates most of its steps accompanies the methodology.

Motivation

Utility Domain's IT-Systems nowadays face different challenges: Liberalization of the energy domain lead to splitting of the former monopolists. The IT-Systems have to be adapted to be compliant with the new market rules, e.g. by providing information non-discriminating for all market participants (European Council and Parliament, 2003).

Another example is the integration of the new renewable energies. The increase of the number of power plants makes the automatic control for a lot more difficult so that automatic decision making becomes a necessity. As for the data, a completely new set of requirements emerges as traditionally data regarding technical equipment was used for informing technical staff and not for automatic decision-making. Therefore the demand regarding data quality rises, as humans are more fault-tolerant than algorithms for automatic control are.

Both the two discussed and further scenarios require a mechanism to provide information about the feasibility, i.e. whether or not the data quality is sufficient for such tasks. We will provide a process model that specifically for the databases of enterprises of the utility domain provides information about their data quality.

Methodologies for Data Quality Management

Several approaches for data quality management have been developed. To put our approach into relationship to those other methodologies, we will classify existing approaches first and give at least one example for every identified class. Afterwards, we will discuss the classification of our own approach in the context of data quality management in the utility domain with focus on data that is provided in the CIM format.

Universal Methodologies for Data Quality Management

Universal methodologies for data quality management structure the process of data quality management without any restrictions regarding their applicability. They can generally be divided into a two phases, where the first phase is used to identify the state of data quality of the databases to be analyzed and a second phase where actions are planned and executed to improve the situation where necessary.

One example of this class of methodologies is CDQM (Complete Data Quality Method) (Batini, Scannapieco, 2006)), which combines the advantages of two other methodologies, TDQM (Total Data Quality Method) and TQdM (Total Quality data Management), by providing both a technical and an economical view on the challenge of data quality management.

CDQM first analyses the interconnections between organizational units. The outcome is a matrix showing the inputs and outputs of data for every unit. Above that, the processes are modeled that are responsible for those data processings.

In the second step, the data quality among other performances of every organizational unit is measured to identify parts where bad data occurs.

Finally, the matrix is completed with costs to improve the data quality. With this information, it is possible to identify the most efficient way to improve the data quality for the whole organization.

Specialized Methodologies for Data Quality Management

As the universal methodologies provide a very general way for data quality management, they need a lot of fine-tuning when applying them to a certain domain. The idea behind specialized methodologies for data quality management is to reduce their applicability and therefore being able to be more precise about the steps to execute to gain a quality-managed database. We will introduce two methodologies in the following, afterwards pointing out their differences.

(Hinrichs, 2002) describes a methodology for data quality management that can be applied to data warehouses. By this specialization, it is possible to make statements about certain referential constraints, as data warehouses always have certain data structures that they are defined by.

(De Amicis, Batini, 2004) describe a methodology for data quality management for the data of the financial domain. By restricting its application to such a domain, it is possible to name certain authorities whose knowledge about the domain makes them experts for estimating certain data regarding their correctness.

Generally speaking, specialized methodologies for data quality management can either be specific for a certain kind of technology or domain. As certain domains tend to use similar technological solutions, this classification is not exclusive.

Putting our Methodology into Context

The methodology we are going to introduce here for data quality management for the utility domain clearly is a specialized methodology as discussed above. Furthermore, its specialization regards the domain, but as mentioned before, that also in some applications has technological implications. In our case, it can often be observed, that utilities prefer distributed information systems e.g. for customer relationship management and asset management. Our approach takes into consideration those implications as shown later on.

Domain Ontologies and their Advantages for Data Quality Management

We will provide several reasons why ontologies are an optimal basis for data quality management. Therefore, we will use the CIM as an example of a domain ontology for the utility domain. Especially when discussing metadata annotation in the second part of this subsection, we refer to the RDF-Serialization of the CIM as introduced before.

Avoiding the Object Identification-Problem

Data quality algorithms' tasks can be described as marking wrong data in a database. Wrong data can come in different appearances: Data can be missing, it can be inconsistent in relation to other data, and it can be wrong (e.g., a negative value for some measurement that can only be positive) or it can be outdated. The fifth possibility is that a real world entity is represented several times in a database. So-called duplicates are also errors.

To find such wrong data it is necessary to have a conceptualized view on the data, i.e. a complete description of the instances to cope with. In other words, it is only possible to apply an algorithm for e.g. duplicate detection in a meaningful way by comparing to instances of the same concept, e.g. transformers, with each other. It is not meaningful to compare two values without their relation to their correspondent instances as the same values appear often in databases without being wrong (e.g., many transformers will have the value "110" as a voltage level).

The task to assign data values to their correspondent instances so that such an instance becomes a meaningful representation of the real world entity is called object identification. In many databases, it is a difficult task to provide such an assignment as the databases' design often follows other design goals like reducing redundancy or being compatible with different software versions. In opposition to those systems, ontologies like the CIM provide a conceptualized view on the domain so that the data schema itself solves the object identification problem. Algorithms for detecting wrong data perform optimally on data that is described in such a way so that the CIM provides an excellent basis for data quality management.

It should be pointed out that while speaking of conceptualization we do not necessarily refer to an OWL ontology that uses all semantical constructs of e.g. OWL 2.0 to ensure its consistency and the consistency of the data of its instances. We rather use the term ontology in the data quality management context as the conceptualized view as discussed above, as the identification of incorrect, inconsistent, missing, outdated, and multiple representation of data is realized by numeric algorithms. The idea behind that is to construct a numeric metamodel for each ontology's concept that holds the information necessary to detect wrong data. Therefore, we avoid several problems that OWL and its open world assumption holds when it comes to the formulation of certain restriction like e.g. the need of existence of certain values.

Seamless Metadata Annotation

Data quality management makes intensive use of metadata annotation. We will give two examples of such tasks and conclude that the RDF-serialization of the CIM is very well suited for data quality management's metadata annotations.

The first example shows the necessity to annotate data at schema level. Beyond the already discussed need for a conceptualized view on data, data quality management also needs information about the data that a conceptualized view cannot deliver. An example are the scales of measurement of primitive data types as the way data is preprocessed for data quality management depends on that information. Therefore concepts are delivered by our own data quality management ontology that allow making statements like "The voltage level of transformers are interval scaled." which interact directly with the CIM's concepts. Ontologies are designed for such interactions contrary to e.g. relational database management systems so that they provide on optimal choice for data quality management.

The second example shows an annotation at instance level. Statements about data quality themselves are metadata as the state an estimation about wrong or correct data. Such a statement could be "The voltage level of the transformer with the name 'Transformer X' seems to be wrong.". The developed data quality management ontology also provides concepts to make such statements about instances of CIM concepts. It shall be pointed out that RDF supports making statements about both concepts and instances optimally.

We have given two examples of different kinds of metadata annotations: One where statements were made on CIM's concepts and one where the annotations applied to instances of CIM's concepts. As the CIM is used in its RDF-serialization both use cases are supported optimally and suits the purpose as basis for data quality management's metadata annotation demands very well. The concepts to formulate those statements are defined in a data quality ontology provided by us.

Case Study: Data Quality Management for Utilities

The case study presented in this subsection shows a real world example where the methodology was applied to an enterprises database management system. We will explain the execution of the methodology's steps by examples and underline the support by the tool.

Introducing VDE and WDE

Our methodology for data quality management for the utility domain is called "VDE" ("Vorgehensmodell zum Datenqualitätsmanagement für Unternehmen der Energiewirtschaft" ~ "Methodology for data quality management for enterprises of the utility domain") and consists of five consecutive steps. Those steps are explained and accompanied by an example in the next subsection. It shall by pointed out that those steps are to be executed consecutively but whenever the outcome of one step is not sufficient for fulfilling the following steps backwards are allowed for improving the outcome similar as in the waterfall model for software development.

VDE is accompanied by WDE ("Werkzeug zur Unterstützung VDEs" ~ "Supporting tool for VDE"), a tool that provides either support for executing VDE's steps or fully automates them. In the following subsection, we will show how WDE fulfills its tasks.

Example Application of VDE and WDE

We will show an example application of how VDE with its supporting tool WDE is used to manage the data quality of a utility's data base management system. The provided use case is a real world example supported by the EWE AG (please visit http://www.ewe.de/). As we are not allowed to show details regarding the enterprise's data, their data schemas, or the outcome of the data quality evaluations, we will provide the description of the methodology's steps sufficiently anonymously.

1. Data selection: A domain expert has to make a selection of data that has to be integrated in the process of data quality management. This means to identify the specific databases of the distributed information system of a utility in question and its subsets that are to be analyzed. Of course, a first attempt could be to integrate all data into such a management, but as data quality management is costly it should be carefully evaluated which data needs data quality evaluation the most.

In our use case, we decided to integrate the data of the concepts "Substation", "Bay", "Switch", "ACLineSegment", and their "Location" and "Asset" information.

2. Mapping original database schemas on CIM concepts: As described above the conceptualized view and the data model provided by CIM respectively by RDF has many advantages for a data quality management approach. We therefore provide a possibility for mapping e.g. schemas of relational database management systems on the CIM. We use a technique named "D2RQ" which is both a mapping language and a tool that executes those mapping instructions. (Bizer & Seaborne, 2004) provide D2RQ.

Figure 13 shows a sample of such mapping instructions. The sample describes the mapping of the CIM concepts "Location" and "GmlPosition", where the further has a property to the latter and the latter has two literals, "GmlPosition.xPosition" and "GmlPosition.xPosition".

This step can be missed out if the data to be taken into account already exists in its CIM representation.

3. Providing necessary data annotations: As already discussed above, the conceptual view of the CIM is beneficial for data quality management, but further information about the data is needed for configuration of the data quality algorithms. Such information is the scales of measurements of the primitive data types.

Figure 13. Sample of mapping instructions for mapping a relational database management schema on the CIM

```
<?xml version="1.0" encoding="UTF-8"?>
<rdf:RDF
    xmlns:rdf="http://www.w3.org/1999/02/22-rdf-syntax-ns#"
    xmlns:rdfs="http://www.w3.org/2000/01/rdf-schema#"
    xmlns:cims="http://iec.ch/TC57/1999/rdf-schema-extensions-19990926#"
    xmlns:map="http://www.informatik.uni-oldenburg.de/dems/mapping#"
    xmlns:d2rq="http://www.wiwiss.fu-berlin.de/suhl/bizer/D2RQ/0.1#">

    <d2rq:ClassMap rdf:about="http://www.informatik.uni-oldenburg.de/dems/mapping#ClassMap_Location">
        <d2rq:uriPattern rdf:datatype="http://www.w3.org/2001/XMLSchema#string">http://iec.ch/TC57/1999/rdf-schema-extensions-19990926#Loc
ation_@@A.XKOORDINATE@@_@@A.YKOORDINATE@@</d2rq:uriPattern>
        <d2rq:class rdf:resource="http://iec.ch/TC57/1999/rdf-schema-extensions-19990926#Location"/>
    </d2rq:ClassMap>
    <d2rq:ClassMap rdf:about="http://www.informatik.uni-oldenburg.de/dems/mapping#ClassMap_GmlPosition">
        <d2rq:uriPattern rdf:datatype="http://www.w3.org/2001/XMLSchema#string">http://iec.ch/TC57/1999/rdf-schema-extensions-19990926#Gml
Position_@@A.XKOORDINATE@@_@@A.YKOORDINATE@@</d2rq:uriPattern>
        <d2rq:class rdf:resource="http://iec.ch/TC57/1999/rdf-schema-extensions-19990926#GmlPosition"/>
    </d2rq:ClassMap>

    <d2rq:PropertyBridge rdf:about="http://www.informatik.uni-oldenburg.de/dems/mapping#PropertyBridge_Location_Location_GmlPositions">
        <d2rq:belongsToClassMap rdf:resource="http://www.informatik.uni-oldenburg.de/dems/mapping#ClassMap_Location"/>
        <d2rq:property rdf:resource="http://iec.ch/TC57/1999/rdf-schema-extensions-19990926#Location.GmlPositions"/>
        <d2rq:refersToClassMap rdf:resource="http://www.informatik.uni-oldenburg.de/dems/mapping#ClassMap_GmlPosition"/>
    </d2rq:PropertyBridge>
    <d2rq:PropertyBridge rdf:about="http://www.informatik.uni-oldenburg.de/dems/mapping#PropertyBridge_GmlPosition_GmlPosition_xPosition">
        <d2rq:belongsToClassMap rdf:resource="http://www.informatik.uni-oldenburg.de/dems/mapping#ClassMap_GmlPosition"/>
        <d2rq:property rdf:resource="http://iec.ch/TC57/1999/rdf-schema-extensions-19990926#GmlPosition.xPosition"/>
        <d2rq:column rdf:datatype="http://www.w3.org/2001/XMLSchema#string">A.XKOORDINATE</d2rq:column>
    </d2rq:PropertyBridge>
    <d2rq:PropertyBridge rdf:about="http://www.informatik.uni-oldenburg.de/dems/mapping#PropertyBridge_GmlPosition_GmlPosition_yPosition">
        <d2rq:belongsToClassMap rdf:resource="http://www.informatik.uni-oldenburg.de/dems/mapping#ClassMap_GmlPosition"/>
        <d2rq:property rdf:resource="http://iec.ch/TC57/1999/rdf-schema-extensions-19990926#GmlPosition.yPosition"/>
        <d2rq:column rdf:datatype="http://www.w3.org/2001/XMLSchema#string">A.YKOORDINATE</d2rq:column>
    </d2rq:PropertyBridge>
</rdf:RDF>
```

Figure 14 shows such annotations, where both the properties "Asset.installationDate" and "Asset.statusDate" of the concept "EquipmentAsset" are marked as interval scaled.

4. Execution of data quality management and compilation of data quality reports: In addition to the annotations shown above there is also the necessity to label correct instances for every concept that was selected in the first step. The labeled data is used for training classifiers that are used to identify incorrect, inconsistent, and missing data as well as duplicates.

The forth step is executed automatically and the data quality reports contain data quality es-

Figure 14. Sample of data annotations showing the annotations of scales of measurement

```
<?xml version="1.0" encoding="UTF-8"?>
<rdf:RDF
        xmlns:rdfs="http://www.w3.org/2000/01/rdf-schema#"
        xmlns:cims="http://iec.ch/TC57/1999/rdf-schema-extensions-19990926#"
        xmlns:rdf="http://www.w3.org/1999/02/22-rdf-syntax-ns#"
        xmlns:dqm="http://www.informatik.uni-oldenburg.de/dems/dataquality#">

        <rdfs:Class rdf:about="http://iec.ch/TC57/1999/rdf-schema-extensions-19990926#EquipmentAsset"/>

        <rdf:Property rdf:about="http://iec.ch/TC57/1999/rdf-schema-extensions-19990926#Asset.installationDate">
                <rdfs:domain rdf:resource="http://iec.ch/TC57/1999/rdf-schema-extensions-19990926#EquipmentAsset"/>
                <rdfs:range rdf:resource="http://www.w3.org/2000/01/rdf-schema#Literal"/>
        </rdf:Property>
        <dqm:PropertyAnnotation rdf:about="http://www.informatik.uni-oldenburg.de/dems/dataquality#PropertyAnnotation_Asset_installationDate">
                <dqm:hasProperty rdf:resource="http://iec.ch/TC57/1999/rdf-schema-extensions-19990926#Asset.installationDate"/>
                <dqm:isMeasurementTypeOf rdf:resource="http://www.informatik.uni-oldenburg.de/dems/dataquality#IntervalType"/>
                <dqm:belongsToClass rdf:resource="http://iec.ch/TC57/1999/rdf-schema-extensions-19990926#EquipmentAsset"/>
        </dqm:PropertyAnnotation>

        <rdf:Property rdf:about="http://iec.ch/TC57/1999/rdf-schema-extensions-19990926#Asset.statusDate">
                <rdfs:domain rdf:resource="http://iec.ch/TC57/1999/rdf-schema-extensions-19990926#EquipmentAsset"/>
                <rdfs:range rdf:resource="http://www.w3.org/2000/01/rdf-schema#Literal"/>
        </rdf:Property>
        <dqm:PropertyAnnotation rdf:about="http://www.informatik.uni-oldenburg.de/dems/dataquality#PropertyAnnotation_Asset_statusDate">
                <dqm:hasProperty rdf:resource="http://iec.ch/TC57/1999/rdf-schema-extensions-19990926#Asset.statusDate"/>
                <dqm:isMeasurementTypeOf rdf:resource="http://www.informatik.uni-oldenburg.de/dems/dataquality#IntervalType"/>
                <dqm:belongsToClass rdf:resource="http://iec.ch/TC57/1999/rdf-schema-extensions-19990926#EquipmentAsset"/>
        </dqm:PropertyAnnotation>
</rdf:RDF>
```

timations on different aggregate levels: At the lowest level, the suspected errors themselves are marked so that lists of errors can be compiled to be corrected by domain experts. At the next level, the ratio between correct and wrong instances is given per concepts. By these listings, ranges with increased data error rates can be identified. The final level is the data quality dimensions, namely correctness, completeness, consistency, and timeliness, where correctness contains the absence of duplicates. The data quality dimensions are defined by the data quality ontology by relating the outcome of the data quality algorithms to the data quality dimensions. Therefore it is possible to adapt the data quality reports by adjusting the ontology accordingly, e.g. making "absence of duplicates" a data quality dimension on its own if this characteristic is especially needful in the respective context.

5. Analysis of data quality reports: Those reports can be used to make decisions like deciding which of several databases should be the leading one or deciding whether money spent to increase the data quality of an enterprise's databases had its positive influence.

It should be pointed out that also the data quality management itself should be evaluated. As the outcome of the data quality management depends on e.g. the labeled data mentioned in step four, it is necessary to decide whether the data quality reports are correct. In case of bad performance the third step needs to be adjusted to improve the data quality management's performance as we already mentioned the steps backwards.

Evaluation and Recommendations for Data Quality Management for Utilities

The use case presented in the previous subsection allows us to draw conclusions regarding the quality of VDE with WDE's support. (Frank, 2006) defines criteria for evaluating methodologies that we will use in the following. Those criteria are divided into four perspectives, namely the economical perspective, the user perspective, the design perspective, and the epistemological perspective.

- Economical perspective: VDE is designed to be applied in enterprises of the utility domain, as it uses the CIM as a domain ontology with its respective vocabulary and little configuration as shown in the steps one to three, so that the costs for applying the methodology are little. Therefore, the ratio between costs and benefit can be evaluated positively.
- User perspective: On the one hand, both VDE and WDE are accompanied by a scientific work that explains motivation, design, and evaluation in detail. These aspects can be evaluated positively. On the other hand, VDE was only applied on a copy of a live system, so that the acceptance by the users cannot be evaluated. It is not possible to except that users have difficulties with accepting the outcome of a data quality evaluation if its evidence them worse success than other users.
- Design perspective: The design decisions for VDE and WDE are discussed in detail in the accompanied work. Furthermore, the methodology is motivated by real world challenges and the vocabulary used for explanation fits the target audience. The design perspective can therefore be evaluated positively.
- Epistemological perspective: A methodology solves a class of problems and not only a specific one; it can be understood as a kind of scientific theory. Considering this, VDE has to be evaluated and critically questioned. As VDE and WDE are accompanied by a scientific work, the

epistemological perspective is covered well.

Overall, VDE is a well fitting approach for the data quality needs for enterprises of the utility domain with its accompanied tool WDE that allows fast setup and quick generations of data quality reports. Especially the CIM proved to be an excellent basis for data quality management approaches.

REFERENCES

Batini, C., & Scannapieco, M. (2006). *Data quality*. Springer-Verlag.

Bizer, C., & Seaborne, A. (2004). *D2RQ-treating non-RDF databases as virtual RDF graphs*. Paper presented at the 3rd International Semantic Web Conference (ISWC2004), Hiroshima, Japan.

De Amicis, F., & Batini, C. (2004). A methodology for data quality assessment on financial data. In *Studies in communication sciences* (pp. 115-136).

Electropedia, I. E. C. (2008). Retrieved from http://www.electropedia.org.

European Parliament and the Council (2003). *Directive 2003/54/EU of the European Parliament and of the Council of 26 June 2003 concerning common rules for the internal market in electricity and repealing Directive 96/92/EC*.

Euzenat, S. (2007). *Ontology matching*. Heidelberg: Springer Verlag.

Frank, U. (2006). *Evaluation of reference models*. In P. Fettke, & P. Loos (Eds.), *Reference modeling for business systems analysis* (pp. 118-140). Idea Group.

Hepp, M. (2007). Possible ontologies: How reality constrains the development of relevant ontologies. *IEEE Internet Computing, 11*(1), 90–96. doi:10.1109/MIC.2007.20

Hepp; M. (2004). *OntoMeter: Metrics for ontologies*. 1st European Semantic Web Symposium (ESWS2004), Heraklion, Greece, May 10-12.

Hevner, A. R., March, S. T., Park, J., & Ram, S. (2004). Design science research in information systems. *Management Information Systems Quarterly, 28*(1), 75–105.

Hinrichs, H. (2002). *Datenqualitätsmanagement in data warehouse-systemen*. Phd thesis, University of Oldenburg, Germany.

Hong Hai, D. (2006). *Schema matching and mapping-based data integration: Architecture, approaches and evolution*. VDM Verlag Dr. Müller.

IEC - International Electrotechnical Commission. (2003). *IEC 61970-301: Energy management system application program interface (EMS-API) – Part 301: Common Information Model (CIM) Base*. International Electrotechnical Commission.

Kostic, T., Frei, C., Preiss, O., & Kezunovic, M. (2004). *Scenarios for data exchange using standards IEC 61970 and IEC 61850*. Cigre Paris 2004. IEEE Publishing.

OFFIS. (2008). *Ontologies for the utility domain*. Retrieved from http://www.offis.de/energie/ontologies

Robinson, G. (2002). Key standards for utility enterprise application integration (EAI). In *Proceedings of the DistribuTech 2002 Miami*. Pennwell.

Shvaiko (2006). *An API for ontology alignment* (Version 2.1).

Uslar, M. (2006). The common information model for utilities: An introduction and outlook on future applications. In R. Eckstein & R. Tolksdorf (Eds.), *Proceedings of the XML-Days 2006 in Berlin, XML-clearinghouse.de* (pp.135-148).

Uslar, M. (2008). Ontology-based Integration of IEC TC 57 Standards. In *Proceedings of the I-ESA 2008 Conference on Interoperability for Enterprise Systems and Applications, Fraunhofer IPK, Berlin.*

Uslar, M., et al. (2009). Untersuchung des Normungsumfeldes zum BMWi-Förderschwerpunkt. *e-Energy – IKT-basiertes Energiesystem der Zukunft.* Ministry of Economics, Germany.

Uslar, M., & Dahlem, N. (2006). Semantic Web technologies for power grid management. In R. Koschke, O. Herzog, K.-H. Rödiger & M. Ronthaler (Eds.), *Informatik 2007: Informatik trifft Logistik, Band 1, Beiträge der 37. Jahrestagung der Gesellschaft für Informatik e.V. (GI) 24.-27. September 2007.* In Bremen, 27(1), Gesellschaft für Informatik, Bonn, Köllen Verlag.

Uslar, Streekmann & Abels (2007). MDA-basierte Kopplung heterogener Informationssysteme im EVU-Sektor - ein Framework. In A. Oberweis, C. Weinhardt, H. Gimpel, A. Koschmider & V. Pankratius (Eds.), *eOrganisation: Service-, Prozess-, Market-Engineering*, 8. Internationale Tagung Wirtschaftsinformatik, 2, Universitätsverlag Karlsruhe.

Chapter 10
Semantic Synchronization in B2B Transactions

Janina Fengel
Hochschule Darmstadt University of Applied Sciences, Germany

Heiko Paulheim
SAP Research CEC Darmstadt, Germany

Michael Rebstock
Hochschule Darmstadt University of Applied Sciences, Germany

EXECUTIVE SUMMARY

Despite the development of e-business standards, the integration of business processes and business information systems is still a non-trivial issue if business partners use different e-business standards for formatting and describing information to be processed. Since those standards can be understood as ontologies, ontological engineering technologies can be applied for processing, especially ontology matching for reconciling them. However, as e-business standards tend to be rather large-scale ontologies, scalability is a crucial requirement. To serve this demand, we present our ORBI Ontology Mediator. It is linked with our Malasco system for partition-based ontology matching with currently available matching systems, which so far do not scale well, if at all. In our case study we show how to provide dynamic semantic synchronization between business partners using different e-business standards without initial ramp-up effort, based on ontological mapping technology combined with interactive user participation.

BACKGROUND

In Germany, academic education is provided by the universities and the universities of applied sciences, with the latter having been entitled to start being active in research about 10 years ago and concentrating on the field of practice-oriented research. In Darmstadt at the University of Applied Sciences, one of the major research topics within the faculty of business administration and economics is the realization of electronic collaboration and the arising business integration requirements. Starting out in the late 1990s with small research projects with partners from both academia and industry, over the years the basis of the e-business integration research group could be established. Presently this group is firmly installed and is working in various projects of different size concentrating on the issues of business integration and intelligent information integration in business information systems. The idea of linking project partners from a university background with partners from the industry has been continuously applied and thus enabled the development of solutions for real-world demands. Thereby the focus is on one of the fundamentals of a market-oriented economy, particularly the matching of demand and supply and the resulting exchange of goods and services. Electronic transaction support enables its execution. However, the issues around integrating the business partners need to be solved, so that they can synchronize their activities wisely. Nowadays, the challenges for enterprises stemming from the dynamics of a globalized market lead to the need of agile management. The fulfillment of this demand does not only require internal business integration, but in particular calls for flexible collaboration enablement in B2B based on meaningful information integration.

Against this background, the research identified for developing a suitable semantic solution led to the creation of the ORBI project. The acronym is created from the project title “Ontologies-based Reconciliation for Business Integration”. The approach is based on the insight that semantic heterogeneity occurs in all kinds of business information systems. Basically, the problem of creating a shared understanding of information arises wherever information to be integrated and subsequently processed is named, formatted or annotated differently.

The project was set-up for developing a conceptual design and implementing a prototypical proof-of-concept for a semantic information system. The idea was that e-business standards can be understood as ontologies. Therefore, ontological engineering methods and tools could be applied for discovering and processing the standards’ semantic content. In order to develop a flexible application for providing semantic support and synchronization between business partners, scientific knowledge had to be linked with practical experiences and demands. A special focus was put on small and medium-sized enterprises, since in this environment the exploitation of market power is not the sole answer to unification efforts. Accordingly, in this context the need for being able to deal with information formatted according to different demands is particularly strong. Under the leadership of the University of Applied Sciences Darmstadt the project consortium assembled included partners from the same university, partner universities, a Fraunhofer research institute, software and consulting companies as well as electronic marketplace providers and industrial partners from different industries. The application for funding the project by the German Federal Ministry of Education and Research was granted under number 1716X04 within the framework “Forschung an Fachhochschulen mit Unternehmen (FHprofUnd)”. This program concentrates on supporting application-driven research collaboration and transfer-oriented cooperations between universities of applied sciences and small and medium-sized enterprises in Germany.

In the following we present our project. First, the research problem is described, followed by a case description presenting the technologies used and problems faced together with the design and implementation of our solution and its application to solve the demand at hand. We close with a discussion and outlook on the current activities.

SETTING THE STAGE

Already for many years the operation of electronic transactions could be supported electronically. The recent high acceptance and spread of web-based technology all over the world led to a quickly growing diffusion of electronic support for a variety of internal and external business conduction.

Semantic Heterogeneity in E-Business

For conducting business, regardless if internally or externally, information needs to be processed, thus being the cause and also the result of business processes. Usually, nowadays the design of business processes aims at facilitating efficient electronic business execution. Interaction with business partners is enabled by way of exchanging information, often transported and recorded in form of business documents, sometimes both electronically and traditionally in paper form (Glushko & McGrath, 2002). In support of this task, often various different business information systems are utilized in combination. Next to systems intended at automating the processing of huge amounts of data, there are also systems aimed at providing communication and decision support (Wigand, Picot, & Reichwald, 1997, pp. 119ff). The linkage of various systems does not automatically lead to seamless processing due to incompatibilities encountered. Furthermore, some business processes even foresee human intervention. Enabling interoperation between applications on the technical and syntactical level is often achieved through Enterprise Application Integration (Linthicum, 1999, pp. 3-4). However, this does not address the question of how to integrate the meaning of the information exchanged. Subsequently, a strong need for integration on a semantic level arose from the wish to enable seamless communication through the various business information systems within enterprises and also across their boundaries. Unfortunately, in applications where typically information from different sources is combined and exchanged, often information is encountered that has been named and formatted differently according to each business partners' individual information processing requirements. In consequence, information exchange can usually only be conducted electronically after extensive initial efforts for mapping data structures and their contents, often done manually for each business relationship.

For easing this task, numerous differing e-business guidelines and specifications have been developed for describing documents, processes or products. Next to official standards, also various proprietary formats are presently in use. As a consequence, even though precautions for seamless transaction processing have been taken by way of using standards, interruptions still occur when information cannot be joined. Thus, the information interoperability problem is only shifted to a higher level: instead of incompatible data structures, electronic business now suffers from incompatible standards. Since it seems unlikely that in near future one globally accepted standard will prevail, a practical solution for coping with the existence of heterogeneous information is needed. Considering the given need for a company to dynamically work ad-hoc with changing business partners in a global market, it is time- and costwise impossible to provide the ramp-up efforts for predefining each information exchange before being able to conduct a business. Therefore, interoperability of the information to be exchanged is required as the basis for focusing on the business instead of concentrating on technological issues.

Information Integration in B2B Transactions

In market economies, market transactions, regardless if conducted traditionally or with electronic support, enable commerce based on trading agreements, thus providing the coordination of demand and supply (Wigand, Picot, & Reichwald, 1997, pp. 22-23). The content of business agreements is usually achieved by way of negotiating (Benyoucef & Rinderle, 2007). Usually, the activities concerning the purchase and sales of consumer goods concentrate on the price for the exchange of standardized goods, whereas often the price, design and service conditions of industrial goods and services are being determined in the course of market transactions by way of negotiating (Hoffmann, 2006, pp. 1-3; Herbst, 2007, pp. 40-42). Such business negotiations do not imply only decisions on a fixed set of attributes, like price or quantity, but enable the configuration of goods' attributes and their characteristics, their price as well as the formulation of payment and delivery terms (Rebstock, Fengel, Paulheim, 2007). As a result, the negotiation positions with their individual characteristics are not pre-defined, but introduced and amended as needed in the course of a negotiation. In the end, the procurement decisions do not depend solely on the supplier's marketing and sales efforts, but are subject to interactive influencing between business partners (Herbst, 2007, p. 1). The conclusion of such a negotiation is usually documented in form of a legal contract, describing all trade information and documenting consensus between the partners.

As a result, electronic negotiation support systems are one of the most complex types of business information systems (Kersten & Lai, 2007, p. 554). This complexity increases considerably further when arbitrarily definable items and attributes can be used in a negotiation (Rebstock & Fengel, 2003). Therefore, such a system has been chosen here as an example showcase for demonstrating the challenges of achieving semantic disambiguity between business partners. In a previous project, the design and implementation of electronic support for such highly complex negotiations led to the creation of a research project on this matter. The result is a web-service-based system called M2N (mobile multi attribute negotiations), enabling electronic support for negotiations covering positions with multiple attributes, regardless if a mobile or a desktop device is used. It allows every party to introduce arbitrary items, attributes, and attribute values, independent of the industry or enterprise size. However, it is not trivially given that both negotiation partners use the same terminology and document structures. This imposed new challenges, since the newly introduced terms may be unknown to the other party and thus require reconciliation (Rebstock, Fengel, & Paulheim, 2008, p. 198).

Hence, an integration solution that allows the parallel use of information named and formatted according to different default guidelines or specifications became necessary. Business partners should be able to continue using their information as is without the need for reconfiguring it for each business transaction or even migrating their data, as this is usually not individually possible for each of the various different business relationships an enterprise is having. Such a support mechanism should provide the matching of communication content on the semantic level and ensure that both parties agree on the same meaning of terms. Thus, business partners are enabled to reconcile their languages, so that their intentions and subsequent actions can be synchronized correctly. Providing such a semantic solution was the aim of the ORBI project.

CASE DESCRIPTION

Business communication and the exchange of information require interoperability on the semantic level inside enterprises and across its boundaries (Bruijn, 2004, pp. 2-3). It denotes the enablement to share and reuse business knowledge by way of integrating heterogeneous sources of information concerning their intended meaning, thus making it compatible. Through interrelating information, semantic integration is achievable involving the identification and explication of logical connections for fusing (Uschold & Menzel, 2005). Potential solutions for the challenges around semantic interoperability and integration have been discussed already for many years (e.g. Kalfoglou, Schorlemmer, Sheth, Staab, & Uschold, 2005;

Alexiev, Breu, Bruijn, Fensel, Lara & Hausen, 2005; Stuckenschmidt, & Harmelen, 2005; Noy, 2004). The use of ontologies has been introduced for reconciling semantically heterogeneous information. For comparing different ontologies, ontology matching methods facilitate the search for ontology elements, which are semantically related on the conceptual level and thus express semantic correspondence. Such semantic relations may serve as references between terms. The process of finding such relations can be automated by means of ontology matching tools. The resulting ontology mappings found are usually not ideal as they may be ambiguous or incorrect. Therefore, for optimization and disambiguation, human involvement is required (Zhdanova, Bruijn, Zimmermann, & Scharffe, 2004). Trading and business execution within enterprises as well as across enterprise borders concerns a clearly distinguishable community with subject expertise. Providing the possibility for community user participation in the process of disambiguation offers a wealth of specific background information concerning the domain context. Tapping into the users' tacit knowledge in an implicit manner allows for its exploitation and combination with existing knowledge such as the automatically derived mappings without requiring tedious additional work. Involving users in a collaborative manner on a case-by-case basis as needed allows for their contribution to the applicability determination of semantic relations.

Combining both automated processing and collaborative user involvement offers the possibility of developing a semantic system for incorporation into existing business processes. It complements the processing power of automated matching with the correctness of manual mapping. With regard to the large amount of information to be reconciled when dealing with e-business standards, thus huge ramp-up efforts are avoidable. Nonetheless, the quality of mappings found this way is assessed and hence improvable, since human support is included. All mappings can be collected and are thus usable of in the course of daily business operation. A dynamic solution can assist humans in resolving misunderstandings or uncertainties about the intended meaning of terms used through suggesting possible explanations. With these, business partners may reconcile the meaning of business content and subsequently their intention at run-time in the course of their interaction. We call this *semantic synchronization*. Supporting the coordination between business partners in such a manner is built on ontology matching supported by user feedback and context information. The purpose of reconciliation can be achieved by establishing references between differing content or structure element terms. In the following we present the theoretical foundations and previous work on which our development is based and show how we leverage these insights for realizing our mediator system.

Ontologies as Semantic Foundations of Business Integration

The vision of the Semantic Web and the approaches for automated information processability lead to the developments in representing knowledge in a web-based manner in structured, machine-processable forms, readable for both humans and computers (Berners-Lee, Hendler, & Lassila, 2001). Meanwhile, such representations are commonly referred to as ontologies (Gómez-Pérez, Fernandéz-López, & Corcho, 2004, pp. 8ff). One of the most popular definitions describes an ontology as "an explicit specification of a conceptualization" (Gruber, 1993). Such a formal specification depicts a part of the world and in doing so defines the meaning of a vocabulary in machine-processable form. In principle, ontologies can be understood as a collection of definitions of elements and the relationships between them. Usually, consensus is established between a group of ontology modellers regarding the capturing and modelling of a domain (Staab, Schnurr, & Sure, 2001). It is jointly decided which specific terms define a unique meaning within a commonly shared vocabulary and how these terms are related (Daconta, Obrst, & Smith, 2003, pp. 181ff).

Ontologies span from light-weight comprising glossaries, thesauri and taxonomies to heavy-weight conceptualizations such as models and formal ontologies expressed in description logic (Gómez-Pérez, Fernandéz-López, & Corcho, 2004, pp. 8ff; Euzenat & Shvaiko, 2007, pp. 29-30). With increasing amount of meaning specified and higher degree of formality, ambiguity decreases, and ontologies become more expressive (McGuiness, 2003; Uschold & Gruninger, 2004, pp. 59-60). Following these notions, one of the most lightweight forms are controlled vocabularies providing listings of terms. Enhanced with their meaning, vocabularies turn into glossaries. Thesauri also contain basic relationships between those terms, such as synonymy or polysemy. When the terms are hierarchically ordered and thereby complemented by subclass relations, the resulting structure turns into a taxonomy. XML and database schemas as well as conceptual models exemplify concepts with their properties and relations. Heavyweight ontologies are formally expressed logical theories and include additional axioms and constraints.

For representation, different languages exist, out of which the XML-based RDF Schema or one of the dialects of OWL are the most popular. Thus, an ontology's content is interpretable by both humans and machines alike, as its meaning is captured entirely in the structure and formal semantics (Bruijn, 2004, p. 68). Consequently, semantics become machine-processable and information from different sources expressed as ontologies can be consolidated. Hence, also business information may be integrated (Stonebraker & Hellerstein, 2001). Furthermore, formal ontologies can be reasoned upon (Blumauer & Pellegrini, 2006). For this purpose, the description logic based OWL DL is often chosen, since the more expressive OWL Full is not decidable (Smith, Welty, & McGuiness, 2004). Based on the relationships contained, inference rules are definable (Saeki & Kaiya, 2006). By means of inference engines, new knowledge can be derived through logical deduction, and thus the ontology further evolves (Antoniou, Franconi, & Harmelen, 2005).

For an enterprise, the general motivation for developing an ontology is the wish to structure its knowledge (Zelewski, 1999). The objective in using ontologies within enterprises or B2B-collaboration networks is to benefit from capturing and sharing knowledge for using and reusing it to solve business tasks, especially for supporting integration efforts within and across enterprise boundaries (Uschold & Gruninger 1996; Bruijn, 2004). Thereby, achieving the same understanding about information is intended, since within information exchanges the information needs to be unambiguous and carry the same meaning for both the sender and the recipient, regardless whether they are humans or computers, for facilitating uninterrupted processing (Wigand, Picot, & Reichwald, 1997, pp. 60ff). As a result, in order to ease business integration, mostly information structures and transaction formats agreed-upon in advance as well as predefined business document contents are in use.

In B2B-e-commerce standards are available for providing this common ground. Very generally, a standard is a set of rules approved by a recognized body for governing a specific situation (ISO, 2004). However, in e-business practice we have to distinguish between de jure standards, applicable by law, and de facto standards, effectively in use without legal authorization and usually developed by expert panels, industry consortia or even individual companies. Therefore, we use the term e-business standards and include official rules as well as non-official specifications and proprietary formats. Often, enterprises apply e-business standards for defining and formatting their information, thus trying to achieve information interoperability through standardization.

Mostly all standards are structured, machine-readable knowledge representations which at least define a common vocabulary and hold some relations between terms, usually subclass-relations. Therefore, in principle, following this point of view, e-business standards can be regarded to be light-weight ontologies (Gómez-Pérez, Fernandéz-López, & Corcho, 2004, p. 86). However, there exists a variety of standards. Some semantic standards focus on the data exchanged. Classifications aim at defining business information on the content level, mostly used for formatting master data by providing unambiguous designations for suppliers and products and their attributes. Often, they are expressed as taxonomies (Rebstock et al., 2008, pp. 45ff). Typically, product classifications are rather basic ontologies, but contain a lot of concepts (Omelayenko, 2001). Other standards focus on the structure level of business information and provide the designations for labeling and sorting the data fields, which in turn can be filled with information formatted according to a certain product classification standard. Such document and transaction standards focus on uniformly representing documents' fields or provide the means for structuring the document flow and thereby focus on the automation of complex workflows in and between enterprises (Rebstock et al., 2008, pp. 55ff). They usually contain many different document types (Omelayenko, 2001). Process standards are not yet very common, but they are intended at providing a uniform representation of business process structures (Rebstock et al., 2008, pp. 62ff). Overall, e-business standards, even if created for the same purpose or same domain, can differ considerably and it seems highly unlikely that one universal, globally accepted standard will become prevailing in the near future (Rebstock et al., 2008, p. 78).

Standard Mismatches

Overall, these e-business ontologies do not match. Following Kalfoglou, Hu, Reynolds, and Shadbolt (2005), ontology mismatches can be distinguished into several categories. Language mismatches stem from the use of different syntactic formats, different degrees of expressiveness of the representation language used or different designations of primitive linguistic constructs. Generally, such linguistic heterogeneity can be solved by means of normalization (Noy, 2004). Mismatches on the ontology level are harder to identify and solve, usually by way of matching (Klein, 2001). This kind of heterogeneity is based on differences in modeling through dissimilar terminology use, evident through the occurrence of synonyms, homonyms, diverse ways of data encoding as well as differing extents in the specification depth and width due to varying granularity and scope. Furthermore, differing modeling styles, designation of different concept names or differing properties next to inconsistencies or incompleteness lead to mismatches. Therefore, it may be non-trivial to find corresponding entities in two ontologies. Figure 1 shows the comparison of two extracts of e-business standards, one incorporating coding as per the official standard called United Nations Standard Products and Services Code (UNSPSC), and points out their language and model mismatches. Both extracts shown model the same domain of paper products. The classes called "writing paper" correspond, but their attributes describing the product number show different designations. Also, the granularity differs by standard B showing a more detailed structuring into subclasses.

In particular in inter-organizational cooperations, very often different standards, i.e., different ontologies, are concurrently in use, thus leading to disruptions in the flow of transactions due to incompatible information (Fensel, 2004). As a consequence, when upon processing transactions business information formatted according to different e-business standards is encountered, it needs to be made understandable and thus interoperable. For providing semantic interoperability, further processing is required, since the interoperability problem which was intended to be solved by use of these e-business ontologies,

Figure 1. Examples of e-business standards mismatches

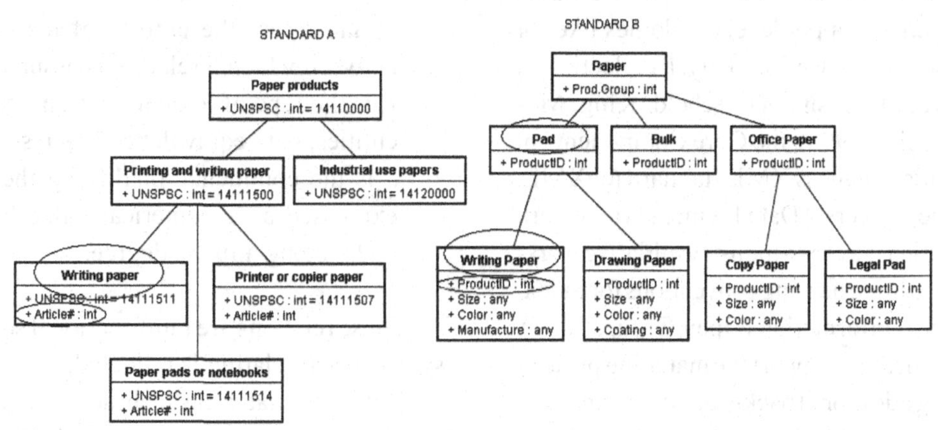

is only transferred onto a higher level (Euzenat & Shvaiko, 2007, p. 11ff).

Therefore, the knowledge contained needs to be consolidated and transformed despite its divergence, even though very often, restructuring one or more of the ontologies involved is hardly feasible (Zelewski, 1999). Usually, within enterprises, existing data models, enterprise vocabularies and ontologies cannot be easily migrated, if at all possible, due to them being in use already. Hence, approaches need to be designed how to cope with the parallel existence of different ontologies and the resulting semantic heterogeneity.

Applying Ontology Matching

Transforming e-business standards into ontologies provides the basis for applying ontological engineering methods and tools. In order to enable working with different ontologies in parallel, they can be related by means of ontology matching, i.e., establishing logical relations between the elements of one or more ontologies for the purpose of comparing and reconciling them. Matching systems try to find pairs of entities from different ontologies with the same intended meaning (Euzenat, Mocan, & Scharffe, 2007, p. 178). Thereby semantic correspondences are looked for, which express equivalence or similarity between elements. In the field of e-business, where standards aim at information unification, such relations can serve as translations. When correspondences are directed, they can serve as mappings between elements of different ontologies (Euzenat, Mocan, & Scharffe, 2007, p. 179). The thus aligned ontologies can remain in their original form, as the mapping may serve as means to a virtual integration. This is especially helpful, as in general, e-business standards cannot be amended according to individual demands once they have been issued.

Ontologies can be analyzed and searched for correspondences by various matching techniques. In general, element based and structure based approaches can be distinguished. The former compare only single elements from the input ontologies, while the latter also include information of those elements' neighborhoods, such as super and sub concepts, or attempt at structural matching of the graphs underlying the ontologies. Structure-based approaches are known for also finding non-trivial correspondences. Furthermore, internal and external approaches can be distinguished. For internal approaches, the only input to the matching system are the ontologies to be matched. External approaches use more sources of information, such as additional upper ontologies or thesauri (Euzenat & Shvaiko, 2007). For e-business, these may be multilingual dictionaries for support in multinational enterprise settings as well as general upper-level ontologies like for example the Enterprise Ontology, a collection of terms relevant to business (Uschold, King, Moralee, & Zorgios, 1998), the Core Components of the Electronic Business XML standard (ebXML, 2007), or the Universal Data Element Framework (UDEF), which is a cross-industry initiative working on determining naming conventions for indexing enterprise information (Open Group, 2007). Such ontologies can support the matching process by providing additional background information, e.g., on synonyms (Ehrig, 2004). Comprehensive overviews of approaches and algorithms can be found in (Euzenat & Shvaiko, 2007, pp. 153ff) and (Kalfoglou & Schorlemmer, 2005).

As a result, the problems encountered upon reconciling different standards as depicted in Figure 1 above can be tackled. Terminology mismatches can be identified using element-based techniques for finding naming variations for concepts, e.g., here the synonyms “ProductID” and “Article#”. A difference in specification, here the coverage of “Writing Paper”, may only be detected by structure-based techniques. In case the term “Pad” is not only used as shown here in the extract, but also for naming an “ink-pad” or a “cushion”, such homonyms would need disambiguation according to their context.

Basically, all matching systems work according to the same principle. The input to the system are two ontologies and optionally a set of already known mapping elements between the input ontologies. Furthermore, external resources like dictionaries, thesauri or related already existing ontologies may support the matching process.

The output is a mapping produced by the system. All mappings can be stored for further use. Following Shvaiko and Euzenat (2005), mappings may be described as tupels

$<e_1, e_2, R, c>$

where

- e_1 and e_2 are the entities of the ontologies between which a relation is assumed,
- R is the type of logical relation between the entities, e.g., equivalence or subsumption,
- c is the confidence qualifying the relation, expressed as a numerical value between 1 and 0 being a fuzzy degree.

These relations are unidirectional so that non-symmetrical relating is reflected.

Ontology matching techniques as described provide the means for relating ontologies and finding mappings between their elements automatically or semi-automatically. Most tools produce a list of related concepts in both ontologies and thus 1:1 mappings. Matching approaches generating complex types of relations implying more than one element from each ontology are being investigated but are not yet widely used (Hu & Qu, 2006). Furthermore, for achieving results of higher quality, there are different approaches for combining matching tools. A combined approach can exploit more possibilities due to the diversity of the various methods utilized. Examples for combined approaches are the CROSI matching system, which uses weighted results from different matching tools and algorithms (Kalfoglou, Hu, Reynolds, Shadbolt, 2005), and the AHP system, which tries to select a matching tool which best fits the input ontologies' characteristics (Mochol, Jentzsch, & Euzenat, 2006). Other approaches try to optimize results by automatically determining optimal parameter sets for matching tools (Lee, Sayyadian, Doan, & Rosenthal, 2007).

The resulting mappings found can be collected for further use and applied as semantic references. In addition, through reasoning, new mappings can be derived. The reconciled ontologies remain unchanged and serve for further reference as intended. Thus, related e-business ontologies can be used in parallel.

Collaborative User Involvement

So far, the results produced by matching tools are not perfect and require user input for quality enhancement. Part of the explanation is the fact, that very often the identification of similarity between entities is futile without knowledge regarding the domain context. Context may be looked at as information characterizing entities, since it contains background knowledge (Keßler, 2007). Usually, context information is not directly available, it is only contained in user expertise. Sometimes it becomes implicitly obvious from the domain specific language utilized within the information system in use, from where it may be extracted. But since an important part of knowledge resides within people's minds only, its capture is beneficial for advancing collaboration (Boone & Ganeshan, 2008). Thus, exploiting the existence of a "wisdom of crowds", a collective intelligence being broader than an individual alone, facilitates knowledge growth through linking and sharing (Ankolekar, Krötzsch, Tran, & Vrandecic, 2007). Through this active participation intensified collaboration can be realized, as implicit knowledge is extracted and becomes usable.

Therefore, technologies for collaboration and semantic technologies can complement each other in this respect (Gruber, 2007). In the given case here, context-sensitive filtering can separate appropriate mappings from inappropriate ones. Hence, an integrated system offers more comprehensive information collection and exchange.

For evaluating the trustworthiness of information, regardless if generated automatically or through user input, rating mechanisms can have a regulating influence. Often, a rating is a user contribution and is intended at ranking information (Mika, 2006, p. 23). However, this requires action on the part of the user. Therefore, as an alternative, the recording of user choices may instead be performed transparently for him and thus prevent additional efforts. In the given case, a rating in a simple form for a semantic reference could be the percentage of choices of a reference in relation to the number of times it has been suggested. Further enhancement of such a rating is derivable from the context in which it was issued, for a ranking according to applicability.

System Design

Over the past years, extensive work has been done in developing ontology engineering tools and frameworks. Building on these foundations, we have developed our ORBI Ontology Mediator as a scalable solution to providing semantic synchronization. It is a framework for supporting the reconciliation of differing terminology based on the use of ontologies. Offering solutions for disambiguation discrepancies, it works as a mediating medium. The basis of our framework is a dynamically growing reference repository that does not require initial manual creation efforts. Depending on the usage scenario, this repository may be set-up for exclusive use within a confined environment or openly on the web.

The ORBI Ontology Mediator allows connecting different mapping, inference and storage tools by an adapter mechanism. References are automatically produced by the connected mapping and reasoning tools and may be added, edited and rated manually. Setting this up in an iterative manner leads to the creation of an evolutionary growing and improving relation collection. The reference repository is accessed via a web service interface, thus allowing integration into arbitrary e-business client applications. Context information from the client application is used to disambiguate different possible mappings for the business term in question. Figure 2 shows the architectural layout. Since the basic concept foresees adapters for coupling existing matching and inference systems, an individual system configuration as desired can be set-up, allowing system combinations or the linking of future developments.

Figure 2. The ORBI ontology mediator's design

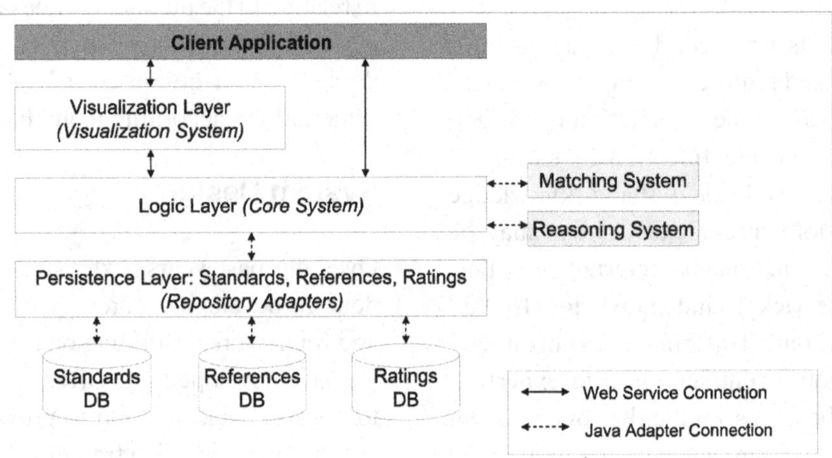

The core system consists of two parts, which are the references and the ratings subsystems. The references subsystem stores the semantic references and the references standards and also calls the matching and inference systems attached. The ratings subsystem is set-up for storing and evaluating the references' ratings together with their context information and calculates the acceptances values. In addition, plug-ins for reporting, access control and digital rights management as well as for converting standards into ontology format and a visualization system for providing graphic, interactive views may be added. The framework is implemented in Java on top of the Jena2 framework and can be accessed by a web service interface, so that it may be integrated with arbitrary applications. It offers a standard interface for daily operation, which is the provision of semantic references, and an expert interface for administration and maintenance purposes. Tools for matching and mapping as well as reasoning can be variably connected by Java adapters. In its present status the system is connected to matching tools as described below. However, the connection to inference systems is only activated in cases of experimental reasoning with small ontologies and mapping collections for deducing, as the scalability of reasoning systems for large-scale ontologies is still an active research field (Schlicht & Stuckenschmidt, 2008).

Context-Sensitive Mappings

Computing and collecting mappings is an iterative process. An initial reference base is established in an automated manner by means of matching and inference tools. Users may contribute to it by actively creating or rating relations themselves. But most importantly, they are giving their implicit feedback for rating of the references available. They are included in the process through observation and rating their choices for or against the usage of a certain semantic relation in a specific context. From these details the applicability of a relation can be measured and put to further use. Enhancing a mapping with a measurement of its applicability extends the description of the semantic relation at hand. For determining the applicability of a reference, context is taken for its disambiguation and subsequent quality enhancement (Rebstock et al., 2008, p. 132ff). This can be achieved unnoticeably to the user in the background. The observation of a user's choice or rejection of a suggested reference can be understood as a rating, either positive or negative, which is stored and used to calculate a reference's acceptance value *a*. With that value, the above definition for mappings is extended to

$<e_1, e_2, R, c, a>$,

where *a* is a dynamically computed value which expresses the acceptance of a reference describing the degree of trust and reputation in the assumed relation. It is calculated from the users' feedback. We call these extended mappings *semantic references.*

Over time, with recurring selections and rejections by a greater number of users, a reference's acceptance value can increase or decrease and could be used by the system, e.g., for ranking query outputs. However, this could lead to the situation that different users may rate the same reference very differently, even though each user can be right within his own context. Therefore, in order to disambiguate references, context-sensitive semantic referencing helps to separate applicable from non-applicable ones by comparing a rating's context to a query's context and weighting the users' ratings accordingly (Rebstock et al., 2008, p. 163). The user's decisions for or against the usage of a certain reference in a certain context are observed for generating positive or negative ratings. As not to impose additional workload onto a user, this is processed in the background transparently to the user.

When comparing an official and a proprietary standard, as shown in Figure 1, this facilitates for example a statement like

<UNSPSCv11.0_Writing paper, STANDARDB_Writing Paper, equal, 1.00, 0.85>,

which reads as "Writing Paper in Standard UNSPSC Version 11.0 and Writing Paper in Standard B are equal with a confidence of 100%, and 85% all of users agreed on this statement".

Since, as mentioned, information formatted and annotated according to a chosen standard cannot easily or flexibly be reformatted without major efforts, knowledge about semantic correspondencies, in particular equivalencies and similarities, can help in dissolving discrepancies. The references are as easy to use as a business dictionary.

Semantic Referencing as Base Process

The combination of semantic technologies and active user participation offers the possibility to generate a knowledge base in a bottom-up manner. Overall, the system is self-learning and can adapt the references collection over time. We call this process *semantic referencing.* A first seed is delivered by automated means. This does not require any expensive, time consuming preparatory work to be delivered by groups of experts. Figure 3 depicts the individual steps and shows the interchange between user and system.

In a first step, e-business standards are converted into a common format for syntactical alignment and turned into ontologies. For example, XSLT transformations can be developed for transforming standards available in XML into OWL. The development of such transformations is a non-trivial task which requires the involvement of subject matter expertise for each standard. As a full explanation would be out of scope of this article, we just give a brief synopsis. In order to transform the standards as-is, a pragmatic approach has been decided upon. Classification categories have been turned into ontology classes with subclass/superclass relations. Even though these taxonomies contain inconsistencies, as shown by Hepp and de Bruijn (2007), the benefit was to obtain rather quickly huge amounts of transformed information. As the focus was on the issue of matching several ontologies, the inherited inconsistencies in some areas of individual ontologies did not seem to have a high impact. For document and process standards transformation the mechanical approaches as presented by Klein, Fensel, Harmelen, & Horrocks (2001) and

Figure 3. Semantic referencing

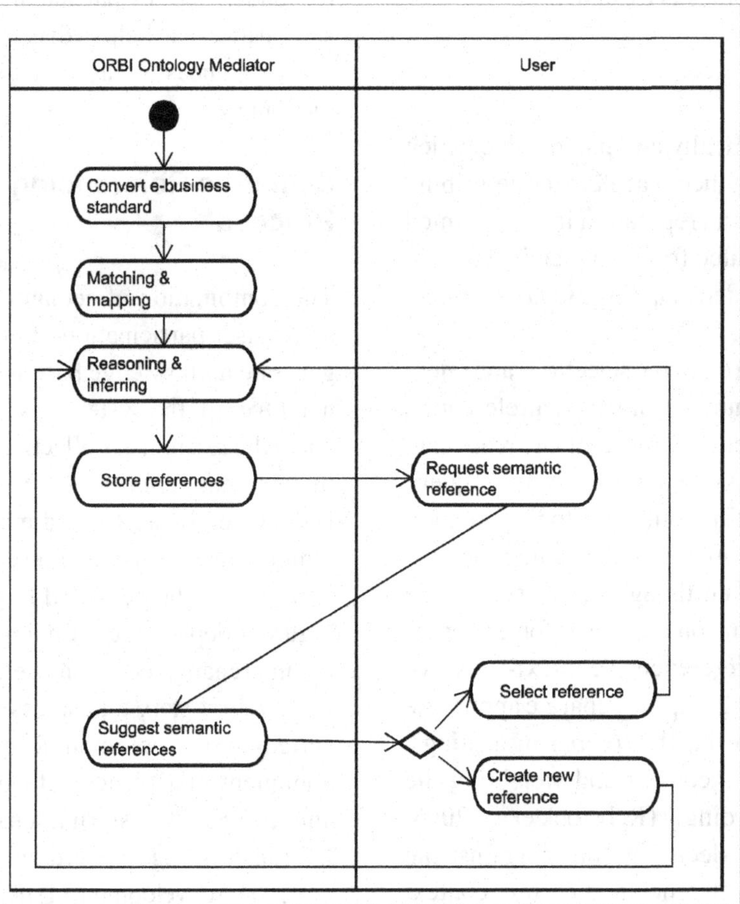

Bohring and Auer (2005) in combination with Garcia and Gil (2007) have been brought together and adapted. For unstructured formats, ontology learning technologies may be applied.

For finding references, matching and mapping is performed without merging or modifying any of the ontologies. The result is an initial set of mappings, which is neither complete nor correct. Further mappings may be deduced by employing reasoning and inference tools, presently depending on the size of the ontologies. All mappings discovered are persisted in the reference repository for further use. In reply to a user query, the mediator system searches the repository like a dictionary and generates a context-sensitive list of suggested references, from which users can choose a reference or, if none of the suggestions fits, create a new one or proceed without a selection from the list. The system observes the users' selections and generates the applicable ratings. The ratings are stored in the ratings repository and are used for calculating the context-dependent acceptance values. Hence, the referencing is performed en passant for the user. Furthermore, this way the system-suggested mappings are presented to the user for evaluation. This reduces the need for domain experts manually checking, as users are taken here as experts in their field of knowledge.

The identification of context information is not a task performed by the ORBI Ontology Mediator, but by the user or the application in which the Mediator is embedded. When using a query interface, users may enter a list of free terms which define their context. When embedding the mediator, the application in which it is embedded can provide those context terms automatically, e.g., by using terms from the document currently edited. Context information is stored and processed as a set of weighted terms. When calculating the context-dependent acceptance value, those sets are compared, and each rating is weighted with the similarity of the context sets. Thus, ratings issued in a similar context receive higher weights than ratings issued in a different context. A typical case of ambiguity resolved by using context information is the occurrence of polysemy and homonymy. All new information entered into the system through these actions evokes the inferring of new references. Thus, the process cycle may begin again, providing self-learning capabilities. Furthermore, the reference collection is extendable by direct input and improvable by way of manipulation such as deleting objectionable references like false positives.

Partitioning for Matching Large-Scale Ontologies

One of the most important tasks the ORBI Ontology Mediator has to fulfil is the automated discovery of mappings. However, current e-business standards are often represented by large-scale ontologies, and only a few of the presently available systems focus explicitly on matching such large-scale ontologies, e.g., the schema matching system COMA++ (Do & Rahm, 2007) and the ontology matching tool Falcon-AO (Hu, Zhao, & Qu, 2006). They address the scalability problem by first partitioning the input ontologies into smaller sub-ontologies and then performing the actual matching task on the partitions. Unfortunately, these tools are often implemented in a way that they consume too much memory to be run on a typical desktop computer. Extensive testing to examine the scalability of the currently available ontology matching tools revealed that matching large-scale ontologies is still a severe unsolved problem (Paulheim, 2008). Furthermore, both of the tools mentioned are monolithic applications which do not allow a combined approach by adding other partitioning algorithms or matching systems.

Nevertheless, the idea of dividing the input ontologies into partitions small enough for processing seems promising. In order to follow the ORBI Ontology Mediator's general idea of leveraging existing work, the matching framework *Malasco* has been developed. Its name is a derivation of the expression "matching large-scale ontologies". The system partitions ontologies for coping with the scalability problem for finding mappings and thus allows the utilization of existing non-scalable tools also on large-scale ontologies, as the matching is carried out on the smaller partitions. The modular design facilitates a flexible coupling of matching and partitioning tools. Thus, the system can be a versatile tool to be tuned according to individual demands of particular applications domains besides e-business, e.g., bioinformatics or cultural heritage. Figure 4 shows the design.

Within the prototypical Malasco implementation in use, three partitioning algorithms have been applied. The first is the islands algorithm (Stuckenschmidt & Klein, 2004). It works in a top-down manner by eliminating connections in the graph underlying an ontology, until that graph falls into pieces of independent islands, which are than regarded as sub-ontologies. The algorithm attempts at choosing those connections for elimination which serve as bridges between strongly connected sub-graphs.

The ε-connections partitioning algorithm (Grau, Parsia, Sirin, & Kalyanpur, 2005), on the other hand, is a bottom-up algorithm. It starts from a set of partitions each containing only one concept from the original ontology, and subsequently merges those partitions.

The third algorithm is a naïve algorithm, which has been implemented to provide a baseline for

Figure 4. Malasco's design

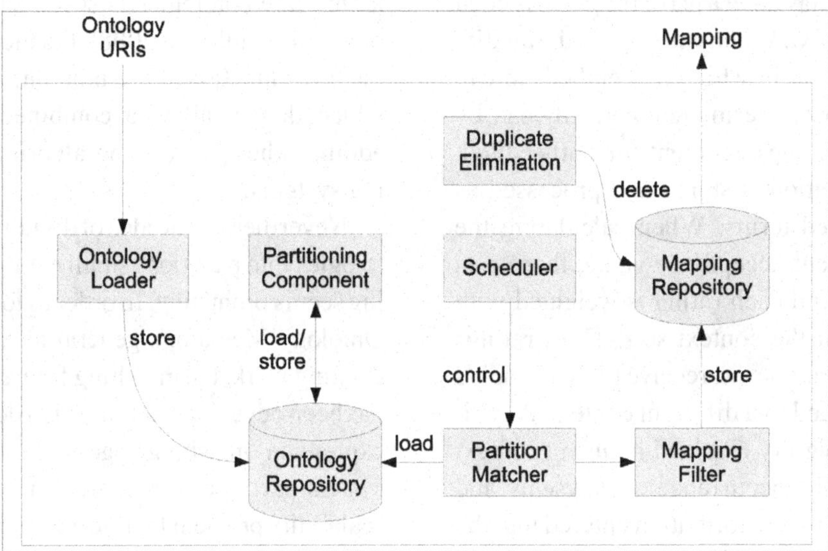

comparing the results. It arbitrarily divides the input ontologies into partitions of a fixed size.

The partitions provided by the partitioning algorithms are then matched by existing matching tools. Since the partitions are smaller than the input ontologies, non-scaleable matching tools may be employed to match those partitions. In the prototypical implementation we have used INRIA (Euzenat, 2004) and FOAM (Ehrig, 2007) as example matching tools, as they are on the one hand well-known and thoroughly evaluated, and on the other hand both proved not to be well-scaleable (Paulheim, 2008). The choice for those partitioning and matching tools and algorithms, however, is not mandatory. Due to Malasco's modular architecture, arbitrary partitioning and matching tools can be used with the system.

The system evaluation has shown that the choice of a particular partitioning algorithm as well as using overlapping partitions has little impact, whereas filtering results using a lower confidence threshold can significantly improve the result quality. Experiments on smaller-scale datasets demonstrated that the quality deviation of mappings produced by Malasco compared to results on unpartitioned ontologies could be reduced to less than 5%. In the field of e-business two rather largely used standards, namely eClass having about 375K triples and UNSPSC with about 83K triples, could not be processed at all by any other matching tool than Malasco, which the ORBI Ontology Mediator is presently set-up with it. Experiments have shown that Malasco is capable of matching those large e-business ontologies by using standard, non-scalable matching tools (Paulheim, 2008). Three key findings resulted. Firstly, when matching large-scale ontologies using the approach described above, the most time-consuming part (about 99% of the total runtime) is the pairwise matching of partitions. In other words, the overhead for partitioning and re-combining the results is neglectable, as can be seen in Figure 5.

Secondly, the result quality (in terms of F-Measure) is up to 97% percent of the results compared to the matching of unpartitioned ontologies. Such an optimization can be achieved by using a simple filter discarding mapping elements below a certain confidence threshold. Other optimization techniques, such as using overlapping partitions, are more costly in terms of runtime and memory consumption, and less effective concerning result

Figure 5. Malasco runtime analysis when matching eClass and UNSPSC. The time axis has a logarithmic scale

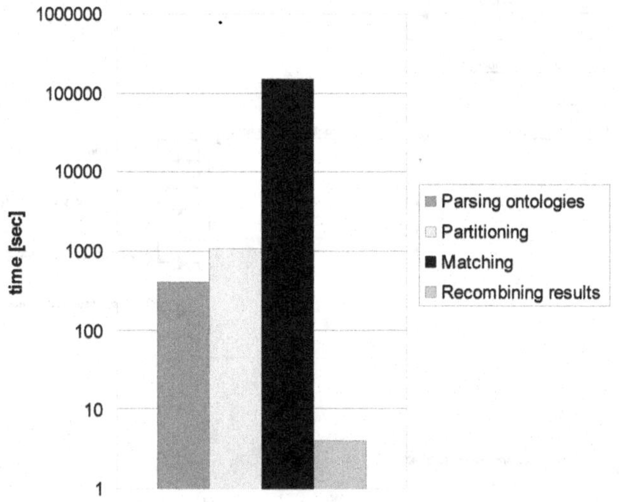

quality. Thirdly, the actual choice for a particular partitioning algorithm has only little influence on the result quality. Thus, the use of a highly sophisticated partitioning algorithm bears only little improvement, compared with using the quick and naïve baseline algorithm. More details on the evaluation of the Malasco system can be found in (Paulheim, 2008).

Achieving Semantic Synchronization in Electronic Negotiations

Putting the ORBI Mediator to work in combination with a business application provides synchronization by way of dynamically resolving semantic mismatches. Resolving ambiguity benefits from the automatedly established reference collection and presents the references found to users for their evaluation. The services offered by the ORBI Ontology Mediator may be called upon as often as necessary. In the course of a business transaction it may be possible that the intended meaning of a business term is subject to mutual discussion and cannot be solved by one of the partners alone. The process may even resemble a negotiation.

As outlined above, electronic negotiation support systems can serve as an example for e-business systems in general. As a practical case for semantic interoperability, the conduction of multi attribute negotiations shows the difficulties in synchronizing information in a system where partners are enabled to introduce arbitrary items, attributes and attribute values into a negotiation and how ontology mapping technology can be applied for providing a solution. The integration of the ORBI services into the M2N negotiation system can assist users in conducting negotiations about items and attributes which are not pre-defined and reach understanding of the content meaning by synchronizing themselves semantically. The basic process is depicted in Figure 6.

When finding a term, an item, or an attribute name or value either with an ambiguous or unknown meaning while working in the negotiation system, users can mark it and request a semantic reference for that element. By querying the ORBI service, business partners can access references between the standards they apply. The answer

Figure 6. Semantic synchronization

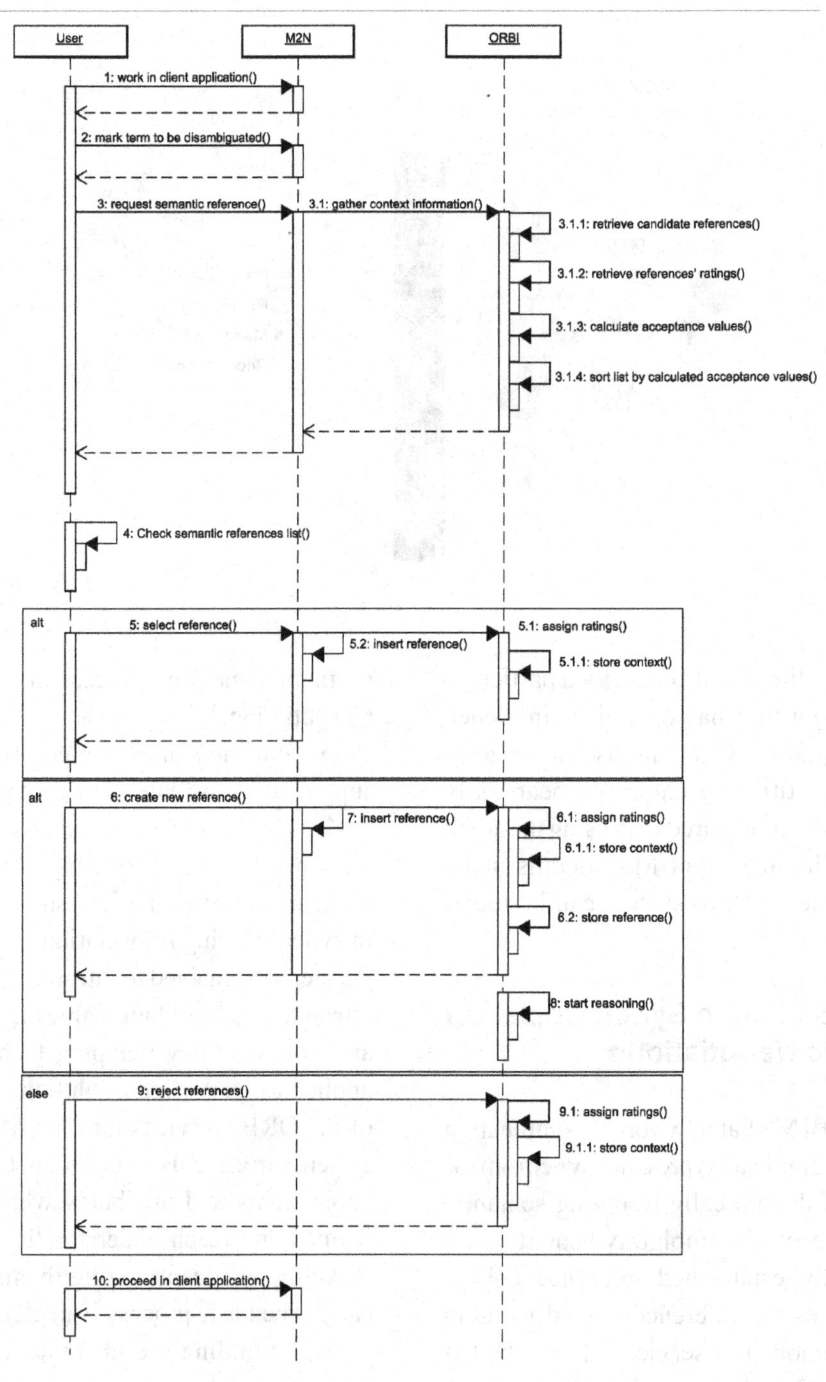

to this query is a list of possible counterparts in the querying user's own standard, sorted by their appropriateness given the user's current context. For ease of use, also queries without the entry of a source or destination term's standard are facilitated by the system. After receiving the list of suggestions, users can choose a reference as seems appropriate, as can be seen in Figure 7.

Figure 7. List of suggested semantic references in ORBI

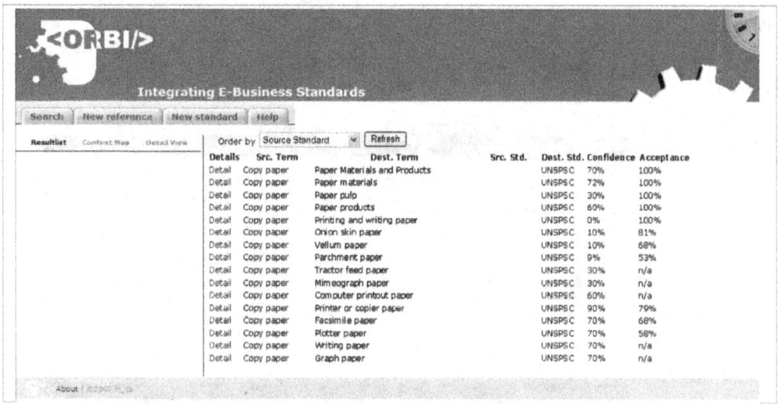

Through selection, the reference is copied over into the negotiation application. Thus, the selected reference becomes an integral part of the negotiated document and can be dynamically negotiated by both partners like any other term such as the price or any quality attribute, until they have agreed on a common understanding of an element's meaning, and, overall, of a negotiated contract's semantics. The reference is being included into the negotiation and the subsequently closed contract, as depicted in Figure 8. Alternatively, users can also create a new reference manually if none of those offered by the semantic synchronization service is appropriate. Thus, the reference collection dynamically grows. The process can be repeated as often as needed by each of the business partners. In doing so, the business negotiation is extended by a subtask, which is clarifying the meaning of a contract element in question by way of negotiating.

Information about the users' interaction with the service is implicitly gathered and used to improve the mapping quality. All references selected retrieve a positive rating with some context information extracted from the current negotiation contract document, all those which have been proposed but not selected, receive a negative one.

In the above example, the semantic synchronization service is integrated directly into the client application, which here is the negotiation support system M2N. Alternatively, users may be supported with semantic references in arbitrary web-based applications by means of using the service's functionality through a browser plug-in. Then users can mark terms in the web pages displayed by the application and retrieve semantic references with the help of the plug-in, hence allowing the user to understand the semantics of unknown terms. Suggested references can be flagged as appropriate or inappropriate and thus, users create feedback. Additionally, as possible within the fix coupled client application, users can also create new references and let the reference collection evolve. Context information to disambiguate different references can be extracted from the web page. This way, semantic synchronization can be integrated into arbitrary web-based applications without having to modify those applications as done in the above case.

Direct access to the Mediator can be obtained through a web-based user interface. For standard queries an interface offering the entry of the term in question is available. For more sophisticated searches, an expert interface allows to directly query the reference repository with preselecting the standards in question and adding the terms for context determination. Figure 9 shows screenshots for the query and the resulting suggested references list.

Figure 8. Addition of semantic reference in M2N

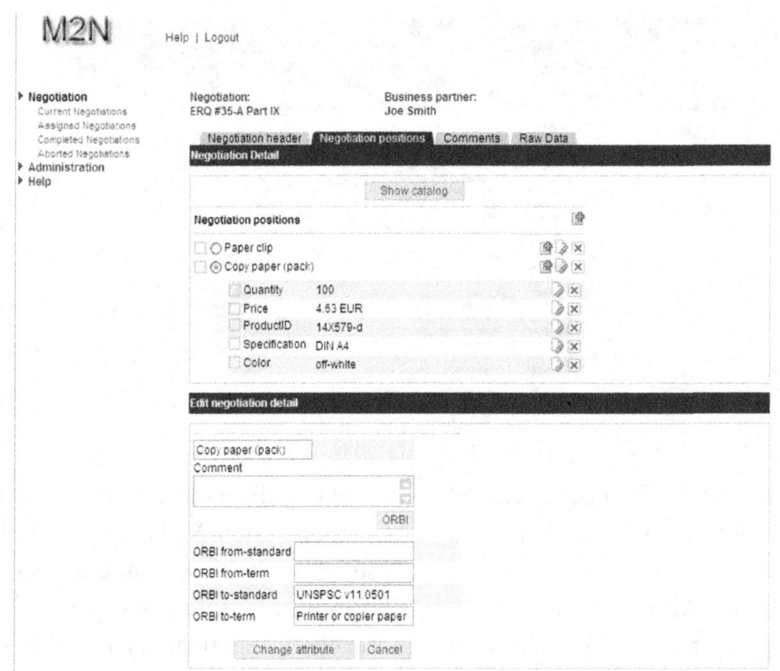

Figure 9. ORBI user interface: extended searching

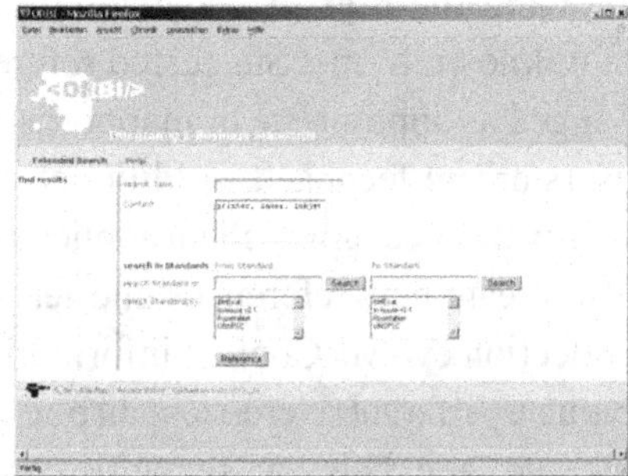

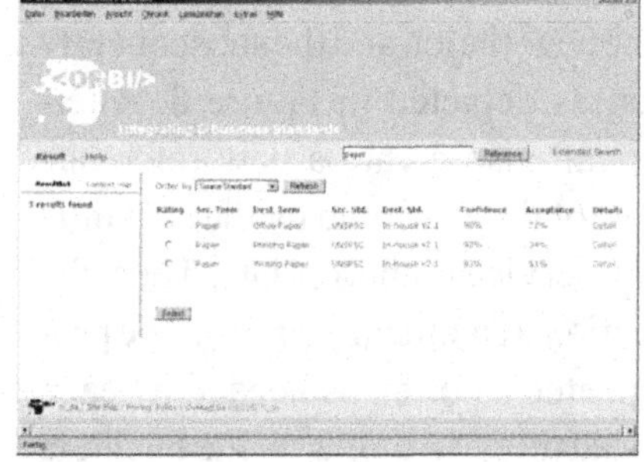

Furthermore, for maintenance and further development an interface is available, allowing the addition of new standards and editing of existing references as may become necessary over time. This user interface foresees active user involvement. With these alternative access possibilities, the ORBI Ontology Mediator may be set up for daily operation and may further be opened for advancing the reference collection.

CONCLUSION AND DISCUSSION

With the ORBI Ontology Mediator and Malasco components developed, we have shown how ontology mapping technology can be applied usefully to achieve semantic interoperability. Both systems are modularily designed, thus facilitating individual configuration. With our example of using ontology matching combined with a partitioning framework in an integration scenario involving large-scale e-business ontologies, its usefulness in solving a real-world demand without initial ramp-up effort could be demonstrated. Through its rating capabilities it is possible to collaboratively include users' expertise for quality enhancement.

In the past, research activities have often concentrated on creating a central ontology (Omelayenko, 2002), or merging existing product classifications into a new umbrella ontology by developing a hierarchic structure of ontologies, connected by mappings (Corcho & Gómez-Pérez, 2001), or integrating different e-business ontologies under one global umbrella ontology like for example WordNet (Kim, Choi, & Park, 2005), or deploying a central ontology for defining mappings (Beneventano, Guerra, Magnani, & Vincini, 2004). In contrast to these approaches, our referencing process allows for continuous growth of the reference collection over time by at the same time being flexibly extendable to changes, enhancements and novel or unexpected standards coming up due to the facilitation of active user input. Unlike as in related efforts, the intention of the ORBI project was to build a reference collection to be used for self-adaptive evolution instead of working with on-the-fly mapping of ontologies (Lopez, Sabou, & Motta, 2006). For disambiguation we use context information, while other approaches assign references to user communities for doing so, as this additionally requires a user management (Zhdanova & Shvaiko, 2006). However, we have also shown that user communities may also be regarded as context information and that thus the ORBI Ontology Mediator may also be used to provide disambiguation of semantic references based on user communities (Paulheim, Rebstock & Fengel, 2008).

One advantage upon incorporating the system is the possibility to automatically generate an initial reference base. Labour-intensive preparation by an expert team developing the ontology mappings can be avoided and subsequently cost incurrence for central editorial tasks. Furthermore, the workload for users for collaboratively giving feedback is reduced through the transparently computable reference rating. Additionally, this passive participation can be combined with active collaboration by including new input or performing maintenance. Such community involvement may help in accepting and adopting the system and ensuring ongoing user support, thus avoiding the acceptance and cost problems that became obvious in the past with attempts at introducing centrally managed knowledge management in enterprises.

We have shown how the service can be integrated into different types of client applications. In principle, the various ways of synchronising as described here are generic and may therefore be applied to any setting involving the matching of large-scale ontologies, e.g., in bioinformatics or health informatics as well as the automatic deployment of semantic web services in service-oriented architectures.

However, the system's usefulness depends not only on the size of the reference collection, but on its acceptance and adoption, as a high usage rate will improve the references' quality quickly and thus offer a benefit and support in a user's daily work. The question of accumulating a critical mass of users has to be faced.

CURRENT CHALLENGES FACING THE ORGANIZATION

Further research activities will include the improvement of user support by ontology visualization techniques, and the use of different ontology mapping and reasoning tools for allowing a quicker growth and improvement of the collection. As existing reasoning tools suffer from the scalability issue as well as matching tools, adapting those reasoning tools for example by partitioning ontologies, as done for ontology matching in the Malasco system, is still an open challenge. Also, a long-time study of a system implementation in full use would allow experimental analysis regarding user reaction and user impact as well as observing semantic inconsistencies occurring in the course of its use and the approaches at solving them.

As the funding for the research project has terminated, presently these works are continued on a much smaller scale. Nevertheless, the insights gained are disseminated by way of publishing and inclusion into the university lectures as well as carried on to related projects for sharing the knowledge acquired.

REFERENCES

Alexiev, V., Breu, M., de Bruijn, J., Fensel, D., Lara, R., & Lausen, H. (2005). *Information Integration with Ontologies*. Chichester, UK: Wiley

Ankolekar, A., Krötzsch, M., Tran, T., & Vrandecic, D. (2007). The Two Cultures Mashing up Web 2.0 and the Semantic Web. In *Proceedings of the 16th International Conference on World Wide Web* (pp. 825–834). DOI 10.1145/1242572.12426842007.

Antoniou, G., Franconi, E., & van Harmelen, F. (2005). Introduction to Semantic Web Ontology Languages. In N. Eisinger & J. Maluszynski (Eds.), *Proceedings of the Summer School: Reasoning Web (LNCS 3564)*. Berlin, Heidelberg, Germany: Springer.

Beneventano, D., Guerra, F., Magnani, S., & Vincini, M. (2004). A Web Service based framework for the semantic mapping amongst product classification schemas. *Journal of Electronic Commerce Research*, *5*(2), 114–127.

Benyoucef, M., & Rinderle, S. (2006). Modeling e-Negotiation Processes for a Service Oriented Architecture. *Group Decision and Negotiation*, *15*, 449–467. doi:10.1007/s10726-006-9038-6

Berners-Lee, T., Hendler, J., & Lassila, O. (2001, May). The Semantic Web. *Scientific American*, 29–37.

Blumauer, A., & Pellegrini, T. (2006). Semantic Web und semantische Technologien: Zentrale Begriffe und Unterscheidungen. In T. Pellegrini & A. Blumauer (Eds.), *Semantic Web Wege zur vernetzten Wissensgesellschaft* (pp. 9–25). Berlin Heidelberg New York: Springer.

Bohring, H., & Auer, S. (2005). Mapping XML to OWL Ontologies. In *Proceedings of 13. Leipziger Informatik-Tage (LIT 2005), Lecture Notes in Informatics (LNI)*. Bonn, Germany: Köllen.

Boone, T., & Ganeshan, R. (2008). Knowledge acquisition and transfer among engineers: effects of network structure. *Managerial and Decision Economics*, *29*(5), 459–468. doi:10.1002/mde.1401

Corcho, O., & Gómez-Pérez, A. (2001). Solving Integration Problems of E-commerce Standards and Initiatives through Ontological Mappings. In *Proceedings of the Workshop on E-Business and intelligent Web at the Seventeenth International Joint Conference on Artificial Intelligence (IJCAI2001)*. Retrieved November 11, 2006, from http://sunsite.informatik.rwth-aachen.de/Publications/CEURWS//Vol-47/corcho.pdf

Daconta, M. C., Obrst, L. J., & Smith, K. T. (2003). *The Semantic Web. A Guide to the Future of XML, Web Services, and Knowledge Management*. Indianapolis, USA: Wiley.

de Bruijn, J. (2004). *Semantic Information Integration Inside and Across Organizational Boundaries* (Tech. Report DERI-2004-05-04A). Innsbruck, Austria: Digital Enterprise Research Institute.

Do, H. H., & Rahm, E. (2007). Matching large schemas: Approaches and evaluation. *Information Systems*, *32*(6), 857–885. doi:10.1016/j.is.2006.09.002

ebXML (2007). *About ebXML*. Retrieved August 06, 2007, from http://www.ebxml.org/geninfo.html

Ehrig, M. (2004). Ontology Mapping – An Integrated Approach. In C. Bussler, J. Davis, D. Fensel, & R. Studer (Eds.), *Proceedings of the First European Semantic Web Conference (LNCS 3053)* (pp. 76-91). Berlin Heidelberg, Germany: Springer.

Ehrig, M. (2007). *Ontology Alignment - Bridging the Semantic Gap. Semantic Web and Beyond. Computing for Human Experience*. New York, USA: Springer.

Euzenat, J. (2004). An API for ontology alignment. In S.A. McIlraith, D. Plexousakis, & F. van Harmelen (Eds.), *The Semantic Web - ISWC 2004, Proceedings of the Third International Semantic Web Conference (LNCS (3298)* (pp. 698-712). Springer.

Euzenat, J., Mocan, A., & Scharffe, F. (2007). Ontology Alignments An ontology management perspective. In M. Hepp, P. De Leenheer, A. de Moor, & Y. Sure (Eds.), *Ontology Management* (pp. 177-206). New York: Springer.

Euzenat, J., & Shvaiko, P. (2007). *Ontology Matching*. Berlin Heidelberg New York: Springer.

Fensel, D. (2004). *Ontologies: A Silver Bullet for Knowledge Management and Electronic Commerce*. Berlin, Germany: Springer.

García, R., & Gil, R. (2007). Facilitating Business Interoperability from the Semantic Web. In W. Abramowicz (Ed.), *Proceedings of the 10th International Conference on Business Information Systems, BIS'07 (LNCS 4439)* (pp. 220-232). Berlin Heidelberg New York: Springer.

Glushko, R. J., & McGrath, T. (2002). Document Engineering for e-Business. In *Proceedings of the 2002 ACM Symposium on Document Engineering*, Virginia, USA.

Gómez-Pérez, A., Fernandéz-López, M., & Corcho, O. (2004). *Ontological Engineering*. London, UK: Springer.

Grau, B. C., Parsia, B., Sirin, E., & Kalyanpur, A. (2005). Modularizing OWL ontologies. In D. Sleeman, H. Alani, C. Brewster, & N. Noy (Eds.), *Proceedings of the 3rd International Conference on Knowledge Capture (K-CAP 2005)*. Retrieved November 03, 2008, from http://www.mindswap.org/2004/multipleOnt/papers/modularFinal.pdf

Gruber, T. (2007). Collective knowledge systems: Where the Social Web meets the Semantic Web. *Web Semantics: Science. Services and Agents on the World Wide Web, 1*(6), 4–13.

Gruber, T. R. (1993). A translation approach to portable ontology specifications. *Knowledge Acquisition, 5*(2), 199–220. doi:10.1006/knac.1993.1008

Hepp, M., & de Bruijn, J. (2007). GenTax: A Generic Methodology for Deriving OWL and RDF-S Ontologies from Hierarchical Classifications, Thesauri, and Inconsistent Taxonomies. In E. Franconi, M. Kifer, & W. May (Eds.), *Proceedings of the 4th European Semantic Web Conference (LNCS 4519)* (pp. 129-144). Berlin Heidelberg New York: Springer.

Herbst, U. (2007). *Präferenzmessung in industriellen Verhandlungen*. Wiesbaden, Germany: Universitäts-Verlag.

Hoffmann, A. (2006). *Interaktionen zwischen Anbietern und Nachfragern bei der Vermarktung und Beschaffung innovativer Dienstleistungen*. Wiesbaden, Germany: Universitäts-Verlag.

Hu, W., & Qu, Y. (2006). Block Matching for Ontologies. In I.F. Cruz, S. Decker, D. Allemang, C. Preist, D. Schwabe, P. Mika, M. Uschold, & L. Aroyo (Eds.), *The Semantic Web - ISWC 2006, 5th International Semantic Web Conference (LNCS 4273)* (pp. 300–313). Berlin Heidelberg New York: Springer.

Hu, W., Zhao, Y., & Qu, Y. (2006). Partition-based block matching of large class hierarchies. In R. Mizoguchi, Z. Shi, & F. Giunchiglia (Eds.), *Proceedings of the The Semantic Web - ASWC 2006*

First Asian Semantic Web Conference (LNCS 4183). Berlin Heidelberg New York: Springer.

ISO. (2004). *ISO/IEC Guide 2:2004 Standardization and related activities – General vocabulary* (8th ed.). Geneva, Switzerland: ISO Press.

Kalfoglou, Y., Hu, B., Reynolds, D., & Shadbolt, N. (2005). *CROSI project final report* (Tech. Report E-Print No. 11717). Southampton, UK: University of Southampton.

Kalfoglou, Y., & Schorlemmer, M. (2005). Ontology mapping: The state of the art. In Y. Kalfoglou, M. Schorlemmer, A.P. Sheth, S. Staab, & M. Uschold, (Eds.), *Semantic Interoperability and Integration: Dagstuhl Seminar Proceedings (No. 04391)* (pp. 1-31)

Kalfoglou, Y., Schorlemmer, W. M., & Sheth, A. P. Staab, Steffen, & Uschold, M. (Eds.) (2005). Semantic Interoperability and Integration. *Dagstuhl Seminar Proceedings 04391 IBFI.* Schloss Dagstuhl, Germany. Retrieved 02. February 2009 from http://www.informatik.uni-trier.de/~ley/db/conf/dagstuhl/P4391.html

Kersten, G. E., & Lai, H. (2007). Negotiation Support and E-negotiation Systems: An Overview. *Group Decision and Negotiation, 16*, 553–586. doi:10.1007/s10726-007-9095-5

Keßler, C. (2007) Similarity Measurement in Context. In *Proceedings of 6th International and Interdisciplinary Conference on Modeling and Using Context (LNAI 4635)* (pp. 277–290). Berlin Heidelberg, Germany: Springer.

Kim, W., Choi, D. W., & Park, S. (2005). Product Information Meta-search Framework for Electronic Commerce. In A. Gómez-Pérez, & J. Euzenat (Eds.), *Proceedings of the European Semantic Web Conference (ESWC 2005), (LNCS 3532)* (pp. 408–422). Berlin Heidelberg, Germany: Springer.

Klein, M. (2001). Combining and relating ontologies: an analysis of problems and solutions. In A. Gómez-Pérez, M. Gruninger, & M. Uschold (Eds.), *Proceedings of Workshop on Ontologies and Information Sharing (IJCAI'01)* (pp. 52-63).

Klein, M., Fensel, D., van Harmelen, F., & Horrocks, I. (2001). The Relations Between Ontologies and XML Schema. *Electronic Trans. on Artificial Intelligence, 2001. Special Issue on the 1st International Workshop Semantic Web: Models, Architectures and Management.*

Lee, Y., Sayyadian, M., Doan, A., & Rosenthal, A. S. (2007). etuner: tuning schema matching software using synthetic scenarios. *The VLDB Journal, 16*(1), 97–122. doi:10.1007/s00778-006-0024-z

Linthicum, D. S. (1999). *Enterprise Application Integration*. Toronto, Canada: Addison-Wesley Professional.

Lopez, V., Sabou, M., & Motta, E. (2006). PowerMap: Mapping the Real Semantic Web on the Fly. In *Proceedings of 5th International Semantic Web Conference (ISWC-2005) (LNCS 4273)* (pp. 414–427). Berlin Heidelberg, Germany: Springer.

McGuiness, D. L. (2003). Ontologies Come of Age. In D. Fensel, J. Hendler, H. Lieberman, & W. Wahlster (Eds.), *Spinning the Semantic Web: Bringing the World Wide Web to Its Full Potential* (pp. 171-193). Cambridge, USA: MIT Press.

Mika, P. (2006). *Social Networks and the SemanticWeb*. New York: Springer.

Mochol, M., Jentzsch, A., & Euzenat, J. (2006). Applying an analytic method for matching approach selection. In P. Shvaiko, J. Euzenat, N. Noy, H. Stuckenschmidt, V.R. Benjamins, & M. Uschold (Eds.), *Proceedings of the 1st International Workshop on Ontology Matching (OM-2006) Collocated with the 5th International Semantic Web Conference (ISWC-2006). CEUR Workshop Proceedings* (Vol. 225) (pp. 37-48). CEUR-WS.org.

Noy, N. (2004). Semantic Integration: A Survey Of Ontology-Based Approaches. *SIGMOD Record, 33*, 65–70. doi:10.1145/1041410.1041421

Omelayenko, B. (2001). Preliminary Ontology Modeling for B2B Content Integration. In *Proceedings of the First International Workshop on Electronic Business Hubs at the Twelfth International Conference on Database and Expert Systems Applications (DEXA-2001)* (pp. 7-13). Washington, D.C., USA: IEEE Computer Society.

Omelayenko, B. (2002). Ontology Mediated Business Integration. In *Proceedings of the 13th EKAW 2002 Conference (LNAI 2473)* (pp. 264-269). Berlin Heidelberg, Germany: Springer.

Open Group. (2007). *The UDEF. The Universal Data Element Framework*. Retrieved August 30, 2008, from http://www.opengroup.org/udef

Paulheim, H., Rebstock, M., & Fengel, J. (2007). Context-Sensitive Referencing for Ontology Mapping Disambiguation. In P. Bouquet, J. Euzenat, C. Ghiaini, D.L. McGuinness, V. Paiva, de, L. Serafini, P. Shvaiko, & H. Wache (Eds.), *Proceedings of the 2007 Workshop on Contexts and Ontologies: Reasoning and Representation (C&O:RR-2007)* (Computer Science Research Report No. 15) (pp. 47-56). Roskilde, Denmark: Roskilde University.

Paulheim. H. (2008). On Applying Matching Tools to Large-Scale Ontologies. *Third International Workshop On Ontology Matching (OM-2008) Collocated with the 7th International Semantic Web Conference (ISWC-2008)*. Retrieved November 03, 2008, from www.dit.unitn.it/~p2p/OM-2008/om2008_poster1.pdf

Rebstock, M., & Fengel, J. (2003). Integrierte elektronische Verhandlungsprozesse auf Basis von ebXML und Web-Services. *HMD Praxis der Wirtschaftsinformatik, 234*(40), 52–60.

Rebstock, M., Fengel, J., & Paulheim, H. (2007). Context-sensitive Semantic Synchronization in Electronic Negotiations. In G.E. Kersten, J. Rios, & E. Chen, (Eds.), *Proceedings of Group Decision and Negotiation (GDN)* (Vol. 2). Montreal, Canada: Interneg Research Center, Concordia University, Montreal.

Rebstock, M., Fengel, J., & Paulheim, H. (2008). *Ontologies-based Business Integration*. Berlin Heidelberg, Germany: Springer.

Saeki, M., & Kaiya, H. (2006). On Relationships among Models, Meta Models and Ontologies. *Presented at 6th OOPSLA Workshop on Domain-Specific Modeling*, Portland, Oregon, USA.

Schlicht, A., & Stuckenschmidt, H. (2008). Towards Distributed Ontology Reasoning for the Web. In *Proceedings of the IEEE/WIC/ACM International Conference on Web Intelligence*. Retrieved 30. January, 2008 from http://ki.informatik.uni-mannheim.de/fileadmin/publication/Schlicht08DistributedOntologyReasoning.pdf

Smith, M. K., Welty, C., & McGuiness, D. (2004). *OWL Web Ontology Language Guide W3C Recommendation 10 February 2004*. Retrieved July 10, 2008, from http://www.w3.org/TR/owl-guide/

Staab, S., Studer, R., Schnurr, H. P., & Sure, Y. (2001). Knowledge Processes and Ontologies. *IEEE Intelligent Systems, 1*(16), 26–34. doi:10.1109/5254.912382

Stonebraker, M., & Hellerstein, J. M. (2001). Content Integration for EBusiness. Proceedings of the 2001 ACM SIGMOD International Conference on Management of Data. *SIGMOD '01 30*(2), 552-560.

Stuckenschmidt, H., & Klein, M. (2004). Structure-based partitioning of large concept hierarchies. In S.A. McIlraith, D. Plexousakis, & F. van Harmelen (Eds.), *Proceedings of the Third International Semantic Web Conference*

(ISWC-2004) (LNCS 3298) (pp. 289-303). Berlin Heidelberg New York: Springer.

Stuckenschmidt, H., & van Harmelen, F. (2005). *Information Sharing on the Semantic Web*. Berlin Heidelberg New York: Springer.

Uschold, M., & Grüninger, M. (1996). Ontologies: principles, methods, and applications. *The Knowledge Engineering Review, 11*(2), 93–155. doi:10.1017/S0269888900007797

Uschold, M., & Gruninger, M. (2004). Ontologies and Semantics for Seamless Connectivity. *SIGMOD Record, 33*(4), 58–64. doi:10.1145/1041410.1041420

Uschold, M., King, M., Moralee, S., & Zorgios, Y. (1998). The Enterprise Ontology. *The Knowledge Engineering Review*, 13.

Uschold, M., & Menzel, C. (2005). *Semantic Integration & Interoperability Using RDF and OWL W3C Editor's Draft 3 November 2005*. Retrieved, 02. February 2008 from http://www.w3.org/2001/sw/BestPractices/OEP/SemInt/

Wigand, R. T., Picot, A., & Reichwald, R. (1997). *Information, organization and management: expanding markets and corporate boundaries*. Chichester, UK: Wiley.

Zelewski, S. (1999). *Ontologien zur Strukturierung von Domänenwissen – Ein Annäherungsversuch aus betriebswirtschaftlicher Perspektive* – (Tech. Report No. 3). Essen, Germany: University of GH Essen.

Zhdanova, A., de Bruijn, J., Zimmermann, K., & Scharffe, F. (2004). *Ontology Alignment Solution v2.0*. (EU IST Esperonto project deliverable (D1.4 V2.0). Retrieved May 30, 2005, from http://www.deri.at/fileadmin/documents/deliverables/Esperonto/Del1.4-V2.0-final.pdf

Zhdanova, A. V., & Shvaiko, P. (2006). Community-Driven Ontology Matching. In Y. Sure, & J. Domingue (Eds.), *The Semantic Web: Research and Applications, Proceedings of the European Semantic Web Conference (ESWC-2006), (LNCS 4011)* (pp. 34–49). Berlin Heidelberg, Germany: Springer.

This work was previously published in the Journal of Cases on Information Technology, Vol. 11, Issue 4, edited by M. Khosrow-Pour, pp. 74-99, copyright 2009 by IGI Publishing (an imprint of IGI Global).

Chapter 11
XAR:
An Integrated Framework for Semantic Extraction and Annotation

Naveen Ashish
University of California-Irvine, USA

Sharad Mehrotra
University of California-Irvine, USA

EXECUTIVE SUMMARY

The authors present the XAR framework that allows for free text information extraction and semantic annotation. The language underpinning XAR, the authors argue, allows for the inclusion of probabilistic reasoning with the rule language, provides higher level predicates capturing text features and relationships, and defines and supports advanced features such as token consumption and stratified negotiation in the rule language and semantics. The XAR framework also allows the incorporation of semantic information as integrity constraints in the extraction and annotation process. The XAR framework aims to fill in a gap, the authors claim, in the Web based information extraction systems. XAR provides an extraction and annotation framework by permitting the integrated use of hand-crafted extraction rules, machine-learning based extractors, and semantic information about the particular domain of interest. The XAR system has been deployed in an emergency response scenario with civic agencies in North America and in a scenario with an IT department of a county level community clinic.

INTRODUCTION

The vision of semantic interoperability on a large-scale, such as that envisioned by the concept of the Semantic Web (Berners-Lee, Hendler & Lassila, 2001), continues to sustain interest and excitement. The availability of automated tools for *semantic annotation* of data on the open Web is recognized as critical for Semantic Web enablement. In the process of semantic annotation we annotate significant entities and relationships in documents and pages on the Web, thus making them amenable for machine processing. The time and investment of marking and

DOI: 10.4018/978-1-60566-894-9.ch011

annotating Web content manually is prohibitive for all but a handful of Web content providers, which leads us to develop automated tools for this task. As an example, consider Web pages of academic researchers with their biographies in free text as shown in Figure 1.

The annotation of significant concepts on such pages, such as a researcher's current job-title, academic degrees, alma-maters and dates for various academic degrees etc (as shown in Figure 1) can then enable Semantic Web agent or integration applications over such data. Such annotation or mark-up tools are largely based on information extraction technology. While information extraction itself is a widely investigated area, one still lacks powerful, general purpose, and yet easy-to-use frameworks and systems for information extraction, particularly the extraction of information from *free text* which is a significant fraction of the content on the open Web. In this chapter we describe XAR, a framework and system for free text information extraction and semantic annotation. XAR provides a powerful extraction and annotation framework by permitting the integrated use of hand-crafted extraction rules, machine-learning based extractors, as well as *semantic* information about the particular domain of interest for extraction. In this chapter we will describe the XAR framework which permits the integrated use of 1) Hand-crafted extraction rules, 2) Existing machine-learning based extractors, and 3) *Semantic* information in the form of database *integrity constraints* to power semantic extraction and annotation.

We have designed XAR to be an open-source framework that can be used by end-user application developers with minimal training and prior expertise, as well as by the research community as a platform for information extraction research. Over the last year we have used XAR for semantic annotation of Web documents in a variety of interesting domains. These applications range from the semantic annotation of details of particular events in online news stories in an overall

Figure 1. Semantic Annotation of Web Content

Professor Deborah Estrin is a Professor of Computer Science with a joint appointment in Electrical Engineering at UCLA, holds the Jon Postel Chair in Computer Networks, and is Founding Director of the NSF-funded Center for Embedded Networked Sensing (CENS). Estrin received her Ph.D. in 1985 in Computer Science from the Massachusetts Institute of Technology, her M.S. in 1982 from M.I.T. and her B.S. in 1980 from U.C. Berkeley. Before joining UCLA she was a member of the University of Southern California Computer Science Department from 1986 through the middle of 2000. In 1987, Professor Estrin received the National Science Foundation, Presidential Young Investigator Award for her research in network interconnection and security. During the subsequent

Professor **<name>** Deborah Estrin**</name>** is a **<title>** Professor**</title>** of Computer Science with a joint appointment in Electrical Engineering at UCLA, holds the Jon Postel Chair in Computer Networks, and is Founding Director of the NSF-funded Center for Embedded Networked Sensing (CENS). Estrin received her **<degree>** Ph.D.**</degree>** in **<PhDDate>** 1985**</PhDDate>** in Computer Science from the **<PhDSchool>** Massachusetts Institute of Technology**</PhDSchool>**, her **<degree>** M.S.**</degree>** in 1982 from M.I.T. and her B.S. in 1980 from U.C. Berkeley. Before joining UCLA she was a member of the University of Southern California Computer Science Department from 1986 through the middle of 2000. In 1987, Professor Estrin received the National Science Foundation, Presidential Young Investigator Award for her research in network interconnection and security. During the subsequent application for internet news monitoring, to the semantic annotation of free text clinical notes as part of a business intelligence application in the health-care domain. This chapter is organized as follows. In the next section we provide an overview of XAR from a user perspective i.e., as a framework for developing extraction applications. We then present the technical details of our approach including the XAR system architecture, algorithmic issues, and implementation details. We present experimental evaluations assessing the effectiveness of the system in a variety of different domains. We also describe use case studies of application development using XAR in two different organizations. Finally, we discuss related work and provide a conclusion.

THE XAR SYSTEM

We first describe XAR from a user perspective i.e., as a framework for developing extraction applications and performing annotation tasks. The extraction step in annotation is treated as one of *slot-filling*. For instance in the researcher bios task, each Web page provides values for slots or attributes such as the job-title, academic degrees, dates etc. The two primary paradigms (Feldman et al., 2002) for automated information extraction systems are (i) Using hand-crafted extraction rules, and (ii) Using a machine-learning based extractor that can be trained for information extraction in a particular domain. Essentially, extraction applications in XAR are developed by using either hand-crafted extraction rules (Feldman et al., 2002) or machine-learning based extractors (Kayed 2006), which are further complemented with semantic information in the form of integrity constraints. We describe and illustrate each of these aspects.

Declarative Extraction Rules

XAR provides the user with a declarative Datalog style extraction rule language using which she can manually specify extraction rules for particular slots. These rules are essentially horn-clauses which state conditions based on which certain tokens get assigned to certain slots in the extraction process. An example of such an extraction rule, continuing with researcher bios domain that we introduced, is:

phd-date(X) ← phd-degree(P), date(X), insamesentence(P,X) **R1** which should be read as follows – "any token in the text that is of *type* date and is *in the same sentence* as another token of the type phd-degree, is a value for the phd-date slot".

The rule head refers to a slot that is to be filled, for instance the rule R1 above is a rule to instantiate the phd-date slot. While we present the rule language in detail in the next section we wish to emphasize a couple of key aspects:

(i) We see that the body of the rule R1 above contains predicates that describe properties of tokens in the text, for instance there are properties such as the type of the token i.e., whether of type date, degree etc. There are also predicates capturing relationships across tokens, for instance whether 2 tokens are in the same sentence etc. A space of such predicates describing properties of tokens and also their relationships is made available *automatically* to the user and she is abstracted from the details of their generation.

(ii) Another key aspect of the XAR rule language is that it provides application developers the ability to represent, and (selectively) exploit features of *multiple* kinds and at different richness levels for information extraction. The rule R1 above illustrated predicates that capture only what are referred to as *shallow features* of the text. Shallow features are basically properties that can be determined by a shallow analysis of the text i.e., through the use of tools such as tokenizers, named-entity or other part-of-speech taggers, etc. The type of a token, its absolute or relative position in the text, etc., are all examples of shallow features. One can also distill what are called *deep features*, which are those obtained after a deeper analysis such as a complete natural language parse of the sentences in the text. A fact such as a token being a verb and another token being the subject of the first token is an example of a deep feature. We claim that there are advantages to having a framework that permits the availability and access to features at *multiple* richness levels, and their selective use in an adaptive fashion. We will look at this aspect in detail in the experimental evaluation section.

Using Machine-Learning Based Extractors

Besides hand-crafted extraction rules, a second paradigm for automated information extraction is the use of machine-learning based extractors and techniques. Typically a machine-learning based extractor is trained by providing the extractor with the slots to be extracted and training examples in the form of extracted data for several cases. The system then induces extraction rules which can be then applied to extract data from other unseen cases. There are several systems in this category such as RAPIER, WHIRL, TIES, LP2, and also CRF-based systems (Kayed, Girgis & Shaalan, 2006) to name a few. The XAR framework provides the option of using any off-the-shelf machine-learning based extractor.

The user essentially has a choice as to whether to use hand-crafted XAR extraction rules or any off-the-shelf machine-learning based extractor for an initial "basic" extraction step. This extraction is then further enhanced with the use of semantic information as integrity constraints.

Semantic Information as Integrity Constraints

The integration of semantic information as integrity constraints with either hand-crafted rule driven extraction or machine-learning driven extraction is one of the key features of the XAR framework. Table 1 below illustrates an example of the utility of integrity constrains in information extraction. We continue with the researcher bios domain, and the first row illustrates a specific portion of text that data is extracted from. The row below provides the results of information extraction for the slots of the PhD, Masters, and Bachelors degrees and their alma-maters and dates using a state-of-the-art extractor. Note that such extraction could have been done by either the hand-crafted XAR extraction rules or a machine-learning based extractor. Some of the extracted values are clearly erroneous. The XAR system then exploits 3 particular integrity constraints that have been specified for the researcher bios domain, namely:

1) The date of any degree is a SINGLE VALUE.
2) A person receives a doctoral degree only *after* his masters degree which in turn is received only after a bachelors degree (true for the same major at least).
3) There is contiguity in the universities or institutions a person attends for his various degrees (true in majority of the cases).

With the knowledge of these 3 constraints the XAR system can correct the erroneous extracted values in to the (correct) values in the last row in Table 1. XAR provides a general purpose framework where 1) In any domain such semantics can be specified by a user as integrity constraints. We consider each semantic annotation task as that involving extracting a *relation*, for instance the researcher bios annotation task is essentially that of populating a researcher-bios relation that has attributes or slots such as an individual's job-title,

Table 1. Semantic Constraints in Extraction

Original Text *He received the PhD degree from Stanford University in 1966 and the BS and MS degrees from the University of Michigan in 1960 and 1961 respectively.*								
PhD	Stanford university	1966	MS	University of Michigan	1960 and 1961	BS	Stanford University	-
PhD	Stanford university	1966	MS	University of Michigan	1961	BS	University of Michigan	1960

academic degrees, alma-maters, etc. 2) The XAR system applies such integrity constraints over basic extraction performed using either hand-crafted rules or machine-learning.

The XAR user interface is illustrated in Figure 2. For any new application the user provides:

(i) A **schema**, which is an SQL (Ullman & Widom, 2007) style schema describing the relation that is to be populated in the process of semantic annotation. The schema specifies the various slots or attributes in the relation to be extracted, the types and classes of such slots, whether single or multi-valued etc. In Figure 3 below we illustrate a schema for the researcher-bios domain.

(ii) Basic extraction powering. This is done using:
   a. A set of hand-crafted **extraction rules**, or
   b. Using an off-the-shelf machine-learning extractor which has to be trained for each new extraction application.

(iii) Semantic information about the relation to be extracted, in the form of **integrity constraints** (Ullman & Widom, 2007). For instance in the researcher bios domain we know that the first computer science degrees were awarded beginning only in the sixties. This is an example of an *attribute level* constraint which is constraining the value that the phd-date attribute can take in the

Figure 2. XAR Interface

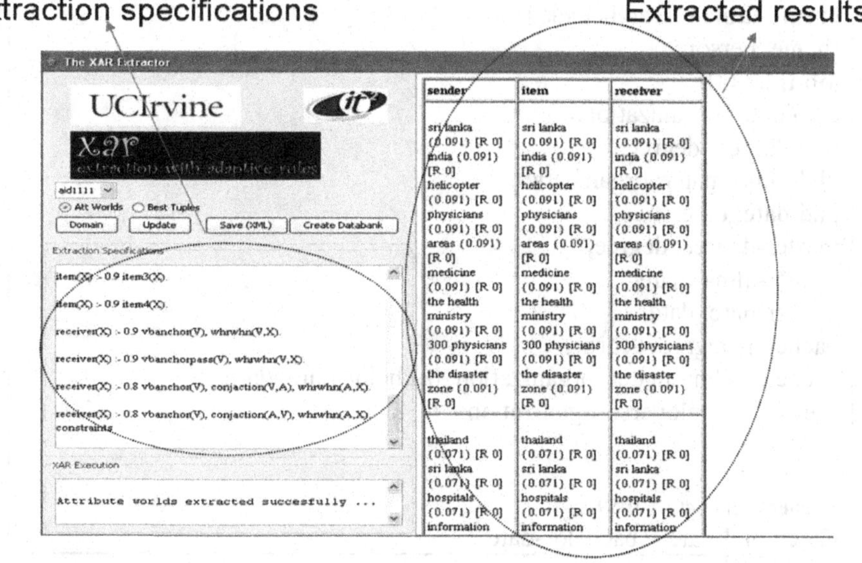

researcher-bios relation. We specify this in the schema below. As an example of another constraint, we know that the year in which a person was awarded a doctoral degree must be greater (later) than the year in which he was awarded a bachelor's degree. This is an example of a *tuple level* constraint where we are specifying semantics *between* two extracted values. Finally we could also have constraints at the level of the relation, called *relation constraints* that ascertain properties that the collection of tuples in a relation must satisfy as a whole. Some integrity constraints for the researcher bios domain are illustrated in Figure 3 below.

The notion of semantics in general is indeed very broad. One can consider semantics of many different kinds and consequently different formalisms to represent it. For instance semantics could be represented in something as simple as a lexicon, to a very complex formalism such as an ontology in an expressive ontology language. We have chosen the formalism of integrity constraints as a means of scoping the semantics we employ in this particular work. Besides, integrity constraints are a database formalism and thus lend themselves naturally to expressing semantics about relations, including relations that are to be extracted.

Integrity constraints in XAR are specified in SQL over the relation representing the information to be extracted. The XAR system extracts information using the application schema, basic extraction in the form of either extraction rules or a trained machine-learning based extractor, and semantic information in the form of integrity constraints. In the next section we provide the technical details of how the framework achieves this.

ARCHITECTURE AND TECHNICAL DETAILS

A schematic overview of the XAR system architecture is provided in Figure 4. The overall extraction process proceeds as follows: for any

Figure 3. Researcher-bios schema and example integrity constraints

XAR Schema and Constraints

```
create table researcher-bios
(name: person,
job-title: title,
employer: organization,
phd-degree: degree,
phd-alma-mater: organization,
phd-date: date,
master-degree: degree,
master-alma-mater,
master-date: date,
bachelor-degree: degree,
bachelor-alma-mater: organization, bachelor-date: date,
previous-employers: organization
)

   check phd-date > 1959
check phd-date > bachelor-date
```

Figure 4. XAR System Architecture

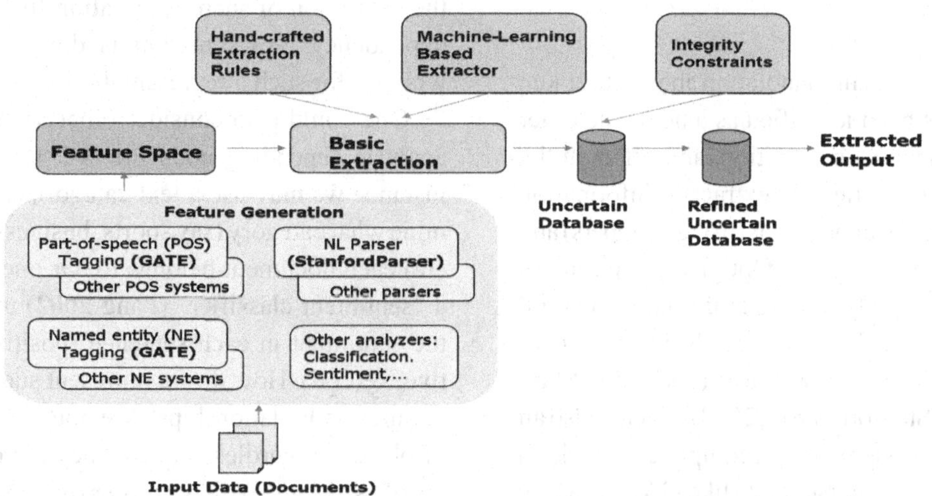

new extraction application and task the system first applies one or more text analyzers that extract different kinds of features from the text. Such features are essentially properties of and relationships amongst significant tokens and entities in the text. Having generated such features, the system then applies one of declarative extraction rules or a machine-learning based extractor to perform basic extraction over the input text data. The output of such basic extraction is stored in an *uncertain* database relation (Dalvi & Suciu, 2005). As a final step, semantic information in the form of integrity constraints is applied to this uncertain relation to *refine* it. This refinement essentially incorporates additional knowledge from the integrity constraints into the uncertain relation. The final extracted output is obtained from this refined uncertain relation.

We describe each of these aspects and steps in detail.

Feature Generation

By default, XAR does a "shallow" analysis of any input text providing features such as the identification of significant tokens and entities, their types, position in the text, sentence demarcation etc. In the current implementation of XAR such shallow analysis is done using GATE (Cunningham, Maynard, Bontcheva & Tablan, 2002), which is an open-source framework for text analysis which we use for the identification of named-entities, other significant tokens, parts-of-speech, etc. Many types of important entities (such as person names, locations, organizations etc) can be recognized with reasonable accuracy and with no user input or training.

Let us consider an example to illustrate the kinds of features that are identified. Consider a sentence such as:

"He was awarded the university teaching excellence award in 1996 for exemplary undergraduate teaching."

An analysis of the above sentence by GATE yields information about tokens in what is called a GATE annotation:

```
AnnotationImpl: id=81; type=Token;
features={category=NN, kind=word,
orth=lowercase, length=5, string=award};
```

```
start=NodeImpl: id=80; offset=226;
end=NodeImpl: id=81; offset=233
```

For instance in the annotation above, the token "award" has been identified as a noun and other properties such as its position, and offset in the text are also identified. We extract the information from such GATE annotations (using wrappers) and represent it in predicates. Optionally, we can use a second text analysis tool, in this case a natural language parser for "deep" analysis of the text. The particular parser we have used is the StanfordParser (StanfordParser, 2008) which is also an open-source system that is a complete (statistical) natural language parser and (like GATE) can be used "as-is" i.e., without any additional user input or training. The StanfordParser can parse the same sentence and provide an output such as:

```
nsubjpass(awarded-3, He-1)
auxpass(awarded-3, was-2)
det(award-8, the-4)
nn(award-8, university-5)
nn(award-8, teaching-6)
nn(award-8, excellence-7)
dobj(awarded-3, award-8)
prep_in(award-8, 1996-10)
amod(teaching-14, exemplary-12)
amod(teaching-14, undergraduate-13)
```

prep_for(awarded-3, teaching-14) which is a *typed dependencies collapsed* representation of the parse tree of this sentence. The typed dependencies representation is essentially a representation of the relationships in the parse tree of a sentence, in relational form. We extract important information about actions of interest from such typed dependencies. For instance in this example, the action "awarded" is of interest. From the typed dependencies we can (in many cases) extract who awarded what and to whom. In fact such associations (subject, object etc.) are typical of literally any action i.e., verb. As with GATE annotations, the extraction of such information from a typed dependency representation is done through a wrapper for such a representation.

One could also consider other kinds of text analysis depending upon the task at hand. For instance we may use a text categorizer to determine what category (say sports, business, politics etc) each document belongs to. Or one may use a "sentiment classifier" (Pang 2002) to classify the sentiment in each sentence (positive, negative, neutral). How do we represent such diverse features and relationships? We note that features of objects, regardless of how they are obtained, are of two kinds. We have *properties* of individual objects and we have *relationships* between objects. Any property then is essentially a 3-ary relationship i.e., we have a certain property of a certain object having a certain value. Relationships on the other hand can be n-ary in general. Any n-ary relationship can however be converted into a set of (n) binary relationships (a unique identifier serves to glue the binary relationships together). We thus represent properties in a FEATURES table (Table 2) with three columns i.e., the object, the property, and the actual value. Relationships are captured in a RELATIONSHIPS table as shown in Table 2 which shows a number of interesting relationships of different kinds.

As a final step, the entries in the FEATURES and RELATIONSHIPS tables are converted to logical predicates representing the same information. The set of predicates capturing properties and relationships for all tokens in all text segments that data is to be extracted from, form the feature databank for that dataset. An important aspect to note is that the two FEATURES and RELATIONSHIPS tables provide a unified representation for features obtained from different kinds of text analyzers and at different semantic levels. In logic database parlance, the feature databank forms what is the extensional database or "EDB".

Table 2. FEATURE and RELATIONSHIP Tables

FEATURE		
OBJECT	***PROPERTY***	***VALUE***
award 1996 1996 d57	type type position category	thing date 33 bio

Basic Extraction

We describe the two options for powering basic extraction in XAR.

XAR Extraction Rules

The first option for achieving basic automated information extraction in XAR is with the use of hand-crafted extraction rules. The XAR extraction rules are essentially Datalog rules with syntactic sugar. Each rule is a horn-clause of the form:

S(X) ← C B1,B2,…,Bm

where ***S, Bi*** s are atoms. ***S***, the head corresponds to a slot to be extracted, the ***Bi*** s are predicates corresponding to conditions based on which tokens are assigned to slots, and ***C*** is an (optional) confidence value [0,1] that is a measure of the precision of the extraction rule. ***C*** reflects the maximum confidence with which we can state that a value inferred for the head predicate ***S*** by that rule is actually a value for the slot corresponding to ***S***. The following are the key features of this rule language:

1. *The rules are essentially horn-clause style rules.* This follows from the rule definition above.
2. The predicates in the body may be either slot predicates or feature predicates.

phd-date(X) ← 0.7 phd-alma-mater(Y), date(X), insamesentence(X,Y) **R2**

The rule R2 above provides an example where in the rule body one of the predicates refers to another slot i.e., phd-alma-mater.

3. A token is assumed to be "consumed" with the application of a rule, unless stated otherwise.

Consider a set of predicates and rules such as:

country(usa)
sender(X) ← country(X) **R3**
receiver(X) ← country(X) **R4**

In a traditional logic program we would infer both sender (i.e., "usa") and receiver (i.e., "usa") to be true after the application of the rules above. In the XAR semantics however a token can be "used" by only one rule. We can infer *either* sender(usa) or receiver(usa) but not both. To clearly define the semantics in such cases we consider any pair of rules whose bodies could be satisfied by the same token(s) as competing rules. A relative priority order must be explicitly specified between any pair of competing rules. For instance in the above example if we gave a higher priority to R3 over R4, we would infer sender(usa) but not receiver(usa). Of course there may be cases where we allow for the same token to be consumed (simultaneously) by more than one rule, i.e., as in regular logic programming. If no explicit order is specified between two competing rules then this traditional semantics is used.

4. Multiple rules are permitted for the same slot.
5. A precision value is (optionally) associated with each rule.

The precision value, if stated explicitly, is interpreted as a lower bound on the confidence that a value inferred by the rule is actually a value for the slot associated with the head of the rule. In rule R2 for instance we have a confidence of (at least) 0.7 that any value inferred by this rule is a value for the slot 'phd-alma-mater'. In case multiple rules infer the same value for a particular slot, we simply associate the precision value that is highest with that value from amongst the different rules that inferred that value. In case no precision value is explicitly stated, it is assumed to be 1. The probabilistic framework is adapted, with simplification, from a general probabilistic logic framework developed in (Lakshmanan & Sadri, 1994) .The work proposes both *belief* and *doubt* rules that capture in horn-clause form why a certain fact should (or should not be) true. A notion of probabilistic confidence (or rather a range defined by a lower and upper bound) is associated with each fact (predicate) and rule. A probabilistic algebra and semantics is also described. In our framework we, at present, use only belief rules i.e., rules that state when a token should be a value for a slot. In extraction there may be room for doubt rules as well though we have not investigated the merits of this yet. We associate confidence values only with rules and not with predicates (i.e., in the rule body) at this point. Again this is a level of detail that we could incorporate in future. The semantics of associating confidence values with inferred values in our framework is simpler as well; we simply associate with each inferred value the highest value amongst the precision values of the rules that led to its inference.

6. Negation is permitted in the rule body.

We allow for writing rules with negated predicates in the rule body (only). However we make the requirement that the set of rules be *stratified* wrt negation (no cyclical dependencies amongst rules that involve negation), this is to ensure consistent fixpoint semantics. For instance:

tempsender1(X) ← anchor(A), who(X,A) **R5**

tempsender2(X) ← anchor(A), immbefore(X,A), not tempsender1(Z) **R6**

illustrates two intermediate rules where R6 is satisfied only if R5 is *not* satisfied.

7. Some predefined predicates are provided for the user's convenience in writing rules.

These include predicates for determining things properties and relationships such as whether one token is before or after another in the text, references to ground values of tokens, choosing the first or last element is a set of tokens, etc.

Application of Rules

A set of rules in the extraction language above can be translated to a regular Datalog program in a straightforward fashion. For instance in the case of token consumption, the capability of prioritizing rules can be achieved in regular Datalog by simply using negation i.e., if a rule R1 has a higher priority than another rule R2, then the body of R2 is augmented with the predicate not R1(X). The association of precision values or support for the user defined predicates can also be provided, we do not provide the translation details here. The complexity of inference with any extraction language is a valid concern. Inference in the extraction language we have described is tractable, in fact the inference can be done in time polynomial in the number of extraction rules and/or the number of tokens or entities in each segment. This is because any set of rules in the XAR extraction language can be translated to a set of rules in regular Datalog, the number of rules in the translated Datalog program being (at most) twice the number of original XAR extraction rules. (Bottom-up) inference in regular Datalog (including Datalog with stratified) negation is polynomial in the number of rules and/or base predicates (Ullman, 1988).

Using a Machine-Learning Based Extractor

The second option for basic extraction is to use any machine-learning based extractor. The XAR framework allows for the integration of any machine-learning base extractor. Any such extractor is treated as a black box and is provided with a set of training examples. The extracted output is represented in an uncertain relation. So far we have integrated in extractors as AutoSlog, RAPIER, and TIES (TIES, 2008).

Uncertain Database Representation

The output of basic extraction, whether done using hand-crafted XAR rules or a machine-learning based extractor, is represented in an *uncertain* database relation. An uncertain database relation (Dalvi & Suciu, 2005) allows for representing uncertainty in database relations where we essentially represent a space of possible relations associated with a probabilistic distribution. In the case of using XAR rules the realization of the intensional database provides us for each head predicate, a set of (zero or more) values that satisfy that predicate each associated with a confidence value. Each such value is then treated as a possible value for the slot that that head predicate corresponds to. At the end of such logical inference we have with each slot associated a set of possible values for that slot, each value associated with a probabilistic confidence. The set of such values is used to generate an *attribute world* associated with that attribute which is a probabilistic space of possible values for that slot. An uncertain database relation representation allows us to capture such attribute worlds for each slot. When using a machine-learning based extractor, many such systems now provide a *set* of possible extracted values for a slot as opposed to a single value. Each such possible value is associated with a confidence score. We translate the set of possible values for each slot and their associated confidences to attribute worlds which are then represented as an uncertain database relation.

An example of an uncertain relation showing a subset of the attributes for the researcher-bios domain is illustrated above, which shows how the uncertainty for the phd-alma-mater and phd-date attributes is represented.

Integrating Semantic Information as Integrity Constraints

At the end of the basic extraction step, using either hand-crafted extraction rules or a machine-learning based extractor, we have the extracted data in an uncertain relation. The application of integrity constraints is essentially a process of *refining* the uncertain extracted relation with the knowledge in the integrity constraints. The refinement results in a recalibrated uncertain extraction relation in which the possibilities inconsistent with the integrity constraints are eliminated. The additional knowledge thus provided by the integrity constraints is taken into account in that instances inconsistent with such constraints are eliminated from consideration.

The general problem of systematically incorporating integrity constraints into uncertain relations is complex. We provide a study of this problem including a scalable practical solution as part of separate work which is described in our technical report on the topic (Ashish, Mehrotra & Pirzadeh, 2008).

Table 3.

name	job-title	phd-alma-mater	phd-date
jim	professor	Oxford University (0.7) University of Oregon (0.3)	1995 (0.6) 1992 (0.4)
mary	scientist	MIT	2000 (0.5) 1995 (0.5)

System Implementation and Availability

The current version of the system is implemented in Java and also incorporates some other off-the-shelf tools. Shallow feature analysis is done using GATE and deep feature analysis is done using the StanfordParser. TuProlog (Denti, Omicini & Ricci, 2001), a Java based prolog engine, is used for the rule language inference. The output of the extraction and eventually the semantic annotation is made available in (i) XML format. Essentially in each document or Web page we put XML tags around the values for the various slots identified, as illustrated in Figure 1. (ii) As RDF triples. Each tuple is treated as a resource. For instance in the researcher bios domain each Web page corresponds to an individual and is treated as a resource. The different slots or attributes to be annotated are essentially properties of each resource and their actual values are the values of these properties. This lends itself to a natural RDF representation and XAR provides the option of saving identified semantic annotations as RDF triples.

An open-source version of XAR has made available for community use under a Creative Commons License. We encourage potential users interested in either developing extraction applications or researching information extraction to consider using this system. The system source code and documentation is available at http://www.ics.uci.edu/~ashish/xar. We have also provided the details of a number of applications developed using XAR including the application schemas, XAR extraction rules, and semantic integrity constraints. We believe this will be illustrative to new users wishing to develop extraction and annotation applications using this framework.

EXPERIMENTAL EVALUATION

As mentioned earlier we have applied XAR for semantic annotation in a number of interesting domains. In some of these domains we have also empirically assessed the effectiveness of the XAR framework for semantic annotation. We have made the empirical evaluations from two primary perspectives: **1) The Extraction Rule Language and Features:** We have provided a comprehensive declarative rule language for extraction. We have also provided a framework where features at multiple semantic levels can be made available and the rule language can exploit such features in a seamless fashion. The first aspect of our evaluation assesses this declarative rule language, we evaluate the effort and complexity of writing extraction rules for different annotation tasks, we also assess the accuracy of the extraction achieved as a result. We then also quantitatively assess the benefits of access to an integrated space of features at multiple semantic levels, **2) The Integration of Semantic Information:** We quantitatively evaluate how the integration of semantic information as integrity constraints improves on the basic extraction done by either hand-crafted rules or machine-learning based systems.

Extraction Domains and Datasets

We have conducted the quantitative assessments on three different real-world datasets and extrac-

Figure 5. Aid-dispatched semantic annotation Extraction Rule Language and Features

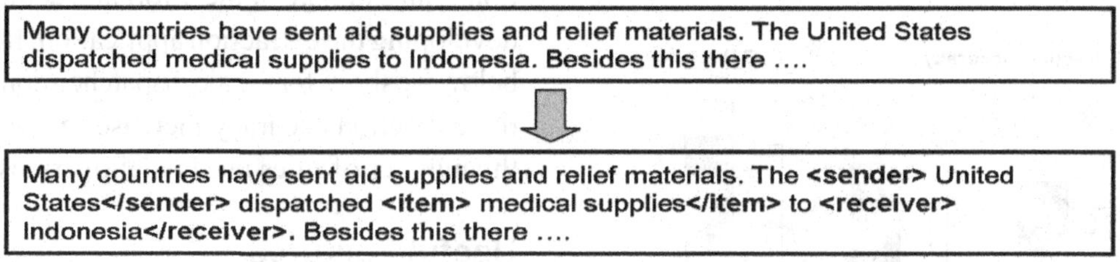

Many countries have sent aid supplies and relief materials. The United States dispatched medical supplies to Indonesia. Besides this there ....

Many countries have sent aid supplies and relief materials. The <sender> United States</sender> dispatched <item> medical supplies</item> to <receiver> Indonesia</receiver>. Besides this there ....

tion tasks, namely a) The researcher-bios extraction task over a corpus of 500 computer science researcher bios on the open Web, b) The MUC-6 (MUC, 1995) task of extracting management succession events (close to a 100 such instances) over a corpus of WSJ news stories, and c) A task of extracting details about instances of aid or relief being or having been dispatched or sent by a country or organization to another in the event of a disaster (see illustration below). This is over a corpus of 4000 online new stories related to the S. E. Asian Tsunami disaster. We will refer to these as the researcher-bios, management-succession, and aid-dispatched tasks respectively.

This evaluation was conducted over the aid-dispatched and management-succession extraction tasks. The following are the schemas for the relations that we extracted.

aid-dispatched (sender: organization country, item: thing, receiver: thing)

management-succession(name: person, company: organization, status [IN/OUT])

Extraction Rules

For each of these extraction tasks we wrote XAR extraction rules based on observations of regular patterns in the text. We considered rule sets of different types i.e., sets of rules over only shallow features, sets of rules over only deep features, and sets of rules over both shallow and deep features. Table 4 provides a listing of some of the XAR extraction rules (of these different types) for the aid-dispatched domain, for the "sender" slot.

We first show (Figure 6) the extraction quality obtained with different sets of extraction rules for the aid-dispatched and management-succession tasks. We provide measures of extraction precision and recall, aggregated over all slots. The results show that we can obtain fairly good extraction quality i.e., in the range of precision and recall as high as 0.7 or above. The number of extraction rules required is reasonable as well. For aid-dispatched, a total of 18 rules are used in the case of shallow rules only, for MUC we use a total of 9 shallow rules. The number of rules required when using deep rules only is much

Table 4. Example of XAR rules for aid-dispatched

Shallow Only Rules
sender(X) ← 0.8 sender1(X).
sender(X) ← 0.6 sender2(X).
sender1(X) ← anchor(V), location(X), before(X,V), insamesentence(X,V), not myout(X).
sender1(X) ← anchor(V), organization(X), before(X,V), insamesentence(X,V), not myout(X).
sender2(X) ← anchor(V), location(X), before(X,V), insamesentence(X,V), not sender1(Z).
sender2(X) ← anchor(V), organization(X), before(X,V), insamesentence(X,V), not sender1(Z).

Figure 6. Extraction accuracies for various sets of rules

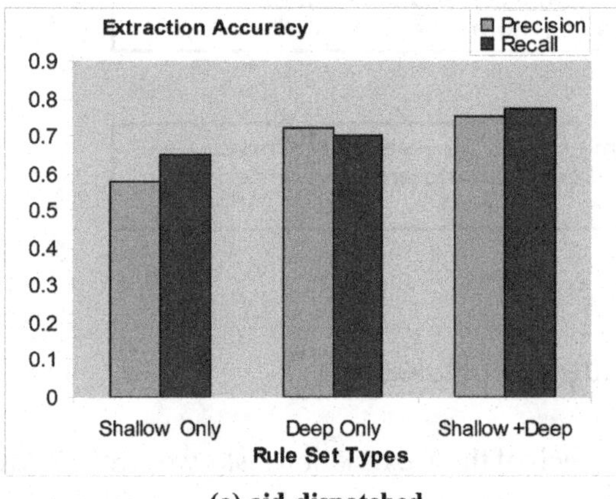

(a) aid-dispatched

(b) management-succession

less, for instance for aid dispatched we use only 3 rules, one rule per slot.

Of course this is because we have access to the semantic predicates where much of the extraction information has already been captured. The combination of both shallow and deep rules provides an even higher boost to the extraction accuracy in both the domains. The reason we see an improvement, over the case of using deep rules only, is that deep rules have their limitations as well. In some cases sentences are quite complex (for instance describing several events or facts) and synthesizing information from the resulting (complex) semantic parse may be difficult.

The number of extraction rules for an application is an estimate of the effort and complexity in developing the extraction application. In Figure 7 below we show, for the aid dispatched domain, how the extraction accuracy increases as we increase the number of rules used (shallow rules only).

Useful Features

In writing rules the user can choose from rules and predicates in such rules of different kinds. For instance we make a distinction between shallow and deep rules and the above rules indicate that deep rules generally capture more information, high accuracy extraction is obtained with relatively much fewer rules. The predicates themselves represent either a feature (property) or a relationship. Such features or relationships can further be of different kinds. Apart from the shallow vs deep distinction, amongst the shallow features we identify the categories of (i) named-entity features, (ii) other part-of-speech features, and (iii) "structural" features such as the position of a token in the segment, which sentence it is part of etc. We make this distinction as different kinds of analyzers are required to extract these different types of features. From an extraction perspective a matter of interest is the relative importance or effectiveness of features of different kinds in extraction.

The usage frequencies (percentage) of the different feature and relationship types, determined by the application of XAR extraction rules in the above domains, are displayed in 7. We observe that features or relationships of each of the four different classes are used with considerable frequency, also there is no one class of features or relationships that is used with overly high or low frequency. One of the design decisions one can make based on this frequency distribution is that relatively equal resources must be invested towards low level text analyzers of all kinds, so that all the above categories of text features are accurately and comprehensively extracted and

Figure 7. Extraction accuracy vs number of rules

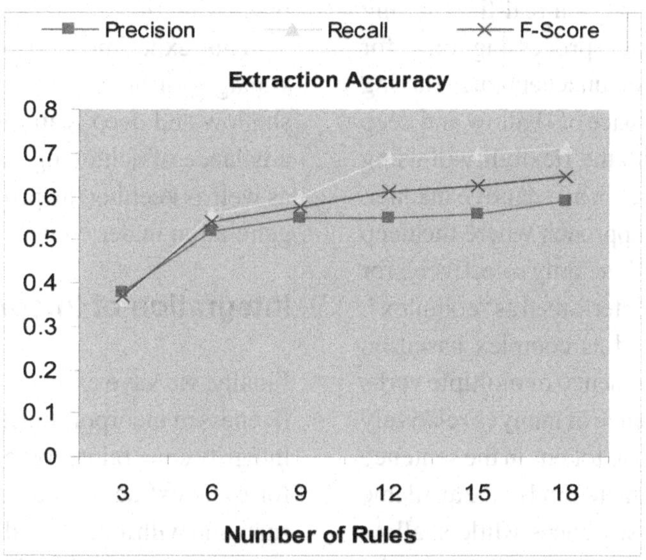

made available to the rule writer. A more skewed distribution, on the other hand, would direct that we bias more resources towards text analyzers that generate features that are more commonly used.

Features at Multiple Semantic Levels

Certainly, writing rules over deep features is simpler where high extraction accuracy can be achieved with using very few rules as demonstrated. One issue however with using deep features is the cost of feature extraction. Deep analysis, such as that based on natural language parsing of any sentence, takes time that is an order of magnitude larger than that required for shallow analysis. Consider the following comparison. The average processing time for shallow feature extraction per sentence, using GATE, is 132 ms. The experiments were conducted on a DELL Inspiron 19200 machine with an Intel Pentium 1.8 GHz processor, 1GB RAM, running Windows XP. Under the same configuration, the average

Figure 8. Frequency of Predicates

Predicate Categories	***Examples***
POS: Part-of-speech features	action(X), to(T), thing(X)
NE: named-entity features	organization(X)
TR: Structural features	position(X,33)
REL-TR: Structural relationships	insamesentence(X,T), before(X,Y)
SEM-TR: Semantic relationships	who(X,Y), what(X,Y)

Type	POS	NE	TR	REL-TR
Freq %	21	27	16	36

processing time per sentence when using the StanfordParser, is 7.8 sec ! In a real-time setting such a high per sentence processing time for feature extraction may be unacceptable. Having access to an *integrated* space of shallow and deep features provides us with the flexibility of using shallow and deep features in an adaptive manner. We have developed an approach where the deep analysis of sentences is done only selectively, for those sentences that are determined as "complex". A sentence is determined as complex based on heuristics, such as the presence of multiple verbs in the sentence, the presence of many (a relatively large number of) entities or tokens in the sentence etc. Deep features are extracted and made available for (only) the complex sentences while shallow features are extracted and made available for the entire text.

Table 5 shows cases where we used different (logical) conditions to flag a sentence as complex, and the associated (total) processing time for feature extraction (for a corpus of 285 documents) and the extraction accuracy achieved. We observe that with the right set of conditions (to determine whether a sentence is complex) one can achieve a fairly high extraction accuracy (albeit not as high as using deep rules for all cases) and still keep the processing time modest. The percentage of sentences identified as complex is also shown, which directly reflects on the total processing time. It should be obvious that such conditions should be chosen carefully, a condition that is too conservative will lead to lower processing time but also lower extraction quality. On the other hand a condition that is too relaxed will lead to higher extraction quality but with a high processing time.

This experiment also demonstrates the advantages of having an integrated space of both shallow and deep features. We are able to strike a balance of achieving high extraction accuracy as well as keeping the processing time for feature generation under control.

Integration of Integrity Constraints

Finally, we have extensively evaluated the effectiveness of incorporating semantic information as integrity constraints. We consider both the options for basic extraction i.e., with hand-crafted XAR rules and with a state-of-the-art machine-learning based extractor and evaluate the improvement in extraction accuracy obtained as a result of incorporating constraints. As this particular aspect of the work is the central topic of other technical reports and papers we do not describe it in detail here. We will summarize the results with the facts that we were able to state meaningful integrity constraints for each of the 3 domains we evaluated here, the number of integrity constraints varied from 6 to over 40 in one of the domains. We achieved a significant increase in extraction accuracy with the incorporation of integrity constraints, achieving about as much as 40% improvement in the F-measure (per slot, averaged over all slots) in one of the domains. We refer to (Ashish, Mehrotra & Pirzadeh, 2008) for a detailed description of these experiments and results.

Table 5.

Complexity condition	Extraction F-Score	% sentences complex	Processing Time (sec)
Multiple verbs in sentence	0.71	55	300
Multiple verbs in certain portion of sentence	0.68	43	234
Multiple verbs, and presence of commas and "and" token	0.64	27	162
Number of entities greater than threshold	0.7	59	318

APPLICATION CASE STUDIES

We describe the use cases of the XAR system in the context of application development for two organizations. The first use case we describe was developed for and in collaboration with the IT department of a city emergency and disaster response government organization. The names and references of both organizations for which use cases are described havc been kept confidential upon request. The organization is responsible for effective and prompt response in natural and man-made disaster situations in the city, it is also responsible for providing information awareness and other services to citizens on a continual basis i.e., even in non emergency situation times. The organization relies significantly on information technologies to provide such services effectively and efficiently. The Disaster Portal (DisasterPortal, 2008) is a flagship example of an internet information service provided by the organization to the city public. One of the important tasks that personnel in such an organization are involved with immediately after or during a disaster is to monitor the spread of rumors among the community regards the disaster. Rumor information such as erroneous or factually wrong reports of serious issues such as the presence or number of casualties, infrastructure damage etc., can have negative consequences in the disaster response. The internet with several online local news sites and other sources is thus also a potential modality for rumors, as such a significant analyst effort is spent is manually monitoring internet information in a disaster. To alleviate this burden we are developing an automated "Internet News Monitoring" module for the Disaster Portal. The task of this module is to poll information at various local internet news sources and indentify key events and facts reported related to a disaster. These include facts such as casualties and injuries, reports of road closures or schools shut downs etc. Events and facts extracted by XAR are then fed into a database that the Disaster Portal can access. In the development of this application the definition of what news events and facts are of interest and what details in these events or facts are of interest was identified by IT analysts at the disaster response organization. Based on these requirements, developers familiar with XAR developed extraction rules for this domain.

The second use case we describe is an application developed for and in collaboration with the IT department of a county level community clinic. This organization provides voluntary health services to underserved populations in the area and receives significant monetary aid as well as aid in the form of food items, medications, etc., from the local community. It relies significantly on the use of IT for tasks such as maintaining databases of patient records, inventories of donated items, referrals of cases to other hospitals and organizations, etc. An important piece of information associated with each patient for each visit is a "clinical note" which is a free form text note of information capturing information about the patient, case history, medications recommended, progress, etc. For aggregate reporting applications, such as an annual report of the organization, thousands of such clinical notes have to analyzed manually. Key details are extracted from the notes, entered into a database and then integrated with other information such as demographic or local geographic information. We developed an application where key details are extracted from clinical notes in an automated fashion using the XAR system.

The experience of application development in both organizations, challenges faced, benefits achieved, and current status are provided in Table 6 below.

As Table 6 shows, both organizations were able to clearly articulate their information integration and consequent semantic annotation requirements. However the application development using XAR was not something that could be achieved by the average analyst in either organization. This highlights that a reasonable level of SQL and logic programming expertise

Table 6. Application Experience

	Requirements and Task Definition	Effort	Reported Benefit	Status
Disaster Response Organization (IT Department)	Organization IT personnel were able to do this without difficulty. Organization personnel not comfortable with rule language and SQL. Task left to XAR developers.	4 man weeks	• Improved coverage of news information. • Significant reduction in news monitoring and analysis time.	Adopted by organization and in active use.
Community Clinic (IT Department)	Organization IT personnel were able to articulate the needs clearly.	6 man weeks	• Improved follow up with individual patients. • Significant reduction in time and effort for aggregate reporting.	Prototype being evaluated by organization.

is required to use the XAR system and that we must develop mechanisms using which the skill level required to use XAR is lowered. The effort in developing these applications, of the order of a few man weeks, is reasonable given the scope of the applications. There is also significant benefit to both organizations. The disaster response organization has integrated access to disparate news information sources for monitoring rumors. The community clinic has automated access to structured information in thousands of clinical notes that further enables integration with other key information. In both cases, there is significant savings in time and effort for annotation tasks that were done manually prior to the application of the XAR system.

RELATED WORK

The problem of semantic annotation has been recognized since the early efforts towards the Semantic Web. (Carr, Bechhofer, Goble & Hall, 2001) and (Kahan, Koivunen, Prod'Hommeaux & Swick, 2001) describe frameworks for semantic annotation of documents in a manual and collaborative fashion. A Dagstuhl workshop on "Machine Learning for the Semantic Web" (Ciravegna, Doan, Knoblock, Kushmerick & Staab, 2005) highlighted the critical need for automated technologies for semantic annotation. KIM (Kiryakov, Popov, Terziev, Manov & Ognyanoff, 2004) is a framework for semantic annotation that exploits domain knowledge as ontologies i.e., the extracted output is improved with the knowledge present in domain ontologies. A similar semantic annotation system is SemTag (Dill et al., 2003) that makes use of the (precompiled) TAP knowledge base for annotation. Earlier efforts include systems such as S-CREAM (Handschuh, Staab & Ciravegna, 2002) that are based on machine-learning techniques for semantic annotation. (Michelson & Knoblock, 2005) is representative of work on automated semantic annotation of semi-structured data such as Web pages. The area of information extraction per se is well investigated with many systems and techniques for automated extraction including that at the slot-filling level. (Kayed et al., 2006) provides an extensive survey of many such systems and approaches. The XAR framework advances these efforts in many ways. First, from a user perspective, it abstracts the user from having to generate features of the text which are essential to any automated extraction over the text. The user can develop extraction and annotation applications at a high level with only a working knowledge of Datalog or Prolog style rules and SQL. Next, we have provided a comprehensive declarative extraction rule language. While many other systems such as DIAL (Feldman et al., 2002), XLog (Shen, Doan, Naughton & Ramakrishnan, 2007), and Lixto (Gottlob, Koch, Baumgartner, Herzog, & Flesca, 2004) provide logic based extraction rule languages, the XAR language provides more comprehensive capabilities. Specifically, we allow for the inclusion of probabilistic reasoning with the rule language, provide higher level predicates capturing text features and relationships, and define and support advanced features such as token consumption and stratified negation in the rule language and semantics. Finally, a pioneering aspect of XAR is that it allows the incorporation of semantic information as integrity constraints in the extraction and annotation process. We have demonstrated, through evaluations in several domains, how the use of integrity constraints improves on the extraction obtained with any existing approaches.

CONCLUSION

In this chapter we described the XAR framework for semantic extraction and annotation. There are several interesting directions of future work. Integrity constraints are but one form of semantic information about a domain. We can consider semantics in the other forms for instance that present in ontologies that could be applied to the task. Or one may also consider semantics that may be present *in* the data itself, for instance patterns that we could mine in the available data and apply it for improving extraction.

Finally, we encourage the community to use the available XAR system for semantic annotation tasks and welcome feedback.

ACKNOWLEDGMENT

The authors wish to acknowledge Pouria Pirzadeh and Zheng Zhang, who led the efforts on the experimental evaluation of the system.

REFERENCES

Ashish, N., Mehrotra, S., & Pirzadeh, P. (2008). *Incorporating Integrity Constraints in Uncertain Databases* (. UCI Technical Report 2008). Retrieved fromOnline at http://www.ics.uci.edu/~ashish/techreporthttp://www.ics.uci.edu/~ashish/techreport

Automatic Content ExtractionA. C. E. (n.d.). http://www.nist.gov/speech/tests/ace/http://www.nist.gov/speech/tests/ace/

Berners-Lee, T., Hendler, J., & Lassila, O. (2001). The Semantic Web. *Scientific American, 284*(5), 34–43.

Carr, L., Bechhofer, S., Goble, C., & Hall, W. (2001). Conceptual linking: Ontology based open hypermedia. *WWW10 Conference Hong Kong.*

Ceri, S., & Gottlob, G., and & Tanca, L. (1989). What you always wanted to know about Datalog (and never dared to ask). *IEEE Transactions on Knowledge and Data Engineering, 1*(1), 1989, pp. 146-66. doi:10.1109/69.43410

Ciravegna, F., Doan, A., Knoblock, C., Kushmerick, N., and & Staab, S. (2005). Machine Learning learning for the Semantic Web. *Seminar 05071 at Schloss Dahstuhl 2005.*

Cunningham, H., Maynard, D., Bontcheva, K., & Tablan, V. (2002). GATE: A framework and graphical development environment for robust NLP Tools and applications. In *Proceedings of the 40th Anniversary Meeting of the Association for Computational Linguistics (ACL'02)*. Philadelphia, July 2002.

Dalvi, N., and Suciu, D. (2005). Foundations of probabilistic answers to queries. Tutorial,. *ACM SIGMOD 2005.*

Denti, E., Omicini, A., & Ricci, R. (2001). tu-Prolog: A Light-Weight Prolog for Internet Applications and Infrastructures. *PADL 2001, Las Vegas, NV.*

Dill, S., Eiron, N., Gibson, D., Gruhl, D., Guha, R., Jhingran, A., et al. (2003). SemTag and Seeker: Bootstrapping the semantic Semantic web Web via automated semantic annotation. *WWW12 Conference Budapest.*

DisasterPortal. (2008). WebRetrieved from: http://www.disasterportal.orghttp://www.disasterportal.org

Feldman, R., Aumann, Y., Finkelstein-Landau, M., Hurvitz, E., Regev, Y., &and Yaroshevich, A. (2002). A comparative study of information extraction strategies. *ACL 2002.*

Gottlob, G., Koch, C., Baumgartner, R., Herzog, M., & Flesca, S. (2004). The lixto data extraction project - back and forth between theory and practice. In *Proc ACM PODS 2004.*

Handschuh, S., Staab, S., and & Ciravegna, F. (2002). S-CREAM: Semi-automatic CREation of Metadata. *EKAW 2002.*

Jayram, T. S., Krishnamurthy, R., Raghavan, S., Vaithyanathan, S., & Zhu, H. (2006). Avatar information extraction system. *A Quarterly Bulletin of the Computer Society of the IEEE Technical Committee on Data Engineering*, 2006.

Kahan, J., & Koivunen, M. Prod'Hommeaux, E., & Swick, E. (2001). Annotea: An open RDF infrastructure for shared web Web annotations. *WWW10 Conference, Hong Kong.*

Kayed, M., Girgis, M. R., & Shaalan, K. F. (2006). A Survey survey of Web information extraction systems. *IEEE Transactions on Knowledge and Data Engineering, 18*, 2006.

Kiryakov, A., Popov, B., Terziev, I., Manov, D., & Ognyanoff, D. (2004). Semantic annotation, indexing and retrieval. *Journal of Web Semantics, 2*(1), 49–79. doi:10.1016/j.websem.2004.07.005

Lakshmanan, L., and & Sadri, F. (1994). Probabilistic deductive databases. *SLP 1994.*

Michelson, M., & and Knoblock, C. (2005). Semantic annotation of unstructured and ungrammatical text. *IJCAI, 2005.*

MUC. (1995). *Proceedings of the 6th message Understanding Conference, MUC-6*, Columbia, MD, 1995.

Naughton, M., Kushmerick, N., & Carthy, J. (2006). Clustering sentences for discovering events in news articles. *ECIR, 2006.*

Pang, B., Lee, L., & Vaithyanathan, S. (2002). Thumbs up? Sentiment classification using machine learning techniques. In *Proceedings of EMNLP*.

Shen, W., Doan, A., Naughton, J., & Ramakrishnan, R. (2007). Declarative information extraction using datalog with embedded extraction predicates. In *Proc ACM SIGMOD 2007.*

StanfordParser. (2008). WebRetrieved from: http://www-nlp.stanford.edu/downloads/lex-parser.shtmlhttp://www-nlp.stanford.edu/downloads/lex-parser.shtml

TIES. 2008. (n.d.). "TIES: Trainable Information Extraction System,". Retrieved from http://tcc.itc.it/research/textec/tools-resources/ties.htmlhttp://tcc.itc.it/research/textec/tools-resources/ties.html

Ullman, J., & Widom, J. (2007). *A first course in database systems*. Prentice Hall, 2007.

Ullman, J.D. (1988). Bottom-up beats top-down for datalog. *ACM PODS 1988.*

Chapter 12
CRUZAR:
An Application of Semantic Matchmaking to e-Tourism

Iván Mínguez
Fundación CTIC, Spain

Diego Berrueta
Fundación CTIC, Spain

Luis Polo
Fundación CTIC, Spain

EXECUTIVE SUMMARY

This chapter describes CRUZAR, a Web application that builds custom tourism routes for each visitor to the city of Zaragoza. This application exploits expert knowledge of the tourism domain (captured in rules and ontologies) and consumes a consolidated repository of relevant tourism resources (RDF instances extracted from different legacy databases: historical buildings, museums, public parks, restaurants, cultural events...). User profiles and interests, as well as user-defined constraints, are modeled with an ontology. A semantic matchmaking algorithm is applied to find the most interesting resources for each profile, and a planner organizes the selections into an optimal route. The authors discuss the main challenges and design choices.

CRUZAR: AN APPLICATION OF SEMANTIC MATCHMAKING TO ETOURISM

The web is a big showcase for tourism. Nowadays, many tourists plan their trips in advance using the information available in web pages. Cities compete against each other to offer the most attractive and complete information and services through the tourism section of their web sites. This competition often leads to information-bloated and multimedia-rich web sites which resemble digital versions of printed brochures.

DOI: 10.4018/978-1-60566-894-9.ch012

Every potential visitor is served with the same information on the web, regardless of his profile. On the other hand, when visitors enter a tourism office in the real world, they can obtain customized information and recommendations based on their profile and desires.

CRUZAR is a web application that uses expert knowledge (in the form of rules and ontologies) and a comprehensive repository of relevant data (instances) to build a custom route for each visitor profile. While some cities have compiled a few predefined routes for the most common profiles (such as "Visit Zaragoza in just three days"), CRUZAR can potentially generate an infinite number of custom routes and it offers a much closer fit for each visitor's profile.

Tourism officials often desire to provide attractive and innovative services to promote the city, its tourism infrastructure and to increase the number of visitors. On the other hand, administrations, like city councils, would like to extract the most profit from the IT resources they already have. However, the deployment of new added value services is often hampered by the issue of integrating data coming from different sources (and parties). Moreover, recent history of the Web has shown increased value of contextualized services and targeted information. We demonstrate how semantic technologies can fulfill both aspects of the challenge: data integration and user contextualization.

There are a number of reasons that make Zaragoza (Spain) an excellent test bed for CRUZAR. In the first place, Zaragoza has a high density of POIs: its city center is packed with remarkable buildings, art galleries, sculptures and historical remains. Even more interestingly, these POIs cover a wide range of artistic styles and ages dating back to the Roman Empire, and therefore, they can attract a wide spectrum of visitors. Zaragoza is one of the biggest cities in Spain, and it enjoys a very dynamic cultural agenda, as well as frequent top-level sport events. Finally, the city council has extensive databases which contain descriptions of all these resources.

The CRUZAR system is split in the following three stages. The complete process is also shown in *Figure 1*:

1. Data Integration. At this stage, a unique access point to all the available tourism information is provided to the system. The result of this process is a coherent and integrated data model, build upon the partial descriptions of resources stored in independent and heterogeneous information repositories of the city council of Zaragoza.
2. Recommendation Algorithm. CRUZAR provides a web form where the user profile is captured, essentially her preferences and the trip context. Preferences, in conjunction with the previous integrated descriptions of tourism resources, are used by CRUZAR to suggest and to recommend the most suitable places for her visit.
3. Planning Algorithm. At this last stage, the system generates a customized route for the visitor. By the way, CRUZAR not only considers the distance between the POIs, but also the subjective interest of tourism resources, previously calculated, the particular circumstances of the trip (number of visitors or trip dates) and other relevant aspects for the route, such as opening and closing time of museums and churches.

The rest of the article is organized as follows. Data acquisition and representation is covered in the next two sections: *Semantic Integration of existing databases* describes how different sources of data were integrated using ontologies and the section *User Profiling* introduces the user profile ontology. *Extending poi and profile descriptions with rules* covers the extension of the data using rules. The route generation algorithm is the subject of *route generation*, while the user-defined constraints are addressed in the section *Route customization*. Section *Related work* reviews some interesting related work,

Figure 1. Resources are first ranked and the planned to create a customized route

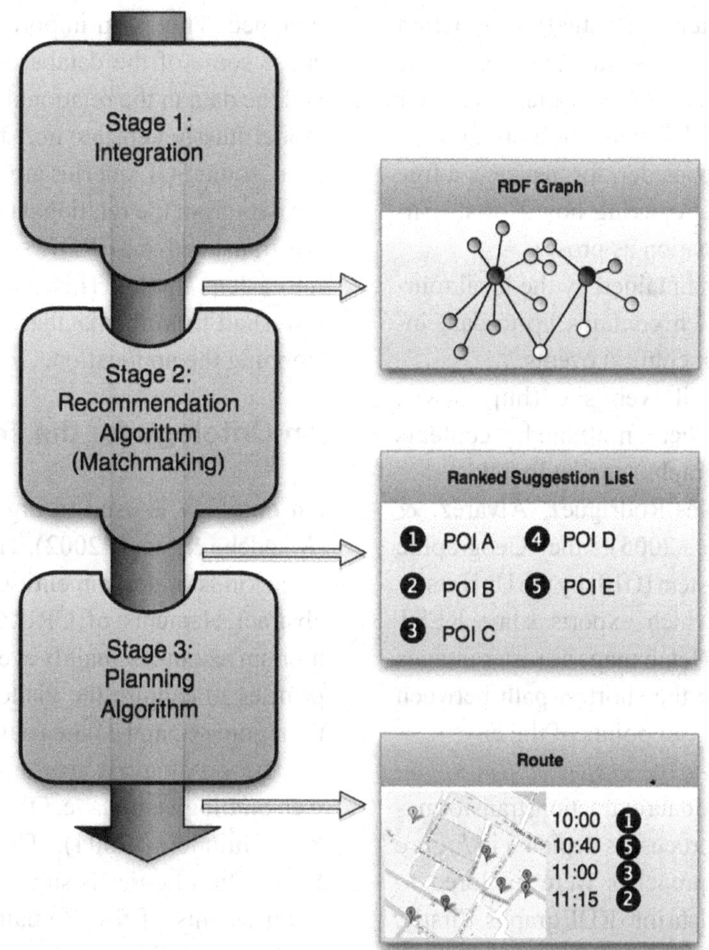

and the section *Discussion and future work* concludes the paper.

SEMANTIC INTEGRATION OF EXISTING DATABASES

The first challenge is to have an integrated and coherent description of each tourism resource from the unconnected partial descriptions already available in different information silos. The completeness and richness of these integrated descriptions are essential for building a successful contextual service. We have chosen RDF (Klyne, Carroll, & McBride, 2004) as the common data model to represent the integrated and partial descriptions of the relevant resources. From the beginning, RDF has been purposely designed to create rich resource descriptions and to provide a clear semantics to merge partial descriptions of the same resource.

Most part of the required information was already available and has to be collected from existing relational databases. Unfortunately, these partial descriptions were locked in independent information repositories:

- The CMS database which feeds the city council web site. This database has the purpose of capturing (textual) information to feed the web. Consequently, some fields are loosely structured, and therefore their conversion to RDF was not a straightforward process (consider, for instance, a free text field titled "opening hours" that contains the information as prose).
- The database maintained by the local tourism office, which contains up-to-date information about cultural events.
- The city council web site (http://www.zaragoza.es), where multimedia contents (mainly photographs) can be found.
- IDEZar (Portolés-Rodríguez, Álvarez. & Muro-Medrano, 2005), the Geographic Information System (GIS) by the University of Zaragoza, which exports some REST web services to fetch maps as raster images and to compute the shortest path between two geo-referenced points of the city.

An overview of the data extraction, transformation and integration process is depicted in *Figure 2*. Two different approaches were explored to transform relational data into RDF graphs. Firstly, an attempt was made to use D2RQ middleware (Bizer & Seaborne, 2004). D2RQ, from the Free University of Berlin, is an excellent tool to create simple RDF wrappers on top of relational databases. However, it cannot address the most challenging adaptations, therefore the adaptation of the relational model to RDF triples was finally achieved by writing *ad hoc* code.

Duplicate detection was another tricky issue: some databases contain complementary and shared data about the same resource. Because of the absence of a shared key to join the data, basic information retrieval techniques were used to spot the duplicates. The set of matched pairs was small enough to perform a manual review. Finally, subclassification was introduced to precisely identify the type of each resource.

It is worth noting that the data were not simply converted to RDF. Instead, the databases were wrapped. This is an important requirement, because some of the databases are updated daily, and the data in the relational model and the RDF model must be kept in sync. At application-loading time, some SQL queries are executed to retrieve the data from the relational model and the results are translated into RDF statements and added into a Jena model. This semantic model can be refreshed from the database at run time without stopping the application.

An Ontology for the Tourism Domain

An ontology is used to organize the RDF data (Maedche & Staab, 2002). This ontology defines three kinds of domain entities that constitute the abstract elements of CRUZAR: 1) Zaragoza's tourism resources, mainly events and POIs, 2) user profiles to capture the visitors' preferences and their context, and 3) the route configuration.

The ontology is expressed using the W3C web ontology language, OWL DL (Smith, Welty, &McGuinness, 2004). The semantics of the Description Logics is suitable for the modelling requirements of this domain. Actually, the DL expressivity of the ontology is *ALCHIF(D)* as we use some OWL property restrictions to describe in detail some core concepts, especially the user profile. Nevertheless, the lack of support for simple rules in OWL DL is still an issue. In our case, inferring the implicit interests of tourist profiles and POIs is not possible using a DL reasoner, therefore we use rules (see section "**Extending POI and Profile Descriptions with Rules**").

The conceptual structure of our ontology is based on the upper-ontology DOLCE (Descriptive Ontology for Linguistic and Cognitive Engineering), but with a practical perspective in mind. DOLCE and its modules (DOLCE-Lite-Plus library), explained in Masolo, Borgo, Gangemi, Guarino, Oltramari, & Scheneider (2002), have been used as a development framework to capture the core concepts and properties of the tourism domain. We also expect that using an upper-ontology will make it easier to map and to extend our ontology with other OWL ontologies or RDF vocabularies (Gangemi, Guarino, Masolo, & Oltramari, 2001). Assuming the ontological commitment of an upper ontology, we delegate some strategic decisions of the conceptual modelling on a philosophical well-founded framework (Guarino & Welty, 2004). Nevertheless, there still remains the identification of the corresponding DOLCE concepts that fit with our modelling aims. Among the different upper-level ontologies, DOLCE specializes in providing specific mechanisms to treat and model "social concepts" (Masolo, Vieu, Bottazzi, Catenacci, Ferrario, Gangemi, & Guarino, 2004), such as the ones needed in this project. Our main decisions were to interpret visitors' profiles as *edns:roles* (DnS module), routes as *pla:execution-plan* (Plan and Task Module) and POIs as *common:geographical-objects* (Common Sense Module). In this sense, we found that DOLCE is a precise domain analysis tool, providing us the guidelines to develop an accurate model.

Figure 2. Information flow in the data extraction, transformation and integration process

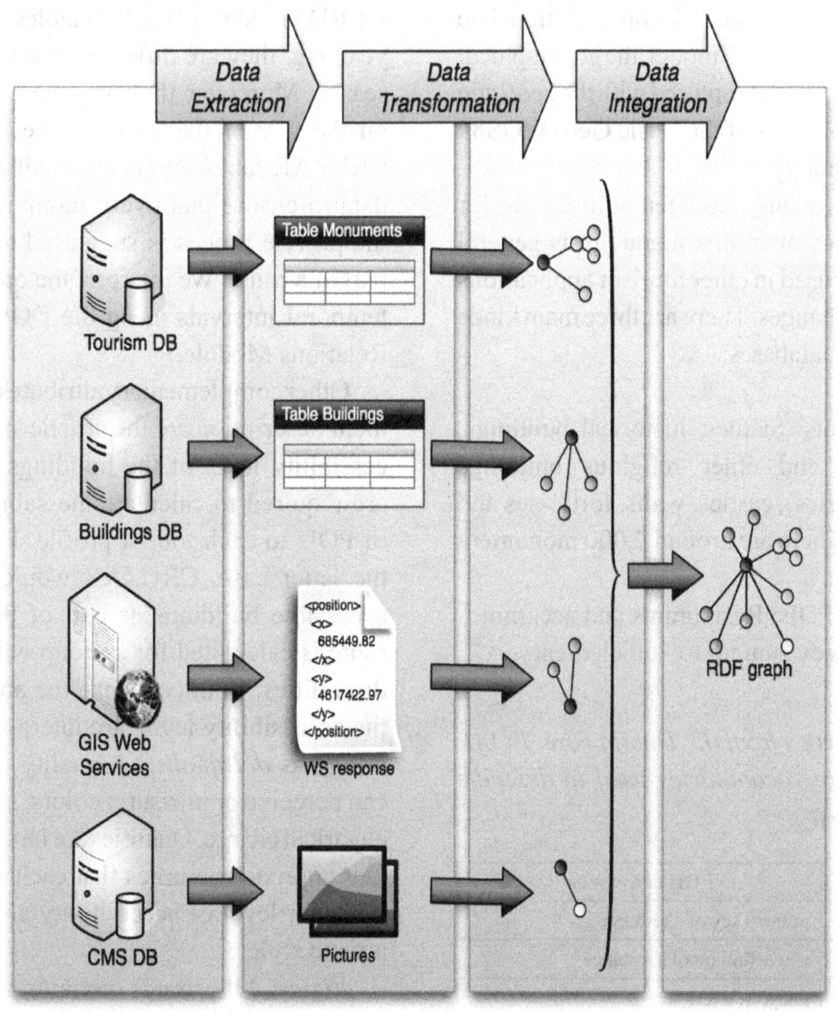

The structure of the aforementioned CMS database fails to meet our strict needs, but on the other hand, it stores a lot of useful information for visitors. The database contains different kinds of resources: green parks, hotels, churches, historical buildings, etc. The purpose of the ontology is to integrate these data in an uniform single model.

The wrappers map the database rows to the corresponding concepts from the ontology, arranged in a hierarchical structure (*rdfs:subClassOf*). The instances of these concepts are the POIs that may be part of the itinerary. Wherever it is possible, we reuse the properties from some well-known RDF vocabularies to describe these resources, see Table 1.

The positions of the POIs were available in the database of the GIS system. In order to translate these positions to the RDF model, the geographical coordinates of POIs are captured with the *geo:long* and *geo:lat* properties of the Basic Geo (WGS84 lat/long) Vocabulary .

The POI taxonomy has been built *ad hoc* for this project. However, this hierarchy is general enough to be reused in other tourism applications with minimal changes. There are three main kinds of POIs in the databases:

- Monuments: Statues, historical buildings, churches and other religious buildings (monasteries), castles, walls, fortresses and palaces. There are around 2,000 monument instances.
- Catering POIs: Restaurants and accommodation. They sum up to 700 elements.

Table 1. Properties from the Dublin core, FOAF and SKOS-Core vocabularies used to describe points of interest

RDF property	POIs description
dc:identifier	primary key of a resource
skos:definition	text definition of a resource
foaf:depiction	image of a resource

- Business POIs: Commercial areas and shopping centers. There are 50 of these in the center of Zaragoza.

The most interesting POIs are the monuments. Some of their attributes are used by the planner to calculate the route. They include an estimation of how long it will take to visit each monument (*zar:visit-duration*) and the objective interest of POIs (*zar:poi-relevance*), that is predetermined by the Zaragoza tourism office. The values of these attributes are entered by the experts of the Tourism Office of Zaragoza. This guarantees a reliable description of monuments. One of the most difficult challenges was the concise representation of the opening times of each monument in the RDF model. These timetables vary during the year, e.g. they are different in summer or winter season. Moreover, the opening times also depend on the day of the week or the bank holidays. CRUZAR takes into account all these temporal data to ensure that every monument is open at the precise time it is suggested to be visited as part of a route. We interpret the opening times as temporal intervals using the DOLCE Temporal Relations Module.

Other complementary attributes of each monument description are the artistic style and the accessibility level of the buildings. These values are required to calculate the subjective interest of POIs to each tourist profile. For instance, in the latter case, CRUZAR would suggest only accessible buildings as part of the route if the route is calculated for a group with people with disabilities. Both concepts, the artistic style and the accessibility level, are interpreted in our ontology as *dol:quality*. A quality is an entity we can perceive or measure: colors, sizes, lengths or electrical charge. Qualities are inherent to entities. Our approach assumes that each monument has a certain level of accessibility and one or more artistic styles.

Figure 3 illustrates our approach, and it provides a complete description of one of Zaragoza tourism resources (POIs). The top layer contains the DOLCE classes that allow to interpret the domain concepts of our ontology. The middle layer is the actual model of the tourism resources: artistic styles, opening times, the type of POIs, etc. Finally, the bottom layer represents the RDF instances organized under the ontology structure.

USER PROFILING

CRUZAR generates a custom tour across the city for each visitor. Therefore, it needs a user profile. In order not to discourage any potential user, the application does not ask them to create a user account. An anonymous profile is created from scratch for each visitor everytime he uses the application (see *Figure 4*). Users are encouraged to describe themselves (i.e, to enter their profile) in the system because there is an immediate and obvious reward: the more complete their profile is, the better the system can fulfill their expectations. Moreover, as the application does not ask for any data that can be (potentially) used to identify the user (such as name, email address, etc.), users are not worried about their privacy.

Regardless of the willingness of the users to enter their profile, filling a web form is not a pleasant task. Therefore, everything in the profile defaults to reasonable values and can be changed later as an add-on in case the user is dissatisfied with the first route proposed by the system. This is an important feature of our application: routes can be generated for every profile, even for unspecific ones, although the application delivers better results for rich profiles.

Visitor profiles are interpreted as social roles. In this way, our model distinguishes between users and profiles, and it does not merge both in the same definition. A user can refine her own profile by modifying some of its attributes to obtain a more customized route. The ontology models a set of relevant elements for profile tailoring. They are split in two disjoint groups: the visitor preferences and the specific context of the visitors. The DL formula in *Figure 5* expresses the set of axioms

Figure 3. The three ontological layers of a POI representation

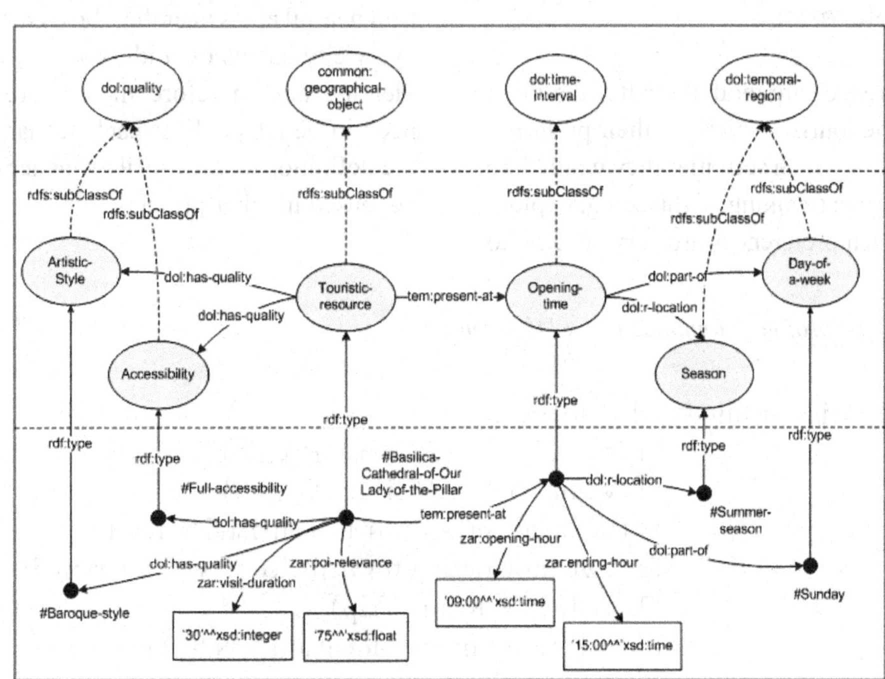

Figure 4. Screenshot of the profile capture form (http://www.zaragoza.es/turruta/Turruta/en/index_Ruta). Even more options can be shown by clicking on the link at the bottom, but only the dates are strictly required.

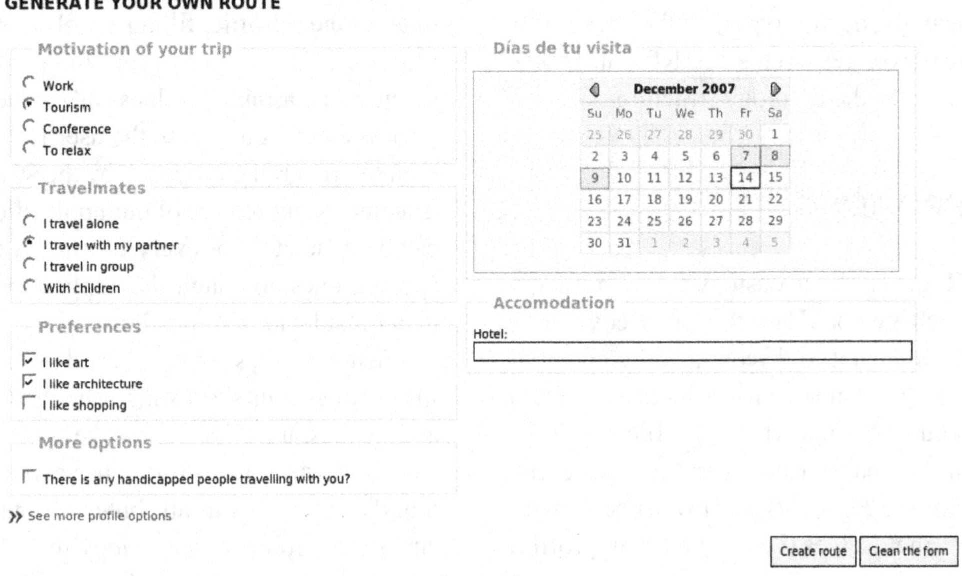

describing the tourist profile in the ontology. More graphically, an equivalent representation of the profile is depicted in *Figure 6*.

Visitor Preferences

Visitor preferences are modelled after the main interests of the tourist: which are their preferred artistic styles, or which activities they would like to do in Zaragoza (walking, sightseeing, explore the town…). All preferences are very specific to and dependent on the characteristics of the city. Zaragoza has one of the most interesting and best preserved cultural heritages in Spain: from Roman ruins, to Baroque and medieval buildings, or beautiful natural areas near the Ebro river. Obviously, every city has its own idiosyncrasy and cultural identity, and therefore the preferences would need to be adapted for each scenario, although the definition of the profile is generic enough to be reused in other projects.

Figure 5. Tourist profile axiomatized in a DL-formula

$$
\begin{aligned}
\text{Tourist-profile} \equiv\ & \text{edns:social-role} \\
& \sqcap (\forall \text{edns:refines.Tourist-Profile}) \\
& \sqcap (\forall \text{edns:covers.Visitors-Group}) \\
& \sqcap (\forall \text{edns:desire-towards.Tourist-Preference}) \\
& \sqcap (\forall \text{zar:not-desire-towards.Tourist-Preference}) \\
& \sqcap (\forall \text{edns:performs.Trip}) \\
& \sqcap (\exists \text{tem:e-temporal-location.Visit-Day})
\end{aligned}
$$

Figure 6. Main components of the tourist profile

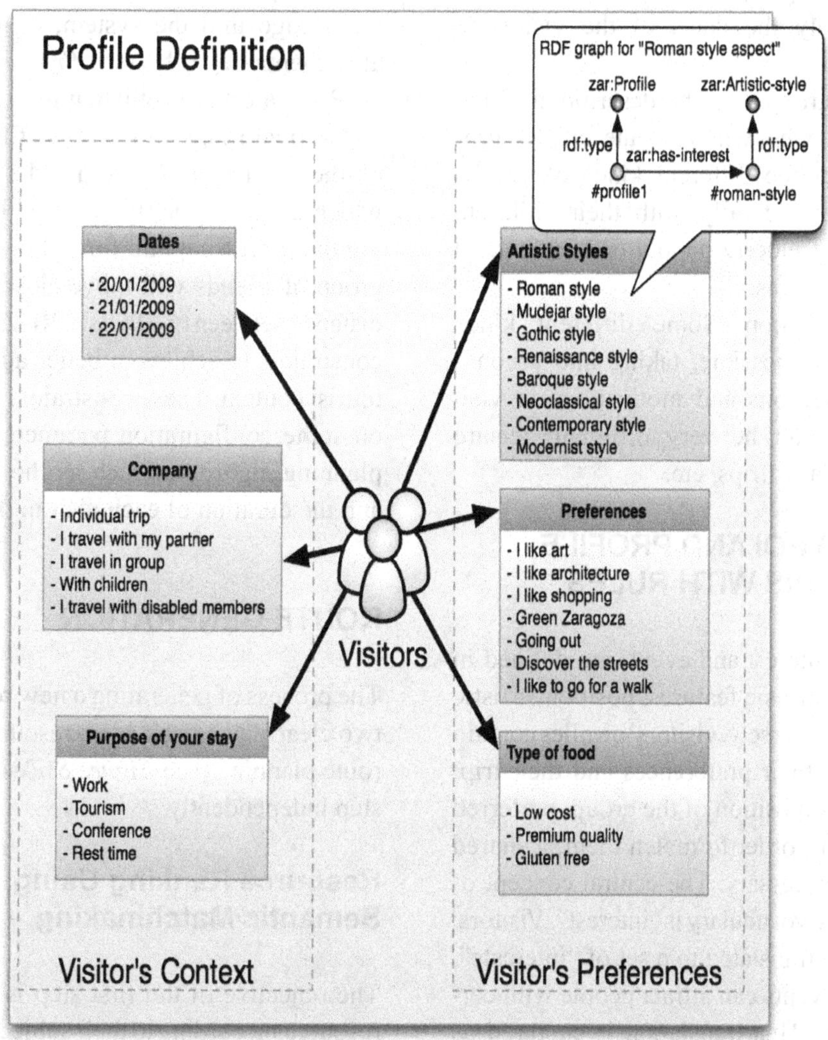

The preferences are modeled as courses of events using the DOLCE module for modal descriptions in combination with the DnS module. Technically, a modal relation, *mod:desire-towards*, is used to express that a profile "desires" certain packages of tourism resources. However, sometimes a profile "desires" not to do some kind of activity or not to visit some kind of places (museums, for instance). Thus, we introduce a new property with the opposite meaning: *zar:not-desire-towards*. This information is later used to raise or lower the relevance of the affected POIs in the matchmaking process.

Visitor Context

The tourist context refers to the specific circumstances of the trip: who is travelling, when does the trip take place, and which are its motivations. This information is part of the definition of the profile as it concerns mainly the route generation.

- Trip dates, i.e., the dates the visitors will stay in Zaragoza. Notice that, as we said above, only the dates of the visits are required.
- Visitors' group, i.e., the description of the collective who will visit the city. A profile can define different kinds of groups of people: a family with their children, a group of elderly people or a individual with disabilities.
- Trip motivation. Some different kinds of trips are possible, taking into account that the reasons and motivations to visit Zaragoza can be very different: leisure trips, business trips, etc.

EXTENDING POI AND PROFILE DESCRIPTIONS WITH RULES

City points of interest and events are defined in terms of their intrinsic features: position, artistic style or date. Conversely, visitors' profiles contain information on their preferences and their trip: arrival date, composition of the group, preferred activities, etc. In order to match them, a shared vocabulary is necessary. The central concept of this intermediate vocabulary is "interest". Visitors' preferences are translated to a set of "interests", and POIs and events can attract people with certain "interests". This translation is captured as production rules, which are executed using the Jena built-in rule engine. These rules are defined by the experts on the domain, i.e., the tourism officers.

There are some "interests" that have straightforward equivalents within both city resources and user profiles. For instance, some buildings are representative of the Baroque architecture, and some visitors may like the Baroque style. Therefore, there is an "interest for Baroque style" in the intermediate vocabulary.

However, there are rules which are not so obvious. For instance, public parks often attract the interest of those travelling with children, but picture galleries will probably bore the kids. It is at this point where domain experts pour their knowledge into the system, writing down the aforementioned rules (see *Figure 7*).

Rules are also useful to infer some constraints of the final route. In many profiles, the context of the tourist implies some desired constraint which is not explicitly declared by the user using the profile capture form. For instance, a big group of friends will move slowly to cover the distance between two POIs. CRUZAR infers these constraints to achieve a better adaptation to the tourist context. These constraints have an impact on some configuration parameters of the route planning algorithm, such as the walking speed and the duration of each visit in the route.

ROUTE GENERATION

The process of generating a new route comprises two clearly distinct stages: resource ranking and route planning (see *Figure 8*). We describe each step independently.

Resource Ranking Using Semantic Matchmaking

The objective of the first step is to rank all the resources according to their subjective interest for each visitor profile. At the end of the matchmaking process, a numerical score is assigned to all the resources to quantify their interestingness.

Initially, each resource has a static score which was decided by the domains experts. This *a priori* score (*zar:poi-relevance*) represents the objective interest of the resource regardless of the profile. A small selection of the most remarkable landmarks of the city have a high static score to ensure they are picked in almost every route generated by the application. The rest of resources are "the long tail" which may arouse the interest of some of the visitors. This static score is the mechanism to counterbalance the pure subjective interest (taking

Figure 7. Two sample rules from the set that translates tourist profiles into interests

```
[ri15:(?p rdf:type zar:Tourist-profile),
     (?p edns:desire-towards zar:Explore-the-city)
     ->
     (?p zar:has-interest zar:Interest-in-architecture),
     (?p zar:has-interest zar:Interest-in-historical-buildings),
     (?p zar:has-no-insterest zar:Interest-in-museums)]

[ri16:(?p rdf:type zar:Tourist-profile),
     (?p edns:desire-towards zar:Go-for-a-walk)
     ->
     (?p zar:has-interest zar:Interest-in-natural-walking),
     (?p zar:has-interest zar:Interet-in-green-sapces)]

[rn2:(?p rdf:type zar:Tourist-profile),
     (?p edns:covers zar:Collective-with-handicapped-people)
     ->
     (?p edns:desire-towards zar:Slow-walking),
(?p edns:desire-towards zar:Long-time-of-visit)]
```

into account only the preferences of the profile). This bias is a business requirement of the tourism officers in order to shape the demand towards the most representative resources of the city (i.e., the landmarks such as the "Basílica del Pilar", the most recognizable postcard of the city).

The semantic matchmaking process is executed individually for each resource, and its outcome is a modulated score for the resource. This value may be lower than or equal to the original one. A high value denotes a close match with the visitor's profile.

Our implementation of the semantic matchmaking algorithm is built after the ideas of Li & Horrocks (2003) and Noia, Sciascio, & Donini (2007). The former defines five categories to measure the match between two instances in Description Logics. The latter uses a penalty function and concept abduction and concept contraction. The penalty function is applied to lower the score of an instance when some constraint is relaxed.

In our implementation, the score degradation depends on the importance of the interest being (miss)matched. Every instance of the interest vocabulary has a "weight", a numerical value that captures the priority of each facet: from those which are "nice to have" (low weight) to those which are "required" (maximum weight). The

Figure 8. General architecture of CRUZAR

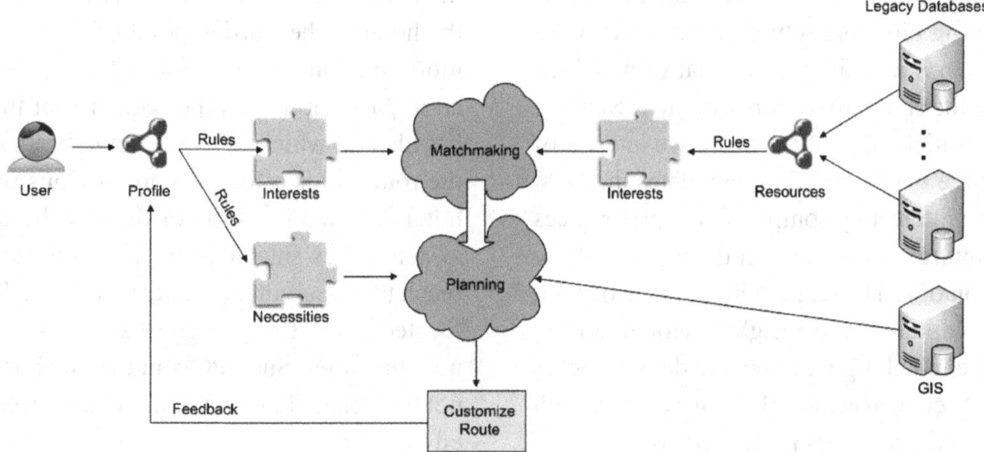

latter are show stoppers: a failure to satisfy the visitor's interest in a required facet will prevent a resource from being part of the route. There are a few of these stoppers; for instance, if the profile contains the sentence "I'm travelling with handicapped people", then the visitor will have "interest for full accessible buildings". Resources that fail to match this "required" interest will not be part of the route.

In order to compute the final, subjective interest of each resource, their interests are matched against the ones from the profile:

- For each interest shared by the profile and the resource, the score of the resource is unaffected.
- For each interest in the profile which is not present in the resource, a penalty function is applied to lower the score of the resource.
- For each negative interest in the profile which is present in the resource, the penalty function is applied as well.

Note that no action is taken for interests that exist in the resource but not in the profile. At the end of the process, resources are ordered by their score. Those that more closely match the visitor's profile will be at the top of the list.

More formally, let K being a knowledge base that contains the semantic descriptions of tourism resources and let p being a tourism profile, the matching functions return for each resource r described in K a positive numerical value which measures the contextual interest of r to p. Starting from the initial value of the objective interest of the resource r, this function modulates the final subjective interest by comparing the preferences of the captured profile p with the aspects of the description of r. The relative importance of each aspect is captured in a weight vector w. In the core of the matching function, the dot product is computed between w and a Boolean vector, which indicates if the aspect is present or not.

Route Planning

After all candidate POIs have been sorted by their subjective interest, a planner algorithm is run in order to create the route. The algorithm aims to balance the quantity and quality (interestingness) of the selected POIs and the distance. Visitors can influence this equilibrium. For instance, those who declare that they "don't mind to walk" will get less packed routes and longer distances between POIs. On the other hand, minimizing the distance is important for physically visitors with disabilities.

Two simplifications were introduced. Firstly, all the movement is on foot. This is consistent with the fact that most of the POIs are enclosed in the central part of the city, in an area of 2.5 square kilometers. Furthermore, many streets in this area are pedestrian-only.

The second simplification assumes that time is split into slots. There are up to five slots per day: morning visits, lunch, afternoon visits, dinner and night activities. Initially, the planner algorithm only cares about the morning and afternoon visits (slots 1 and 3), and it tries to pack them with POIs. Restaurant recommendations for lunch and dinner (slots 2 and 4) are picked later, taking into account the final point of the route in the previous slot. The algorithm simply provides suggestions for the last slot by querying all the available events for each night.

CRUZAR asks the visitors for the name of their hotel. This information is used to include the hotel as the starting point of the route in the morning. Thus, the location of the hotel can have an impact not just on the sequence of the visits, but also on which POIs are actually included in the route. This effect is more obvious when the hotel is in the outskirts of the city, because the system takes into account the time needed to reach the city center (where most of the POIs are located), and it may suggest some POIs located near the hotel. Such POIs in the outskirts would not be included in a route if the hotel were in the city center.

Due to response time constraints, a greedy algorithm is used to compute a nearly optimal solution for route calculation. A function of the distance and the interest is used as the heuristic to drive the algorithm.

ROUTE CUSTOMIZATION

The route proposed by the system is offered to the user using an accessible, information-rich interface (see *Figure 9*) that includes: the sequence of selected POIs, a tentative timetable for each day, a map highlighting the POIs, suggestions of other interesting places near the route, and two sets of recommended restaurants near the last POI of the route (a set for lunch and another one for dinner). Complementary activities, such as events (music concerts, sport events, etc.) and shopping, are also suggested. Almost every piece of information is hyperlinked to a comprehensive description of the resource (these descriptions are the outcome of the aforementioned databases).

For each POI in the route, visitors can request an explanation on why it was picked by the algorithm. We consider this information is valuable for the visitor, because she can have an insight of how the system works, and therefore, she can learn to use it more productively. Moreover, these explanations highlight the shared aspects between the user profile and the POI, so the visitor can know in advance what she would probably like from the POI.

Users can interact with the generated route in a number of ways. They can "ban" individual POIs, either because they do not like them or because they have already seen them during a previous visit to the city. There is also a "not now" option for each POI; when used, the system modifies the plan so that particular POI is moved to a different time slot. For visitors specially interested in a certain POI, there is also an option to manually pick the POI and force its inclusion in the route, even if it was given a low score by the matchmaker. Finally, there is also an option to skip a time slot; this may be useful for visitors who must attend a part-time meeting.

User-entered and inferred constraints are represented using an RDF vocabulary. This makes it possible to link them to profiles and routes, and to store them in the same RDF repository. Actually, all the information managed by the application (profiles, routes, constraints) is represented in RDF, and stored for anonymous off-line analysis and perfective maintenance of rules and algorithms.

RELATED WORK

Our review of the related work focuses on three topics: 1) recommender and planning systems for tourism, 2) domain ontologies for tourism and 3) general approaches to resource matching.

Regarding recommender and planning systems, there are several approaches that take into account the tourist profile to build queries in order to retrieve relevant resources by filtering and enlarging the result set. Linden, Hanks, & Lesh (1997) describe a flight planning system in which the successive refinement capture of the user preferences delivers the most suitable trip plan. Mirzadeh, Ricci, & Bansal (2004) and Jannach (2006) explore how to relax the constraints of a query to increase the number of resources without loosing the query´s ultimate objective. Taking into account the interactions among users in collaborative systems, Ricci (2002) proposes a new method to generate recommendations.

The most significative initiative to create a shared ontology in the tourism domain is the Harmonise ontology, developed by the EU Tourism Harmonisation Network (HarmoNet). The aim of this ontology is to remove the interoperability gap that exists in the European tourism market by allowing interoperation using different industry standards (Hepp, Siorpaes, & Bachlechner, 2006).

Figure 9. Detail of a route (http://www.zaragoza.es/turruta/Turruta/en/index_Ruta). Information from different sources is merged in a consistent user interface

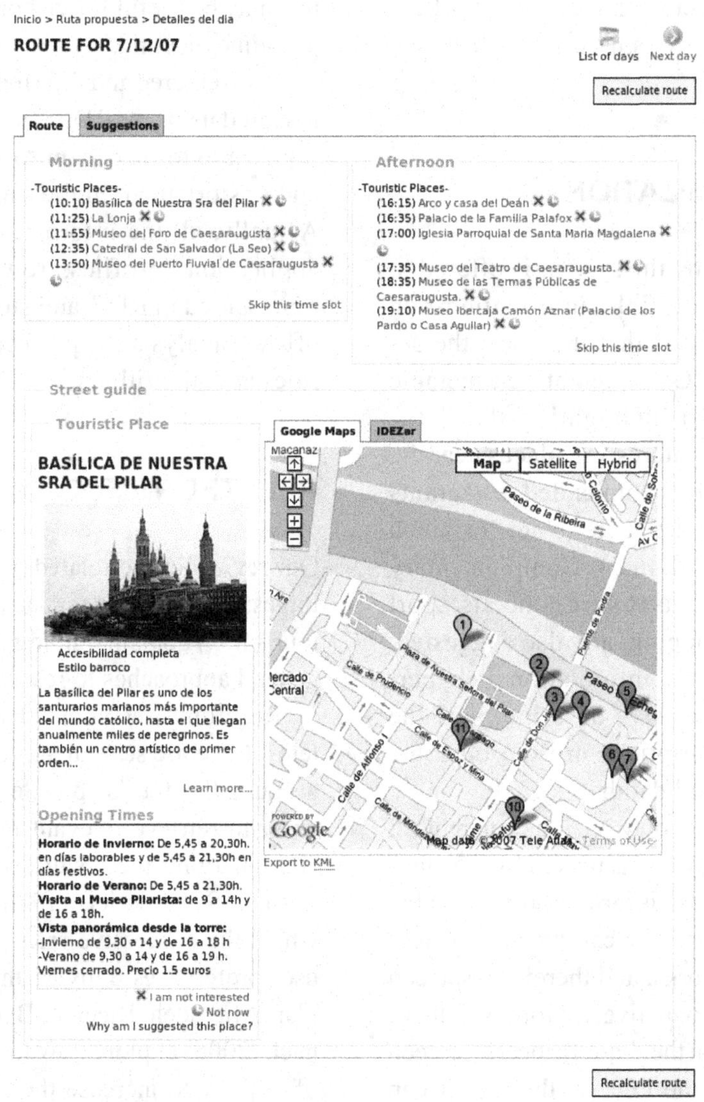

Harmonise covers accommodation facilities, events and activities, with a special focus on the latter. Nevertheless, the unavailability of this ontology in the public Web discouraged us from using it as the basis for our ontology. Instead, we chose the upper-level ontology DOLCE. Moreover, our ontology reaches a deeper and richer description of Zaragoza resources, and more importantly, of the visitor profiles (the visitor preferences and the context and circumstances of her trip).

Finally, a lot of research has been done on matching and correlation algorithms. Our work is closed to the approaches based on Description Logics. Paolucci, Kawamura, Payne, & Sycara (2002) firstly defined four levels of matching between different concepts (unary predicates). Li & Horrocks (2003) extended this classification with a new level that takes into account the shared features of each pair of concepts. These approaches provide a logical interpretation of correlation between resources, but the results lack the granularity demanded by our scenario where a quantitative ranking is required. Our work is inspired by the work of Colucci, Noia, Sciascio, Donini, & Mongiello (2003), and Noia et al. (2007), which respectively define the abduction and contraction techniques and the penalty functions. The aim of these techniques is to evaluate the level of matching between two concepts by accounting the number and relevance of the constraints that must be relaxed to facilitate their match.

DISCUSSION AND FUTURE WORK

We described CRUZAR, an application created for one of the largest cities in Spain (the application is already deployed in the city council web servers http://www.zaragoza.es/turruta/Turruta/en/index_Ruta). Semantic web technologies are put into practice 1) to integrate and to organize data from different sources, 2) to represent and to transform user profiles and tourism resources, and 3) to capture all the information about the generated routes and their constraints. CRUZAR has been prominently available in the website of the City Council of Zaragoza for the International Expo 2008, that took place there.

The main benefits of providing customized tourism information are, on the one hand, time saving when planning a trip a new city and, on the other hand, a higher probability of enjoying the visit. These benefits are well understood by tourism officials even before the age of tourism planning on the Web. Traditionally, tourism offices have staff who assist prospective and in-place visitors to help them in the configuration of their trip. CRUZAR can be seen as an extension of this effort to the Web, by providing guidance for visitors in the abundance of available information and recommendations on the most suitable places with respect to their preferences and trip circumstances. In addition, CRUZAR allows its users to build a complete and customized plan for the trip in a few seconds, even if they are newcomers to the city of Zaragoza.

We apply a matchmaking algorithm to objects described in RDF, and we pipe the results to a planner algorithm. The final result is a custom tourism route across the city, different for each visitor profile. Although all the information pieces were already available from different sources, CRUZAR merges them in a consistent user interface. Moreover, at the same time, it offers an innovative service for visitors to plan their trip in advance, exploiting expert knowledge. These features are often used as exemplars to illustrate the potentiality of the Semantic Web.

We use RDF to represent all the data consumed, managed or produced by the application. It can be argued that there are some kinds of information that may be more efficiently captured using other data structures. However, we plan to exploit the data with SPARQL, a query language for RDF datasets (Prud'hommeaux & Seaborne, 2008). SPARQL is not just a query language but also a protocol to access the data from any point in the Web. By providing a SPARQL endpoint (i.e., a web service that complies to the SPARQL protocol), we allow third party applications to take full benefit of our effort to integrate the data of the city council of Zaragoza. Also, our model can be easily extended with new data sources if necessary. Plans have been made to consume the integrated RDF model in small widgets as part of a new generation, customizable and multi purpose user interface.

The RDF model has proven adequate to describe resources and events, but it falls short to capture visitor profiles and interests. For our purposes, the main limitation is the absence of negative clauses. As a result, we duplicated some properties ("has-interest"/"has-no-interest"). Integration of ontologies and rules is feasible with current tools for simple cases like ours. However, for the general case, it would be desirable to have a standard. This is still ongoing work by W3C (Boley, Hallmark, Kifer, Paschke, Polleres, & Reynolds, 2008), (Bruijn, 2008).

The semantic matchmaking process we have successfully applied to the eTourism domain can prove useful for other domains. To name a few, we envision its application for the discovery of semantic web services (Keller, Lara, Lausen, Polleres, Predoiu, & Toma, 2005), for context-aware user interfaces for the web (particularly for the mobile web) and for e-Commerce sites. We plan to release a generic framework for semantic matchmaking. Using this framework, it will be possible to easily re-use and customize the matchmaking algorithm in new applications.

A first tuning of the algorithms (route planning and matchmaking) has been carried out by domain experts of the city council. Nevertheless, we plan to evaluate the user satisfaction by collecting feedback and mining the record of the application activities (profiles, preferences, routes, most often requested POIs, etc.). It is worth noting that the system is deterministic: for the same profile (interests, preferences and dates) the resulting route is exactly the same. Actually, for prototypical profiles (such as the ones described in a touristic brochure), the route suggested by the system is remarkably similar to the predefined ones provided by the tourism office. This fact provides a first criterion to evaluate the quality of suggestions made by CRUZAR.

Finally, we are exploring the integration of web services as data sources in our application. This would be particularly useful to include real-time information on public transport and the availability of the accommodation options.

ACKNOWLEDGMENT

We are grateful to the staff of the Web Office of the Zaragoza City Council (http://www.zaragoza.es), in particular, to María Jesús Fernández and Víctor Morlán for their critical support for this project and for providing an invaluable showcase for web technologies. We are also grateful to Maria José Pérez, Pedro Álvarez and Francisco J. López (University of Zaragoza) for providing access to the geospatial data stored in the local GIS of Zaragoza City Council.

REFERENCES

Bizer, C., & Seaborne, A. (2004). *D2rq - Treating non-RDF Databases as virtual RDF graphs*. Paper presented at the meeting in Iswc2004.

Boley, H., Hallmark, G., Kifer, M., Paschke, A., Polleres, A., & Reynolds, D. (2008). *RIF Core (W3C Working Draft)*. Retrieved from http://www.w3.org/TR/rif-core/

Colucci, S., Noia, T. D., Sciascio, E. D., Donini, F. M., & Mongiello, M. (2003). Concept abduction and contraction in description logics. In D. Calvanese, G. D. Giacomo, & E. Franconi (Eds.), *Description logics (Vol. 81)*. CEUR-WS.

de Bruijn, J. (2008). *RIF RDF and OWL compatibility* (W3C Working Draft). Retrieved from http://www.w3.org/TR/rif-rdf-owl/

Gangemi, A., Guarino, N., Masolo, C., & Oltramari, A. (2001). Understanding top-level ontological distinctions. In *Proceedings of the 2001 ijcai workshop on ontologies and information sharing, Seattle, USA*.

Guarino, N., & Welty, C. A. (2004). An overview of ontoclean. In S. Staab & R. Studer (Eds.), *Handbook on Ontologies* (p. 151-159). Springer Verlag.

Hepp, M., Siorpaes, K., & Bachlechner, D. (2006). *Towards the Semantic Web in e-tourism: Lack of semantics or lack of content?* Poster presented at the 3rd Annual European Semantic Web Conference. Budva, Montenegro.

Jannach, D. (2006). Techniques for fast query relaxation in content-based recommender systems. In C. Freksa, M. Kohlhase, & K. Schill (Eds.), *Ki 2006 Vol. 4314* (p. 49-63). Springer.

Keller, U., Lara, R., Lausen, H., Polleres, A., Predoiu, L., & Toma, O. (2005). *Semantic Web service discovery* (Tech. Rep. No. WSMX Deliverable D10). DERI Innsbruck. Retrieved from http://www.wsmo.org/TR/d10/v0.2/

Klyne, G., Carroll, J., & McBride, B. (2004). *Resource description framework (RDF): Concepts and Abstract Syntax* (W3C Recommendation). W3C. Retrieved from http://www.w3.org/TR/rdf-concepts/

Li, L., & Horrocks, I. (2003). *A software framework for matchmaking based on Semantic Web technology*. In *Proceedings of the World-Wide Web conference*. Budapest, Hungary.

Linden, G., Hanks, S., & Lesh, N. (1997). Interactive assessment of user preference models: The automated travel assistant. In C. P. A. Jameson & C. Tasso (Eds.), In *User Modeling: Proceedings of the Sixth International Conference* (pp. 67-78). Springer Wien.

Maedche, A., & Staab, S. (2002). Applying Semantic Web technologies for tourism information systems. In K. Wöber, A. Frew, & M. Hitz (Eds.), *Proceedings of the 9th international conference for information and communication technologies in tourism, enter 2002*. Springer.

Masolo, C., Borgo, S., Gangemi, A., Guarino, N., Oltramari, A., & Schneider, L. (2002). *Wonderweb deliverable d17. the wonderweb library of foundational ontologies and the dolce ontology* (Tech. Rep.). ISTC-CNR.

Masolo, C., Vieu, L., Bottazzi, E., Catenacci, C., Ferrario, R., Gangemi, A., & Guarino, N. (2004). Social roles and their descriptions. In D. Dubois, C. Welty, & M.A. Williams (Eds.), *Proceedings of the Ninth International Conference on the Principles of Knowledge Representation and Reasoning* (pp. 267-277), Whistler, Canada.

Mirzadeh, N., Ricci, F., & Bansal, M. (2004). Supporting user query relaxation in a recommender system. In K. Bauknecht, M. Bichler, & B. Pröll (Eds.), *Ec-web Vol. 3182* (p. 31-40). Springer.

Noia, T. D., Sciascio, E. D., & Donini, F. M. (2007). Semantic matchmaking as non-monotonic reasoning: A description logic approach. *Journal of Artificial Intelligence Research, 29*, 269–307.

Paolucci, M., Kawamura, T., Payne, T. R., & Sycara, K. P. (2002). Semantic matching of Web services capabilities. *The Semantic Web — ISWC 2002 Vol. 2342* (pp. 333-347). Springer.

Portolés-Rodríguez, D., Álvarez, P., & Muro-Medrano, P. (2005). IDEZar: An example of user needs, technological aspects and the institutional framework of a local SDI. In *Ec gi and gis workshop, esdi setting the framework.*

Prud'hommeaux, E., & Seaborne, A. (2008). *SPARQL query language for RDF* (W3C Recommendation). W3C. Retrieved from http://www.w3.org/TR/rdf-sparql-query/

Ricci, F. (2002). Travel recommender systems. *IEEE Intelligent Systems*, (November-December): 55–57.

Smith, M. K., Welty, C., & McGuinness, D. L. (2004) *OWL Web Ontology Language Guide* (W3C Recommendation). W3C. Retrieved from http://www.w3.org/TR/owl-guide/

Chapter 13
Data Integration in the Geospatial Semantic Web

Patrick Maué
Westfälische Wilhelms-Universität, Münster, Germany

Sven Schade
Westfälische Wilhelms-Universität, Münster, Germany

EXECUTIVE SUMMARY

Geospatial decision makers have to be aware of the varying interests of all stakeholders. One crucial task in the process is to identify relevant information available from the Web. In this chapter the authors introduce an application in the quarrying domain which integrates Semantic Web technologies to provide new ways to discover and reason about relevant information. The authors discuss the daily struggle of the domain experts to create decision-support maps helping to find suitable locations for opening up new quarries. After explaining how semantics can help these experts, they introduce the various components and the architecture of the software which has been developed in the European funded SWING project. In the last section, the different use cases illustrate how the implemented tools have been applied to real world scenarios.

INTRODUCTION

A careful assessment and selection of relevant information retrieved from the World Wide Web (WWW) is crucial for potentially precarious decision making tasks. Geographical (or geospatial) data created by national mapping agencies or globally acting companies is the relevant information in the case of geospatial decision making. Such information is most often served as compiled and sometimes interactive maps. Processing such data, for example to run a geospatial analysis, requires raw data. Using a case example from the mining industry, we are going to explain in this chapter how Semantic Web technologies facilitate the task of finding such geospatial data sets and assessing their usefulness for the intended application. We also show how semantics simplify loading and visualizing of this data using generic desktop clients.

Geospatial decision making requires the acquisition of relevant data sets beforehand (Longley et al., 2005). The notion of Geographic Information Retrieval (GIR) (Larson, 1996) is commonly used to summarize all the tasks needed to acquire geospatial data from the WWW by using search engines or catalogs implemented especially for managing such data. Most information is captured in form of text-based documents, which makes searching using keywords and text-indexing search engines very efficient. Geospatial data comes with additional dimensions: Space, i.e. the geographical extent of the represented entities, is one apparent characteristic. Special catalogs have been implemented to deal with the spatial component of such data by adding interactive maps to search dialogs. Time is another important aspect (Longley et al., 2005). The data yields information about entities or phenomena in the real world which is continuously moving on in time and changing its state. Hence, making geospatial data available in the Web poses various challenges to the data provider. The major standardization organization in the domain of geospatial applications, the Open Geospatial Consortium (OGC), introduced standardized catalog interfaces which support basic GIR functionalities. Instances of these catalogs are, together with other OGC-conformal Web Services serving or processing geospatial data, embedded in Spatial Data Infrastructures (SDI). In (Nebert, 2004) the basic principles of SDIs are introduced; various components of SDI and the potential benefits of Semantic Web technologies are further discussed later in this chapter.

Standards specifying how to access and use GIR systems are limited to the technical level. They define how to encode the queries, what parameters are allowed, and which operations the catalog should implement. They do not, however, suggest how a user formulates the query. The properties of geospatial data (space, time, and theme) can all be individually queried. But the task of asking the right question to retrieve this information is still a challenging one. It seems to be so simple, though. A user defines a region by drawing a box on a map, selects a point in time using a calendar, and specifies a theme by choosing a category or typing in some search terms. But especially keywords and categories suffers from the information asymmetry (Akerlof, 1970) between the searching user and the data provider. Language is, by nature, ambiguous and imprecise. Semantic conflicts (i.e. heterogeneities) and varying background knowledge impair every discovery task and can decrease the usefulness of the GIR system tremendously. And the success of systems depending on user interaction is measured by its usefulness.

Let us consider a common example. In a mining context, a team of experts is searching for a suitable location for a new quarry (more details about this use case are discussed in the following section). Many regulations constrain the potential areas; the region could be a protected area due to conservation, water protection zones, or national monuments. Before getting to a decision, the experts have to consider this additional data bearing potential conflicts with regulations. Considering relevant information made available in the Web is challenging. Experts looking for potential conflicts due to unknown regulations would probably have no problem to define the spatial and temporal extent of the data they are looking for. Selecting appropriate keywords for discovery is more difficult. Search engines are often limited to combinations of keywords; the so called Boolean search queries (Manning et al., 2008). Too few and too general keywords like "protected area" yield too much results. Specific, but also usually required terms like "ZNIEFF" (or Zones Naturelles d'Intérêt Ecologique Faunistique et Floristique) are unknown to the experts. They are experts in their own domain, but have no knowledge in others. In a next tedious step, they have to extend and reformulate the query until the search results in a manageable number of hits. Next, they have to browse through the remaining results, probably with the result that the requested information is not even included. More sophisticated IR systems are clearly needed to improve efficiency, and the Semantic Web is the promising emergent technology to address this issue.

In addition to the challenging task to find the relevant information, the decision makers have to include the different stakeholders in the process. Results of geospatial decision making can have a severe impact on the living conditions of the local population, especially if it ends up in opening a new quarry. NIMBY (Not In My Back Yard) issues (McAvoy, 1999) have to be carefully considered when planning new sites which might potentially have a negative impact on the neighborhood. Typical examples include waste disposal and utility facilities, nuclear power plants, or, as in the example, industrial sites like quarries.

Public Participation GIS (PPGIS) are one potential solution to involve the citizens already in the planning phase, with the goal to minimize the potential conflicts with the local population. A GIS in this case refers to a Geographic Information System, which comprises tools to query, analyze, modify, and visualize geospatial data. According to the International Association for Public Participation, one of the core values of public participation is, that it "is based on the belief that those who are affected by a decision have a right to be involved in the decision-making process". The Web is obviously the ideal platform for both, the decision makers and the local population. Here they can publish their information and arguments, and they can try to coordinate the planning process. But we already mentioned that the Web demands for expertise to find even trivial information. How can we ask these people to participate if already the first step is too challenging for many?

One key requirement for useful GIR systems is to support users in formulating sophisticated queries. They should provide intuitive user interfaces telling the user about the possibilities to ask more precise questions. They should be able to incorporate users being experts in their own field, but novices in information retrieval. In this chapter we introduce the results from the European funded SWING Project (more info at: http://wwww.swing-project.org), which was targeting the integration of Semantic Web technologies to facilitate discovery, evaluation and usage of geographic information in the Internet, with the ultimate goal to merge the Semantic Web and SDIs. One goal of the project was to develop an application which enables the experts to create and publish decision-support documents. Its functionality includes the dynamic discovery and integration of interoperable Semantic Web Services. The targeted technological development in SWING will help to:

1. enhance the efficiency of data collection by integrating existing data,
2. sustain the availability of acquired information through Semantic Web Services,
3. semi-automate data integration and analyses, and thus
4. save time and money, while improving the quality, significance and coherence of the assessments.

An ultimate goal would be an evolution towards a domain expert application fully operational as a natural resources management and assessment system. In the project, we elaborate on one use case: geologists and engineers searching for potential locations to open up a new quarry.

The following section will introduce the quarrying use case. BRGM, the French geological survey, is responsible for the exploration and management of potential quarry sites in France. We discuss the range of relevant information needed to assess if one spot might be suitable for quarrying or not. Afterwards, we elaborate on the notion of the Geospatial Semantic Web, and how its technologies can support the tasks from the quarrying use case. The framework developed within the SWING Project is illustrated afterwards. We briefly go through the architecture and explain how the different components interact to produce the decision-support documents needed by BRGM's clients. The chapter is concluded with a walk-through explaining how the new tools can support the user to formulate the right search query and to create maps helping them in their daily decision-making tasks.

A Story about Quarries

Aggregates like gravel or crushed rock have a two-fold purpose all over the world. Together with sand it serves as main component of concrete. It also forms stable foundations for buildings and tracks. Aggregate sources are either alluvial deposits (sand and gravel) or hard rocks such as sandstone, limestone, and crystalline rocks like granite, which are excavated using blasting and crushing methods. Demand for aggregates is mostly driven by the construction activity, and new roads or buildings are continuously needed. According to Amil (2008), non energy quarrying has been a growing industry in the European Union, India, and Russia between 2007 and 2008. In the year 2006, the U.S. production of crushed stone reached 1.72 billion metric tons (Willett, 2006), with a total value of $13.8 billion. In the EU27 around 17 000 enterprises were 2004 engaged in the non-energy mining and quarrying industry, with in average turnover of 36 billion € and around 290.800 employees (eurostat, 2006). These numbers render the sector of non-energy mining and quarrying in the EU27 to the largest macro-regional markets in the world (Tertre, 2007). The steady demand does require a continuous exploration and installation of new quarries for aggregate exploitation. Reasons are, amongst others, the depletion of existing sites and tremendous costs to transport aggregates to remote construction sites. Quarrying companies are therefore trying to minimize the distance between potential sites for quarries and consumption sites, which are usually urbanized areas with construction sites. But finding a suitable quarry site is not simply a matter of looking at the geology on site and calculated transport costs to a consumer. Regulations due to conservation, water pollution control, or patrimony protection limit potential quarry sites. A sustainable and profitable exploitation of natural resources has to consider not only a sufficient availability and quality of needed resources like limestone, granite, or sand. The companies also have to be aware of the society needs, and the economic and environmental consequences of their extraction, transformation and transport of the produced goods.

Geospatial decision-support for sustainable planning and prognoses of the impact on urban development, spatial occupation, wildlife protection, etc., has become a multi-disciplinary exercise. It has to account for long-term perspectives and multi-stakeholder viewpoints at local, regional, national and even the continental scales (COM, 2003, 2000). Decision makers have to find and integrate as much relevant information as possible. They have to analyze the data to assess its economical, environmental and public concerns. Finally, results have to be presented to stakeholders in an open review process. We require an application framework which enables aggregation of relevant information in one map. Figure 1 shows two examples which support the geospatial decision making process. The left picture lists existing locations of sand quarries in the lower Normandy, France. Next to it, potential conflicting areas are visualized. Later in this chapter we discuss the tool which has been used to create these maps, and how Semantic Web technologies had helped.

Nowadays, with immediate access to nearly all the information ever existed, it is nearly impossible to solve the task to create these maps without

Figure 1. Examples for decision-support documents in the quarry domain

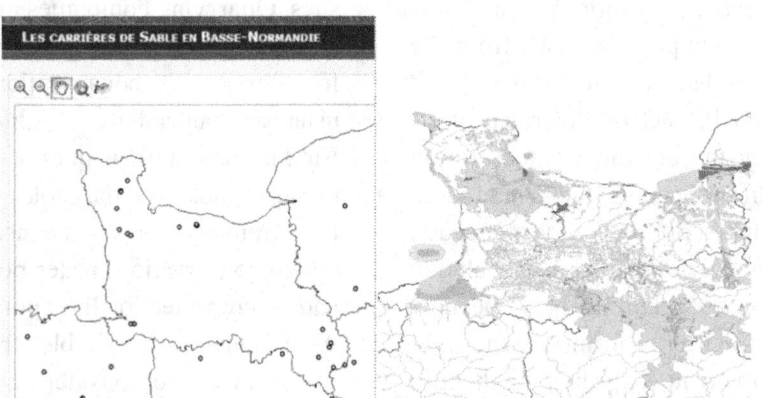

any support. Relevant data are scattered around the Web. It is created, maintained and served by the different responsible public institutions. It comes in many different data formats, which often requires specialized applications to visualize its content. And it often lacks any meaningful description allowing for assessing its usefulness for certain geospatial decision-making tasks. Hence, creating decision-support maps aggregating relevant information is a challenging task.

The French geological survey BRGM (acronym for Bureau de recherches géologiques et minières) is an example for a public authority responsible for creating and publishing such maps. In the SWING project, BRGM provided the use case and related data sources. This French public institution is responsible for advice and expert assessments to French authorities, national and international organizations, and companies, for the definition and realization of policies related to geosciences. In our example, BRGM's experts have to create maps which integrate all relevant information like geology, transportation infrastructure, and potential conflicts with communities and regulation. The traditional approach of the specialists, mostly geoscientists, is the creation of reports by performing the following three steps:

1. Acquire relevant information, usually in form of data files, from different providers,
2. structure and prepare these files and analyze the contained information in a GIS,
3. and produce reports with maps like in Figure 1 to wrap up the findings.

In the mineral resources domain, a typical discovery task (Step 1) requires contacting about twenty different partners (including geologists, hydrologists, engineers, public authority, and citizens), identifying available information, defining an exchange strategy, and ensuring efficient local integration. The experts have to deal with an ever increasing amount of relevant information, and have to face the increasingly complex challenge of finding and successfully integrating it. And the work of BRGM represents just one case of many (Klien et al.., 2005).

In the last decade much of this data has been made available as Web Services, following the principles of Service-Oriented Architectures (SOA) (Erl, 2005). This trend has been taken into account for the specification of the INSPIRE Directive (INSPIRE, 2007), which defines a European Spatial Data Infrastructure built on top of network services for the provision of geospatial data. By encapsulating data or processing-functionality in network services such as Web Services, re-usability has been tremendously improved. The publish-find-bind-paradigm explains best the basic principles of a SOA and, consequently, a modern SDI. A geospatial Web Service is *published* by registering it to a catalog. Using the catalog functionality, a potential service consumer can *find* the requested service. Since the service interfaces are standardized, he can immediately integrate (*bind*) the Web Service into an application. From an end users perspective, it doesn't make a difference if data comes as file from the hard drive or as data stream from a Web Service. In this manner, access to data which bears information about, for example, water protection sites, can be easily integrated in the tools the geo-scientist from BRGM have to use to create the decision-support documents.

The members of the OGC (and ISO TC/211) specify implementation standards for geospatial Web Services embedded in SDIs. These standards clarify the semantics of a Web Service's behavior and define a homogeneous structure for data encodings. The OGC developed the *Geography Mark-up Language* (GML) as data modeling and encoding standard. These data models are only homogeneous at the structural level. OGC also specified the Web Feature Service (WFS) as a set of service interfaces for the access of (geospatial) vector data, which enables smooth integration and visualization of such data in desktop GIS. We call two Web Services *interoperable* if they can communicate and exchange data without the need for adapting the data. The introduced standards ensure syntactic and structural interoperability, but they miss capabilities which make *semantic interoperability* possible.

The lack of semantic descriptions of provided content is addressed by Semantic Web Services (SWS). SWS are "Self-contained, self-describing, semantically marked-up software resources that can be published, discovered, composed and executed across the Web in a task driven automatic way" (Arroyo et al.., 2004). To semantically describe a Web Service, a comprehensive knowledge in logics, ontologies, metadata, and various specification languages is required. Two major impediments for realizing the Semantic Web Service vision therefore are (1) the lack of Web Services that are semantically described, and (2) the lack of development tools that can hide the complexity and automate the creation of the necessary semantic mark-up. Once we have implemented and published semantically enabled geospatial Web Services, semantic-enabled IR and semantic validation of work flows can be realized. How these two applications can benefit from the Geospatial Semantic Web is discussed in the following section.

Semantic Geospatial Web: Challenges and Techniques

We already introduced the notion of Geographic Information Retrieval (GIR) systems, and how they suffer from the lack of sophisticated discovery and evaluation techniques. Boolean search queries are sufficient means to retrieve text-based information, but they are often too imprecise and ambiguous to let untrained users efficiently find the needed information. Technologies developed for the Semantic Web (Berners-Lee et al., 2001) promise to overcome most of these challenges. Egenhofer (2002) extended its notion by introducing a spatial and temporal dimension and called it the Geospatial Semantic Web. The supply of geospatial data within a SDI is managed by Web Services. Depending on the nature of the data, we distinguish between different OGC Web Service specifications (and therefore ways to access the data): Web Feature Services (WFS) serve vector based data, such as a street network or Quarry point locations. Web Processing Services (WPS) are meant to process geospatial data, e.g. merging two datasets, or running a geospatial analysis. These standards have been identified as relevant for the SWING project, but various other standards exist and are listed on the OGC Web site.

We did not consider all special characteristics of geospatial data within the project. But we want to highlight one particular property, which we think one has to be aware of before discussing potential applications. Geospatial data bears information about (physical) entities in geographic space, the space we humans walk and live every day. People searching, for example, data about rivers or quarries have a specific, abstract idea about this topic. The creation of such concept grounded in the real world is based on an observation (you know about rivers because you have seen one, at least on pictures). Hence, it is reasonable to assume that we can support our users by visualizing a formal representation of such conceptualization (Lutz & Klien, 2006). It is then just a matter of selecting the appropriate concepts, detailing the relations, and querying the GIR system for data which best matches the query's conceptualization.

Once a user is able to formulate semantic queries by not only using keywords, but actual concepts and relations from the domain knowledge (Figure 2), a reasoning engine (assuming the query is encoded in machine-interpretable format) can infer if the query matches one or more registered Web Services (Lutz & Klien, 2006). If query processing is realized on this level, we might overcome some of the typical semantic problems contemporary search engines are still struggling with.

But depending on the background of the user, the conceptualizations used for the semantic queries can differ significantly. The engineers might see a river as part of the transportation infrastructure, since ships are cheap means to transport the aggregates. From an environmental perspective rivers are ecosystems which have to be protected. Some believe rivers are simply obstacles they have to cross on their way to work. One particular specification of the River concept can therefore not exist. Creating and formalizing it should take these different perspectives into account. The user should not only be able to select a concept. He should also be able to limit possible interpretations of the concept, e.g. by saying he is interested only in Rivers which are navigable. The required conceptualizations are therefore complex structures, which should not only include the vocabulary and some basic relations between the individual concepts, but also formalisms to constrain the possible interpretations.

An ontology is formal specifications of such a conceptualization (Gruber, 1995), or better, "an engineering artefact, constituted by a specific vocabulary used to describe a certain reality, plus a set of explicit assumptions regarding the intended meaning of the vocabulary words" (Guarino, 1998). Ontologies comprise basically four main components: categories, relations, individuals, and the axioms putting constraints on the relations. This is a rather simple definition, but it already explains the main difference to less powerful representations like dictionaries,

Figure 2. The developed user interface integrating keyword-based, spatial, and semantic query tools

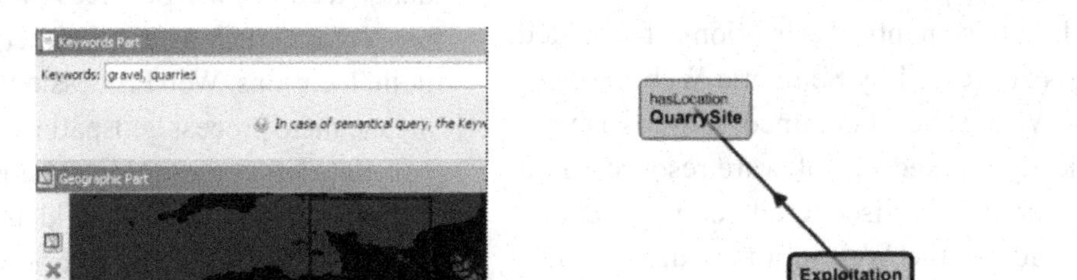

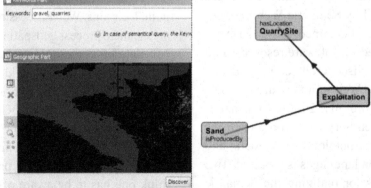

controlled vocabularies, and taxonomies. Due to their flexibility, ontologies can be applied to every application suffering from language ambiguity. Reasoning algorithms can infer solutions, as long as the ontologies are specified in languages based on a formal deductive system (Baader, 2003). Inference can be as simple as creating new facts from transitive relations, but also as complex as matching complex logical statements using techniques like Query Containment (Calvanese et al., 1998).

The following list introduces key problems where ontologies and reasoning methods were successfully applied. The first group includes conflicts caused by the information asymmetry between the searching user and the data provider (Akerlof, 1970; Manning et al., 2008):

- **Application-specific knowledge:** Sometimes specific terms are only used within one particular application. For example, a Web Service description listing its served data as znieff_v2006 areas is only understood by specialists knowing where to find the Web Service documentation. Untrained users would fail to discover the data, although it contains the needed information. Without a further description using a more commonly understood language, the use of this data is constrained to a very limited user group. Having elaborated semantic descriptions linked to the data provides a solution to this challenge.
- **Hierarchical knowledge:** Probably the most common issue in GIR is due to the different levels of expertise between provider and requester. Someone looking for excavation sites might choose terms like "excavation" or even "mining". The specialist publishing the data will likely use more specialized terms, like "Gravel pit" or "opencast mining". Searching based only on keywords would yield no results here. Since one term is more specific then another, they can be simply associated on the conceptual level using taxonomic relationships. A reasoner-supported IR system can then infer a match using, for example, subsumption reasoning.
- **Multilingual community:** BRGM is the French geological survey, the ontology engineering group is from the University of Münster, Germany, and the ontologies were all documented in English. Concepts at the domain level support labels in different languages; this makes it possible to match a user's query and service description even if the chosen languages differ. Of course, this assumes that terms in different languages all refer to the same concept. The German term "Steinbruch" does not necessarily bear the same meaning as the American English term "quarry" or the British English term "stone pit". Depending on the required complexity of the knowledge, language-specific concepts might need to be introduced as well.

In addition to variations in expertise, the ambiguity of natural language is one additional source of problems impairing the usefulness of geographic information in the Web. Language is driven by one's personal background, which is heavily influenced by society, culture, profession, and much more. If data should not be limited to one community, we need to solve the resulting semantic heterogeneities as well (Saeed, 2003). Prominent examples are synonyms and homonyms. The latter refers to words having a multiple meaning (e.g. a "mine"). And if two terms denote the same object (e.g. "open pit mine" and "quarry"), they are commonly explained as synonymous. In both cases, reasoning and consistent ontologies help to avoid these ambiguities. We do not argue that these problems can only be addressed using ontologies, since they are sometimes claimed to be unnecessarily complex and tedious to create. They are by no means the only solution for more efficient GIR systems. Different levels of hierarchy might, for example, be also resolved using a thesaurus like GEMET (European Environment Information and Observation Network)', which serves synonyms and hypernyms for a defined collection of terms.

Semantic annotations link geospatial data to ontologies capturing the domain knowledge. But before we explain these annotations, we have to introduce architectures for ontologies. We distinguish between local and global ontologies. Local ontologies are used in a particular application and are not shared or publicly available. Global ontologies, on the other hand, are available to everyone, and do not contain any individual, application-specific knowledge. Concepts in local ontologies have to be linked to global concepts to make them useful, for example, to let the reasoner decide if two local concepts used in different applications are denoting the same real world object. Local ontologies are often Application Ontologies, since they comprise concepts used for a specific application (see Guarino (1998) for a full specification). We are only concerned about geospatial resources (data and processes) provided by OGC Web Services, we therefore use the term *Resource Ontology* here. The *Domain Ontology* is a globally shared conceptualization used across different applications. The Foundational Ontology (or Upper Level Ontology) sits on top of domain ontologies, and allows for bridging between the different domains. This level of ontologies is not yet fully specified, and requires more research before being useful for applications.

Attaching a meaningful description to an arbitrary resource is commonly described as an annotation. Without them, non-textual information like images, videos, or music could not be discovered in the Web. In the case of Web Services, the descriptions like the OGC *getCapabilities*-document are the annotations describing the functionality of the service (e.g. the operations and parameters). Semantic annotations extend this notion by attaching descriptions encoded as ontologies to the data. The strict distinction between Domain Ontologies which try to capture one community's perspective of the real world, and the application-specific resource ontologies which model the very specific inner workings of a particular dataset or process, is fundamental for the understanding of semantic annotations. Information exchange requires commitment of all parties to the global knowledge modeled in the Domain Ontology. On the local level each participant can model the Resource Ontology in a way which suits his purpose. Forcing him to use only domain concepts will result in losing valuable application specific knowledge. Relating the local application-specific knowledge to global ontologies allows for keeping these local models as well making the served data findable for reasoner-supported GIR systems. In Figure 3 we present a conceptual overview of the semantic annotations idea. The *Resource Metadata*, e.g. the *getCapabilities*-document describing the data model of a *Resource* like a Web Feature Service, is linked to the Resource Ontology using a *Model Reference*. The service provider can decide how precise these references have to be: he can either choose to link each element in the XML schema describing the output data to the corresponding concept, or simply link the complete output of one service operation as one entity to a concept. The Resource Ontology represents this data model. Using a rule-based approach, the resource ontology concepts are then related to the domain ontologies. The following listings show the model references linking from a feature type schema to the resource ontology, and the rules used to link the resource concept to the domain ontology.

Figure 4 and Figure 5 depict one approach how the model reference can be technically realized. In Figure 6 the WSML axiom with the domain reference is listed. Here, we explicitly stated what the value of the attribute siteName refers to (it identifies the site). Creating and maintaining these rules is rather challenging and certainly too complex for domain experts.

One major goal of the project was the implementation of a discovery and resource manage-

Figure 3. Semantic annotations overview

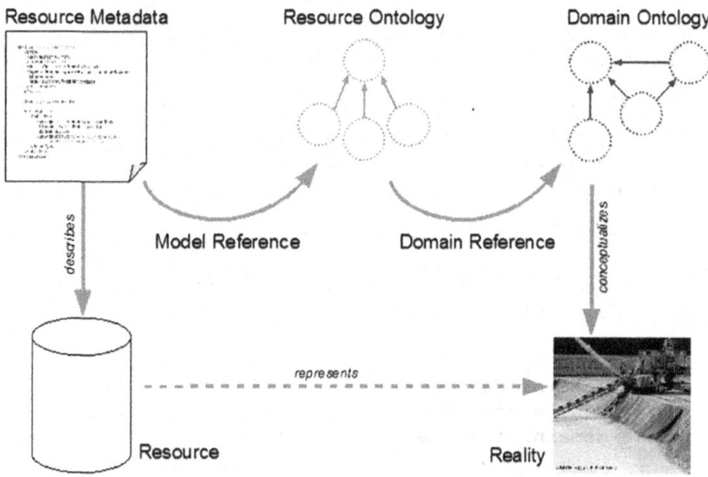

Figure 4. Linking the Data Model to the Resource Ontology

```
<element name="sites"
      type="qua:sitesType"
      sawsdl:modelReference="res:sites">
<complexType name="sitesType">
< … >
  <element name="msGeometry" type="gml:GeometryPropertyType"
  <element name="FactoryName" type="string"/>
< … >
```

Figure 5. The Resource Ontology, representing the Data Model

```
concept sites subConceptOf gml#FeatureType
      msGeometry impliesType (0 1) gml#GeometryPropertyType
      FactoryName impliesType (0 1) _string
```

ment tool which is also usable for computer illiterate persons like the geoscientists working for BRGM. Ontologies are encoded in logic languages which require expert knowledge to understand, not to mention to formulate the queries. IR supported by ontologies does therefore depend heavily on intuitive user interfaces which hide away the complexity of the ontologies. In Figure 7 (left) the WFS serving locations of construction sites is going to be related to a domain concept.

The concept ConstructionSite is linked to the local concept sites representing the Feature Type. We made the relation between location and construction site explicit by also stating that the value of the attribute msGeometry (represented as local concept msGeometry) is the Location of the ConstructionSite. With this approach we are now able to elaborate on the inner relations between attributes and entities. But still, the user is only aware of the concepts and its properties, visualized

Figure 6. Rules including the domain references linking the Resource Ontology to the Domain Ontology

```
axiom annotateSites
 definedBy
      /* specify feature with properties */
      ?x memberOf site and
      ?x[msGeometry ofType ?x_attr1] and
      ?x[FactoryName ofType ?x_attr2] and

      /* selection of relevant domain concept */
      ?site memberOf domain#ConstructionSite and
      ?location memberOf domain#Location and
      ?siteName memberOf domain#Identifier and

      /* linking local to global*/
      annot#domainReference(?x_attr1, ?location) and
      annot#domainReference(?x_attr2, ?siteName) and
      annot#domainReference(?x, ?site) and

      /* specify relationship between attributes */
      domain#names(?siteName, ?site) and
      ?site[hasLocation ofType ?location].
```

as edges to other concepts. He does not have to cope with complex formulas as in Figure 6.

In the query in Figure 7 (right), the requester states that he is looking for a Web Service providing information about Quarries. In addition, the served data about the Quarries should include attributes for the maximal allowed production rate, as well as the production capacity. The production capacity is measured in metric tons per year. The encoding in the WSML abstract syntax is produced in the background by the visualization tool (since the code itself is too complex to write for the domain experts). From a technical point of view, a query is an axiom like the rules used for the model reference (see Figure 6). In the end, a semantically supported discovery simply matches the rules in the query with the all annotations, and returns all web services whose annotated output

Figure 7. Annotation of FeatureType sites (left) and Formulation of Query (right)

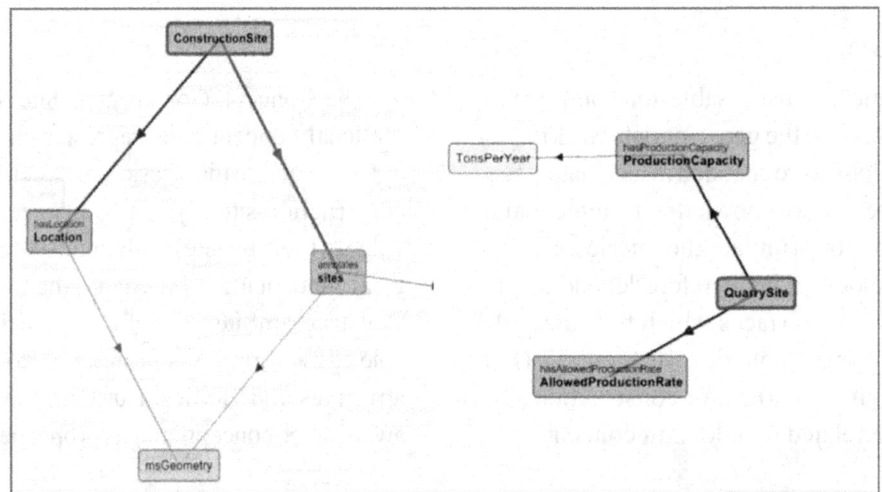

data models logically match (not necessarily equal) the query.

Semantically Supported Geospatial Decision Making

In the SWING Project we investigated how we can integrate Semantic Web technologies and SDIs (Roman & Klien, 2007). The benefits discussed above required beforehand a collection of carefully engineered domain ontologies and the implementation of an intuitive user interface to let the domain experts perform the semantic annotations. Only then can we leverage discovery and integration beyond Boolean search techniques and exploit the expressiveness of the ontologies. Seven organizations were involved in the project, each with its own field of expertise. In Figure 5, an overview of the individual work packages and contributions is given. BRGM provides the data and the services, as well as the supporting use case. The Semantic Technology Institute (STI) at Universität Innsbruck offered the required reasoning framework; the engine used to execute the service compositions comes from DERI Galway. At the Institute for Geoinformatics (IfGI) at the University of Münster, we engineered the ontologies needed for the use case and implemented tools facilitating ontology creation and maintenance. The Department of Knowledge Technologies at Joseph Stephan Institute (JSI) is responsible for the tools supporting the annotation process. ERDAS Inc. supplied the adapted catalog software used for the Web Service discovery. SINTEF implemented the Service Composition Studio, which is used to combine existing Web Services to sophisticated workflows.

The objectives for using ontologies are manifold. They form the basis for *semantic annotations* of service metadata and data models, help the user in *formulating requests* (also called goals), support *discovery* of geospatial data and geo-processing services, and enable the *specification of workflows* for service execution. We selected WSMO, the Web Service Modeling Ontology (Fensel et al., 2006), as Semantic Web Services framework to deal with the targeted issues. Four entities make up the WSMO:

- Ontology provides the terminology used by other WSMO entities to describe the relevant aspects of the domains of discourse.

Figure 8. The SWING Project consortium

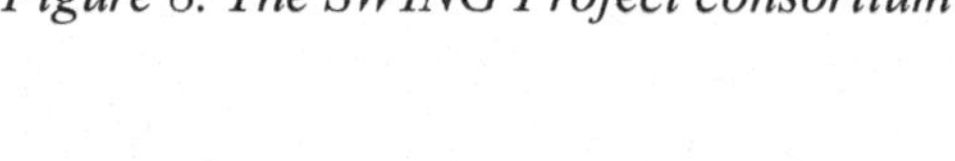

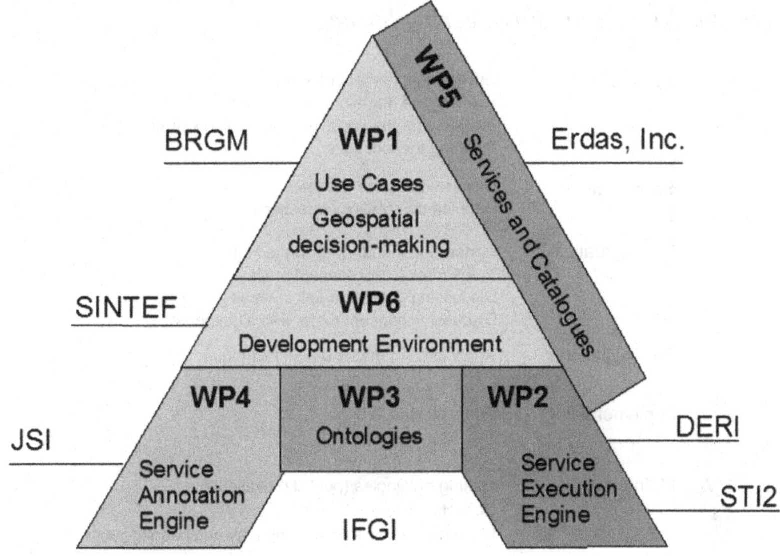

- WebService represents computational entities providing access to services that, in turn, provide some value in a domain.
- Goal captures any aspect related to a user request.
- Mediator enables harmonization using mappings between two entities (e.g. ontologies).

As illustrated in Figure 8, the ontologies have been an integral component for nearly every component. Hence, a mature engineering process has been applied. External sources like scientific articles or standards specifications served as secondary knowledge sources; although the domain experts from BRGM have been the primary source (Klien et al., 2007). We followed the METHONTOLOGY, a common methodology for ontology engineering. It suggests five phases: Specification, Conceptualization, Formalization, Implementation and Maintenance. A detailed explanation can be read in (Gomez-Perez et al., 2004). The relation of these phases and the knowledge acquisition with domain experts is depicted in Figure 6. The ontologies have been implemented in WSML-Flight (de Brujn et al., 2006). This dialect of WSML is based on the logic programming paradigm (Nilsson & Maluszynski, 1995). Reasoning transforms the abstract WSML syntax into Datalog, a (syntactical) subset of the well established logic programming language Prolog. The reasoning is therefore (compared to other solutions) very efficient.

The architecture including all components which have been developed and extended in the project is sketched in Figure 10. MiMS, the Mineral Resource Management System, is the end user tool developed by BRGM. MiMS is a rich client used for annotating, registering and discovering OGC Web Services. It has been developed in Java, with BRGM's domain expert as end user in mind. It is capable of arranging geospatial data in various views and exporting maps as interactive Web pages which, in the end, are the decision support documents made available to the experts and the public. Annotating a Web Service is supported by Visual OntoBridge (VOB), a tool integrated into MiMS *(1)* (illustrated in Figure 7), which is able to link graph representations of the data with the concepts from the Domain Ontologies. The domain ontologies are managed and served *(3)* by the concept repository (CORE) developed by IFGI. Since CORE serves Domain Ontologies using the WSML/RDF syntax, VOB simply uses

Figure 9. All steps for the Knowledge Engineering Strategy

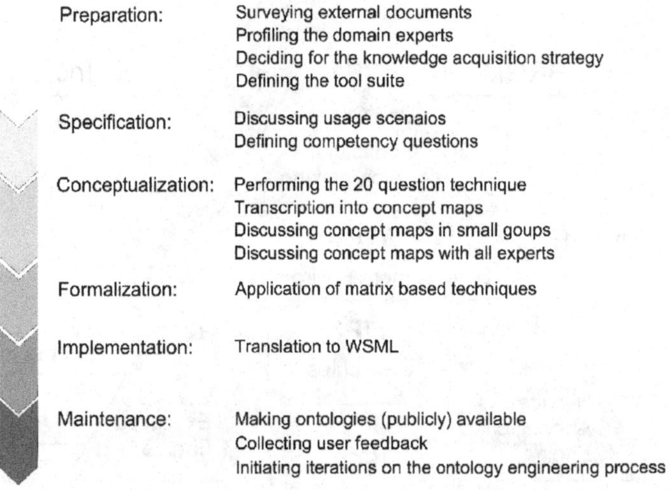

Figure 10. The simplified SWING Architecture

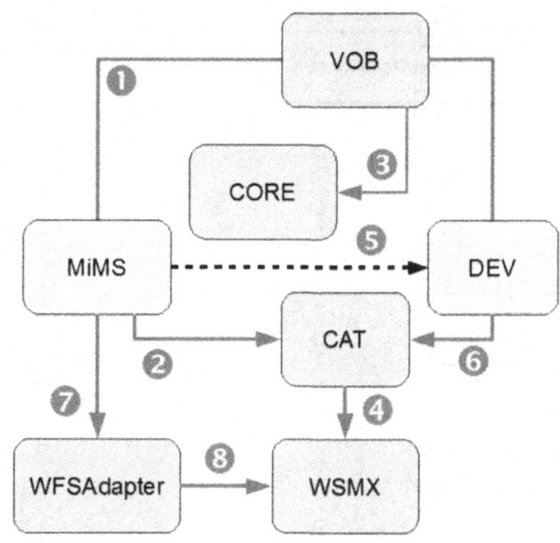

a common RDF library to parse and visualize the formalized knowledge. Users can discover Web Services in MiMS using the catalog CAT *(2)*, and directly semantically annotate them with VOB by linking the concepts from the local Resource Ontology to one or more concepts in the global Domain Ontology. The CAT component is an extended implementation of the standardized OGC CSW interface, which supports keyword-based and spatial search queries (see Figure 2 showing MIMS accessing this interface).

Annotating an existing web service with VOB requires the existence of the application-specific Resource Ontology. It comprises a representation of the data model, such as the Feature Type schema of Web Feature Service, as well as the rules with the annotations. This ontology is then used by the WSMO WebService which contains the rules linking the local concepts to the global domain concepts. Both, the Resource Ontology and an initial version of the WebService, are created automatically by transforming the existing Web Service description and data schema documents into the according WSML representation. Ongoing work investigates the use of explicit annotations like SAWSDL (Kopecký et al., 2007) in the source documents like the GML data schema or the WSDL documents. Once the annotation has been performed, the user can register it to CAT. It forwards the WSML part to WSMX *(4)*, which needs the annotations for the semantic-enabled discovery.

VOB is not only used to annotate already existing Web Services. It does also support the user in creating the semantic queries. He simply selects the wanted concepts within the visualized graph and adds them to the query. VOB is then generating a WSML Goal containing the query in its WSML representation, which is then forwarded to CAT. CAT acts as repository of Web Services which provides means to search and register usual OGC Web Services as well as Semantic Web Services described using WSML. The catalog itself does not include any reasoning capabilities, the user Goal is therefore forwarded *(4)* to the Web Service Execution Environment (WSMX). This component has a local repository of WSMO Web Services; it is therefore able to match the incoming Goal with the available WebServices. A match in this case means, that a user's query (the Goal) is fully realized by the WebService. The Goal is contained in the WebService, we therefore refer to this search strategy as Query Containment (Calvanese et al., 1998; Ullman, 1996). Details of the implementation can be found in (Hoffman et al., 2008; Schade et al., 2008).

If the desired geospatial resource is not available, the BRGM specialists have to create it themselves by sending a request *(5)* to the experts using DEV. One assumption in the project is that all required data is already somewhere supplied by a Web Service. Creating new resources is therefore a matter of finding these Web Services, for example in our CAT *(6)*, and combining them in the right order. DEV, realized by the Composition Studio from SINTEF (see Figure 11 for a screenshot), is used to generate such workflows. Based on a variant of UML 2.0 activity diagrams (Jeckle et al., 2005), users can simply compose workflows by dragging Web Services into the diagram; connecting two Web Services means

Figure 11. Web Service Composition for the first Use Case

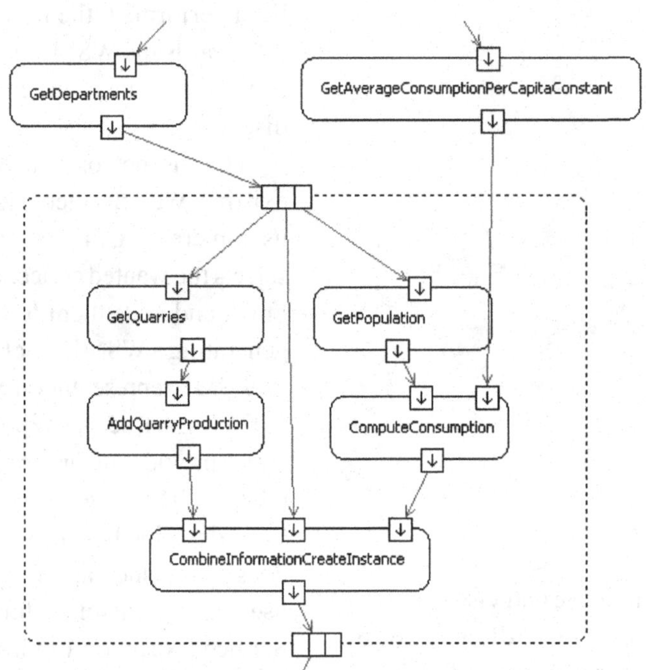

that the output of one serves as input for the other Web Service. Following the philosophy of Model-Driven Architectures (MDA, explained in OMG, 2004 and Kleppe et al., 2003), the workflow model is abstracted and therefore independent from the executable workflow language. The tool is supposed to export the diagram into various languages, in the project we focused on compositions based on abstract state machines (ASM, see also Roman et al., 2008). A comparison of this approach with the more commonly used (but not explicitly semantic) BPEL is provided in (Gone & Schade, 2007). The WSMO ASM is modeled as a part of the WebService which is called Choreography. The composition itself is, depending on the output, again an OGC-compatible Web Service like the WFS. The WFS adapter provides the standardized interfaces usable by MiMS *(7)*, but as soon as someone requests data from such a WFS, this request is forwarded *(8)* to a WSMX instance which executes the composition. Users like the geoscientists from BRGM are therefore not even aware of these complex processes. The result of the composition, for example the aggregated map showing conflicts between potential quarry sites and existing water protection zones, is visualized in MiMS just like any other geospatial resource.

This very brief description of all tools developed within SWING is hardly exhaustive, but a thorough discussion is clearly out of scope of this chapter. The tools are all either part of products (CAT), established open source projects (WSMX, IRIS) or made available for download on the project partner's website (MiMS, DEV, both including VOB). Note that the given URLs are subject to change in the future. Videos of all tools in action have been made available on the project website (http:://www.swing-project.org).

Walking through the Use Cases

At the beginning of the chapter we discussed the need for technologies which simplify the information retrieval process. Geospatial decision making, in particular the question where to open a new quarry, has to include many different stakeholders: the specialists coming from geology, water management, conversation, or the traffic infrastructure, as well as the local population which, at the end, is most affected by these decisions. One way to achieve this goal is the creation of decision support documents, which are then disseminated to all relevant parties. These documents can form the basis for discussions, with the ultimate target to let al.l voices participate in the decision making process, and to include every relevant piece of information.

MiMS is used to aggregate all relevant information and to create such decision support documents. The digital maps documenting the decision-making process are then made available to the public. Domain experts, although untrained regarding information retrieval, are now able to consider all relevant information in the Web due to the support of Semantic Web technologies. And as important, citizens, potentially organized in non-governmental organizations, can produce such relevant information, semantically annotate it, and make it available to the decision makers. And they have, of course, access to the published decision support documents as well.

In this section, we present three use cases which have been taken as examples during the project. The use cases cover the requested discovery and annotation of Web Services, as well as the generation, deployment and execution of application-specific service compositions. Thereafter we discuss more complex scenarios illustrating further benefits of our approach.

In the first scenario, BRGM's geologists were asking for large-scale information about the production and consumption of aggregates in France. Such information acts as initial supportive material to decide whether new quarries might be needed. One of the implemented WFS served geospatial data about existing quarries, with information about the location, the exploited material, and more. This service has been annotated by the domain experts using VOB. In the same manner, services providing aggregate consumption data of French administrative units such as departments have been semantically described and registered to the semantically enabled catalog. Once we had Web Services prepared and published, the MiMS enabled the experts to query the catalog for discovery. The classical OGC catalog interface required simply to specify the needed region on a map. In

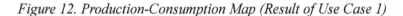

Figure 12. Production-Consumption Map (Result of Use Case 1)

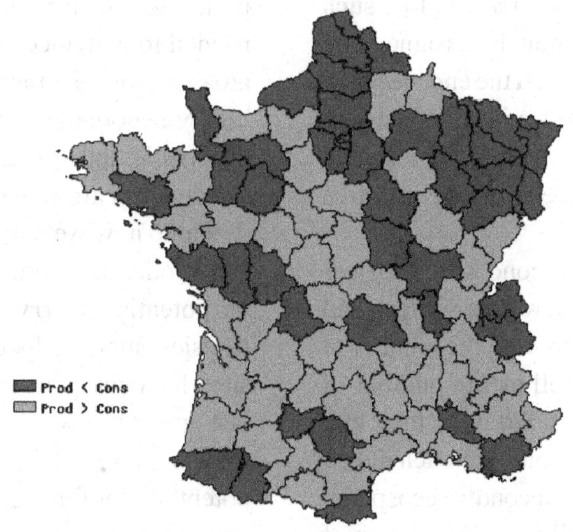

the next step, they started VOB to semantically enrich the classical query by selecting appropriate concepts from the domain ontologies. Following this approach the geoscientists using MiMS were able to find the relevant information, in this case Web Services with information about production and consumption of aggregates.

But they actually asked for a map which aggregates the data from these two sources. In the next step they therefore had to create a Web Service composition where this information is automatically created. With the help of the Composition Studio, this composition (see Figure 11) has been created and again published to the catalog. The geologists were then able to discover this newly created Web Service and finally to publish the requested information on a map (see Figure 12).

This first scenario illustrated how available data sources can intuitively be annotated using the graph-based VOB, how VOB can be combined with classical clients for spatial search, and how a complex service composition can be seamlessly integrated into standard GIS clients. In a second scenario, we looked at integrating the constraints for opening a new quarry. Due to legal obligations and regulations, it is forbidden to open new quarries in urban areas, at locations of protected habitats, or close to historical monuments. Many of these conflicts may be resolved by negotiation. In total BRGM has to deal with a list of 84 such constraints, each of which may be assigned one of four levels of negotiability. At the end, decision makers have to be provided with a 'constraint map', which summarizes constrained areas and associated negotiability levels for a given area of interest.

The challenge for the second scenario was therefore threefold: Many new data sources had to be discovered, which increased the number of required annotations, as well as the number of required domain ontologies. We were therefore able to test the scalability of our approach developed for the first use case. Secondly, geospatial processing was required, like the calculation of buffers around sites of historical monuments. This required annotation and discovery of processing functionality, which is considerably more complex than for data models only (Hoffmann et al., 2008). Next to descriptions of input and output data types, it demands for specifications of applied operations, constraints on service inputs, and dependencies between the in- and outputs (Lutz, 2007). Related approaches have been developed and implemented within the SWING project. Detailed information is available in the SWING deliverables (Hoffmann et al., 2008; Schade et al., 2008). Third, we had to develop a service composition in the Composition Studio to create the requested data.

This composition of the second use case is considerably more complex then the one developed for the first scenario: Features from various sources have to be discovered and requested, connected to levels of negotiability, and intersected. The example in Figure 13 shows parts of the decision-support documents (a website) created with MiMS. On the left, various constraints have been selected (all representing various kinds of protected areas). The map on the right gives a summary of the selected constraints for the area of Brasse-Normandie in France. It is an overlay of relevant regulations in this particular region. Depending on the level of negotiability, the experts can now infer how much effort is possibly needed to convince the opposing parties. Green areas are of negotiability level 4, which means highly negotiable, yellow indicates level 3, less negotiable, and level 2, in red, is hardly negotiable. White areas are free of constraints.

Up to now we have numbers on consumption and production, and maps showing constraints on potential quarry locations. We still miss a decision-support document suggesting potential sites for new quarries. Hence, in the third and last use case we focused on aggregating the information of the first two use cases to locate potential sites for aggregate quarries. A new large construction project, in our example a new air-

Figure 13. Client view of the quarry constraint summary (Result of Use Case 2)

port near Caen (France), has been initiated. Raw materials are required, and it has to be decided where to get them from. First, the experts need to check if existing quarries nearby can provide enough raw materials (for a rational price). If not, they need a synthetic map presenting the available natural resources and the constraints applied on them. Finally, they need a summary map resulting from a multi-criteria analysis and presenting the ranking of the best locations to open new quarries or using existing ones (Tertre et al., 2008). In addition to the basic requirement for geological layers with the requested minerals and the input from the first two use cases, we now have to consider the potential transportation costs as one additional factor. The assessment of these costs depends on the transportation network. Such data is typically provided by third party actors, for example the local surveying agency. But the provided data usually doesn't bear exactly the required information, such as the assessment if the present road network supports transporting goods with heavy trucks. In this case we require data mediation, i.e. the identification of data model heterogeneities (Rahm & Bernstein, 2001), the definition of transformation rules (Lehto, 2007) and the execution of these rules on a specific data set (Curtis & Müller, 2006; Donaubauer & Schilcher, 2007). Transport costs are used to rank the final result, which may either by quarries able to serve the requested supply or locations for opening a new quarry.

The needle in the right part of Figure 14 specifies the location of a new infrastructure project within the French department Brasse-Normandie. In this case, 100 tons of alluvion (sediments like sand, silt, or gravel) is requested for the construction of a new airport. Potential locations for opening a new quarry are displayed on the map. For clarity we added red cycles indicating the ranked locations. Rank 0 indicates the best location for opening a new quarry, rank 1 the second best, and so on.

Looking Back, Moving Forward

In the current state of the project (early 2009), we have successfully implemented all needed components and realized the three use cases, We were able to integrate all the different components in one large workflow, starting from the geologist working at BRGM pressing the "Search"-Button

Figure 14. Client view used to determine best locations for opening a new quarry (Result of Use Case 3)

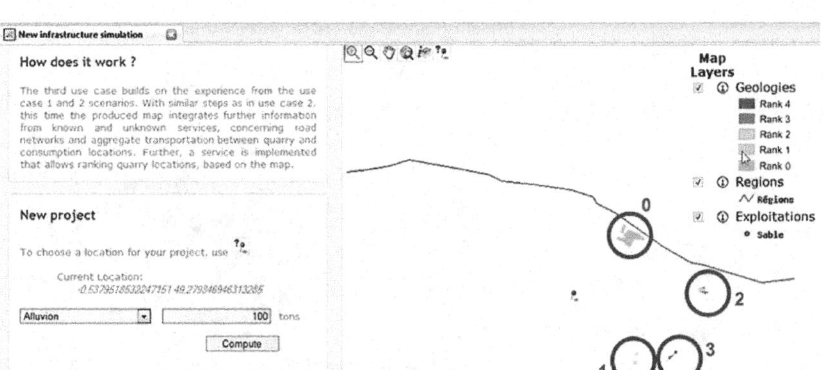

to the invocation of a complex workflow using the reasoner-supported semantic execution engine. In this book chapter we wrapped up the ongoing work, with a focus on geospatial decision-making and its implications on stakeholders. The use cases are sufficiently generic to cover different scenarios besides quarrying. Every geospatial decision making tasks requires consideration of different information sources. Every decision-maker has to be aware of possible conflicts which can impair the realization of the decision. With the proposed solution and the implemented technologies we are now able to offer a generic framework which takes these challenges into account. And since we always had the end user in mind, we were able to focus on user interfaces which let everyone, including the geologists from BRGM, use these technologies.

At the time of writing, the funding phase of the project is ending, and with it the active development of some of the components. Setting up the whole infrastructure is not an easy task to accomplish, and some results (especially the performance of the reasoning for both, discovery and execution of workflows) have not been completely satisfactory. Certainly, to recognize that Semantic Web technologies can be applied to real life applications and don't depend on tiny toy examples has been one of the main outcomes of the project. This success distinguishes it from the many other research projects targeting the further development of Semantic Web technologies. Some developments within SWING even exceeded this goal and will be further pushed forward in the years to come. Ontology engineering is a tedious task prone to fail if it relies on such close collaboration as it has been practiced in the project. Supporting the engineers by looking at the inner relationships of the data (Klien 2007b), using algorithms mining relevant documents fetched from the Web, or directly integrating user feedback (Maué 2007), is a promising approach and will be further investigated. Since workflow execution didn't meet our expectations, future work (then conducted in follow-up projects) has to focus on solutions with better performance. Additionally, the integration of semantic annotations and reasoning capabilities in OGC-conformal geospatial catalogs has been recognized as being an important step for the future of SDIs. Future implementations will hopefully realize some of the principles developed and studied in the work presented in this chapter, making the idea of a Geospatial Semantic Web accessible to everyone not as far-fetched anymore as it has been at the beginning of our research project. From a scientific point of view, many interesting results have been developed within SWING.

In the last phase, an extensive evaluation together with representatives of BRGM, the French government, and relevant companies has been conducted. In a workshop, the toolkit has been presented and used by the different stakeholders, and feedback forms have been filled out by all parties. The results are summarized in the SWING Experience Report (Urvois, 2008) available from the project website. One noteworthy concern has been raised by some of the potential end users. Semantic Web technologies can certainly support the domain experts to perform their daily tasks, and this is commonly acknowledged. But on the other hand the processes and underlying assumptions used to (automatically) create the decision-support documents remain hidden and therefore unclear to the user. It is argued that Semantic Web technologies for professional use will only be accepted if we find ways to ensure transparency, and to communicate to the end-user what the reasoning engine has decided (and why).

In this chapter we have presented the results of the European SWING project. After discussing the notion of Geospatial-Decision making and the related challenge of acquiring relevant geographic information from the Web, we went into more details about the quarrying use case in the second section. We discussed the daily struggle of BRGM's geologists to provide decision-support maps helping the decision-makes to find suitable locations for quarries. We introduced Semantic Web technologies as key technology to simplify the task to find the relevant information. We then discussed the developed components and the architecture, and finally went through the use cases to explain how the implemented tools can be applied to real world scenarios.

ACKNOWLEDGMENT

This work was supported by the IST Programme of the European Community under SWING (FP6-026514). Special thanks go to all project partners and colleagues who helped us to achieve the results presented in this book chapter. We also appreciate the valuable comments by the reviewers.

REFERENCES

Akerlof, G. (1970). The Market for "Lemons": Quality Uncertainty and the Market Mechanism. *The Quarterly Journal of Economics, 84*(3), 500, 488.

Amil, D. (2008). *Industrial production indices - global developments.* Statistics in focus. EUROSTAT.

Arroyo, S., Lara, R., Gómez, J. M., Berka, D., Ding, Y., & Fensel, D. (2004). Semantic Aspects of Web Services. In *Practical Handbook of Internet Computing.* Baton Rouge: Chapman & Hall and CRC Press.

Baader, F. (2003). *The Description Logic Handbook: Theory, Implementation and Applications.* Cambridge University Press.

Berners-Lee, T., Hendler, J., & Lassila, O. (2001). The Semantic Web. *Scientific American, 284*(4), 43, 34.

Calvanese, D., De Giacomo, G., & Lenzerini, M. (1998). On the Decidability of Query Containment under. *Constraints*, 149–158.

COM. (2000). *Promoting sustainable development in the EU non-energy extractive industry.* Communication from the Commission (COM).

COM. (2003). *Towards a thematic strategy on the sustainable use of natural resources.* Communication from the Commission (COM).

Curtis, E., & Müller, H. (2006). *Schema Translation in Practice.* Snowflake Software.

de Brujn, J., Lausen, H., Polleres, A., & Fensel, D. (2006). The Web Service Modeling Language WSML: An Overview. In *Proceedings of 3rd Eu-*

ropean Semantic Web Conference, Lecture notes in computer science. Berlin: Springer.

Directive 2007/2/EC of the European Parliament and of the Council of 14 March 2007 establishing an Infrastructure for Spatial Information in the European Community (INSPIRE). *(2007).*

Donaubauer, A., & Schilcher, M. (2007). *mdWFS: A Concept of Web-enabling Semantic Transformation.* Aalborg University, Denmark.

Egenhofer, M. (2002). Toward the Semantic Geospatial Web. In *GIS '02: Proceedings of the 10th ACM international symposium on Advances in geographic information systems* (S. 4, 1). ACM Press.

Erl, T. (2005). *Service-Oriented Architecture (SOA): Concepts, Technology, and Design*. Prentice Hall PTR.

EUROSTAT. (2006). *Non-energy mining and quarrying*. EUROSTAT.

Fensel, D., Lausen, H., Polleres, A., Brujn, J. D., Stollberg, M., & Roman, D. (2006). *Enabling Semantic Web Services: The Web Service Modeling Ontology*. Springer.

Gomez-Perez, A., Corcho, O., & Fernandez-Lopez, M. (2004). *Ontological Engineering: with examples from the areas of Knowledge Management, e-Commerce and the Semantic Web. First Edition (Advanced Information and Knowledge Processing)*. Springer.

Gone, M., & Schade, S. (2007). Towards Semantic Composition of Geospatial Web Services – Using WSMO in Comparison to BPEL. In *Proceedings of 5th GI Days – Young Researchers Forum*, ifgi Prints. Münster, Germany.

Gruber, T. (1995). Toward principles for the design of ontologies used for knowledge sharing. *Int. J. Hum.-Comput. Stud., 43*(5-6), 928, 907.

Guarino, N. (1998, June 6-8). Formal ontology and information systems. In N. Guarino (Ed.), *Proceedings of FOIS'98, Trento, Italy*, (pp. 3-15). Amsterdam: IOS Press.

Hargittai, E. (2002). Second-Level Digital Divide: Differences in People's Online Skills. *First Monday*, *7*(4).

Hoffmann, J., Steinmetz, N., & Fitzner, D. (2008). *2.4 - Semantic Web Geoprocessing Services*. SWING Project Deliverable.

Jeckle, M., Rupp, C., Hahn, J., Zengler, B., & Queins, S. (2005). *UML 2 glasklar*. Hanser Fachbuchverlag.

Kleppe, A., Warmer, J., & Bast, W. (2003). *MDA Explained: The Model Driven Architecture(TM): Practice and Promise*. Addison-Wesley Object Technology Series. Addison-Wesley.

Klien, E. (2007). A Rule-Based Strategy for the Semantic Annotation of Geodata. *Transactions in GIS. Special Issue on the Geospatial Semantic Web, 11*(3), 437–452.

Klien, E., Lutz, M., & Kuhn, W. (2005). Ontology-Based Discovery of Geographic Information Services-An Application in Disaster Management. *Computers, Environment and Urban Systems (CEUS)*.

Klien, E., Schade, S., & Hoffmann, J. (2007). *3.1 - Ontology Modeling Requirements*. SWING Project Deliverable.

Kopecký, J., Vitvar, T., & Bournez, C., & Joel Farrell. (2007). SAWSDL: Semantic Annotations for WSDL and XML Schema. *IEEE Internet Computing, 11*(6), 60–67. doi:10.1109/MIC.2007.134

Larson, R. (1996). Geographic Information Retrieval and Spatial Browsing. *GIS and Libraries: Patrons. Maps and Spatial Information, 124*, 81.

Lehto, L. (2007, May 8-11). Schema translations in a web service based sdi. In M. Wachowicz & L. Bodum (Eds.), *Proceedings of AGILE, Aalborg, Denmark.*

Longley, P., Goodchild, M., Maguire, D., & Rhind, D. (2005). *Geographic Information Systems and Science*. John Wiley & Sons.

Lutz, M. (2007). Ontology-Based Descriptions for Semantic Discovery and Composition of Geoprocessing Services. *GeoInformatica, 11*(1), 36, 1.

Lutz, M., & Klien, E. (2006). Ontology-based retrieval of geographic information. *International Journal of Geographical Information Science, 20*(3), 260, 233.

Manning, C. D., Raghavan, P., & Schütze, H. (2008). *Introduction to Information Retrieval*. Cambridge University Press.

Maué, P. (2007, September 26-28). Collaborative metadata for geographic information. In *Proceedings of the 1st Conference on Social Semantic Web, Leipzig, Germany*. CEUR Proceedings, ISSN 1613-0073, online CEUR-WS.org/Vol-301/Paper_7_Maue.pdf.

McAvoy, G. E. (1999). *Controlling Technocracy: Citizen Rationality and the Nimby Syndrome (American Governance and Public Policy)*. Georgetown University Press.

Nebert, D. (2004). *Developing Spatial Data Infrastructures: The SDI Cookbook*. GSDI.

Nilsson, U., & Maluszynski, J. (1995). *Logic, Programming and Prolog*. John Wiley & Sons Inc.

Object Management Group (OMG). (2004). *UML 2.0 Superstructure Specification*. Framingham, Massachusetts.

Rahm, E., & Bernstein, P. (2001). A survey of approaches to automatic schema matching. *The VLDB Journal, 10*, 334–350. doi:10.1007/s007780100057

Roman, D., Kifer, M., & Fensel, D. (2008). WSMO Choreography: From Abstract State Machines to Concurrent Transaction Logic. In *Proceedings of 5th European Semantic Web Conference (ESWC2008).*

Roman, D., & Klien, E. (2007). SWING - A Semantic Framework for Geospatial Services. In *The Geospatial Web: How Geobrowsers, Social Software and the Web 2.0 are Shaping the Network Society*. Springer.

Saeed, J. (2003). *Semantics (Introducing Linguistics)*. Wiley-Blackwell.

Schade, S., Kien, E., Maué, P., Fitzner, D., & Kuhn, W. (2008). *Report on Modeling Approach and Guideline*. SWING Project Deliverable.

Shneiderman, B. (2001). Design: CUU: bridging the digital divide with universal usability. *interactions, 8*(2), 15, 11.

Tertre, F., Bercker, J., & Lips, A. (2007). *Use Case Definition and I&T Requirements*. SWING Project Deliverable.

Tertre, F., Langlois, J., & Urvois, M. (2008). *Use Case 3*. SWING Project Deliverable.

Ullman, J. (1996). The Database Approach to Knowledge Representation. AAAI Press, MIT Press.

Urvois, M. (2008). *D1.3 - SWING Experience Report*. SWING Project Deliverable.

Willett, J. C. (2006). *2006 Minerals Yearbook - Stone, Crushed*. U.S. Geological Survey.

This work was previously published in the Journal of Cases on Information Technology, Vol. 11, Issue 4, edited by M. Khosrow-Pour, pp. 100-122, copyright 2009 by IGI Publishing (an imprint of IGI Global).

Chapter 14
An Ontology-Based GeoDatabase Interoperability Platform

Serge Boucher
Université Libre de Bruxelles, Belgium

Esteban Zimányi
Université Libre de Bruxelles, Belgium

EXECUTIVE SUMMARY

This chapter presents an ontology-based platform enabling automatic translation between a large number of geographical formats and data models. It explains the organizational motivations for developing this system, the technologies used, how its architecture and processing components were developed, what it achieves and where it still needs improvement. Since current off-the-shelf description logic reasoners are unable to process the large ontologies involved in this system, this platform uses a custom mapping algorithm that scales gracefully and still computes the required information to effect translation between supported data formats. The authors believe that the lessons learned during this project and discussed in this chapter will prove especially useful to interoperability practitioners contemplating the use of semantic technologies for enabling large-scale integration across organizational boundaries.

INTRODUCTION

Achieving efficient data conversion and integration between information sources has always been crucial for extracting maximum value from database assets, and is one of the most important areas of research for us at the CoDE department of ULB. This case presents one of the results of this research, a platform for interoperating geographical information sources, developed upon request from one of our industrial partners.

DOI: 10.4018/978-1-60566-894-9.ch014

BACKGROUND

The client for this interoperability platform is responsible for the evaluation and development of the weapons systems used by one of Europe's national armies. Historically, the geographical databases used in the various weapon systems deployed by the defense forces were the responsibility of each arm. For example, the Army was solely responsible for procuring the cartographical data used to feed *moving map* devices installed in tanks and other land attack vehicles. Warships, on the other hand, are equipped not with moving maps but with *chartplotters*, and the data they used was the responsibility of the Navy. While from a technological perspective both these devices are very similar to each other, (as well as to GPS receivers now present in many cars) for historical reasons they tend to use completely different data formats. The Army and the Navy were thus simultaneously tasked with the development of data sets to accommodate subtly different use cases and physical formats. Predictably, they came up with schemas that had large intersecting areas of expressivity but yet presented many subtle differences that made them completely incompatible. Over the years, this problem was repeated again and again, and today the terabytes of cartographical information critical to the army's operations are stored in dozens of different formats, with each pair of them exhibiting design differences, some fundamental and some gratuitous, which makes data conversion between them extremely difficult.

The previous paragraph might give the impression that the army managers and executives who allowed such a situation to occur have been incredibly shortsighted. This, however, couldn't be farther from the truth. As is so often the case in the computer science industry, a long series of sensible decisions has led to a collection of legacy systems that are ill adapted to current and future needs. A little background knowledge on the history of weapon systems helps explain why.

Military Cartography

Cartographical systems are used by the military at all stages of operations, sometimes directly by humans and sometimes as an input to a largely unsupervised computer process. These various cartographical systems have to accommodate a large disparity of user interface and timing constraints, from relatively slow systems limited by the speed of human reasoning, to the most stringent real-time constraints current technology can offer. At one end of this scale lie the maps and charts used by higher command for planning strategic operations. These have relatively lax timing constraints, and are thus supported mostly by paper charts on which physical markers are laid, due to the very convenient user interface these offer. A bit further down the scale, we find the systems that power *situation rooms,* where tactical operations are directed. Response times here are measured in minutes, and computerized systems are expected to show a representative, real-time updated view of the tactical situation in a field hundreds of kilometers wide. Here the main bottleneck remains human reaction time. Space constraints being relatively lax, powerful computers and large screens can be used to their full potential. Still further down the scale, tank pilots use the aforementioned moving maps to get a better understanding of the tactical situation in their close vicinity. Reaction times here are measured in seconds, and space is extremely limited. Towards the end of our scale we find terrain-following autopilots, used in many warplanes and cruise missiles. Those are quintessential real-time systems: any delay in retrieving needed information or computing the appropriate trajectory leads to either overshooting the altitude bound and risking detection by enemy forces, or failing to pull up in time and crashing into the ground.

Computerized cartographical information systems started being designed for the military in the nineteen-seventies and eighties, when available computing power was extremely scarce by today's standards. At that time, getting such a system to work reliably was a big enough challenge. Its suitability for future needs and compatibility with other existing systems were, quite simply, out of scope. For example, designing an embedded moving map that could accommodate many different data formats and be upgraded in the future to support other formats was deemed impossible. However expensive converting available datasets to the format imposed by the system might prove, at least it was technologically feasible.

In addition to the technological constraints of the time, operational realities help explain why so many different formats came to exist. The various embedded systems were often *designed* in isolation because they were expected to *operate* in isolation. A moving map inside a tank shows a representation of the tank's surroundings. A computerized situation map in a command and control room shows a representation of the entire theatre of operations. While it is obviously desirable that these two views be coherent with each other, it is much more important for them to be as close as possible to reality. Given the different technological constraints imposed on the two systems, it makes sense that the data sets they rely on would be created and updated independently from each other, and it would fall on the users to resolve any incoherence that may reveal itself during usage.

These circumstances have largely changed. Computing power is now much more plentiful, and human work comparatively more expensive, leading all industrial IT departments to shift more and more toward automation. This is especially true in the military of European nations, who are under growing political pressure to become more efficient. While in the past independence between military branches justified the work duplication described above, military commands are now expected to pool their resources at the national and trans-national levels. Indeed, NATO powers have made tremendous efforts at technology sharing: for example, weapon systems like air-launched missiles are now designed to be interchangeable between member armies, and global infrastructure projects are now pooled across nations, as in the Skynet satellite network (Amos, 2007). In this context, armies are now expected to make use of data sets available from allied countries rather than recreating them in-house. Obviously the organizational factors that lead to multiple incompatible formats were equally present in those other countries, which means that the number of different cartographical formats used by all NATO countries is substantially greater than that used inside any single country. However, there now is a rationale for enabling interoperability between all those formats.

Given this situation, our client had over the past decade launched many small research projects exploring the possibilities for interoperating some of those formats, leading to the project studied in this case. Most of these projects centered on problems found in specific conversions, e.g. converting VMAP2i data to VMAP1 ("Vector Product Format," n.d.) is difficult because they store data at different scales and automatic geometrical generalization is still an open research problem. (Chan, 2002) While these small projects revealed that in some cases automatic translation could never be expected to produce satisfactory results, they also showed that the general approach was worth pursuing further. It was thus decided to study approaches to provide a unified solution to all the agency's data cartographical data translation needs. This case discusses the results of this study.

CASE DESCRIPTION

Having described the organizational and managerial context of this case, we now present the technical specifications for the system we designed and its implementation. We start with a very brief primer on geographical databases, then present useful previous work on the subject of geographi-

Figure 1. Sample Geographical Dataset – Graphical View

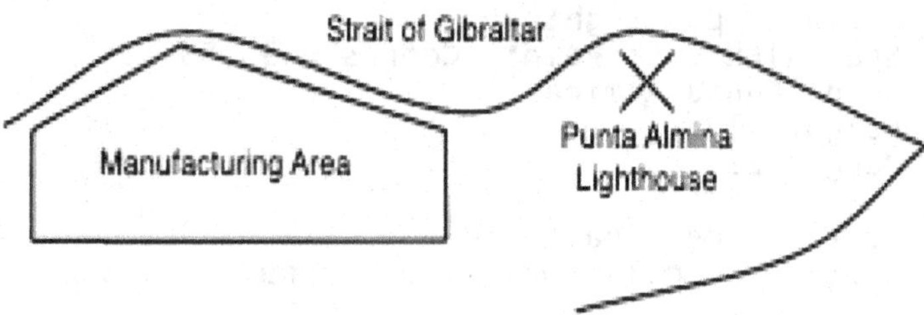

cal database interoperability. We then describe the high-level specification of our translation service and finally discuss how semantic technologies were used to effect the actual translation.

Geographical Databases

In the most general sense, a geographical database is any structured collection of information that has some geographical component. Many subcategories exist: geographical coordinates can be two- or three-dimensional, and the information can be stored either as raster or vector data. The distinction is similar to the one between bitmap and vector image formats: raster formats are better suited for representing information sampled on a closely spaced grid (e.g. patterns of rain over an area) while vector formats work better for resolution independent data (e.g. a map showing buildings and roads). Efficiently storing and processing significant amounts of geographical data is a challenging problem, which has lead to the development of Geographical Information Systems, or GIS, which serve the same purpose for geographical data that RDBMS do for relational data. Popular systems include Oracle Spatial and ArcGIS among others. ("Oracle Spatial," n.d.)

Our system processes two-dimensional vector geographical datasets representing cartographical data. Conceptually, these can be thought of as unordered lists of features, where a **feature** is a representation of some real-world object, e.g. the mountain Everest or the Golden Gate Bridge. Figure 1 presents a small example dataset containing three features: a coastline, a lighthouse and an industrial area.

Each feature in such a dataset has an associated **spatial extent**, which describes its geometry. In a 2D database, this extent can have up to 2 dimensions. Features with 0 dimensional (resp. 1, 2) spatial extents are called point features (resp. linear, area features). On Figure 1, the lighthouse is a point feature, the coastline a linear feature and the industrial area an area feature. In addition to the spatial extent, most features have a number of **properties**, which store additional information about the feature. Examples of such information are: the name of a city, the height of a tower, or the type of activity that occurs in a given area.

While some GIS allow the creation of an arbitrary list of features, geographical databases are vastly more useful when they follow some kind of **schema** or **data model**. A geographical database schema specifies a list of **feature types** that features can belong to, e.g. Lighthouse, Coastline, Ocean, and a list of **properties** that can be applied to these features with associated domains and ranges. The **domain** of a property is the set of feature types that it can be applied to, e.g. features of type Tower can have a property Height, while features of type Ocean cannot. The **range** of a property describes the kind of value that this property can take. This range can be either a data type, e.g. accepted values for the property Name are alphanumerical strings, or a discrete set of enumerated values, e.g. the values allowed for TypeOfIndustrialArea are: Production, Refining, Manufacturing, etc. In the rest of this chapter we

Figure 2.

```
FeatureType: Lighthouse
SpatialExtent: Point, Coords = 35,53...
Name: Punta Almina
Height: 148
Range: 22

FeatureType: Coastline
SpatialExtent: LineString, Coords = 35,5...

FeatureType: WaterBody
SpatialExtent: Polygon, Coords = 35,3...
Name: Strait of Gibraltar

FeatureType: Industrial Area
SpatialExtent: Polygon, Coords = 35,53...
TypeOfIndustrialArea: Manufacturing
```

will use the term **concept** to mean any of feature type, property, or enumerated property value. The set of concepts defined in a data model and the relationships between them determines the expressiveness of this data model, i.e. the set of physical realities that it can accurately represent.

Below is a simplified excerpt showing how a geographical information system would store the dataset drawn in Figure 1 above:

Geographical Database Heterogeneities

Like relational databases, two different cartographical data formats can exhibit different levels of heterogeneity. The most obvious is the **physical** level: some formats are stored in (collections of) flat files, others in relational databases, still others in XML. This level is the one most easily dealt with: writing converters between physical data formats is tedious, but it only has to be done once for each physical format, and either the conversion can be done without loss of information, or the information losses are easily found, described and understood. Next comes the **logical** level, which describes differences in structure between two data models. While quite troublesome for relational databases, this doesn't appear for the formats we had to process because they all share a common structure: the feature-attribute-extent hierarchy described in the previous paragraph. Geographical databases have a unique heterogeneity level that is not present in traditional relational databases: the **geometric** level. Equivalent features in two different formats sometimes are described with different types of spatial extents. For example, one format may allow arbitrary curves for linear features while another only allows straight lines. One format may store the location of a building as a simple point, while another would store its entire footprint as an area feature. While dealing with those heterogeneities is an active research problem that may never be completely solved in the general case, it is entirely orthogonal to the problem of semantic heterogeneity, so we won't discuss it further here. The **semantic** level is the last and most important level of heterogeneity. It deals with the actual meaning of the terms used in the schema specification. Consider the term "lighthouse", which appears in many cartographic format specification: many land cartography formats define (sometimes implicitly) a "lighthouse" as any tall building that was once used for marine navigation, focusing on the building's aspect as seen in daylight from a short distance. On the other hand, a maritime format such as AML defines lighthouse as any structure that supports a light currently used for navigation, focusing on how the object appears at night from the sea. Some formats don't define "lighthouse" at all, considering that real-world lighthouses can be modeled using a more general feature type such as Tower or Building. Solving the translation problems caused by these semantic heterogeneities in an automatic fashion was the main goal of the research project discussed in this case.

Related Work

Substantial work has been done on using semantic technologies to help process geographical data, starting with quantitative spatial reasoning using predicates based on Allen calculus (Allen, 1983) and its 2D extensions. (Cohn, 1992) The long-term goal of spatial reasoning is to find a formal logical representation for general spatial relationships that can be used for inference and reasoning, a goal that has proven quite difficult to attain. (Dutta, 1989) More recently, focus has shifted to exploring ways of embedding geographical information in Web 2.0 and semantic web applications. Standardized geographical ontologies are being engineered (Defne, 2004; Goodwin, 2005) and research on building the geospatial semantic web is active. (Aufaure, 2008) None of these are however addressing database interoperability per se. There has been significant research on using ontologies for spatial database integration, often to help domain experts find feature mappings that will be used for building the converters. Our work focuses on a different problem – using ontologies built by domain experts to enable automatic translation – on which much research still needs to be done. (Hakimpour, 2003)

Also related to this case are results on automatic ontology alignment, both for geographical (Bucella, 2007; Dolbert 2008) and general ontologies. (Euzenat, 2007) These however tend to focus on automatically mapping concepts based on their linguistic and structural similarity, which is not our focus here. We rely on domain experts to define concepts and focus on streamlining the conversions between multiple formats. One pioneering application of ontology-based interoperability was developed for the description of manufacturing processes, leading to the standardization of the Process Specification Language. ("Process Specification Language", 2003) Ontologies have also been used to facilitate (non-geographical) relational database interoperability, most notably in the QuONTO project. (Acciari, 2005)

As far as we know, the system presented here is the first attempt to develop an automated translation platform for cartographical systems based on semantic web technologies.

System Design

The goal of this research project was to prove that universal data access and conversion could be implemented across all studied formats at reasonable cost, and to evaluate the level of data quality that could be expected from an entirely automated process. This means that the user interface specifics of the final visualization system were out of scope: to prove that some AML data can be shown on an embedded VMAP1 viewer, we don't need access to the actual viewer.[1] We only need to convert the data to VMAP1, ensure that it meets the VMAP1 specification and evaluate the resulting data quality on a viewer program that allows visualizing VMAP1 data. We were thus able to make our system's interface extremely simple. It is implemented as a Web Service that accepts one single type of request, containing the location of the source data set and an identifier for the target format. The result of this request is the converted dataset. A high-level view of this process is presented in Figure 3 below.

Translation is performed using a two-layer approach, dealing first with physical then with semantic heterogeneities. The first step consists of translating the source data to the Geography Markup Language, ("GML", n.d.) which is an XML language standardized by the Open Geospatial Consortium. It has been designed to provide a

Figure 3. High Level System Interface

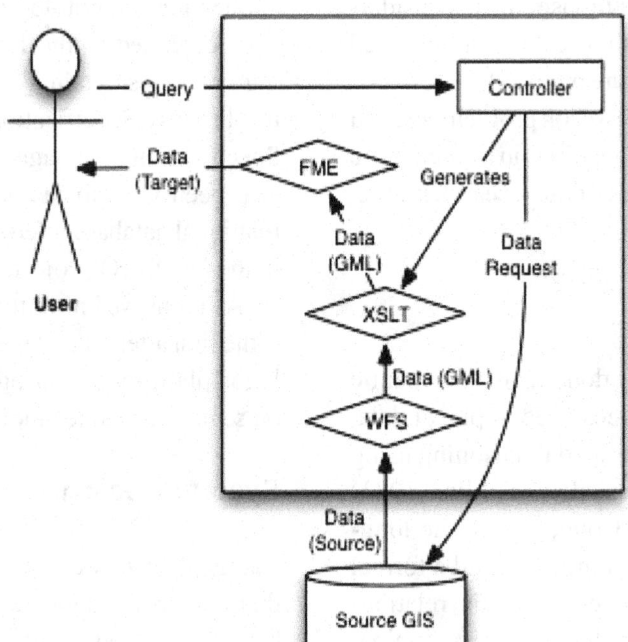

universal physical representation of geographical data to enable interchange between different GIS applications.

We use different tools for the two translation directions. To convert the source data to GML, we use a Web Feature Service. This is another OpenGIS standard that specifies a web service that outputs GML data. Current WFS implementations are available for most common geographical databases, including all the formats that we had to process. The other side of the conversion, from GML to target data format, was less straightforward. Using Safe Software's Feature Manipulation Engine ("FME Server", n.d.), we implemented a converter for each target format that takes GML as input. At the end of the translation process, the main Web Service controller calls the appropriate converter, which outputs the final dataset in the target data format.

Having resolved physical heterogeneities using GML converters, the hard task of converting the source GML to another GML that matches the target format semantics remains to be done. Since GML is an XML format, the most natural tool to process it is XSLT. The problem, however, is to economically generate one XSLT stylesheet for each pair of source and destination formats when the number of formats is large. This is where making the semantics of each data format explicit becomes invaluable. The remainder of this section describes this process in detail.

Semantic Translation

The goal of this project was to enable automatic translation between any two datasets stored in a known, but large, number of different formats. Figure 4 below illustrates two naïve approaches for achieving this goal.

The first solution, pictured on the left, is to manually implement a converter for each pair of formats. This solution allows the implementer

Figure 4. Two Approaches for Translating Between Many Different Schemas

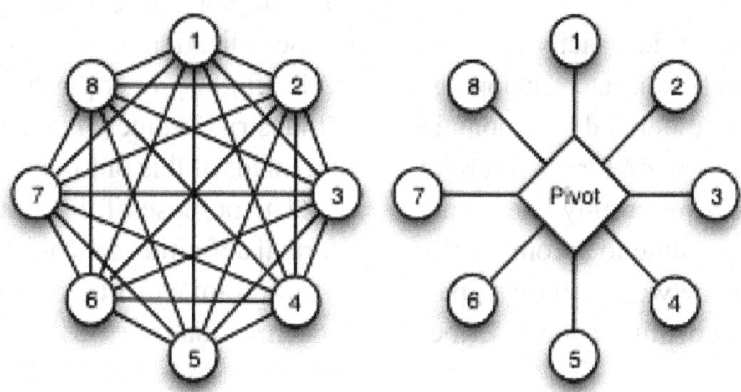

to tweak each and every translator and thus potentially provides the best translation quality. However, it has the obvious drawback that for *n* different formats it requires *n(n-1)* individual translators, making it prohibitively expensive when the number of formats is large and likely to grow in the future. Our case study currently has dozens of formats with new ones added each year, making this option unviable.

Another naïve possibility is to build a central pivot format, which is expressive enough to encompass all the others and to translate each format to and from it, as depicted on the right-hand side of Figure 4. This approach sounds very attractive in theory, since it seems to solve the problem with comparatively little work: the only requirement is to define a single new data schema and to implement a two-way convertor for each of our original formats. However, closer examination reveals that it doesn't actually work: even setting aside the huge complexity involved in creating and maintaining the very expressive pivot schema, this approach fails to solve the underlying translation problem.

Inasmuch as there are intersections between the expressivenesses of the original formats — and if there are none, data translation is both trivial and useless — a pivot format expressive enough to represent any possible data from the original formats will necessarily afford many different ways to represent the same information. For example, if format A represents a lighthouse using a specific feature type called Lighthouse while format B instead relies on the generic feature type Building with a qualifying attribute BuildingFunction valued as Lighthouse, then the pivot format needs to define both Lighthouse and Building feature types as well as a BuildingFunction property with Lighthouse as one of its possible values. Now, translating towards the pivot format is easy: we just map each original feature type to the equivalent pivot feature type. However, the opposite transformation is much more complicated. Since a real-world lighthouse could be represented in the pivot format using either its specific Lighthouse feature type or using the generic Building with an associated BuildingFunction of Lighthouse, the pivot-to-target converter has to handle both cases. More generally, each pivot-to-format converter has to be aware of all other existing formats, and thus the pivot format does not solve our translation problem at all.

Thus, neither of these two approaches work: manually implementing individual converters requires a workload that rises quadratically in the number of formats, and while the pivot approach seems to require only linear workload it fails to address the actual translation problem. However, studying these two failed solutions suggests an attractive possibility: what if there was a way to build the $n(n-1)$ converters with only linear workload?

Our system attempts to do exactly that. By describing each individual format using mappings from its concepts to those defined in a domain ontology — which can be done for each format independently and thus requires only linear time in total — it becomes possible to automatically generate data converters between any given pair of formats. The remainder of this section describes the entire process.

Ontology Building

The cornerstone of our approach is a domain ontology, which is an OWL ontology that describes all real-world concepts relevant to the domain of cartography. It is grounded on three disjoint taxonomies: one for feature types, one for properties, and one for property values which describes the generalization/specialization relationships that exist between those real-world concepts. For example, the Factory feature type is a special kind of Building, the hasIndustryCategory property is a specialization of the hasUse property, and the OilRefining property value is a special case of the "Industrial" value. Figure 5 below shows a small fragment of this ontology.

The purpose of this ontology is to provide a formal definition for concepts that appear in each of the formats to be translated. These formats' specifications are most often *flat*, i.e. they define a list of feature-types with only implicit relationships between them. A format might define different feature-types for Lighthouse, Tower and Building, and while it is obvious from reading the specifications that a Lighthouse is a special kind of Tower which is a special kind of Building[2], this knowledge is not present in the original schemas in machine-readable form. Hence we spell it out in the Domain Ontology.

With this knowledge formally stated in the domain ontology, it can be used to describe all features and properties appearing in each format.

Figure 5. Fragment of Domain Ontology

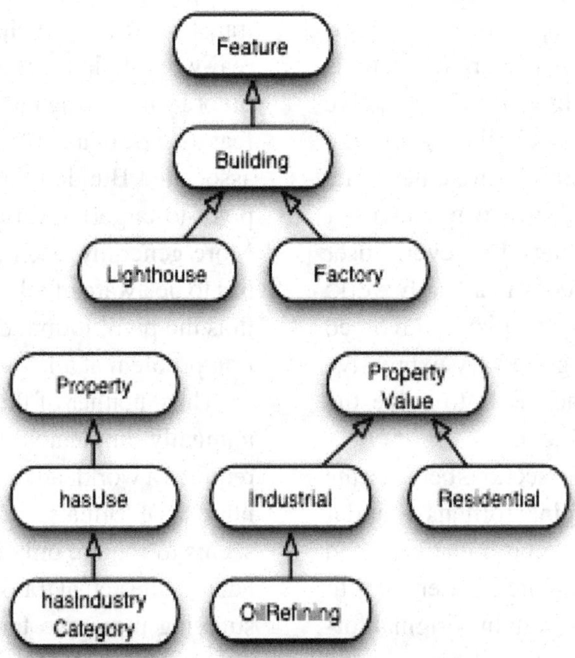

After expressing each format schema in OWL form, by creating a "format ontology" that defines an OWL concept for each feature type, property, and property value defined in the format, we write a mapping between these format-specific OWL concepts and the concepts defined in the domain ontology. This step gives tangible meaning to the feature types specified in each format: if a land cartography format defines the feature type Lighthouse as a tower-shaped building that sits near the sea but may not be used for marine navigation anymore, this feature type will be mapped to the domain ontology concept HistoricLighthouse. A Lighthouse feature type defined in a maritime cartography format might however refer to any building that contains a light source used for navigation: this feature type would be mapped to the domain concept LandBasedNavigationalAid. A feature type defined as having the shape of a traditional lighthouse and being used for navigation would be mapped to the domain concept Lighthouse, which is subsumed by both previous concepts. An example of such format-to-domain mapping is shown in Figure 6 below:

The way these ontologies are built does not matter much. Best practices dictate that the domain ontology should be created by trained ontology engineers with input from domain experts, and each format-specific ontologies and mappings should be created by specialists in each of these formats with support from the engineers who created the domain ontology. Our team developed the prototype ontologies used for this project after close examination of all format specifications and with occasional support from experts in these formats. In the end, the only important thing is for the domain ontology to ensure sound translations of feature types when direct format-to-format mappings don't exist. Each "A subsumes B" relationship in the domain ontology means that while translating from a format that defines B to one that does not, A is a reasonable substitute.

Translation Algorithm

Given an ontology formally defining domain concepts and mappings linking format-specific concepts to those definitions, designing an algorithm to translate data between any pair of formats is reasonably straightforward. The basic idea is as follows. Feature types, properties and property values are treated separately but similarly. Each of these concepts needs to be mapped to some concept in the target format, if at all possible. When a fully equivalent concept exists in the target format, the mapping is trivial. Otherwise,

Figure 6. Format-to-Domain Mapping

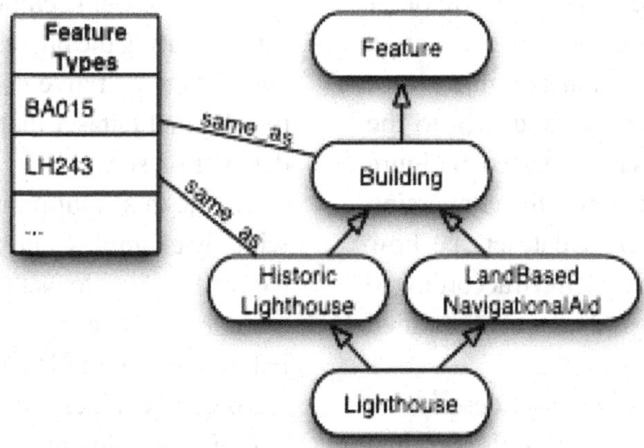

Figure 7. Translation Process Overview

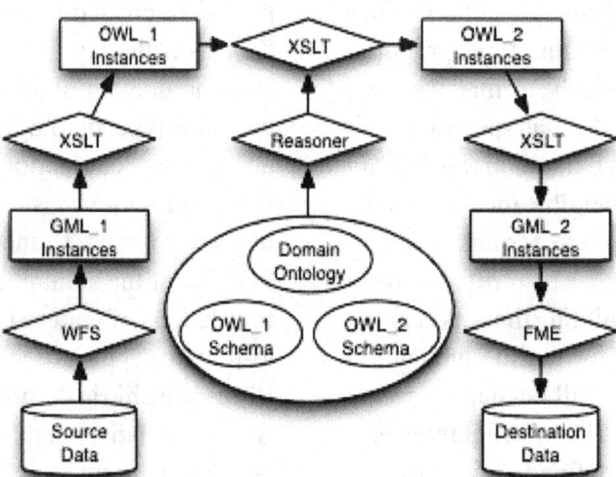

we look for a more general concept by walking up the domain ontology breadth-first until we encounter a concept that is defined in the target format. If we find one, it is mapped to the source concept. If we don't, then a mapping cannot be found, thus information about this concept is not expressible in the target format and we are forced to drop it. The following describes the translation process in more detail.

As seen earlier, the very first step is to convert the source dataset from its native format to GML, which is a straightforward process, handled by an industry-standard Web Feature Server. Then, this GML dataset is converted to OWL instances belonging to the source format ontology. This OWL dataset is then processed to obtain another OWL dataset where instances belong to the target format ontology. It is then again straightforward to convert this dataset to GML and then to the target format. This process is illustrated in Figure 7. Obviously, the difficult step is the conversion between source and target OWL datasets, i.e. how can we express the knowledge defined according to the original concepts using only concepts defined in the target format.

Our first approach was based on description logics reasoning. In theory, loading the original OWL dataset in a DL reasoner along with the source, domain and target ontologies reduces the conversion problem to an instance-retrieval problem: doing a series of instance retrieval queries on all the concepts defined in the target format would yield a dataset containing all the knowledge from the original dataset that is expressible with the concepts defined in the target format. For example, if the source data set contained a Lighthouse, and the destination data format defined a Building feature type, and the domain ontology stated that Building subsumes Lighthouse, then loading all ontologies in a reasoner, classifying the merged ontology and doing an instance retrieval on the Building concept defined in the destination schema would return our Lighthouse from the source data set. Repeating the process with all the other target concepts would give us all the information from the original dataset that can be expressed in the destination schema.

While this solution is elegant and works well with toy examples, current reasoning technology has scaling problems that make it impractical for our purpose. The cartographical formats we studied define thousands of feature types, properties and property values. Combining format ontologies with the domain ontology yields a data structure that is much too large to be classified by current tableaux-based reasoners.

There is, however, a workaround. We designed an algorithm that walks the source format ontology tree to generate a mapping between source and destination format, and store this mapping as an XSLT file. Once this is done, data conversion only requires executing this XSLT with the OWL source instances as input. The main drawback of this approach is its lack of generality. Firstly, our algorithm only processes the OWL constructs we used and thus can't handle general OWL-DL ontologies. Secondly, given that XSLT is not specifically an OWL processing technology, and that a given OWL ontology has many different XML serializations, our XSLT has to make a number of assumptions on how the OWL was serialized. Thus it cannot handle general OWL/XML files. In practice, it only works on OWL files generated by our GML-to-OWL converters.

The payoff for this lack of generality is that our algorithm does not suffer from the combinatorial explosion of all-purpose OWL-DL reasoners and thus is orders of magnitude faster in our case. Due to the way they're engineered and the characteristics of our domain, our ontologies have a very clean structure that allows very efficient processing if the processor is aware of this structure. This is not the case for tableaux-based reasoners, which don't make any assumption on how ontologies are built. Our algorithm works as follows:

For each feature type present in our source format, we walk the domain ontology to try to find a mapping with a feature type in the destination format. If the domain class equivalent to our source format feature type has an equivalent destination format feature type, then we have a direct mapping. If this is not the case, we walk the domain ontology upwards and breadth-first, starting at source feature-type, until we find a domain class with an equivalent destination feature class. If we encounter *#Feature* (the super-concept of all feature types in the domain ontology) before we've found a mapping, then this source feature type is not expressible in the target format.

A similar procedure is followed to generate property and property-value mappings. All three sets of mappings are then serialized as XSLT templates which, when executed, translate source OWL instance data into target OWL instance data.

Extensions

While the algorithm described above is the essential idea behind our translation platform, as presented it can only handle simple one-to-one feature mappings, which is too simplistic for many of the conversions we had to handle, so a number of extensions were created to handle the more complicated cases. This subsection presents some of these implemented extensions.

The first extension deals with a type of mapping we call *conditional mapping*. Some formats use the same feature types for conceptually different entities and distinguish between them using different values for a qualifying property. For example, a lighthouse is represented in VMAP2i by using the feature type Building and setting the property hasBuildingFunctionCategory to 82. This is expressed in our format-domain mapping by using an OWL restriction, as shown on Figure 8 below. When writing the XSLT transform for such a mapping, our algorithm generates an appropriate selector (when the restriction appears in the source format) or writes out the property value and inhibits transforms on conflicting properties (when the restriction appears in the destination format).

While this type of conditional mapping is easily expressible in OWL, others are not. Some formats require conditions on DataType properties, e.g. a tower higher than 150 meters should be represented using the Skyscraper feature type. To deal with these mappings, we extend the OWL restriction syntax as shown below:

Lastly, we have only discussed here the semantic aspects of data conversion. Our translation

Figure 8. Conditional Mapping

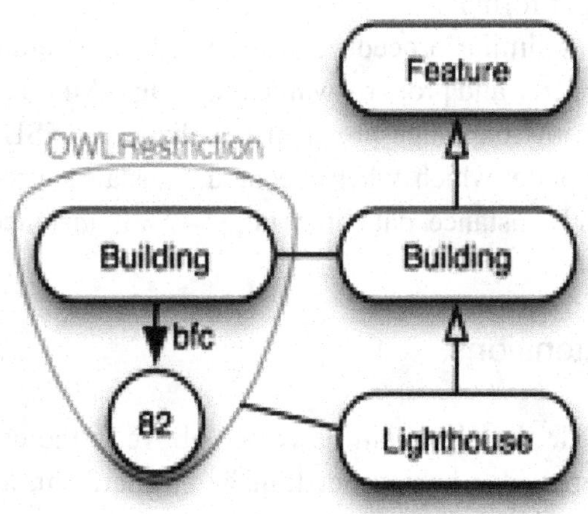

engine also deals with units of measures as well as geometric aspects such as specialization and generalization, scale-dependent linear approximations and point-area conversions, but these are out of scope for this chapter.

DISCUSSION

This section explains in more depth the choices we made while designing this system and experiences we learned during early prototype testing. The first subsection discusses our choice of ontology modeling language. The second subsection explains at length the differences between the role of our domain ontology and the data model of pivot format approaches. While our approach has the obvious benefit of making cartographical formats interoperate with an amount of work that rises linearly in the number of formats, instead of quadratically, it does have a few drawbacks, which we discuss in the third subsection. Finally, the fourth subsection discusses the performance of our system and strategies for optimization.

Semantics

It should be noted that our use of semantic technologies differs from the one envisioned in the early views of the semantic web on at least two points. Firstly, we don't reuse any existing ontologies. Secondly, our use of OWL is somewhat unorthodox: although we only use a relatively small subset of the OWL vocabulary, some of its constructs are given slightly different semantics than they have in OWL-DL, which might be misleading for someone accustomed to working in this language. Obviously, the right design for a computer system is the one that is best at performing its current and future tasks, not the one that is "purer" in the technologies it uses, but given the intent of this book and the ongoing debate on those issues in the semantic web community we think it worthwhile to explain the reasoning behind those design choices.

Our decision not to reuse existing ontologies is easy to explain: no suitable ontology could be found. While the number of formally defined and publicly available OWL and RDF files is certainly rising, there are still many domains that are not adequately covered by available ontologies, and military cartography is one of them. Although the ontologies published by Ordnance Survey ("Ordnance Survey Ontologies," n.d.) were

Figure 9.

```
<owl:Restriction>
      <owl:onProperty rdf:resource="height"/>
      <owlext:hasValueSuperiorTo>
            150
      </owlext:hasValueSuperiorTo>
<owl:Restriction>
```

initially identified as good candidates for reuse, they are heavily tied to the data models used by the organization and reusing them for our domain ontology ultimately would have caused too many problems.

Our use of OWL deserves further discussion. In any project using semantic technologies, careful consideration should be given to the ontology language used. Some projects are best served by RDF/RDFS. Others will require some level of OWL. Some models are best expressed in OWL-Full, but standard DL reasoners only work with strict OWL-DL. In any case, it is obviously desirable to respect the standard semantics of OWL constructs: this makes the ontologies easier to document and facilitates integration with other semantic web projects.

In our case, the original plan was to use OWL-DL — originally one of our goals was to evaluate how description logics reasoning could help resolve geographical database heterogeneities. As explained above, the size of our ontologies made this approach difficult, but this was not the only problem: the constraints of OWL-DL made some modeling situations tricky. For example, some properties accept enumerated values in some formats but unstructured string values in others. The logical way to model this in OWL is to use an ObjectProperty in the first case and a DatatypeProperty in the second. When these are linked to the domain ontology, we get a subproperty relationship between an ObjectProperty and a DatatypeProperty. This is not allowed in OWL-DL, and for a very good reason: lifting this restriction leads to an undecidable logic. However, in our case this modeling choice is reasonable and its meaning is easy to understand.

Because of those problems, using off-the-shelf reasoners on this project would have required substantial pre- and post-processing steps, adding significant complexity to the system with little benefits in return. We thus decided to stick with the more natural models and find a way to exploit them to their fullest, leading to the translation algorithm that is the main topic of this case.

It can be argued that our system uses a good part of the OWL syntax while giving it different semantics, which might be confusing for people accustomed to pure OWL-DL. However, a more accurate view is that our ontologies are really RDF ontologies that happen to use many components of the OWL vocabulary — after all, any OWL ontology is also an RDF ontology. OWL provides many constructs that are perfectly suited for our modeling purposes. For example, OWLRestriction is a natural fit for our conditional mappings, and while it would certainly have been possible to achieve the same result using ad hoc RDF predicates, reusing OWL ensures that our ontologies can be edited using standard OWL editors and eases the learning curve for any one familiar with OWL. Our system gives to nearly all OWL constructs the semantics they have in OWL-DL—the only exception is subPropertyOf, for the reason explained above, and this is thoroughly explained in the project's internal documentation.

It should be noted that the practice of using OWL notation without OWL-DL semantics is used in many well known projects, notably Friend-of-a-friend. (http://www.foaf-project.org/)

Pivot Formats and Domain Ontologies

We gave a number of talks on the project and approach described in this case, and one question came up often enough that it deserves some discussion in these pages: how is our approach different from the pivot format approach shown in Figure 4? Looking at the translation process described in Figure 7, one can't help noticing that the domain ontology in our system acts very much like the pivot format of Figure 4. Indeed, it contains all concepts that might appear in all supported formats and is the central reference point for generating inter-format mappings and thus translating data between different formats. How, then, is our approach different

Figure 10. Excerpt from Domain Ontology and Related Pivot Format

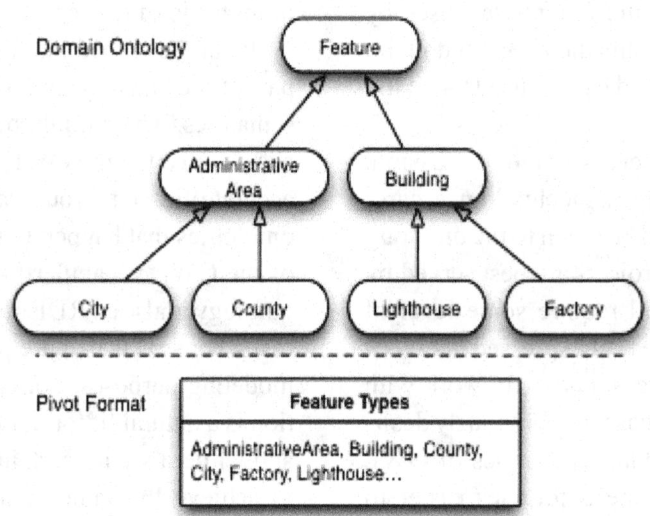

than the pivot format one and why doesn't it suffer from the same drawbacks?

The answer has to do with the fundamental definition of an ontology, and specifically with what an ontology is not. An ontology is a formal specification of knowledge, not a data model, which is what the pivot format is.[3] A data model is only a set of building blocks that can be used to describe the world. An ontology, on the other hand, actually describes the world, in a machine-readable way. To illustrate, let's consider what a domain ontology and a data model might say about the real world concepts of Building and Lighthouse.

As we can see on Figure 10 above, both ontology and data model acknowledge that in the world of cartography there exist things known as buildings and lighthouses. The data model provides two corresponding feature types that can be used by a human modeler to represent instances of these structures present at some location in the physical world. This, however, doesn't help at all when we are given a Lighthouse instance in some format and we want to express it in another format that only defines the Building feature type.

On the other hand, the domain ontology does more than acknowledge the existence of these two feature types: it formally states that all Lighthouses are Buildings. This knowledge proves very useful when we want to represent a Lighthouse in a format that only defines Building.

The advantages of the domain ontology are even more obvious when we consider that other formats can be added to the system some time after the initial implementation. Assume that we add a format that defines the feature type Tower, which does not exist in any previous format and is thus not defined in our domain ontology or in the pivot format. Obviously they have to be modified, yielding the revised version of Figure 11 below.

With the pivot format approach, we are in trouble: we have to revise all existing pivot-to-target-format converters so that they accept instances of the Tower feature type as Buildings. With the domain ontology, however, nothing changes: since the subsumption relation is transitive, it still contains the knowledge that all Lighthouses are Building (as well as Towers), and conversions from formats that define Tower to those that don't will work as expected.

More formally, the kind of knowledge stored in our domain ontology is *monotonous*, i.e. add-

Figure 11. Adding a Tower Concept in Domain Ontology and Pivot Format

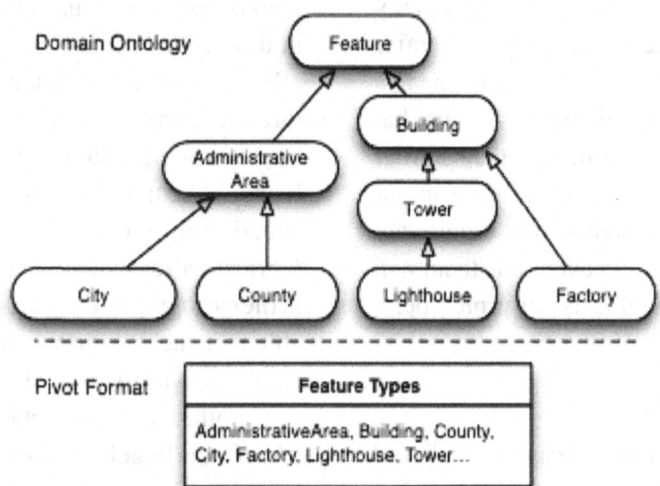

ing new concepts from new formats to the system does not invalidate previous knowledge.[4]

It sometimes happens that the new format uses the name of some existing domain ontology concept with a different meaning. Imagine our system only deals initially with terrestrial formats, and the domain ontology contains a Lighthouse concept, a sub-concept of Tower that represents all tower-shaped buildings situated near a coastline that were originally built to facilitate night-time maritime navigation. While this is the definition generally used for land maps, in most maritime cartography formats a Lighthouse refers to a currently active land-based navigational light, regardless of the shape of the building it sits in. When adding such a maritime format to our system, obviously we can't map its Lighthouse concept to the domain ontology concept of the same name: we have to define a new concept that matches the definition of Lighthouse as used in maritime cartography, which we might call MaritimeLighthouse. One could argue that the original Lighthouse domain ontology concept was badly named, and that the right solution is to rename it to LandLighthouse, change all existing format-to-domain mappings, and create a new Lighthouse concept that only applies to features that fit both maritime and land definitions. Such a change obviously breaks monotonicity: adding a new format broke existing knowledge.

Obviously, nothing forces us to do this: while the original name of the Lighthouse concept might have been badly chosen, its semantics are well defined. It is perfectly okay to leave the concept as it is, add a comment to the ontology documenting the fact that it only refers to Lighthouses as defined in land cartography, and create the new concept as LandAndMaritimeLighthouse. After all, the system does not care about the names given to domain ontology concepts. On the other hand, if this issue occurs often, it seems doubtful that we can keep adding comments to misnamed existing concepts and creating new equally misnamed concepts for the sake of backward compatibility without at some point getting stuck with a domain ontology that is impossible to maintain.

This problem of imperfect concept names is revealing of a larger issue: the domain ontology is a software artifact of significant size and complexity, and it is bound to evolve. As ontology evolution is still an active research area (Noy, 2004) and best practices for documenting ontologies are still being developed, keeping the domain ontology up-to-date and well documented while many formats are added to the system will likely raise some challenges. While dealing with change in a complex system is always difficult, the fact that ontology engineering is less mature than similar disciplines like relational data modeling might lead to unpredictable problems. How significant these will be and how best to overcome them will be studied while the client tests our prototype.

Limitations

Our approach to inter-format mapping is based on one core assumption: if a source concept has no equivalent in the target format, it should be mapped to a more general concept, or not at all. For example, if the source format defines a feature type for towers, and the destination format has no feature type for tower but has one for buildings, then Tower instances are converted to Building instances. If none of the parent concepts of Tower in the domain ontology are defined in the target format, then Tower instances are simply dropped during translation.

While this seems like a sensible approach, it should be noted that it cannot handle cyclical mappings. Imagine that there exists three concepts A, B, C defined in three different formats, and that a domain expert tells us that A should be translated into B, B into C and C into A. Our system cannot effect those translations: it is impossible to structure the domain ontology in such a way that the translation algorithm generates those mappings. It should be noted that we did not encounter this situation in our case, and that we cannot even fabricate a reasonable example of such features in the cartography domain. However it is conceivable that such a situation might arise if the same approach was to be used in other domains.

Another core assumption is that property value mapping is largely independent from feature type mapping. Thus our system is a bit awkward at mapping properties whose meaning depends on which feature they're associated with. Consider a translation from format A to format B, with features *A1* and *A2* mapping to features *B1* and *B2*, and some object property *ap* defined in format A with a domain that includes *A1* and *A2*. Assume that property value *ap1* should map to property value *bp1* when it is applied to *A1*, but to *bp2* when it is applied to *A2*, as is shown on Figure 12 below.

Our system can handle such a case, but only if we create two ad hoc domain ontology concepts: one that maps to A1 with property *ap* equal to *ap1*

Figure 12. Feature-Dependent Property Value Mapping

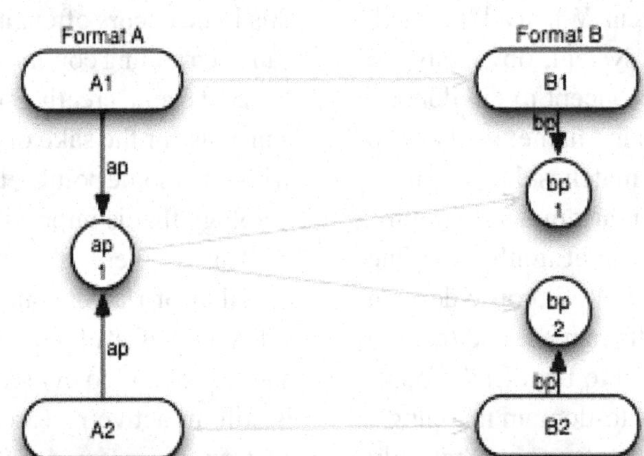

Figure 13. Domain Ontology for Feature-Dependent Property Value Mapping

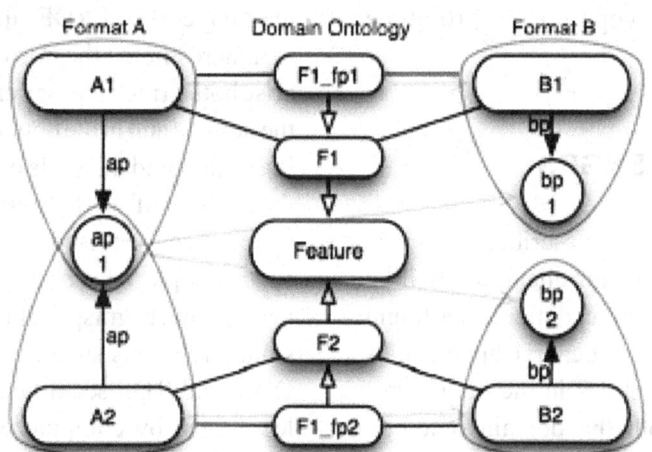

and to *B1* with property *bp* equal to *bp1*, and one that maps to *A2* with property *ap* equal to *ap1* and to *B2* with property *bp* equal to *bp2*, as seen on Figure 13.

If there are two such properties then we need four domain ontology concepts, and the number rises exponentially. If this situation occurs often, we risk a class explosion in our domain ontology, which would become very difficult to maintain. We would argue that having the semantics of property values depend on their subject type is bad data model design, and it seldom occurred in the formats we used for our case study, but this consequence of our approach could still be a problem in some cases.

Performance

Performance is an important concern in any translation architecture that deals with huge amounts of data. Our system converts data by using XSLT, a technology that is not known for its scalability, and any conversion requires three successive transforms, so for large datasets it certainly isn't the fastest approach. In practice this turned out to be not much of a problem. Due to the nature of our datasets, each unique feature can be translated independently. Moreover, the XPath expressions appearing in our stylesheets only refer to very local XML nodes — typically the current node's direct children or parent. These two factors mean that the translations run much faster than one would expect and can handle very large datasets: in our tests, the overall time spent on XML processing was small compared to the final conversion from GML to the target physical format.

It should also be noted that nothing in our translation architecture forces us to use XSLT. Mappings are generated as object-oriented data structures, and these could conceivably be converted to any translation mechanism. We currently support two: XSLT, which given the availability of our data in XML format was deemed the easiest to implement, and a plain text format that is not executable but has proven invaluable for evaluating the quality of our mappings and communicating with domain experts. If the system needed to be optimized past the point where XSLT became a bottleneck, it would be reasonably easy to use e.g. STX, SAX or JavaCC (https://javacc.dev.java.net/) instead. If even that proved too slow, we could even get rid of GML altogether without changing the mapping algorithm. This would allow substantial performance gains in the cases where source and target physical formats happen to be the same. These performance optimizations, however, were out of scope for our prototype implementation.

CURRENT CHALLENGES

The demonstrator system described above is currently being tested by our client and will be iteratively modified to correct deficiencies found during testing. While the general approach is sound, adding functionalities in the main algorithm and refining both the domain ontology and the different format ontologies will augment the usefulness of the system by improving the translations' data quality.

Since the domain and format ontologies were engineered by computer scientists with limited domain knowledge, it is fair to say that they are currently far from perfect. While this is mainly a consequence of this project's limited budget and its exploratory nature, some of the difficulties encountered seem like a direct consequence of our usage of semantic technologies. The consensus among knowledge representation experts is that ontologies should be created by collaboration between domain experts and ontology engineering specialists, (see for example: Gómez-Péres, 2004) however the specifics of such collaboration are rarely spelled out. It is easy to conceive of many arrangements that sound as if they should work. One possibility is for domain experts to assume most of the ontology creation work after having been briefed by ontology engineers on the rudiments of ontology engineering and associated tools. Alternatively, ontology engineers can build the ontology from some semi-formal description of the target domain, eventually asking domain experts for clarification whenever they need it. We mostly used the latter strategy, which required a lot of back and forth between ontology engineers and domain experts and thus made the process of ontology engineering slower than initially expected. We made some attempts to use the first strategy but these were frustrated by the relatively steep learning curve of RDF and OWL. It is very easy to underestimate the misunderstandings that will arise both in the ontology engineers' conception of the domain and in the domain experts' understanding of the fundamentals of ontology engineering. After years of working in computer science, we were often surprised at how difficult it is for smart people who have little computer science background to grasp the precise semantics of even simple relations such as is-a or owl:Restriction. OWL and RDF seem like difficult languages to learn even by computer science standards, and while we can hope that at some point tools will be developed that lower the learning curve of ontology engineering, these tools do not exist yet.[5] It seems to us that any project that requires substantial ontology engineering effort and deals with a complex domain will benefit from very careful study of these issues.

A future challenge for the prototype is support for real data integration, i.e. going beyond 1-to-1 data translation and offering the possibility of merging information stored in different data sources. While the system's architecture was designed with this goal in mind, and limited ad hoc merging can be performed, the current implementation does not support it in the general sense. Specifically, there is no way to get all the information relevant to a given region of space in a single query. Supporting this use case would require permitting the user to express such a query in a dataset-independent way, querying all the available datasets with adequate translations of this query, translating all results to the destination format and finally merging them. The current system only supports the "translation" step of this process. Both merging geographical datasets without introducing duplicate features and ensuring good performance of such distributed queries are difficult problems.

CONCLUSION

All in all, the implemented prototype has shown that building and maintaining an industrial-strength system to support universal data access across all the formats used by our client will require a lot more study, design and implementation work. It has also opened the way for more ambitious use cases like data integration, which will also require significant advances to meet operational requirements. The goal of this project, however, was not to build a perfect system, but to explore ways in which current state of the art information technology could be used to allow cost-effective access to geographical databases across numerous formats and database schemas. While languages and tools for formal description and processing of the semantics of a database schema are still in their infancy, this project has shown that their use in an industrial setting can in some cases provide efficient and cost-effective solutions to large-scale infrastructural problems that initially seem intractable. While it is fair to say that knowledge representation still has a lot of room for improvement, it is also true that it is now mature enough to be used in an industrial context. Those who are prepared to invest enough time and effort to climb the inevitable learning curve of this emerging technology will likely find in it tremendous value for improving existing data infrastructure systems.

REFERENCES

Acciarri, A., Calvanese, D., De Giacomo, G., Lembo, D., Lenzerini, M., Palmieri, M., & Rosati, R. (2005). QuOnto: Querying Ontologies. In M. M. Veloso, S. Kambhampati (Eds.), *20th National Conference on Artificial Intelligence* (pp. 1670-1671). Menlo Park: AAAI Press.

Allen, J. F. (1983). Maintaining knowledge about temporal intervals. *Communications of the ACM, 26*(11), 832–843. doi:10.1145/182.358434

Amos, J. (2007). British Skynet satellite launched. *BBC News*. Retrieved November 10, 2008, from http://news.bbc.co.uk/2/hi/science/nature/6434773.stm

Aufaure, M. A., Baazaoui, H., Ben Ghezala, H., Claramunt, C., & Hadjouni, M. (2008, May). *Towards a personalized spatial web architecture*. Paper presented at "Semantic Web meets Geospatial Applications" workshop, Girona, Spain.

Buccella, A., & Cechich, A. (2007). Towards integration of geographic information systems. *Electronic Notes in Theoretical Computer Science, 168*, 45–59. doi:10.1016/j.entcs.2006.08.023

Chan, E. P. F., & Chow, K. K. W. (2002). On multi-scale display of geometric objects. *Data & Knowledge Engineering, 40*(1), 91–119. doi:10.1016/S0169-023X(01)00051-9

Cohn, A., Cui, Z., & Randell, D. (1992). A spatial logic based on regions and connection. In Nebel, B., Rich C., & Swartout W. R. (Eds.), *3rd International Conference on Principles of Knowledge Representation and Reasoning (KR'92)* (pp. 165-176). Boston, MA: AAAI Press.

Datasheet, O. S. (n.d.) Retrieved February 10, 2009, from http://www.oracle.com/technology/products/spatial/htdocs/data_sheet_9i/9iR2_spatial_ds.html

Defne, Z., Islam, A., & Piasecki, M. (2004) *Ontology for geography markup language (GML3.0) of open GIS consortium (OGC)*. Retrieved on November 10, 2008 from http://loki.cae.drexel.edu/~wbs/ontology/2004/09/ogc-gml.owl

Dolbear, C., & Hart, G. (2008, March). *Ontological bridge building - Using ontologies to merge spatial datasets*. Paper presented at the "AAAI Spring Symposium on Semantic Scientific Knowledge Integration, Stanford, CA.

Dutta, S. (1989). Qualitative spatial reasoning: A semi-quantitative approach using fuzzy logic. In A. Buchman, O. Günther, T.R. Smith, & Y.F. Wang (Eds.), *First symposium on design and implementation of large spatial databases* (pp. 345-364). Berlin, Germany: Springer.

Euzenat, J., & Shvaiko, P. (2007) Ontology Matching. New York, NY: Springer-Verlag.

Format, V. P. (VPF) Overview. (n.d.) Retrieved September 22, 2008, from http://www.nga.mil/portal/site/nga01/index.jsp?epi-content=GENERIC&itemID=a2986591e1b3af00VgnVCMServer23727a95RCRD&beanID=1629630080&viewID=Article

GML 3.1.1 Standard. (n.d.). Retrieved October 10, 2008, from http://www.opengeospatial.org/standards/gml

Gómez-Péres, A., Fernández-López, M., & Corcho, O. (Eds.). (2004). *Ontological engineering: with examples from the areas of knowledge management, e-commerce and the Semantic Web*. New York, NY: Springer-Verlag.

Goodwin, J. (2005). *Experiences of using OWL at the ordnance survey.* Paper presented at OWL: Experiences and Directions Workshop, Galway, Ireland. Retrieved October 12, 2008 from http://www.mindswap.org/2005/OWLWorkshop/sub17.pdf

Hakimpour, F. (2003). *Using ontologies to resolve semantic heterogeneity for integrating spatial database schemata*. Ph.D. thesis. Zurich, Switzerland: Zurich University.

Noy, N., & Klein, M. (2004). Ontology evolution: Not the same as schema evolution. *Knowledge and Information Systems*, *6*(4), 428–440. doi:10.1007/s10115-003-0137-2

Ordnance Survey Ontologies. (n.d.). Retrieved June 17, 2008, from http://www.ordnancesurvey.co.uk/oswebsite/ontology/

Process Specification Language. (2003) Retrieved February 3, 2009, from http://www.mel.nist.gov/psl/

Server Overview, F. M. E. (n.d.). Retrieved August 15, 2008, from http://www.safe.com/products/server/overview.php

ENDNOTES

1 Even if we wanted access to the actual hardware, we would not have gotten it. The precise capabilities of some of these systems are classified and the army only issues security clearances when absolutely necessary.

2 More precisely, the specialization relationships hold not between the feature types themselves but between the real-world entities they're meant to represent. Since in the geographical database each Feature has only one feature type, the sets of Lighthouses and Towers in the database itself are distinct, even though in the real world all Lighthouses are Towers. Ironically, format specification documents often encourage modelers to always use the most specific feature type suitable to represent a given real-world feature, but they almost never spell out the specialization relationships that exist between feature types, perhaps assuming them to be obvious.

3 The word "format" in "pivot format" is somewhat unfortunate in this context. A data format generally defines both a data

model and a physical storage format. Since all translations in this project start and end in the same physical format (i.e.: GML), the pivot would likely use it as well, and its only relevant aspect would be its data model.

4 Note that this is not true of general OWL-DL ontologies, which can be made inconsistent and thus unusable by adding new axioms. Pure RDF/RDFS ontologies, however, are monotonous.

5 Graphical ontology editors such as Protégé and TopBraid help the reader abstract himself from OWL syntax but still require a deep understanding of description logics to be used successfully.

Compilation of References

Abecker, A., Bernardi, A., Hinkelmann, K., Kuhn, O., & Sintek, M. (2000). Context-aware, proactive delivery of task-specific knowledge: The KnowMore project. [ISF]. *International Journal on Information Systems Frontiers, 2*(3/4), 139–162.

Acciarri, A., Calvanese, D., De Giacomo, G., Lembo, D., Lenzerini, M., Palmieri, M., & Rosati, R. (2005). QuOnto: Querying Ontologies. In M. M. Veloso, S. Kambhampati (Eds.), *20th National Conference on Artificial Intelligence* (pp. 1670-1671). Menlo Park: AAAI Press.

Aggarwal, R., Verma, K., Miller, J. A., & Milnor, W. (2004). Constraint driven web service composition in METEOR-S. In *Proceedings of IEEE SCC.*

AIAG MOSS Project. (2008). *MOSS conceptual model (a UML model).* Retrieved February 9, 2009, from http://syseng.nist.gov/poc/repo/trunk/conceptual-model/moss.mdxml

AIAG MOSS Project. (2009). *MOSS message mapping.* Retrieved February 9, 2009, from http://syseng.nist.gov/moss/moss-views/msgview?msg=DELJIT&select=1185&open=1202*1219#1185

Akerlof, G. (1970). The Market for "Lemons": Quality Uncertainty and the Market Mechanism. *The Quarterly Journal of Economics, 84*(3), 500, 488.

Alani, H., & Brewster, C. (2005). Ontology ranking based on analysis of concept structures. In *Proceedings of the 3rd International Conference on Knowledge Capture (K-Cap'05),* Banff, Canada (pp. 51-58).

Alani, H., Dasmahapatra, S., Gibbins, N., Glasser, H., Harris, S., Kalfoglou, Y., et al. (2002). Managing reference: Ensuring referential integrity of ontologies for the Semantic Web. In *Proceedings of the 13th International Conference on Knowledge Engineering and Knowledge Management (EKAW'02),* Siguenza, Spain (pp. 317-334).

Alexiev, V., Breu, M., de Bruijn, J., Fensel, D., Lara, R., & Lausen, H. (2005). *Information Integration with Ontologies*. Chichester, UK: Wiley

Allen, J. F. (1983). Maintaining knowledge about temporal intervals. *Communications of the ACM, 26*(11), 832–843. doi:10.1145/182.358434

Amil, D. (2008). *Industrial production indices - global developments*. Statistics in focus. EUROSTAT.

Amos, J. (2007). British Skynet satellite launched. *BBC News*. Retrieved November 10, 2008, from http://news.bbc.co.uk/2/hi/science/nature/6434773.stm

Ankolekar, A., Krötzsch, M., Tran, T., & Vrandecic, D. (2007). The Two Cultures Mashing up Web 2.0 and the Semantic Web. In *Proceedings of the 16th International Conference on World Wide Web* (pp. 825–834). DOI 10.1145/1242 572.12426842007.

Antoniou, G., Franconi, E., & van Harmelen, F. (2005). Introduction to Semantic Web Ontology Languages. In N. Eisinger & J. Maluszynski (Eds.), *Proceedings of the Summer School: Reasoning Web (LNCS 3564)*. Berlin, Heidelberg, Germany: Springer.

Arroyo, S., Lara, R., Gómez, J. M., Berka, D., Ding, Y., & Fensel, D. (2004). Semantic Aspects of Web Services. In *Practical Handbook of Internet Computing.* Baton Rouge: Chapman & Hall and CRC Press.

ASC. (2009). *Accredited standards committee, ANSI X12*. Retrieve February 9, 2009, from http://www.x12.org

Ashish, N., Mehrotra, S., & Pirzadeh, P. (2008). *Incorporating Integrity Constraints in Uncertain Databases* (. UCI Technical Report 2008). Retrieved fromOnline at http://www.ics.uci.edu/~ashish/techreporthttp://www.ics.uci.edu/~ashish/techreport

ATHENA. (2003). *A3 knowledge support and semantic mediation solutions (2004), European integrated project*. Retrieved August 2008, from http://www.athena-ip.org

ATHENA. (2007). *B5.10 - inventory visibility subproject: IV&I end-to-end interoperability demonstration including conformance testing demonstration*. Retrieved August 2008, from http://xml.aiag.org/athena/resources/WD.B5.7.6—InteropAndConformanceTestDemo.pdf

Aufaure, M. A., Baazaoui, H., Ben Ghezala, H., Claramunt, C., & Hadjouni, M. (2008, May). *Towards a personalized spatial web architecture*. Paper presented at "Semantic Web meets Geospatial Applications" workshop, Girona, Spain.

Automatic Content ExtractionA. C. E. (n.d.). http://www.nist.gov/speech/tests/ace/http://www.nist.gov/speech/tests/ace/

Baader, F. (2003). *The Description Logic Handbook: Theory, Implementation and Applications*. Cambridge University Press.

Barkmeyer, E. J., & Kulvatunyou, B. (2007). *An ontology for the e-kanban business process* (NIST Internal Report 7404). Retrieved August 2, 2008, from http://www.mel.nist.gov/msidlibrary/doc/NISTIR_7404.pdf

Barwise, J., & Seligman, J. (1997). Information flow: The logic of distributed systems (Cambridge Tracts in Theoretical Computer Science 44). Cambridge, UK: Cambridge University Press.

Basili, R. V., Shull, F., & Lanubile, F. (1999). Building knowledge through families of experiments. *IEEE Transactions on Software Engineering, 25*(4), 456–473. doi:10.1109/32.799939

Batini, C., & Scannapieco, M. (2006). *Data quality*. Springer-Verlag.

Bazzanella, B., Bouquet, P., & Stoermer, H. (2009). *A cognitive contribution to entity representation and matching* (Tech. Rep. DISI-09-004). Ingegneria e Scienza dell'Informazione, University of Trento.

Beneventano, D., Guerra, F., Magnani, S., & Vincini, M. (2004). A Web Service based framework for the semantic mapping amongst product classification schemas. *Journal of Electronic Commerce Research, 5*(2), 114–127.

Benyoucef, M., & Rinderle, S. (2006). Modeling e-Negotiation Processes for a Service Oriented Architecture. *Group Decision and Negotiation, 15*, 449–467. doi:10.1007/s10726-006-9038-6

Bergamaschi, S., Castano, S., & Vincini, M. (1999). Semantic integration of semistructured and structured data sources. *SIGMOD Record, 28*(1). doi:10.1145/309844.309897

Berners-Lee, T., Hendler, J., & Lassila, O. (2001). The Semantic Web. *Scientific American, 284*(5), 34–43.

Bernstein, P. A., Melnik, S., & Churchill, J. E. (2006). Incremental schema matching. U. Dayal, K.-Y. Whang, D. B. Lomet, G. Alonso, G. M. Lohman, M. L. Kersten, S. K. Cha, & Y.-K. Kim (Eds.), *Proceedings of the 32nd International Conference on Very Large Data Bases* (Vol. 32) (pp. 1167-1170). Seoul, Korea. PA: VLDB Endowment.

Besana, P., & Robertson, D. (2007). How service choreography statistics reduce the ontology mapping problem. In *Proceedings of ISWC*.

Bicer, V., Laleci, G. B., Dogac, A., & Kabak, Y. (2005). Artemis message exchange framework: Semantic interoperability of exchanged messages in the healthcare domain. *SIGMOD Record, 34*(3), 71–76. doi:10.1145/1084805.1084819

Bizer, C., & Seaborne, A. (2004). *D2RQ -treating non-RDF databases as virtual RDF graphs*. Paper presented at the 3rd International Semantic Web Conference (ISWC2004), Hiroshima, Japan.

Blumauer, A., & Pellegrini, T. (2006). Semantic Web und semantische Technologien: Zentrale Begriffe und Unterscheidungen. In T. Pellegrini & A. Blumauer (Eds.), *Semantic Web Wege zur vernetzten Wissensgesellschaft* (pp. 9–25). Berlin Heidelberg New York: Springer.

Bock, C., & Gruninger, M. (2004). *PSL: A semantic domain for flow models, Software and Systems Modeling.*

Bohring, H., & Auer, S. (2005). Mapping XML to OWL Ontologies. In *Proceedings of 13. Leipziger Informatik-Tage (LIT 2005), Lecture Notes in Informatics (LNI).* Bonn, Germany: Köllen.

Boley, H., Hallmark, G., Kifer, M., Paschke, A., Polleres, A., & Reynolds, D. (2008). *RIF Core (W3C Working Draft).* Retrieved from http://www.w3.org/TR/rif-core/

Bonifacio, M., Bouquet, P., & Traverso, P. (2002). Enabling distributed knowledge management. Managerial and technological implications. *Informatik/Informatique, 3*(1).

Boone, T., & Ganeshan, R. (2008). Knowledge acquisition and transfer among engineers: effects of network structure. *Managerial and Decision Economics, 29*(5), 459–468. doi:10.1002/mde.1401

Bouquet, P., Magnini, B., Scrafini, L., & Zanobini, S. (2003). A SAT-based algorithm for context matching. In *Proceedings of the 4th International and Interdisciplinary Conference on Modeling and Using Context (Context03).*

Bouquet, P., Stoermer, H., Niederee, C., & Maña, A. (2008). Entity name system: The backbone of an open and scalable Web of data. In *Proceedings of the IEEE International Conference on Semantic Computing, ICSC 2008, number CSS-ICSC.* Washington, DC: IEEE.

Brauer, F., Schramm, M., Barczyński, W., Loeser, A., & Do, H.-H. (2008). Robust recognition of complex entities in text exploiting enterprise data and NLP-techniques. In *Proceedings of the ICDIM '08.*

Brickley, D., & Guha, V. (2004). *RDF vocabulary description language 1.0: RDF schema.* W3C Recommendation.

Broder, A. (2002). A taxonomy of Web search. *SIGIR Forum, 36*, 3–10. doi:10.1145/792550.792552

Broder, A. Z. (2000). Identifying and filtering near-duplicate documents. In *COM 0: Proceedings of the 11th Annual Symposium on Combinatorial Pattern Matching* (pp. 1-10). Berlin, Germany: Springer-Verlag.

Buccella, A., & Cechich, A. (2007). Towards integration of geographic information systems. *Electronic Notes in Theoretical Computer Science, 168*, 45–59. doi:10.1016/j.entcs.2006.08.023

Buitelaar, P., Wennerberg, P. O., & Zillner, S. (2008). Statistical term profiling for query pattern mining. In D. Demner-Fushman, S. Ananiadou, K. B. Cohen, J. Pestian, J. Tsujii, & B. Webber (Eds.), *ACL BioNLP Workshop Current Trends in Biomedical Natural Language Processing* (p.114). Columbus, Ohio. PA: Association for Computational Linguistics.

Calvanese, D., De Giacomo, G., & Lenzerini, M. (1998). On the Decidability of Query Containment under . *Constraints*, 149–158.

Carr, L., Bechhofer, S., Goble, C., & Hall, W. (2001). Conceptual linking: Ontology based open hypermedia. *WWW10 Conference Hong Kong.*

Carroll, J., & Klyne, G. (2004). *RDF concepts and abstract syntax.* W3C Recommendation.

Ceol, A., Chatr-Aryamontri, A., Licata, L., & Cesareni, G. (2008). Linking entries in protein interaction database to structured text: The FEBS letters experiment. *FEBS Letters, 582*(8-9), 1171–1177. doi:10.1016/j.febslet.2008.02.071

Ceri, S., & Gottlob, G., and & Tanca, L. (1989). What you always wanted to know about Datalog (and never dared to ask). *IEEE Transactions on Knowledge and Data Engineering, 1*(1), 1989, pp. 146-66. doi:10.1109/69.43410

Chalupsky, H. (2000). Ontomorph. A translation system for symbolic knowledge. In A.G. Cohn, F. Giunchiglia, & B. Selman (Eds.), *7th Intl. Conf. on Principles of Knowledge Representation and Reasoning KR'2000* (pp. 471-482). Breckenridge, Colorado. PA: Morgan Kaufmann Publishers.

Chan, E. P. F., & Chow, K. K. W. (2002). On multi-scale display of geometric objects. *Data & Knowledge Engineering, 40*(1), 91–119. doi:10.1016/S0169-023X(01)00051-9

Charikar, M. S. (2002). Similarity estimation techniques from rounding algorithms. In STOC 02: Proceedings of the thirty-fourth annual ACM symposium on Theory of computing (pp. 380-388). New York: ACM.

CIDX. (2003). *CIDX overview*. Retrieved February 2, 2009, from http://www.cidx.org/AboutCIDX

Cimino, J. J., & Barnett, G. O. (1993). *Automatic knowledge acquisition from MEDLINE 32*(2) . *Methods of Information in Medicine*, 120–130.

Ciocoiu, M., Gruninger, M., & Nau, D. (2001). Ontologies for integrating engineering applications . *Journal of Computing and Information Science in Engineering, 1*, 45–60. doi:10.1115/1.1344878

Ciravegna, F., Doan, A., Knoblock, C., Kushmerick, N., and & Staab, S. (2005). Machine Learning learning for the Semantic Web. *Seminar 05071 at Schloss Dahstuhl 2005.*

Cohn, A., Cui, Z., & Randell, D. (1992). A spatial logic based on regions and connection. In Nebel, B., Rich C., & Swartout W. R. (Eds.), *3rd International Conference on Principles of Knowledge Representation and Reasoning (KR'92)* (pp. 165-176). Boston, MA: AAAI Press.

Colucci, S., Noia, T. D., Sciascio, E. D., Donini, F. M., & Mongiello, M. (2003). Concept abduction and contraction in description logics. In D. Calvanese, G. D. Giacomo, & E. Franconi (Eds.), *Description logics (Vol. 81).* CEUR-WS.

COM. (2000). *Promoting sustainable development in the EU non-energy extractive industry.* Communication from the Commission (COM).

COM. (2003). *Towards a thematic strategy on the sustainable use of natural resources.* Communication from the Commission (COM).

Conroy, C. (2008). Towards semantic mapping for casual web users. In *Proceedings of the 7th International Semantic Web Conference (ISWC) doctoral consortium, Karlsruhe (DE)* (LNCS 5318, pp. 907-913).

Corcho, O., & Gómez-Pérez, A. (2001). Solving Integration Problems of E-commerce Standards and Initiatives through Ontological Mappings. In *Proceedings of the Workshop on E-Business and intelligent Web at the Seventeenth International Joint Conference on Artificial Intelligence (IJCAI2001).* Retrieved November 11, 2006, from http://sunsite.informatik.rwth-aachen.de/Publications/CEURWS//Vol-47/corcho.pdf

Cunningham, H., Maynard, D., Bontcheva, K., & Tablan, V. (2002). GATE: A framework and graphical development environment for robust NLP Tools and applications. In *Proceedings of the 40th Anniversary Meeting of the Association for Computational Linguistics (ACL'02).* Philadelphia, July 2002.

Curtis, E., & Müller, H. (2006). *Schema Translation in Practice.* Snowflake Software.

Daconta, M. C., Obrst, L. J., & Smith, K. T. (2003). *The Semantic Web. A Guide to the Future of XML, Web Services, and Knowledge Management.* Indianapolis, USA: Wiley.

Dalvi, N., and Suciu, D. (2005). Foundations of probabilistic answers to queries. Tutorial,. *ACM SIGMOD 2005.*

Datasheet, O. S. (n.d.) Retrieved February 10, 2009, from http://www.oracle.com/technology/products/spatial/htdocs/data_sheet_9i/9iR2_spatial_ds.html

De Amicis, F., & Batini, C. (2004). A methodology for data quality assessment on financial data. In *Studies in communication sciences* (pp. 115-136).

de Bruijn, J. (2004). *Semantic Information Integration Inside and Across Organizational Boundaries* (Tech. Report DERI-2004-05-04A). Innsbruck, Austria: Digital Enterprise Research Institute.

de Bruijn, J. (2008). *RIF RDF and OWL compatibility* (W3C Working Draft). Retrieved from http://www.w3.org/TR/rif-rdf-owl/

de Bruijn, J., Ehrig, M., Feier, C., Martín-Recuerda, F., Scharffe, F., & Weiten, M. (2006). Ontology mediation, merging and aligning. In J. Davies R. Studer, & P. Warren (Eds.), *Semantic Web Technologies: Trends and Research in Ontology-based Systems*. PA: Wiley.

de Brujn, J., Lausen, H., Polleres, A., & Fensel, D. (2006). The Web Service Modeling Language WSML: An Overview. In *Proceedings of 3rd European Semantic Web Conference*, Lecture notes in computer science. Berlin: Springer.

Dean, M., & Schreiber, G. (2004). *OWL Web Ontology Language: Reference*. W3C Recommendation.

Deerwester, S., Dumais, S., Landauer, T., Furnas, G., & Harshman, R. (1990). Indexing by Latent Semantic Analysis. *Journal of the American Society for Information Science American Society for Information Science*, *41*(6), 391–407. doi:10.1002/(SICI)1097-4571(199009)41:6<391::AID-ASI1>3.0.CO;2-9

Defne, Z., Islam, A., & Piasecki, M. (2004) *Ontology for geography markup language (GML3.0) of open GIS consortium (OGC)*. Retrieved on November 10, 2008 from http://loki.cae.drexel.edu/~wbs/ontology/2004/09/ogc-gml.owl

Dell'Erbaa, M., Fodor, O., Ricci, F., & Werthner, H. (2002). HARMONISE: A solution for data interoperability. In J. Monteiro (Ed.), *Proceedings of the Second IFIP Conference on E-Commerce, E-Business, E-Government (I3E 2002)* (pp. 433-445). Norwell, MA: Kluwer.

Dennet, D. C. (1987). *The Intentional Stance*. Cambridge, MA, The MIT Press.

Denti, E., Omicini, A., & Ricci, R. (2001). tuProlog: A Light-Weight Prolog for Internet Applications and Infrastructures. *PADL 2001, Las Vegas, NV.*

Dill, S., Eiron, N., Gibson, D., Gruhl, D., Guha, R., Jhingran, A., et al. (2003). SemTag and Seeker: Bootstrapping the semantic Semantic web Web via automated semantic annotation. *WWW12 Conference Budapest*.

Ding, L., Finin, T., Joshi, A., Pan, R., Cost, R., Peng, Y., et al. (2004). Swoogle: A search and metadata engine for the semantic web. In *Proceedings of the 13th ACM Conference on Information and Knowledge Management* (pp. 652-659).

Directive 2007/2/EC of the European Parliament and of the Council of 14 March 2007 establishing an Infrastructure for Spatial Information in the European Community (INSPIRE). *(2007).*

DisasterPortal. (2008). WebRetrieved from: http://www.disasterportal.orghttp://www.disasterportal.org

Do, H. H., & Rahm, E. (2007). Matching large schemas: Approaches and evaluation. *Information Systems*, *32*(6), 857–885. doi:10.1016/j.is.2006.09.002

Do, H.-H., & Rahm, E. (2002). COMA: A system for flexible combination of schema matching approaches. In *Proceedings of the 28th International Conference on Very Large Databases (VLDB'02),* Hong Kong, China.

Doan, A., Madhavan, J., Domingos, P., & Halevy, A. (2002). Learning to map between ontologies on the Semantic Web. In *Proceedings of the 11th International World Wide Web Conference (WWW 2002)*, Hawaii, USA.

Doan, A., Madhavan, J., Domingos, P., & Halevy, A. (2003). Ontology matching: A machine learning approach. In S. Staab & R. Studer (Eds.), *Handbook on ontologies in information systems* (pp. 397-416). Berlin Heidelberg, PA: Springer-Verlag.

Dolbear, C., & Hart, G. (2008, March). *Ontological bridge building - Using ontologies to merge spatial datasets*. Paper presented at the "AAAI Spring Symposium on Semantic Scientific Knowledge Integration, Stanford, CA.

Donaubauer, A., & Schilcher, M. (2007). *mdWFS: A Concept of Web-enabling Semantic Transformation.* Aalborg University, Denmark.

Dutta, S. (1989). Qualitative spatial reasoning: A semi-quantitative approach using fuzzy logic. In A. Buchman, O. Günther, T.R. Smith, & Y.F. Wang (Eds.), *First symposium on design and implementation of large spatial databases* (pp. 345-364). Berlin, Germany: Springer.

Dwork, C., Kumar, S., Naor, M., & Sivakumar, D. (2001). Rank aggregation methods for the Web. In *Proceedings of the 10th International Conference on World Wide Web* (pp. 613-622).

Dzbor, M., Takeda, H., & Vargas-Vera, M. (Eds.). (2005). *Proceedings of the UserSWeb: Workshop on End User Aspects of the Semantic Web (UserSWEB'05), CEUR (137)WS*. Retrieved from http://sunsite.informatik.rwth-aachen.de/Publications/CEUR-WS//Vol-137

ebXML (2007). *About ebXML*. Retrieved August 06, 2007, from http://www.ebxml.org/geninfo.html

Egenhofer, M. (2002). Toward the Semantic Geospatial Web. In *GIS '02: Proceedings of the 10th ACM international symposium on Advances in geographic information systems* (S. 4, 1). ACM Press.

Ehrig, M. (2004). Ontology Mapping – An Integrated Approach. In C. Bussler, J. Davis, D. Fensel, & R. Studer (Eds.), *Proceedings of the First European Semantic Web Conference (LNCS 3053)* (pp. 76-91). Berlin Heidelberg, Germany: Springer.

Ehrig, M. (2007). *Ontology Alignment - Bridging the Semantic Gap. Semantic Web and Beyond. Computing for Human Experience*. New York, USA: Springer.

Ehrig, M., & Staab, S. (2004). QOM - quick ontology mapping. In *Proceedings of the 3rd International Semantic Web Confernece (ISWC'04)*, Hiroshima, Japan (LNCS 3298, pp. 683-697).

Ehrig, M., Staab, S., & Sure, Y. (2005). Bootstrapping ontology alignment methods with APFEL. In *Proceedings of ISWC*.

Electropedia, I. E. C. (2008). Retrieved from http://www.electropedia.org.

Erl, T. (2005). *Service-Oriented Architecture (SOA): Concepts, Technology, and Design*. Prentice Hall PTR.

European Parliament and the Council (2003). *Directive 2003/54/EU of the European Parliament and of the Council of 26 June 2003 concerning common rules for the internal market in electricity and repealing Directive 96/92/EC*.

EUROSTAT. (2006). *Non-energy mining and quarrying*. EUROSTAT.

Euzenat, J. (2004). An API for ontology alignment. In S.A. McIlraith, D. Plexousakis, & F. van Harmelen (Eds.), *The Semantic Web - ISWC 2004, Proceedings of the Third International Semantic Web Conference (LNCS (3298)* (pp. 698-712). Springer.

Euzenat, J., & Shvaiko, P. (2007). *Ontology matching*. Heidelberg: Springer-Verlag.

Euzenat, J., & Valtchev, P. (2004). Similarity-based ontology alignment in OWL-lite. In *Proceedings of ECAI*.

Euzenat, J., Mocan, A., & Scharffe, F. (2008). Ontology alignments: An ontology management perspective. In M. Hepp, P. De Leenheer, A. De Moor, & Y Sure (Eds.), Ontology management: semantic web, semantic web services, and business applications (pp. 177-206). New York: Springer.

Eysenbach, G. (2001). An ontology of quality initiatives and a model for decentralized, collaborative quality management on the (semantic) World Wide Web. *Journal of Medical Internet Research*, *3*(4), e34. doi:10.2196/jmir.3.4.e34

Fagin, R., Kumar, R., & Sivakumar, D. (2003). Efficient similarity search and classification via rank aggregation. In *Proceedings of the ACM SIGMOD International Conference on Management of Data*.

Feldman, R. (2006). *Tutorial: Information extraction, theory and practice*. Tutorial presented at the ICML.

Feldman, R., Aumann, Y., Finkelstein-Landau, M., Hurvitz, E., Regev, Y., &and Yaroshevich, A. (2002). A comparative study of information extraction strategies. *ACL 2002*.

Fellbaum, C. (1998). *WordNet: an electronic lexical database*. MIT Press.

Fensel, D. (2004). *Ontologies: A Silver Bullet for Knowledge Management and Electronic Commerce*. Berlin, Germany: Springer.

Fensel, D., Lausen, H., Polleres, A., Brujn, J. D., Stollberg, M., & Roman, D. (2006). *Enabling Semantic Web Services: The Web Service Modeling Ontology*. Springer.

Flater, D. (2004). *Automated composition of conversion software*. Retrieved August 2, 2008, from http://www.mel.nist.gov/msidlibrary/doc/nistir7099.pdf

Format, V. P. (VPF) Overview. (n.d.) Retrieved September 22, 2008, from http://www.nga.mil/portal/site/nga01/index.jsp?epi-content=GENERIC&itemID=a2986591e1b3af00VgnVCMServer23727a95RCRD&beanID=1629630080&viewID=Article

Frank, U. (2006). *Evaluation of reference models*. In P. Fettke, & P. Loos (Eds.), *Reference modeling for business systems analysis* (pp. 118-140). Idea Group.

Galperin, M. Y. (2008). The molecular biology database collection: 2008 update. *Nucleic Acids Research, 36*, D2–D4. doi:10.1093/nar/gkm1037

Gamma, E., Helm, R., Johnson, R., & Vlissides, J. M. (1995). *Design patterns: Elements of reusable object-oriented software*. Boston, MA: Addison Wesley.

Gangemi, A., Guarino, N., Masolo, C., & Oltramari, A. (2001). Understanding top-level ontological distinctions. In *Proceedings of the 2001 ijcai workshop on ontologies and information sharing, Seattle, USA*.

Ganter, B., & Wille, R. (1999). *Formal concept analysis: Mathematical foundations*. Berlin, Germany: Springer.

García, R., & Gil, R. (2007). Facilitating Business Interoperability from the Semantic Web. In W. Abramowicz (Ed.), *Proceedings of the 10th International Conference on Business Information Systems, BIS'07 (LNCS 4439)* (pp. 220-232). Berlin Heidelberg New York: Springer.

Giles, J. (2005). Internet encyclopaedias go head to head. *Nature, 438*(7070), 900–901. doi:10.1038/438900a

Giunchiglia, F. McNeill, F., Yatskevich, M., Pane, J., Besana, P., & Shvaiko, P. (2008a, November). Approximate Structure-Preserving Semantic Matching. In *Proceedings of "ODBASE 2008"*, Monterrey, Mexico.

Giunchiglia, F., & Walsh, T. (1989, August). Abstract theorem proving. In *Proceedings of "11th international joint conference on artificial intelligence (IJCAI'89)* (pp 1372-1377).

Giunchiglia, F., & Walsh, T. (1992). A theory of abstraction. *Artificial Intelligence, 57*(2-3). doi:10.1016/0004-3702(92)90021-O

Giunchiglia, F., Sierra, C., McNeill, F., Osman, N., & Siebes, R. (2008b). Deliverable 4.5: Good Enough Answers Algorithm. *Techincal Report, OpenKnowledge*. Retrieved November 2008 from www.openk.org.

Giunchiglia, F., Yatskevich, M., & McNeill, F. (2007). Structure preserving semantic matching. In *Proceedings of the ISWC+ASWC International workshop on Ontology Matching (OM)* (pp. 13–24).

Giunchiglia, F., Yatskevich, M., & Shvaiko, P. (2007). Semantic matching: Algorithms and implementation. *Journal on Data Semantics, IX*.

Gligorov, R., Aleksovski, Z., ten Kate, W., & van Harmelen, F. (2005). Accurate and efficient html differencing. In *Proceedings of the 13th IEEE International Workshop on Software Technology and Engineering Practice (STEP)* (pp. 163–172). IEEE Press.

Gligorov, R., Aleksovski, Z., ten Kate, W., & van Harmelen, F. (2007). Using google distance to weight approximate ontology matches. In *Proceedings of WWW*.

Glushko, R. J., & McGrath, T. (2002). Document Engineering for e-Business. In *Proceedings of the 2002 ACM Symposium on Document Engineering*, Virginia, USA.

GML 3.1.1 Standard. (n.d.). Retrieved October 10, 2008, from http://www.opengeospatial.org/standards/gml

Goble, C., & Stevens, R. (2008). State of the nation in data integration for bioinformatics. *Journal of Biomedical Informatics, 41*(5), 687–693. doi:10.1016/j.jbi.2008.01.008

Gómez-Péres, A., Fernández-López, M., & Corcho, O. (Eds.). (2004). *Ontological engineering: with examples from the areas of knowledge management, e-commerce and the Semantic Web.* New York, NY: Springer-Verlag.

Gone, M., & Schade, S. (2007). Towards Semantic Composition of Geospatial Web Services – Using WSMO in Comparison to BPEL. In *Proceedings of 5th GI Days – Young Researchers Forum*, ifgi Prints. Münster, Germany.

Goodwin, J. (2005). *Experiences of using OWL at the ordnance survey.* Paper presented at OWL: Experiences and Directions Workshop, Galway, Ireland. Retrieved October 12, 2008 from http://www.mindswap.org/2005/OWLWorkshop/sub17.pdf

Gooneratne, N., & Tari, Z. (2008). Matching independent global constraints for composite web services. In *In Proceedings of WWW* (pp. 765–774).

Gottlob, G., Koch, C., Baumgartner, R., Herzog, M., & Flesca, S. (2004). The lixto data extraction project - back and forth between theory and practice. In *Proc ACM PODS 2004.*

Grau, B. C., Parsia, B., Sirin, E., & Kalyanpur, A. (2005). Modularizing OWL ontologies. In D. Sleeman, H. Alani, C. Brewster, & N. Noy (Eds.), *Proceedings of the 3rd International Conference on Knowledge Capture (K-CAP 2005).* Retrieved November 03, 2008, from http://www.mindswap.org/2004/multipleOnt/papers/modularFinal.pdf

Gruber, T. (1995). Toward principles for the design of ontologies used for knowledge sharing. *Int. J. Hum.-Comput. Stud., 43*(5-6), 928, 907.

Gruber, T. (2007). Collective knowledge systems: Where the Social Web meets the Semantic Web. *Web Semantics: Science . Services and Agents on the World Wide Web, 1*(6), 4–13.

Gruber, T. R. (1993). A translation approach to portable ontology specifications. *Knowledge Acquisition, 5*(2), 199–220. doi:10.1006/knac.1993.1008

Grüninger, M., & Uschold, M. (1996). Ontologies: Principles, methods and applications. *The Knowledge Engineering Review, 1*(2), 93–155.

Gruninger, M. (2003). Ontology of the Process Specification Language. In S. Staab (Ed.), *Handbook of Ontologies and Information Systems (pp.* 599-618). Berlin: Springer-Verlag.

Gruninger, M., & Fox, M. S. (1995). Methodology for the Design and Evaluation of Ontologies. *Workshop on Basic Ontological Issues in Knowledge Sharing.* IJCAI-95, Montreal.

Gruninger, M., & Kopena, J. (2004). Semantic Integration through Invariants. *AI Magazine, 26,* 11–20.

Gruninger, M., & Menzel, C. (2003). Process Specification Language: Principles and Applications. *AI Magazine, 24,* 63–74.

Guarino, N. (1998, June 6-8). Formal ontology and information systems. In N. Guarino (Ed.), *Proceedings of FOIS'98, Trento, Italy,* (pp. 3-15). Amsterdam: IOS Press.

Guarino, N., & Welty, C. A. (2004). An overview of ontoclean. In S. Staab & R. Studer (Eds.), *Handbook on Ontologies* (p. 151-159). Springer Verlag.

Guinchiglia, F., Shvaiko, P., & Yatskevich, M. (2004). S-Match: An algorithm and an implementation of semantic matching. In *Proceedings of 1st European Semantic Web Symposium (ESWS'04),* Crete, Greece, (pp. 61-75).

Haase, P., Ehrig, M., Hotho, A., & Schnizler, B. (2006). Personalized information access in a bibliographic peer-to-peer system. In S. Staab, & H. Stukenschmidt (Eds.), Semantic Web and peer-to-peer (pp. 143-158). Heidelberg: Springer.

Haase, P., Schnizler, B., Broekstra, J., Ehrig, M., van Harmelen, F., & Menken, M. (2004). Bibster – a semantics-based bibliographic peer-to-peer system. *Journal of Web Semantics, 2*(1), 99–103. doi:10.1016/j.websem.2004.09.006

Hakimpour, F. (2003). *Using ontologies to resolve semantic heterogeneity for integrating spatial database schemata.* Ph.D. thesis. Zurich, Switzerland: Zurich University.

Halaschek-Wiener, C., Golbeck, J., Schain, A., Grove, M., Parsia, B., & Hendler, J. (2005). Photostuff - an image annotation tool for the Semantic Web. In *Proceedings of the 4th International Semantic Web Conference poster session.*

Hameed, A., Preece, A., & Sleeman, D. (2004). Ontology reconciliation. In S. Staab (Ed.), *Handbook on ontologies* (pp 231-250). Berlin, Germany: Springer-Verlag.

Handschuh, S., Staab, S., and & Ciravegna, F. (2002). S-CREAM: Semi-automatic CREation of Metadata. *EKAW 2002.*

Hargittai, E. (2002). Second-Level Digital Divide: Differences in People's Online Skills. *First Monday, 7*(4).

He, B., & Chang, K. C. (2003). Statistical schema matching across Web query interfaces. In *Proceedings of SIGMOD Conference* (pp. 217-228).

Hearst, M. A. (1998). Automated discovery of Wordnet relations. In Ch. Fellbaum (Ed.), *WordNet: An electronic lexical database.* Cambridge, PA: MIT Press.

Hepp, M. (2007). Possible ontologies: How reality constrains the development of relevant ontologies. *IEEE Internet Computing, 11*(1), 90–96. doi:10.1109/MIC.2007.20

Hepp, M., & de Bruijn, J. (2007). GenTax: A Generic Methodology for Deriving OWL and RDF-S Ontologies from Hierarchical Classifications, Thesauri, and Inconsistent Taxonomies. In E. Franconi, M. Kifer, & W. May (Eds.), *Proceedings of the 4th European Semantic Web Conference (LNCS 4519)* (pp. 129-144). Berlin Heidelberg New York: Springer.

Hepp, M., Siorpaes, K., & Bachlechner, D. (2006). *Towards the Semantic Web in e-tourism: Lack of semantics or lack of content?* Poster presented at the 3rd Annual European Semantic Web Conference. Budva, Montenegro.

Hepp; M. (2004). *OntoMeter: Metrics for ontologies.* 1st European Semantic Web Symposium (ESWS2004), Heraklion, Greece, May 10-12.

Herbst, U. (2007). *Präferenzmessung in industriellen Verhandlungen.* Wiesbaden, Germany: Universitäts-Verlag.

Hevner, A. R., March, S. T., Park, J., & Ram, S. (2004). Design science research in information systems. *Management Information Systems Quarterly, 28*(1), 75–105.

Hinrichs, H. (2002). *Datenqualitätsmanagement in data warehouse-systemen.* Phd thesis, University of Oldenburg, Germany.

Hirst, A., & Budanitsky, G. (2006). Evaluating Wordnet-based measures of lexical semantic relatedness. [Cambridge, PA: MIT Press.]. *Computational Linguistics, 32*(2), 13–47.

Hoffmann, A. (2006). *Interaktionen zwischen Anbietern und Nachfragern bei der Vermarktung und Beschaffung innovativer Dienstleistungen.* Wiesbaden, Germany: Universitäts-Verlag.

Hoffmann, J., Steinmetz, N., & Fitzner, D. (2008). *2.4 - Semantic Web Geoprocessing Services.* SWING Project Deliverable.

Hong Hai, D. (2006). *Schema matching and mapping-based data integration: Architecture, approaches and evolution.* VDM Verlag Dr. Müller.

Hu, W., & Qu, Y. (2006). Block Matching for Ontologies. In I.F. Cruz, S. Decker, D. Allemang, C. Preist, D. Schwabe, P. Mika, M. Uschold, & L. Aroyo (Eds.), *The Semantic Web - ISWC 2006, 5th International Semantic Web Conference (LNCS 4273)* (pp. 300–313). Berlin Heidelberg New York: Springer.

Hu, W., & Qu, Y. (2006). Block matching for ontologies. In *Proceedings of ISWC.*

Hu, W., Zhao, Y., & Qu, Y. (2006). Partition-based block matching of large class hierarchies. In R. Mizoguchi, Z. Shi, & F. Giunchiglia (Eds.), *Proceedings of the The Semantic Web - ASWC 2006 First Asian Semantic Web Conference (LNCS 4183).* Berlin Heidelberg New York: Springer.

ICC. (2008). *International Chamber of Commerce, INCOTERMS, rules at the core of world trade.* Retrieved

November 10, 2008, from http://www.iccwbo.org/incoterms/id3045/index.html

IEC - International Electrotechnical Commission. (2003). *IEC 61970-301: Energy management system application program interface (EMS-API) – Part 301: Common Information Model (CIM) Base*. International Electrotechnical Commission.

IEEE. Computer Society. (2004). *Guide to the software engineering body of knowledge*. Retrieved February 10, 2009, from http://www.swebok.org/

INCOSE. (2009). *International council on systems engineering (INCOSE), guide to the systems engineering body of knowledge*. Retrieved February 10, 2009, from http://www.incose.org/practice/guidetosebodyofknow.aspx

Isaac, A., Matthezing, H., van der Meij, L., Schlobach, S., Wang, S., & Zinn, C. (2008). Putting ontology alignment in context: usage scenarios, deployment and evaluation in a library case. In *Proceedings of the 5th European Semantic Web Conference (ESWC), Tenerife (ES)* (pp. 402-417).

ISO. (2004). *ISO/IEC Guide 2:2004 Standardization and related activities – General vocabulary* (8th ed.). Geneva, Switzerland: ISO Press.

Ives, Z., Halevy, A., Mork, P., & Tatarinov, I. (2004). Piazza: Mediation and integration infrastructure for Semantic Web data. *Journal of Web Semantics, 1*(2), 155–175. doi:10.1016/j.websem.2003.11.003

Jannach, D. (2006). Techniques for fast query relaxation in content-based recommender systems. In C. Freksa, M. Kohlhase, & K. Schill (Eds.), *Ki 2006 Vol. 4314* (p. 49-63). Springer.

Jayram, T. S., Krishnamurthy, R., Raghavan, S., Vaithyanathan, S., & Zhu, H. (2006). Avatar information extraction system. *A Quarterly Bulletin of the Computer Society of the IEEE Technical Committee on Data Engineering*, 2006.

Jeckle, M., Rupp, C., Hahn, J., Zengler, B., & Queins, S. (2005). *UML 2 glasklar*. Hanser Fachbuchverlag.

Jena Rule Language. (2007). *Jena rule language*. Retrieved August 2008, from [REMOVED HYPERLINK FIELD]http://jena.sourceforge.net/

Johnson, H. L., Cohen, K., B., Baumgartner, W.,A., Jr., Lu, Z., Bada, M., Kester, T., Kim, H., & Hunter, L. (2006). Evaluation of lexical methods for detecting relationships between concepts from multiple ontologies. Pac. Symp. *Biocomputing*, 28-39.

Kahan, J., & Koivunen, M. Prod'Hommeaux, E., & Swick, E. (2001). Annotea: An open RDF infrastructure for shared web Web annotations. *WWW10 Conference, Hong Kong.*

Kalfoglou, Y., & Hu, B. (2005). CMS: CROSI mapping system - results of the 2005 ontology alignment contests. In *Proceedings of the K-Cap'05 Integrating Ontologies workshop,* Alberta, Canada.

Kalfoglou, Y., & Hu, B. (2006). Issues with evaluating and using publicly available ontologies. In *Proceedings of the 4th International EON workshop,* Edinburgh, UK.

Kalfoglou, Y., & Schorlemmer, M. (2003). IF-Map: an ontology mapping method based on information flow theory. *Journal on Data Semantics, I.*

Kalfoglou, Y., & Schorlemmer, M. (2003). Ontology mapping: the state of the art. *The Knowledge Engineering Review, 18*(1), 1–31. doi:10.1017/S0269888903000651

Kalfoglou, Y., & Schorlemmer, M. (2003b). IF-Map: An ontology mapping method based on information flow theory. *Journal on Data Semantics, 1*, 98–127.

Kalfoglou, Y., & Schorlemmer, M. (2005). Ontology mapping: The state of the art. In Y. Kalfoglou, M. Schorlemmer, A.P. Sheth, S. Staab, & M. Uschold, (Eds.), *Semantic Interoperability and Integration: Dagstuhl Seminar Proceedings (No. 04391)* (pp. 1-31)

Kalfoglou, Y., Hu, B., Reynolds, D., & Shadbolt, N. (2005). *CROSI project final report* (Tech. Report E-Print No. 11717). Southampton, UK: University of Southampton.

Kayed, M., Girgis, M. R., & Shaalan, K. F. (2006). A Survey survey of Web information extraction systems.

IEEE Transactions on Knowledge and Data Engineering, 18, 2006.

Keller, U., Lara, R., Lausen, H., Polleres, A., Predoiu, L., & Toma, O. (2005). *Semantic Web service discovery* (Tech. Rep. No. WSMX Deliverable D10). DERI Innsbruck. Retrieved from http://www.wsmo.org/TR/d10/v0.2/

Kersten, G. E., & Lai, H. (2007). Negotiation Support and E-negotiation Systems: An Overview. *Group Decision and Negotiation, 16*, 553–586. doi:10.1007/s10726-007-9095-5

Keßler, C. (2007) Similarity Measurement in Context. In *Proceedings of 6th International and Interdisciplinary Conference on Modeling and Using Context (LNAI 4635)* (pp. 277–290). Berlin Heidelberg, Germany: Springer.

Kim, W., Choi, D. W., & Park, S. (2005). Product Information Meta-search Framework for Electronic Commerce. In A. Gómez-Pérez, & J. Euzenat (Eds.), *Proceedings of the European Semantic Web Conference (ESWC 2005), (LNCS 3532)* (pp. 408–422). Berlin Heidelberg, Germany: Springer.

Kiryakov, A., Popov, B., Terziev, I., Manov, D., & Ognyanoff, D. (2004). Semantic annotation, indexing and retrieval. *Journal of Web Semantics, 2*(1), 49–79. doi:10.1016/j.websem.2004.07.005

Klein, M. (2001). Combining and relating ontologies: an analysis of problems and solutions. In A. Gómez-Pérez, M. Gruninger, & M. Uschold (Eds.), *Proceedings of Workshop on Ontologies and Information Sharing (IJCAI'01)* (pp. 52-63).

Klein, M., Fensel, D., van Harmelen, F., & Horrocks, I. (2001). The Relations Between Ontologies and XML Schema. *Electronic Trans. on Artificial Intelligence, 2001. Special Issue on the 1st International Workshop Semantic Web: Models, Architectures and Management.*

Kleppe, A., Warmer, J., & Bast, W. (2003). *MDA Explained: The Model Driven Architecture(TM): Practice and Promise*. Addison-Wesley Object Technology Series. Addison-Wesley.

Klien, E. (2007). A Rule-Based Strategy for the Semantic Annotation of Geodata. *Transactions in GIS . Special Issue on the Geospatial Semantic Web, 11*(3), 437–452.

Klien, E., Lutz, M., & Kuhn, W. (2005). Ontology-Based Discovery of Geographic Information Services-An Application in Disaster Management. *Computers, Environment and Urban Systems (CEUS).*

Klien, E., Schade, S., & Hoffmann, J. (2007). *3.1 - Ontology Modeling Requirements*. SWING Project Deliverable.

Klusch, M., Fries, B., & Sycara, K. (2006). Automated semantic web service discovery with OWLS- MX. In *Proceedings of AAMAS.*

Klyne, G., Carroll, J., & McBride, B. (2004). *Resource description framework (RDF): Concepts and Abstract Syntax* (W3C Recommendation). W3C. Retrieved from http://www.w3.org/TR/rdf-concepts/

Kopecký, J., Vitvar, T., & Bournez, C., & Joel Farrell. (2007). SAWSDL: Semantic Annotations for WSDL and XML Schema. *IEEE Internet Computing, 11*(6), 60–67. doi:10.1109/MIC.2007.134

Kostic, T., Frei, C., Preiss, O., & Kezunovic, M. (2004). *Scenarios for data exchange using standards IEC 61970 and IEC 61850*. Cigre Paris 2004. IEEE Publishing.

Kotoulas, S., & Siebes, R. (2007). Deliverable 2.2: Adaptive routing in structured peer-to-peer overlays. *Technical report, OpenKnowledge*. Retrieved November 2008 from www.openk.org.

Lakshmanan, L., and & Sadri, F. (1994). Probabilistic deductive databases. *SLP 1994.*

Larson, R. (1996). Geographic Information Retrieval and Spatial Browsing. *GIS and Libraries: Patrons . Maps and Spatial Information, 124*, 81.

Lee, Y., Sayyadian, M., Doan, A., & Rosenthal, A. S. (2007). etuner: tuning schema matching software using synthetic scenarios. *The VLDB Journal, 16*(1), 97–122. doi:10.1007/s00778-006-0024-z

Lehto, L. (2007, May 8-11). Schema translations in a web service based sdi. In M. Wachowicz & L. Bodum (Eds.), *Proceedings of AGILE, Aalborg, Denmark.*

Leitner, F., & Valencia, A. (2008). A text-mining perspective on the requirements for electronically annotated abstracts. The FEBS letters experiment. *FEBS Letters, 582*(8-9), 1178–1181. doi:10.1016/j.febslet.2008.02.072

Lenat, D. (1995). Cyc: A large scale investment in knowledge infrastructure. *Communications of the ACM, 38*, 11.

Li, L., & Horrocks, I. (2003). *A software framework for matchmaking based on Semantic Web technology.* In *Proceedings of the World-Wide Web conference.* Budapest, Hungary.

Libes, D., Barkmeyer, E. J., Denno, P., Flater, D., Steves, M. P., Wallace, E., & Feeny, A. B. (2004). *The AMIS approach to systems integration* (NISTIR 7101). Retrieved August 2, 2008, from http://www.mel.nist.gov/msidlibrary/doc/nistir7101.pdf

Linden, G., Hanks, S., & Lesh, N. (1997). Interactive assessment of user preference models: The automated travel assistant. In C. P. A. Jameson & C. Tasso (Eds.), In *User Modeling: Proceedings of the Sixth International Conference* (pp. 67-78). Springer Wien.

Linthicum, D. S. (1999). *Enterprise Application Integration.* Toronto, Canada: Addison-Wesley Professional.

Loeser, A., Barczyński, W., & Brauer, F. (2008). What's the intention behind your query? A few observations from a large developer community. In *Proceeding of the IRSW.*

Longley, P., Goodchild, M., Maguire, D., & Rhind, D. (2005). *Geographic Information Systems and Science.* John Wiley & Sons.

Lopez, V., Sabou, M., & Motta, E. (2006). PowerMap: Mapping the Real Semantic Web on the Fly. In *Proceedings of 5th International Semantic Web Conference (ISWC-2005) (LNCS 4273)* (pp. 414–427). Berlin Heidelberg, Germany: Springer.

Lozano-Tello, A., & Gomez-Perez, A. (2004). ONTOMETRIC: A method to choose the appropriate ontology. *Journal of Database Management, 15*(2), 1–18.

Lutz, M. (2007). Ontology-Based Descriptions for Semantic Discovery and Composition of Geoprocessing Services. *GeoInformatica, 11*(1), 36, 1.

Lutz, M., & Klien, E. (2006). Ontology-based retrieval of geographic information. *International Journal of Geographical Information Science, 20*(3), 260, 233.

Madhavan, J., Bernstein, P. A., Kuang, C., Halevy, A., & Shenoy, P. (2003). Corpus-based schema matching. In *Proceedings of the IJCAI'03 Workshop on Information Integration on the Web (IIWeb-03),* Acapulco, Mexico.

Madhavan, J., Bernstein, P., Chen, K., Halevy, A., & Shenoy, P. (2005). Corpus-based schema matching. In *21st International Conference on Data Engineering Proceedings* (pp. 57-68).Tokyo, Japan. PA: IEEE Computer Society.

Maedche, A., & Staab, S. (2000). Discovering conceptual relations from text. In W., Horn (Ed.), *Proceedings of the 14th European Conference on Artificial Intelligence* (pp. 321-325). Amsterdam, PA: IOS Press.

Maedche, A., & Staab, S. (2002). Applying Semantic Web technologies for tourism information systems. In K. Wöber, A. Frew, & M. Hitz (Eds.), *Proceedings of the 9th international conference for information and communication technologies in tourism, enter 2002.* Springer.

Magnini, B., Speranza, M., & Girardi, C. (2004). A Semantic-based Approach to Interoperability of Classification Hierarchies: Evaluation of Linguistic Techniques. In *20th International Conference on Computational Linguistics* (p. 1133). Geneva, Switzerland. PA: Association for Computational Linguistics. Falconer, S., M., Noy, N., & Storey, M.A.D. (2006). Towards understanding the needs of cognitive support for ontology mapping. In P. Shvaiko, J. Euzenat, N.F. Noy, & H. Stuckenschmidt (Eds.), *Proceedings of the ISWC'06 International Workshop OM-2006* (Vol. 225). Athens, Georgia. PA: CEUR-WS.org

Manning, C. D., Raghavan, P., & Schütze, H. (2008). *Introduction to information retrieval*. Cambridge, UK: Cambridge University Press.

Masolo, C., Borgo, S., Gangemi, A., Guarino, N., Oltramari, A., & Schneider, L. (2002). *Wonderweb deliverable d17. the wonderweb library of foundational ontologies and the dolce ontology* (Tech. Rep.). ISTC-CNR.

Masolo, C., Vieu, L., Bottazzi, E., Catenacci, C., Ferrario, R., Gangemi, A., & Guarino, N. (2004). Social roles and their descriptions. In D. Dubois, C. Welty, & M.A. Williams (Eds.), *Proceedings of the Ninth International Conference on the Principles of Knowledge Representation and Reasoning* (pp. 267-277), Whistler, Canada.

Maué, P. (2007, September 26-28). Collaborative metadata for geographic information. In *Proceedings of the 1st Conference on Social Semantic Web, Leipzig, Germany.* CEUR Proceedings, ISSN 1613-0073, online CEUR-WS.org/Vol-301/Paper_7_Maue.pdf.

Mbanefo, O. (2006). *Comparaison expérimentale d'algorithmes d'alignement d'ontologies*. Unpublished TER manuscript. Grenoble (FR): Université Joseph Fourier.

McAvoy, G. E. (1999). *Controlling Technocracy: Citizen Rationality and the Nimby Syndrome (American Governance and Public Policy)*. Georgetown University Press.

McGuiness, D. L. (2003). Ontologies Come of Age. In D. Fensel, J. Hendler, H. Lieberman, & W. Wahlster (Eds.), *Spinning the Semantic Web: Bringing the World Wide Web to Its Full Potential* (pp. 171-193). Cambridge, USA: MIT Press.

McGuinness, D., Fikes, R., Rice, J., & Wilder, S. (2000). The chimaera ontology environment. In *Proceedings of the Seventeenth National Conference on Artificial Intelligence and Twelfth Conference on Innovative Applications of Artificial Intelligence* (pp. 1123-1124.) PA: AAAI Press / The MIT Press.

Melnik, S., Garcia-Molina, H., & Rahm, E. (2002). Similarity flooding: A versatile graph matching algorithm and its application to schema matching. In *18th International Conference on Data Engineering* (pp. 117-128).

Melnik, S., Garcia-Molina, H., & Rahm, E. (2002). Similarity flooding: A versatile graph matching algorithm and its application to schema matching. In *Proceedings of the 18th International Conference on Data Engineering (ICDE)* (pp. 117-128).

MetCapp Utilities Manual. (1994).*The Institute of Advanced Manufacturing Sciences.* Cincinnati, Ohio. SAP Library. Retrieved on November 17, 2008 from http://help.sap.com/saphelp_erp60_sp/helpdata/en/e1/8e5134 1a06084de10000009b38f83b/frameset.htm

Michelson, M., & and Knoblock, C. (2005). Semantic annotation of unstructured and ungrammatical text. *IJCAI, 2005.*

Mika, P. (2006). *Social Networks and the Semantic Web.* New York: Springer.

Miletic, I., Vujasinovic, M., Ivezic, N., & Marjanovic, Z. (2007). Enabling semantic mediation for business applications: XML-RDF, RDF-XML, and XSD-RDFS transformation. In R. J. Goncalves (Ed.), *Enterprise interoperability II, new challenges and approaches* (pp. 483-494). Berlin, Germany: Springer-Verlag.

Miller, G. A. (1990). WORDNET: An online lexical database. *International Journal of Lexicography, 3*(4), 235–312. doi:10.1093/ijl/3.4.235

Milo, T., & Zohar, S. (1998). Using schema matching to simplify heterogeneous data translation. In *Proceedings of the 24rd International Conference on Very Large Data Bases (VLDB'98),* New York, NY, USA (pp. 122-133).

Mirzadeh, N., Ricci, F., & Bansal, M. (2004). Supporting user query relaxation in a recommender system. In K. Bauknecht, M. Bichler, & B. Pröll (Eds.), *Ec-web Vol. 3182* (p. 31-40). Springer.

Missikoff, M. (2000). *OPAL a knowledge based approach for the analysis of complex business systems* (Internal report). Laboratory of Enterprise Knowledge and Systems, IASI-CNR, Rome.

Missikoff, M., & Taglino, F. (2007). *athena document D.A3.1 - part 3, the ATHOS user manual* Retrieved February 2, 2009, from http://www.athena-ip.org

Mochol, M., Jentzsch, A., & Euzenat, J. (2006). Applying an analytic method for matching approach selection. In P. Shvaiko, J. Euzenat, N. Noy, H. Stuckenschmidt, V.R. Benjamins, & M. Uschold (Eds.), *Proceedings of the 1st International Workshop on Ontology Matching (OM-2006) Collocated with the 5th International Semantic Web Conference (ISWC-2006). CEUR Workshop Proceedings* (Vol. 225) (pp. 37-48). CEUR-WS.org.

MUC. (1995). *Proceedings of the 6th message Understanding Conference, MUC-6*, Columbia, MD, 1995.

Nau, D. Muñoz-Avila, H., Cao, Y., Lotem, A., & Mitchell, S. (2001). Total-order planning with partially ordered subtasks. In B. Nebel (Ed.), *Proceedings of the International Joint Conference on Artificial Intelligence (IJCAI-2001)*. New York: Morgan Kaufmann.

Naughton, M., Kushmerick, N., & Carthy, J. (2006). Clustering sentences for discovering events in news articles. *ECIR, 2006.*

Naumann, F. (2002). *Quality-driven query answering for integrated information systems* (LNCS 2261). Berlin, Germany: Springer-Verlag Inc.

Nebert, D. (2004). *Developing Spatial Data Infrastructures: The SDI Cookbook.* GSDI.

Nejdl, W., Wolf, B., Qu, C., Decker, S., Sintek, M., Naeve, A., et al. (2002). Edutella: A P2P Networking Infrastructure Based on RDF. In *Proceedings of the 11th Worldwide web conference, Honolulu (HA US)* (pp. 604-615).

Nilsson, U., & Maluszynski, J. (1995). *Logic, Programming and Prolog.* John Wiley & Sons Inc.

Noia, T. D., Sciascio, E. D., & Donini, F. M. (2007). Semantic matchmaking as non-monotonic reasoning: A description logic approach. *Journal of Artificial Intelligence Research, 29*, 269–307.

Noy, F. N., & Musen, M. (2002). PROMPTDIFF: A fixed-point algorithm for comparing ontology versions. In *Proceedings of the 18th National Conference on Artificial Intelligence, (AAAI'02),* Edmonton, Alberta, Canada (pp. 744-751).

Noy, N. (2004). Semantic Integration: A Survey of Ontology-Based Approaches. *SIGMOD Record, 33*, 65–70. doi:10.1145/1041410.1041421

Noy, N. (2004). Tools for mapping and merging ontologies: In Staab, S & Studer, R, (Eds.). *Handbook on Ontologies* (pp. 365-384). Springer-Verlag.

Noy, N., & Klein, M. (2004). Ontology evolution: Not the same as schema evolution. *Knowledge and Information Systems, 6*(4), 428–440. doi:10.1007/s10115-003-0137-2

Noy, N., & Musen, M. (2000). PROMPT: Algorithm and tool for automated ontology merging and alignment. Artificial Intelligence. In *Proceedings of the Seventeenth National Conference on Artificial Intelligence* Austin, TX. PA: AAAI Press.

Noy, N., & Musen, M. (2001). Anchor-PROMPT: Using non-local context for semantic matching. In *Proceeding IJCAI 2001 workshop on ontology and information sharing* (pp. 63-70). Washington, USA. PA: AAAI Press.

Noy, N., & Musen, M. (2003). The PROMPT suite: Interactive tools for ontology merging and mapping. *International Journal of Human-Computer Studies, 59*(6), 983–1024. doi:10.1016/j.ijhcs.2003.08.002

Noy, N., Sintek, M., Decker, S., Crubezy, M., Fergeson, W., & Musen, M. (2001). Creating Semantic Web contents with Protege-2000. *IEEE Intelligent Systems, 16*(2), 60–71. doi:10.1109/5254.920601

O'Hara, K., & Shadbolt, N. (2001). Issues for an ontology for knowledge valuation. In *Proceedings of the IJCAI'01 workshop on E-Business and the Intelligent Web,* Seattle, WA, USA.

Oaks, S., Travaset, B., & Gong, L. (2002). JXTA in a nutshell. Sebastopol, CA: O'Reilly.

OASIS. (2001). *Organization for the advancement of structured information systems (OASIS) ebXML business process specification schema version 1.01.* Retrieved

February 7, 2009, from http://www.ebxml.org/specs/ebBPSS.pdf

OASIS. (2002). *Organization for the advancement of structured information standards. Message service specification version 2.0.* Retrieved February 9, 2009, from http://www.ebxml.org/specs/ebMS2.pdf

Object Management Group (OMG). (2004). *UML 2.0 Superstructure Specification.* Framingham, Massachusetts.

Object Management Group. (2009). *Meta object facility (MOF) 2.0 query/view/transformation, V1.0.* Retrieved February 9, 2009, from http://www.omg.org/spec/QVT/1.0/

OFFIS. (2008). *Ontologies for the utility domain.* Retrieved from http://www.offis.de/energie/ontologies

Ogden, C., & Richards, I. (1923). *The meaning of meaning: A study of the influence of language upon thought and of the science of symbolism.* San Diego, CA: Harcourt Brace Jovanovich.

Omelayenko, B. (2001). Preliminary Ontology Modeling for B2B Content Integration. In *Proceedings of the First International Workshop on Electronic Business Hubs at the Twelfth International Conference on Database and Expert Systems Applications (DEXA-2001)* (pp. 7-13). Washington, D.C., USA: IEEE Computer Society.

Omelayenko, B. (2002). Ontology Mediated Business Integration. In *Proceedings of the 13th EKAW 2002 Conference (LNAI 2473)* (pp. 264-269). Berlin Heidelberg, Germany: Springer.

Open Applications Group. (2003). *Open application group.* Retrieved February 1, 2009, from http://www.openapplications.org

Open Group. (2007). *The UDEF. The Universal Data Element Framework.* Retrieved August 30, 2008, from http://www.opengroup.org/udef

Ordnance Survey Ontologies. (n.d.). Retrieved June 17, 2008, from http://www.ordnancesurvey.co.uk/oswebsite/ontology/

Oundhakar, S., Verma, K., Sivashanugam, K., Sheth, A., & Miller, J. (2005). Discovery of web services in a multi-ontology and federated registry environment. *Journal of Web Services Research, 2*(3).

Palopoli, L., Terracina, G., & Ursino, D. (2003). DIKE: A system supporting the semi-automatic construction of cooperative information systems from heterogeneous databases. *Software. Practice, 33*(9), 847–884.

Pang, B., Lee, L., & Vaithyanathan, S. (2002). Thumbs up? Sentiment classification using machine learning techniques. In *Proceedings of EMNLP.*

Paolucci, M., Kawamura, T., Payne, T. R., & Sycara, K. P. (2002). Semantic matching of Web services capabilities. *The Semantic Web — ISWC 2002 Vol. 2342* (pp. 333-347). Springer.

Paulheim, H., Rebstock, M., & Fengel, J. (2007). Context-Sensitive Referencing for Ontology Mapping Disambiguation. In P. Bouquet, J. Euzenat, C. Ghiaini, D.L. McGuinness, V. Paiva, de, L. Serafini, P. Shvaiko, & H. Wache (Eds.), *Proceedings of the 2007 Workshop on Contexts and Ontologies: Reasoning and Representation (C&O:RR-2007)* (Computer Science Research Report No. 15) (pp. 47-56). Roskilde, Denmark: Roskilde University.

Paulheim. H. (2008). On Applying Matching Tools to Large-Scale Ontologies. *Third International Workshop On Ontology Matching (OM-2008) Collocated with the 7th International Semantic Web Conference (ISWC-2008).* Retrieved November 03, 2008, from www.dit.unitn.it/~p2p/OM-2008/om2008_poster1.pdf

Portolés-Rodríguez, D., Álvarez, P., & Muro-Medrano, P. (2005). IDEZar: An example of user needs, technological aspects and the institutional framework of a local SDI. In *Ec gi and gis workshop, esdi setting the framework.*

Process Specification Language. (2003) Retrieved February 3, 2009, from http://www.mel.nist.gov/psl/

Prud'hommeaux, E., & Seaborne, A. (2008). *SPARQL query language for RDF* (W3C Recommendation). W3C. Retrieved from http://www.w3.org/TR/rdf-sparql-query/

Prud'hommeaux, E., & Seaborne, A. (2008). *SPARQL query language for RDF.* W3C Recommendation.

Rahm, A., & Bernstein, A. (2001). A survey of approaches to automatic schema matching. *The Very Large Databases Journal, 10*(4), 334–350. doi:10.1007/s007780100057

Rebstock, M., & Fengel, J. (2003). Integrierte elektronische Verhandlungsprozesse auf Basis von ebXML und Web-Services. *HMD Praxis der Wirtschaftsinformatik, 234*(40), 52–60.

Rebstock, M., Fengel, J., & Paulheim, H. (2007). Context-sensitive Semantic Synchronization in Electronic Negotiations. In G.E. Kersten, J. Rios, & E. Chen, (Eds.), *Proceedings of Group Decision and Negotiation (GDN)* (Vol. 2). Montreal, Canada: Interneg Research Center, Concordia University, Montreal.

Rebstock, M., Fengel, J., & Paulheim, H. (2008). *Ontologies-based Business Integration.* Berlin Heidelberg, Germany: Springer.

Resnick, P., & Zeckhauser, R. (2002). Trust among strangers in Internet transactions: Empirical analysis of eBay's reputation system. *Advances in Applied Mircroelectronics, 11.*

Ricci, F. (2002). Travel recommender systems. *IEEE Intelligent Systems*, (November-December): 55–57.

Robertson, D. (2004). A lightweight coordination calculus for agent systems. In Declarative Agent Languages and Technologies (pp. 183–197).

Robertson, G., Czerwinski, M. P., & Churchill, J. E. (2005). Visualization of mappings between schemas. In *Proceedings SIGCHI Conference on Human factors in Computing Systems* (pp. 431-439).

Robinson, G. (2002). Key standards for utility enterprise application integration (EAI). In *Proceedings of the DistribuTech 2002 Miami.* Pennwell.

Roman, D., & Klien, E. (2007). SWING - A Semantic Framework for Geospatial Services. In *The Geospatial Web: How Geobrowsers, Social Software and the Web 2.0 are Shaping the Network Society.* Springer.

Roman, D., Kifer, M., & Fensel, D. (2008). WSMO Choreography: From Abstract State Machines to Concurrent Transaction Logic. In *Proceedings of 5th European Semantic Web Conference (ESWC2008).*

Rosse, C., & Mejino, J., L. (2003). A reference ontology for bioinformatics: the foundational model of anatomy. *Journal of Biomedical Informatics*, (36): 478–500. doi:10.1016/j.jbi.2003.11.007

Rousset, M.-C., Adjiman, P., Chatalic, P., Goasdoué, F., & Simon, L. (2006). Somewhere in the semantic web. In *Proceedings 32nd International Conference on Current Trends in Theory and Practice of Computer Science (SofSem), Merin (CZ)* (LNCS 3831, pp. 84-99).

Saeed, J. (2003). *Semantics (Introducing Linguistics).* Wiley-Blackwell.

Saeki, M., & Kaiya, H. (2006). On Relationships among Models, Meta Models and Ontologies. *Presented at 6th OOPSLA Workshop on Domain-Specific Modeling,* Portland, Oregon, USA.

Schade, S., Kien, E., Maué, P., Fitzner, D., & Kuhn, W. (2008). *Report on Modeling Approach and Guideline.* SWING Project Deliverable.

Scheduler, I. L. O. G. 6.3 Reference Manual, ILOG, Inc. (2008).

Schlenoff, C., Gruninger, M., & Ciocoiu, M. (1999, December). The essence of the Process Specification Language. *Transactions of the Society for Computer Simulation, 16*(4), 204–216.

Schlicht, A., & Stuckenschmidt, H. (2008). Towards Distributed Ontology Reasoning for the Web. In *Proceedings of the IEEE/WIC/ACM International Conference on Web Intelligence.* Retrieved 30. January, 2008 from http://ki.informatik.uni-mannheim.de/fileadmin/publication/Schlicht08DistributedOntologyReasoning.pdf

Schumacher, K., Sintek, M., & Sauermann, L. (2008). Combining metadata and document search with spreading activation for semantic desktop search. In *Proceedings 5th European Semantic Web Conference (ESWC), Tenerife (ES)* (pp. 569-583).

Server Overview, F. M. E. (n.d.). Retrieved August 15, 2008, from http://www.safe.com/products/server/overview.php

Shadbolt, N., O'Hara, K., & Crow, L. (1999). The experimental evaluation of knowledge acquisition techniques and methods: History, problems, and new directions. *International Journal of Human-Computer Studies*, *51*, 729–755. doi:10.1006/ijhc.1999.0327

Sharma, A. (2006). Lightweight synchronization of ontologies. Unpublished Master's thesis. Aachen (DE): RWTH.

Shasha, D., & Zhang, K. (1997). Approximate tree pattern matching. In *Pattern Matching Algorithms* (pp. 341–371). Oxford University Press.

Shen, W., Doan, A., Naughton, J., & Ramakrishnan, R. (2007). Declarative information extraction using datalog with embedded extraction predicates. In *Proc ACM SIGMOD 2007.*

Shneiderman, B. (2001). Design: CUU: bridging the digital divide with universal usability. *interactions, 8*(2), 15, 11.

Shvaiko (2006). *An API for ontology alignment* (Version 2.1).

Shvaiko, P., & Euzenat, J. (2005). A survey of schema-based matching approaches. *Journal on Data Semantics,* (4), 146-171.

Smith, B. (2004). Beyond concepts: Ontology as reality representation. In *Proceedings of the International Conference on Formal Ontology and Information Systems (FOIS 2004),* Turin.

Smith, M. K., Welty, C., & McGuiness, D. (2004). *OWL Web Ontology Language Guide W3C Recommendation 10 February 2004*. Retrieved July 10, 2008, from http://www.w3.org/TR/owl-guide/

Sonntag, D. (2007). Embedded Distributed Text Mining and Semantic Web Technology. In *Proceedings of the NATO Advanced Study Institute Workshop on Mining Massive Data Sets for Security.* PA: NATO Publishing.

Sonntag, D. (2008). Towards dialogue-based interactive semantic mediation in the medical domain. In *Proceedings Third International Workshop on Ontology Matching (OM-2008) collocated with the 7th International Semantic Web Conference.* Karlsruhe, Germany. PA: CEUR-WS.org

Sonntag, D., Engel, R., Herzog, G., Pfalzgraf, A., Pfleger, N., Romanelli, M., & Reithinger, N. (2007). SmartWeb Handheld. Multimodal interaction with ontological knowledge bases and semantic web services (extended version). In T. Huang, A. Nijholt, M. Pantic, & A. Plentland, (Eds.), *LNAI Special Volume on Human Computing* (Vol. 4451). Berlin, Heidelberg, PA: Springer Verlag.

Staab, S., & Stukenschmidt, H. (2006). *Semantic Web and peer-to-peer.* Heidelberg: Springer.

Staab, S., Studer, R., Schnurr, H. P., & Sure, Y. (2001). Knowledge Processes and Ontologies. *IEEE Intelligent Systems, 1*(16), 26–34. doi:10.1109/5254.912382

StanfordParser. (2008). WebRetrieved from: http://www-nlp.stanford.edu/downloads/lex-parser.shtmlhttp://www-nlp.stanford.edu/downloads/lex-parser.shtml

Starbucks, W. H. (1993). "Watch where you step!" or Indian starbuck amid the perils of academe (Rated PG). In A.G. Bedeion (Ed.), *Management Laureates* (Vol. 3) (pp. 65-110).

Steels, L., & Kaplan, F. (1999). Bootstrapping grounded word semantics. In T. Briscoe (Ed.), *Linguistic evolution through language acquisition: Formal and computational models.* Cambridge, UK: Cambridge University Press.

Stonebraker, M., & Hellerstein, J. M. (2001). Content Integration for EBusiness. Proceedings of the 2001 ACM SIGMOD International Conference on Management of Data. *SIGMOD '01 30*(2), 552-560.

Straccia, U., & Troncy, R. (2005). oMAP: Combining classifiers for aligning automatically OWL ontologies. In *Proceedings of WISE.*

Stuckenschmidt, H., & Klein, M. (2004). Structure-based partitioning of large concept hierarchies. In S.A. McIlraith, D. Plexousakis, & F. van Harmelen (Eds.),

Proceedings of the Third International Semantic Web Conference (ISWC-2004) (LNCS 3298) (pp. 289-303). Berlin Heidelberg New York: Springer.

Stuckenschmidt, H., & van Harmelen, F. (2005). *Information Sharing on the Semantic Web.* Berlin Heidelberg New York: Springer.

Sure, Y., Maedche, A., & Staab, S. (2000). Leveraging corporate skill knowledge - from ProPer to OntoProPer. In *Proceedings of the 3rd International Conference on Practical Aspects of Knowledge Management (PAKM2000),* Basel, Switzerland.

Tai, K.-C. (1979). The tree-to-tree correction problem. *Journal of the ACM, 26*(3). doi:10.1145/322139.322143

Tang, J., Li, J., Liang, B., Huang, X., Li, Y., & Wang, K. (2006). Using Bayesian decision for ontology mapping. *Journal of Web Semantics, 4*(1).

Tertre, F., Bercker, J., & Lips, A. (2007). *Use Case Definition and I&T Requirements.* SWING Project Deliverable.

Tertre, F., Langlois, J., & Urvois, M. (2008). *Use Case 3.* SWING Project Deliverable.

TIES. 2008. (n.d.). *TIES: Trainable Information Extraction System.* Retrieved from http://tcc.itc.it/research/textec/tools-resources/ties.htmlhttp://tcc.itc.it/research/textec/tools-resources/ties.html

Ullman, J. (1996). The Database Approach to Knowledge Representation. AAAI Press, MIT Press.

Ullman, J., & Widom, J. (2007). *A first course in database systems.* Prentice Hall, 2007.

Ullman, J.D. (1988). Bottom-up beats top-down for datalog. *ACM PODS 1988.*

UN/CEFACT. (2009). *United Nations directories for electronic data interchange for administration, commerce and trade.* Retrieved February 9, 2009, from http://www.unece.org/trade/untdid/welcome.htm

Urvois, M. (2008). *D1.3 - SWING Experience Report.* SWING Project Deliverable.

Uschold, M. (2003). Where are the semantics in the Semantic Web? *AI Magazine, 24*(3), 25–36.

Uschold, M., & Grüninger, M. (1996). Ontologies: principles, methods, and applications. *The Knowledge Engineering Review, 11*(2), 93–155. doi:10.1017/S0269888900007797

Uschold, M., & Gruninger, M. (2004). Ontologies and Semantics for Seamless Connectivity. *SIGMOD Record, 33*(4), 58–64. doi:10.1145/1041410.1041420

Uschold, M., & Jasper, R. (1999). A framework for understanding and classifying ontology applications. In *Proceedings of the IJCAI-99 Workshop on Ontologies and Problem-Solving Methods (KRR5),* Stockholm, Sweden.

Uschold, M., & Menzel, C. (2005). *Semantic Integration & Interoperability Using RDF and OWL W3C Editor's Draft 3 November 2005.* Retrieved, 02. February 2008 from http://www.w3.org/2001/sw/BestPractices/OEP/SemInt/

Uschold, M., King, M., Moralee, S., & Zorgios, Y. (1998). The Enterprise Ontology. *The Knowledge Engineering Review,* 13.

Uslar, M. (2006). The common information model for utilities: An introduction and outlook on future applications. In R. Eckstein & R. Tolksdorf (Eds.), *Proceedings of the XML-Days 2006 in Berlin, XML-clearinghouse.de* (pp.135-148).

Uslar, M. (2008). Ontology-based Integration of IEC TC 57 Standards. In *Proceedings of the I-ESA 2008 Conference on Interoperability for Enterprise Systems and Applications, Fraunhofer IPK, Berlin.*

Uslar, M., & Dahlem, N. (2006). Semantic Web technologies for power grid management. In R. Koschke, O. Herzog, K.-H. Rödiger & M. Ronthaler (Eds.), *Informatik 2007: Informatik trifft Logistik, Band 1, Beiträge der 37. Jahrestagung der Gesellschaft für Informatik e.V. (GI) 24.-27. September 2007.* In Bremen, 27(1), Gesellschaft für Informatik, Bonn, Köllen Verlag.

Uslar, M., et al. (2009). Untersuchung des Normungsumfeldes zum BMWi-Förderschwerpunkt. *e-Energy – IKT-basiertes Energiesystem der Zukunft.* Ministry of Economics, Germany.

Uslar, Streekmann & Abels (2007). MDA-basierte Kopplung heterogener Informationssysteme im EVU-Sektor - ein Framework. In A. Oberweis, C. Weinhardt, H. Gimpel, A. Koschmider & V. Pankratius (Eds.), *eOrganisation: Service-, Prozess-, Market-Engineering,* 8. Internationale Tagung Wirtschaftsinformatik, 2, Universitätsverlag Karlsruhe.

van der Aalst, W. M. P., & ter Hofstede, A. H. M. (2005). YAWL: Yet Another Workflow Language. *Information Systems, 30*(4), 245–275. doi:10.1016/j.is.2004.02.002

Vintar, Š., Todorovski, L., Sonntag, D., & Buitelaar, P. (2003). Evaluating context features for medical relation nining. In *Proceedings Workshop on Data Mining and Text Mining for Bioinformatics at the 14th European Conference on Machine Learning.* Berlin, Heidelberg: Springer Verlag.

Wang, J. T.-L., Zhang, K., Jeong, K., & Shasha, D. (1994). A system for approximate tree matching. *IEEE Transactions on Knowledge and Data Engineering, 6*(4), 559–571. doi:10.1109/69.298173

Weber, N., & Buitelaar, P. (2006). Web-based otnology learning with ISOLDE. In *Proceedings of the Workshop on Web Content mining with Human Language, International Semantic Web Conference (ISWC'06),* Athens, USA.

Wenger, E. (1998). *Communities of practice: The key to knowledge strategy.* Cambridge, UK: Cambridge University Press.

Wennerberg, P. O., Buitelaar, P., & Zillner, S. (2008a). Towards a human anatomy data set for query pattern mining based on wikipedia and domain semantic resources. *In Proceedings Workshop on Building and Evaluating Resources for Biomedical Text Mining at LREC.* Marakesch. PA:ELDA.

Wennerberg, P., Zillner, S., Moeller, M., Buitelaar, P., & Sintek, M. (2008b). KEMM: A knowledge engineering methodology in the medical domain. In C. Eschenbach & M. Grüninger (Eds.), *Proceedings 5th international conference on formal ontology in information Systems (FOIS).* PA: IOS Press.

Wigand, R. T., Picot, A., & Reichwald, R. (1997). *Information, organization and management: expanding markets and corporate boundaries.* Chichester, UK: Wiley.

Wilks, Y., Webb, N., Setzer, A., Hepple, M., & Capitzone, R. (2005). Machine learning approaches to human dialogue modelling. In *Advances in natural multimodal dialogue systems.* Amsterdam: Kluwer Academic Publishers.

Willett, J. C. (2006). *2006 Minerals Yearbook - Stone, Crushed.* U.S. Geological Survey.

World Wide Web Consortium. (2000). *Simple object access protocol, (SOAP) 1.1.* Retrieved February 9, 2009, from http://www.w3.org/TR/2000/NOTE-SOAP-20000508/

World Wide Web Consortium. (2004). *RDF vocabulary description language 1.0: RDF schema.* Retrieved August 2008, from http://www.w3.org/TR/rdf-schema/

Wu, F., & Weld, D. (2008). Automatically refining the Wikipedia infobox ontology. In *Proceedings of the 17th International Conference on World Wide Web* (pp. 635-644).

Zaihrayeu, I. (2006). *Towards peer-to-peer information management systems.* PhD thesis. Trento, IT: University of Trento.

Zelewski, S. (1999). *Ontologien zur Strukturierung von Domänenwissen Ein Annäherungsversuch aus betriebswirtschaftlicher Perspektive* (Tech. Report No. 3). Essen, Germany: University of GH Essen.

Zhdanova, A. V., & Shvaiko, P. (2006). Community-driven ontology matching. In Y. Sure, & J. Domingue (Eds.), *The Semantic Web: Research and Applications, Proceedings of the European Semantic Web Conference (ESWC-2006), (LNCS 4011)* (pp. 34–49). Berlin Heidelberg, Germany: Springer.

Zhdanova, A., de Bruijn, J., Zimmermann, K., & Scharffe, F. (2004). *Ontology Alignment Solution v2.0.* (EU IST Esperonto project deliverable (D1.4 V2.0). Retrieved May 30, 2005, from http://www.deri.at/fileadmin/documents/deliverables/Esperonto/Del1.4-V2.0-final.pdf

About the Contributors

Yannis Kalfoglou is a Technology Innovation Consultant with RICOH Europe Plc, and a Visiting Senior Research Fellow with the University of Southampton. He has published extensively in the field of semantic interoperability and integration and he is a pioneer in ontology mapping technology. He holds a PhD in Artificial Intelligence from the University of Edinburgh and several years post doctoral experience in the field of Artificial Intelligence, Knowledge Engineering and Management and the Semantic Web. He participated in national and international funding programmes on the use of AI technologies on the Web. He led industrially funded projects on the provision of services in the field of semantic interoperability. He participates in several programme committees for national and international research consortia and he has consulted venture capitalist funds on the use of semantic technologies.

* * *

Naveen Ashish is a Senior Computer Scientist with Calit2 at UC-Irvine. His research interests and expertise are in areas such as information integration, semantic-web, information extraction, ontologies, and semi-structured data management and he has authored many highly cited publications in these areas. He received a PhD in Computer Science from the University of Southern California, Los Angeles in 2000, and a BTech in Computer Science from IIT, Kanpur, India in 1993. Prior to UC-Irvine, he worked at NASA Ames Research Center. He is a founding member of the UCI Center for Biomedical Informatics.

Wojciech Michał Barczyński is a PhD candidate at SAP Research where he is a member of the Data Management & Analytics team. He started his PhD at Hasso-Plattner-Institut in Potsdam, in the field of Unstructured Data Management with the focus on providing "explain why" for Information Extraction systems. His interests are: Information Extraction, Semantic Technologies, Data Mining, and application of these technologies in the context of Business Intelligence. Since 2008, he is a member of OKKAM project – a large European project about providing unique identifiers for entities. He is working on two SAP use cases: Community Self Support and Business Intelligence over unstructured data. Wojciech received M. Sc. (polish "mgr inż.") in computer science in 2006 from the Wroclaw University of Technology on Electronic Faculty with specialization in Data Processing Engineering.

Ed Barkmeyer has an M.S. degree in Applied Mathematics and forty years' experience in the computer sciences, covering a wide range of topics, including compilers, operating systems, database systems, communications, systems simulation and real-time control. Since 1981, Mr. Barkmeyer has been involved in manufacturing systems integration activities at NIST, as a principal architect and implementor of distributed systems, and as a principal analyst in information interchange among manufacturing software systems - engineering, planning, control, and supply-chain operations. He is currently working in automating software integration processes using systems engineering and artificial intelligence methods. Mr. Barkmeyer represents NIST on national and international standards bodies in the areas of interface specification, information modeling, process modeling and data interchange.

Diego Berrueta Muñoz holds a MSc in Computer Science by the University of Oviedo. He was awarded with two intermediate and two final awards to the best qualifications. At the present moment, he studies for his PhD degree at the same university. He coordinates the Semantic Web Unit at the CTIC Foundation R&D department, where he is involved in national and European research projects. As part of his participation in the Semantic Web Deployment Working Group at W3C, he has edited a W3C Technical Report and reviewed the RDFa specifications.

Paolo Besana is a post doctoral researcher at the University of Edinburgh. He is currently working on Safe and Sound project funded by EPSRC and in collaboration with Cancer Research UK, aiming at creating a distributed approach to medical decision support systems. Previously he worked in the EU-funded OpenKnowledge project, whose target was the dynamic integration of the components and services in open, peer-to-peer systems. He holds a degree in Telecommunication Engineering from the Politecnico of Milano, and has recently discussed his PhD on the use of interaction models to simplify dynamic ontology matching.

Stefano Bocconi studied Engineering at the University of Florence, Italy, specialization Control Theory, and graduated in 1994 with full marks. He then worked in software development as a free-lancer as well as employed by Olivetti and Alcatel-Lucent till 2001. From 2002 till 2006 he did a PhD about automatic video editing at the CWI research center in Amsterdam. From 2006 till 2008 he joined the Computer Science department of the University of Turin, Italy, working on model-based diagnosis and video mash-ups. Since 2008 he is working at the European project OKKAM about unique identifiers for entities, focusing on two use cases in scientific publishing and news publishing.

Serge Boucher, received the Computer Engineering degree (2004) and the Diplôme D'Études Approfondies in Computer Engineering (2005) from the Université Libre de Bruxelles, Belgium (ULB). He is currently in charge of the LOBSTER research project on Location-Based Semantic Web Services, funded by the region of Walloonia. He studies new approaches in ontology engineering and matching, and prepares a doctorate thesis that studies the introduction of Semantic Web technologies and Web Services in geographical database systems.

Paolo Bouquet is Associate Professor at DISI since 2004. His main research areas are: knowledge representation and management, semantic interoperability, formal theories of context and contextual reasoning. His results are published as articles in several international journals, and were presented as papers at many international conferences. He has been responsible for the research unit of the University of Trento of national and European projects. He is currently the Coordinator of the European FP7 Integrated Project OKKAM. Paolo organized several international workshops and conferences, including the CONTEXT conference series, the workshops on Meaning Coordination and Negotiation, and the workshop series on Identity and Reference.

Paul Buitelaar (PhD Computer Science 1998, Brandeis University, USA) is a senior research fellow and head of the DERI Unit for Natural Language Processing. Before joining DERI in 2009, he was a senior researcher at the DFKI Language Technology Lab and co-head of the DFKI Competence Center Semantic Web in Saarbrücken, Germany. His main research interests are in language technology for semantic-based information access. He has been a researcher and/or project leader on a number of national and international funded projects, e.g., on concept-based and cross-lingual information retrieval (MuchMore), semantic navigation (VIeWs), ontology-based information extraction and ontology learning (SmartWeb); (THESEUS MEDICO), semantic-based multimedia analysis (K-Space). A current focus is also on ontology libraries and ontology search (OntoSelect) as well as on the integration of linguistic information in ontologies (LingInfo, LexInfo).

Peter Denno has a B.S. in Mathematics and twenty five years' experience in the research and development of advanced software solutions for manufacturing. His work has included constraint-based engineering design, AI techniques for factory scheduling and process planning, and supply chain integration. Since 1994, Mr. Denno has been with NIST, where he has been involved with projects in systems engineering and systems integration. He participates in international standards development and served as Editor of an ISO standard for information mapping, Express-X. He currently leads NIST's participation in the AIAG MOSS project, an automotive industry effort to improve the performance of long-distance manufacturing supply chains through more effective information exchange.

Reiner Dumke holds a M.Sc. degree in mathematics (1971), a Ph.D. degree in "Efficiency of programming in data base projects" (1980) and has gained a postdoctoral lecture qualification in "Macro Languages" in 1989. Since 1994 he is a full professor in Software Engineering and fills the chair position for the Software Engineering Group at the Otto von Guericke University of Magdeburg, Germany. Prof. Dumke is an active member of german and international professional communities (IEEE, GI, ACM, DASMA) and a frequent speaker at various conferences. His research interests include software quality assurance, web engineering, formal specification, distributed systems design, agent technologies, and e-learning.

Jérôme Euzenat is a senior research scientist at INRIA Grenoble Rhône-Alpes and Laboratoire d'Informatique de Grenoble (LIG). He leads the Exmo team investigating the exchange of formal knowledge mediated by computers. He is particularly interested in the relationships between representations including abstraction, granularity, versioning and transforming representations. He holds a PhD and habilitation in computer science, both from Grenoble 1 University. More on http://exmo.inrialpes.fr/~euzenat

Janina Fengel is a research associate at the University of Applied Sciences in Darmstadt, Germany. She works in research projects in the Electronic Business Integration research group (e-big), located at the Faculty of Economics and Business Administration. Previously, after completing a commercial apprenticeship, she worked for several years in the travel and software industry before pursuing her degree. She holds an MSc in Business Administration from the University of Applied Sciences in Darmstadt, specializing in information management. Her research interests focus on the application of semantic technologies for business integration and issues of collaborative business.

Fausto Giunchiglia is professor of Computer Science at the University of Trento, ECCAI Fellow. Previously studied or had positions at: University of Genoa, Stanford University, Edinburgh University, IRST (Trento). Academic and scientific track: more than fifty journal papers; around two hundred publications overall; more than thirty invited talks in international events; program or conference chair of more than ten international events, editor or editorial board member of around ten journals, among them: Journal of Autonomous Agents and Multi-agent Systems, Journal of applied non Classical Logics, Journal of Software Tools for Technology Transfer, Journal of Artificial Intelligence Research.Fausto was member of the IJCAI Board of Trustees (01-11), President of IJCAI (05-07), President of KR, Inc. (02-04), Advisory Board member of KR, Inc., Steering Committee of the CONTEXT conference.

Fabian Gruning Fabian Grüning studied computer science at the University of Oldenburg, Germany. From 2005 on he started to work as a research assistent at the OFFIS - Institute for Information Systems both in third party founded projects as well as teaching. He currently finishes his PhD-Thesis "Data Quality Management for the Utility Domain" which contains a process model for data quality management that is adjusted to meet the requirements companies of the utility domain have for efficient application of a data quality management in the specific domain. It is accompanied by a supporting tool that automizes the steps of the process model.

Michael Gruninger is an Assistant Professor in the Department of Mechanical and Industrial Engineering at the University of Toronto, and is the head of the Semantic Technologies Laboratory. He returned to after spending five years as an Assistant Research Scientist in the Institute for Systems Research at the University of Maryland College Park and also a Guest Researcher at the National Institute for Standards and Technology (NIST). Before that, Michael was a Senior Research Scientist in the Enterprise Integration Laboratory of the Department of Mechanical and Industrial Engineering at the University of Toronto. Michael received his Ph.D. and M.Sc. in Computer Science at the University of Toronto and his B.Sc. in Computer Science at the University of Alberta. His current research focuses on the design and formal characterization of theories in mathematical logic and their application to problems in manufacturing and enterprise engineering.

Bo Hu is a researcher in SAP Research (CEC Belfast). He received his PhD in Computer Science from the Robert Gordon University, Aberdeen in 2004. Between 2002 and 2008, He worked as a Research Fellow in the Intelligence, Agent, Multimedia Group (IAM), School of Electronics and Computer Science, University of Southampton. His main research interest is in knowledge management, Semantic Web, context modelling and context awareness, and the application in e-learning and e-healthcare.

Martin Kunz, born in 1980, received his MS in Computer Science form the Otto-von-Guericke-University Magdeburg, Germany, in 2004. Since January 2005, Martin Kunz has been research scientist at the University of Magdeburg in the Software Engineering Group on the topic of software measurement infrastructures. The combination of Service-oriented architectures with semantic description of services has been his method of choice and prepared the ground for new solutions in this regards. Martin

Kunz has been published over 40 scientific papers and journal articles regarding software measurement, semantic descriptions and software quality.

Patrick Maué has graduated in Geoinformatics in 2006. At the time of writing (early 2009), he is employed as research associate the Institute for Geoinformatics in Münster, Germany. He is and has been involved in several research projects related to the semantics of geographic information and its applications. His research if focusing on the users of Geographic Information (GI), and how semantics can help to improve GI re-usability across different information communities. He has authored and co-authored various publications in the fields of Geospatial Semantic Web and the emerging field of GI in the Social Web.

Onyeari Mbanefo currently works with Coface Services, developing software programs used for credit insurance and debt management. She holds a Masters degree in Computer Engineering from Grenoble 1 University.

Fiona McNeill completed a PhD with the Mathematical Reasoning Group at the University of Edinburgh in 2006, in which she developed the Ontology Refinement System (ORS). Since then she has been a research associated in the MRG. From 2006-2008, she worked on the OpenKnowledge project, in which she primarily focussed on good enough answers and matching and on the testbed of emergency response flooding. Since the end of the OpenKnowledge project she has been working on a 3-year ONR grant, focussing on knowledge evolution and management of knowledge from disparate sources.

Sharad Mehrotra is a Professor in the School of Information and Computer Science at University of California, Irvine. He is the Director of the newly created UCI Center for Emergency Response Technologies (CERT) and was the Principal Investigator of the NSF-funded "RESCUE" project on information technologies for disaster response. His research expertise is in the data management and distributed computing areas where he has made many pioneering contributions. He received his PhD in Computer Science from the University of Texas, Austin in 1993. He is a recipient of numerous best paper awards including the SIGMOD best paper award in 2001.

Steffen Mencke, born in 1978, holds a M.Sc. degree in Computer Science (2005) and a Ph.D. degree from the Otto-von-Guericke-University of Magdeburg, Germany. The german state of Saxony-Anhalt awarded him a scholarship to work on his Ph.D. thesis about "Proactive Ontology-Based Content Provision in the Context of e-Learning", which he successfully defended in 2008. His research interest covers the Semantic Web, agent technology, e-Learning and Software Engineering. Steffen Mencke has published over 45 scientific papers and journal articles as well as several books and book chapters.

Iván Mínguez Pérez holds a Technical Engineer's degree in Computing by the University of Oviedo. He is currently taking the Official Master of Web Engineering (University of Oviedo) and has a long experience in Web Development issues, especially Semantic Web. Since January 2007, he develops his professional career as a member of the R&D Department, in CTIC Foundation (Spain).

Fabian Neuhaus is a guest researcher at the National Institute of Standards and Technology. His current research focus is on the development of foundational ontologies as well as application ontologies for supply chains in the manufacturing domain. Fabian received his Ph.D in Philosophy at Humboldt University, Berlin.

Juan Pane received his degree in Informatics Engineering from the National University of Asuncion - Paraguay. His major research interests include trust and reputation models, semantic matching and collaborative models in social interactions, the latter of which is the main focus of his current PhD studies at the University of Trento in Italy.

Heiko Paulheim works as a research associate at SAP Research CEC Darmstadt with his research focus on semantic web and ontologies. He has worked in both academic and applied research as well as in commercial software development. His research interests encompass a large variety of applications of semantic web technologies, including ontology engineering, ontology matching, semantic annotation, ontology-based systems integration, and ontology-driven software development, as well as engineering-oriented problems such as developing frameworks and infrastructures for ontology-based software. Heiko Paulheim holds an MSc in Computer Science from Technische Universität Darmstadt (Darmstadt University of Technology).

Luis Polo Paredes holds a Master Degree in Linguistics by the University of Oviedo. He also receives an Advanced Studies Diploma by the Philosophy Faculty at the University of Oviedo, where he studies his PhD degree. Since March 2005, he develops his professional career as a member of the R&D Department, in CTIC Foundation (Spain), where he coordinates the Semantic Web Unit. He is involved in several national and European research projects.

Michael Rebstock studied business in Germany and the UK and holds a PhD from Mannheim University. Before joining Darmstadt University of Applied Sciences' Faculty of Economics and Business Administration as a Professor of Business Computing in 1995, he worked as a consultant for two leading consulting companies. Michael Rebstock heads the Electronic Business Integration research group (e-big) at Darmstadt University of Applied Sciences. He is a member of the Steering Committee of the Special Interest Group 'Modeling of Business Applications' (WI-MobIS) of the German Computing Society (GI) and a regular contributor to and reviewer for scientific journals and conferences on business computing.

Sebastian Rohjans Sebastian Rohjans has joined the OFFIS - Institute for Information Systems in late 2008. He holds a computer science degree from the University of Oldenburg with a minor in business and wrote his thesis about ontology-based integration. He is now working in industrial setting projects having the same scope. His research interests include semantic web services, the OPC unified architecture and ontology based mediation.

Dmytro Rud holds a diploma in International Economics from the Donetsk National Technical University, Ukraine (2001) and a M.Sc. degree in Computer Science (Software Engineering) from the Otto-von-Guericke-University of Magdeburg, Germany (2005). In December 2008 he has successfully defended his Ph.D. thesis titled "Evaluation and ensuring of performance of orchestrated service offerings". Currently he works as a software engineer at the InterComponentWare AG in Walldorf (Baden), Germany.

Sven Schade is a third year PhD student in the Geoinformatics group of Prof. Werner Kuhn, University of Muenster (Germany). He holds a diploma in Geoinformatics since 2004 and works on data model semantics and translation. He was and is involved in international research projects and teaching dealing with Spatial Data Infrastructures (SDI), Semantic Web Technology, and Ontology Engineering. He spent 6 months as an intern at the SDI group of the Joint Research Centre (JRC) of the European Commission in Ispra. Responsibilities are in the area of service-based architectures for geospatial information, data quality, and sensor networks.

Arun Sharma is an Investment Associate at TLcom Capital Partners, a London-based technology venture capital firm. He is particularly interested in identifying European investment opportunities that bring innovation to the global technology and media markets. His past experiences range from computer science research to investment banking. He holds an MSc in Computer Science from RWTH Aachen University.

Daniel Sonntag is a senior research scientist at the Intelligent User Interface Department (IUI) at DFKI. He received a doctor's degree in computer science and a diploma (Msc.) in computational linguistics from Saarland University in Saarbrücken, Germany. Daniel has worked in natural language processing, text mining, interface design, and dialogue systems for over 10 years and has been affiliated with DFKI, Xtramind Technologies, and Daimler/Chrysler Research. His current research interests include multimodal interface design, ontology-based question answering, and semantic search engines. At the moment he is working on a situation-aware dialogue shell for semantic access to media and services in the THESEUS research program. MEDICO is one of the major use cases for the integration of semantic technologies.

Heiko Stoermer works as a post-doctoral researcher in the area of Knowledge Management and Information Systems at the University of Trento, Italy. He holds a university degree in Business Computing, and was awarded with a PhD in Computer Science for his work on Identity and Reference on the Semantic Web in 2008. His research interests include information integration, semantic interoperability and contextual knowledge representation. He has (co-) authored a number of international scientific publications, acted as a reviewer for important international conferences and is co-organizer of several workshops. Currently, he is devoting most of his time to his position as Technical Director of the European FP7 Integrated Project OKKAM, which he co-founded.

Mathias Uslar Since 2004, after having finished his studies of informatics with a minor in legal informatics and business, Mathias Uslar joined the OFFIS –Institute in Oldenburg Germany where he is working in the Utility Informatics branch. His main interests are standardization and utility EAI. He also brings in his expertise to both national and international standardization boards. He is also the director of the Center for It Standards in the Energy Domain, abbreviated CISE (http://www.ccise.de)

Pinar Wennerberg is a research scientist at Siemens Corporate Technology-Knowledge Management Department, where she is also pursuing her PhD in computer science. She received a diploma (Msc.) in computational linguistics from the Ludwig-Maximilian University in Munich, Germany and a diploma in English Language and Literature (BA) from the University of Istanbul, Turkey. Pinar has been working in knowledge representation and semantic modelling, natural language processing, text mining and in multi-lingual web technologies for several years. Prior to Siemens, she has been working as a research scientist for the European Commission in the Web Intelligence group. Her current focus is in biomedical ontology research within the context of the THESEUS-MEDICO project, and particularly in the application of biomedical ontologies to unstructured text, e.g., ontology-driven information extraction from biomedical corpora. A further focus is in the alignment of large biomedical ontologies such as those on anatomy and radiology.

Sonja Zillner is a research scientist at Siemens Corporate Technology Knowledge Management Department. She received her Diploma in Mathematics and Psychology from the Albert Ludwig University of Freiburg and her PhD in Computer Science from the Technical University of Vienna. Sonja has been initiating, leading and participating in external and internal research projects focusing on semantic applications in the medical domain. Her current focus lies in the domain of medical knowledge representation and medical decision support systems. Moreover, she is doing research and consulting in the area of change management, innovation, and "improvisation as mindset".

Esteban Zimányi is a professor and director of the Department of Computer & Decision Engineering of the Université Libre de Bruxelles (ULB). He started his studies at the Universidad Autónoma de Centro América, Costa Rica. He received a B.Sc. (1988) and a doctorate (1992) in computer science from the Faculty of Sciences at the ULB. During 1997, he was a visiting researcher at the Database Laboratory of the Ecole Polytechnique Fédérale de Lausanne, Switzerland. His current research interests include the semantic web and web services, bio-informatics, geographic information systems, spatio-temporal databases, and data warehouses.

Index

D

E

F

G

H

I

J

K

T

U